AppleScript: A Comprehensive Guide to Scripting and Automation on Mac OS X

Hanaan Rosenthal

friendsof

DESIGNER TO DESIGNER™

an Apress® company

AppleScript: A Comprehensive Guide to Scripting and Automation on Mac OS X

Credits

Lead Editor
Chris Mills

Technical Reviewer
Bill Cheeseman

Editorial Board
Steve Anglin, Dan Appleman,
Ewan Buckingham, Gary Cornell,
Tony Davis, John Franklin,
Jason Gilmore, Chris Mills,
Dominic Shakeshaft,
Jim Sumser

Project Manager
Sofia Marchant

Copy Edit Manager
Nicole LeClerc

Copy Editor
Ami Knox

Production Manager
Kari Brooks-Copony

Production Editor
Ellie Fountain

Compositor
Katy Freer

Proofreader
Liz Welch

Indexer
John Collin

Artist
April Milne

Cover Designer
Kurt Krames

Manufacturing Manager
Tom Debolski

To Johanne

CONTENTS AT A GLANCE

PART THREE: THE WILD WORLD OF APPLESCRIPT

CONTENTS

Chapter 8: Variables 231

CONTENTS

Chapter 10: Teaching your script to make decisions. 305

Chapter 11: The assembly line: Creating repeat loops 321

Chapter 13: Working with files 429

Chapter 14: Working with the clipboard 497

Chapter 15: Turn errors in your favor 509

PART THREE: THE WILD WORLD OF APPLESCRIPT

Chapter 19: AppleScript amenities in Mac OS X 595

Chapter 20: Scripting additions and extendibility 615

Chapter 21: The fundamentals of automating applications . . . 637

Chapter 22: Debugging scripts 653

Chapter 25: Scripting Apple apps 697

Chapter 26: Scripting data and databases 717

ABOUT THE AUTHOR

 **Hanaan Rosenthal:** OK, so who are we kidding, this part is not some facts concerning the author's life, but rather where I get to write good stuff about myself. So, here I go with some info about myself and how I got to be a scripter:

I started with computer graphics when I was 10 years old. I got a Sinclair 8-bit computer, wrote a couple of graphic programs and a game for it, and published a newsletter that had a one-issue life span.

When I got to Providence, RI, from Israel at twice that age, I fell in love with Macs after taking a course at the Rhode Island School of Design. I quit my job delivering candy, bought a Mac II with $2,435 of the $2,500 my wife and I had in the bank, and became a computer graphics consultant. In 1996 I started scripting professionally, and my first $100K+ job came in 1998. This project turned into a disaster when the president of the company I was creating the system for decided to kill the project and blame it on me. Now it's all but a funny memory, since over the past eight years I have had the pleasure of creating some pretty cool systems for some pretty neat people from companies such as Fidelity Investments, The Hartford, Wellington Management, Showtime Networks, *The Boston Globe*, and others.

During that time I also met with John Thorsen and the rest of the folks from TECsoft Developers Consortium (TDC), which is a national consortium of AppleScripters.

Some of my early clients were financial companies from the Boston area for which I created different graphing and document generation systems (all AppleScript based!). These jobs led to an AppleScript-based graphing engine I invented that allows me to add custom graphing capability to any AppleScript system. The daily stock graphs in *The Boston Globe*, for instance, are created using one of these systems.

Now, as always, I mix consulting with other things I love such as caring for my two sweet kids, whom Johanne and I homeschool, pouring concrete countertops, renovating historical homes, and rooting for the Boston Red Sox.

ABOUT THE TECHNICAL REVIEWER

 **Bill Cheeseman** lives in Quechee, Vermont. He is well known in the AppleScript community as webmaster of The AppleScript Sourcebook site (www.AppleScriptSourcebook.com) and in the Cocoa community as the author of Cocoa Recipes for Mac OS X—The Vermont Recipes (www.stepwise.com/Articles/VermontRecipes). He is the author of two AppleScript utilities for Mac OS X, PreFab UI Browser and PreFab UI Actions (www.prefab.com/scripting.html). He has programmed extensively in a variety of languages on a long succession of Apple II, Apple III, and Macintosh computers. In his spare time, he is a trial lawyer specializing in intellectual property, and environmental and commercial insurance coverage litigation.

ACKNOWLEDGMENTS

I would like to thank a few people for making this effort possible. The first thanks I owe to my family who were there every step of the way: Johanne, my wife, who told me I could write a book and was there for me whenever I was roaming the house aimlessly in search of a sentence, and also to my kids, Aylam and Olivia, who tallied the page count and graciously named the book "That dumb book my dad wrote about AppleScript" (the publisher didn't bite).

I owe thanks to Bill Cheeseman, who kept me honest and didn't hold back. This book would not have been the same without Bill's deep understanding of the subject matter, which I can only hope to possess. I also drew from the knowledge of people such as Emmanuel Lévy, Shirley Hopkins, Mark Munro, and the folks from TDC who turned every simple question into an election-year debate.

I also owe thanks to the many people at Apress and friends of ED who were on top of everything from the direction of the book to crossing the t's and dotting the i's. I'd like to thank Ami and Ellie and the rest of the folks who worked on this book, for managing to find even the most obscure inaccuracies, and to Chris and Sofia, who whenever I sat there idle with nothing to do cheered me up with one form or another that I had to fill out.

PREFACE: WHAT MAKES APPLESCRIPT UNIQUE AND WHAT WILL MAKE THIS BOOK YOUR FAVORITE?

One issue that keeps coming up in the AppleScript world is the place of scripting between recording macros and programming from scratch. Is scripting more like programming with C++, or more like creating Photoshop Actions or FileMaker scripts? This question doesn't have one answer, but it does have some interesting aspects. First, let's establish some facts: AppleScript is an object-oriented programming language that has both depth and beauty in its own right, and an unlimited potential for expandability by scriptable applications and scripting additions. While AppleScript can be used for more straightforward tasks like applying one or two transformations to a mass of files, it shines brightest when taken to a higher level. You only start to tap into the power of AppleScript when you start branching and looping.

Figuring out, however, what AppleScript resembles the most is missing the point. The best aspect of AppleScript is also what makes it like no other programming language. In other programming languages you write programs, mostly a standalone package of code with some supporting files. The program has an interface that the user does something with, and some result is produced. All that happens as part of that package. What makes AppleScript different is that what we create with AppleScript is not so much a program, but rather a robot that uses other people's programs. Imagine being a graphic designer with some modest scripting capability. Now imagine that you have to superimpose a transparent logo at the corner of 1000 images for an online catalog. Manually, this would take you three days; however, using AppleScript, you fashion yourself a robotic arm complete with a motor, a trigger, and some controls, which does the job in 12 minutes. Next, you detach the cool gadget from your arm, build it two legs, and set it loose with a remote control. Now, it does the boring repetitive job of three people. You have created an employee that works at phantom speed, is 100% accurate, and doesn't need health insurance. In fact, when I meet with clients I ask them to describe to me the ideal human position they would like the script to function as, instead of a program they need; the scripter's job is to teach the Mac to do the work of that person, using the exact same applications the human employee would have used. While other programming languages create programs that need a human operator, in AppleScript you create a super-operator that uses these programs with a speed and precision like no one has ever imagined.

So, what possessed me to take on the task of writing what is undoubtedly the longest book ever written about AppleScript? It started with reading David Blatner's *Real World QuarkXPress 3* book in the early 90s. This book inspired me because it was written in such a way that any novice could open it up and learn from it, but at the same time, the subject matter was advanced enough to keep even the power users happy. Ever since getting involved with AppleScript, I wanted to do the same for this programming language.

What sets this book apart is that it combines a substantial reference alongside in-depth explanation and real-world examples. This combination of features isn't so much trying to be everything for everyone as create a complete experience.

Another thing I noticed in other books was that they distributed the share of discussion between subjects based on the subject's complexity, not its usefulness. These subjects were organized according to the role they played in the language. That has never made sense to me, and I set out to change it. This book is not about the AppleScript language but rather about the scripter. It is organized from the viewpoint of a person who needs to do real things with the language. This philosophy shows itself in a few ways: first, the subjects you will find can be described as "things people want to do," things such as work with files, manipulate strings, create interfaces, etc. In each chapter I cover all aspects related to the issue at hand, while giving it the attention it deserves based on how much it is used in the real world, not how many properties and related commands it happens to have. Second, all information relevant to a specific topic is discussed, but is then taken a step further: it gives you the opinion of a professional scripter (that would be me) on what actual uses this feature has, what related tricks there are, what are the potential problems, and more. The chapters also include real-world examples that shed light on every feature from several different directions. My thought was, If I know it, I will write it. There is so much more to a programming language such as AppleScript than meets the eye, and I wanted you to know as much of it as possible.

About the scripts that come with the book: you can download the scripts for the book from www.customflowsolutions.com. Go to that site and click the AppleScript book link to get to the download area.

The scripts are divided into two groups: figure scripts and copy scripts. The figure scripts are the scripts that appear in the screen shots in the book and they match the number of the screen shot. The copy scripts are the scripts that appear in the copy and have a script number above them, such as Script 3-5, which will be script 5 in Chapter 3.

RESOURCES

Following are some resources you can refer to for more information about AppleScript:

Apple's own AppleScript web pages (www.apple.com/applescript) are full of information, sample scripts, and links to other resources. If you are interested in scripting different Apple applications such as iTunes, iPhoto, Mail, etc., then refer to the special application pages listed in www.apple.com/applescript/apps/. The resources page lists about 50 links to websites, books, consultants, and more.

For making some AppleScript friends and getting your questions answered, you can join the AppleScript users mailing list. Join the list by going to www.lists.apple.com/mailman/listinfo/applescript-users.

Outside the Apple-sphere there are a few great websites dedicated to AppleScript. Chief among them is MacScripter.net. MacScripter.net has a few sections including the most complete database of scripting additions, AppleScript code shared by other scripters, a BBS, and other features. Another great website is Bill Cheeseman's The AppleScript Sourcebook (www.applescriptsourcebook.com). The AppleScript Sourcebook is known for Bill's detailed explanation of different topics. Following software updates from Apple related to AppleScript, this website is the place to look for explanations of what these updates involve.

For AppleScript training, the best place to go is www.tecsoft.com. John Thorsen, the founder of TECSoft, has been training on AppleScript since the beginning of time and has trained thousands of people on the subject. John also provides online training as well as a training CD for AppleScript.

There are many other AppleScript-related websites that I haven't included. Please see the "links" page in Apple's AppleScript website and the other two websites I mentioned for a complete listing of related sites.

PART ONE **READ ME FIRST**

1 INTRODUCTION

What are scripts for?

AppleScript is for Macintosh automation, and so scripts you write can automate tasks you would otherwise have to perform with the mouse and keyboard.

While you can use AppleScript to automate almost anything you can do with the mouse and keyboard, you probably wouldn't want to. So what would you want to automate? The answer to this question falls under two broad categories: small things and big things.

The main difference between big scripts and small scripts is the amount of thought and planning required. When writing small scripts, you start out by . . . writing the script. As the script progresses, you add more functions, more lines, and you go back and fix and debug until things work. Big systems require planning. You have to carefully consider the users, the environment, the different triggers for things the system will do. You have to deal with data sources, small interfaces, return on investment, and all these things that can kill your efforts just as you start to get excited.

Automating small things

Small scripts are the way one usually starts to become familiar with AppleScript. AppleScript lets you easily create a script, test it, save it as an application, and start using it. This quick turnaround for truly useful utilities is part of the winning recipe that made AppleScript so great.

A few years ago I was teaching a Photoshop class, and during my five-minute break a colleague told me of a problem a client of his, a prepress house, was having. The client couldn't print lines in Quark XPress documents that were thinner than 0.25 point, and was spending hours correcting every document that came in. By the end of my break I had written the following script, saved it as an application, and handed it back to him. The script went like this:

```
tell application "QuarkXPress 4.01"
   tell every page of document 1
      set width of (every line box whose width < 0.25) to 0.25
   end tell
end tell
```

The prepress shop was thrilled for the "utility" we scrambled to program for them.

Now, since the client got this one for free, and I gave it away, return on investment can't be measured in terms of money. But just for kicks, we can figure it out if we assume it took a person ten minutes to manually fix an average client file, and that this prepress facility went through ten files a day. Using these numbers, the time investment paid for itself 5000 times over during the first year. Sounds a bit over the top, but it's not. Little AppleScript efforts can make a big difference.

Automating big things

While AppleScript doesn't sweat the small stuff, it can be the base for large-scale custom integrated systems. As far as what to automate, you *could* automate any task that has a repeatable logic, and if the cost of automation is less than the amount of money you save, and it usually is, the task will be worth automating. A repeatable logic is logic that can be applied successfully to similar, but not identical, subjects, and produces a predictable outcome, based on the uniqueness of the subject.

For example, here is a process that is not so suitable for automation:

> *You take the client's instructions file, you read them, and figure out what corrections the client wanted. If the client wanted the image to be color-corrected, you open the image in Photoshop and apply curves until it looks better. Otherwise, just correct the typos.*

This process is much too arbitrary and relies on the operator's human qualities such as the ability to perform color correction and correct typos.

Here is a better candidate for automation:

> *When you get a job from a client, search for the client in the database to locate the job information. If the job is marked "urgent," e-mail the imaging room to expect it within ten minutes. Open the InDesign document and verify that all the fonts were provided. Make sure that the document contains the number of pages indicated in the electronic job ticket; if it doesn't, make a note in the database and e-mail the client. When done, make a copy of the job folder to the archive folder on the server, and send another copy to the "in" folder on the production server. Repeat for all jobs that arrived last night.*

Now this is a process that AppleScript was made for. Besides having programmatic elements such as a repeat loop for applying the process for all jobs and some branching, the process itself is clear, logical, and can be applied to any client job that comes in.

If we look into the previous process, we see that quite a bit of it happens in applications. The operator has to know how to use FileMaker for searching and entering data; InDesign for checking fonts, pages, etc.; and the Finder for moving folders around. Controlling these and many others applications is one of AppleScript's main strengths. AppleScript can give applications commands and get information from applications, such as the data in a FileMaker Pro record or the number of pages in an InDesign document.

AppleScript is also ideal for performing repetitive tasks. For instance, how would you like to show up at work one morning and realize that your job for that day is to go through 200 TIF images in a folder, add a black frame to each one, and export them as JPEGs? Then, you must create a PDF file with all the images, four-up, with the image name under each image. Sounds like hard work? Your reward for job-well-done just might be another folder the next day . . .

While not very sophisticated, this process is very repetitive. A script can do it for you while you take a walk to the cafeteria and back.

Where's AppleScript?

For about ten years now, every Mac that shipped with System 7.11, also known as System 7 Pro, had everything needed to use AppleScript. No special installs, hardly any configuration issues from Mac to Mac, and a basic array of scriptable applications that grew rapidly, and still does.

What it means is that writing scripts and installing and running them on other Macs requires transporting the script file alone, and not a whole array of other resources; everything you need is there.

What's truly remarkable about the expandable nature of AppleScript is that most of the language resides inside the actual applications you automate. For better or worse, the level to which applications are automatable and the ease in which you can include them in an automated solution is largely up to the software vendor. It is up to the development team of every application to implement scriptability for any feature they imagine someone will want to automate.

It wasn't until a few years ago that Adobe jumped on the scripting bandwagon and started incorporating AppleScript into their widely used graphics program. Adobe Illustrator 9 was the first major Adobe app to be scriptable, followed by InDesign, which started out boasting a comprehensive scripting vocabulary, and finally Photoshop 7 came out of the box scriptable as well.

As it stands, the very existence of AppleScript depends on the applications that support it. Making an application scriptable doesn't mean simply checking the Make Scriptable option in the Compile dialog box.

> *When writing Cocoa applications, there is a basic scripting dictionary that can be easily made available; however, in order to allow scripters to automate their applications, developers must put a good amount of thought, planning, and development time into the scriptability of their applications.*

To make an application scriptable, developers have to create special terminology for each feature they want to make scriptable and come up with an object model for the application. That can add up to many hours and can't be done as an afterthought. However difficult, software developers see good return on their investment when companies integrate their applications into automated solutions. This alone ties that application to the client and lowers the chances that the client will dump their application for a competing product.

How are scripts written?

You can't write and run AppleScript scripts from any text editor. To write scripts you need to use a special script editor that will allow you to write the script, check syntax, compile the script, run it, and save it as an application.

To start, you may want to use Apple's own free Script Editor. Script Editor is a little application that comes preinstalled and ready to use with every Mac system. Although Script Editor has been around for years, it is only in version 2. Despite the low number, the program is pretty robust and will allow you to do anything you need to start with AppleScript. Besides Apple's Script Editor application, there are a few commercially available AppleScript editors that have enhanced editing and debugging features.

> **Third-party script editors:** Other AppleScript editors include Late Night Software's Script Debugger (www.latelightsw.com) and Smile (www.satimage-software.com), which is a commercial scripting program, but is also available as a free download. See more about Smile in Chapter 28.

As you're writing a script, you can compile it right from the script editor. Even if you save it as a droplet or an application, it can be changed, recompiled, and run right from the script window. This makes your scripts (or other people's scripts for that matter) easy to look at and try.

Where do scripts reside and how do they run?

Scripts can be saved anywhere! It is up to you where you want to save scripts you create. This flexibility leaves you wide open to create your own super-organized script storage system, and, of course, allows you to create a holy mess.

Some applications have special folders, usually called Scripts, and if you place your scripts there they will appear in some script menu. For instance, if you've installed the Mac OS X script menu, the first item in the menu opens your personal scripts folder. This folder is found in the Library folder in your own home folder, and any scripts or folders you put there will appear under the Script menu in the menu bar. The Script menu also lists scripts found in the Scripts folder in the general Library folder on the startup disk. Folders found in these Scripts folders are shown as submenus.

More and more software vendors realize that adding a Scripts menu to their applications is more than letting the user create their own script; it also allows them to quickly add "features" to their applications that otherwise would take timely programming resources.

For example, BBEdit has a script menu with some useful scripts that perform some editing functions.

AppleScript file format

Where scripts do get a bit confusing is in their file format. Although you write scripts using text, and when you reopen a saved script the text is usually there, the script is actually saved as special tokens that are interpreted by the AppleScript component when the script is run.

This "what you see is not what you saved" situation will usually go unnoticed by the scripter, unless there's some version issue, or usually an application or scripting addition issue. What you have to remember is that the AppleScript language, as we discussed earlier, is composed largely of the terminology that scriptable applications contain for their own scriptability. An application can add hundreds of commands and objects to AppleScript, each with their own arguments and properties. For a script to compile properly, it needs the applications that are referenced in it present and open. In fact, if an application referenced in your script isn't present when you try to open the script, you will either have to give up until you install it, or trick AppleScript to think some other application is that missing one. If you do trick AppleScript, you will have a hard time changing the AppleScript code you wrote for that application since it will appear as hard-to-read special codes inside double angle brackets (known as Apple events code) instead of the easy-to-read English-like AppleScript text you're used to.

So how can all that affect you and your script? The main reason why you won't be able to see your code properly is that the application, scripting addition, or application's AppleScript plug-in isn't available. If the application is open but is lacking a plug-in, the script will open but won't display correctly.

> Some applications, mainly from Adobe, don't incorporate their scripting terminology into the actual application, but rather have a plug-in manage all the AppleScript-related activity.

Rest assured, however, that the actual script is fine. The next time you open it with the target application open, it will return to its old self and compile properly.

So what formats can a script be saved as? There are three main kinds of script files: regular compiled script, which is the native AppleScript file format, and scripts saved as plain text or as applications. On top of that, OS X added a new option for saving compiled scripts and script applications called "bundle." Bundles are folders that appear and behave as files. You can read more about them in Chapter 23.

1

For most purposes, your script will start as text, but will be most likely saved as a compiled script file. Later on the script can be saved as an application and installed somewhere. A script may remain in its AppleScript format (nonapplication) state if it's either loaded into another script or used in an application that is "attachable."

> *An attachable application is one that can have scripts attached to it, usually via a* Scripts *menu.*

There are also two kinds of applications: regular application and applets. A regular application runs the script when you double-click it, and quits after the script is done. A droplet can also respond to files being dropped on it. This is useful for a script that processes files or folders.

When saving a script as an application, you can't specify whether you want it to be a droplet or a normal application. Instead, AppleScript determines that based on the contents of your script. Basically, if you told AppleScript what to do in case some files are dropped on it, it will become a droplet; otherwise, it will be a normal application. We will discuss all that in detail in later chapters.

So, why then would you ever save a script as text? There are a few reasons. One, saving and opening scripts as text doesn't require that the script gets compiled. This is very useful when something stops you from compiling the script, namely, an error in your AppleScript text. Also, when I send scripts to be used on other Macs, I try to send them in text format. Getting the script as text forces the other person to open them in Script Editor and compile them on the Mac on which the script will eventually run. This helps iron out issues that may stem from using a slightly different version of application and gives the script a chance to see where all the applications are located on the new Mac.

Another format-related option you have is to save a run-only version of the script. This will allow the script to run, but no one will be able to read it. Distributing a script as run-only is useful when you want to protect the rights to your proprietary code.

The golden triangle: AppleScript language, application scriptability, and the scripts you write

We looked at the role of applications' scriptability earlier. Now, how does that scriptability work with the AppleScript language and with the actual scripts you write?

All this is very much like any other spoken language, say, English. We have the base language that has verbs, nouns, adjectives, and some rules. We can use English to talk, but what we say has to have some context in order to be interesting and for us to relate to others. This is where different subjects come in, and I mean big subjects; subjects that have their own lingo. Take for example military speak, computer geek speak, or medical language. They all are English, but each has its own special words, some of which no one outside of the business can understand. More than that, they add meaning. Take for example the following sentence: "Put your masks on, the operation is about to begin." It means two completely different things whether you're a surgeon or a sergeant, and if you're a computer geek it means nothing!

The same with AppleScript: the language does give us the command *make* and the object *document*, which are known to most applications, but simply writing *make document* has no meaning unless you point it to an application that knows what to do with it. And this application will have its own way of dealing with that command, which is different than the way another application was told to deal with it.

OK, so now we have AppleScript with some programming basics and applications that contain their own nouns, also known as objects, and verbs, called commands. Where does that leave you and your blank script editor window? Well, you can use all these indiscriminately: mix AppleScript core terms with application objects, or use AppleScript to crunch data taken from an application's object properties.

Out of all these, perhaps the most exciting thing you can do (if you're the type of person who can get excited by a programming language) is to create your very own commands and objects. You create commands by writing handlers and objects by bundling those handlers along with some properties in script objects.

Let's see if we can get into the spirit of procreation (getting excited by the last section should help some). What if your script's purpose is to automate the creation of a catalog? What you might have is one string of commands, starting at the top going down, telling the different applications what to do. First you have some database commands for gathering the information, then you use some AppleScript commands to clean and format the text and add some dollar signs to numbers, etc., followed by some repeat loops and conditional statements (*if, then*) that dump all that text into the page layout program.

OK, that's not fair. When you start out you just want to get things done and you don't care really how. While I still think you should start this way, I do want you to have a mental idea of how you should be writing scripts once you get over the initial euphoria that overcomes you every time your computer does something for you, and you have to run and get a cup of coffee just so you can tell everyone that "the script did that by itself while I . . . while I . . . was getting a cup of coffee!"

The better script model

So how would you make the orderly chain of commands different, and why? For the second question there are a few answers. The quick and dirty on it is that well-written scripts are more portable and flexible. They're easier to change, and making a change can mean improving the way multiple scripts run. Also, your code becomes more reusable, which is a major part of being a profitable scriptwriter.

And how are better scripts written? While Chapter 24 is dedicated to healthy scriptwriting, I wanted to touch upon the "better script" model in general terms.

Teaching the script new commands

Let's start with redundant code. Redundant code is code that performs nearly identical operations in many places in the script. For instance, in our catalog automation script, you may have some code that goes to the database and gets some information from a field, say, the price of an item. Then, the script adds a $ sign to the number and inserts it in a named text frame in the page layout application. These operations strung together take up, say, 30 lines of code, and they repeat in about five places in your script.

You can make your script much better by your own command! How about a command that goes by the name "get_data_from_database_format_it_and_insert_into_layout".

This command you write yourself is called a handler or a subroutine. It is placed separately from the script, but its functionality is available from anywhere in the script.

When you decide to start writing your own commands, or handlers, your script will be suddenly divided into two parts: the first part will contain the list of things that the script should do, and the second part, a detailed description of how to do each thing.

For the sake of our example, you create the command by first describing to the script what to do whenever you tell it to "get data from database, format it, and insert into layout." Then you can execute that command from anywhere in your script, or even other scripts. This allows you to get data from the database, format it, and insert it into the layout using a single line instead of 30 lines.

Calling handlers is similar to asking someone for a cup of coffee: with three words you asked them to perform about 20 separate operations.

When you're just starting to script, creating subroutines appears to be an added complication that you may not be quite ready for. Later on, however, writing and calling subroutines can become one of the most important things you will do. Organizing your scripts with subroutines makes them efficient and easy to read and edit. It also makes your code much easier to reuse in other scripts.

Handlers will be covered in more detail in the following chapter and in Chapter 18, which is dedicated to the subject.

Packaging your commands into script objects

Now let's look at yet another way to organize your script.

Let's assume that you've created a whole bunch of subroutines, some for replacing data in the page layout application, some to get data and record data in the database, and some for general purposes. What this situation calls for is the creation of script objects. One script object can deal with the database commands, one with the page layout stuff, and the rest of the subroutines can be just a part of your script as they are now.

What you've done is the equivalent of creating your own applications. You can talk to those parts of your script as if they were stand-alone units, or better yet, you can easily use these units in other scripts.

While script objects can help you organize a complex system, many scripters stay away from them. You owe it to yourself to try to understand the different ways script objects can be used, and to try at some point to utilize script objects in your solutions. You will find that script objects are fun and satisfying to use, and can give you an edge as a script writer.

One way to look at script objects is as a separate script file. Imagine saving a part of your script in a separate file, then loading it into your main script and running it from there. This can have a few advantages: it makes your main script smaller and more manageable, and the same script object can be loaded into and used by different scripts.

You can also create script objects right inside your main script. This approach is useful when you want a part of your script to act more like an object, rather than just code that executes. If your script controls a board game such as checkers, for example, each piece on the board can be controlled by a script object. Since all the game pieces are identical, they can all start out from the same script object. That object can have properties such as *side*, which can be "black" or "white"; *position*, which can be "A3," etc.; and whether the piece is a queen or not. At the start of the game the script object for each piece is created and initialized with position and other values. During the game you can target different pieces with commands such as *eat_left()* or *set is_queen to true*, etc.

Wrapping up

So what have we looked at thus far? We saw that while AppleScript provides a rich language to work with, in order to talk to someone who can get real things done we need an application.

Then, we can start creating our own commands, and finally, combine these commands into our own script objects.

In the following chapter we will go into the language in more detail. Later on in the book, we will explore each facet of the language on its own.

PART TWO **HOW TO APPLESCRIPT**

2 STARTING TO SCRIPT— ALL OVER AGAIN

OK, all you "been scripting for a year and think I can script the New York City traffic light system" people, listen up. Although this chapter covers fundamental AppleScript concepts, it is written also for you. There's nothing better than to reread about that stuff you think is way behind you. Like any other complex subject, AppleScript has a lot of levels, and in order to understand more and get up to the next level, you sometimes have to start fresh and pretend you know nothing.

Script concentrate: Just add water!

In the following section, we'll write a script that contains in it some of the basic AppleScript constructs. Then we'll run the script and try to understand what happened line by line. This script will be a bit longer than your usual "Hello World" script, but once we sift through all the lines you'll be on top of it! Here's what the script will do:

Get a random number and use it to create a name for a folder. Create the folder in the Finder, name it, and then delete it if the user clicks Yes in a dialog box.

This part here will go over many big AppleScript issues. Don't get stressed if it's too much; just go with the flow, read the text, and do the exercises. All of the points covered here will be repeated in great detail throughout the book.

OK, let's start:

Open Script Editor. You can find it in the AppleScript folder of your Applications folder (unless the system administrator thought it was a game and deleted it in last night's software raid).

Before we continue, here's a little Script Editor primer:

The main window is divided into two parts: the top is the area where you can write your script and the bottom is divided into three tabs. The tabs in the bottom area of the script window are Description, Result, and Event Log. Both the Result and the Event Log tabs are essential for debugging. The toolbar contains buttons for your basic AppleScript functions: Record, Stop, Run, and Compile. That's all for now, let's start scripting.

In the blank new Script Editor window that should be staring you in the eye right now, type the following two words:

    random number

See Figure 2-1.

The text you typed should be formatted with the font Courier. This is because it has not been compiled yet.

To check your syntax, either press the ENTER key, or click the Compile button.

Figure 2-1.
The noncompiled script in the
Script Editor window

You're welcome to enter, but please, do not return: The ENTER key on the
Mac, to all you Windows migrants, is not the same as the RETURN key. The RETURN
key is used to start a new line, and the ENTER key is used for other things, like
compiling a script in Script Editor. To tell between them, simply read what they
say and apply the following cryptic rule: the ENTER key has the word "Enter" on
it, and the RETURN key has "Return" written all over it.

Once you compile the script, the font and possibly the color of the text changes. Suddenly
AppleScript understands what you're saying. Well, it understands what you're saying given
you speak properly, of course.

We're going to take a second to see what happens when you press the Compile button.
Before that, we will save the random number script as text to the desktop. Saving the
script as text does not require you to compile the script. To save the script as text, choose
Save As from the File menu, and specify Text from the File Format pop-up menu. We'll get
back to that script later on.

To better understand the difference between correct syntax and usable code, let's try the
following:

Start yet another script by choosing New from the File menu, and write the following:

```
It's time to go
```

When you try to compile this script, you get an error. We will ignore the specific error and
just note that what you typed didn't adhere to the AppleScript syntax. In other words, if
you were in Greece and couldn't speak Greek, but tried to say something you just read in
the dictionary, the response of the Greek you're trying to communicate with will be something along the lines of "Hah?"

Back to AppleScript now, let's delete the words "to go" and end up with

```
It's time
```

Now the script compiles just fine. All excited, let's try to run it.

Now what you said was actually a sentence in Greek, but with no real meaning. The Greek will now smile at the poor foreigner and move on.

Even if the script compiles, it still doesn't guarantee that it'll run! In order for the script to run, it has to be a correctly written AppleScript expression.

Being able to compile a script does, however, ensure that you can save it as a compiled script. If you can't compile it, and there may be other reasons for that, you may have to save it as plain text until you figure out what went wrong.

OK, back to our random number script. If you closed it, open it up, and if you want to start over, start a new script window and type random number.

Now let's run the script and see what happens.

As far as folders suddenly synchronizing, catalogs being created, or your iMac suddenly doing the Macarena, I can't say that anything really happened. However, the script did run.

Take a peek at the Result area. If it's hidden, display the pane by dragging the horizontal divider line with the grab bar up until the pane at the bottom fills about a third of the window. The Result area shows us the script's result. And since the script has only one line, the result is the result of that one line.

What you got is a decimal number somewhere between 0 and 1, which is the result of the *random number* command. In this context, *random number* is also an expression, since it is responsible for the result of the script line.

Much like any other language, expressions and results are the building blocks of AppleScript. Take for instance the following situation: My goal is to play squash, and here is how I went about it:

I checked what day it is, and the result of that expression was Thursday. I can play on Thursday! I checked the time; it was still early enough. I called my buddy and he could play. Every single action I took had a result that led to my next action. In this case, the positive result of each step led to the next step; however, I could have collected all the results regardless of their orientation, and evaluated them all at the end to see if squash will work out. I could have a list that read

```
Day OK?
Time OK?
Partner OK?
```

At the end, I could read the list, and if I had three OKs, I'd go and play.

In order for that to happen, I need to store the results someplace. This "someplace" is another form of expression called a variable. A variable is a word you can make up that holds a value you can use later in the script. A script without variables is like a bucket with a hole at the bottom. You can put a lot in it, but since nothing is retained, you can't utilize the script information you were given at an earlier point.

With that said, let's put the random number we picked into a variable so that we can go back to it later in the script. To do that, change the single line in the script to

```
set my_random_number to random number
```

The *set* command assigns the result of the expression, in this case the *random number* command, into the *my_random_number* variable. Later in the script we will use the value that is stored in that variable to name a folder.

For now, let's add the number 100 to the end of the line to make it

```
set my_random_number to random number 100
```

The number that follows the *random number* command is an optional parameter. That means that you can choose to omit it or include it. There are other optional parameters to the *random number* command that we'll look at later on. The number parameter that follows the command makes the *random number* command return a whole number (also called an integer) between 0 (zero) and that number, instead of a decimal number (also referred to as a real number).

To move on to the next line, press *RETURN* and then the following:

```
my_random_number as text
```

This expression includes coercion (which means conversion, in programmer language), from a number to text. When *my_random_number* was created, its value was a number, since the result of the *random number* command was a number. This is all OK, but for this script we won't need that number to use for calculations or other number-related stuff, but rather for including in a name of a folder. For that we need text.

You might be asking yourself, Why should AppleScript care if a value is number or text? The answer is that AppleScript cares about type of value far less than other programming languages, which may make your first few scripts easier to swallow, but can create some confusion later on as you start trusting AppleScript's ability to guess whether you wanted a number or text, etc. In fact, since we later will tack that random number to the end of the folder name, which is a string, AppleScript will convert the number to text on its own. Much more on that later, so hang on.

Now run the script. Before, the result was just a number; now the number appears in double quotes. Double quotes are the distinguishing characteristic of text, or to use a more programming-like term, a string.

The last line, again, needs to be put in a variable for later use. What we'll do now, however, is just put it back in the same variable. This is good if you don't need the value in its previous form. Keep the first line of the script, but change the last line you wrote into

```
set my_random_number to my_random_number as text
```

Now we can build the string that will be used to name the folder. Type the following new line at the end of the script:

```
Set folder_name to "Folder number " & my_random_number
```

Your script should now look like the one in Figure 2-2.

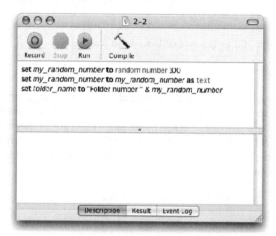

Figure 2-2.
The script so far

The last expression connected two text strings together. Or in other words, concatenated them. The & character, when put between two strings, returns the two strings as a single string. This is also an expression, one that includes the concatenation operator.

Run the script and see that the result is "Folder number 35" (assuming that the random number is 35).

The next and fourth line in our script will speak directly to the Finder:

```
tell application "Finder" to make new folder at desktop
```

This expression does two things: first, it involves a command, a direct order to make something real happen—to create a folder on the desktop. Second, it also returns an AppleScript-like result: a reference to the new folder.

This reference isn't text or a number, and it is most likely going to be unusable for other applications in its current form. However, it will give us a way to refer to that new folder we just made. We can grab that Finder object reference by adding a fifth line that puts the result of the previous line into a variable:

```
set my_folder to the result
```

Run the script and let's see what happens. The result you get is in the following lines:

```
folder "untitled folder" of folder "Desktop" ¬
of folder "hanaan" of folder "Users" of startup disk
```

This is what's called a Finder reference to a file. While this will work now, as soon as we run the line that will change the name of the folder, this reference will be useless. It's a bit like telling someone who's never seen you that you are going to be the guy with the beard, and then going right away and shaving it off! You are still you, but the description you gave is no good.

For that we can try to use the alias data type. Change the last line to

```
set my_folder to the result as alias
```

Now, when running the script for the first time, the last line returns

```
alias "Macintosh HD:Users:hanaan:Desktop:untitled folder:"
```

Any subsequent time you run the script, the resulting folder's name will be untitled folder 2, untitled folder 3, etc. This name difference will be reflected in the result of the script as well.

This unique reference works much like aliases in the Finder: it knows what file you're talking about even if it has been moved or renamed! This will come in handy.

Let's talk to the Finder again; write the following sixth line:

```
tell application "Finder" to set the name of my_folder to folder_name
```

What we did here is used the two variables we collected earlier in our script, *folder_name* and *my_folder*, to rename the folder we created.

In the seventh line we're going to ask the user to decide if s/he wants the folder deleted. Type the following line:

```
display dialog ("Delete new folder "& folder_name & "?") buttons
{"Yes", "No"}
```

The *display dialog* command has a few optional parameters, of which we will use the string that is the dialog's text and the buttons. By default a dialog box has two buttons: OK and Cancel.

Notice a couple of things:

1. We put the *("Delete new folder "& folder_name &"?")* operation in parentheses. While we didn't have to, it keeps things a little more organized, just like in math.
2. The result of a dialog box is a record. We won't get into records now, but just know that from that record we can understand what buttons the user pressed and other dialog-related stuff.

The following line we will add to the end of our script will put the dialog result into a variable. You can display the dialog box and collect the result into a variable in a single line, but not now.

```
set dialog_command_record to the result
```

The next few lines look inside the dialog result to determine if the user answered yes or no, and acts accordingly.

```
if button returned of dialog_command_record is "Yes" then
    tell application "Finder" to delete my_folder
end if
```

Notice that the variable *my_folder* knows what folder we mean even though the folder's name was changed earlier on. Your script should now look like the script in Figure 2-3.

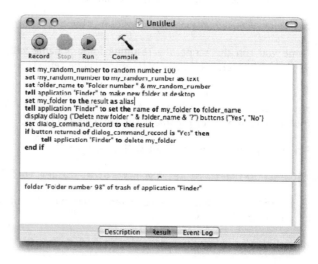

Figure 2-3. The script so far

More results with less talk

Let's discuss again the way AppleScript relates to expressions and results. We know that almost every line has a result that can be trapped. This is because every line is a statement. There are statements that do not return results, but they are the exception.

A statement can contain a single operation, or multiple operations, and return a single result. For instance, you can write the following:

```
set x to 3 + 4
set y to x * 5
set z to y - 37
set final_number_I_actually_want to z / 15
```

Or, you can make it a more math-like operation, and write

```
set final_number_I_actually_want to (((3 + 4) * 5)-37) / 15
```

The second choice may be a bit more confusing if you're not used to math, but it will be between 20% and 40% faster. That is because AppleScript has to only do the math without setting all these variables.

On top of that, the first example created three variables that we don't really need: x, y, and z. If we have to separate the operations into lines, we can either reuse the variable, or simply refer to the result of the previous line:

```
3 + 4
result * 5
result - 37
set final_number_I_actually_want to result / 15
```

Variable speed

Variables are the memory of AppleScript. Anytime you want to figure something out and use it later, you assign your conclusions to a variable. That value can be retrieved later and used anywhere in the script, simply by mentioning the variable.

Besides assigning values to variables, your job is also to name them. Naming variables logically can save you a lot of frustration later on. The variable name is called an identifier.

The basic rules for naming identifiers are these:

- Must start with a character
- May contain characters, digits, and an underscore (_)

Identifiers are case insensitive; however, when you've used a variable once in a script, AppleScript will remember how you typed it, and anywhere else that you use it, AppleScript will change the case of the letter to match the same pattern you used the first time.

Unlike many other programming languages, AppleScript allows you to assign any type of data to any variable. In other languages, when you create an identifier, you also tell it what data type it will hold. In AppleScript, you can create a variable and assign a text value to it, and later replace that value with a number. Makes no difference.

Let's try some variable things. Open a new Script Editor window and type the following:

```
set the_city to "Providence"
```

Since the word "Providence" is in quotes, AppleScript knows that it's literal text, or a string, and not an identifier. The identifier *the_city* now has the string value "Providence" assigned to it.

Let's type another line:

```
set the_state to "Rhode Island"
```

Now we can do something with these variables. Type a third and fourth line:

```
set my_greeting to "Hello, I live in " & the_city& ", " & the_state
display dialog my_greeting
```

See Figure 2-4.

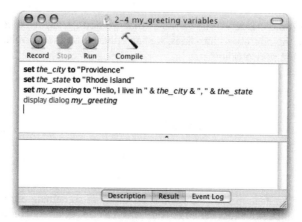

Figure 2-4.
The two variables assembled into a string that's assigned to a third variable

We use the & character to connect, or concatenate, the different strings, both the ones that are specified literally and the strings that are stored in the variables.

When you run the script, the dialog box displays the final greeting. See Figure 2-5.

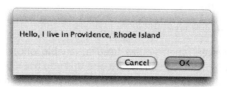

Figure 2-5. The script's resulting dialog box

Variables have a scope in which they're good. Outside of that scope they don't mean much. A bit like taking your cell phone to France and trying to make a call. If you didn't set up the phone to work there, it will most definitely not.

For now, we're not going to France, so there's nothing to worry about. But later on we will discuss in great detail the implications of using variables in handlers, global and local variables, and properties.

Values come in many classes

Value classes in AppleScript refer to the different ways we have to look at information. Information may be a number, it may be text, it may be either true or false, or it may be a reference to an object somewhere. Whatever it is, it's not only the actual value that makes a difference, but also the class of that value.

The basic classes are very logical:

Text

Also called a string, text is just that: a bunch of characters strung together. A string always has double quotes on either side. Here are some strings:

```
"A"
"My oh my! "
"IT IS SO ST&@%*"
"75"
```

Notice that even though we have the number 75, since it is in quotes, it is a string.

To concatenate strings together, you use the & character. For instance, the result of *"to"* & *"day"* is *"today"*.

The ampersand, or concatenation operator, can be used as a regular character inside a string if it is enclosed in quotes, as shown here:

```
"AT" & "&" & "T" --> "AT&T"
```

There are other types of strings, which we will discuss later.

Number

Numbers come in two flavors: integer and real. An integer is always a whole round number, and a real number can be either whole or decimal.

When performing math operations, you can mix and match reals and integers; however, the result will always be a real.

```
8.5 + 70 = 78.5
1.75 + 1.25 = 3.00
```

Boolean

Boolean is one of the most-often-used value classes. A Boolean value can be either true or false.

```
3 = 5 --> false
"BIG" is "big" --> true
disk "Macintosh HD" exists --> true
```

Tell me about it

The *tell* statement is AppleScript's way to get the attention of the object we want to direct commands to. Imagine a school, and you are a fly on the wall at the dean's office. The dean has a helper named AppleScript, who's in charge of making sure that the dean's commands get to the right place.

The first command the dean gives is "I need the report by tomorrow." The helper looks at him baffled; something is missing!

Oh, the dean finally got it: "Tell the student in the second seat in the first row of Ms. Steinberg's class that . . . I need the report by tomorrow." That's better.

Unless you're using statements that contain only AppleScript commands and objects, you have to use the *tell* statement to direct AppleScript to the right object. See, that object is the one containing the command, so just throwing the command out there or directing it to the wrong object will most likely generate an error.

For instance, if we happen to be scripting InDesign and we want to get the font of some text, we need to use the *tell* command to direct AppleScript to the text frame that is found on the page that is found in a specific document. If we tell the page to get the name of the font, we will get an error.

The many faces of tell

While using the *tell* statement is required, there are a few variations to how you can do it. They all work the same, but some are better than others in different situations. The main difference between the different ways of using the *tell* statement is in readability versus number of lines you use, so most of the decision is left up to you.

So what are the different ways to *tell*?

Let's get back to our dean. The dean used a long sentence that included the target object (the student) and the command in a single line: "Tell the student in the second seat in the first row of Ms. Steinberg's class that I need the report by tomorrow."

From that statement we can start to understand the school's object model (which is essential if it was a scriptable application), which is this: the main object is a school, in the school we have classroom objects, and each has a teacher. We can refer to the classroom by the teacher name! Also, each classroom has seats arranged in rows, and each seat has a student. That student has a name, age, and other useful school-related properties.

Now that we understand the object model a bit better, we realize that the dean could have also said to his helper AppleScript: "Tell Ms. Steinberg's class to tell the first row to tell the student in the second seat that the report is due . . ."

Notice how things got reversed? Now, instead of starting from the last object, we start at the top and go down: tell the class, followed by the row, followed by the seat, while before it was the seat that is in the row that is in the class.

How about a real example? Open Script Editor and type the script shown in Figure 2-6. Notice the ¬ character at the end of the first line, after the word "of." You get it by pressing *Option+Return*.

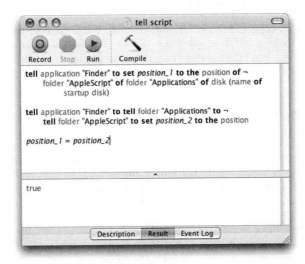

Figure 2-6. Use *Option+Return* to insert the line break character.

Look at the two different ways we target or request information to a specific folder. In the first one we use the *set* command directly after the first *tell* statement, and the specific folder is described as part of the *set* command.

In the second one, we place the *set* command at the end, after we singled out the folder.

Continuation character

Back to the little ¬ creature. This character is AppleScript's continuation character and is used to split long lines into more manageable chunks. It's used for readability only and has no effect on the script result.

You can insert the continuation character without also inserting a new line, by pressing *Option+L*.

Comparing results

One more thing we did in that script is comparing to see if the two results we got from the two lines were identical. For that we used the *equals* comparison operator. An operation that uses the comparison operator may have one of two results: true or false. In other words, the operation returns data of class Boolean. Comparison operators can be written in many ways that perform the same; for instance, we could have used "is equal to" instead of the simple = sign. Much more on operations and operators in Chapter 9.

Objects you can tell things to

Back to our main track here, the *tell* statement. Let's look at some so-called objects that like to be referred to with the *tell* statement.

The main type of object is your run-of-the-mill scriptable application. Anytime you want to send commands to an application, you have to start with the *tell* statement. Later on you will also see how you can load handlers or script objects into a variable, and that variable will become an object that likes to be told things.

Telling in blocks

The dean scratches his head. He realized that two more students from that same class owe him different reports. Now, when instructing his trusted helper, AppleScript, he may not want to use the entire reference to the student. Instead, he can start with "While you're in Ms. Steinberg's class, tell the kid in row 2, seat 4, the student in row 6, seat 1, and the student in row 3, seat 2 that they have reports due."

See, when writing scripts, many times you will want to single out an object and then use a few commands on it. What you won't want to do is use the entire object reference (file 1 of folder 4 of folder applications . . .). Instead, you can use a *tell* block. Here is how:

In a *tell* block, we start by singling out the object or objects we want to affect, then we give one or a few commands, and we finish with the line *end tell*.

For instance, in our Finder example, we got the folder's position. What if we want to get the modification date of the folder as well? Here is how we can do that: we start with the *tell* block. Write the lines shown in Figure 2-7 and click the Compile button.

Figure 2-7.
Your first *tell* block

The second line starts with a double dash. This makes it into a comment, which AppleScript ignores.

Now, add the lines shown in Figure 2-8.

Figure 2-8. Adding more levels to the *tell* block

Notice how each level of the *tell* block starts with the word "tell," ends with the word "end," and all the lines in between are indented for readability.

Now add the statements that get some properties from the folder, and from items that are in the folder. Figure 2-9 shows the final script.

Figure 2-9. The final script with the *tell* blocks

When you run the script, the result shows only the last line's result; however, the rest of the data you collected is safe and sound in the variables *file_list*, *time_folder_was_created*, and *time_folder_was_changed*.

More on Script Editor

One of the improvements OS X's AppleScript provided is the new Script Editor; it has many nice new features that are covered throughout the book. It has a customizable Aqua tool-bar that gives you access to the main features, and easy access to results, the event log, and their respective histories.

Event log

The event log is the Result feature on steroids, and can be found in the tab at the bottom of the Script Editor window. The event log logs the events that AppleScript sends, the object the commands are sent to, and the result returned by the object. In Figure 2-10 you can see the preceding script and the log it created when running.

The script in Figure 2-10 shows how your commands are translated and boiled down to a single *tell* block. Also you can easily see all the results the different statements had, only without the variables that store the result.

Figure 2-10. The response of the event log

Result history

If every script has a result, the Result History feature keeps track of them all in chronological order.

Choose Result History from the Window menu and click the clock-shaped History button. Figure 2-11 shows the Result History window.

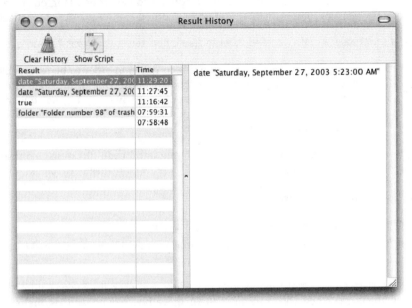

Figure 2-11. I ran the random number script multiple times, and the result history captured them all.

Script description

Clicking the Description tab at the bottom part of the script window in Script Editor reveals a large text field. You can write a description for your script and format it using the Format menu. Change the type size, font, and color as you like.

You can have that formatted text appear in a dialog box every time your script application is launched. To display the dialog box at launch, check Startup Screen when you save the script as an application.

Toolbar

You can customize the toolbar by choosing Customize Toolbar from the View menu, or by CONTROL-clicking the toolbar and choosing Customize Toolbar from the contextual menu.

My favorite is the ability to make the icons smaller, or make them go all together. You can also choose to add icons for a bunch of other features. The toolbar can be hidden altogether by clicking the pill-shaped hide toolbar button at the right of the script window's title bar.

Recording scripts

Here's recording in a nutshell: you press the Record button in Script Editor, do some stuff in another application, and everything you do is recorded in the AppleScript language.

OK, if it's that easy, why do we need to write a script ourselves ever again? Good question.

While recording is nice, not every application is recordable. In order to be recordable, an application has to get a time-consuming programming boost. One of the main efforts of the AppleScript team with OS X implementation of the technology was not only on the core of AppleScript, but also on the ease in which software vendors can implement script-ability and recordability in their own applications.

When you record scripts, you get a computer-generated code. It doesn't contain any repeat loops, handlers, conditional statements, or easy-to-manage *tell* blocks. For the most part, recording scripts is great if you can't figure out how to script a specific aspect of an application. For instance:

- In OS X Jaguar, the Finder isn't yet recordable, but . . .
- In OS X Panther, the Finder is at least partially recordable, which can make your life a little easier.

To test it, start a new script window in Script Editor and click the Record button in the toolbar. Then, create new windows, move them, move files around, and see the recorded actions.

As you can tell, some basic actions do not get recorded, such as closing windows and moving and duplicating files.

Spaces don't count

Extra spaces and tabs will be cleaned up when you check syntax, so don't bother with them. Also, indentation will happen automatically.

You can, for readability's sake, leave some blank lines here and there. AppleScript will leave those alone.

To add text that you want the script to ignore, precede it with a double dash. This will compile as a comment.

Adding comments is essential if you want to understand what either you yourself meant when you wrote that script a couple of months ago, or worse, if someone else has to figure out what your code tries to achieve. It is amazing how even our own scripts can become a jungle of code after a while.

Another reason to comment scripts is that when you're creating scripts that are part of a large system, these comments will be a part of your technical specifications. Clients take well to scripters who comment their scripts.

Understanding applications' scriptability

As we talked about earlier, the success of AppleScript greatly depends on AppleScript implementation by independent software vendors, much like the success of OS X depends on the support and implementation of the same software vendors.

While the quality and thoroughness of AppleScript implementation in applications is up to the individual vendors, there are a few rules they all go by, and for the most part, many applications have shown a beautiful object model and a rich set of commands.

One of the main areas on which the AppleScript team is spending development resources is helping developers streamline and ease the burden of making their applications scriptable.

The application scripting dictionary

The application dictionary contains a listing and some descriptions of the application's entire array of objects and commands. A dictionary is your first stop for anything to do with the scriptability of a specific application. For me, it's also a way to divide applications into the two major groups they fall into: scriptable and nonscriptable.

The dictionary for any scriptable application can be viewed in Script Editor by choosing Open Dictionary from the File menu, and choosing an application from the application list. The dictionary of the selected application will be displayed in the dictionary window. Figure 2-12 shows the dictionary of the Finder.

As you can see in Figure 2-12, an application's dictionary is segmented into suites. The suites are organized in a logical way in order to help you find the information you need.

In each suite you will find both classes and commands. Classes are the object types and commands are the AppleScript commands of that application that are related to the suite.

Classes in the dictionary

Each object type, or class, is listed in its respective suite, a listing that includes specific details about that class.

There are two main types of information you will find for every class. The first type of information is *elements*. Under the *elements* heading are listed the potential elements a class could have once it is an actual object in the application. For instance, among the elements of the *folder* class are folder, file, alias, clipping, etc. Disk is not an element of the *folder* class since a folder can never contain an object of the class *disk*.

The other type of information listed for a given class is that class's properties. Properties can be read using the *get* command, and changed using the *set* command. Not all properties can be set, however. Properties that are denoted with *r/o* are read only, and therefore can't be changed, only read.

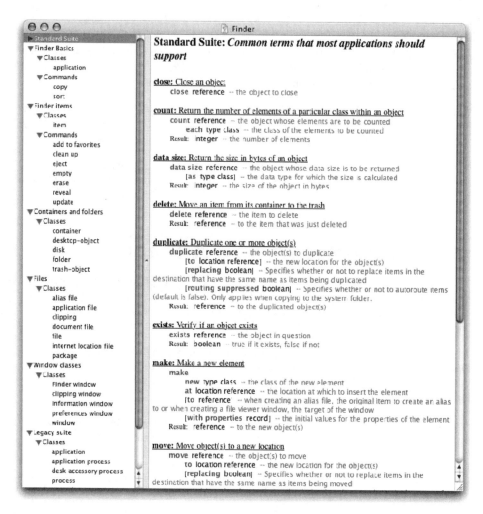

Figure 2-12. The Finder's dictionary as shown in Script Editor

Commands in the dictionary

The commands in the dictionary are listed along with a brief description, followed by the command's syntax and parameters. The optional parameters are listed in square brackets.

Following is an example taken from the Finder's dictionary. The example shows the listing of the *update* command:

```
update: Update the display of the specified object(s)
to match their on-disk representation
update  reference -- the item to update
```

```
    [necessity boolean] -- only update if necessary (i.e. a finder ¬
window is open).  default is false
    [registering applications boolean] -- register applications.
default is true
```

The description of the *update* command is great. You read it and there's no doubt of what the command does.

The required parameter for the command is the reference to the object you want to update.

The optional parameters are *necessity*, which is explained well, and *registering applications*, which I have no idea what it's good for or what it does. The dictionary author either got a bit lazy, or simply didn't know the answer either.

At their mercy

While dictionaries are invaluable for any scripter, they are sometimes badly written and incomplete. Not that they lack commands or classes, but many times dictionaries are written as an afterthought, not taking into account the immense difference a good dictionary can make to the scripter who tries to automate that application. The amount of details and level of clarity that is invested in dictionaries is solely up to the dictionary authors, and the range of acceptable detail is high. For instance, when the properties are listed for a specific class, the dictionary usually mentions something in regard to the value that property accepts. Some properties only accept a list, string, or number; some can accept only specific keywords that are part of that application, such as the *owner privileges* property of the *item* class in the finder. The values can be read only, read write, write only, or none. If the dictionary doesn't specify them, you have to backwards-engineer objects to see what they are set to in order to use the property in your script. While the Finder's dictionary does list these options, some dictionaries lack basic information, a thing that can make scripting very frustrating.

Another thing that dictionaries lack by nature is class-command links. The dictionary does not show you which class accepts which commands. For instance, the Finder dictionary contains the class *window* and the command *duplicate*, but that doesn't mean that you can duplicate a window. How commands and classes interact is information you have to get in other places such as books, Internet lists, or sample scripts that come with the application.

The object model

Perhaps the most compelling part of application scriptability is its object model.

The idea of an object model is that a higher-level object can have elements. These elements are objects by themselves, possibly of a different kind or class, and these objects may have elements of their own. Usually, the number of elements can be anywhere from zero and up, but sometimes applications will allow only one child element per object.

This type of hierarchy is called containership hierarchy, since it describes what objects contain which elements, and which elements are contained by what objects.

Let's look at Adobe InDesign's object model as an example: the InDesign *application* object has a high-level object element called *document*. As you know, you can have multiple documents. The document is also an object in its own right, and can have its own child elements such as spreads, layers, etc. Spreads can have many pages, each page has text frames, guides, etc. The document, in other words, contains these pages, layers, etc.

Like many other applications, in InDesign, you can ask for the object model in reverse as well: the parent of a specific text frame may be a specific page, etc. As you may have guessed, any object may have only one parent object. Figure 2-13 shows a partial view of InDesign's containment hierarchy. By looking at it you can clearly see what objects have the capacity to contain elements of which classes.

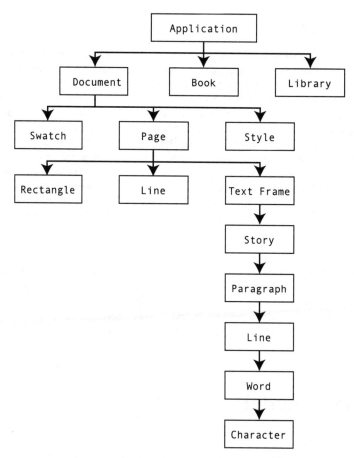

Figure 2-13. InDesign's containment hierarchy

Well, I guess that AppleScript is a single parent world where everyone is an object and the value can be found only in his or her property; sad.

Objects and class inheritance

Class inheritance is not the same as containment hierarchy. Class inheritance describes how classes share similarities with classes that inherit their attributes. Understanding class inheritance can allow you to refer to a narrower or broader range of objects, as you see fit. For example, you may ask the Finder to delete items in one of the following three versions:

1. Delete every item of disk 1.

2. Delete every file of disk 1.

3. Delete every document file of disk 1.

These three statements are different such that the first one will delete the broadest range of objects, which will include any folder or application on disk 1, since they are also items. The second version will delete only files, not folders, but will still delete applications, since the *application* class is also a descendent of the *file* class. The third version is the narrowest. Every document file is also a file and also an item, but not every file or item is a document file.

A class is a group of like objects. For instance, in the Finder, there's an *item* class. This class includes files, folders, applications, and every other item you can have in a hard disk somewhere. The *item* class has a subclass called *container*. The *container* is a subclass of the *item* class. A folder is both an item and a container; a file on the other hand is an item, but not a container. In InDesign, a *page item* is a class of which rectangle, text frame, and graphic line are all members.

In order to understand how classes work, we have to look at the way they inherit properties from one another. Every class has a super class. This super class is the class that is higher on the chain. It's a more basic and generic version of all subclasses that spawn off of it. This is not the same as parent and child objects, since parent and child objects, as described earlier, may be from different classes.

Let's look at a real-life analogy to classes. Take dogs; dogs are a class. The dogs class has a few subclasses: terriers, herding dogs, poodles, etc. The dogs class is also a part of another class, mammals, which makes the mammals class the dogs class's super class. The mammals class by itself is a subclass of the class living beings. That last class, living beings, is the top super class; any subclass of the living being class by default inherits all of its properties. For instance, all living beings are born, then they live, and then they die. That is true for mammals, dogs, and terriers. However, every member of the dogs class walks on four legs, which is not true for all members of the mammals class, which is the dogs class's super class.

In the application InDesign, we have a class called *base page item properties*. This class has all the properties that are shared by all of its subclasses: *page item, oval, rectangle, graphic line, polygon, text frame, image, PDF, EPS, group,* and *master page item*.

Classes and commands

Classes also share commands with their subclasses. For instance, the Finder's *item* class understands commands such as *duplicate* and *delete*. That ability to understand these commands also passes to all of the *item* class subclasses such as *file*, *folder*, etc.

Classes may be a bit intimidating in the beginning, and you may be asking yourself just how essential it is to get that info down. Well, classes are very important, and although you should be grateful they exist and define and make life more organized, don't kill yourself trying to understand them right now. You can take care of a dog just fine without dwelling on the evolutionary reasons for the existence of its tail.

What makes an object what it is?
A look at object properties

Properties is where the relationship between a class of objects and the objects themselves becomes clear. While a class has all the properties that all objects of that class have, the objects themselves have something the class doesn't: values. For example, in the Finder we have a class *File*. That class has a property called *File Type*. The class however is not an actual file; it's only a theoretical idea. On the other hand, a file on the hard disk is a real file, and the property *File Type* of that file actually has a value, which tells us the file type of that particular file.

Object properties are much like people properties. We all share the same set of properties in the class human, it's just that the values are different for each of us. For instance, we have a height property. Each one of us has a number we can give the nurse at our annual checkup. This number is written on the form at the specific place and used for some health-related voodoo. In AppleScript, object properties are used in similar ways: there are objects, let's say files in the Finder. In our script, we pinpoint the file we want to deal with and we inspect its properties. We figure out that the size property of the file is 2MB. We write that in our script in a variable and later use it in some AppleScript voodoo.

There are two ways to see which object properties AppleScript has access to. One is the application's AppleScript dictionary, and the other is the *get properties* command.

When you use the dictionary in Script Editor, you can click any item under the Classes disclosure triangle. The right side of the screen will then show you the properties of the class you clicked (remember, class is another word for object type, so a class has all the properties of all the objects that are a part of that class).

Figure 2-14 shows the FileMaker Pro 7 dictionary in Script Editor.

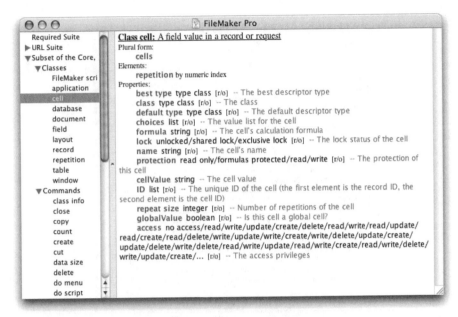

Figure 2-14. The FileMaker Pro dictionary shown in Script Editor. The *cell* class is clicked on the left and all of the *cell* class properties are showing on the right.

The advantage of using the dictionary to examine a class's properties is that the dictionary often comes with helpful hints. As you can see in Figure 2-14, the FileMaker Pro dictionary has a nice explanation after each property. This can be an invaluable source of knowledge, especially because it is not always obvious what type or range of value the property will agree to. After every property in the dictionary either the data type or actual values you can use are specified. For example, the FileMaker dictionary shows you that the *lock* property of the *cell* class can have one of the following three values: *unlocked*, *shared lock*, or *exclusive lock*.

Get properties

Getting the properties of an object or class using the *get properties* command is a bit different. Not only do you get the list of property names, but you also get the value of each property for a specific object.

Let's try and get the properties for a single file in the Finder. We will first need to identify the file whose properties we want to get. To do that we're going to use the *choose file* command, which returns an alias reference to the file. After putting that alias result in a variable, we will ask the Finder to get us the properties of that file. Create a new script window and type the four lines shown in Figure 2-15.

Figure 2-15. The properties of a chosen file

The result of the script is a record that contains about 30 properties associated with the file class, and their values that apply to the actual file you chose.

While the *get properties* statement seems like its own little command, it is not. The command is actually the verb "get," while the word "properties" is simply another object property. Some object properties return a number, such as *size*; some return text, such as *name*. The *properties* property returns a record that includes all of the other properties. We will discuss records in detail later on, but for now, just imagine the record as a list of values with their labels. Each piece of data has the identifying label that tells us what the data stands for, and the actual value. Looking at the file properties we got (Figure 2-15), we can see that the chunks of data are separated by commas, but each chunk is separated by a colon. Here is a part of it:

```
name:"first book script", index:3, displayed name:"first book script",
name extension:"", extension hidden:false
```

You can easily tell that the value of the property *name* is *"first book script"*, the index is *3*, extension hidden is *false*, etc.

The *properties* property exists in most objects in most applications, so it's almost a sure bet that you will get the results you want if you try it. All you have to make sure of is that you have a valid object reference (see "How to talk to objects so they listen" later in this chapter).

Read only

As you look at a class's properties in the dictionary, some properties will have "r/o" written next to them. These properties are read only, which means that you can ask to see their value, but you can't change it.

While initially it appears to be a questionable restriction, some properties were simply not meant to be tampered with or are naturally unchangeable. Let's take for example the scriptability of the Address Book application. When you create a new person, that person gets a *creation date* property. While being able to use AppleScript to get the creation date of a person is nice, it would not make any sense if you could change that date; it would no longer be the creation date, but just any date.

If you try to change the value of a read-only property, as in the script shown in Figure 2-16, you get an error as shown in Figure 2-17.

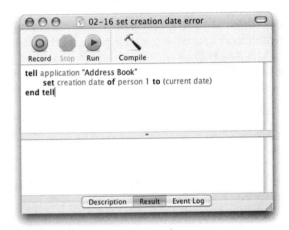

Figure 2-16. A lame attempt at changing a read-only property

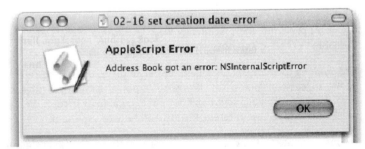

Figure 2-17. Trying to set the *creation date* property of a person generates an error.

Property, inheritance, and class!

Remember that confusing "class" discussion we had a couple of pages ago? Well, let's try and recall some of it.

We saw that objects belong to classes, and classes may have subclasses and super classes. We also separated them from the containment hierarchy, which is the way objects may be elements of other projects (like a text frame is an element on a page). Classes are for classification purposes only, but they have a very strong connection with object properties. So, take a dose of virtual dope and dive in:

How are properties inherited from super classes? OK, take a mental look at your entertainment center's media organizer. It has lots of tapes, CDs DVDs, VHS tapes, etc. What name can we use to describe *all* those things? How about media units? Good, now what characteristics can we define that will make sense for all media units? Type of media (that may include CD, DVD, VHS, etc.), length of time, genre, format, language, etc. Now let's look at one of the media unit types. How about DVD movies? DVD movies are a subclass of the media unit class, and media units are the super class of the DVD movies class. If we look at all the distinctive properties of a DVD movie, we'll find that some are unique to DVDs, such as ratio (3:4 or 16:9), or whether the movie is subtitled or not. Other properties, however, are inherited from the media unit class. In fact, the DVD movie class inherits *all* of its super class properties.

The point is that classes and inheritance of properties is not some far-fetched programming concept; it's a concept that can be found anywhere in the programming language of life.

Every class inherits all of the properties of its super class: the *text frame* class has all of the properties of its *page item* super class; the *folder* class has all of the properties of the *container* super class, etc.

How to talk to objects so they listen

As we already know, in order to have your commands obeyed, you must address the recipient correctly. In AppleScript, there are many ways to address objects in a way that will make them eligible to receive and obey your commands.

These ways of pointing to an object are called reference forms. Mastering reference forms is crucial to the success of your script. If you can't point to the right object using the appropriate reference form, your script will not be as reliable as it could be. The coming section will help you understand reference forms and how to use them.

Let's go back for a minute to the dean at our made-up school. The dean's job today is to assign extracurricular duties to students. Before naming the duties that need to be carried out (command) he needs to identify the students who will perform the tasks. Based on what we know so far, he can finger each student individually: tell the student in seat 4 of row 8 of Mr. Popokovich's class that his duty is dishwashing at the cafeteria. Or, in slightly different words: the duty of student of seat 4 of row 8 of Mr. Popokovich's class is dishwashing. While this is all good, our poor dean will realize soon enough that in order to name all the students and duties for the day, he will need to spend the entire afternoon assigning duties! He needs a better system.

Object names

2

Many applications allow you to name, or label, objects. The name of the object makes it easier to refer to it; however, it is up to you to name it in the first place. Object names are simply another property of the object. Just like, say, the width of the object, its position, its size, or color; the object's name is just one more piece of information that you can use to get the object's attention.

Some applications, such as the Finder, have a natural naming structure already in place. Also in Adobe Illustrator you can use the Layers palette to name objects, a name that can be later used in a script to refer to that object.

The use of object names or labels can prove invaluable when automating graphics applications: assigning a graphic frame on an InDesign page the label "chart" will allow your script to later import the image chart.EPS into that frame. If you've done your job, then there will be one page item labeled "chart" on that page, and the script will work even if you move that frame around.

One thing to remember about naming or labeling objects is that referencing those objects using the name still depends a whole lot on the way the application has implemented the object model. Here are a few examples:

In the OS X Finder, objects actually have a few name-related properties on top of the *name* property, such as *display name* and *name extension*. Also in the Finder, you can only work with files in a single folder at a time, so writing

```
delete every file whose name contains "temp"
```

will only delete files in the folder you're referring to, not the entire hard drive.

In InDesign and in Illustrator you can refer to all objects in the entire document that have a certain name, but InDesign will omit the items that are a part of a group.

May I see some ID please?

While names are useful, some applications use an additional identifier for objects: unique ID.

Unlike naming and labeling objects, an object's unique ID is assigned by the application and is a read-only property, which means that you can't change it, only look at it. That aspect of a unique ID is what makes is so useful: while the name of the object can be changed by either a script or in the user interface, an ID is created automatically when the object is created, and stays with the object until it is deleted, or the page it's on is deleted.

Unique IDs are an essential reference form since, unlike the *name* and *index* properties, they are truly unique. You have to be aware that the *id* property for a particular object may change the next time you launch the application. Also, the format of the property may change from application to application. In InDesign, object IDs are a three-digit integer or higher. In Address Book, a person's ID may look like this: 03CEBE56-CA2B-11D6-8B0C-003065F93D88:ABPerson.

Applications that assign IDs to objects are InDesign, Quark, FileMaker, Address Book, iCal, BBEdit, and more. However, these applications do not: Mail, Illustrator, Photoshop, Safari, and Excel.

Every . . . whose

The *whose* clause, also known as the test reference form, is one of the most powerful programming constructs in the AppleScript language. It gives you the ability to group objects into subsets out of a larger set of objects based on their shared attributes. OK, so that was loaded. Let's break it down. Whenever you examine any group of objects, some of them are similar in different ways. If a folder contains 50 files, 20 of them may be TIFF files, 10 may be aliases, 8 may be larger than 10MB, and some may be older than a month. On an InDesign page you may have 30 page items: 10 of them may be lines, 22 may have a stroke of 1 point, and 20 may have a blue fill. Notice that I named properties that are unrelated: in the Finder, the same file can be over 10MB and under a month old, and may or may not be a TIFF file.

This way of grouping objects allows you to easily and logically refer to just the objects you want to affect.

Our dean, for instance, had a thought: "I can simply say 'Every student whose grade average is C or lower has dishwashing duty today.'" Ouch! Way too mean, but it would have worked.

In some applications, however, you can use an unlimited combinations of *whose* clauses and commands. Here are a few:

Script 2-1

```
tell application "InDesign CS"
  tell page 1 of document 1
    delete every text frame whose contents is " "
  end tell
end tell
```

The entire set we reference here is the set of text frames on page 1. Using the *whose* clause, we can single out the text frames that contain no text and delete them.

Script 2-2

```
set the_folder to path to documents folder from user domain
tell application "Finder"
```

```
        duplicate (every file of the_folder whose size is greater than ¬
            (2 * 1000000))
    end tell
```

In the Finder, the set of objects is all the files in the documents folder. The script though only wants to duplicate the files that are larger than 2MB.

Script 2-3

```
    tell application "FileMaker Pro"
      tell table  "guests" of database "party"
        set kids_list to cell "name" of every record whose cell "age" is ¬
            less than 12
      end tell
    end tell
```

In this script, we will end up with a list of names of all the party guests who are younger than 12.

When you work with an application that doesn't support the *whose* clause, you have to settle for slower, clumsier repeat loops.

Index and range reference forms

The *index* and *range* reference forms both use integers to reference objects. To use the *index* reference form, you type the class name followed by the position of the specific object you want. For instance, to get the first file of the second folder you can type file 1 of folder 2. The *index* reference form uses the order of the object, in the way the application defines that order. In the Finder, for instance, the files are arranged alphabetically. In page layout applications the order of page elements is determined based on their stacking order: the topmost item is always item 1. Some objects' order, such as pages, is easy to determine.

The *index* reference form is especially useful when working with an application's documents. Even if the extent of it is the use of *tell document 1*, it saves the scripter from having to figure out the document's name or ID.

The *index* reference form works from the back as well by specifying negative numbers. The last item is also item -1, one before last is item -2, etc.

Another way to use the *index* reference form is with number words such as first, second, and third, like this: third application file of last folder.

The *range* reference form is a variation of the *index* reference form. It allows you to reference an entire range of objects, instead of one object at a time. You do that by specifying the index of the first item in the range you want, followed by the word "thru," and then followed by the index of the last item in the range: pages 3 thru 6, files 1 thru 10, etc.

Ranges are often used when scripting different aspects of text. The following script extracts a portion of a file's name:

Script 2-4

```
tell application "Finder"
   tell folder "In" of disk "Jobs"
      tell file 1
         set job_number to (characters 3 thru 9 of name of it) ¬
            as string
      end tell
   end tell
end tell
```

Relatives

Relative reference refers to references that rely on a position of another object. For instance, the reference paragraph after paragraph 3 requires that paragraph 3 will be a valid reference in order for it to be valid itself. If there's no paragraph 3, then you can't use the reference paragraph after paragraph 3 or the paragraph before paragraph 3.

The following example loops through the paragraphs in the first TextEdit document and creates a document that is a reverse version of the document where the first paragraph is last, the last is first, etc. The way the script works is by always using the *paragraph after . . .* reference form. The reference of the last paragraph according to the script is

```
paragraph after paragraph after paragraph after paragraph
after paragraph after paragraph 1 of document 1
```

This is due to the fact that I had five lines in the front document.

Here is the entire script:

Script 2-5

```
1. tell application "TextEdit"
2.    tell document 1
3.       set paragraph_count to count (get paragraphs of it)
4.       set current_paragraph to a reference to paragraph 1 of it
5.       set reverse_text to ""
6.       repeat with i from 1 to paragraph_count
7.          if i is equal to paragraph_count then
8.             set reverse_text to current_paragraph & return & ¬
                 reverse_text
9.          else
10.            set reverse_text to current_paragraph & reverse_text
11.         end if
12.         set current_paragraph to (a reference to paragraph after ¬
               current_paragraph)
```

```
13.      end repeat
14.   end tell
15.   set new_document to make new document at end
16.   set text of new_document to reverse_text
17. end tell
```

Objects and commands they understand

As a general rule, different objects are designed to respond to different commands. For instance, the *rectangle* object can understand the *rotate* command, while the *page* object unfortunately can't.

While it's basic for scripting to know what objects can handle which commands, and as important to know how to phrase the command in a way that will give you a result and not an error, it's sometimes difficult to find that connection.

The dictionary is not much help on that matter. It lists all the events (commands) and all the classes (objects), but doesn't make a connection between them.

The best place to go for that information is to the scripting guide that comes with most scriptable applications, or to sample code that ships with the application.

Making your own commands

Do you know those people who start on a subject, like how their day went, but they get entangled in the small details, which bring up little related thoughts and more details, and soon enough you forget where they started and they forgot where they were going with the conversation? OK, so I can be like that sometimes, but the last thing I want is to have my scripts behave like that as well.

So how can we organize our scripts to be more punctual and stick to the point?

When you write scripts, you use statements. Those statements have some purpose that is bigger than the individual statement itself. For instance, when you need a part of the script to create a folder, you may want to first figure out if a folder with that name already exists at that location. Part of getting all that done may be to write a statement that returns the list of files in a folder, a statement that renames a folder, a statement that creates a folder, etc.

The result is that even though you had a single purpose in mind, that purpose got translated into quite a few lines of AppleScript code. Wouldn't it be nicer if we had a single command that checks if a folder exists, renames it if it does, and then makes a folder?

While there's no such command in AppleScript to date, AppleScript does give you the chance to create one! This means that *you* can create the command that does all that, and then, in your script, you can just tell that command to execute, or in AppleScript words, call that command.

Creating your own commands, also called handlers or subroutines, will have a positive effect on the organization, readability, flexibility, portability, and modificationability of your script (OK, so I made up a word—it's my book, after all . . .) We will discuss the implication of handlers on scripts in later chapters.

There are two ways to write handlers in AppleScript. You can either use positional parameters or labeled parameter handlers. The easier form is positional parameters, and therefore we will start by creating those. In Chapter 18 we will get into labeled parameter handlers as well.

For now, let's look at the basic anatomy of a handler.

A handler has two aspects: the handler definition and the handler call. The call is simply stating the name of the handler, possibly including a few parameters. A handler call may look like this: *my_command()*.

The term *my_command* is not a part of AppleScript. Beside bragging rights for your handler, you also have naming rights. That's true, you get to give your handler any name that is not a reserved word. You should also make sure that the name of the handler is descriptive.

Start a new script window and type the handler call in, like in Figure 2-18.

Figure 2-18.
A handler call

Now run the script, and you'll get the result shown in Figure 2-19.

Figure 2-19. When the script looked for the handler definition and couldn't find it, it generated an error.

The script found a command but didn't know what to do with it. This is our fault; we never shared with the script the specifics of the plan. Let's do that now.

Add a couple of blank lines and add the following lines (see Figure 2-20):

```
on my_command()
--command here!
end my_command
```

Figure 2-20.
The handler definition

The lines we added are the "wrap" for the handler definition. Whatever AppleScript code we add between those lines will be the code that AppleScript will execute when the *my_command* handler is called.

To see it run, let's insert a simple *display dialog* command into the *my_command* handler.

Insert the following line between the *on my_command()* and *end my_command* lines:

```
display dialog "Hello Handler!"
```

See Figure 2-21.

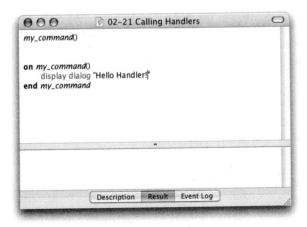

Figure 2-21. The script
runs, the *my_command*
handler is called,
and the code in the
handler is executed.

What will happen if the handler is never called? Try commenting the calling line: insert two dashes before the line that calls the handler.

```
--my_command()
```

Now run the script and see that nothing happens. Handler definitions that never get called just sit there and do nothing.

Even though handlers are thoroughly covered in Chapter 17, they are an important enough subject to touch on a few different items in the next sections.

Handlers can deal with arguments

The handler we created is designed to display the same dialog box every time, which is good if that's what we want. However, what if we want the same dialog box, but different text every time? Or even different buttons? Let's give it a whirl.

When you want a handler to process different information each time it runs, you need to somehow supply it that information. This is done using arguments that are passed inside the parentheses. We will start with one argument for the dialog box text and then add another one for the button's text.

An argument you pass to a handler is touched on at least twice if you want the script to run, and a third time or more if you want the argument to be used in the handler.

The way to pass an argument to a handler is by creating a special variable name and placing it in the parentheses in the first line of the handler definition. This variable is called a *parameter variable* because a parameter value passes to it during the handler call.

When the handler runs, any value that is found in the parentheses of the handler call will be the value of the parameter variable in the handler's definition.

To see all that work, type the variable name dialog_text in the handler definition parentheses. Then, to supply the value for that variable, type "Hello!", including the quotes, in the handler call's parentheses. Your script should look like the one in Figure 2-22.

If you run the script now you will see that the dialog box still says "Hello Handler!". To make the dialog box display the text we give it when we call the handler (Hello!), we need to replace the text in the *dialog* command with the variable that contains the text we passed from the handler call. That would be the variable *dialog_text*.

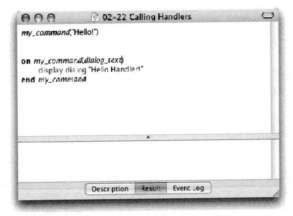

Figure 2-22. When the handler *my_command* is called, the variable *dialog_text* in the handler is going to be replaced with the text "Hello!" from the handler call line.

Figure 2-23 shows how the revised script will look.

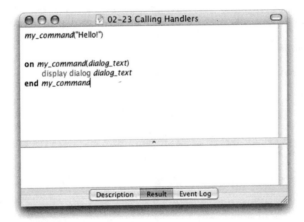

Figure 2-23. The parameter variable *dialog_text* is used in the *display dialog* command. The string "Hello!" specified in the handler call is passed to the parameter variable *dialog_text*, and is later used in the handler.

Try to run the script.

Now, copy the line of script that calls the handler (the first line in the script), and paste it in a new line just below. Change the argument text in the second line to "Goodbye . . .". See Figure 2-24.

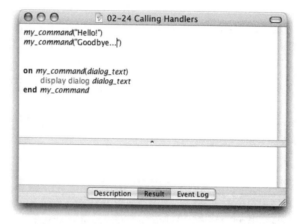

Figure 2-24. The same handler is called twice.

When you run the script now, the same handler will be called twice, each time with a different message.

To add a second parameter that will be used for the button name, you have to add a comma followed by the second parameter variable in the first line of the handler definition:

```
on my_command(dialog_text, button_text)
```

Just for kicks, try to run the script . . . see Figure 2-25.

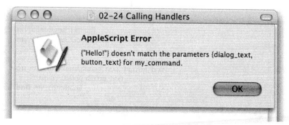

Figure 2-25. The error says that while the handler definition has two parameter variables, the handler call specifies only one.

To fix that, add a comma and a string in quotes, one after the word "Hello!" and one after the word "Goodbye . . ." in the two handler calls. See Figure 2-26.

Also, notice the *buttons* addition to the *display dialog* command.

Run the script and see the dialog box appears twice with a different button each time.

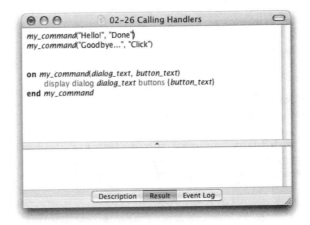

Figure 2-26. Another parameter variable has been added to both the handler call and definition and used as the button name.

Handlers return results

The next handler we will write will do a little calculation for us and return the result of the calculation.

While handlers can return results, they don't always, and even if they do, you don't always need to use that result.

If we don't specify the result we want the handler to return, it will automatically return the result of the last line on the handler. For instance, in the last part we ran a handler that displayed a dialog box. The last statement of the handler returned the following result:

```
{button returned:"Click"}
```

Therefore, the entire handler returned that same result. Not that we care, however, since we didn't trap that result, intend to do anything with it, or care if it comes back as a particular data type.

In the next mini-script we'll create a handler that returns a result. In fact, that handler will be completely useless unless it returns that result since it's going to do nothing other than calculate some numbers. If the result is lost, the handler is useless.

So how do we trap the result of a handler? Simple: we assign it to a variable. For instance, if we have a handler that calculates the distance between two cities, we might call it in the following way:

```
set the_distance to calculate_distance("Providence, RI", ¬
"San Francisco, CA")
```

Whatever the result is (which is hopefully the distance between the two cities) will be assigned to the variable *the_distance*.

Try the following example:

Script 2-6

```
set year_born_dialog_result to ¬
   display dialog "What year were you born in?" ¬
   default answer "19XX" buttons {"OK"}
set year_born to text returned of year_born_dialog_result
set the_person_age to get_person_age(year_born)
display dialog ("Then you must be " & the_person_age & " years old")

to get_person_age(year_born)
   set year_born_as_date to date ("1/1/" & year_born)
   set the_age_in_seconds to ¬
        (current date) - year_born_as_date
   set the_age to the_age_in_seconds / 60 / 60 / 24 / 365
   set the_age to round the_age
   return the_age
end get_person_age
```

In the example, the result of the *get_person_age* handler call on line 3 is assigned to the variable *the_person_age*.

A few things to notice: first, in the handler call we use the same variable as in the handler parameter variable. It may or may not be the same variable. As discussed in an earlier section, a variable used inside a handler is completely separate from variables used outside of the handler, unless a variable is declared as global or as a property. We will discuss that in further detail later on. Second, the first word in the handler declaration is "to" instead of "on." These words can be used interchangeably.

> In line 6 of the preceding script we create a date that is formatted like this: *M/D/YYYY*. This should work on any Mac whose date format in International preferences has not been changed. If the date format has been changed, then this script may not work.

Since so far we worked with positional parameter handlers, the order of the parameter variables and the values that are passed to them in the handler call have a material importance. If you flipped them around, the value you intended to use for one variable will be assigned to a different one. This may return an error, or worst, the wrong result, which will send you into a mad search for what went wrong.

This was an introduction to variables. Much more on that subject appears throughout the book, and specifically in Chapter 8, which is dedicated to variables.

3 VALUES

I love the big

```
et my_string to "tic-tac-toe
et my_list to every character of my
et my_new_string to ""

epeat with the_character in my_lis
    --display dialog the_character
    if the_character as string is "t"
        set my_new_string to my_
    else
        set my_new_string to my_
    end if
nd repeat
isplay dialog my_new_string
```

Record   Stop   Run   Compile

```
set text_file_path to (choose file) a
set file_text to read file text_file_p
set text item delimiters to {return}

set database_records_list to every
repeat with i from 1 to (count iter
    set the_database_record to it
    set text item delimiters to tab
    set field_list to every text iten
    set the_name to item 1 of fiel
```

Values are the bits of information that we use when we talk AppleScript: the numbers we use, the text we display or store in different ways, dates and times we calculate different things with, and any other piece of information.

When we speak the AppleScript language, it's important to notice the distinction between giving commands and the information that we use to make the command mean something. Just like when we speak English, we can have this exchange:

"Hey what time is it?"

"Hmmm . . . It's quarter of four, I need to get to the bank before it closes and withdraw $60 to pay Dan and Gail for helping me paint."

In AppleScript this would have been the following (although this is not a real script):

```
set time_bank_closes to date "5/22/2003 4:00 PM"
set time_to_get_to_bank to 15
set time_left_until_bank_closes to ¬
time_bank_closes - current date - 18 minutes
if time_left_until_bank_closes > time_to_get_to_bank then
    set my_money to withdraw 60 from bank
    set list_of_people_to_pay to {"Dan", "Gail"}
    give (my_money / 2) to (item 1 of list_of_people_to_pay)
    give (my_money / 2) to (item 2 of list_of_people_to_pay)
end if
```

In the preceding example we gave a few commands, such as *set*, *withdraw*, and *give*, (which are commands found in the application Life, yet to be scriptable . . .). The commands themselves, however, don't mean much without the values we attach to them: dates and times that represent the bank closing time, amount of money I have to withdraw, and the list of people I have to give it to.

These values, or bits of information, get their meaning not only from the data itself, but also from the *type* of information they represent. For instance, the money I have to pay Dan and Gail is stored in the script as a number. The significance of that is there are certain things I can do with numbers that I can't do with text, for instance, math! I could take the amount I withdrew and divide it by 2. I also did some math with the dates to figure out if I'm too late to get to the bank. The result of these calculations was a number as well.

What about the people I had to give money to? Each one of them was represented as text, or a string in AppleScript terms. The names of the two people, however, were clumped together in what we call a list, which we will look at in a bit.

The different types of data we use in AppleScript are called classes, and the pieces of data are referred to as values. In AppleScript, then, the types of information we use are called value classes.

While in AppleScript there are about 14 value classes, and some of these divide into even smaller groups, there are a handful that we use constantly: numbers, text, and Boolean. Boolean, the only class that may need a basic introduction, is a value class that can have one of two values: true or false.

The fourth one I want to cover alongside number, text, and Boolean is list; as I mentioned earlier, a list isn't really a single piece of information, but rather a cluster of information. A list is made out of items, and each item can be a value from any value class.

A list is a sort of a compound value class that is infinitely useful. It is dynamic, which means you can add items to it, and you can retrieve individual items from it at any time. We will delve more into lists in a bit, and explore its many uses throughout the book.

Stringing characters

3

One of the things you will find yourself doing a lot in AppleScript is working with text in one way or another. The following sections look at the many aspects of text manipulation in AppleScript.

What can we do with text?

While the official word for text I'll use in the book is "string," it is basically text. The *string* value class is an ordered string of characters. In order to distinguish a string from other value classes and from variable identifiers, we wrap strings with straight quotes:

"Hello World!" is a string, while *hello_world* is an identifier, or a variable name.

You can assign strings to a variable using either the *copy* or *set* commands:

```
set my_greeting to "Hello World!"
```

This line assigns the text "Hello World!" to the variable *my_greeting*.

The same result using the *copy* command would look like this:

```
copy "Hello World!" to my_greeting
```

The length of a string is limited only by your computer's memory.

The character set you can use in a string is a different issue though. As simple strings go, they can include 256 different characters. In fact, you can ask for any character's ASCII value. In OS X, though, different applications may return values in a class called Unicode text. Unicode text is a relative of string, but instead of being based on the single-byte pattern, it uses two bytes for many characters. Now what's a byte between friends, you ask, and really what is the difference?

OK, so let's start with electronics 101: a byte has how many bits? 8. A bit can be how many different values? 2. A bit can be either on or off. That means that when we have 8 of them, and each one can be either on or off, we increase the number of variations. How many variations do we get? You figure it out, manually:

Take a piece of ruled paper and make eight columns. Now, write a zero at the top of each column. In the binary language, you wrote the number zero! Now, write seven zeros and a one. Next row: six zeros, a one, and a zero. This is actually the number 2 in the binary system. Continue writing the numbers down until you either get to the number 11111111, or you feel like resorting to calling me names. In any case, here is how your page would look like:

00000000

00000001

00000010

00000011

00000100

00000101

00000110

00000111

00001000

00001001

00001010

00001011

. . . . . .

11111111

and so on . . .

If you got to the end and counted the rows, you will discover that you have a total of 256 rows. Hmm . . . sounds familiar. It works this way since each byte has 8 bits, the maximum number of combinations 8 bits can have in the binary system is 256, and hence the 256 characters in the ASCII table.

Another way to figure that out is by using this formula: 2^8=256.

Where else does the number 256 appear? In images, of course. The idea is the same: in an 8-bit image, each pixel has 8 bits to its disposal; therefore the image can only have 256 different shades. A 24-bit image is an image that's made of three 8-bit images, usually a red one, a green one, and a blue one. Enough of that though.

As for Unicode text, it has 2 whole bytes to use for most characters. That means that instead of the 256 characters, it has, well, let's look at our formula: 2^16=65,536. That's right, a double-byte character can have 65,536 different characters.

Why do we need these variations? Well, each variation is assigned a different character. Here is how it works. In a single-byte text system, such as the plain old string we use in AppleScript, every character is assigned a byte of memory, so we can have 256 characters. While that's just about enough for use on one computer, when we need to start communicating with other platforms and other languages, the 256-character system falls short. For that reason, most applications will return strings to AppleScript in the Unicode string format.

What it means to you, the lone scripter, isn't much, since AppleScript for the most part makes sure to convert between plain strings and Unicode text. That conversion in AppleScript is called coercion. To coerce is to convert values from one class to another. More on coercion later. While AppleScript and OS X in particular are moving towards Unicode parity, there are still many glitches. Some commands don't understand Unicode, and some don't return string values in Unicode. This, however, is becoming better with every release of the OS and will hopefully become seamless within a year or two.

Special string characters

While you can include any one of the 256 ASCII characters in a string, some of them need a slightly different treatment. For instance, take double quotes. Since a double quote is the character that specifies the start and end of a string, how can you include quotes in a string? If you write

```
set my_string to "Click on the file named "Read me" and open it"
```

AppleScript will get confused and think that the string ends at the second double quote mark: set *my_string* to "Click on the file named ", and what comes after that won't compile.

The error you get, shown in Figure 3-1, is almost philosophical. I'm glad that AppleScript at least found itself . . .

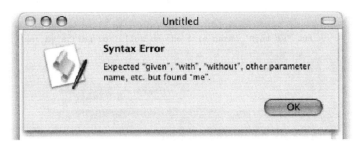

Figure 3-1. AppleScript expected "without" but found "me".

The error is meaningless, since we messed up on the quotes front. The first thing you do when an error makes no sense is check if you left some quote open somewhere.

To properly include a quote in the string, you escape it with a backslash, also known as the escape character. The backslash is found to the right under the *DELETE* key on US keyboards.

To property assign the text to the variable as we tried to previously, you write

```
set my_string to "Click on the file named \" Read me\" and open it"
```

Now, however, we have a second problem: how do we include the backslash character? For instance, if we want to display a dialog box asking users not to use the backslash character, we will need to use it ourselves. To do that we will simply escape it with another backslash character:

```
Display dialog "Don't use the \\ character"
```

See Figures 3-2 and 3-3 for how to show the backslash character inside double quotes. Fancy stuff!

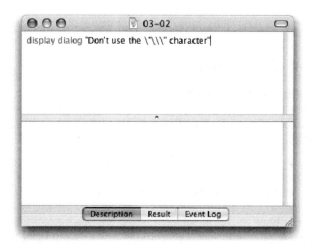

Figure 3-2. The code

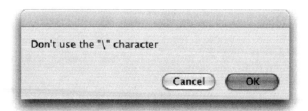

Figure 3-3. The resulting dialog box

Other characters you should know about are the tab and return characters. These two characters won't give you a hard time, just the opposite; there are a few ways to include them in a string. You can simply use the words *tab* and *return* respectively outside the double quotes. If you type the word "return" or "tab" inside double quotes, they will appear spelled out instead of as the sign they represent. Another way to include these characters is by typing \r for return and \t for tab (see details that follow). Both \r and \t will be replaced with returns and tabs as soon as you compile the script; see Figures 3-4 and 3-5.

Figure 3-4. The script before compiling

Figure 3-5. The script after compiling

The other way you can refer to the return and tab characters is by using their constants. There are actually three constants: space, tab, and return. They're used like variables, but the AppleScript language predefines them. Just as with variables, you can't use these three constants in quotes.

They're useful when we use the concatenation operator to connect a few strings together:

```
set my_own_menu to "coffee" & tab & "$1.15" & return & "donut" & ¬
    tab & "$0.65".
```

The funny thing about the space, tab, and return constants is that you can actually set their values in a script to something other than their originally intended values, as in this example:

```
set space to "-"
return "space" & space & "station"
```

The result is "space-station", not "space station".

That change, however, applies only to that script.

ASCII's a sure thing

Think about how neat it is to be able to describe characters without typing the character itself. Think about characters that don't even appear on the keyboard, or characters that you got out of some PC text file. In AppleScript they look like gibberish, or like nothing at all.

To identify a character, you can ask for its ASCII number, and then use the number instead of the character. You do that using the Standard Additions commands, *ASCII number* and *ASCII character*.

The *ASCII number* command takes a string as the parameter and returns a result in the form of a number from 0 to 255. The number it returns is the ASCII number of the first character of that string. For instance, the statement *ASCII number space* will return 32, which is the ASCII number of the space character.

The opposite command is *ASCII character*. The *ASCII character* command accepts a number between 0 and 255 as the argument, and returns the character that has that ASCII number. For instance, the statement *ASCII character 36* will return $.

Try the following script; see the resulting dialog box in Figure 3-6.

```
display dialog "I love the big " & ASCII character 240
```

While executing the script, AppleScript replaces the *ASCII character 240* statement with the Apple logo character.

Figure 3-6. The dialog box with ASCII character 240

A string operation

You'd think that performing operations on strings would return different strings as results. In fact, only one string operator returns a string. That operator is the concatenation operator, or in other words, the "put two or more strings together to perform a single, longer string" operator.

The rest of the operations you can apply to strings use comparison operators. That means that their result is a Boolean: either true or false—for example, checking if "a" comes before "b", or if the string "Angel food cake" contains the string "food".

The concatenation operator is specified in scripts by using &.

The concatenation operator can work on strings and on lists, and it's up to you to ensure that you know whether the operations you perform with the concatenation operator are supposed to return a list or a string. On top of that, you have to make sure that the result the operation returns is the result you wanted.

What happens here in a sense is that we pay for the AppleScript programming language relaxed syntax. In many other languages, you have to declare, or dimension, variables before you use them, and also specify the value class for that variable (whether it will hold a real, an integer, text, etc.).

We already saw the concatenation operator at work, but let's look at a couple of issues with it:

Concatenating strings returns a string result. That makes sense. What else would it return?

Well, try the following in a new script window:

```
set the_price to "$" & 6
```

The result is "$6".

The difference here is that we concatenated a string to a number. AppleScript took the liberty to coerce the number into text, so the result is the same as if we treated the 6 as text in this way:

```
set the_price to "$" & "6"
```

Same result.

However, let's see what happens when we switch places:

```
set the_price to 6 & " Dollar"
```

The result this time is different. Since the first operand (the item we operate on) is a number and not a string, AppleScript figures that it would be safer to return a list instead of a string. The result then is a list of two items, a number and a string:

```
{6, " Dollar"}
```

To prevent that from happening, we have to include a coercion operator: *as*.

The operator *as* coerces the resulting value into a different value class. In this case, we can write

```
set the_price to 6 & " Dollar" as string
```

which will return "6 Dollar".

We can also coerce the number into string by itself, and therefore the entire statement will result in a string:

```
set the_price to (6 as string) & " Dollar".
```

In both instances the result is a single string: "6 Dollar".

What about the other operators? Well, there are many operators that compare either two strings or pieces of a string to other strings.

These operators are =, ≠, >, ≥, <, ≤, *starts with*, *ends with*, *contains*, and *is contained by*.

Let's start with the simple ones. It's easy to understand how we can see if strings are equal; consider the following operations:

```
"Ice cream" = "carrot"
```

returns false.

```
"Me" ≠ "You"
```

returns true.

These two operators alone have multiple variations, cooked up in the name of making the AppleScript language more like a casual spoken language versus a programming language. These variations are shown in the following script:

Script 3-1

```
"Ice cream" is "carrot"
"Ice cream" equals "carrot"
"Ice cream" is equal to "carrot"
"Me" is not "You"
"Me" is not equal to "You"
```

How about the following statement:

```
"555-1212" = "5551212" --> false
```

or

```
"ASCII" = "ascii" --> true
```

The result of the first operation is false while the second one is true. That is because AppleScript makes assumptions about what special issues you may want to consider or ignore while comparing text. You should not only be aware of these issues, but also always keep in mind that AppleScript's assumptions can be overruled with special clauses that allow you to ignore or consider certain conditions.

Considering and ignoring

There are a few string-comparison-related consideration clauses. They are (in alphabetical order) case, diacriticals, hyphens, expansion, punctuation, and white space. Other consideration clauses exist, but don't relate directly to strings.

All the following samples are part of **Script 3-2**.

Let's start with a simple example of the *case* clause.

To use the *case* clause, or any other consideration clause, we have to wrap our statement in the following way, using either the word "ignoring" or "considering," depending on our intention:

```
considering case
    "A" = "a"
end considering
```

The result of the preceding script snippet will be false.

The default AppleScript behavior is to ignore the case of characters, so asking AppleScript to consider the case of characters will yield a different result. Simply stating

```
"A" = "a"
```

will return true, and since AppleScript ignores characters' case by default, the following statement will return true as well:

```
ignoring case
    "A" = "a"
end ignoring
```

The deal with the diacritical, hyphen, and punctuation consideration clauses is a bit different. Each one of these refers to a set of special characters that can be ignored when comparing strings. All are true by default, so using them in a *considering* clause won't change the result, but using them in an *ignoring* clause will.

The *ignoring diacriticals* clause allows you to ignore any accent marks, so that the following statement returns a true result:

```
ignoring diacriticals
    "Résumé" = "Resume"
end ignoring

result: true
```

The *ignoring hyphens* clause allows you to ignore hyphens in the text:

```
ignoring hyphens
    "stand-alone" = "standalone"
end ignoring
result: true

ignoring hyphens
    "1-800-555-1212" = "18005551212"
end ignoring
result: true
```

Note, however, that the *ignoring hyphens* clause will only ignore plain hyphens created with the minus key, not any typographical dashes such as an en dash or em dash.

The *ignoring punctuations* clause allows you to ignore any punctuations marks. These marks are . , ? : ; ! \ ' " `. And in words: period, comma, question mark, colon, semicolon, exclamation point, backslash, single quote, double quote, and that other character you get when you press that key at the top left.

```
ignoring punctuation
    "That's all, right? Now!" = "Thats all right now"
end ignoring
result: true
```

The *ignoring white spaces* clause allows you to ignore spaces, tabs, and return characters when comparing strings.

```
ignoring white space
    "Space craft" = "Spacecraft"
end ignoring

result: true
```

The most obscure variation of the *ignoring* clause is probably used more in languages where combined characters, such as Æ, æ, Œ, and œ, are used.

```
ignoring expansion
    "Æ" = "AE"
end ignoring

Result: true
```

Also, since case isn't considered, the following will be true:

```
ignoring expansion
"Æ" = "æ"
end ignoring
```

A quick note regarding finding these characters on the keyboard: as a protest to the elimination of the venerable Key Caps, I've developed my own system that includes opening text edit and frantically pressing as many keys as possible while holding different modifier keys. This system isn't so good if you want to trace the key combination for later use.

Using a single *considering* or *ignoring* clause may get you what you need, but what if it takes more than one? For that you can use multiple parameters, and even nest clauses. Let's take a look.

Say you want to evaluate words that may or may not include either dashes, spaces, or accents marks. Let's assume that we want to evaluate a student's response to a test question. While we need the answer spelled correctly, we want to be lenient when it comes to spaces, dashes, accents, etc.

Here is how we can evaluate the accuracy of the answer:

```
ignoring white space, hyphens and diacriticals
    set is_answer_correct to student_answer = actual_answer
end ignoring
```

This will ensure that if the answer was El Niño, the responses elnino, El nino, Elñino, and El-Nino would also register as correct.

Another way to state the same intention is by nesting the different consideration clauses like this:

```
ignoring white space
    ignoring hyphens
        ignoring diacriticals
            set is_answer_correct to student_answer = actual_answer
        end ignoring
    end ignoring
end ignoring
```

What if you did want to consider the case of the answer, but wanted to give some slack over the accents? Your statement would look like this:

```
considering case but ignoring diacriticals
    a = b
end considering
```

"My Dad" comes before "Your Dad"

Much like the = operator, the different variations of the greater than and less than operators always return a result as a Boolean. That means that the result of using an operator can be either true or false. Before embellishing on the variations of the same basic operators, we need to understand how a certain character is considered to be greater than another.

In general, all 256 characters in the ASCII table are ordered based on how they would appear in an English language dictionary. Here is the order of characters in which they will appear if sorted:

ASCII Number	Character	ASCII Number	Character	ASCII Number	Character
32	(space)	107	k	182	∂
33	!	108	l	183	Σ
34	"	109	m	184	Π
35	#	110	n	185	π
36	$	111	o	186	∫
37	%	112	p	187	a
38	&	113	q	188	o
39	'	114	r	189	Ω
40	(	115	s	190	æ
41	)	116	t	191	ø
42	*	117	u	192	¿
43	+	118	v	193	¡
44	,	119	w	194	¬
45	-	120	x	195	√
46	.	121	y	196	ƒ
47	/	122	z	197	≈
48	0	123	{	198	Δ
49	1	124	|	199	«
50	2	125	}	200	»
51	3	126	~	201	…
52	4	127		202	
53	5	128	Ä	203	À
54	6	129	Å	204	Ã

ASCII Number	Character	ASCII Number	Character	ASCII Number	Character
55	7	130	Ç	205	Õ
56	8	131	É	206	Œ
57	9	132	Ñ	207	œ
58	:	133	Ö	208	–
59	;	134	Ü	209	—
60	<	135	á	210	"
61	=	136	à	211	"
62	>	137	â	212	'
63	?	138	ä	213	'
64	@	139	ã	214	÷
65	A	140	å	215	◊
66	B	141	ç	216	ÿ
67	C	142	é	217	Ÿ
68	D	143	è	218	⁄
69	E	144	ê	219	€
70	F	145	ë	220	‹
71	G	146	í	221	›
72	H	147	ì	222	fi
73	I	148	î	223	fl
74	J	149	ï	224	‡
75	K	150	ñ	225	·
76	L	151	ó	226	‚
77	M	152	ò	227	„
78	N	153	ô	228	‰
79	O	154	ö	229	Â

ASCII Number	Character	ASCII Number	Character	ASCII Number	Character
80	P	155	õ	230	Ê
81	Q	156	ú	231	Á
82	R	157	ù	232	Ë
83	S	158	û	233	È
84	T	159	ü	234	Í
85	U	160	†	235	Î
86	V	161	°	236	Ï
87	W	162	¢	237	Ì
88	X	163	£	238	Ó
89	Y	164	§	239	Ô
90	Z	165	•	240	
91	[	166	¶	241	Ò
92	\\	167	ß	242	Ú
93	]	168	®	243	Û
94	^	169	©	244	Ù
95	_	170	™	245	ı
96	`	171	´	246	ˆ
97	a	172	¨	247	˜
98	b	173	≠	248	¯
99	c	174	Æ	249	˘
100	d	175	Ø	250	˙
101	e	176	∞	251	˚
102	f	177	±	252	¸
103	g	178	≤	253	˝
104	h	179	≥	254	˛

ASCII Number	Character	ASCII Number	Character	ASCII Number	Character
105	i	180	¥	255	ˇ
106	j	181	μ		

To determine in a script which one of two strings comes before the other, you can use any of the following operators:

        "a" comes before "b"

or

        "a" < "b"

or

        "a" is less than "b"

Similarly, the following operators checks whether the first parameter is greater than the second, or appears later in the sorting chain:

        "a" comes after "b"

or

        "a" > "b"

or

        "a" is greater than "b"

You can also use some of the comparison operators that have "or" built right into them:

        "a" ≥ "b"

or

        "a" is greater than or equal to "b"

or

        "a" ≤ "b"

or

        "a" is less than or equal to "b"

Sorting text

In the spirit of putting characters in order, let's try to analyze a script that takes a list of strings and creates a new list, with the same strings in order.

First, here is the script. Note that this script snippet is a prime candidate for a subroutine. The parameter will be the list we want to sort, and the returned result will be the sorted list. For now, though, we will just concentrate on the code itself and not how it may fit in a script.

I must also note that I did not write this script. This is one of the many useful subroutines found in the AppleScript Guidebook. These scripts were for the most part written by Sal Soghoian, the renowned AppleScript product manager from Apple Computer.

Let's see how the script works:

Script 3-3

```
1.  set the index_list to {}
2.  set the sorted_list to {}
3.  repeat (the number of items in my_list) times
4.    set the low_item to ""
5.    repeat with i from 1 to (number of items in my_list)
6.      if i is not in the index_list then
7.        set this_item to item i of my_list as text
8.        if the low_item is "" then
9.          set the low_item to this_item
10.         set the low_item_index to i
11.       else if this_item comes before the low_item then
12.         set the low_item to this_item
13.         set the low_item_index to i
14.       end if
15.     end if
16.   end repeat
17.   set the end of sorted_list to the low_item
18.   set the end of the index_list to the low_item_index
19. end repeat
```

Breaking up strings

A large part of working with text is being able to break apart a string and evaluate different pieces of it.

One obvious way to break a string is into its characters. Since a string is made of characters, the length of the string is also the number of characters it has in it.

Actually, length is a string property. You use it to get a string's character count. Here is how you do that:

```
length of "rope"
```

The result is a number, in this case, the number 4, since the word "rope" has four characters.

In addition to the *length* property, we can also use the *count* command to get the number of characters of a string. The *count* command can work on strings, lists, and records, and also inside many applications. For instance, you can use the *count* command to get the number of records in a FileMaker database, or the number of files in a folder.

Characters

So far, however, neither the *length* property nor the *count* command manages to break the string apart. To break a string into characters, we have to use the word "character" along with the *get* command:

```
get characters of "tic-tac-toe"
```

We can also drop the word "get", and write

```
characters of "tic-tac-toe"
```

Or make it more explicit, and write

```
get every character of "tic-tac-toe"
```

In any case, the result will be the same, and the class of the result, meaning the type of data we get back from the statement, is a list. The list will contain all the characters of the string, with each character taking up one item in the list.

```
{"t", "i", "c", "-", "t", "a", "c", "-", "t", "o", "e"}
```

This is useful when you want to evaluate each character and perform an action based on specific characters. For instance, having the string broken down into a list of characters can be useful if we wanted to take a string and replace every instance of the character "t" with the string "sl". However, there's a faster way to perform such replacement, as we will see later on.

We will start with a variable with a string value, and then add another variable that will hold a list containing every character of the string in the first variable:

```
set my_string to "tic-tac-toe"
set my_list to every character of my_string
```

At this point, the value of the variable *my_list* is

```
{"t", "i", "c", "-", "t", "a", "c", "-", "t", "o", "e" }
```

Next we will create a simple repeat loop that will loop through the characters and add each one to an empty string variable. If the character is "t", however, the script will replace it with "sl".

We start by defining the empty string variable:

```
set my_new_string to ""
```

But why do we have to do that? Shouldn't AppleScript be able to create a variable on the fly? Why are we suddenly forced to define the variable? The answer is that in the next few lines of code we'll need to add to the variable *my_new_string*. The way we add to variables is by setting a variable to itself and then adding anything else on top of it. For instance:

```
set the_name to "Jack"
set the_name to the_name & " B. Back"
```

The result is that the variable *the_name* has the value "Jack B. Back" assigned to it.

Anyway, back to our script.

As you can see in Figure 3-7, we defined the three variables that will be used in the script, and created the skeleton of the repeat loop.

Figure 3-7. The variables are defined and a repeat loop skeleton has been created.

Since we will discuss repeat loops in detail later on, for now I just want you to understand that when we use *in* inside a repeat loop statement, the repeat variable, in this case *the_character*, will be assigned the next list item at every loop revolution. To test the functionality of it, let's add a *display dialog* command inside the loop.

```
display dialog the_character
```

Now run the script, which should look like the one in Figure 3-8.

Figure 3-8. A temporary *display dialog* command has been added.

When you run the script, a dialog box will be displayed for each character in the string. That should make the function of the *repeat* statement a bit clearer.

Now that we did that, comment out the *display dialog* command. This way you can quickly get back to it later if you need to.

Next we will explain to the script what to do if the character happens to be a "t," and what to do if it's not.

Add the following lines inside the *repeat* statement:

```
if the_character as string is "t" then
    set my_new_string to my_new_string & "sl"
else
    set my_new_string to my_new_string & the_character
end if
```

Your script should look like the one in Figure 3-9.

Figure 3-9. A conditional statement reacts differently if the character is "t."

The conditional statement checks if the repeat loop variable *the_character* happens to be a "t." If it is, then the script adds "sl" to the *my_new_string* variable. If it's any other character, the character itself is added to the *my_new_string* variable. The value of the variable *the_character* has to be coerced into a string since it is really "item *n* in a list," instead of a string.

As we discussed earlier, we add to a variable by setting it to itself, and concatenating (adding) more text to it:

```
set my_new_string to my_new_string & "sl"
```

The last statement of the script, for lack of other use for our new and improved string, will be

```
display dialog my_new_string
```

You may be surprised to find out that the result hasn't changed; it is still "tic-tac-toe"! This is due to AppleScript looking at the variable *my_character* as an item in a list instead of a string. To remedy that we can force AppleScript to look at the text itself. We do that by adding "text of" to the *if* statement; like this:

```
if text of the_character is "t"
```

Now the dialog box should be like the one in Figure 3-10.

slic–slac–sloe

Cancel   OK

Figure 3-10. The dialog box showing the resulting variable *my_new_string*

Another way we could've remedied this little problem is by coercing *the_character* variable into a string:

```
if (the_character as string) is "t"
```

Picking the pieces

So now we know that AppleScript can split a string into characters. What we also need to know is how to extract chunks of strings for use in our script.

To put it in context, slicing up strings and turning chunks of them into new strings is one thing that as a scripter you will do all the time: figuring out what date a job is due based on the date embedded in the file name, parsing out text files and using the information there, cleaning out unwanted characters taken from different sources, formatting phone numbers, etc. The list is endless.

The first and most used tool we have is the ability to extract a number of characters from a string by specifying the starting and ending character. This method is called the index reference form, since you refer to a character (in this case) by its position among the other characters.

An easy example would be

```
character 3 of "AppleScript"
```

As you must have guessed already, the result of the preceding statement is a string class with a value of "p".

And since we're talking AppleScript here, and not some other no-fun programming language, we can also write

```
third character of "AppleScript"
```

The result, as you can imagine, is the same.

And if we can refer to the third character, then we surely can refer to the first character, which would've made it cruel and unusual to not allow us to ask for the last character or character before last character of "AppleScript".

Try this:

```
character before last character of "AppleScript"
```

OK, so the only person I know that actually uses these terms in programming is Sal himself (AppleScript product manager at Apple), but then again, I don't go out much.

Another thing that makes AppleScript a language more suitable for use by humans is that the first character in a string, or the first anything for that matter, is referred to as 1, not 0. This is known as a one-based index instead of zero-based.

Let's go back a step and look at the term "last character." Of course, using this kind of syntax is useful for that very last character, or even the one before it, but what about the one before that? You're in luck, because AppleScript has the perfect solution! The last character is also known to AppleScript as character -1 (that is, negative one). The reason why this is so cool and so useful is that you can use a number to look for a specific character counting from the end of the string, not the beginning. Using that negative-index reference style we can write

```
character -3 of "AppleScript"
```

which will return the character "i".

For your reference, Figure 3-11 shows you different ways you can refer to different characters in a string.

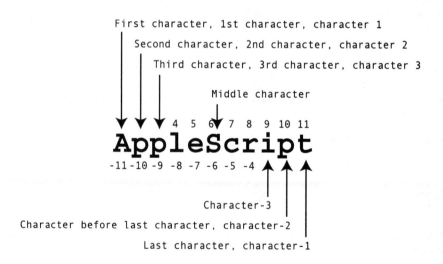

Figure 3-11. Referring to characters in a string

Looking at Figure 3-11 you can also see that the word "middle" is a valid reference, although I've never used that one.

Another way to refer to a character is to use the arbitrary reference form: *some*. The *some* reference form returns a random character from a string, which is another reference form I've never used. I prefer to go the formal route and first derive a random number, and then use that number to refer to a character by index:

```
set my_string to "AppleScript"
set my_random_number to random number from 1 to (length of my_string)
set my_random_character to character my_random_number of my_string
```

OK, so now that I look at it, it does seem neater to just write

```
set my_string to "AppleScript"
set my_random_character to some character of my_string
```

What was I thinking of all these years? Oh well, as long as I don't tell anyone . . .

Chunk at a time

Now that we know all about picking the right character, what about a bunch of characters?

What if we got a file name into a string, and we know that the client's account number is a six-digit number starting from the third character?

OK, so the string is "JB445091_UTFg12.sit". To extract the account number out of it, we can write the following statement:

```
set job_file_name to "JB445091_UTFg12.sit"
set account_number to characters 3 thru 8 of job_file_name
```

The first thing you notice is that the word "thru" (which stands for through) isn't spelled out. Say "thank-you" to the AppleScript team for locking the grammar police in the closet that day. As one who uses the word "thru" in quite a few AppleScript statements, I know I'm grateful.

The second twist is that although (or should I say altho) asking for a single character as we saw earlier returned a value as a string, when you ask for a few characters using the *thru* expression, the result is returned as a list of characters. That means that the value of the variable *account_number* from before will be

```
{"4", "4", "5", "0", "9", "1"}
```

The same is true for when you want all of the characters.

Both statements that follow will produce the same result, which is a list with all the characters from the string:

```
get every character of "AppleScript"
get characters of "AppleScript"
```

Result:

```
{"A", "p", "p", "l", "e", "S", "c", "r", "i", "p", "t"}
```

So in order to get the result as a string we can either ask for the text of it:

```
set account_number to text 3 thru 8 of job_file_name
```

or, as we saw earlier (though I doubt you were paying attention :-)), we can simply coerce the resulting list into a string:

```
set account_number to characters 3 thru 8 of job_file_name as string
```

I know what you're thinking: since it's a number we're trying to get here, why wouldn't we just ask for it as an integer? After all, a list of characters can be coerced into a string, and a string containing numbers can be coerced into an integer, right? Well, sort of. First, a list, and even a list of numbers, can't be coerced into a number. What you could do, though, is coerce the list into a string, and then into an integer in this way:

```
set account_number to (characters 3 thru 8 of job_file_name as string) ¬
    as integer
```

The first set of parentheses produces a string, and the *as integer* at the end converts that string into an integer.

That same result could have been written in three lines for better readability in this manner:

```
characters 3 thru 8 of job_file_name
result as string
set account_number to result as integer
```

In the preceding example we didn't store the result of each line in a variable; we didn't even need to reuse the same variable. The *result* variable holds the resulting value of every statement by default, and that saves us the trouble of using the *set* command.

Another point that we will discuss later is that the error-free execution of that script depends on the extracted characters being all digits. More on that when we talk about numbers.

Words

As would be expected, we can also break down text into individual words. Doing this will also return a list, but unlike breaking text into characters where the integrity of the text remained, breaking text into words cleans out any characters that are considered word delimiters.

Let's start with a little example. Write the script from Figure 3-12 and execute it.

Figure 3-12. A string being broken into words

When you run the script the obvious happens: the result is a list in which each item is a word. What you may not notice right away you're sure to notice in the example shown in Figure 3-13.

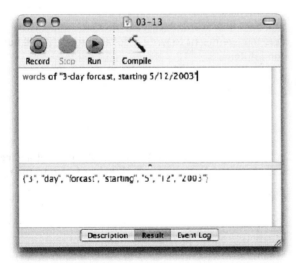

Figure 3-13. Breaking text into words eliminates the delimiters.

Notice that I use words of *and* get every word of *interchangeably. They produce the same result.*

When you ask for the words of a string, you get a list of the words, but the dashes, commas, slashes, etc. are nowhere to be seen.

The characters that are used as built-in word delimiters are

! \ " ( ) ' : ; ? [ ] { } « » " " ' ' —

The following characters are considered to be words on their own, and even if they're found right next to another valid word, they will be counted as their own item:

& * + > < @ \ \ ^ _ ` | ~ ° £ § • ¶ ß ® © ™ ´ ¨ ≠ ∞ ± ≤ ≥ ¥ µ ∂ ∑ ∏ π ∫ ª º Ω ¿ ¡ ¬ √ ƒ ≈ ∆ ÷ ◊ – ⁄ ‹ › ‡ ‚ „ ‰

For instance, *words of "you&me"* has no delimiters and therefore should return a list with a single item. However, AppleScript recognizes the ampersand (&) as a word, and therefore gives it its own list item. The result will therefore be

        {" you ", "&", "me"}

One more area where AppleScript shows intelligence in the way it breaks apart words is when it deals with US currency marks, periods, and commas. When used in text, the dollar sign ($), cents sign (¢), and percent sign (%) are all considered their own words. This means that writing

        words of "Seven$Flat"

will return

        {"Seven", "$", "Flat"}

However, if AppleScript recognizes that we meant to write a dollar amount, it will bunch the $ sign with the number in one list item:

        words of "pay me $10"

returns

        {"pay", "me", "$10"}

This only works if the dollar sign is to the left of the number, unlike the percent and cent signs, which will be considered a part of the same word only if they're found to the right of the number.

        words of "10%"

returns

        {"10%" }

but . . .

        words of "%10"

returns

        {"%", "10"}

When used between two digits, commas and periods suddenly give up their delimiter role and jump in as part of the word. Take this statement for example:

```
words of "to get $1,000,000.50, you must give 100%."
```

returns

```
{"to", "get", "$1,000,000.50", "you", "must", "give", "100%"}
```

Notice that the period and comma that are a part of *"$1,000,000.50"* were left as part of the dollar amount, but the comma that comes right after that amount and the period at the end of the sentence were used as delimiters and are not a part of anything in the resulting list.

Paragraphs

Very much like breaking strings into words, we can break them into paragraphs. The logic behind a paragraph is much simpler: the first paragraph in the string starts at the beginning of the string, and ends at the first carriage return character, which is ASCII character number 13. If there's only one paragraph (and there's always at least one paragraph, even if the string is empty!), then that one paragraph ends at the end of the string.

The rest of the paragraphs (if there are more than one) start right after the carriage return and end right before the next one. The last paragraph ends at the end of the string.

Take for example the script in Figure 3-14. We started with a simple string that included four paragraphs, and asked AppleScript to return every paragraph. The result is a list in which every list item contains one paragraph.

Figure 3-14. AppleScript breaks a string into paragraphs.

What would happen, though, if we try to merge the paragraphs back into a string again? See Figure 3-15.

Figure 3-15. A list of paragraphs coerced into a string become a single paragraph.

Why did that happen? Why is it that when we take a string, break it into paragraphs, and then merge them back into a string right away we get one long paragraph? Because of the fact that when AppleScript broke down the string into a list, each list contained only the paragraph itself and not the carriage return character itself. We will discuss a quick solution for that in the item delimiters discussion later on.

Words and paragraphs in the real world

That is, for those of us who consider AppleScript to be the real world . . .

From my experience, looking at the words and paragraphs components of strings can be extremely useful. Breaking down a text file into paragraphs and looping through them is essential, and asking for every word of some text is great for finding the information you need.

As an exercise, let's create a little script that will parse some text and use the information.

The script is a rendition of a script I actually use for scheduling purposes.

One of my large clients has scheduling software that sends me e-mails whenever I'm scheduled to be part of a meeting. The e-mails are well formatted, and their content is predictable and reliable. It contains in plain text information about the location and time of the meeting, and some other general information.

What I need to do is parse that e-mail and create an event in my iCal calendar.

We will start by creating the script as a single flow, from top to bottom. The beginning will gather the text from the message in Apple's Mail application. Then, we will extract the actual meeting information out of that text, and we will end by adding a new event to iCal with the information we collected.

After we're done, we will take a minute to better organize the script into subroutines. One subroutine will gather the text, the other will extract the data, and the third will apply it to iCal.

If you grade a script based on code efficiency, the script we're about to write is probably an 8 out of 10. There are slight variations that would've worked just as well or better, but for now I'd like to focus on using words and paragraphs to accomplish the job.

Mail to iCal script

We will start by extracting the information from Mail. What we will assume is that there's a message selected, and that it contains text formatted to our expectation. If this was a script we had to distribute to users in our company, or make it public in any way, over 50% of the code would have been related to idiot-proofing the script: making sure the user selected a message, making sure the user selected the right message, making sure the user knows what the script will do, etc. Everything short of making sure their Mac is plugged in. Idiot-proofing your code takes time and makes the script more cumbersome, but it ensures that different errors are filtered back to the user as friendly little comments such as "Oh great one, please note that in order to select a message you must have Mail open, and then you must click the message you choose to select. For clicking instructions, please refer to your user manual."

This script, however, will be 100% functional without any error capturing.

Now for the script.

Like most applications, the mail application gives us access to the *selection* property. The *selection* property belongs to the application object, and therefore can be accessed from within the initial application *tell* block.

In Mail, like other applications, the *selection* property is a list, even though in our case it holds only a single item. That item is the message, and we need to reference it in order to get its text.

Before you start writing here, make sure that the Mail application is running and that you have a single application selected. What you may also want to do is to type the content of the message from the text that follows and send it to yourself. The message you will get will serve as the script subject.

I realize that you might not be using Mail. If you don't, you can skip the start and just set the string variable you will see in a minute to the message text. This way you will bypass Mail and get right to cleaning the text.

All this, by the way, isn't just logistics that relate strictly to learning AppleScript from my book; these are different things you should do while writing actual scripts. Creating dummy data, creating objects in application to use in testing, etc.

Let's look at the *selection* property first. Write the following lines and run the script:

```
tell application "Mail"
    get selection
end tell
```

The result is a list containing one item. Now let's change the script to reference the first item of the list:

```
tell application "Mail"
    get item 1 of (selection as list)
end tell
```

Now the result isn't a list, but rather the item itself.

Why did I put *selection* in parentheses? Well, Mail got a bit picky with me and this calmed it down a little. Sometimes applications get confused and need you to describe what you want more clearly by surrounding objects in parentheses.

Now let's go all the way and extract the text.

In Mail, every message has a *content* property that includes all the text of the message. You can see that in Mail's dictionary.

> *We'll discuss dictionaries and application objects and properties in detail in Chapter 21.*

What we need is to get the *content* property of the selected message into a variable. Here is how:

```
tell application "Mail"
    set the_message to item 1 of (get selection as list)
    set message_text to content of the_message
end tell
```

Here is the content of the message. You can either e-mail it to yourself, or just assign it to the *message_text* variable without calling Mail at all.

Message text (with added carriage return marks for looks . . .):

Meeting Reminder¶

Subject: Preapproval of the meeting proposed in the initial proposal draft¶

When: Friday, March 2, 2001, 8:30 AM - 9:30 AM (GMT-05:00) Eastern Time¶

Where: Break Room in the Marketing Wing

Notice that there are four paragraphs and that the meat or nutritional part is concentrated in paragraphs 2, 3, and 4.

Let's add the lines of code that assign the contents of these paragraphs to different variables. We will make the identifiers of these variables as descriptive as we can:

```
set message_subject_line to paragraph 2 of message_text
set message_dates_line to paragraph 3 of message_text
set message_location_line to paragraph 4 of message_text
```

Now we can start to turn the text into the information we need.

If we examine iCal's dictionary we can see that there's an *event* object. That object is the object we need to create. An *event* object has about 12 properties, out of which we only care about four: *start date*, *end date*, *summary*, and *status*.

Of these four properties, two need a value of the class *Date*, one is a string (summary), and the *status* property uses a custom class that can be one of four values: *none*, *cancelled*, *tentative*, or *confirmed*.

All this information can be found in the iCal application AppleScript dictionary. Here's an excerpt from the iCal dictionary that shows these properties of the *event* class:

```
summary Unicode text  -- The event summary
start date date  -- The event start date
status none/cancelled/tentative/confirmed  -- The event status
end date date  -- The event end date, if defined
```

Notice that although the *status* property uses values that are words, these words are not strings—they're custom application values that fit this particular property of the *event* class; got it?

Anyway, our job is to end up with four variables that hold the data from these four properties. We'll call these variables *start_date*, *end_date*, and *the_summary*. OK, so there are only three variables. For the *status* property we will just use the *confirmed* value.

The next portion of the script will mold the plain text we got from the message into data that will fit into these variables.

We'll start with the easy one: summary. The summary is just a text description, and I believe that the text in the *message_subject_line* and *message_location_line* variables is perfect. Let's concatenate them and assign the result to the *the_summary* variable:

Add the following line:

```
set the_summary to message_subject_line & return &
message_location_line
```

Now we need to attend to the dates. Let's start by breaking down the *message_dates_line* variable into words. To do that we can type a temporary line that will return the words of the string value of the *message_dates_line* variable.

At the end of the script type

```
words of message_dates_line
```

Run the script, copy the result, and paste it in any text editor, or into a blank script window. We will use that text as a reference, which will allow us to see what the different words are and their order.

The result should be a list with 15 items:

```
{"When", "Friday", "March", "2", "2001", "8", "30", "AM", "9", ¬
    "30", "AM", "GMT", "00", "Eastern", "Time"}
```

A quick analysis reveals that words 3, 4, and 5 contain the date; words 6, 7, and 8 make up the start time; and words 9, 10, and 11 make up the end time.

In AppleScript, a *date* object can contain both date and time. In fact, if you don't specify a time, AppleScript assigns midnight of that date as the time.

In that case, we can create two strings; one will have the date and the start time, and the other the same date and the end time. The AppleScript trick we'll use later is that we'll convert that string into a *date* class just by adding the word "date" before the string.

First though, we need to assemble the strings.

Script 3-4

```
set the_meeting_date to ¬
    word 3 of message_dates_line & space & ¬
    word 4 of message_dates_line & ", " & ¬
    word 5 of message_dates_line as string
set the_start_time to ¬
    word 6 of message_dates_line & ":" & ¬
    word 7 of message_dates_line & space & ¬
    word 8 of message_dates_line as string
set the_end_time to ¬
    word 9 of message_dates_line & ":" & ¬
    word 10 of message_dates_line & space & ¬
    word 11 of message_dates_line as string
```

Although adding the *as string* coercion parameter at the end is optional, I add it just to remind myself of the class of the variable. This also prevents confusion later if, say, you want to start the concatenation with an integer. Now AppleScript will give you back a list, not a string. Using *as string* at the end of operations that need to return strings is well worth it.

Let's examine the variables we created:

Add the line

```
return the_meeting_date
```

What you will get is a string containing the date only. You can do the same with the other variables to examine their values for accuracy.

In the next two lines, we will concatenate the date and each of the strings containing the start time and end time, and coerce them into a *date* class.

```
set start_date to date (the_meeting_date & space & the_start_time ¬
    as string)
set end_date to date (the_meeting_date & space & the_end_time ¬
    as string)
```

Run the script and see how AppleScript has formatted the date into its own date format. As long as you give AppleScript some sort of a date containing at least the month, day, and year, it'll take it from there and make it into a date it can understand.

OK, so it seems like we have all the information we need, neatly formatted into dates, text, etc. Now let's create the event in iCal.

iCal's AppleScript object model starts with the *application* class, which has a *calendar* subclass, which has an *event* subclass. For that reason, we can't create an event just in iCal's main *tell* block; instead we must talk to an existing *calendar* object. Since a working iCal application must have at least one *calendar* object, we can safely use the reference of *calendar 1*. Here is the *tell* block we will use in order to talk to iCal's calendar:

```
tell application "iCal"
    tell calendar 1
        --command here
    end tell
end tell
```

I always complete the *tell* blocks first before inserting the command. This is a way to eliminate nagging little typos that will steal more debugging time than they deserve.

Now, type the following line in the *tell* block:

```
make new event at end with properties ¬
    {start date:start_date, end date:end_date, ¬
    summary:the_summary, status:confirmed}
```

The statement we added starts with the *make* command. The direct parameter is an event, which is the class of the object we're creating; we want the event created at the end, making it the last event to be entered. Also, as part of the *make* command statement, we can specify object properties. This is a fast and efficient way to set the start date, end date, etc. Notice that all four properties we cared about now have a value.

If you left any lines in your script that start with the word "return" and are not in a sub-routine (we don't have any subroutines here yet . . .), then comment these lines out by adding a double dash before them (--). A line that starts with the *return* command will stop the script's execution.

Now run the script and see if it worked!

As promised, we're going to take a minute and streamline our linear script into three sub-routines. We will cover subroutines extensively in later chapters; however, it's important to get there with a wee bit of an "I already did it" feeling. So here we go.

The quick-and-dirty idea behind what we're about to do is to segment the linear script into logical operations. Each operation will be determined based on its function, and may con-tain as few or as many lines of AppleScript code as needed. In our example, we will have three subroutines, each one dealing with one of the following tasks:

1. Get the message text from Mail.
2. Extract and format the information.
3. Create the new event in iCal.

In our example, we'll see that each subroutine has three main components: the subroutine identifier, which is the name of the subroutine; the parameters it takes; and the result it returns.

Our first subroutine will have no parameters, but it will return an important result: the text of the currently selected message in Mail. The second subroutine will take that same mes-sage text that was the result of the previous subroutine and will return the start and end dates and the summary.

The third subroutine will take the three resulting values (start/end dates and summary) and use them to create the new event in iCal.

Figure 3-16 shows you how the new script will be organized. Notice the three subroutine calls at the top, and how the body of each subroutine reflects almost perfectly the chunk of the original script that performed its function.

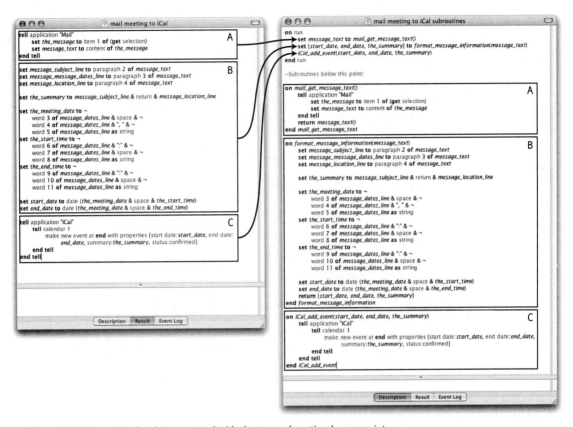

Figure 3-16. The original script compared with the new subroutine-happy script

Notice also in the new script that we put all of the three subroutine calls inside of the *run* handler. Any lines of code that exist inside the *run* handler will execute when the script is either launched as an application, or set to run from inside the script editor. The *run* handler is implied if not supplied, which means that if you don't include the *run* handler, AppleScript will consider any stray line of code that is not in any other handler part of the *run* handler. The script would run the same whether it includes or doesn't include the *run* handler. However, since we're in "being organized" mode, it's appropriate to include the *run* handler too.

Look at the content of the finished script that follows and make the needed changes to your script to bring it to that point.

Here's the code of the new script:

Script 3-5

```
1. on run
2.    set message_text to mail_get_message_text()
3.    set {start_date, end_date, the_summary} to ¬
format_message_information(message_text)
4.    iCal_add_event(start_date, end_date, the_summary)
5. end run


6. --Subroutines below this point:

7. on mail_get_message_text()
8.    tell application "Mail"
9.       set the_message to item 1 of (get selection)
10.         set message_text to content of the_message
11.      end tell
12.      return message_text
13. end mail_get_message_text

14. on format_message_information(message_text)
15.      set message_subject_line to paragraph 2 of message_text
16.      set message_message_dates_line to paragraph 3 of message_text
17.      set message_location_line to paragraph 4 of message_text

18.      set the_summary to message_subject_line & return & ¬
            message_location_line

19.      set the_meeting_date to ¬
20.      word 3 of message_dates_line & space & ¬
21.      word 4 of message_dates_line & ", " & ¬
22.      word 5 of message_dates_line as string
23.      set the_start_time to ¬
24.      word 6 of message_dates_line & ":" & ¬
25.      word 7 of message_dates_line & space & ¬
26.      word 8 of message_dates_line as string
27.      set the_end_time to ¬
28.      word 9 of message_dates_line & ":" & ¬
29.      word 10 of message_dates_line & space & ¬
30.      word 11 of message_dates_line as string

31.      set start_date to date (the_meeting_date & space & ¬
            the_start_time)
32.      set end_date to date (the_meeting_date & space & the_end_time)
33.      return {start_date, end_date, the_summary}
34. end format_message_information

35. on iCal_add_event(start_date, end_date, the_summary)
36.      tell application "iCal"
37.          tell calendar 1
```

```
38.          make new event at end with properties ¬
39.      {start date:start_date, end date:end_date, ¬
40.      summary:the_summary, status:confirmed}
41.        end tell
42.      end tell
43. end iCal_add_event
```

Text item delimiters

Yet another AppleScript pearl, *text item delimiters* is an AppleScript global property, and it's useful for a whole range of text manipulations.

The *text item delimiters* property is used primarily in two situations: when splitting strings into lists, and when combining list elements into a single string.

Splitting strings with text item delimiters

By default, AppleScript's *text item delimiters* is set to an empty string {""}, which means that asking for every text item of a string is the same as asking for every character of a string. See Figure 3-17 for an example.

Figure 3-17. Every text item here returns a list of characters. The fact that the *text item delimiters* property is set to an empty string makes AppleScript understand that every single character, including spaces, punctuation marks, etc., appears as an item in the resulting list.

Where things start to get exciting is when you set AppleScript's text item delimiters to a different value.

Let's take a phone number that a user entered into a dialog box. The entry was 800-555-1212. Now, let's see what happens when we change AppleScript's *text item delimiters* property to "-".

Start a new script window and enter the following script text:

```
set text item delimiters to "-"
get every text item of "800-555-1212"
```

As you can tell from Figure 3-18, the delimiters themselves are discarded, while anything in between them gets put into list items.

The once single string with text "chunks" separated by a character we called a delimiter, is now a list where each text chunk is a single list item.

"800-555-1212" changed to {"800", "555", "1212"}

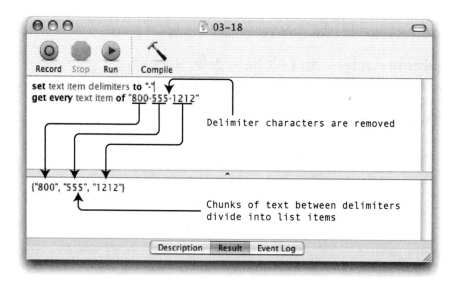

Figure 3-18. Changing the text item delimiters property to a dash.

Combining lists

The other function of the *text item delimiters* property is to act as padding when combining a list into a single string.

Let's take the list we created in the last part:

```
{"800", "555", "1212"}
```

Start a new script window and write a script like the one in Figure 3-19.

Figure 3-19. When the *text item delimiters* property is set to an empty string, the list items just squish together.

Now, let's give the *text item delimiters* property a different value. Change the first line in our script to look like the one in Figure 3-20.

Figure 3-20. Now that the *text item delimiters* property is set to an asterisk (*), when we join the list items into a string, the *text item delimiters* property value is used as padding between the items.

What you may be asking yourself is where the plural in delimiters come from. Can we set the *text item delimiters* property to multiple delimiters? Well, we can, but nothing will really happen with them. Just like the fact that your bank's deposit slip has place for seven digits where you write the amount, AppleScript's delimiters is a bit about a promise. While you can currently set AppleScript's text item delimiters to a list of strings, AppleScript will only look at the first one and ignore the rest.

The text items delimiter can be set to a multicharacter string. In the following script, the *text item delimiters* property is set to the string "mississippi":

Script 3-6

```
set text item delimiters to "mississippi"
set the_secret_message to ¬
    "memississippiet mississippime mississippiamississippit" & ¬
    "fimississippive"
set the_items to text items of the_secret_message
set text item delimiters to ""
set the_message to the_items as string
-->"meet me at five"
```

Setting the text item delimiters property

Until now whenever we wanted to change the value of the *text item delimiters* property, we just referred to it by name. However, this worked because we weren't talking to any application at the time. In other words, we weren't in any application's *tell* block.

If you try the script in Figure 3-21, you will get an error. The error, shown in Figure 3-22, let's you know that the Finder doesn't have a *text item delimiters* property, and therefore can't change it.

Figure 3-21. Trying to set the value of the *text item delimiters* property

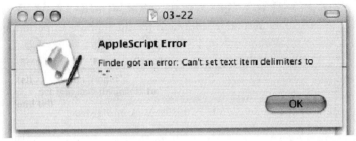

Figure 3-22. The error resulted from running the script from Figure 3-21.

Trying to use commands and set properties that belong to an object you happen to not be talking to at the time is a common error that can lead to a wild goose chase, or should I say a wild bug chase . . .

What happened is a bit like saying, "George, your laces are untied." George looks confused, since he's wearing rubber boots. "Oh, I meant Jim's laces!" Now we're being clear.

In this case, we need to specify that the property we want to set belongs to AppleScript rather than to the Finder, which we happen to be addressing at the moment.

Figure 3-23 shows how we can set AppleScript's property inside any application's *tell* block.

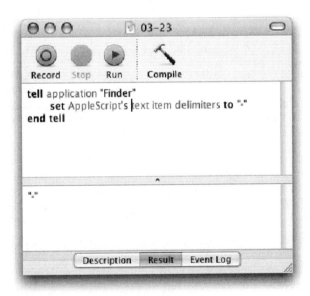

Figure 3-23. Setting the value of the *text item delimiters* property inside an application *tell* block

Text delimiters in the real world: Search and replace

One use of the *text item delimiters* property is for the purpose of performing a simple search and replace on strings inside AppleScript.

The way we go about it is by setting the value of the *text item delimiters* property to the character or text we want to replace, and split the text we want to search in, into a list. This will remove the search character. Next we will set the *text item delimiters* property to the replacement character, and combine the list back into a string.

For our example, we will convert a file path from AppleScript format to a UNIX-style string reference. In AppleScript, we refer to files by separating the folder tree with colons in this way:

"Macintosh HD:Users:hanaan:Desktop:Picture 1.PDF"

The same path in UNIX will be

"Macintosh HD/Users/hanaan/Desktop/Picture 1.PDF"

We need to take the first string and replace the colons with slashes. Here is the script that will do that:

Script 3-7

```
set the_file_path to "Macintosh HD:Users:hanaan:Desktop:Picture 1.PDF"
set text item delimiters to {":"}
set the_file_path_items to every text item of the_file_path
set text item delimiters to {"/"}
set the_UNIX_file_path to the_file_path_items as string
```

In line 1 we put the file path in the form of a string into a variable. While AppleScript doesn't care if you make operations on the value or on a variable holding the value, in reality you will rarely operate on raw strings without first assigning them to variables. This way your code isn't littered with text and numbers that you need to hunt for all over if it needs to be changed, or rather when it needs to be changed.

In line 2 we set the value of the *text item delimiters* property to a colon (:). The actual value we set the *text item delimiters* property to is a list of strings rather than a single string. Although setting this property to a single string works today, it is more correct to specify a list of strings since at some point AppleScript may support multiple text item delimiters, and a list has a somewhat better chance of surviving that transition.

In line 3 we split the string into a list, which leaves us with the text and without any of the colons.

In line 4 we change the text item delimiters to "/".

In line 5 we coerce the list of string items into a single string. We do that by adding the *as string* operator at the end. This uses the text item delimiter, which is now set to a slash (/), as padding between the different list items. The list then becomes a string again, but instead of any occurrence of the colon, we now have a slash.

While the script works OK and does what we wanted it to, there's a small job that we neglected to do. It's called cleanup. Now I don't care if you're sitting in your high-school-year pajamas among piles of laundry and the cereal bowl from this morning and yesterday's morning still on your desk, but when it comes to scripting, not cleaning up after yourself can cause your scripts to be almost as much of a maintenance nuisance as they are a timesaver.

Our cleanup job in this case has to do with returning the value of the *text item delimiters* property to the same state we found it in. The operation will have two parts: remembering what the text item delimiter was set to before we started meddling with it, and setting it back to that value at the end.

Through that process we may never know what the actual value is, but that doesn't matter. It's like borrowing your friend's car for the day. You should come with a CD jewel box marked CD_I_found_in_the_car. As you get in the car, put your friend's CD in there. At the end of the day, before you return the car, take the CD out of that box and pop it back into the CD player. It makes no difference what CD it was, just that it was there when you started out.

Here is what we will do with the script:

Start a new script line before the current first line of the script. This new first line will store the original text item delimiter in a variable of our choice.

```
set the_original_text_item_delimiter to text item delimiters
```

The final step will be to restore the value of the *text item delimiters* property back to the original value. But what is that original value? Makes no difference, as long as you know where you put it! Add the following line to the end of your script:

```
set text item delimiters to the_original_text_item_delimiter
```

And, as always, we can't quite leave until we properly turn our bits of code into a useful subroutine.

The parameter for the subroutine, or in other words, the information the subroutine will work on, will be the AppleScript style path as a string. The subroutine will return a string containing the converted UNIX-style path.

To convert the script we've written so far into a subroutine we can call from anywhere, we can start by wrapping it in a subroutine package:

Add the following line to the beginning of the script, before the first line:

```
to convert_this_path_to_unix_style(the_mac_style_path)
```

Notice that I used the word "to" and not "on." These two words are interchangeable as beginning of subroutines.

The last line before the end will be the statement that returns the final value. This will be the value that will be returned as the result of the subroutine call statement.

After what is now the last line of the script, type the following line:

```
return the_UNIX_file_path
```

If you don't add the *return* statement at the end, the subroutine will return the result of its last statement, which is in this case the value of the *the_original_text_item_delimiter* variable.

The last line we will add will have one word: "end."

We only have to type end, and AppleScript figures out which compound statement we're ending, and finish the line for us when it compiles our script.

By now we have a subroutine that can be called, and will return a result. However, is it the result we expected? Not really. That is because the subroutine is still processing the same path we gave it as a string, and not the parameter it receives when it is called. See, the point of this subroutine is that you can give it any file path and it'll convert it to a UNIX path. To make our subroutine do that, we must make a little tweak in the middle.

The line that sets a variable to the literal string is unnecessary. The variable it sets, which is used later on in the subroutine, will be replaced with the variable that holds the value supplied when the subroutine is called. This variable is called a parameter variable.

Figure 3-24 shows the finished script.

Figure 3-24. The finished script

One final note about the cleanup we did here. In my scripts, I always get the *text item delimiters* property back to an empty string, as a single item in a list: {""}. This way I know what to expect. An empty string as the only item in a list is the default value of that property, and always getting it back to that value is a good idea.

Reading and using tab-delimited text files

In the following exercise we will use AppleScript to read a tab-delimited text file as if it were a database table. Well, actually, a tab-delimited text file is just that. What gives the text meaning is knowing what each column stands for.

The feel-good part of tab-delimited text files is that they're easy to handle. There's no code, no characters to omit, no hidden characters, just data separated by tabs. The way data is arranged in a tab-delimited text file is just the same as in a database: there are records, fields, and cells. In the text file, each paragraph is a record, each column is a field, and the cells are the text separated by tabs.

For our project's purposes, we will use a text file exported from FileMaker Pro. Granted, we can use AppleScript to get the data right out of FileMaker Pro, but let's assume that we get the data in that form from our company's headquarters.

Figures 3-25 and 3-26 show how the data looks in FileMaker and when opened in a text editor.

Figure 3-25. The data in the source FileMaker Pro database

Figure 3-26. The data as text in BBEdit text editor; the little gray triangles represent tabs and the line with the 90° angle is the return character.

Our script will read the file, loop through the records (paragraphs), and display a little dialog box with a message saying something like "Jane, 29 years old, can be reached at 401-837-1123 at home in Providence."

Our first task is to identify the file and read its contents. The result will be a string variable that will contain the entire text contents of the file.

There are a few ways to identify the file you want. It can be in a folder that the script is aware of, or the file can be dropped on a script droplet. What we're going to do here is let the user choose the file, and process it from there.

The command *choose file* is perfect for that. It's very simple to use, and it returns a file reference.

A file reference isn't a string, although it can be coerced into a string. I personally use strings as much as possible, as they are much more flexible. You can add them to text files as script preferences, precede them with the word "alias," "folder," or "file" to create an instant file (or folder) reference, and anyway, some applications require a string, not a file reference as parameters to commands.

Figure 3-27 shows some file references and string variables.

Figure 3-27. A string compared with file and alias references

We will spend quite a bit of book real estate on file references and working with files, so if it's not all clear here, don't beat yourself up (unless, of course, it causes you pleasure).

So what we'll do here is convert every file reference right into a string as soon as we get it, and back into a file reference when we have to.

To thoroughly enjoy this exercise, create yourself a little text file with data similar to the one in Figure 3-26. Save that file as plain text (not RTF) on the desktop.

Let's start with the *choose file* command:

Start a new script window and type the following:

```
choose file
```

Compile the script and run it. AppleScript opens the normal Mac open dialog box and allows you to specify any file, just like in Figure 3-28.

Choose the file you made and click the Choose button.

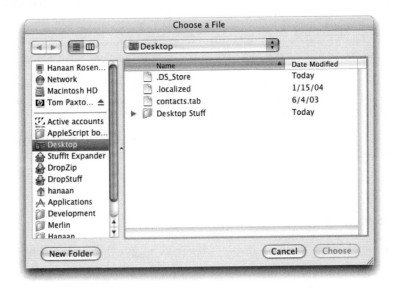

Figure 3-28. The Choose a File dialog box

Now examine the result: the result of that statement containing the *choose file* command is an alias. Let's add *as string* to the end of the statement:

```
choose file as string
```

Now that you run the script the result is a string with out the word "alias" preceding it.

Speaking of results, we need a home for the resulting string. What better place than a variable. Add the variable name with the *set* command to the beginning of the line like this:

```
set text_file_path to choose file as string
```

The next line will read the file and put the text in a variable:

```
set file_text to read file text_file_path
```

The shorter way to do that is simply have a single line that says

```
set file_text to read (choose file)
```

This statement actually performs three commands: it chooses a file, which returns a file reference; then it reads the file, which returns a string; and at the end, it also doubles as an assignment command, and it assigns the resulting text it read from the file to a variable.

It's great fun trying to see how few lines you can use to perform different actions, although others might not agree. John Thorsen, a longtime AppleScript developer and trainer, tries to stretch each command on as many lines as he can. He says that he does it for readability reasons, but I suspect that he does that because he charges his clients by the line :-).

In any case, we got to the point where we have the text in a variable and we can start playing with it.

What we will do from here, in general terms, is loop through each record, and as we do that, split the record and use the information in the cells to build our personalized message.

In AppleScript terms, there are two ways to extract the records: the obvious choice would be to use the paragraph element as we loop through the text. However, since we're in a text item delimiters kind of mood, we should use that one instead.

Let's break the text into a list, where each record is in one list. Write the next line of the script like this:

```
set text item delimiters to return
set database_records_list to every text item of file_text
```

Now we can loop through the items in the list.

Look at Figure 3-29 to see our progress, and the result we get when we break the text into list items.

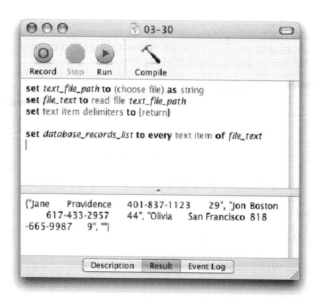

Figure 3-29. While the result in the result window may be a bit hard to understand, you can make out the items that are separated by a comma. Notice how each item is surrounded with double quotes. That's what is telling us that it's a list of strings.

Now we'll loop through the records. Add the following line to your script:

```
repeat with i from 1 to (count items of database_records_list)
```

What does *i* stand for? Well *i* is the repeat variable. In this type of repeat, its value is a number that changes with each loop. In the first loop, *i* will have a value of 1, in the next loop, a value of 2, etc. This can be a useful variable and in many cases you make different mathematical operations with it to figure out frame positions, grids, and other graphical aspects.

What will *i* do for us now? Well, we can use it to get the correct item of the *database_records_list*.

Add the following three lines:

```
set the_database_record to item i of database_records_list
display dialog the_database_record
end repeat
```

Now run the script and see what happens. Every record turns into a string and displays in a dialog box like in Figure 3-30.

Figure 3-30. The database record as a string

Now we need to break each record into a list that will contain the fields. Add a blank line before the *display dialog* line and insert the following lines:

Script 3-8

```
set text item delimiters to tab
set field_list to every text item of the_database_record
set the_name to item 1 of field_list
set the_city to item 2 of field_list
set the_telephone to item 3 of field_list
set the_age to item 4 of field_list
set the_message_text to ¬
    the_name & ", " & the_age & ¬
    " years old, can be reached at " & ¬
    the_telephone & " at home in " & ¬
    the_city as string
```

Now, change the *display dialog* line to display the message instead of *the_database_record*:

```
display dialog the_message_text
```

Refer to Figure 3-31 for the finished script. Figure 3-32 shows one of the dialog boxes you get when running the script.

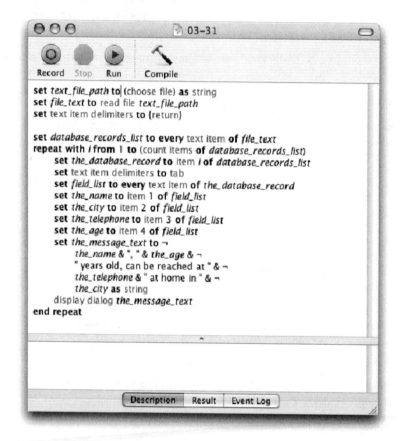

Figure 3-31. The finished script

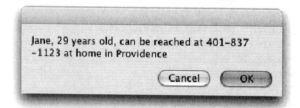

Figure 3-32. The dialog box resulting from running the script

Copy and set

I mentioned using the *set* command to assign a value to a variable. We also saw earlier that the *copy* command produces the same result. Take a look at these two examples:

```
set the_variable to "Value"
```

works the same as

```
copy "Value" to the_variable
```

This scenario is true for single values, such as strings, numbers, etc. The situation is different when working with list items. Consider the following scenario:

```
set my_list to {1, 2, 3}
set my_other_list to my_list
set item 2 of my_list to "a"
--> my_other_list = {1, "a", 3}
```

In the preceding script, we start with a simple list of three items: {1, 2, 3}. Then we set the variable *my_other_list* to the variable *my_list*.

The crucial detail here is that the variable *my_other_list* is not set to the value of the list *my_list*, which would be {1, 2, 3}, but rather to the variable itself. As you can see, when any list item changes in *my_list*, as happens in line 3 of the script, the value of *my_other_list* is affected as well.

This situation is called data sharing, and is used when you want two variables that point at the same place in memory. To get around data sharing, all you have to do is use the *copy* command when assigning lists, like this:

```
set my_list to {1, 2, 3}
copy my_list to my_other_list
set item 2 of my_list to "a"
--> my_other_list = {1, 2, 3}
```

In the second variation of the preceding script, the variables *my_list* and *my_other_list* are separate. Setting an item in one list does not change the other list.

More on value assignment

Remember having fun with shorter scripts that do more with less? Well here's one for you: in the preceding script, we used five lines of code to assign the fields' content to the four variables. First, we put them all in a list, then we broke them down to the individual items. There's a better way to do that. If you set a list of variables to a list of values, each variable in the list gets the corresponding value in the value list assigned to it. Observe the following line:

```
set {a,b,c} to {"why","not","today"}
```

The result is that a = "why", b = "not", and c = "today". Pretty cool. We could have used this trick in our script like the one shown in Figure 3-33.

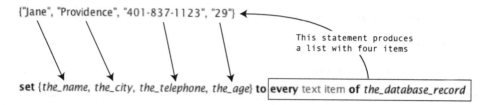

Figure 3-33. Using a single line to assign each item of a list to a separate variable.

As noted in the "Copy and set" section earlier, there is a slight difference between using the *set* and *copy* assignment commands when we assign lists to variables. In the example shown in Figure 3-33, it doesn't really matter if we use the *copy* or *set* commands, because what we're assigning here is the strings that are elements of the list to individual variables. The list itself never gets assigned like it does in the longer version shown in Figure 3-31.

Offset

The *offset* command is useful for figuring out where a certain substring starts in another string. This command is a bit limited, but for small operations it can come in handy.

The result of the *offset* command is an integer that contains the first instance of the substring in the main string.

Here's a simple example of the *offset* command:

```
offset of "@" in "info@apple.com"
```

The result is 5.

In Figure 3-34 we use the *offset* command to figure out a domain name in an e-mail address.

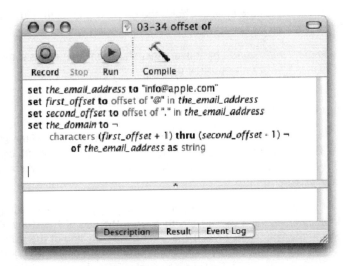

Figure 3-34. Using the *offset* command to get the domain off of a string

Of course, if the e-mail address were info@apple.store.com, our script would have still returned "apple", while our intent was probably to get "apple.store".

A solution to this problem could involve using the text item delimiters we looked at earlier. Following is the script that returns the correct domain, with or without additional periods:

```
set the_email_address to "info@apple.store.com"
set first_offset to offset of "@" in the_email_address
set text item delimiters to {"."}
set email_address_items to text items of the_email_address
set domain_length to (length of (last item of email_address_items)) + 1
set text item delimiters to {""}
set the_domain to ¬
    characters (first_offset + 1) thru -(domain_length + 1) ¬
        of the_email_address as string
```

The main change we made in this script is that we use the text item delimiters and the *every text item* statements in order to get the length of the domain. We figure that if we split the whole e-mail into chunks by using the period as a delimiter, the last chunk will be the "com" or "net", etc.

In line 5 we assign the length of that last chunk to a variable.

Line 5 has a pretty complex statement. This statement could've been broken down to two or three lines, which would have made it more legible. It could have read

```
get last item of address_items
get length of result
set domain_length to result + 1
```

Anyhow, now the variable *domain_length* holds the length of the "com" plus 1 to account for the period.

The variable *domain_length* comes back in another statement that needs some analyzing in line 7. Let's look at the complex portion of it:

```
characters (first_offset + 1) thru -(domain_length + 1) of ¬
    the_email_address
```

We start with *(first_offset + 1)*. Remember that *first_offset* holds the offset of the @ character. In our example it would have a value of 5. If we start the domain from the fifth character, we will get the @ as part of our domain, so we must add 1 to it, which is where we get the *(first_offset + 1)* operation.

The second part is also neat: *-(domain_length + 1)*. The purpose of the minus sign is to let AppleScript know that we want to start counting from the end of the string. Remember that character -1 is the last character, or 1 character before the end of the string. Now, we know that the *domain_length* variable has a value of 4 (length of "com" +1), that means that if we get the characters up to the fourth character from the end, we will *still* get that darn period as part of our result. That's why we need to add 1 yet again to the *domain_length*. We put it in parentheses so that it evaluates as a number, and only then becomes negative.

Line 7 could also have been broken into three lines in this manner:

```
set start_character_offset to first_offset + 1
set end_character_offset to domain_length + 1
set the_domain to ¬
    characters start_character_offset thru -end_character_offset ¬
    of the_email_address as string
```

Note that using a character range statement such as *character x thru y of the_string* returns a list of characters, not a string, which is why we need to coerce the result into a string at the end. Now what else do we have to take into account when joining a list into a string? Text item delimiters, of course! Not only that, but at the start of the script we changed the text item delimiters to a period. After line 5 and before line 7 (how about say, line 6) we need to set the text item delimiters back to an empty string in a list: {""}.

Power wrap-up

This section summarizes the chapter in an intensive-reference style. Use this part to look up facts related to the chapter without the chatter.

Strings and variables

Assign strings to a variable.

```
set x to "some text"
copy "some text" to x
```

In order to include quotes in your string, use the \ (backslash) character to "escape" them, like this:

```
set x to "Press the \"OK\" button"
--> x = Press the "OK" button
```

3

Escape character

You also have to escape the backslash if you want to include it in a string, like this:

```
set x to "This is a backslash: \\"
--> x = This is a backslash: \
```

Including tabs, returns, and spaces

To include tabs and returns in strings, you can use \t and \r, respectively.

```
set tab_delimited_text to "Name\tCity\rJoan/tNew York/rJames\tAtlanta"
--Result:
Name  → City
Joan  → New York
James → Atlanta
```

Outside of the quotes you can specify the tab, space, and return characters using their names, like this:

```
set tab_delimited_text to "Name" & tab & "City" & return & "Joan"
& tab & "New" & space & "York"
--Result:
Name → City
Joan → New York
```

The constants *space*, *tab*, and *return* can be set to other values; however, this is not recommended.

ASCII numbers and characters

Use the *ASCII character* command to get the character associated with a particular ASCII position.

```
ASCII character 36
--> "$"
```

The *ASCII number* command works the opposite way: you provide the character and the result is the character that fits the position in the ASCII table.

```
ASCII character "$"
--> 36
```

String operators

The main operator used with strings is the concatenation operator, the ampersand: &.

The two operands are strings, but the right operand can be any value class that can be coerced into a string.

The following line concatenates (links together) the string to the left of the operator and the string to the right of it.

```
"Apple" & "Script"
--> "AppleScript"
```

If the left operand is not a string, the result of the operation is a list, not a string.

```
"$" & 5
--> "$5"
5 & "$"
--> {5, "$"}
```

Comparing strings

Strings can also be compared with the following operators: =, ≠, >, ≥, <, ≤, *starts with*, *ends with*, *contains*, and *is contained by*.

```
"Apple" = "Orange" --> false
```

With the >, <, ≥, and ≤ operators, the larger character is the character that appears later in the alphabet.

```
"A" > "B" --> false
```

Considering and ignoring

You can consider and ignore different attributes of the text to sway the comparison results in different ways. Look for the section "Considering and ignoring" for details.

Length

You can get the length of a string in two ways:

By using the *length* property of the string:

```
length of "Charles River" --> 13
```

Or by using the *count* command:

```
count "my marbles" --> 10
```

String parts

A string has built-in parts. These parts are characters, words, paragraphs, and text items. Asking for the parts of a string returns a list with each such part as a list item.

```
characters of "particles" --> {"p", "a", "r", "t", "i", "c", "l", ¬
    "e", "s"}
words of "James: 'would you give-up!'" --> {"James", "would", "you", ¬
    "give-up"}
paragraphs of "line 1
line 2
line 3"
--> {"line 1", "line 2", "line 3"}
```

Notice that the separators are not a part of the result. The words list has no punctuation and the paragraph list has no return characters.

Text item delimiters

Text items of a string are the parts of any string, separated by the current text item delimiters. While the text item delimiters can be set to a list of strings, only the first string will be used.

The default text item delimiters value is {""}, which is an empty string in a list.

You script with text items as you would words and characters.

```
text items of "abc" --> {"a", "b", "c"}
```

Changing the value of the *text item delimiters* constant changes the result.

```
set text item delimiters to {"b"}
text items of "abc" --> {"a", "c"}
set text item delimiters to {"@"}
text items of "george@jungle.com" --> {" george", " jungle.com"}
set text item delimiters to {"i"}
text items of "Mississippi" --> {"M", "ss", "ss", "pp", ""}
set text item delimiters to {"stop"}
text items of "helpstopmestopJoe" --> {"help", "me", "Joe"}
```

Setting the *text item delimiters* value inside an application *tell* block requires that you use the following syntax:

```
set AppleScript's text item delimiters to ...
```

It is also recommended that after setting the *text item delimiters* property in your script, that you set it back to the default of {""}.

Offset command

The *offset* command returns the offset of a substring in a string. The offset is the number of characters from the beginning of the right operand string that the left operand string first appears in:

```
offset of "s" in "Music" --> 3
offset of "Ang" in "Los Angeles" --> 5
offset of "a" in "1-800-555-1212" --> 0
```

The last statement's result is 0 because the string "1-800-555-1212" does not contain the string "a".

Details previously . . .

The last part of this chapter is a summary of the entire chapter. For more details on any of the items here, refer to earlier sections in this chapter.

4 DOING THE MATH: ALL ABOUT NUMBERS

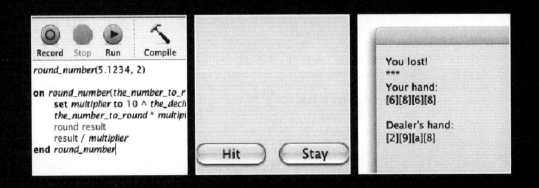

In AppleScript, math is not the purpose, but rather a tool. No matter what you are trying to achieve, you will need to manipulate numbers. This chapter looks at numbers in AppleScript and how to use them to get the results you want.

Massaging numbers

One of the great challenges in writing complex scripts is dealing with numbers and math. In AppleScript programming, though, your job is not to figure out the solution to a math problem, but rather to figure out how to present the problem to AppleScript in a way that it will be able to return a useful result.

AppleScript supports two kinds of numbers, or rather we should refer to them as two classes of numbers: reals and integers.

Integers are whole numbers without a decimal fraction, and with no potential of ever getting one. Integers can, however, be negative numbers.

Real numbers have a decimal point, even if it's ceremonial, like in the case of the real 1.0. It's equal in value to the integer 1, but it is a real nonetheless.

When specifying numeric values (a snooty way of saying "numbers"), you're not allowed to use commas, etc. Here are some examples:

Script 4-1

```
class of 2003 --> Integer
class of 1.5 --> real
class of "1000" --> string
"1000" as integer --> 1000
"1000" as real  --> 1000.0
"1,000" as integer --> error
```

When we do math, some operations return results as real and some as an integer. The implications aren't great because you can process both reals and integers interchangeably without choking AppleScript.

There are some statements that demand whole numbers as parameters, and using a real with a fraction will return an error, but these are obvious enough, such as

```
repeat 1.5 time
--Loop here
end repeat
```

Real big

Real numbers have the tendency to be written using exponential notation. You can write them this way, but they get converted to this most irritating format when the script is compiled.

Try to write the following in a new script editor window:

    10000.0

When you compile the script, the number will change to

    1.0E+4

4

The mathematical equivalent is 1.0 * 10^4.

In other words, AppleScript tells you, "I moved the decimal point four spots to the left. Move the decimal point back, and you have your 10000 back."

Watch how easy it is to apply the decimal-shifting technique:

If we take the number 123456789.987654321 and compile it in a script window, it will be displayed as 1.23456789987654E+8. All we have to do is shift the decimal point eight spaces to the right to get the number 123456789.987654.

What? Oh . . . the last three digits after the decimal point . . . oh stop being so picky! Why do you need that precise a number anyway?

The same decimal-shifting idea works with negative exponential numbers. That doesn't mean that the number itself is negative, just the direction of the decimal point. Example:

1.0E-4 is actually 0.0001. Notice the decimal point moved four spots to the right. Move the decimal and you get the number.

In order to become part of that heartless form of displaying numbers, a real number has to either be lower than 0.0001 or higher than 10000; otherwise, it is displayed as is.

Rounding numbers

Rounding numbers is an important aspect of scripting and programming. While the *round* command rounds the number you give it to a nearby whole number, there are many more things you can do with the command if you only make some modifications to it.

To start, let's look at the *round* command in detail.

The parameter you supply it is a real number. This makes sense, since an integer is already round.

The result returned by the *round* command is an integer. Actually, the *round* command is the definition of the difference between integers and reals: integers are round and reals are (usually) not. I write *usually* because I'm not sure if 1.0 is considered round or not. Hmm.

To test the basic function of the *round* command, start a new script window and type each of the following lines:

```
round 1.5 --> 2
round 2.2 --> 2
round -6.4 --> -6
```

You can fine-tune the result of the *round* command by using the *rounding* parameter. There are five possible constant values to the *rounding* parameter, if you choose to use any. The constants are *up*, *down*, *toward zero*, *to nearest*, and *as taught in school*. If you simply use the *round* command without specifying the *round* parameter, AppleScript will use the *to nearest* logic, as described a little later in this chapter.

Rounding up

As it sounds, *rounding up* will always round to the next higher integer. Examples:

```
round 1.1 rounding up --> 2
round 5.5 rounding up --> 6
round -2.9 rounding up --> -2
```

Rounding down

The opposite of *rounding up*, *rounding down* will always return the next lower integer. Examples:

```
round 1.7 rounding down --> 1
round 5.5 rounding down --> 5
round -2.1 rounding down --> -3
```

Rounding toward zero

The *rounding towards zero* constant acts the same as *rounding down* with positive numbers, and with negative numbers it acts like the *rounding up* constant would.

Rounding to nearest or as taught in school

As far as what was taught in school, well, I hate to say that I was probably chasing butterflies the day they taught that . . . but I'll make an effort to explain it anyhow.

Rounding to nearest is the default answer that will be used if none other is specified. *Rounding to nearest* acts as you would expect, other than with the rounding in-between numbers: numbers and a half. When you try to round 0.5, 2.5, 56.5, etc. the *rounding to nearest* option will round towards zero. This is done that way, as explained in the AppleScript Language Guide, to avoid cumulative errors.

Rounding as taught in school, on the other hand, will round numbers and a half away from zero.

Rounding to other increments

When you simply round a real number, you get a whole number, or an integer, as a result. That's good for some things, but let's look at two other scenarios that are related to rounding numbers, but can't be achieved directly with the *round* command.

Scenario 1: What if we want to round a real to have no more than a certain number of digits after the decimal point?

Take for example currency formatting. If we need to calculate a price, we need only two decimal points. If I'm automating a catalog and I need to use AppleScript to calculate the 7% RI state sales tax on a product that costs $4.99, the total cost with tax will be $5.3393. Rounding that number will give me $5, but what I want to show is $5.34, right?

Scenario 2: What if the script needs to start with an integer and get that integer's previous number, which is a multiplication of 1000? For instance, let's assume that I have a product number of 55782. Using the product numbering scheme I can teach AppleScript that the category number for that product is 55000. Sure, I can coerce it into a string, take the first two digits, and tack on "000" at the end:

```
characters 1 thru 2 of (the_product_number as string) & "000" as string
```

But we're out of luck: this is the numbers section, and the strings section of the book is way over, so we're stuck having to find a solution using the *round* command.

The solution to both scenarios I mentioned previously involves dividing and multiplying the number before and after rounding it. To be more specific, here is how we would solve each of the needs described in scenarios 1 and 2:

Let's start with the scenario 1 solution. When we analyze the finished script in Figure 4-1, we can see that there are two mathematical operations that involve first multiplying by 100 on line 4, and then dividing by 100 at the last line. This forward-and-back action is the foundation of our script.

Figure 4-1. The script that rounds currency to only two decimal points

Let's look at the script line by line:

Script 4-2

```
set the_price to 4.99
set the_tax_rate to 0.07
(the_price * the_tax_rate) + the_price
result * 100
round result rounding as taught in school
set price_with_tax to result / 100
```

In lines 1 and 2 we assign values to some variables we will use in the script. This is a good idea even if the values never change. For instance, if the tax rate will always be 7%, we should still assign it to a variable. This gives it a meaning and makes your script clearer and more flexible, especially if that value is used in multiple spots in your script.

From line 3 until line 6 we don't assign any variables. Instead, we rely on the built-in *result* variable that automatically holds the result of the previous statement. We do that since we don't care for the intermediate results. We don't care to store the result of line 4, which happens to be 533.93. We need that resulting value for the following operation, not beyond it. The result of line 3 is used in line 4, the result of line 4 is used in line 5, and the result of line 5 is used in the final operation in line 6.

In line 3 we calculate the actual price with tax. This results in a number with too many decimal points, a problem we will need to remedy.

In line 4 we multiply the result by 100. We do this because any real number with two decimal points multiplied by 100 should be whole. To figure out the number to use, we can raise 10 to the power of the number of digits we want. Get it? We want to end up with two decimal points, so we do 10^2 to get 100.

To make that result whole, we round it in line 5; we use the *rounding* parameter with the value *as taught in school* to ensure that a price ending with a half a penny rounds to the next penny up.

To give the resulting number its two decimal points back, we divide it by 100 in line 6.

Generally, as you as a math-whiz already know, if you take a number (n) and first multiply it by another number (say m) and then divide it by that same number (m), you get your original number back. We're counting on that fact, but we're adding a little twist: we round the number in the middle.

This solution is not complete, though. What if our original price number was 4.5? Using these operations would still return 4.5 and finally end up looking like this: "$4.5". Try to add lines of code that will see if that's the issue and add the extra zero if needed. Hint: you can't do that with numbers, only strings!

Scenario 2 is similar, but the crucial difference is that we first divide the number then round it, and only then remultiply it.

As you can see in Figure 4-2, I tried to condense the operations from the last script into a single script line.

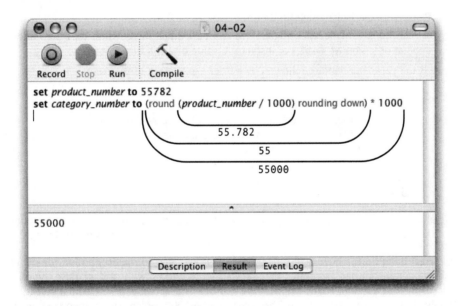

Figure 4-2. Figuring out the product category from the product number

Since we don't have script lines to specify the order of operations, we have to rely on good old parentheses.

The first operation is in the innermost set of parentheses:

```
product_number/1000
```

The result is 55.782

The result is then processed by the second set of parentheses:

> round (product_number/1000) rounding down

We round down since even product number 55999 still belongs to category 55000. This way, the number 55.782 rounds down to 55.

The final operation returns the number to its original length:

> (round (product_number/1000) rounding down)*1000

which returns 55000.

Rounding handler

To cap off the rounding discussion we're going to put together a handler that will be in charge of rounding numbers.

The handler will accept two parameters:

- The number to round in the real value class.
- The number of decimal points. This will be a small integer that tells the handler what precision we want. For instance, a value of 2 will turn 1.66667 to 1.67.

Here is the complete handler followed by a brief explanation of the steps:

Script 4-3

```
on round_number(the_number_to_round, the_decimal_precision)
    set multiplier to 10 ^ the_decimal_precision
    the_number_to_round * multiplier
    round result
    result / multiplier
end round_number
```

We already discussed steps 2 through 4 earlier. We multiply the number we want to round, then we round it, and divide it by the same number to get it back to its original range.

The neat thing here is how we got to that number we need to multiply and divide by. We use the number of decimal points that we wanted to end up with, and we raise the number 10 by that number. For example, if we want to end up with three decimal places, we would do this calculation: $10 \char`^ 3$. The result will be 1000, which will be then used in the rounding, as seen in Figure 4-3.

Figure 4-3 shows the handler, a statement calling that handler, and the result.

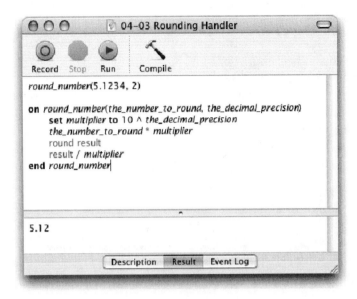

Figure 4-3. The handler and the handler call

In the example, the real value 5.1234 is passed along with 2 as the number of decimal spaces. The result is 5.12.

Scripting at random

Now what's a programming language without the ability to generate random numbers? Like other languages, AppleScript has a command for generating random numbers, and a number of strong parameters to make it work for you in many ways.

Random number result

The *random number* command returns a result that can be either an integer or a real. Whether the result is a real or integer depends on whether the parameters you provided are reals or integers.

In any case, the *random number* command generates a single number result.

Parameters

The *random number* command can be used as is without any parameters. The result in that case is a real number between 0 and 1 as shown in Figure 4-4.

Figure 4-4. The random number command used without parameters

The first parameter you can use is a number, either a real or an integer, following the command. Try this:

        random number 5

The result is an integer between 0 and 5.

Now try this:

        random number 5.0

Now the result is a real with 12 decimal spots, also between 0 and 5.

You can also use the range parameters *from* and *to*; try this:

        random number from 20 to 30

or

        random number from 20.0 to 30.0

If you combine parameters, only the first one will be used. For instance, the following command will generate an integer from 0 to 3:

        random number 3 from 20.0 to 30.0

The final parameter is a bit obscure. The syntax for it is

        random number [any other parameters] with seed number

The *with seed* parameter associates a random number with the seed number. This allows you to either get the same random number every time or ensure getting a different random number.

OK, so these two statements seemed to be contrary to the concept of random numbers. Aren't random numbers supposed to always be random? Well, yes. Sometimes, however, you will be getting a random number that is a repeat of the last random number AppleScript returned. This is due to the seed used.

To get the same "random" number every time, simply use the same seed number:

```
random number with seed 100
```

The result will always be 0.716641089949.

Now, try this script:

```
random number from 100000 to 999999 with seed (current date)
```

Using the current date as the seed ensures that the seed is different every time, and therefore that the number you're getting is truly random.

Blackjack!

To cap off this short random number section, I thought it would be appropriate to invite you for a little game of blackjack.

In order to keep the script within a length that can work OK for the book, I simplified a few rules. In our AppleScript blackjack, the cards keep their value: for instance, Ace is always 1, Jack is 11, King is 13, etc.

If this is too much for your purist-self, I suggest that you add the necessary lines of code to make the game complete. This will involve scenarios for whether the different aces are 1s or 11s, etc.

As for my script, here's how I went about it:

There are two players: the dealer and you. Each of you has a hand of cards. The information regarding that hand is kept in a record. Each of you have your own record that includes two items: total, to see if either of you passed 21, etc., and a string I called "hand" that's used to show you the cards you have, and the dealer's hand at the end of the game. In that string, cards may appear like this: [5][K]. That means you have a 5 and a King.

Here is how the player's record may look like:

```
{total:18, hand:" [10] [8]"}
```

This way, the statement that follows can be used if the script needs to show either the player or the dealer's hand:

```
display dialog (display of dealer)
```

Here is the complete script, followed by a breakdown and description.

Script 4-4

```
1. set card_marks to {"[A]", "[2]", "[3]", "[4]", "[5]", "[6]", ¬
2.    "[7]", "[8]", "[9]", "[10]", "[J]", "[Q]", "[K]"}
3. set dealer_hand to {total:0, hand:""}
4. set player_hand to {total:0, hand:""}

5. --setup dealer hand
6. set total_this_draw to 0
7. repeat
8.     set drawn_card to random number from 1 to 13
9.     set total_this_draw to total_this_draw + drawn_card
10.    set hand of dealer_hand to ¬
11.        (hand of dealer_hand) & ¬
12.        (item drawn_card of card_marks) as string
13.    if total_this_draw > 21 then
14.        set dealer_lost_round to true
15.        set total of dealer_hand to total_this_draw
16.        exit repeat
17.    else if total_this_draw ≥ 17 then
18.        set dealer_lost_round to false
19.        exit repeat
20.    end if
21. end repeat

22. --Draw first two player cards
23. set total_this_draw to 0
24. repeat 2 times
25.    set drawn_card to random number from 1 to 13
26.    set total_this_draw to total_this_draw + drawn_card
27.    set hand of player_hand to ¬
28.        (hand of player_hand) & ¬
29.        (item drawn_card of card_marks) as string
30. end repeat

31. if dealer_lost_round then
32.    display dialog "You won! "
33.    return
34. end if

35. set player_lost_round to false
36. repeat
37.    set final_display to "* * *" & return & ¬
38.        "Your hand:  " & (hand of player_hand) & return & return & ¬
39.        "Dealer's hand:  " & (hand of dealer_hand) as string
40.    if total_this_draw > 21 then
41.        display dialog ¬
42.            "You lost! " & return & final_display buttons {"OK"}
```

```
43.        exit repeat
44.    else
45.        display dialog "Your hand:" & return & ¬
46.            (hand of player_hand) buttons {"Hit", "Stay"}
47.        if button returned of result is "Stay" then
48.
49.            if total of player_hand > total of dealer_hand then
50.                display dialog ¬
51.                    "You won! " & return & final_display buttons {"OK"}
52.                return
53.            else
54.                display dialog ¬
55.                    "You lost!" & return & final_display buttons {"OK"}
56.                return
57.            end if
58.        else
59.            set drawn_card to random number from 1 to 13
60.            set total_this_draw to total_this_draw + drawn_card
61.            set hand of player_hand to (hand of player_hand) & ¬
62.                (item drawn_card of card_marks) as string
63.        end if
64.    end if
65. end repeat
```

We start the script by setting up some basic variables.

The first is a list of cards the way they should display. As you can see, the items in the list correspond to the card numbers. This way, if the drawn card is 12, for instance, we can ask for item 12 of *card_marks*, and get the string "[Q]". We'll use that to build the graphical (kind-of) display of the hands.

```
set card_marks to {"[A]", "[2]", "[3]", "[4]", "[5]", "[6]", "[7]", ¬
    "[8]", "[9]", "[10]", "[J]", "[Q]", "[K]"}
```

We also initialize the dealer's hand and the player's hand.

```
set dealer_hand to {total:0, hand:""}
set player_hand to {total:0, hand:""}
```

We continue by picking cards for the dealer. We simply repeat in a loop until the dealer's card total reaches 17 points or more. If the dealer got over 21, s/he instantly loses.

```
--setup dealer hand
set total_this_draw to 0
repeat
    set drawn_card to random number from 1 to 13
    set total_this_draw to total_this_draw + drawn_card
    set hand of dealer_hand to ¬
        (hand of dealer_hand) & ¬
        (item drawn_card of card_marks) as string
```

Get that last statement? *drawn_card* is an integer from 1 to 13 (random, of course). Item *drawn_card* of *card_marks* is the string that shows how we want the card to look; for instance, if the number drawn is 1, then item 1 of *card_marks* will be "[A]".

```
if total_this_draw > 21 then
    set dealer_lost_round to true
    set total of dealer_hand to total_this_draw
    exit repeat
else if total_this_draw ≥ 17 then
    set dealer_lost_round to false
    exit repeat
end if
end repeat
```

The preceding logical statement first checks if the card total exceeded 21. If it did, the dealer has lost. If it reached 17, but didn't go beyond 21, then the dealer rests. In both these cases the script is instructed to leave the repeat loop. If it wasn't instructed to do so, the repeat loop would last forever.

The next segment of the script starts up the player's hand by drawing the first two cards, and adding them to the player's total.

```
--Draw first two player cards
set total_this_draw to 0
repeat 2 times
    set drawn_card to random number from 1 to 13
    set total_this_draw to total_this_draw + drawn_card
    set hand of player_hand to ¬
        (hand of player_hand) & ¬
        (item drawn_card of card_marks) as string
end repeat
```

OK, so the next statement can come before the player's cards are drawn. In it, we check if the dealer lost. If true, the player is notified of the victory.

```
if dealer_lost_round then
    display dialog "You won!"
    return
end if
```

Next, we create a similar loop to the repeat loop that built the dealer's hand, but here, we interupt the loop with a dialog box asking the player to either hit or stay.

If the player stays, the script checks if s/he won. If not, the player gets another card, and here we go again.

```
set player_lost_round to false
repeat
```

The following statement creates a general string that contains the dealer's hand and the player's hand. This string will be used in dialog boxes that inform the player of either a loss or a win.

```
set final_display to "* * *" & return & ¬
    "Your hand:   " & (hand of player_hand) & return & return & ¬
    "Dealer's hand:   " & (hand of dealer_hand) as string
if total_this_draw > 21 then
    display dialog ¬
        "You lost! " & return & final_display buttons {"OK"}
```

Figure 4-5 shows the resulting dialog box.

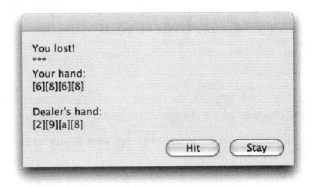

Figure 4-5. You lost!

```
exit repeat
    else
        display dialog "Your hand:" & return & ¬
            (hand of player_hand) buttons {"Hit", "Stay"}
```

See the resulting dialog box in Figure 4-6.

Figure 4-6. The player is prompted for the next move.

```
        if button returned of result is "Stay" then
            if total of player_hand > total of dealer_hand then
                display dialog ¬
                "You won! " & return & final_display buttons {"OK"}
                return
            else
                display dialog ¬
                "You lost!" & return & final_display buttons {"OK"}
                return
            end if
        else
            set drawn_card to random number from 1 to 13
            set total_this_draw to total_this_draw + drawn_card
        set hand of player_hand to (hand of player_hand) & ¬
            (item drawn_card of card_marks) as string
        end if
    end if
end repeat
```

So what now? Well, in order to prove your super AppleScript ability, I challenge you to make the following improvements and e-mail them to me (Hanaan@mac.com):

Make the 11, 12, and 13 cards (Jack, Queen, and King) have a value of 10, not their actual card value as I've programmed them.

Make the Ace, or 1, have a value of either 1 or 11. This can be quite a challenge since you will need to run an unknown number of scenarios to determine what the dealer's best number under 21 is, and when the player went over his/her limit.

Put the whole game in a repeat loop and assign a starting cash allowance of, say, $1000. Give the player the ability to bet money on each game and add or subtract the bet amount at each round.

You do the math

Although numbers can be used in many ways that require not more than some counting skills, when we think numbers, we think math.

I personally love math and look forward for those challenging operations a script may require.

The operators you can use with numbers are the familiar ones such as addition, subtraction, division, etc., and some less often used ones such as div and mod.

The math operators we can use on numbers are +, -, *, /, ^, *div*, and *mod*.

There are also the good-old comparison operators, but these don't return a number; rather they return a result in the Boolean value class. Here are the comparison operations you can use with numbers: =, ≠, >, ≥, <, ≤.

Comparing with logic

Logical operators can be quite boring when used one at a time. However, when you gang them up, you can create some mighty powerful, and also rather confusing, statements. My ASP programmer friend Steve says that I use JSL to write my scripts. JSL stands for **J**ob **S**ecurity **L**anguage.

A simple expression may look like this:

the_age ≥ 18

which means "Is the value of the variable *the_age* equal to or greater than 18?" This expression may return a true or false. But, that's not all!

What if we need to write a statement that will approve or reject a credit card application? Now we need to check for a number of true-or-false expressions such as age, household income, bankruptcies, credit ratings, current debt, etc.

We can use Boolean operators such as *or, and, not,* etc. to combine simple expressions into a compound statement.

This statement may look something like the one in Figure 4-7.

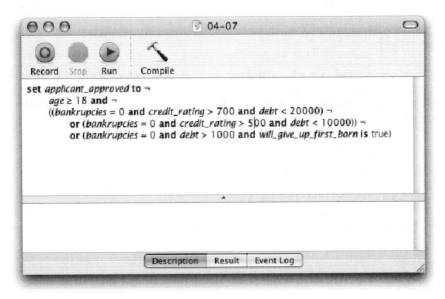

Figure 4-7. A compound statement that uses multiple comparison operations and some Boolean operators.

One of the important factors that makes the formula in Figure 4-7 work is the use of parentheses.

While you don't always need to add parentheses, they make your scripts more legible. Many times the lack of properly placed parentheses will break the script. It may still compile OK but will return an error when executed.

It is best to enclose each expression in its own parentheses. The preceding script could have been improved from

```
(bankruptcies = 0 and credit_ratings > 500 and debt > 10000)
```

to

```
((bankruptcies = 0) and (credit_ratings > 500) and (debt > 10000))
```

Another aspect of script readability that can help here is the use of soft returns. AppleScript assumes that any script line ending with the character ¬ continues on the next line.

You get the ¬ character by pressing OPTION+L or OPTION+RETURN.

Using soft returns, the preceding statement from may look like this:

```
((bankruptcies = 0) and ¬
    (credit_ratings > 500) and ¬
    (debt > 10000))
```

Basic math

In the following section we will create a handler that takes a list of numbers and returns a record with a few mathematical facts regarding the list. The resulting record will include the list average, the highest number, and the lowest number in the list. If you fed the following list to the handler:

```
{10, 3, 5, 4, 13}
```

you'll get this record as the result:

```
{average:7.0, high:13, low:3}
```

Here is the complete script:

Script 4-5

```
1.  math_facts({10, 3, 5, 9, 13})

2.  on math_facts(numbers_list)
3.      try
4.          set high_number to item 1 of numbers_list
5.          set low_number to item 1 of numbers_list
6.          set numbers_total to 0
7.          repeat with i from 1 to count numbers_list
8.              set the_number to item i of numbers_list
```

```
9.                if the_number is greater than high_number then copy ¬
        the_number to high_number

10.               if the_number is less than low_number then copy ¬
        the_number to low_number
11.             set  numbers_total to numbers_total + the_number
12.          end repeat
13.          set the_average to (numbers_total / (count numbers_list))
14.          return ¬
        {average:the_average, high:high_number, low:low_number, ¬
    errored:false}
15.      on error
16.          return {average:0, high:0, low:0, errored:true}
17.      end try
18. end math_facts
```

The script is fairly simple, so instead of explaining it line by line I will just go over what was done here.

I started by creating three variables. These variables, for the most part, will hold the values that we will return in the handler's result. The variables are *high_number*, *low_number*, and *numbers_total*, which will be used to get the list average at the end.

The repeat loop between lines 7 and 12 is the main loop that goes through the numbers in the list and analyzes each number to see if it fits in the high number or low number spots, and to add it to the numbers total.

Notice that although I could have created a *repeat* with *the_number* in *numbers_list*, I chose to go with the traditional *repeat* using *i* as an integer from 1 to the number of numbers in the list. There are a couple of reasons for that. The first reason is that I just like to have an *i* variable counting the loops. I may not need it in the current version of the handler, but in the next version I may want to add more features that will require the loop increment. Why change the script later if I can start it with a loop increment to begin with?

The other reason is even more pressing. When you use a repeat loop where the repeat variable is the value of the list item, the variable isn't really the value of the list item. Try the following script:

```
repeat with x in {"a", "b", "c"}
   if x = "b" then display dialog "yes"
end repeat
```

In the second loop we should've gotten a message, right? Oh well . . . more on that when we discuss repeat loops in Chapter 11.

At the end of our handler we create the average number by dividing the numbers total by the number of numbers.

Then we return the entire record containing the high number, low number, and average.

Also notice that the entire handler is wrapped with a *try* statement. This is to ensure that there's a consistent response even if the list supplied as a parameter includes a string.

Notice that even if there's an error, the record still contains the same elements as in normal operation. Handlers are much easier to use and manage if they always return a result in the same value class, and in that case, if the record has the same elements.

mod and div

The final math example we'll look at uses the *mod* and *div* operators. Although *mod* and *div* are used less than other math operators, when you need them they really shine.

mod and *div* deal with how many instances of a number can fit inside a different number without breaking. For instance, *div* can tell you that 2 can fit three times in 6.5, while *mod* will tell you that after you fit 2 in 6.5 3 times, the rest will be 0.5.

Why is this so great? Here are a few examples of how your script can take advantage of *div* and *mod*:

You need to impose four postcards per page, and the number of postcards changes from job to job. If a job has 27 postcards, how many whole pages will you need?

How about the following calculation:

```
set whole_pages to 27 div 4
if 27 mod 4 > 0 then set whole_pages to whole_pages + 1
```

27 div 4 will return 6, since 4 fits 6 times in 27. Then, if the remainder is zero, it means that the division is perfect, like if we had 24 postcards. But if the remainder is more than 0, then you need to add a page.

Or how about taking a number of seconds and showing them as minutes and seconds:

```
set seconds to 735
set minutes to seconds div 60
set extra_seconds to seconds mod 60
set the_time to minutes & ":" & extra_seconds as string
```

Reversing numbers

To convert a number from positive to negative, simply add the minus sign before it, even if the number is in a variable:

```
set my_balance to 500
set my_opposite_balance to -my_balance
```

In this situation, the minus operator is used as a unary operator.

Folder kitchen timer

Anyway, in our next example script we will convert an ordinary folder into a kitchen timer. The folder's name will change every second to reflect the remaining time. At the end, iTunes will pick a random track and play it.

Here is the script in its entirety:

Script 4-6

```
1. set get_minutes_dialog to display dialog ¬
   "How many minutes?" default answer "120"
2. set timer_minutes to text returned of get_minutes_dialog as integer

3. tell application "Finder" to set the_folder_reference to ¬
   (make new folder at (path to desktop folder) with properties ¬
   {name:"Timer"}) as alias
4. repeat with the_minute from (timer_minutes - 1) to 0 by -1
5.     set hrs_left to the_minute div 60
6.     set min_left to the_minute mod 60
7.     set hrs_text to add_zero(hrs_left)
8.     set min_text to add_zero(min_left)
9.     repeat with sec_left from 59 to 0 by -1
10.        set sec_text to add_zero(sec_left)
11.        set displayTime to hrs_text & ";" & min_text & ";" & sec_text
12.        tell application "Finder" to set name ¬
       of the_folder_reference to displayTime
13.        delay 1
14.    end repeat
15. end repeat

16. tell application "iTunes"
17.     play some track of library playlist "library" of source 1
18. end tell

19. on add_zero(the_number)
20.    if the_number < 10 then
21.        return ("0" & the_number as string)
22.    else
23.        return (the_number as string)
24.    end if
25. end add_zero
```

The script utilizes one custom handler called *add_zero*, whose purpose is to convert an integer into a string while ensuring that if the integer has only one digit it will be proceeded by a zero. This has to be done as a string since if you ask AppleScript for 01 as integer or as real, the preceding zero will be disregarded.

If you have some basic understanding of handlers, you know that they can accept parameters and return values. This handler accepts a single integer parameter and it returns a string. If the handler is fed the integer 5, it'll return "05".

The *add_zero* handler sits at the end of our script (lines 19–25), and we call it to perform three times during the execution of the script.

The script starts by asking the user to set the timer to any number of minutes, and then in line 2, AppleScript takes the text the user typed in the dialog box and converts it into an integer.

This integer will be the starting point of the script. Just like setting a real kitchen timer, the first thing is telling the timer how many minutes the timer has to be set to.

Line 3 of the script talks directly to the Finder. The Finder is instructed to make a new folder with a specific name.

I want you to notice a couple of things regarding the syntax of that statement. One is that there's no *tell* block; both the command and the application reference are in the same line. I did that because I needed the Finder to do one thing only.

The second neat thing about this statement is that it assigns a reference to the new folder not as the usual Finder reference that will include the name of the folder, but rather as an alias reference.

Since Chapter 13 is dedicated to file references, for now I'll just add that the alias-style reference to the folder we created allows us to later change the name of the folder again and again, and the alias reference will always remain accurate.

Also notice the use of parentheses. Every expression is surrounded with parentheses to direct AppleScript to the order we would like the expressions executed in, and to keep general order.

What comes next in the script is the main repeat loop starting at line 4 and ending on line 15. This repeat loop starts from the number of minutes and counts down to 0, stepping −1 step at a time.

Actually, just like a real timer, the loop starts from one minute lower than the requested number, plus 59 seconds.

Lines 5 and 6 are where we take the current number of minutes and separate that number into hours and minutes. Here's how that's done, assuming for a second that there are 135 minutes left:

```
set hrs_left to 135 div 60
```

This statement will return 2, since 60 fits two times in 135.

```
set min_left to 135 mod 60
```

This statement will return 15, since after we take all the whole 60s out of 135 two times, or 120, the remainder that doesn't fit is 15.

These two statements repeat for each minute that passes, and they're followed by the handler calls that add a leading zero to the number of hours or minutes, if needed.

The repeat loop starting on line 9 counts the seconds for each minutes. Like the last loop, it starts from 59, the number of remaining seconds, and ends at 0.

Inside that second loop, the seconds are being formatted with the *add_zero* handler, and then concatenated with the hours and minutes to form a single string that contains the time left formatted as we like it. I used a semicolon, but you can also use a period or dash—anything other than a colon, which should be the separator of choice if you could use it in a folder name.

Next, line 12 names our timer folder with the newly formed name, line 13 delays the script by a minute, and the entire process starts over.

After the repeat loop has ended, you can choose any method of alert. I ask iTunes to play some track. The term *some* tells AppleScript to pick a random track.

Conclusion

No matter what you do in AppleScript, numbers and math are everywhere. Page layout automation, database interaction, system administration—all require some dealing with numbers. Some of my graphic-intensive scripts even forced me to pick up a trigonometry book and figure out triangles' sines and cosines.

Throughout the book we will be attacking number problems and using the very concepts covered in this chapter.

Power wrap-up

This section summarizes the chapter in an intensive-reference style. Use this part to look up facts related to the chapter without the chatter.

Types of number values

AppleScript supports two types of number values: real and integer.

A real number is a number with a decimal point, while an integer is any whole number.

```
class of 120 --> Integer
class of 3.8 --> Real
class of 99999 --> Integer
class of 1000.0 --> Real
```

Coercing numbers

You can coerce real numbers or integers into strings.

```
30 as string --> "30"
1.25 as string --> "1.25"
```

Integers can be always coerced into real numbers.

```
2 as Real --> 2.0
```

A real number can be coerced into an integer only if it has no fraction.

```
4.0 as Integer --> 4
4.0001 as Integer --> error
round 4.4 as integer
```

Large numbers

When working with numbers that total five digits or more, including any decimal places, AppleScript displays the numbers using exponential notation, instead of their normal form.

The number 10000.0, for instance, will be displayed as 1.0E+4.

See the section "Real big" in this chapter for an explanation on how to decipher the exponential notation code.

Rounding numbers

The *round* command takes a real number and rounds it.

The *rounding* parameter determines how rounding is decided on by AppleScript. There are five constants that can be used with the *round* command: *up*, *down*, *toward zero*, *to nearest*, and *as taught in school*.

Following are examples of using each one.

Simple rounding uses the default parameter *round to nearest*:

```
round 1.5 --> 2
```

Rounding up:

```
round 1.1 rounding up --> 2
round -2.9 rounding up --> -2
```

Rounding down:

```
round 5.5 rounding down --> 5
round -2.1 rounding down --> -3
```

The *rounding towards zero* constant acts the same as rounding down with positive numbers, and with negative numbers it acts like rounding up would.

The *rounding as taught in school* constant acts the same as the default rounding, *to nearest*. The only difference is with numbers and a half: 1.5, -2.5, etc. These numbers will be rounded away from zero.

```
round 5.5 rounding as taught in school --> 6
round -2.5 rounding down --> -3
```

Random numbers

The *random number* command is a part of the Standard Additions.

In its basic form, the *random number* command generates a random number between 0 and 1.

```
random number --> 0.295602678734
```

The *random number* command has a few parameters: *from, to*, and *with seed*.

The *from* and *to* parameters specify to the command the number range in which the returned random number has to be in.

```
random number from 1 to 10 --> 5
random number from 1 to 10 --> 3
random number from 1 to 10 --> 1
```

The parameter *with seed* determines where the random number is going to be pulled out of in the pool of numbers stored in the computer's memory.

Using the same seed will return the same number on all computers.

```
random number with seed 100 --> 0.716641089949
```

To ensure a different random number is returned, use the current date as the argument for the *with seed* parameter.

```
random number with seed (current date) --> truly random number ¬
from 0 to 1
```

Math operators

AppleScript supports the following math operators: +, -, *, /, ^, *div*, and *mod*.

```
set new_number to 5 + 12 --> 17
set new_number to 9 - 3 --> 6
set new_number to 10 * 4 --> 40
set new_number to 12 / 4 --> 3
set new_number to 3 ^ 2 --> 9 (nth power)
```

The *mod* operator returns the number of times the right operand fits whole into the left operand. In the following example, without breaking, 5 fits twice into 13.

```
13 div 5 --> 2
```

The *div* operator returns the remainder of the *mod* operation.

After you take 5 out of 13 twice, you are left with 3.

```
13 mod 5 --> 3
```

The *div* and *mod* operators can be used in scripts in some clever ways. See the "mod and div" section in this chapter.

Comparison operators

AppleScript supports the following comparison operators: =, ≠, >, ≥, <, ≤. These operators can use their written forms as well: *is equal to*, *is not equal to*, *is greater than*, *is greater than or equal to*, *is less than*, *is less than or equal to*.

These operators always return a Boolean result: either true or false.

Details previously . . .

The last part of this chapter is a summary of the entire chapter. For more details on any of the items here, refer to earlier sections in this chapter.

CHAPTER 5

PICKING UP DATES

```
···set the_prompt to "Pick a file and
···set the_file_path to choose file with
···set file_info to info for the_file_path
···set the_date to creation date of file
set the_date to date "Saturday, Apr
```

```
date "Saturday, April 5, 2003 6:00:
```

```
et file_info to info for the_file_path
et the_date to creation date of file_info
set the_date to date "Saturday, April 5,
et file_age_in_seconds to (current date)

et weeks_old to file_age_in_seconds div
et left_over_seconds to file_age_in_seco

et days_old to left_over_seconds div da
et left_over_seconds to left_over_secona

et hours_old to left_over_seconds div ho
et left_over_seconds to left_over_secona

et minutes_old to left_over_seconds div
et left_over_seconds to left_over_secona
```

```
t to ¬
with prompt "Pick a folder to clean"
n to the_folder_path as string


 display dialog ¬
at how how many weeks old?" defaul
xt returned of weeks_dialog) as inte


 date
ls to weeks_old * weeks
 date · weeks_old_in_seconds
```

As you're about to find out, the *date* class in AppleScript is versatile and has many hidden aspects worth exploring. This chapter covers working with dates, the *date* object properties, and simple and complex date operations.

The date class and date object

In AppleScript, a single value class, the *date* value class, holds information about a specific second in time. That second includes information about the date, time, weekday, month, year, etc.

To create a date value we use the word "date," and following it we specify the date with a string. The format of the string has to resemble a date to be recognized, but AppleScript is fairly lenient about the exact format, and will fill in the blanks if needed.

To create a simple date, start a new window in Script Editor and type the following:

```
date "2/3/03"
```

> In certain situations you will find that some computers don't compile statements containing dates. This situation can happen when the user's date format in System Preferences is ordered differently than you intended (year first, etc.), and you have specified a four-digit year. This buggy behavior may cause some concern when planning for wide distribution of your scripts.

Now compile the script. As you can see in Figure 5-1, AppleScript takes the liberty of formatting your date, and adding on to it the time, which is by default midnight of the date you specified. You can, of course, specify your own time, and this is the time AppleScript will use.

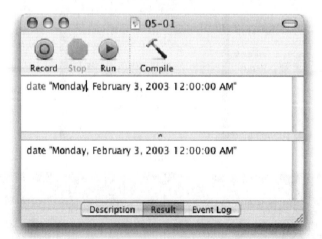

Figure 5-1. The date "2/3/03" compiled

Now try this:

```
date "2/3/03 1:54 PM"
```

AppleScript compiles this one as follows:

```
date "Monday, February 3, 2003 1:54:00 PM"
```

Date and time format

The format of the date string that AppleScript uses when it compiles the date you give it is derived from the settings in the International panel of System Preferences (not the Date and Time panel!).

Figure 5-2 shows the Formats tab in the Mac OS X System Preferences panels, which you can use to modify the format of the date and time.

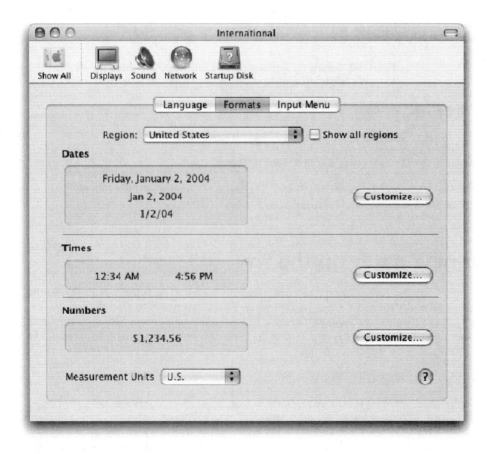

Figure 5-2. The Formats tab in Mac OS X System Preferences

The fact that the user of the computer on which the script runs is able to change the date format makes it unreliable for many purposes. For instance, if you want to extract the weekday out of the date, you should be able to use the string manipulation shown in Figure 5-3.

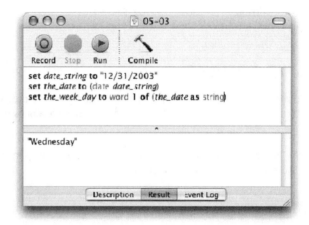

Figure 5-3. Getting the weekday out of a date may work, unless the user has changed his/her date formats in the International panel of System Preferences.

In the example shown in Figure 5-3, line 2 will result in the following value:

    date "Wednesday, December 31, 2003 12:00:00 AM"

When converted to a string, the first word is "Wednesday."

This issue, however, becomes moot when you become familiar with the different properties of the *date* object. We'll discuss those in a bit.

Forming dates on the fly

AppleScript does have a few default behavior patterns it uses to convert your date strings into a *date* object. These are important when your script needs to take different values and make up *date* objects out of them. For instance, your script may need to create a *date* object that has the first day of the month, or let the user input a date and make sure AppleScript understands it.

The following strings will all compile properly into *date* objects:

    date "03/03/03" --> date "Monday, March 3, 2003 12:00:00 AM"
    date "0" --> date "Monday, May 31, 2004 12:00:00 AM"
    date "5/1/2002" --> date "Wednesday, May 1, 2002 12:00:00 AM"
    date "Feb 28 5:50 AM" --> date "Monday, February 28, 2005 12:00:00 AM"
    date "3:30" --> date "Monday, May 31, 2004 3:30:00 AM"
    date "May" --> date "Saturday, May 1, 2004 12:00:00 AM"

Here are some of the rules AppleScript will use to compile these strings into dates:

In general, AppleScript will do its best to fill in the blanks. Since the *date* object includes a date and a time down to the second, AppleScript has to add something to most date strings you give it.

- If you specify only a date without the time, the default time will be midnight on the date you specified. If you didn't specify AM or PM, AppleScript will treat your time as if you wrote the time in 24 hours format. That means that the default will be AM, other than 12:00, which will compile as PM.

- If you specify only a time without the date, AppleScript uses the date on which the script was compiled.

Here are the preceding date strings with their compiled version:

        date "03/03/03"

compiles as

        date "Monday, March 3, 2003 12:00:00 AM"

AppleScript had to tack on the time, which is, by default, midnight.

        date "0"

This compiles as

        date "Wednesday, July 2, 2003 12:00:00 AM"

AppleScript uses the date the script was compiled. This book is my only alibi for any crime that happened on that date . . .

        date "5/1/2002"

compiles as

        date "Wednesday, May 1, 2002 12:00:00 AM"

Whereas

        date "Feb 28 5:50 AM"

compiles as

        date "Monday, February 28, 2005 12:00:00 AM"

Oops! What happened here is that the year hasn't been specified. AppleScript then took the first digit we intended to use for the time and used it for the year, The minutes we specified appear to have been ignored . . .

        date "3:30"

compiles as

        date "Wednesday, July 2, 2003 3:30:00 AM"

The time was understood as 3:30 AM, and the date, again, is the date the script was compiled on.

```
date "May"
```

compiles as

```
date "Thursday, May 1, 2003 12:00:00 AM"
```

AppleScript used the first day of May on the current year.

More ways to specify dates

OK, so I admit that until writing this book I was not aware of the following type of statement. What it allows you to do is tack the time from one date onto the date of another. You do that in one of two ways.

The first one takes the time from the first date and the date from the second one.

The following script creates a date that points to 5 PM of the current date:

```
date "5:00 PM" of (current date)
```

The other way is to specify the date first relative to the time.

```
date "6:30 AM" relative to date "September 1, 2003"
```

If you enter that literal expression and compile it, AppleScript will change it to a single date.

```
date "Monday, September 1, 2003 6:30:00 AM"
```

However, if you use variables, this may be very useful, as in the following example:

```
set the_date to (current date)
set the_time to "4:00 PM"
date the_time relative to the_date
--> date "Monday, May 31, 2004 4:00:00 PM"
```

The result shown depends on the date you run it.

User-supplied date

In the following example, we'll create a script snippet that prompts the user to enter a date, then we will see if the date is valid. If the date is not valid, we will force the user to reenter it. If it is valid, we will give the user a chance to reenter it.

There are two basic ways to insist that a user does something to your specifications. One is to create a subroutine that asks for user input. This way, if you inspect the user's response and it's not good, you can have the subroutine call itself until the user complies, and at that point the subroutine can return a result to the calling statement.

The method we're going to use here, however, is a repeat loop.

The script enters a repeat loop with no specified end. The user is only allowed out of the loop if the data s/he provided has tested OK.

Notice that the script that follows starts with a plain *repeat* and ends with *end repeat*. Also notice that the only way out of the loop is in line 9, which executes only if the user clicked OK to a dialog box.

Here is the script:

Script 5-1

```
1. repeat
2.   display dialog "Enter date" buttons {"OK"} ¬
     default button 1 default answer "MM/DD/YYYY"
3.   set user_date to text returned of result
4.   try
5.     set the_date to date user_date
6.     display dialog ("You have chosen:" & return & ¬
       (date string of the_date))
7. buttons {"Try again", "OK"} default button 1
8.     if (button returned of result) = "OK" then
9.        exit repeat
10.      end if
11.   on error
12.      display dialog ¬
     "Invalid date, please try again using the format \"MM/DD/YYYY\"" ¬
     buttons
13. {"OK"} default button 1 with icon stop
14.   end try
15. end repeat
```

Line 2 of the script asks the user to enter a date and gives a format to follow. Figure 5-4 shows the dialog box. The format in the dialog box is just a part of the dialog text.

Figure 5-4. The input dialog box asking the user to enter a date

Line 3 assigns the user's typed text to one of the only two variables: *user_text*. The value of *user_text* is a string that was returned from the *dialog* command.

So how do we check if the date is valid? We try to coerce it into a *date* value class. We're counting on the fact that if the date is not valid, trying to coerce it into a *date* class will return an error. Therefore, we put the whole command into a *try* block.

That *try* block actually takes over the rest of the script. It starts on line 4 and ends on line 12. If anything goes wrong between lines 5 and 9, the *on error* part will be executed. We start by attempting to coerce the string the user entered into a *date* class. That happens right after the beginning of the *try* statement, and is the statement we expect will generate an error if the date is invalid.

If the date string the user supplied coerced properly into a *date* class, we continue by asking the user if that was really the date s/he meant to enter. Maybe s/he mistyped something, or AppleScript had a different idea of what date was intended.

So on line 6 we display an interesting dialog box, which can be seen in Figure 5-5. Part of the dialog message is the property *date string* of the *date* object. We'll discuss this and other *date* object properties later on; however, the *date string* property is a string that holds the date portion of the *date* object.

Figure 5-5. The dialog box confirming the date entered by the user

Line 7 checks if the user clicked OK to confirm that the date is fine. If the user approved the date, then line 8 executes and exits the repeat loop, and therefore allows the script to continue.

current date

The *current date* command is part of the Standard Additions that come with the Mac OS. It takes no parameters, and returns a value in the *date* value class.

```
current date
--result: date "Wednesday, July 2, 2003 10:15:09 PM"
```

When used as part of a larger operation, the *current date* command likes to be enclosed in parentheses. Actually, AppleScript is quite aware of that and will many times enclose it with parentheses when the script is compiled.

The usefulness of the *current date* command never ceases to amaze me. Just imagine how many times a day you turn to someone to ask what time or what date it is . . .

OK, so its usefulness goes beyond knowing the current date and time. For one, it's a way to get a unique time stamp on which you can perform several operations. You can use the result of the current date to figure out the time it takes to run a script, as shown in the following example:

```
set script_start_time to (current date)
--your script here
--more script
--a few more statements...
set script_end_time to (current date)
set script_time_in_seconds to script_end_time - script_start_time
display dialog "The script took " & script_time_in_seconds & ¬
    " seconds to run!"
```

time to GMT

Another date-related command, *time to GMT*, returns the time difference between the time zone of the computer that runs the script to Greenwich mean time. The result is returned in seconds, which means that in order to extract any useful information out of it, like the number of hours, you have to divide it by the number of seconds in an hour.

As you will see later in this section, AppleScript has the number of seconds in an hour built into a constant called *hours*. That means that, if the time zone is properly set on your computer, the following script will return the time difference between your time zone and GMT:

Script 5-2

```
set time_difference to (time to GMT) / hours
set time_difference to round time_difference
if time_difference < 0 then
  set time_difference to -time_difference
  set the_message to "You are " & time_difference & " hours behind GMT"
else if time_difference > 0 then
  set the_message to "You are " & time_difference & " hours after GMT"
else
  set the_message to "Your time zone is GMT"
end if
display dialog the_message
```

We start the script by getting the time difference and dividing it by the constant hours, whose value is 3600, which is the number of seconds in an hour (more about that specific constant later in this chapter).

The conditional statement that starts on line 3 and ends on line 10 forms a different message whether the time zone of the user is before GMT, after it, or the same.

If the time zone is before GMT, then the *time_difference* value has to be made positive for the dialog message. That happens on line 4:

```
set time_difference to -time_difference
```

Adding the minus sign before a number means it will be used as a unary operator, and it turns a positive number into a negative and a negative number into positive.

Date object properties

So we decided that parsing the date as a string to extract the individual pieces such as the month, weekday, hour, etc. wasn't such a good idea. For these items we turn to the properties built right into the *date* object.

class property

The first property is *class*. The value of that property is always *date*.

The *class* property is useful to check if the value of a variable is of class *date*.

year

The *year* property is an integer representing the four-digit year of the given date.

```
year of (current date)
result: 2003
```

month

The *month* property contains the name of the month of the given date. The value of the *month* property isn't a string or a number, rather one of the following 12 constants: *January, February, March, April, May, June, July, August, September, October, November,* or *December*.

You can coerce the *month* property into a string, and finally, in the AppleScript release 1.9.3 that ships with OS X 10.3 (Panther), you can coerce the *month* property into a number, and compare the order of months.

weekday

The *weekday* property can contain one of these constants: *Sunday, Monday, Tuesday, Wednesday, Thursday, Friday,* or *Saturday*.

The following script will return the month containing the first Friday the 13th of a given year:

Script 5-3

```
set the_year to 2004
repeat with i from 1 to 12
    set date_string to i & "/13/" & the_year as string
    set the_date to date date_string
    if weekday of the_date = Friday then
        return month of the_date
    end if
end repeat
```

Notice lines 3 and 4. Line 3 creates a string with the months changing based on the loop, the day of month is 13, and the year is specified at the start of the script. In its first repeat loop that string will look like this:

```
"1/13/2004"
```

Line 4 coerces that string into a class date, and line 5 checks if the weekday of that date happens to be Friday. If it is Friday, the name of the month is returned.

Try and have a month list and have the script add all the Friday the 13th months of the year to that list.

time

Unlike the date-related properties we've seen so far, the *time* property of a *date* object is just a long integer. It represents the number of seconds that have passed since midnight of the given date.

```
time of (current date)
result: 73793
```

To extract any meaningful information out of that number, we have to make some mathematical or comparison operations. We'll do a bunch of them later on in the "Doing math with dates" section.

date string

The *date string* property is a string that contains the date portion of the *date* object.

The date part in the Formats tab of the International panel of System Preferences, shown in Figure 5-2, determines the exact format of the *date string* property.

```
date string of (current date)
--result: "Wednesday, July 2, 2003"
```

5

short date string

This property first came out with AppleScript version 1.9.3, which shipped with Panther.

The *short date string* property is a string that contains a short version of the date portion of the *date* object.

The date part in the Formats tab of the International panel of System Preferences, shown in Figure 5-2, determines the exact format of the *short date string* property. You can make several adjustments such as adding leading zeros to the day and month.

time string

The *time string* property is a string that contains the time portion of the *date* object.

The time part in the Formats tab of the International panel of System Preferences, shown in Figure 5-2, determines the exact format of the *time string* property.

```
set date_string to "1pm"
        time string of date date_string
        --result: "1:00:00 PM"
```

Useful date-related constants

In order to assist you in performing date arithmetic, AppleScript was fitted with a few date-related constants. These constants mean that you can use them in the script without having to remember their numerical value.

Here are the constants and their values:

minutes = 60

hours = 3600

days = 86400

weeks = 604800

Just to get the idea, type the following script and run it:

```
display dialog weeks
```

Now what exactly do these numbers mean, and what are they good for? When you're performing operations on dates, you can get results in three flavors: if you compare dates, you get a Boolean value. When you're adding to or subtracting a period of time from a date, you get another date, but when you check the difference between two dates, the result is an integer that indicates the number of seconds between these two dates.

Let's look at the last two scenarios.

If I want to check what the date's going to be three weeks from today, I could use the following script:

```
(current date) + 1814400
```

The number 1814400 is the number of seconds in 3 weeks. Now, I don't expect to want to remember that, let alone figure out the number of seconds in, say, 5 weeks, 3 days, and 2 hours! So, since the constant *weeks* is equal to the number of seconds in one week, the same result can be gotten like this:

```
(current date) + (weeks * 3)
```

Here are some expressions that return a true value:

```
days * 7 = weeks
24 * hours = days
(date "1/1/2004") - (date "1/1/2003") = 52 * weeks + days
```

So, where are the *years* and *months* constants? Well, the number of seconds in a month or in a year isn't constant; therefore they couldn't become AppleScript constants.

Expect much more fun with these constants in the next section.

Doing math with dates

When performing operations on dates, the result can be one of three classes: *date*, *integer*, or *boolean*. Well, actually, the *as* operator can be also used on dates to coerce them into strings, but that's not really math . . .

Returning a Boolean

As with numbers, dates can be compared. You can use the *is equal to* operator to see if two dates are equal.

```
set the_date_string to "7/27/2003"
set the_date to date the_date_string
if (current date) = the_date then
  display dialog "happy birthday"
end if
```

So you may expect that the script, if ran on July 27, 2003, will display a dialog box, right? Hmm, maybe not.

See, when you run line 2 of the preceding script, the resulting date would be

```
date "Sunday, July 27, 2003 12:00:00 AM"
```

That means that only if the script runs at exactly midnight will you get the dialog box.

There are a few ways to remedy this problem. One is to compare the day, month, and year separately.

You can also take the date portion of the *(current date)* command, and convert that into a date. This will give you today's date, at midnight.

Here is how that might work:

Script 5-4

```
set the_date_string to "7/27/2003"
set the_date to date the_date_string
set todays_date_string to date string of (current date)
set todays_date to date todays_date_string
if todays_date = the_date then
  display dialog "happy birthday"
end if
```

You can also use the *comes after* and *comes before* operators with dates:

```
set the_date_string to "7/27/2003"
set the_date to date the_date_string
(current date) comes after the_date
```

In this case, there's still a chance that you will not get the intended result. In the preceding script, anytime after midnight (or zero in the morning) of July 27 will be considered after *the_date*.

Here's an example script that looks at a version of a file in both the server and on the hard drive. If the hard drive version of the file is newer, the file is copied over the server version:

Script 5-5

```
1. set backup_folder_path to "Backup:files:"
2. set file_folder_path to "Macintosh HD:Users:hanaan:Documents:"
3. set file_name to "proposal.pdf"
4. --get modification date of the original file
5. set file_info to info for alias (file_folder_path & file_name)
6. set original_modification_date to modification date of file_info
7. --get modification date of the original file
8. set file_info to info for alias (backup_folder_path & file_name)
9. set backup_modification_date to modification date of file_info
10. if original_modification_date comes after ¬
    backup_modification_date then
11. tell application "System Events"
12. duplicate file (file_folder_path & file_name) to ¬
13. folder backup_folder_path with replacing
14. end tell
15. end if
```

A few points regarding the preceding script:

First, as usual, I like to keep paths to files and folders as strings. This allows me to concatenate them and coerce them into alias file or folder references as I wish.

In lines 5 and 8 I use the command *info for* to get file information. This command is great since it's part of the Standard Additions, which means that you don't have to use it in a Finder *tell* block.

Calculating time differences

When you want to see the time difference between two dates, AppleScript gives you a result in *integer* class. The resulting integer is the number of seconds between the two dates. At first it looks a bit funny, especially when trying to figure out things like Frank Sinatra's age:

```
set date_born to date "Sunday, December 12, 1915 12:00:00 AM"
set date_died to date "Thursday, May 14, 1998 12:00:00 AM"
set seconds_lived to date_died - date_born
```

The result (2.6009856E+9) of that script tells us that Frank lived for a little over 2.6 million seconds. There are two main ways to make that number make some more sense.

If we want to know how many days or weeks were in that period, we can use AppleScript's built-in constants: *minutes*, *hours*, *days*, and *weeks*.

The following script will ask users for their birthday and tell them how long they lived:

Script 5-6

```
1. set the_dialog to display dialog "Enter your date of birth" ¬
   default answer "" buttons {"weeks", "days"}
2. set birthday_string to text returned of the_dialog
3. set increment_chosen to button returned of the_dialog
4. try
5.   set birthday to date birthday_string
6. on error
7.   display dialog "Bad date format, birthday boy!"
8.   return
9. end try
10. set age_in_seconds to (current date) - birthday
11. if increment_chosen = "weeks" then
12.   set age_in_weeks to round (age_in_seconds / weeks) rounding down
13.   display dialog "You have been alive " & age_in_weeks & " weeks"
14. else
15.   set age_in_days to round (age_in_seconds / days) rounding down
16.   display dialog "You have been alive " & age_in_days & " days"
17. end if
```

This method works well with predictable increments such as weeks or days. However, if we just want to know the age in years, then we would be better off comparing the date components: *year*, *month*, and *day*. We have to compare all three since comparing years only may leave you with the wrong answer. Look at this example:

```
set birthday to date "Wednesday, October 31, 1979 12:00:00 AM"
set today to date "Thursday, July 10, 2003 12:00:00 AM"
set age to (year of (today)) - (year of birthday)
```

The script returns a result of 24, which is the difference between 1979 and 2003. However, the dude won't turn 24 for three more months!

Now, we could use the following trick:

```
set birthday to date "Wednesday, October 31, 1979 12:00:00 AM"
set today to date "Thursday, July 10, 2003 12:00:00 AM"
set age_in_days to (today - birthday) / days
--The result is 8653.0
set age_in_years to age_in_days div 365.2425 —23 years
set extra_days to age_in_days mod 365.2425 —252(+) days
```

The number 365.2425 is the number of days (on average) per year, taking into account leap years.

Another method would be to compare the years *and* the months.

If the month in your birthday comes after the month in today's date, then you have to reduce the year difference by one. However, if the months are the same, then the day has to be compared, and the same rule applies: if the day in your birthday comes after the day in today's date, then you have to reduce the year difference by one. If the days are the same, then guess what: it's your birthday!

Thanks to the improvements Panther or OS X 10.3 brings us, we can now compare the month of a date without going to the extreme measures of finding the numerical value of the month using list manipulations, etc.

Here's how we can go about that script:

Script 5-7

```
set birthday to date "Wednesday, October 31, 1979 12:00:00 AM"
set today to date "Thursday, July 10, 2003 12:00:00 AM"
set age_in_years to (year of today) - (year of birthday)
if (month of birthday) comes after (month of today) then
    set age_in_years to age_in_years - 1
else if (month of birthday) is equal to (month of today) then
    if (day of birthday) comes after (day of today) then
        set age_in_years to age_in_years - 1
    else if (day of birthday) is equal to (day of today) then
        set today_is_my_birthday to true
    end if
end if
```

File age script

In the following exercise, we will create a script that allows the user to choose a file and will then tell the user the age of the file in weeks, days, hours, and minutes.

We will make handsome use of the four constants we looked at earlier, and also look at the *mod* and *div* operators.

The script starts when we ask the user to pick a file, and then we extract the date out of it, as shown in Figure 5-6.

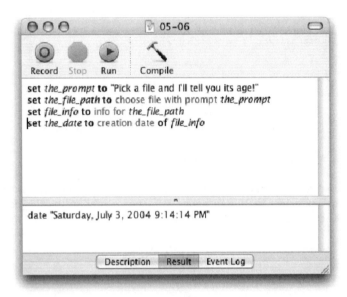

Figure 5-6. The first four lines of the script have one purpose: to get the creation date of the chosen file.

While these four lines will eventually make up the beginning of our script, they might be in the way while we develop the rest of the script. What we want to do is to copy the result of these four lines (shown in the result panel in the script window in Figure 5-6), and temporarily assign it to the *the_date* variable. This will allow us to skip the *choose file* step when we create the script. True, we may want to test our script on more than one date, but having one date for testing can give you consistent results throughout the initial development stage.

In the script shown in Figure 5-7, I have commented the first four lines, and inserted a temporary line as described previously.

Figure 5-7. The script's second stage

Next, we will get the difference between the creation date and the current date. We do that by simply subtracting the file's creation date, now stored in the *the_date* variable, from the date returned from the *current date* command. This step is shown in Figure 5-8.

Figure 5-8. Subtracting a date from another date produces an integer result that is the number of seconds passed between the two dates.

The result we got was 22031214; twenty-two million and some odd seconds. The rest of the script will involve parsing that number of seconds into weeks, days, hours, and minutes.

We start parsing from the large chunks down. To figure out how many weeks fall within that number of seconds, we use the *div* operator.

```
22031214 div weeks --> 36
```

The result to this statement should give us the whole number of weeks. We could of course divide the number of seconds by the *weeks* constant, but we would have gotten a decimal number instead of simply the number of weeks:

```
22031214 / weeks --> 36.427271825397
```

We also need to know what the leftover number of seconds is after we extracted the number of whole weeks. We get that leftover number by using the *mod* operator, like this:

```
22031214 mod weeks --> 258414
```

The result, 258414, is the number of seconds left after we deducted the 36 weeks.

Figure 5-9 shows the script with the new statements extracting the number of weeks and the time remaining without the weeks.

Figure 5-9. The fourth stage of our date script extracts the number of weeks and the leftover seconds.

Next, we will repeat our last two lines, but now with the *days*, *hours*, and *minutes* constants. Figure 5-10 shows these lines of code.

```
000                         05-10
--set the_prompt to "Pick a file and I'll tell you its age!"
--set the_file_path to choose file with prompt the_prompt
--set file_info to info for the_file_path
--set the_date to creation date of file_info
set the_date to date "Saturday, April 5, 2003 6:00:49 PM"
set file_age_in_seconds to (current date) - the_date

set weeks_old to file_age_in_seconds div weeks
set left_over_seconds to file_age_in_seconds mod weeks

set days_old to left_over_seconds div days
set left_over_seconds to left_over_seconds mod days

set hours_old to left_over_seconds div hours
set left_over_seconds to left_over_seconds mod hours

set minutes_old to left_over_seconds div minutes
set left_over_seconds to left_over_seconds mod minutes


46


              Description   Result   Event Log
```

Figure 5-10. Variables have been put in place for the days, hours, and minutes.

Our next step is to combine all the variables into a single message we can use to inform the end user of the files—age.

We do that with simple concatenation, as shown in Figure 5-11.

The other step that was done in the script in Figure 5-11 is the reinstatement of the initial script lines that allow the user to choose a file.

So, if you want to know if the monster chasing you through a dark forest is a vampire, throw some beads on the ground. If he's a true vampire he'll be compelled to stop and pick them up. And if you are a true programmer, you will not relax until you rewrite the end of this script to make sure that the final message doesn't read "1 hours".

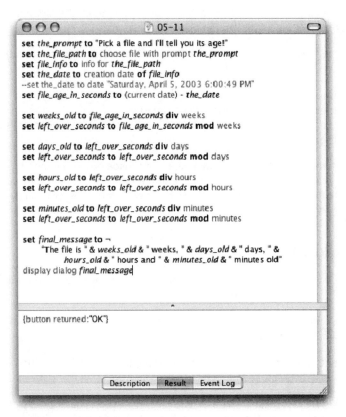

```
set the_prompt to "Pick a file and I'll tell you its age!"
set the_file_path to choose file with prompt the_prompt
set file_info to info for the_file_path
set the_date to creation date of file_info
--set the_date to date "Saturday, April 5, 2003 6:00:49 PM"
set file_age_in_seconds to (current date) - the_date

set weeks_old to file_age_in_seconds div weeks
set left_over_seconds to file_age_in_seconds mod weeks

set days_old to left_over_seconds div days
set left_over_seconds to left_over_seconds mod days

set hours_old to left_over_seconds div hours
set left_over_seconds to left_over_seconds mod hours

set minutes_old to left_over_seconds div minutes
set left_over_seconds to left_over_seconds mod minutes

set final_message to ¬
    "The file is " & weeks_old & " weeks, " & days_old & " days, " &
            hours_old & " hours and " & minutes_old & " minutes old"
display dialog final_message
```

```
{button returned:"OK"}
```

Description | **Result** | Event Log

Figure 5-11. All the variables we collected in the script are put into a single string and displayed to the end user.

Using dates to get more dates

As we've just seen, when we test the difference between two dates, we get an integer. Similarly, we can add or subtract an integer from a date and get another date.

This can be useful for several purposes. For instance, you can have a script look in a folder and delete every file that's over three weeks old. Here is the statement that will test whether to trash the file or not:

```
if (file_modification_date + (3 * weeks)) > (current date) then...
```

The expression *(3 * weeks)* evaluates as an integer that stands for the number of seconds in three weeks, since the constant *weeks*, as discussed earlier, evaluates as 604800, which is the number of seconds in one week.

In a script I recently created, I had to figure out the date of the last day of any given month. Here's how I used date calculations to achieve that:

The variable *the_month* is an integer from 1 to 12 and it stands for the month whose last day I want.

```
set the_month to 4
set the_year to year of (current date)
set the_date to date ((the_month + 1) & "/1/" & the_year as string)
set the_date to the_date - (1 * days)
```

Note the statement on line 3. We build a date that's made out of the month plus one, and the day is 1. That gives us the first day of the following month. In line 4 we subtract a day from the date to get the last day of the previous month, which happens to be the date we were looking for.

Deleting old files

Let's use the same motif as we did earlier with the file's creation date. This time, however, we will look at a file's modification date.

Let's create a script that looks at a folder's contents and deletes every file that's older than a specified number of weeks.

What we will need is to prompt the user to enter the number of weeks. Then, we will need to calculate the date that is that number of weeks ago. We'll call that date *expiration_date*.

Then, we take the modification date of each file. If it is less than our expiration date, it means that the file is over that number of weeks old and we can delete it. For our purposes, instead of deleting the file, we can just set its label to red (which requires you to use OS X 10.3 or higher).

Creating the script

In this script we will use a property that will hold the path to the folder we want to clean out. This property will be kept as a string, not a file reference since a string is more flexible and we're less likely to mess up with it.

The script will start by checking if that path is valid, or in other words, if the folder specified actually exists.

If the folder does not exist, the user will be prompted to choose a different one.

While this is the way the script will start, we will write that portion at the end. In our last example we started with the file-choosing portion, later commented it out for development purposes, and reinstated it at the end. Both ways work OK. For testing purposes we should create a folder and put some assorted files in it.

There are two ways to create this script. We can either rely on scripting additions such as *info for* and *list folder*, or use the system events scripting, which is very much like scripting the Finder.

While working with files is documented in Chapter 13, we should note that if we do want to use *list folder* and *info for* it'll mean that we have to get a list of all the items in the folder, then we have to loop through them, testing each one to see if it's a file and not a folder, and finally test the date and set the label if needed. This will create a lengthy and slow repeat loop.

Instead, we will use system events, which allows us to utilize the *whose* clause. Using the *whose* clause, we can condense the entire repeat loop into a single line of code!

One problem with system events, though, is that while they support deleting files, they do not support labels. For that reason I will write my script using the Finder instead. The final version, which does not use Finder file labels, can be switched back to system events scripting.

Before we start programming the Finder, we need to have a folder path to work with for testing purposes and an integer indicating the number of weeks old the file has to be in order to be marked.

While the integer isn't a big issue, a path may be a bit irritating. Not that I can't trust myself to spell out the full path; however, I have saved myself some time by creating a little lazy workaround.

> If you're using Script Debugger, you can just drag and drop the folder on your script. This will create an alias reference to the folder.

For the workaround, start a new script, type the command choose folder, and run the script.

The *choose folder* command will force you to choose a folder and return a path to that folder, as shown in Figure 5-12.

Figure 5-12. The result of the *choose folder* command

The script in Figure 5-12 is a throwaway script. We copy the resulting string only (without the word "alias") to our real script, and close this one without saving.

Our script starts with two variables: *the_folder_path*, which holds the path pointing to the folder we want to clean, and *weeks_old*, which will be the integer specifying how many weeks old the file has to be to be deleted (or have its label changed in our case . . .).

Figure 5-13 shows the initial stage of our script.

Figure 5-13. The initial stage of the clean folder script

Our next step is to script the part that calculates the date that is x weeks ago. I used 12 weeks in my script, which ensures me that some of the files in my test folder will be affected and some will not.

The date calculation statement is rather simple, and like many other statements in AppleScript, it can be written out on a single line or spread out over several lines. The single-line version is shown here:

```
Set too_old_date to (current date) - (weeks_old * weeks)
```

The multiline version is a bit longer but is more flexible and easier to understand. This is important if you want to return to this script some months down the road and understand what you wrote. Commenting your script may also help.

```
Set this_date to current date
Set weeks_old_in_seconds to weeks_old * weeks
Set too_old_date to this_date - weeks_old_in_seconds
```

> It's always fun to see in just how few lines you can write your script.

The following part of the script will be telling the Finder to treat the old files. Here is how it'll look:

Script 5-8

```
tell application "Finder"
  tell (every file of folder the_folder_path ¬
    whose creation date comes before too_old_date)
    set label index to 2
  end tell
end tell
```

Notice how we can use a single statement to address only the files we want. In the final version of the script, the statement that now says *set label index to 2* will simply say *delete*.

Figure 5-14 shows the script with the added statements.

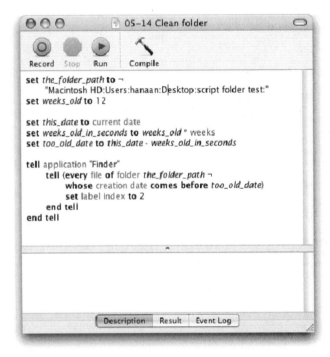

Figure 5-14. The script with the added Finder statements

Adding the user interaction portion

The final stage of the script will be getting the end user involved. We need to make sure that s/he understands what the script will do. We will also allow the user to change the settings that are stored in script properties, these being the folder that will be cleaned and the number of weeks.

We start by promoting the first two variables into properties with an initial value. Then, we check the current value of the properties. Remember that, even though we assign a value to the properties when we write the script, this value will be changed by user activity and the new values will stick.

After the properties are declared, the first real part of the script will be checking if the folder is valid, and making sure that the number of weeks specified isn't zero. If all is well, we will show a dialog box reminding the user that the files in a specific folder that are older than a specific date will be deleted.

When we get the OK (OK button, that is), we will go ahead with the process.

Figure 5-15 shows the script with the added properties and conditional statement.

Figure 5-15. The user interaction portion has been added.

Let's see what was added to the script and what is still missing.

The *verify folder* section (shown in the following code) uses a trick that builds on the fact that an invalid file path will return an error if you coerce it into an alias. This means that if the variable *the_folder_path* does not contain a valid path, an error will be generated. The error will be captured, and instead of an error message, the user will be asked to choose a different folder. This part happens in the portion between the *on error* and *end try* lines. You can read more about error handling in Chapter 15.

Script 5-9

```
--verify folder
try
    alias the_folder_path
on error
    set the_folder_path to ¬
    choose folder with prompt "Pick a folder to clean"
    set the_folder_path to the_folder_path as string
end try
```

The *verify weeks* section (shown in the following code) checks if the *weeks_old* property is less than 1. What it doesn't do is verify that the user entered a value that can be coerced into an integer. If the user tried to be funny and typed Five, for instance, the script would choke when trying to coerce the result into an integer.

Script 5-10

```
--verify weeks
if weeks_old < 1 then
    set weeks_dialog to display dialog ¬
        "Delete files that how how many weeks old?" default answer "5"
    set weeks_old to (text returned of weeks_dialog) as integer
end if
```

The next thing that we did was create the message to allow the user to bow out of the deal and cancel. For this we used three new variables: *folder_name*, *short_date*, and finally, *the_message*.

The value of the *folder_name* variable is the value attached to the name label in the record returned from the info for command. I know, this was a mouthful. The chapter dealing with files thoroughly explains this command.

The *short_date* variable is assigned the *short date string* property of the date, which we figured out earlier in the script.

Finally, the variable *the_message* collects the last two variables with a bunch of other text into a coherent message used in the *display dialog* command. The dialog box is shown in Figure 5-16.

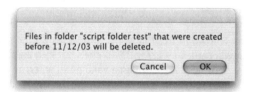

Figure 5-16. The dialog box informing the user of the action that follows

A few things to notice about the *dialog* statement:

First, the entire statement is inside a *try* block. This is done because if the user clicks Cancel, instead of returning a button clicked "cancel" result, AppleScript returns an error. The error is error −128 user canceled, and the only two ways to avoid it are specifying buttons other than Cancel, or trapping the error with a *try* statement as we did here. Anyway, if we change the button's name, we have to test which button the user pressed; but in this case, if there's no error, the user must have pressed the OK button.

Another thing to notice is the use of quotes in the dialog text. If you look at the script, you will notice that in order to display a quote mark in the dialog box, we need to escape it, or in other words, to put a backslash before it: \ ".

Following is the part of the script specifying the variables and displaying the dialog box:

Script 5-11

```
set folder_name to name of (info for alias the_folder_path)
set short_date to short date string of too_old_date
set the_message to "Files in folder \"" & folder_name ¬
    & "\" that were created before " & short_date & " will be deleted."
try
    display dialog the_message
on error
    return
end try
```

Formatting time

Now, you may want to use the time difference results you extracted (see scripts 5-9 through 5-11 . . .) for your own good as a scripter and never report on them to the end user during runtime. If, however, you do decide to put that information somewhere, which is usually a good idea, you may want to format it a little. Since the time is returned as seconds, anything under 3 minutes or so is fairly comprehensible. For example, take 130 seconds—well, we know it's a bit over 2 minutes. But what if the process took 1519 seconds? You may want to provide the end user or system administrator some more understandable results, for instance, 0:25:19. Let's look at the handler that will format an integer containing a number of seconds into a nice-looking string:

We'll devise a strategy first. We will need to break down seconds into hours, minutes, and seconds. For each we will have a string variable. Even though these start as integer values, we will end up reporting on them as a string. The variables we'll use are *h*, *m*, and *s*.

Also, we will be better off dealing separately with times that are an hour or longer, times that are a minute or longer, or finally, times that are shorter than a minute.

Each portion will be responsible for setting values to the *h*, *m*, and *s* variables, and the final line of the script will concatenate them with a colon as a delimiter.

Figure 5-17 shows the skeleton of the script.

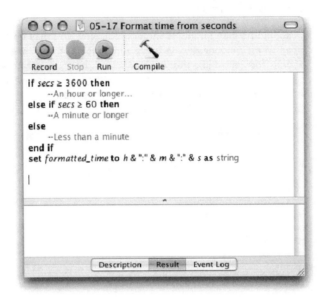

Figure 5-17. The skeleton of the "format time from seconds" script

Notice that the script is basically one big conditional statement. It is separated on the basis of the seconds variable being an hour or more, a minute or more, or under a minute.

Another thing to notice right away is that we use the number 3600 for an hour, and 60 for a minute. Actually, AppleScript helps us out by giving us constants we can use instead of these numbers. There are four time-related constants, and they're all covered later on in this section. For now, we will look at two of them: the constant *hours* has the value 3600 assigned to it, and the constant *minutes* is by default 60. This is as if AppleScript anticipated your needs here and created these two variables for you.

So are they constants or variables? Well, a bit of both. They are constants in the way that they are available from AppleScript out of the box, but they are like variables since you may assign any value to them. However, there's no reason to. More on that subject later in this chapter.

So with that said, we can make our script read better by replacing the number 3600 with the constant *hours*, and the number 60 with the constant *minutes*.

Let's continue with the actual script. Next, we'll attack the simplest part: what happens if the number of seconds is less than a minute.

In that case, hours should be 0 and minutes should be 0. Now you may be asking yourself, "What would happen when we concatenate these zeros into a string?" We certainly don't want to see 20 seconds formatted like this: 0:0:20. We will, later on, create a little handler that will add a zero before the number if it has only one digit. For now, we just need to set the *h* and *m* variables to 0. Figure 5-18 shows our progress so far.

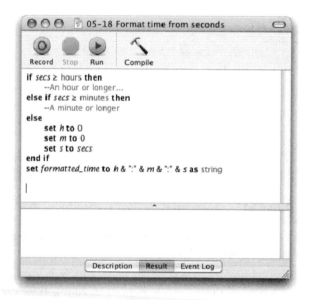

Figure 5-18. The script with the time constants and the first portion filled in

In building the following two portions of the script, we will make some cool use of the *mod* and *div* commands. Here's a little reminder of what they do and the way we will use them: the *div* command returns the number of times that the right operand fits into the left operand. In this case, we can use it to extract the minutes out of the *seconds* number. For instance, if the total seconds is 130, we can do *130 div 60*. The result will be 2, which would tell us that 60 fit twice into 130. Now what about the rest? If the number 60 fits twice in 130, then the remainder is 10. To get that remainder, you can use the *mod* operator: *130 mod 60* returns the leftovers of *130 div 60*. Figure 5-19 shows the next portion of our script, where we added the portion dealing with numbers between 1 minute and 1 hour.

Figure 5-19. Note the use of *mod* and *div* in figuring out the minutes and seconds. Hours are still 0.

In the script shown in Figure 5-19, I also added a test at the top. I set the *secs* variable, which is the number of seconds I want to evaluate. Also notice that the resulting string has the number of minutes shown as 2 and not 02, as we will soon have it.

The final portion of the script, the portion that deals with numbers 3600 and up, is similar to the second portion, just that we have to go through the *div* and *mod* exercise twice, once for the hours and once for the minutes.

We start by extracting the number of hours with the *div* operator. The *mod* operator allows us to get the number of seconds left over. This number is then treated the same way as in the second section. Figure 5-20 shows the script in its almost-complete form.

Figure 5-20. The part that deals with number of seconds 3600 or larger is added.

Now we get to aesthetics. If you look at the result of the script in Figure 5-20, the string's value indicates 3 hours, 2 minutes, and 5 seconds. While the result is correct, we would like to display it as 3:02:05.

What we need is a little handler that will tack on a 0 before numbers that have one digit, numbers that are less than 10.

The handler will take a number, in this case between 0 and 60, and will return a string consisting of two digits. If the number is 10 or greater, it will be simply coerced into a string. If it is less than 10, a 0 character will be jammed in front of it. Here's what our handler will look like:

Script 5-12

```
on make_two_digit(the_number)
  if the_number is less than 10 then
    set the_result to "0" & the_number as string
  else
    set the_result to the_number as string
  end if
end make_two_digit
```

You could go ahead and make this handler more sophisticated and allow a number to have any number of digits, but that's up to you.

Watch, though, how we call the handler: instead of calling it on a separate line, we just embed the call into the statement that concatenates the seconds, minutes, and hours. Instead of

```
set formatted_time to h & ":" & m & ":" & s as string
```

we write

```
set formatted_time to ¬
    h & ":" & ¬
    make_two_digit(m) & ":" & ¬
    make_two_digit(s) as string
```

You may also add a 0 to the *h* variable, if you want.

The final touch is converting the entire script into a handler. The handler will accept a single integer value, and will return a string showing the formatted time. The final script is shown in Figure 5-21.

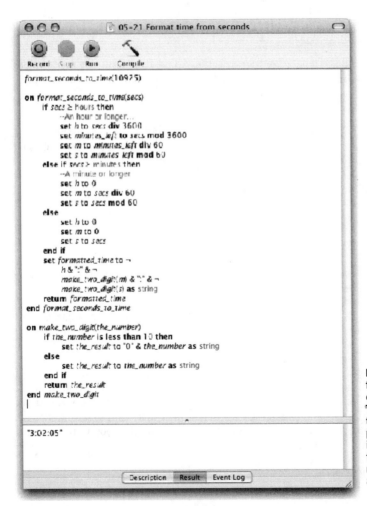

Figure 5-21. The final script is made out of two handlers. The first handler takes an integer parameter. The result is that number formatted in hours, minutes, and seconds as a string.

Last day of the month

In some cases, such as reporting on financial information, we need AppleScript to know the date of the last day of a given month.

Now, getting the first day is not a problem. Say we have an integer variable called *the_month*. This variable is set to the number 7, indicating that we want some date in July. To get the first day, all we have to do is concatenate a string and tack the word "date" before it:

Script 5-13

```
set the_year to year of (current date)
set the_month to 7
set the_day to 1
set next_month to the_month + 1
set last_day_string to next_month & "/" & the_day & "/" & ¬
    the_year as string
set last_day to date last_day_string
set last_day to last_day - (1 * days)
```

The preceding script is quite simple: we start by setting some variables (using literal values in the script is just bad form), so lines 1 through 3 set the *day*, *month*, and *year* variables.

Line 4 figures out for us the next month.

In line 5 we build a string that initially points to the first day of the following month. All we have to do in line 7 is subtract one day (in seconds) from the first day of the following month. The result is the last day of the month we started with.

```
date "Thursday, July 31, 2003 12:00:00 AM"
```

Alarm clock script

The script presented in this section used to wake me up every morning when I had to be in Boston for a few months.

Like a few other scripts we looked at earlier, this one is composed of a single endless repeat loop. Line 45 of the script exits that loop after iTunes finishes playing the wakeup song.

If you check the script, you'll see that it has a few other *exit repeat* statements that lead you out of other endless loops. These are more related to user interaction than to dates. The user interaction trick forces the user to enter a valid value into the dialog box, and this trick is explained in Chapter 12. The basic idea behind it is that you repeat indefinitely, until you manage to coerce the user-entered text into the value class you want such as a number or a date, as it is in this case.

Let's go over the script's parts:

In lines 3–6, we choose the song file and extract the file's name into a variable. Note that we only have the user choose a file if the property *wakeup_tune_file_path* is set to the default settings of *missing value*. That means that these lines will only be executed the first time the script runs. Later on in the script, in lines 26, 27, and 28, we give the user a chance to change the song file.

The following part, which starts on line 7 and ends on line 23, allows you to figure out and verify the wakeup time and date.

We start with line 7 where we simply figure out the date of tomorrow:

```
set tomorrow_date to (current date) + (1 * days)
```

We will later apply a new time to the date of *tomorrow_date*.

Line 8 starts a repeat loop that ends on line 23. The purpose of that loop is to qualify the text the user typed as a valid date. The user was not only asked to provide a time, but also a time string, like "7:00 am", that can be coerced into a date.

The script first stores the string the user entered into the *requested_time* variable. Then it will try to coerce the *requested_time* value of the *requested_time* variable into a date. This happens in lines 13 through 22. If the coercion is successful, AppleScript will exit the repeat loop (line 15). If the coercion fails, the *try* statement will capture the error and the *on error* statement portion will be executed.

At this point, we start a new *try* statement. This time it is meant to allow the user to cancel. We ask the user to enter a new date, but we give him/her a way out this time. If the Cancel button is pressed, the *display dialog* command will generate an error this time, and the script will stop. This happens on lines 19 and 20.

Line 25 will then collect all the information and will use a self-terminating dialog box to let the user know when the clock is going to play which song, and allow the user to change the tune that'll play. This dialog box is shown in Figure 5-22.

Figure 5-22. The script displays a dialog box that allows the user to change the song. The dialog box will give up (close by itself) after 15 seconds.

Lines 22 through 31 allow the user to change the song file.

The final part of the script starts on line 33 and ends on line 49.

It is again an endless repeat loop that exits only when the date stored in the variable *wakeup_date* is smaller than the current date.

```
if (current date) > wakeup_date then...
```

The script

Following is the script in its entirety:

Script 5-14

```
1. property wakeup_tune_path : missing value
2. property requested_time : "7:00"
3. if wakeup_tune_path is missing value then
4.    set wakeup_tune_path to choose file with prompt ¬
   "Pick a wakeup tune" of type {"MPG3"}
5. end if
6. set song_name to name of (info for wakeup_tune_path)
7. set tomorrow_date to (current date) + (1 * days)
8. repeat
9.    set wake_dialog to display dialog ¬
   "Enter time you want to wake up:" default answer ¬
   requested_time buttons {"stop", "OK"} default button "OK"
10.    if button returned of wake_dialog is "Stop" then return
11.    set requested_time to text returned of wake_dialog
12.    date requested_time
13.    try
14.       set wakeup_date to date requested_time of tomorrow_date
15.       exit repeat
16.    on error —no good date
17.       try
18.          display dialog "Enter time again"
19.       on error
20.          return
21.       end try
22.    end try
23. end repeat
24. repeat
25.    display dialog "The song \"" & song_name & "\"" & return & ¬
   "should wake you up on: " & return & wakeup_date buttons ¬
   {"Change Song", "•"} default button "•" giving up after 15
26.    if button returned of result is "Change song" then
27.       set wakeup_tune_path to choose file with prompt ¬
   "Pick a wakeup tune" of type {"MPG3"}
28.       set song_name to name of (info for wakeup_tune_path)
29.    else
30.       exit repeat
31.    end if
32. end repeat
33. repeat
34.    if (current date) > wakeup_date then
35.       tell application "QuickTime Player"
36.          try
37.             close every movie
38.          end try
```

```
39.        open wakeup_tune_path
40.        tell movie 1
41.            set sound volume to 300
42.            play
43.        end tell
44.      end tell
45.      exit repeat
46.    else
47.      delay 10
48.    end if
49. end repeat
```

Power wrap-up

This section summarizes the chapter in an intensive-reference style. Use this part to look up facts related to the chapter without the chatter.

The date value class

The *date* value class is a value class intended to store, keep track of, and manipulate dates.

A value of the *date* class has information about the year, month, day, day of week, hour, minute, and second.

The date value is more of an object with properties rather than a simple value.

The way a given date will look when compiled is dependent upon the settings in the International panel of System Preferences.

Specifying dates

The following statement:

```
date "2/3/03"
```

will compile like this:

```
date "Monday, February 3, 2003 12:00:00 AM"
```

AppleScript is pretty loose in the values it will accept as a valid date. All the following strings compile properly when converted to dates:

```
date "03/03/03" --> date "Monday, March 3, 2003 12:00:00 AM"
date "0" --> date "Monday, May 31, 2004 12:00:00 AM"
date "5/1/2002" --> date "Wednesday, May 1, 2002 12:00:00 AM"
date "Feb 28 5:50 AM" --> date "Monday, February 28, 2005 12:00:00 AM"
```

You can also marry a date and a time using either the *of* or *relative to* operators.

```
date "5:00 PM" of (current date) --> date "Monday, May 31, 2004 5:00:00
PM"
```

Or

```
date "6:30 AM" relative to date "September 1, 2003"
--> date "Monday, September 1, 2003 6:30:00 AM"
```

current date

The *current date* command is a part of the Standard Additions. It returns the current date and time using the *date* value class:

```
current date --> date "Monday, May 31, 2004 12:18:38 PM"
```

When mixing the *current date* command in a longer statement, AppleScript requires you to place the command in parentheses.

```
set tomorrow_date to (current date) + days
```

time to GMT

The *time to GMT* command returns an integer that stands for the number of seconds between the time set on the computer running the script and Greenwich mean time.

```
time to GMT --> 14400
result / hours --> -4.0
```

date class properties

The *date* class contains the following properties: *year, month, day, weekday, time, date string, short date string,* and *time string*.

Examples follow:

```
year of (current date) --> 2004
month of (current date) --> May
```

The following script returns the day of the month:

```
day of (current date) --> 31
```

The following script returns the day of the week as a constant value, not as a string:

```
weekday of (current date) --> Monday
```

The following script returns the number of seconds passed from midnight last night:

```
time of (current date) --> 55956
```

Date constants

The constants *minutes, hours, days,* and *weeks* help you manipulate dates. Each one has a numerical value:

- *minutes* = 60, the number of seconds in a minute
- *hours* = 3600, the number of seconds in an hour
- *days* = 86400, the number of seconds in a day
- *weeks* = 604800, the number of seconds in a week

See earlier sections in this chapter for script samples using these constants.

Comparing dates

The same operators used to compare numbers can be used to compare dates: =, ≠, >, <, ≥, ≤. Operations using these operators return a Boolean result. When comparing dates, later dates count as larger. Following is an example:

```
set theDate to "1/1/2000"
(current date) > date theDate --> true
```

The = and ≠ operators aren't really useful with dates, since only two dates that are identical to the second will be considered equal.

Calculating time differences

Subtracting one date from another date produces a result that is the number of seconds between the two dates.

```
set theDate to "1/1/2000"
set time_lapse to (current date) - date theDate --> 139323057
set days_passed to round (time_lapse / days) rounding down
```

The result of 139323057 is the number of seconds passed between 1/1/2000 and time of writing. The last line returns the number of days instead of seconds.

Changing dates

To change a date into another date, you have to either add seconds to it or subtract seconds from it. Doing so is much easier when using the date constants *minutes, hours, days,* and *weeks.*

The result of each of the following script statements is always a *date* class.

The following statement returns the date three weeks from today:

```
(current date) + (weeks * 3)
```

The following script returns yesterday's date:

```
(current date) - days
```

Details previously . . .

The last part of this chapter is a summary of the entire chapter. For more details on any of the items, refer to sections earlier in the chapter.

CHAPTER 6

LISTS AND RECORDS

```
***
1. employment form.pdf
2. mailer east.pdf
3. mailer west.pdf
4. meeting summary.pdf
5. User manual.pdf


File type: GIFf
***
1. Headquarters map.gif
2. International logo.gif
3. logo.gif
4. small logo.gif
|
```

Headquarters map.gif   International log

Brochure   Layout

mailer east.pdf   mailer west.p

Create brochure   Create mail

```
ID solute rotation angle:0.0, absolu
bsolute vertical scale:100.0, id:65
lement:nothing, all graphics:{}, all |
nd cap, end join:miter end join, fil
:L.20040610.E.indd" of applicatio
f page id 420 of spread id 403 of
nDesign CS", gap tint:-1.0, geomet
47.553999999997, 868.0), text
ift line end:none, stroke color:swat
pplication "InDesign CS", stroke we
l 420 of spread id 403 of docume
S", miter limit:4.0, nonprinting:fals
verridden master page item:nothir
rame preferences:text frame prefe
```

Lists and records are the nonvalue-class value classes. Although they're considered value classes like strings, integers, etc., in truth they're simply a compilation of other values.

Imagine a list as a clothes hanging rack. The rack can be empty, but it can also have a few items hung on it. The items can be of different types, and you can look them over and pick the item you want to use. You can take items off the rack and put others on it.

The only problem with that rack is that the only way to define the item you want to work with is by its position on the rack. Today I will wear the shirt on the third hanger, the pants from hanger 12, and my socks must be on hangers 6 thru 7.

It is the same with a list—you can have an empty list that can sit and wait for you to add items to it; you can start with a predefined list, such as a list with the names of the 12 months; and you can also create lists out of application objects like the names of every file in a specific folder, or ID of every text frame on a given page, etc. So a list is a flexible and expandable storage solution. Each item in the list, as it's called, can hold a value of any value class.

In other programming languages lists are referred to as arrays, and they can, for the most part, include any number of elements, but only from a single value class. For instance, an array will have only text elements. A list in AppleScript can have text strings, numbers, dates, and, yes, other lists as items.

As we've seen in our scripts in previous sections, a list is surrounded by curly brackets and the items, if any, are separated by a comma. You can see a few examples of lists in Figure 6-1.

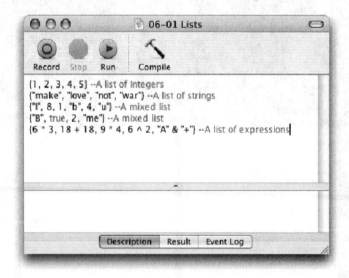

Figure 6-1. Different lists assigned to variables. The last list has five items, and each one is an expression.

So what is a record, then? A record is similar to a list, but every item is labeled. This makes it easier to find items because their order isn't important, but it also limits the things you can do with it.

If we look back to our rack example, in the list scenario, I could have grabbed the contents of hanger 3 thinking it was my hat, but if in an earlier script statement I hung my boxer shorts there, it could get pretty interesting. If my hanger rack was a record, I could have just asked the script to hand me the hat off my clothes hanger.

A record in AppleScript is also wrapped in curly brackets, and each item is still separated by a comma, but each item now has two parts: the label and the value itself.

One common place you see a record is in the result returned from the *display dialog* command. Figure 6-2 shows a *display dialog* command along with the resulting record.

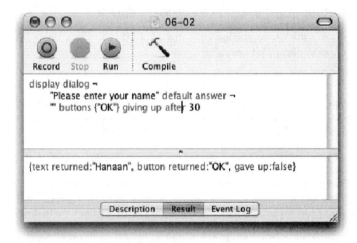

Figure 6-2. A statement with the *display dialog* command, along with the resulting record below

This record result allows me to get different information: for instance, what text did the user type, or whether the dialog gave up or not. As will be explained in detail in Chapter 12, the *give up* parameter closes down the dialog box if the user hasn't responded in the specified number of seconds.

More on lists

The best way to start with a list is to create an empty one. The syntax we use to create a new list and assign it to a variable also happens to be the syntax we use to erase all the items from a list:

```
set my_list to {}
```

The double curly brackets with nothing in between represent the empty list.

Adding items to a list

There are two ways to add items to a list, each with advantages and limitations.

The best way to append an item to the end of a list is to use the following syntax:

```
set end of the_list to the_item
```

This is the fastest way and the most efficient memory-wise, and since appending an item to the end of a list is one of the more common list-related tasks, you will find yourself using it quite a bit.

The other method of adding to a list is to reassign the list to a variable, along with the new item.

The operator we use to do that is the concatenation operator: &.

Whenever you use the concatenation operator on a list, you get a single list as a result. Here are a few examples of list operations:

Script 6-1

```
set new_list to {1, 2, 3} & {4 ,5 ,6 }-->  {1, 2, 3, 4 ,5 ,6}
set list_1 to 1 & 2 & 3 & 4 & 5 & 6-->  {1, 2, 3, 4 ,5 ,6}
set list_2 to "a" & "b" & "c" & "d" -->  "abcd"
```

Oops . . . what happened here? *list_1* ended up as a list, but *list_2* ended up as a string.

Remember that the concatenation operator works on strings as well as on lists, and if you're trying to concatenate a string to another string or to a number, the result will always be a string, unless, of course, you add the coercion operator *as*. So, let's try that again:

```
set list_2 to "a" & "b" & "c" & "d" as list-->   {"a", "b", "c", "d"}
```

That's better.

Getting items from a list

Once we have either built a list or gotten a list returned as a result, we need to be able to extract items out of it.

In the following example, I created a list with six items, assigned it to the variable *my_list*, and then extracted items out of it in various ways:

Script 6-2

```
set my_list to {1, 2, 3, 4 ,5 ,6}
item 3 of my_list --> 3
first item of my_list = item 1 of my_list --> 1
last item of my_list = item -1 of my_list --> 6
middle item of my_list --> 3
```

You can also use the term "some" to get a random item from a list.

```
set winner_name to some item of lottery_entry_list
```

You can also get a range of list items from the same list using the *thru* operator:

```
items 2 thru 5 of {1, 2, 3, 4 ,5 ,6}
--result: {2, 3, 4 ,5}
items -2 thru -1 of {"a", "b", "c", "d", "e"}
--result: {"d", "e"}
```

This range technique is also the only way to delete an item from a list. Here is how you do it:

To delete an item from the middle of a list, say the third item from a five-item list, you use this method:

```
set the_list to {"a", "b", "c", "d", "e"}
set remove_item to 3
set new_list to (items 1 thru (remove_item - 1) of the_list) ¬
& (items (remove_item + 1) thru -1 of the_list)
```

Here it is in a more literal form:

```
set new_list to (items 1 thru 2 of the_list) ¬
& (items 4 thru 5 of the_list)
```

It is, however, safe to assume that you can't predict whether the item we'll want to remove is in the middle and not the first or last item. So for that, we have to create a conditional statement that checks where the item is in the list. Check out Figure 6-3 for how that can be done.

Figure 6-3. Removing an item from a list

And as usual, I can't leave well enough alone, and I'm compelled to turn this script into a useful little handler that you can use in your own scripts. See Figure 6-4 for the handler version.

Figure 6-4. A handler for removing an item from a list

Now there's another way to get the same result that appears much cleaner from a scriptwriting standpoint. If you look at the solution presented in Figure 6-5, you can see that the same result can be achieved with far fewer lines of code.

This is misleading, though, since if the handler will have to remove an item from a long list, with, say, a few dozens items, there will be a significant speed difference. Whenever you can avoid looping, you should. Looping means just that, doing the same thing over and over.

Figure 6-5. A solution for removing an item from the list appears neater but will take far longer to execute.

List by class

As we saw earlier, a list can contain items from any value class. What AppleScript allows you to do is create another list that contains all the list items of a specific class. This allows you to extract numbers, text, etc. from a list that may contain multiple value classes.

All you have to do is ask for that class of a list:

```
text of {"I" ,"Love" ,"You" ,2} --> {"I" ,"Love" ,"You"}
```

If your list contains expressions, such as mathematical or string operations, the resulting list will have the result of that expression, not the expression itself:

```
integers of {1000 - 999, 1 + 1, -97 + 100} --> {1, 2, 3}
```

This method appears to be a good way to figure out valid numbers in a phone number, for instance.

Script 6-3

```
set the_phone_number to "(800) 555-1212 "
set the_phone_number_characters to characters of the_phone_number
-- Result: {"(", "8", "0", "0", ")", " ", "5", "5", "5", "-", "1", ¬
    "2", "1", "2"}
integers of the_phone_number_characters
-- Result: {}
```

This, however, will not work as you expect, since integers that are enclosed in quotes are still strings . . .

List properties

Being a bit more complex than other value classes, the *list* value class has a few neat properties that allow you to get different variations of the list. The properties are *class*, *length*, *rest*, and *reverse*.

The *class* property is always the same:

```
Class of {1, 2, 3}
--result is list
```

Here are the other properties:

6

Length

The length of the list is the number of items it has. Figure 6-6 shows that the *length* property of the given list is 4.

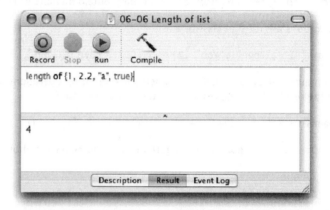

Figure 6-6. Length of list

Asking for the *length* property returns an identical result as using the *count* command on the list.

```
length of {1 ,2 ,3} = count items of {1 ,2 ,3}
```

Rest

The rest of a list is all the items of the list without the first item.

```
rest of {"don't", "talk", "while", "you", "eat"}
--result: {"talk", "while", "you", "eat"}
```

The string "don't", which was the first item in the list, has been removed.

Reverse

Just like it sounds, the *reverse* property of a list presents the same items in reverse order.

```
reverse of {"start", "middle", "nearly there", "finish"}
--result: {" finish", "nearly there", "middle", "start"}
```

Treating one list item at a time

Often the purpose of collecting items into a single list is so you can later go through that list and do something with each item. Take cooking, for instance: you start by standing in front of the potato bin, going through each potato, putting only the nice ones in your bag. You created a list of potatoes called *nice_potato_list*. Then you go home and peel each potato. You loop through the list, remove defects, if any, and peel each one.

See, you create a list and then loop through it to treat each item. This happens quite a bit in scripting, so our example later on will deal with that scenario.

There are two ways to get at every item of a list in succession, and both involve creating a repeat loop.

The idea is to repeat an action, and have the same variable take on the value of the next item in the list. The example that follows turns the second part of our potato example into a script:

```
set potato_list to {"small potato", "nice potato", "banged potato"}
repeat with the_potato in potato_list
    tell application "kitchen"
        peel the_potato
    end tell
end repeat
```

In the preceding example we start with a list of potatoes. As we loop through the list, with each repetition the variable *the_potato* takes on the value of the next item in the list, until the list is over.

In the next example, the *repeat* variable is a number, not a list item. For that reason, we must add another line that assigns the next list item to our variable:

```
set potato_list to {"small potato", "nice potato", "banged potato"}
repeat with i from 1 to (length of potato_list)
    set the_potato to item i of potato_list
    tell application "kitchen"
        peel the_potato
    end tell
end repeat
```

In this example, the value of the *repeat* variable *i* is 1, then 2, then 3; therefore the variable *the_potato* is set first to item 1 of *potato_list*, then item 2, and then item 3.

There are advantages of using this method versus repeating with a variable in a list, which we'll discuss in the "List of lists" section later in this chapter.

List operations

We already looked at the concatenation operator and saw how we can use it to put list items together into a single list.

The other list operators are, for the most part, comparison or containment operators, and they all return a Boolean value.

6

Comparing lists

As with any other value class, you can compare two lists to see if they're equal or not. You can't, however, check if a list is greater or smaller than another.

```
{1,2,3} = {1,2,3}
--result is true, (I know, this is a shock).
```

Comparing portions of lists

List comparison doesn't end in comparing whole lists. You can check if parts of a list match with parts of another list. The operators you use to do that are *starts with*, *ends with*, *contains*, and *is contained by*.

Let's examine these operators:

starts with and ends with

The *starts with* operator can check if a list starts with either another list or any other class. The following statements will all return true:

```
{1, 2, 3, 4} starts with 1
{1, 2, 3, 4} starts with {1}
{1, 2, 3, 4} starts with {1, 2}
{1, 2, 3, 4} starts with {1, 2, 3, 4}
```

The next statement, however, returns false:

```
{"abc", "def", "ghi"} starts with "a"
```

The last statement was false because in order to see whether a list starts with a specific string or ends with a specific string, you have to use the entire string in the comparison operation.

The following statement will return true:

```
item 1 of {"abc", "def", "ghi"} starts with "a"
```

The difference is that here we're using the *starts with* operator on item 1 of the list, which happens to be a string. What we're doing here in fact is this:

```
"abc" starts with "a"
```

The *ends with* operator works the same, but this time compares the last item of a list, or if the operand is a list, the *ends with* compares the last items of the given list.

contains

Use the *contains* operator to see if a list contains either a single value or another list. If a list either starts with or ends with a value, then it definitely contains it.

Here's an example using the *contains* statement. This script checks if the startup disk contains the documents folder. Of course, there are other ways to check that, but we're in list mode right now.

The script will first create a list using the *list folder* command, and then checks to see if the default folders are part of that list.

```
set folder_list to list folder (path to startup disk) ¬
    without invisibles
if folder_list contains "Applications" and ¬
    folder_list contains "Desktop" and ¬
    folder_list contains "Library" and ¬
    folder_list contains "System" and ¬
    folder_list contains "Users" then
    display dialog "Startup disk has all key folders"
else
    display dialog "Startup disk is missing some key folders"
end if
```

After line 1 executes, the result is a list with the names of every file and folder of the startup disk as its items.

Line 2 checks to see if the list contains a series of strings. Since we separated each *contains* statement with the Boolean operator *and*, the comparisons operate independently, and only if all items that are checked are contained in the list does the startup disk get the OK.

is contained by

The *is contained by* operator checks whether the left operand, which can be a list or a single value, is contained by the list in the right operand. Here's an example:

```
{1, 2} is contained by {1, 2, 3} --> true
{"a", "c"} is contained by {"a", "b", "c"} --> false
{1, 2} is contained by {1, 2, 3} --> true
"treasure" is in (words of "treasure chest") --> true
```

As you can see, the term *is in* can be used instead of *is contained by*.

Commands that produce a list

Asking AppleScript for multiple elements of an object or a value returns a list. A simple example of that is

```
characters of "abc"
--result: {"a", "b", "c"}
```

The same statement can also use the word "every":

```
every character of "abc"
```

The same situation of getting a list of elements as a result is heavily used when scripting applications with a strong object model.

When talking to applications, not only can you ask for a list of objects, which are usually elements of a higher-class object, but you can also ask for one property of all these elements, and you can also filter the elements you get with the *whose* clause.

While we will discuss this in much more detail in later chapters that deal with scripting applications, here are a few examples.

```
tell application "Finder"
    set big_file_name_list to name of every file of folder x ¬
    whose size > 10000.
end tell
```

Result: a list where each item is a string that contains a file name. All file names in the list belong to files larger than 10MB.

Applications can also return lists of references to objects, not only values such as numbers and text. Figure 6-7 shows how InDesign returns a list of references to text frames. Notice how each reference is using the ID of the text frame, and every parent object up the chain of command.

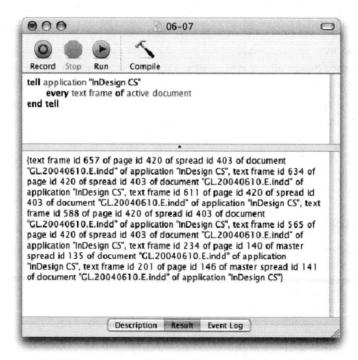

Figure 6-7. InDesign returned a massive list of references to text frames. Despite its size, the list contains only six items.

Another common command that returns a list is the *list folder* command. This command is a part of the standard additions, and its purpose is to return a list of file names enclosed by a folder.

As seen in Figure 6-8, the *list folder* command returns a list of file names only, not the whole path. To do something with the files in following statements, you have to concatenate the folder path to each of the file names in the list.

Figure 6-8. The *list folder* command with its result

The *list folder* command doesn't distinguish between different types of files, or even between folders, etc. You can, however, specify whether you want the list to include invisible files or not.

Figure 6-9 shows a typical set of statements that gets a list of file names using the *list folder* command, and then repeats in the list and treats each file.

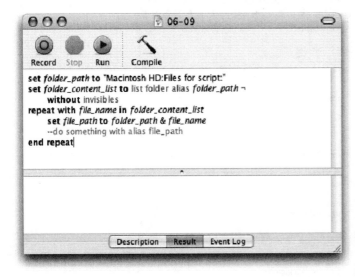

Figure 6-9. The *list folder* command is used in combination with a repeat loop.

List of lists

Let's get fancy now. If list items can belong to any value class, they can also be lists themselves. Not only that, but creating a list of lists is a very useful form of scripting.

We discussed the usefulness of a list in solving the need for an expandable storage space: a list of files in a folder, for instance. We don't always know how many files we're going to have when the script runs, so instead of putting every file name in its own variable, which does rarely happen, we create a single list and make each file name an item in that list.

Now, what if we're looking to tackle a more complex problem? What if we need to create a report that will list all files in a particular folder by file type, and have a header above each file list that will consist of the file type? Figures 6-10 and 6-11 show the sample folder and the report the script should generate.

Figure 6-10. The sample folder

Figure 6-11. The report the script will generate

Here's the final script:

Script 6-4

```
1.  set the_folder to (choose folder) as string
2.  set master_file_list to list folder alias the_folder ¬
    without invisibles
3.  set types_list to {}
4.  set types_of_files_in_master_list to {}
5.  repeat with i from 1 to count master_file_list
6.      set file_name to item i of master_file_list
7.      set file_info to get info for file (the_folder & file_name)
8.      set file_type to file type of file_info
9.      copy file_type to end of types_of_files_in_master_list
10.     if file_type is not in types_list then
11.         copy file_type to end of types_list
12.     end if
13. end repeat
14. set list_of_file_lists to {}
15. repeat with i from 1 to count types_list
16.     set temporary_list to {}
17.     repeat with j from 1 to count master_file_list
18.         set the_file_name to item j of master_file_list
19.         set the_file_type to item j of types_of_files_in_master_list
20.         set comparison_type to item i of types_list
21.         if comparison_type is equal to the_file_type then
22.             copy the_file_name to end of temporary_list
23.         end if
24.     end repeat
25.     copy temporary_list to end of list_of_file_lists
26. end repeat
27. --format report
28. set report_text to ""
29. repeat with i from 1 to count types_list
30.     set the_type to item i of types_list
31.     set list_of_files_of_that_type to item i of list_of_file_lists
32.     set report_text to report_text & "File type: " & the_type & ¬
    return & "***" & return
33.     repeat with j from 1 to count list_of_files_of_that_type
34.         set the_file_name to item j of list_of_files_of_that_type
35.         set report_text to report_text & j & ". " & ¬
            the_file_name & return
36.     end repeat
37.     set report_text to report_text & return & return
38. end repeat
39. --Show report
40. tell application "TextEdit"
41.     make new document at beginning with properties ¬
    {text:report_text, name:"File Report"}
42. end tell
```

6

The main challenge in understanding the script, and in writing it too, is the different list variables.

Let's go over the different lists this script creates and deals with:

The first list is *master_file_list*. This is simply a list where each item is a name of a file in the chosen folder. The number of items then will be the same as the number of files in the folder.

The list *types_of_files_in_master_list* will be a parallel list to *master_file_list*. It'll have the same number of items, but in this list, each item will have a file type. The two lists correspond in a way that if you take the same item number, one list will contain a file's name, and the other list will contain this file's type. Synchronized lists is a simple way to build database functionality for runtime purposes. Figure 6-12 shows the two lists side by side. The windows you're looking at are taken from Late Night Software's Script Debugger, which has some great views of lists, records, and other compound values.

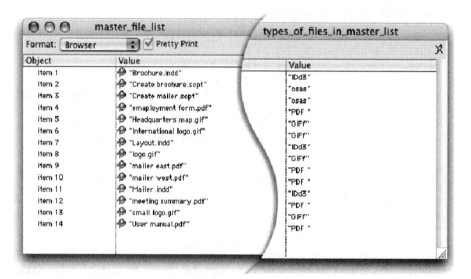

Figure 6-12. The lists *master_file_list* and *types_of_files_in_master_list* are compared.

So what is *types_list* responsible for? The *types_list* list variable will have a single item for each unique file type. Since the folder I chose contains files of four different types, the *types_list* list will contain four items by the end.

These three list variables collect their values in the first repeat loop from line 5 to line 13.

In line 14 we introduce a new list variable: *list_of_file_lists*. This list will have as many items as the *types_list*. Each of the items will be a list by itself that will include the names of files whose file type is the corresponding item in the *types_list* variable. Figure 6-13 illustrates how the script is designed with corresponding lists.

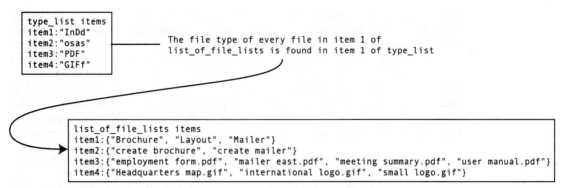

```
type_list items
item1:"InDd"
item2:"osas"                    The file type of every file in item 1 of
item3:"PDF"                     list_of_file_lists is found in item 1 of type_list
item4:"GIFf"
```

```
list_of_file_lists items
item1:{"Brochure", "Layout", "Mailer"}
item2:{"create brochure", "create mailer"}
item3:{"employment form.pdf", "mailer east.pdf", "meeting summary.pdf", "user manual.pdf"}
item4:{"Headquarters map.gif", "international logo.gif", "small logo.gif"}
```

Figure 6-13. The synchronization between the *type_list* and *list_of_file_lists* variables

A key to understanding the structure shown previously is that AppleScript isn't aware of any link between the two lists, nor is it responsible to maintain their synchronicity. This job is up to you, and it takes planning and confidence. Confidence, because you unleash your script to gather information and collect two separate lists, and at the end you expect that these two lists will match.

From line 15 to line 26 we actually have a double repeat loop. The first loop loops through the type lists. The second loop loops through the entire *master_file_list*. What happens in the loop is that the type from the type list, which is assigned in line 20 to the variable *comparison_type*, is compared with the type of the file, which is assigned in line 19 to the variable *the_file_type*.

The names of all the files that match the current comparison file type are collected in line 22 to the list variable *temporary_list*. Notice the conditional statement between lines 21 and 23.

Line 25 is key. In that line, the temporary list is tacked onto the end of the *list_of_file_lists* variable. Since this happens once in the repeat loop starting on line 15, and this loop repeats the number of times that is equal to the number of items in *types_list*, then the result is that the variable *list_of_file_lists* will have, by the end, as many items as the *types_list* variable; each item is a list by itself.

In the next portion of the script, a string variable called *report_text* is created (line 28). This variable slowly gathers text that accounts for the report. After all, the report isn't a list, rather a string of text.

Following the introduction of the *report_text* variable, we start a repeat loop that is almost identical to the repeat loops in the previous section. Here, however, instead of creating the *list_of_file_lists* variable, we're using the values in it to generate the report.

Now, whenever you look at your script and see that two parts of it are almost identical, you start wondering whether you could have done OK with only one of them, slightly more bloated. Meaning if in one part of the script we collect the data we need to use in the report, and in the other part of the script we use the data we collected, couldn't we have just used the data the first time around? Couldn't we just generate the report as we're collecting the information? Wouldn't it be faster and more efficient?

6

203

Yes and yes, but! Yes, we probably could have just generated the report without creating the elaborate lists. Yes, doing so would have created a faster script. Looking for the but? Well here we go: first, it's not always better to create faster, smaller, and more efficient scripts. When Apple tried to create a faster, smaller, and more efficient Mac, it called it the Cube, and a little bit later it called it off. Part of what makes Power Macs great, in contrast to the Cube, is the large door on the side that makes the entire inside accessible. This helps on a few levels: it helps you add RAM, replace the hard drive, or just admire all that fun-looking stuff. It helps Apple's (number one in the industry) technical support troubleshoot and fix your Mac, and it helps Apple's engineers create the Mac in the first place.

The same lessons are true for the scripts you write. Sometimes you have to spread it out a little to make it better. The construction of our script clearly distinguishes between data collection and structure, and the final output of that data. This is important, since now that you have two cool parts to your script, you can actually turn them into handlers, and call them something like *data_collection* and *file_report*. Now, they become their own independent objects that can be expanded upon and used in other scripts as well.

See, the construction of that script wasn't an arbitrary attempt to make the script longer and therefore more legible, rather an attempt to separate the input branch (data collection) from the output branch (report making).

Due to the database field–like nature of a list, it is a natural choice for collecting and temporarily storing data.

Records

While lists are wild things with items only you and god know that they contain, records are also a collection of items, but here, each item is meticulously labeled.

Figure 6-14 illustrates the differences between a list and a record.

Figure 6-14. A list and a record with the same values in each item

Like a list, a record has items that can be counted using either the record's *length* property or the *count* command:

```
length of {name: "Bob", age: 24, married: true, income: 55000}
count {name: "Bob", age: 24, married: true, income: 55000}
```

Both of these statements return 4.

Getting record items

Let's go back to *the_dude* with the following assignment statement:

```
set the_dude to {name: "Bob", age: 24, married: true, income: 55000}
```

If we want to use in our script some of the information from the record assigned to the *the_dude* variable, we have to know the record labels. Since there's no real way to get the labels during runtime, scripting records can become a fairly planned-out static sort of thing.

Figure 6-15 shows how to get a value from a record.

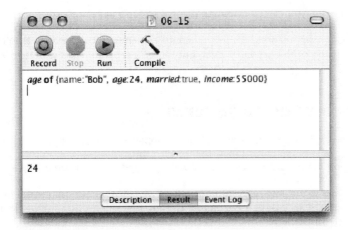

Figure 6-15. Getting a value from a record using that item's label

Records are useful when you have a static set of information that you use in the script, and you would rather clump that information into a single variable instead of dividing it into multiple single-value variables.

Records shortfalls

While we can count the items in a record, we can't ask to see an item by index.

Figure 6-16 shows the error we get when we try to get item 2 of a record.

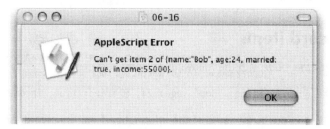

Figure 6-16. Trying to get an item of a record based on its index (position) generates an error.

Another problem with implementing records in a script is that you can't add items to them during runtime.

As you'll see later, you can concatenate records to form larger records.

When working with records, it's important to remember that records aren't simply an improved version of the list value class, but rather a separate class with its own uses and limitations.

Where records do make sense

One function that records fill really well lies in application scriptability.

Whenever you ask for properties of any object, you get a record containing all properties.

Figure 6-17 shows the vast range of information we get when we ask for the properties of a text frame from an InDesign document. Getting these items as a list would surely confuse even the best scripter.

Getting the properties of an object as a record is also useful while creating the script or for familiarizing yourself with the application's object model.

Another place where you will find a record to be a useful tool is when you write scripts that someone else has to not only run, but also open and understand.

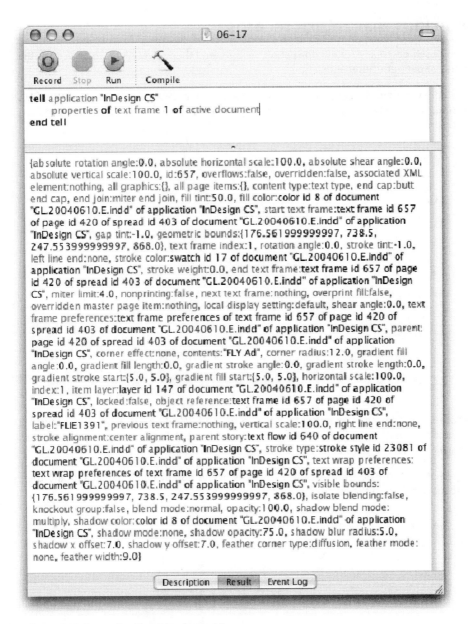

Figure 6-17. Properties of an InDesign text frame

Records make scripts much more legible, and using them will make the job of the poor scripter who'll have to take over your job a wee bit easier (oh, what the heck, let him fry).

Commands that return records

Being a self-describing set of information, records lend themselves nicely to be used as the result of different commands.

The command *info for* accepts a file reference as parameter, and returns all of that file's attributes. Figure 6-18 shows the attributes of the file Picture 1, which is created by taking a screen shot.

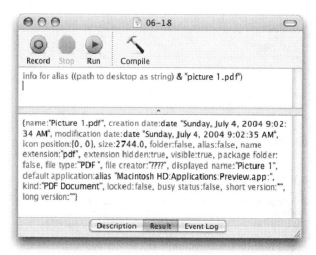

Figure 6-18. The result of the *info for* command

Another old favorite is the *display dialog* command. What's neat about this particular command is that depending on the parameters you give it, the record you get as a result may have different items in it.

Figures 6-19 and 6-20 show two different uses of the *display dialog* command and their respective results in the *record* value class.

Figure 6-19. The *display dialog* command with the *default answer* parameter used

Figure 6-20. The *display dialog* command with the *giving up* parameter used

Notice how the *display dialog* command returned a different result in Figures 6-19 and 6-20. It is up to you to know what result to expect and how to deal with it when it comes.

Comparing records

Records can only be compared to other records. You can see if two records are equal or not and see if a record contains or is contained by another record. Though the AppleScript language guide claims that you can use the *starts with* and *ends with* comparison operators on a record, I found no evidence of that. It makes sense that these operators aren't used since the order of a record plays no role in comparisons.

For instance, the following statement will return true as a result regardless of the fact that the items are ordered differently:

```
{model: "Focus", year: "2000"} = {year: "2000", model: "Focus"}
```

The following two statements are also true:

```
{model: "Focus"} is contained by {year: "2000", model: "Focus"}
{year: "2000", model: "Focus"} contains {model: "Focus"}
```

Concatenating records

You concatenate records the same way you concatenate lists: by using the concatenation operator, &. Following is a simple record concatenation operation:

```
{model: "Focus", year: "2000"} & {size: 2}
--result: {model: "Focus", year: "2000", size: 2}
```

If the two records share one or more properties, they will merge into a single item whose value is taken from the record on the left.

```
{model: "PB17", RAM: 512} & {RAM: 256, speed: 1000}
--result: {model: "PB17", RAM: 512, speed: 1000}
```

Notice how both records contained the property *RAM*, but the result threw away that property from the right-side operand.

Coercing records

Directly, you can only coerce a record into a list.

```
{model: "Focus", year: "2000", size: 2} as list
--result: {"Focus", "2000", 2}
```

Creating records on the fly

Creating a compound value on the fly is usually the specialty of a list. Records are usually planned and predefined by nature.

However, since this is a comprehensive book, I thought I'd add a slick way to create a record on the fly, with custom labels and all. All we'll do is concatenate text into a string that looks like a record and then run that text as a script.

Figure 6-21 shows a simplified no-frills version of that method.

Figure 6-21. A string converted into a record

If the record you're trying to create includes strings, you must escape the quote with a backslash. Figure 6-22 shows an example of taking two lists, one of the record labels and one of the record values, and turning them into a single record value.

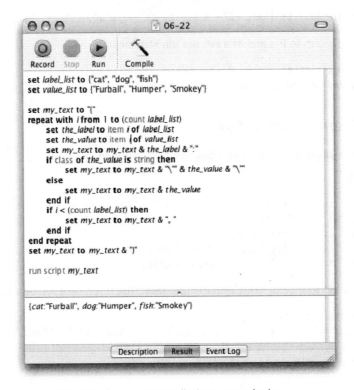

```
set label_list to {"cat", "dog", "fish"}
set value_list to {"Furball", "Humper", "Smokey"}

set my_text to "{"
repeat with i from 1 to (count label_list)
    set the_label to item i of label_list
    set the_value to item i of value_list
    set my_text to my_text & the_label & ":"
    if class of the_value is string then
        set my_text to my_text & "\"" & the_value & "\""
    else
        set my_text to my_text & the_value
    end if
    if i < (count label_list) then
        set my_text to my_text & ", "
    end if
end repeat
set my_text to my_text & "}"

run script my_text
```

{cat:"Furball", dog:"Humper", fish:"Smokey"}

Figure 6-22. Coercion of a compex list into a record value

Power wrap-up

This section summarizes the chapter in an intensive-reference style. Use this part to look up facts related to the chapter without the chatter.

Lists

The list data type is a container that may contain no items, one item, or multiple items from any other data type. The following list has three items, each one being a string:

```
{"Boston", "Atlanta", "San Francisco"}
```

An empty list looks like this:

```
{}
```

Manipulating lists

To add an item to a list or link two lists, use the concatenation operator.

```
set new_list to {"A", "B"} & {1, 2, 3} --> {"A", "B", 1, 2, 3}
```

To add a single item to the end of a list, use this statement:

```
set new_list to {1, 2, 3}
set end of new_list to 4 --> {1, 2, 3, 4}
```

Getting items from a list

You can get a single item from a list using the item's position in the list.

Script 6-5

```
set city_list to {"Boston", "Atlanta", "San Francisco"}
set the_city to item 2 of city_list --> "Atlanta"
first item of city_list --> "Boston"
last item of city_list --> "San Francisco"
item -1 of city_list --> "San Francisco"
```

You can also get a range of items with the *thru* term. The result here will be a list:

```
set city_list to of ¬
 {"Boston", "Atlanta", "San Francisco", "Providence", "Seattle"}
set the_city to items 2 thru 4 of city_list
--> {"Atlanta", "San Francisco", "Providence"}
```

Comparing lists

You can compare two lists, or a list with a possible list item.

```
{1, 2, 3} contains 2 --> true
{1, 2, 3} starts with 2 --> false
{1, 2, 3} ends with 3 --> true
```

List of lists

A list whose items are also lists is a list of lists.

```
{{1, 2, 3}, {10, 20, 30}, {100, 200, 300}}
```

List properties

To get the list without the first item, use the *rest* property.

```
rest of {"Atlanta", "San Francisco", "Providence"}
Result --> {"San Francisco", "Providence"}
```

The *reverse* property contains the same list in reverse order.

```
reverse of {"Atlanta", "San Francisco", "Providence"}
Result --> {"Providence", "San Francisco", "Atlanta"}
```

Records

A record is a list where each item has a descriptive label.

```
{name: "Burt", age: 30, member: true}
```

Record labels can't contain spaces; however, terms defined in an application's dictionary that has a space may be used as a record label in a record created by that application.

You can't get a record's item by position, only by label.

```
age of {name: "Burt", age: 30, member: true} --> 30
```

Comparing records

You can check whether two records are equal, or whether a record contains, or is contained by, another record. Following are a few examples:

```
{name: "Burt", age: 30, member: true} = {age: 30, name: "Burt", ¬
    member: true}
Result --> true
```

The preceding statement returns true because AppleScript puts no emphasis on the order of the items in a record.

```
{name: "Burt", age: 30, member: true} contains {name: "Burt"} --> true
{name: "Burt"} is contained by {name: "Burt", age: 30, member: true} ¬
    --> true
```

Concatenating records

Concatenate records by using the concatenation operator.

```
{name: "Burt", age: 30, member: true} & {position: "President"}
Result --> {name: "Burt", age: 30, member: true, position: "President"}
```

If both operands contain the same label, then the value from the left operand will be used.

Coercing records

A record can be coerced into a list, in which case the labels will be stripped.

Details previously . . .

The last part of this chapter is a summary of the entire chapter. For more details on any of the items here, refer to earlier sections in this chapter.

CHAPTER 7
GIVING COMMANDS

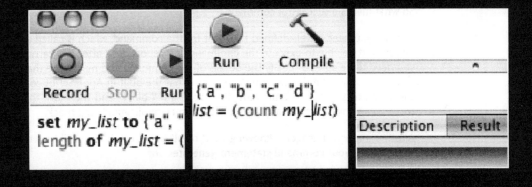

If you had to choose a friend from ancient Greece, Socrates may be an interesting choice. You two could sit down for hours reflecting on and discussing the state of things. However, if you needed someone who can get things done, someone in command, you'd probably want to move a few hundred years into the future to ancient Rome, and consider someone like Julius Caesar.

AppleScript is more like Caesar than like Socrates; it rules the Mac OS kingdom. When AppleScript talks, most statements it uses contain a command, and after stating most of those, it'll wait there until it gets a result. The AppleScript language is used to get results, to get things done. And since AppleScript has no mouse or keyboard, it gets things done by giving commands. Interestingly enough, the commands AppleScript was given at the factory are few: *copy*, *count*, *get*, *run*, *set*, and *error*. So where does the complexity lie? Remember that most of the AppleScript language comes from applications' scriptability. Applications have many more commands built into them. InDesign, for example, has about 80 of its own commands, FileMaker Pro has about 30, and Photoshop has over 65 commands.

Note that there are many other command-like terms used in AppleScript. How these terms are categorized isn't all that important, so here I will stick to the five commands listed in the AppleScript Language Guide. I did list a sixth such command, which is the *error* command, but it will be described in Chapter 16, which is dedicated to errors.

The goal is to draw a broad enough base of understanding commands that anytime you want to start automating a new application, the learning curve won't be as steep. You will be able to start focusing on the subject of your automation rather than on struggling with simple things that refuse to work.

The anatomy of a command

Commands, even in life, are not just meaningless sentences you throw around. Commands have a purpose, and any one of a few things can make them not work.

So what makes a successful command?

To start, you need a well-defined recipient for the command, which is called a target. That target must be able to execute the command and report back after it is carried out. Then, you need to be able to specify the details of the command and make sure that your recipient understands the details. You should note that the built-in AppleScript commands and some scripting addition commands don't have a *tell* block, and therefore the "target" of these commands is not an application object in an application's *tell* block.

Another important aspect is knowing what result to expect, if any, and how to process an error in case your command statement generates one.

Let's start with the command itself. As we saw earlier, AppleScript has only six built-in commands. The rest belong to either an application or scripting addition, or to a script object. Script object commands are usually commands that you have full control of, mainly because you can write them yourself.

When you do (and you will), you will have intimate knowledge of their inner working, and also how to make them error-out. As we discuss creating your own commands in more detail, we will also look at ways to make sure you don't lose yourself in an unmanageable mess of commands, to the point where they're unusable.

Commands you make yourself, also called handlers and subroutines, are very cool. They're written using AppleScript, and they are your discount-fare ticket to becoming a power-user. We will discuss them in great detail later in the book.

For now, though, we will try to focus on AppleScript commands and application commands.

Who made you boss?

One of the important aspects of a good command, as we said earlier, is a good target. Something that will understand the command and give you a result back. In the case of the six AppleScript commands, the target is AppleScript, so the command can be used without specifying a target object.

Let's look at the five commands:

copy and set

copy and *set*, as they're used in AppleScript, are usually found in assignment statements. Assignment statements are statements that assign a value to a variable. Although the way the two commands go about assigning values is in reverse to each other, the result they produce is in most cases the same.

Using copy and set

Since assigning values to variables is one of the most basic things we do in AppleScript, we should pay some attention here.

If we go back to our last analogy that said that variables are like AppleScript's knowledge and memories, using the *set* and *copy* commands in AppleScript is like your making a mental note of important information that is presented to you. Consider the following:

I walk down the hall when I see a co-worker with someone I don't recognize. "Hanaan," he says, "I'd like you to meet Jena. She's the new marketing director, she was transferred here from Salt Lake." I say "Hello," shake hands and think to myself, "Man, is she cute! I've got to remember her name." So I make a mental note of her face, and assign her information as single values into variables:

```
set the_name to "Jena"
set the_origin to "Salt Lake"
set the_position to "marketing director"
```

OK, I've got it down. The next day I meet her in the cafeteria. "Hi," I say, "How's day two treating you?"

"Oh hi," she answers.

I quickly pull out the information I gathered the day before, and compile a completely generic sentence, personalized to impress:

Set my_next_sentence to "So "& the_name & "were you also the " & the_position & " when you worked at our " & the_origin & "office?"

I say my_next_sentence, and . . .

"What a pathetic guy," she thinks, "He actually remembered all this information just to impress me? I got to copy 'Hanaan' to my 'people_I_should_avoid' list."

OK, so that wasn't the result I was hoping for, but nevertheless, without the use of variables and assigning values to them, all I would've had was "Hi, you're that person who was transferred from our other office to fill a position here." Even worse.

What's even more unique about the assignment commands *set* and *copy*, is that they not only assign a value to a variable, but they can also define the variable. That means that I was not planning to store Jena's name until I met her. I wasn't walking around knowing that I will need to remember information about a new person.

The same happens in a script. You may start the script by initializing some variables such as the current date and name of the startup disk, but as you advance in the script, more values will become needed, and along with them you will need to define more variables.

So where is the difference between *copy* and *set*? It would be bad if two out of the five commands in AppleScript do the exact thing!

The difference is that in some cases the *set* command allows for two variables to share the same value, while the *copy* command always makes a copy of the data before stuffing it into the second variable.

This, however, is only true in cases where the value we set is a list, a record, or a script object.

Let's look at some *set* and *copy* examples:

In the most basic form, *set* and *copy* assign a value of any class to a variable. That value can then be later retrieved by using the variable's identifier. The identifier, just for clarification, is the actual word you used to name the variable.

```
set the_user_name to "George"
```

is the same as

```
copy "George" to the_user_name
```

However, things are different when we start dealing with values in a list or record.

copy and set examples

Let's try a simple exercise:

```
set my_list to {1, 2, 3}
set your_list to my_list
set item 3 of my_list to 10
```

We start with a list of three numbers. Then we assign that list to another variable. Now we have two list variables: *my_list* has the value {1,2,3} assigned to it, and *your_list* has *my_list* assigned to it.

Now, what would you expect will happen to *your_list* when I change *my_list*? Put expectations aside; when we assigned *my_list* to *your_list*, we didn't set *your_list* to the value of *my_list*, but rather as a reference to *my_list*. That means that changing *my_list* also changes *your_list*.

At the end of the preceding script, both *my_list* and *your_list* will have the value of {1, 2, 10}.

To me, that situation sort of beats the purpose of assigning a variable to another variable. The point is that you can have one variable keep the original value and the other hold the value that will get changed. If I wanted two variables to remain synchronized, I would, well, use only one variable.

In order to assign the list value of one variable to a second variable, you can use the *copy* command instead of the *set* command.

Here's how the script would look:

```
set my_list to {1, 2, 3}
copy my_list to your_list
set item 3 of my_list to 10
```

In the preceding script, the value of *my_list* will be {1, 2, 10}, while *your_list* will remain {1, 2, 3}.

copy in applications

In AppleScript, the meaning of a command is determined by the object that receives it. That means that while you're inside an application's *tell* block, the *copy* command may get a different meaning.

For one, many applications include the *copy* command without any parameters. A statement that is made solely of the *copy* command will act as if you chose Copy from the Edit menu.

Typically, when an application allows you to use the *copy* command to copy selected items to the clipboard, the target application has to be in the front. You can use the *activate* command for that, or you will quickly encounter the error message in Figure 7-1.

Figure 7-1. Many applications have to be front-most to execute the *cut*, *copy*, and *paste* commands.

While it's easy to see if you forgot to add the *activate* command before using the *copy* command (the script stops during testing . . .), user behavior is almost impossible to predict. Take for instance a scenario where you have a whole bunch of commands that target Adobe Illustrator. Before all these commands execute, you include the *activate* command, which brings Illustrator to the front. If at any point the user gets bored and decides to check e-mail or browse the Web while the script is running, the script will stop when the *copy* command executes.

There are a few things you can do. First, place the *activate* command right before the *copy* command. This will shorten the time the impatient user has to switch back away from your target application.

Another thing you can do is to trap the error and alert the user that s/he shouldn't be messing with his/her Mac while the script is running. Another dialog box solution is to display a dialog box for three seconds, telling the user not to interfere. You can use the *giving up* parameter of the *display dialog* command to have the dialog box display for a specific period of time.

The script that follows illustrates the methods previously outlined:

Script 7-1

```
1. tell application "Adobe Illustrator 10"
2.  tell document 1
3.    set selected of every text art item to true
4.  end tell
5.  activate
6.  try
7.    display dialog "The script can't be interrupted!" ¬
   buttons {"•"} giving up after 3
8.    copy
9.  on error error_message number error_number
10.   if error_number is 9002 then
11.     display dialog "Hey buddy, don't mess with your Mac while ¬
   the script is running!"
```

```
12.   end if
13.   end try
14.   make new document
15.   paste
16.   end tell
```

Other applications require that you specify a target object for the *copy* command, as shown in the following script:

```
tell application "BBEdit 6.5"
    copy text of window 1
end tell
```

count

The *count* command returns the number of items in a list, a record, or a string. Here are some simple examples:

Script 7-2

```
count "abc" -->3
count {10,20,30,40,50} --> 5
count items in {"alef", "bet", "gimel", "dalet"} --> 4
count {name: "Jerry", occupation: "singer", outlook: "greatful", ¬
    status: "dead"}
Result: --> 4
```

Another way to get the number of characters in a string or the number of items in a list or in a record is by tapping into these classes' *length* property. As you can see in Figure 7-2, the *count* command will return an identical result to that value's *length* property.

Figure 7-2. my_list has four items, therefore the *length* property of it is equal to the result of the *count* command when using *my_list* as a parameter.

count for looping

One of the most common uses of the *count* command comes in handy when constructing repeat loops. Many times, when you create a repeat loop, you need to treat items that are part of a list. Since these items are treated one at a time, the *count* command helps us figure out how many times we need to loop.

```
set user_list to list folder "Macintosh HD:Users:"
repeat with i from i to (count user_list)
    set the_user to item i of user_list
    --do something with the_user
end repeat
```

Counting application objects

Another way to use the *count* command is to get the number of elements of an application. The result can be used for looping through and treating each object, or for other purposes within the script. This command becomes even more useful when used with the *whose* clause.

There's a small twist, however, in using the *count* command inside applications: the application may have its own *count* command that requires different syntax. So just how complicated can that get? Not too complicated at all. See, what most people do is never deal with the application's syntax, which varies from application to application. Instead, you can just get a reference of *every* object of a specific class into a list and count the list. You can do that in a single statement, and there are a few advantages: the syntax is similar from application to application, and you can use the *whose* clause to narrow down the range of objects you're counting.

The FileMaker example that follows uses both FileMaker's own *count* command and AppleScript's version:

Script 7-3

```
tell application "FileMaker Pro"
    --Application's count command:
    count database "clients" class record
    count record 1 class field
    --AppleScript's count command:
    count (every record of database "clients")
    count (records of database "clients" whose cell 1 > 0)
end tell
```

In the preceding example, lines 3 and 4 use FileMaker's *count* command. You can see that the syntax requires that you specify an object and a class. The object is the object whose elements you want to count, and the class you specify is the class of the elements you want to count. Line 3 counts the record elements of the database *"clients"* object.

Line 6 does the same thing using AppleScript's *count* command. Line 7 also uses AppleScript's *count* command, but with the *whose* clause, which helps narrow down the counted objects to only the records whose cell 1 is greater that 0 (sounds just like AppleScript . . .).

Also, when compiling the script, AppleScript adds parentheses around the *every object* reference. This is to make it clear that this part of the statement returns a list, and AppleScript counts the list.

InDesign has taken a similar approach to FileMaker, where you specify the object whose elements you want to count, and the type of objects you want counted. The following script counts the pages of document 1:x:

```
tell application "InDesign 2.0.2"
  count document 1 each page
end tell
```

get

While you don't see the actual word "get" of the *get* command, the *get* command itself is used in many statements that you write.

The *get* command is used slightly differently in AppleScript than in scripting applications. In AppleScript, the *get* command returns the resulting value from an expression into the *result* variable, while an application returns a value related to one of its objects to the same *result* variable.

If you forgot, *result* is a variable built into AppleScript, and any value that is returned by any expression is assigned to this variable.

Like the *get* command, the *result* variable usually goes unnoticed. However, it's important to understand what role these two terms play in your scripts.

The get command in AppleScript

Consider the following script statements, which you'll hardly ever see in actual scripts (not created for demonstration or training):

```
get item_cost * sales_tax
set item_price to result
```

In the preceding example, the first statement gets the value of a simple mathematical expression and assigns it, automatically, to the *result* variable. The second statement assigns the value of the *result* variable to a more permanent variable, because as you imagine, the next statement will most likely alter the value of the *result* variable once more.

The same two-line script snippet shown previously can be written, and most commonly is, using a single assignment statement with no mention of the words "get" and "result":

```
set item_price to item_cost * sales_tax
```

The difference is that in the two-line example, we explicitly use the *get* command, while in the one-liner, and in most real-world applications, we will not.

Getting values inside applications

When working inside an application's *tell* block, the use of the *get* command doesn't change much. Instead of returning a value resulting from an expression such as *2 + 2*, or *item 2 of my_list*, it returns a value related to one of its objects.

```
tell application "InDesign 2.0.2"
  get document 1
  copy result to my_document
end tell
```

In the preceding script, we get the *document* from InDesign and assign it to the *my_document* variable.

The same can be achieved in the following script:

```
tell application "InDesign 2.0.2"
  set my_document to document 1
end tell
```

The application uses its own version of the *get* command, passes the resulting value to AppleScript, and AppleScript then assigns it to a variable.

Real-world use of the get command

Theoretically, you can script successfully for many years without knowing that the *get* command even exists. The *get* command, as shown previously, returns a result to AppleScript, after which it is your job to do something with it.

There are some times when certain applications will get picky when you try to combine too many commands in one statement.

For instance, let's look at the caveats of the following general statement:

```
tell application "some app" to set n to ¬
  (count pages of document 1) * (count documents)
```

In the preceding statement, AppleScript actually processes a few commands: it first gets the pages of document 1, counts the result, does the same for getting and counting the document objects, and multiplies the two results. While this should theoretically work, an application may have an issue with it.

The solution may be to either break down the commands into individual lines or use the two explicit *get* commands. Following are three possible ways to write the preceding script. Out of the three, the second one strikes a good balance between legibility and functionality.

Version 1: Lay it all out there.

```
tell application "some app"
    set document_pages to get pages of document 1
    set application_documents to get documents of it
    set page_count to count document_pages
    set document_count to count application_documents
    set n to page_count * document_count
end tell
```

Version 2: Let's not overdo it . . .

```
tell application "some app"
    set page_count to count (get pages of document 1)
    set document_count to count (get documents of it)
    set n to page_count * document_count
end tell
```

Version 3: All in one line

```
tell application "some app" to ¬
    set n to (count (get pages of document 1)) * (count (get documents ¬
    of it))
```

run

The *run* command has two functions: running an application, which is hardly ever done by itself, and running a script object.

Running applications

Every time AppleScript goes into an application's *tell* block and starts to execute commands, the *run* command is set to that application.

For example, the following script:

```
tell application "Script Editor"
    make new document
end tell
```

Is actually seen by AppleScript as

```
tell application "Script Editor"
    run
    make new document
end tell
```

This scenario suggests that the *run* command really isn't that useful, which is true.

You can, however, choose to send the *run* command to an application that's not running at the time. Instead of using the *run* command inside the *tell* block, you can use it to specify the full path to the application. This helps if you suspect that more than one copy or one version of the same application exists on the Mac. Here's how you do that:

```
run application "Macintosh HD:Applications:AppleScript:Script
Editor.app:
```

launch

The *launch* command is technically an application command and not one of AppleScript's commands. It works similarly to the *run* command with one difference you should be aware of.

When you use the *run* command to start up an application, the application will start, and a new blank document will be created. If you use the *launch* command instead, a new document is not created.

```
tell application "BBEdit 6.5" to launch
```

Power wrap-up

This section summarizes the chapter in an intensive-reference style. Use this section to look up facts related to the chapter without the chatter.

Application commands and AppleScript commands

Most commands you will use in your scripts will be commands that are defined in applications' dictionaries. AppleScript has only six built-in commands. These are *copy, count, get, run, set,* and *error*.

Application commands need a target object on which the command operates. AppleScript's built-in commands and scripting addition commands have targets, but they are not real objects.

set and copy

The *set* and *copy* commands assign values to variables.

```
set the_variable to "value"
copy "value" to the_variable
```

These commands work the same other than with lists. In this case, AppleScript uses data sharing, which makes the same list shared by two variables.

get

The *get* command is used to get values from variables and from applications' object properties. The *get* command is hardly ever used explicitly, but is one of the most used commands in its implied form.

The two following statements produce the same result:

```
get item 2 of {100, 110, 120} --> 110
item 2 of {100, 110, 120} --> 110
```

run and launch

Both the *run* and *launch* commands will open an application that is not running.

The *run* command will create a new document after starting the application, and the *launch* command will not.

Details previously . . .

The last part of this chapter is a summary of the entire chapter. For more details on any of the items here, see the full chapter.

7

ular	12
Regular	12
Demibold R	12
Regular	12
Regular	12
Regular	12

```
property user_name : ""
if user_name is "" then
    display dialog "Enter name:" d
    set user_name to text returne
end if
display dialog ("Hello " & user_nam
```

{button returned:"OK"}

Hello Be

In AppleScript, and most other programming languages, variables are made of two parts: the identifier and the value. The identifier is a name that describes the value, but the value is what you actually want to use. Here's an example:

```
set first_name to "Sponge"
```

In the preceding example, we assign the value "Sponge" to the variable *first_name*. If we want to either retrieve the value of that variable or assign a different value to it somewhere else in the script, we use the identifier *first_name*. When the script is run, AppleScript evaluates the identifier and returns the variable's value.

Picture variables as a container on your desk. The container has a label on it that says, "today's newspaper". What would you imagine would be found in this container? We would surely expect to find today's newspaper. Will that be the case every day, though? Well, let's say that our script is instructed to go to the stand before you get to work, get the newspaper for you, and put it in that container. Will that paper be the same every day? Well, yes and no. The size, shape, and look, or format, will be the same, but the information will not. When asked what's in that container, you can either say, "This is the newspaper from July 23, 2003," which will be accurate today, but not tomorrow. See, the variable label, or identifier, as referred to by AppleScript, is (or should be) the accurate *description* of the variable's value, while the value is the information itself. When you open that newspaper, what you care about is the news collected up to last night, which can be found in that specific newspaper you're holding. That information is the value, the stuff you use.

How are variables created?

In AppleScript, there are a few ways in which you can define variables in certain points of the script. The most widely used form of defining a variable is through an assignment statement with either the *set* or *copy* commands.

Another way to create variables is by declaring a property or a global variable. The main difference between the two is that when declaring a global variable, you don't assign a value to it, but you do assign a value to a property.

It is important to understand that while you can implicitly declare a local variable anywhere in the script by simply assigning a value to it, global variables and script properties have to be explicitly declared. This declaration occurs in the first part of the script before the run handler. The start of a well-structured script may look like this:

Script 8-1

```
property identifier1:"starting value"
property identifier2:"starting value"
global identifier3, identifier4
on run
   local identifier5, identifier6
   --statements
end run
```

Assignments and declarations

So we agreed that a variable is a container that holds specific information, like, for example, the "Employee of the Month" spot on a company's bulletin board. Let's take a second to imagine how that spot was created. The office manager came up with the idea, and the assistant printed the header that says "Employee of the Month" and posted it. The variable has been declared. The actual name of the employee of the month won't be posted there until next month. When it is, then the variable will be assigned a value.

```
--declare the variable:
global employee_of_the_month
--or
local employee_of_the_month
--assign a value to the variable:
set employee_of_the_month to "Fred Flintstone"
```

Does that mean that you have to declare a variable before assigning a value to it? Not always.

As you saw in the preceding script, there are two main kinds of variables: global variables and local variables (we will get into the specific differences between them later in "How variables live and die").

Basically, when you don't declare a variable, it naturally becomes a local variable. To define a global variable, you must declare it as such:

```
global my_variable
```

8

How to name variables

Variables are defined by you when you write the script. Variable identifiers, or the actual word you use to assign or get a value from a variable, is a word that you make up yourself, and there are syntax rules you have to follow in order for your variable to work. Once you considered all the basic no-no's in variable naming, you are pretty much on your own.

What's good is that you don't usually have to wait until runtime to discover if your variable name can't be used. For the most part, the script would simply not compile.

Basic variable naming rules

Here are the things to avoid when deciding on a name, or identifier, for a variable:

Basic no-no's

The following rules are easy to learn because if you break them, the script will simply not compile.

Rule 1: An identifier can't start with a digit or contain spaces, dashes, or any other non-alphanumeric characters.

Here are a few good variables:

```
my_total_solitare_score
x
RatioBetweenTaxibleIncomeAndCharitableContribution
```

And some bad ones:

```
2_times_dose
price*tax
first&last
```

More obscure naming rules

The following rules are a bit more problematic since they will only reveal themselves as problems during runtime. Even then, though, they're easy to detect and fix:

Rule 2: An identifier can't be the same as a reserved word.

AppleScript has several words it reserves for its own use. These words, as you can imagine, can't be used as variable or handler identifiers. AppleScript also has its own variables, such as PI, space, hours, etc. These are different from reserved words. Trying to set the value of a predefined variable has the potential of messing up your script, while trying to use a reserved word as a variable will generate an error when the script tries to compile.

Instead of listing all these words just for the purpose of remembering not to use them, you can simply use AppleScript's built-in syntax coloring:

In Script Editor, and virtually all other script editors, you can use the preferences to set AppleScript's syntax coloring and formatting. These attributes, shown in Figure 8-1, are actually global, which means that if you use more than one AppleScript editor, the changes will affect both.

Anyway, notice the categories Language keywords, Application keywords, and Variables and subroutines names. If you make them different, you will notice right after compiling your script whether the variables you typed have the color and formatting you assigned to the Variables and subroutines names category.

Figure 8-1. Apple's Script Editor allows you to set AppleScript's syntax coloring in the preferences pane.

Rule 3: A handler's identifier can't be used as a separate variable identifier.

In your own scripts, you are the name giver to both variables and subroutines, so not repeating the same name shouldn't be hard. It may be a slight problem if you inherit a long script that you now have to maintain; however, the first time you test the script the issue will probably reveal itself and will be resolved.

As a rule, I always name my variables with word caps, and my handlers with underscore separators, like this:

```
this_is_my_handler(argumentPassedToIt)
```

Safe naming tactics

Try to make your variables and subroutine names stand out. I always use at least two words in my variable identifiers. This way I can tell them apart from other elements. The syntax coloring is a big help, too.

Break all the rules!

OK, so now that we recited all the rules and know them perfectly, I'll give you the invisibility cloak that'll allow you to bypass all those rules! Use spaces, start with a number, and use reserved words, anything you want!

All you have to do is wrap your identifier in a pair of straight lines, like this:

```
|my variable|
```

This shields the variable from any naming rules.

Values and references

We use variables in scripts to hold values. When we need that value, we use the variable's identifier, and the script treats it as if it is the value itself. In fact, the identifier is an expression that returns the value stored in the variable.

This works fine with normal value classes such as strings, numbers, lists, etc. What about other computer things, more real things like a folder on the hard disk or a text frame in InDesign? Can we set variables that hold these things? Not really, but close enough.

While we can't take the entire chunk of data that makes a folder and cram it into a variable, we can create a variable that holds a *reference* to that folder.

In fact, referring to applications' objects is a major part of scripting, and being able to store these references in variables is very important.

While each application has its own reference forms, it's not that hard to figure out. All we have to do is use the same reference form we use when we want to do something to an object: we have to follow the object hierarchy.

Script 8-2

```
tell application "Finder"
    set my_folder to folder "Applications" of disk "Macintosh HD"
    delete my_folder
end tell
```

In the preceding script, we assign to the variable *my_folder* a reference to the folder Applications of disk Macintosh HD. This allows us to work with that folder later on, or as line 3 of the script shows, use the variable to delete the folder.

We can also more explicitly say that we want a reference to an object instead of the object itself.

```
tell application "InDesign cs"
    set my_page to (a reference to page 2 of document 1)
end tell
```

As a shortcut, you can also use *ref* instead of *a reference to*. AppleScript will fill in the rest when you compile the script.

```
tell application "InDesign cs"
    set my_doc to ref document 1
end tell
```

While testing your script you want to learn about the forms different applications use to return object references to you. If you're not careful, when you turn to use the reference it is no longer current and will return an error.

Figure 8-2 shows a script that changes the name of a folder and then tries to delete it.

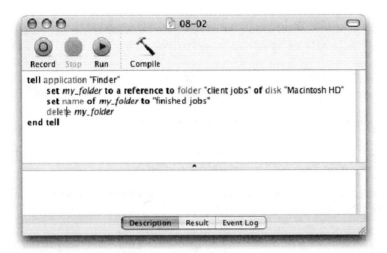

Figure 8-2. The Finder will return a reference to a folder, then use the reference to rename the folder and then delete it.

When this script runs, it generates an error, shown in Figure 8-3, on the *delete* command. The reference worked OK to rename the folder but not to delete it. Why is that?

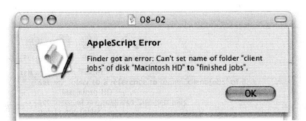

Figure 8-3. The Finder got an error trying to delete the folder referred to in the variable.

To understand we have to look at the reference the script gave us in the line where we assign the reference to the variable. Figure 8-4 shows that line and the result.

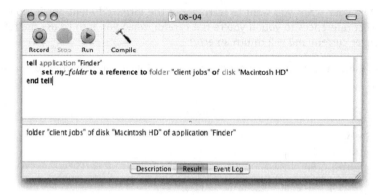

Figure 8-4. The result of the assignment statement

As you can see, the reference the Finder gave us has the folder name in it. This makes the reference obsolete the second we renamed the folder.

In the Finder, we would be much better off if we coerced the reference form into an alias class, like in the script shown in Figure 8-5.

Figure 8-5. A Finder reference to an item is coerced into an alias reference.

An alias reference remains current even as the file or folder it points to changes name or location. In fact, it works just like the aliases in the Finder.

More on file references in Chapter 14.

This is, however, just the way the Finder works. Other applications have their own object reference issues.

As we've already seen, Adobe InDesign is an example of good scripting implementation. Every object in InDesign has a property called *object reference*; this property returns a reference to the object. If this seems redundant to you, then you're onto something.

If we got close enough to the object to get its object reference property, then we must already have some sort of a reference to the object. It's a bit like asking, "What was the color of King Arthur's white horse?" Well, not really, because the reference InDesign returns is most likely not the same reference you used to get to the object to ask for that property. Figure 8-6 shows how you ask for that object reference and what you get in return.

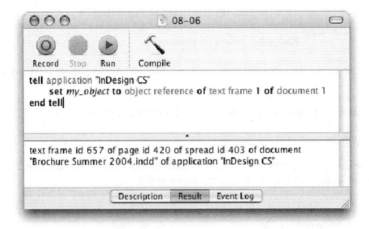

Figure 8-6. The object reference property in InDesign

Notice that the object reference we used to get to the object wasn't very stable. If a new object was created, or a page inserted, our reference wouldn't hold. However, the value of the *object reference* property uses the unique ID of the spread, page, and text frame, so even if you change the stacking order or add pages, the reference would still be good.

How variables live and die

So far we know that assigning a value to a variable allows you to retrieve that value later on. That is true to some extent, but as your scripts become more sophisticated, you will need to understand for what, where, and how long variables are good.

As we stated earlier in the chapter, when you simply assign a value to a variable, you are actually getting AppleScript to perform two actions: declare the variable and assign a value to it.

The variable that was created, however, has been declared as a local variable, by default.

Local variables are good until you start creating your own commands, or in other words, defining handlers.

Let's examine the following example to better understand what I mean:

```
set user_name to "Ben"
display dialog ("Hello " & user_name & "!")
```

When you run the script, AppleScript displays the dialog box shown in Figure 8-7.

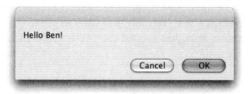

Figure 8-7. Hello Ben dialog box

Line 1 of the script declared the local variable *user_name*, and then assigned the value "Ben" to it.

Line 2 displayed a dialog box that used the value stored in the variable.

So far so good.

What we're going to try now is to put the *display dialog* statement from line 2 in the preceding script into a subroutine. This is the way it will look:

Script 8-3

```
set user_name to "Ben"
say_hello()
on say_hello()
  display dialog ("Hello " & user_name & "!")
end say_hello
```

The subroutine is declared between lines 3 and 5. It is called to action on line 2.

If you try to run the preceding script, you will get the error shown in Figure 8-8.

Figure 8-8. Apparently, the variable *user_name* has not been declared.

So what went wrong? We did specifically assign a value to the *user_name* variable in line 1, so why did line 4 return the error it did? Because our local variable was good in the body of the script, but not inside any handlers.

The scope of a local variable—and since we didn't specify otherwise, *user_name* was a local variable—is the current handler only.

What handler is that exactly? It's the *run* handler. The *run* handler can be left out, but it is always implied. Our script could have explicitly specified the *run* handler as shown in Figure 8-9.

Figure 8-9. The run handler, which was implied in the last script, is described explicitly here.

Now, looking at the script in Figure 8-9, things come into focus a bit. The *user_name* variable was declared in the *run* handler and therefore not recognized in the *say_hello* handler.

There are a few ways to remedy the problem and they divide into two main solutions:

You can either tell the handler what the variable is by passing it as an argument, or tell all handlers in the script what the variable is and then avoid any issues with any handler that may want to use that variable.

Up front, the second choice appears to make more sense. Why pass a variable as an argument to multiple handlers when you can just announce it once to all handlers? The main reason is portability. May not seem like a big deal at the start, but later on, when you try to take those brilliant handlers you created and use them in a different script, figuring out which global variables or properties are used by the handler may just put you in the seat of a surgeon trying to separate conjoined twins.

As many variables as a handler may need, it is almost always better to pass them as arguments rather than declare them as global variables, especially if the reason for it is blatant laziness.

8

Passing variables to handlers

There are a couple of ways to create handlers and therefore a couple of ways to pass variables to handlers. The two methods will be covered extensively in Chapter 17, but here's a primer for passing variables the simple way.

To pass a variable, you include it in the parentheses following the handler name. Figure 8-10 shows how that can be done.

Figure 8-10. Passing the *user_name* variable to the *say_hello* handler

While this example works, it is a bit misleading. What we're passing isn't the variable, but rather the value of the variable. The *user_name* variable in the *run* handler is completely separate from the one in the *say_hello* handler. The two scripts that follow show other ways of passing a value to a handler:

Script 8-4

```
on run
    set user_name to "Ben"
    say_hello(user_name)
end run
on say_hello(somebody)
    display dialog ("Hello " & somebody & "!")
end say_hello
```

In the preceding script, the handler call passes the *value* of the variable *user_name*. The *say_hello* handler receives the value and assigns it to the *somebody* variable, where it is used in the handler.

Script 8-5

```
on run
    say_hello("Ben")
end run
on say_hello(somebody)
    display dialog ("Hello " & somebody & "!")
end say_hello
```

In this script, we don't pass a variable at all. What we do is simply pass the value itself.

Passing multiple values

To pass multiple values to a handler, providing you use positioned parameters and not labeled parameters (until now we only dealt with positional parameters), you must separate the values you pass in the handler call with commas, and do the same with the parameter variables in the handler definition. The handler call must have a single value for each parameter variable in the handler definition.

You must not confuse that with a list, however. The parameters are passed as single values. You could pass a list as a value to the handler, but it will be put into a single variable. More on that when we cover handlers in Chapter 18.

Properties

We discussed the ability of global variables to be visible to all handlers. Another way to make a value visible to any handler in the script is to assign it to a property. Properties are just what they say they are: properties of the script. Much like an application object that may have properties such as *name* and *version*, a script is an object that can have its own properties.

For instance, if you're creating a script that is responsible for backing up some files to the server, one of its properties may be the destination folder for the backed-up files.

Both global variables and properties share another important feature: when the script assigns a different value to a property, the property will retain that value even after the script is done running. That means that the script can remember values you give it from run to run. Remember, this is true for both global variables and script properties.

If you open the script, however, you will not see the new value assigned to the property. If you open the script and recompile it, the values of the properties will be reset to the original values you gave them.

8

To try it, type the script in Figure 8-11 and save it as an application. Then run the script a few times.

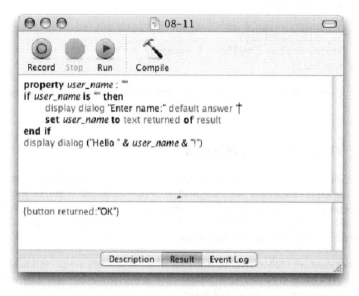

Figure 8-11. This script has a property that will retain its value from run to run.

When you run the script for the first time, the value of the *user_name* property is "", or a blank string. The second line in the script picks up on that and asks users to enter their name.

The fourth line assigns the text the user typed to the property *user_name*. From this point on, the script has the value embedded into it, and the way this particular script is structured, the user has no way to reenter the name. The script in Figure 8-11 verifies that the user typed the right name, and gives him/her the chance to enter a new name.

There's always a big question as to whether to use properties or variables. In truth, there's no functional difference between them, especially when dealing with relatively simple scripts.

As with global variables, it is strongly advised to weigh carefully before adding properties. Since they're mainly used for specific functions of the script, if you try to reuse them later in other scripts you may run into trouble separating the properties you need from the ones you don't.

When are properties a good idea?

In the following sections we look at three instances in which utilizing script properties can be very useful.

Top-level variables

Once in a while there are pieces of information that belong at the top of the script. For instance, I always include a *debugMode* property, which has a Boolean value. Certain functions I want performed only if I'm debugging, but I would hate to forget to turn them off before I put the script to use, or worse, send it to a client. So any debugging-related function I just wrap in a *if debugMode then* block, and all I have to do in order to turn them all off is to set the *debugMode* property to false.

Script object properties

While we will cover this issue in detail when we talk about script objects, I thought it would be appropriate to discuss the aspect of properties in script objects in this chapter.

A script object is a script you write and save, and later on tell other scripts to use it as if it were an application. You can either call different handlers in that script or just tell it to run, which in this case will invoke the *run* handler of the script.

Before we get into properties, here's how you call a script:

Assume that you saved a script named "commands.applescript" in your hard drive. This will be the script that loads and runs it:

```
set my_script to load script file "Macintosh HD: commands.applescript"
tell my_script to run
```

See, that was so easy.

So what do properties have to do with all that? Well, if you properly organize the scripts you want to load, then each script should have its function: you can have different scripts that are a collection of commands for a specific application, or a script that's in charge of performing file operations, etc. For these scripts, having appropriate properties is perfectly acceptable since the properties are a part of the function the script is supposed to perform, so the chance that you will want to separate handlers from this script and reuse them somewhere else is slim: instead, you can load this script to the other script.

User preferences

OK, so making the user open the script and make changes is the last thing you want. However, some situations just call for it. Take for example a droplet script that creates titles in Illustrator and exports them as TIFF files. The user indicates that s/he may want to change the font the script uses sometime down the road. Well, you could go ahead and build a way for that user to gracefully change the font, but that would be one more thing that can get broken later and . . . you're already out the door . . . so you add the *title_font* property to the top of the script and tell the user to change it later on to a different font.

While I do that sometimes, I don't like to for obvious reasons. Anytime you let the end user mess with your scripts you're asking for trouble, and besides, it's hardly as nice as facilitating a way for the user to change some script settings.

8

Your script's preferences pane

Unless you go for an AppleScript Studio application, you can't really create a preference pane with radio buttons, etc.; however, you can present a series of dialog boxes intended for collecting different settings from the user.

The idea is to present a single dialog box at the beginning with three buttons: Cancel, in case the user didn't mean to launch the script; a Run button used for normal operation, which should also be the default button; and last, a Settings button for changing some preferences.

If the user clicks the Settings button, s/he will be presented with a series of dialog boxes whose results will supply values to the script's properties.

In our next example, we'll pretend we have an Illustrator script that replaces variables with data in a template and applies the font specified in the *title_font* property. The template file path is specified in the *template_path* property.

The only twist in this script is that if the file specified in the template path property doesn't exist, we will force the user to pick one.

Here's how I would do that:

Script 8-6

```
1. property title_font : ""
2. property template_path : ""

3. on run
4.     set template_file_exists to check_if_path_exists(template_path)
5.     if not template_file_exists or title_font is "" then
6.         get_user_settings()
7.         set got_settings to true
8.     else
9.         set got_settings to false
10.    end if
11.    if not got_settings then
12.        display dialog "Run the script or change settings?" buttons ¬
    {"Quit", "Settings", "Run"} default button "Run"
13.        set dialog_result to button returned of result
14.        if dialog_result is "Quit" then
15.            return
16.        else if dialog_result is "Settings" then
17.            get_user_settings()
18.        end if
19.    end if
20.    --REST OF YOUR SCRIPT HERE...
21. end run

22. to get_user_settings()
```

```
23.    choose file with prompt ¬
            "Pick an Illustrator template" of type {"PDF "}
24.    set template_path to result as string
25.    tell application "Adobe Illustrator 10"
26.        set font_list to get name of every text face
27.    end tell
28.    choose from list font_list with prompt ¬
            "Pick a font for the title"
29.    set title_font to result as string
30. end get_user_settings

31. to check_if_path_exists(the_file_path)
32.    try
33.        alias the_file_path
34.        return true
35.    on error
36.        return false
37.    end try
38. end check_if_path_exists
```

In the preceding script, we have a *run* handler and two custom handlers: one is in charge of collecting settings from the user, and the other one checks if a file path passed to it actually exists on the hard disk. It does that by trying to coerce the file path into an alias reference. If the file doesn't actually exist, then the coercion statement will generate an error. We capture the error in line 35, and return false.

Back to the script itself, in line 4 we check if the currently set template path exists. In line 5, if either the file wasn't there or the font is still set to an empty string, then we force the user to choose new settings.

We also create a local variable called *got_settings*. This variable indicates whether we forced the user to pick a specific setting, so that we don't ask him/her again if s/he wants the settings changed.

If the *got_settings* variable is false, that means that the user didn't yet get the chance this time around to pick settings, so we display the dialog box that allows the user to pick the settings.

Predefined variable

AppleScript's predefined variables, *return*, *space*, *tab*, and *pi*, are global variables with a preset value. Although I'd like to see this list grow, the variables that are in the list can be quite useful, and some are essential.

The first four predefined variables are useful for text and math manipulations; however, they aren't essential, and have the same value assigned at all times (unless you discover that you can change it . . .).

The other variables, *it*, *me*, and *result*, are a bit more sophisticated. *it* and *me* are references, and *result* can be anything.

Here are the details:

return

The *return* variable's default value is the return character. It's useful for text concatenations.

Although you can set *return* to any value you choose, you probably shouldn't, unless you're playing a practical joke on someone. In that case, start the script with statements that change return to a tab value, tab to space, and space to return. Then, give it to a friend to debug.

Here's an example of using the *return* variable:

```
set names_message to "Peter" & return & "Paul" & return & "Mary"
```

The result:

```
"Peter
Paul
Mary"
```

Here's another, more flexible way to perform the same general function:

Script 8-7

```
set names_list to {"peter", "paul", "mary"}
set names_message to ""
repeat with i from 1 to (count names_list)
  set the_name to item i of names_list
  set names_message to names_message & i & ". " & the_name & return
end repeat
display dialog names_message
```

In line 5, we concatenate a bunch of text into a single string, and add it onto itself in a *repeat* loop. The last item we add in each loop is *return*, which adds another line to the string.

In scripts where I use this a lot and want a shorter version of *return*, I create a global variable called *cr* for carriage return. Then I add the following statement:

```
set cr to ascii character 13
```

From that point, I can use *cr* as I would the *return* character.

space and tab

Just like the *return* variable, the *space* and *tab* predefined variables hold a one-character string.

The value of the *space* variable is a single word space, or ASCII character number 32, and the value of the *tab* variable is a single character string with one tab character, or ASCII character number 9.

Using these variables produces the same result as typing the actual character, or using the command *ASCII character* with their respective numbers. They are very useful, though, since by looking at a string with a few spaces, or tabs, you can't always see right away what characters are used, and how many of them.

The following script handler uses the *tab* and *space* variables to trim them from the start or end of a string. It takes one argument, which is the string you want trimmed.

Script 8-8

```
1. on trim_spaces(the_text)
2. repeat
3.    if the_text starts with space or the_text starts with tab then
4.        set the_text to rest of characters of the_text as string
5.    else
6.        exit repeat
7.    end if
8. end repeat
9. repeat
10.    if the_text ends with space or the_text ends with tab then
11.        set the_text to characters 1 thru -2 of the_text as string
12.    else
13.        exit repeat
14.    end if
15. end repeat
16. end trim_spaces
```

pi

The *pi* variable has the value 3.14159265359 assigned to it. You can use it anywhere you do math with trigonometry.

The following script calculates the amount or ribbon you would need to tie around a given number of pies:

Script 8-9

```
on how_much_ribbon(pie_count, pie_radius)
    set pie_circumference to pie_radius * pi
    set ribbon_length to pie_circumference * pie_count
    --add 10% to compensate for bow-tie at end
    set ribbon_length to ribbon_length * 1.1
    return round ribbon_length
end how_much_ribbon
```

Reference variables

The value class of the following two variables is an object reference:

it

The *it* variable refers to the current target of the *tell* block. The *it* variable is mostly implied and used literally for readability.

Figure 8-12 shows a script using InDesign.

In the script, the variable *it* has been placed inside the InDesign *tell* block, therefore the value of the *it* variable is a reference to the application.

Figure 8-12. The value of the *it* variable is a reference to the application InDesign.

So when is the *it* variable used, and when is it implied?

Consider the following script, which is a variation on the script in Figure 8-12:

Script 8-10

```
tell application "InDesign CS"
   name of active document
   tell active document
      name
      get name of it
   end tell
end tell
```

In the preceding script, the results of line 2, line 4, and line 5 are identical. This is because when you just name a property, AppleScript returns the value stored in that property of the object targeted by the *tell* block, in this case, the inner *tell* block.

So, in line 2 we ask for the name of active document, and we get it. In line 3 we target the active document with a *tell* block. Lines 4 and 5 are identical; they both ask for the *name* property of the active document, just that line 5 is more explicit.

You could've also used *name of it* or *get name* instead.

While the *it* variable can be implied instead of written out, in many cases you would want to use it in order to make your script read more easily. Saying

```
if name of it is "Document 1"
```

is much nicer than

```
if name = "Document 1"
```

me

The variable *me* refers to the script object. The script object is the main script you're running. Any handlers you wrote or properties are commands and properties of the script object, which separate them from the application commands. There aren't many distinct uses for the *me* variable; however, the few uses it has repeat quite a bit throughout the script, and they're not easily replaceable with other syntax.

path to me

One of the nice uses of the *me* variable is using the *path to me* command. The *path to me* command returns the path to the script application. This is very useful in making your scripts find files that they count on for execution.

Say that you have a script that generates a text file called settings as part of its execution. The script needs a reliable folder to write the file to and find the file for reading.

One solution is to use one of OS X's many unmovable folders in the user's library folder, or other places. This, however, complicates things, because if the script is stopped from being used on a specific Mac, you either have to hunt for these files, or just leave your mess all over.

Another solution is to get the user to always put the script folder in the root directory or on the desktop or somewhere you can teach your script to find. This is also not so good since, well, you just made a crucial mistake: you counted on the user to listen to your instructions . . .

Here's a solution that has worked for me with many different projects:

I create a folder that I designate as the main folder. This folder can have any name, and the user can also change the name and it wouldn't matter.

Then, I create a folder structure, and yes, I do have to ask the user not to rename folders in there. In this case, I might have a folder in the main folder called scripts where I put my scripts. I have a settings folder and a utilities folder where I usually put my application script that the user launches. I also have a folder I call system where I put files I absolutely don't want the user to touch. Figure 8-13 shows the sample folder structure I described.

Figure 8-13. A sample automated system folder structure

Now, let's see how this works.

To create a settings file all I need is the path to the settings folder. Since I told the user to put the main folder anywhere, I can't count on a specific location. I have to do an inside job in order to find the location.

The following script creates a few variables whose string values describe the location of different folders in my folder structure:

Script 8-11

```
tell application "Finder"
    set main_folder_path to container of container of (path to me) ¬
        as string
end tell
set settings_folder_path to main_folder_path & "settings:" as string
set system_folder_path to main_folder_path & "system:" as string
```

In line 2 we get the container of container of *path to me*. The container of *path to me* is the folder the script is in. This is the utilities folder. The container of that folder is the main folder. From there, I have to simply concatenate the names of the other folder to the *main_folder* variable to get paths to other folders.

Let's assume for a minute that the main folder is located in the root directory of the hard disk. In this case, the following expressions will return the results right below them:

```
path to me
--> alias "Macintosh HD:Main Folder:utilities:Launch me..."
container of path to me
--> alias "Macintosh HD:Main Folder:utilities:"
container of container of path to me
--> alias "Macintosh HD:Main Folder:"
```

This main folder can be put anywhere and named anything. Thanks to the *path to me* command, we can always locate it from within the utility script.

Tell me something

The *me* variable also comes in handy when you want to call a handler from within an application *tell* block.

If you try to run the script shown in Figure 8-14, you will be presented with the error message shown in Figure 8-15. The reason is that when you call a subroutine, AppleScript sees it as a command, and checks to see if the current target of the *tell* block understands that command. If it doesn't, you get an error.

Figure 8-14. Calling a handler from within the Finder *tell* block returns an error.

Figure 8-15. The error you get from calling a command within an application *tell* block

I always get a kick from the message, "can't continue." I guess what I want is more details, something like, "Can't continue because my feet hurt," or something.

Anyway, the reason why the Finder just couldn't continue the command was because the Finder doesn't have a *say_hello* command in its dictionary.

Who does? The script. What you have to do in this case, or whenever you want to call a handler from within an application *tell* block, is to specify that the command belongs to the script, and not the application. Figure 8-16 shows how that's done.

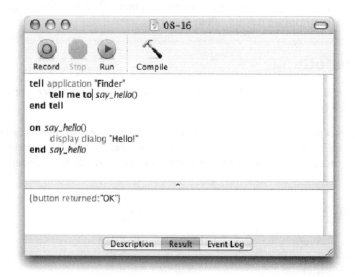

Figure 8-16. To call a handler that belongs to the main script from within an application's *tell* block, you have to target the script using the *me* variable.

The other way to do it, which is a bit shorter and nicer, is to just add the word *my* before the command.

```
tell application "Finder"
    my say_hello()
end tell
```

My property

Another problem you may encounter is when you try to retrieve values of properties whose names are used both as a property in your script and as a property in the application.

Take for example the following script:

Script 8-12

```
property name : "Olivia"
tell application "Finder"
   tell file 1 of disk "Macintosh HD"
      display dialog (get name as string)
   end tell
end tell
```

In line 4 we want to get the property *name* and display its value in a dialog box. The dialog box displays the name of file 1 of disk Macintosh HD.

If we want the dialog box to display the property name defined in the script itself, we must specify it using one of the following forms:

```
get name of me
get my name
```

Either way, the name "Olivia" will be displayed, not the name of the file.

result

The *result* variable is the most often updated, and most used variable in AppleScript. The result of every statement that you run, given the statement returns a result at all, is that the returned value is assigned to the *result* variable.

Examine the simple statement in the script in Figure 8-17.

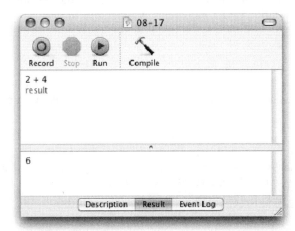

Figure 8-17. The result variable is assigned the value resulting from the previous statement.

Watch line 1 of the script in Figure 8-17. It contains a simple mathematical expression that isn't assigned to any specific variable, it is simply expressed to the air. But, thanks to the *result* variable, the value it returned is safe. The value 6 that was returned from the statement in line 1 was put in the *result* variable. Line 2 retrieves the value of the result variable and shows that it is 6.

Power wrap-up

This section summarizes the chapter in an intensive-reference style. Use this part to look up facts related to the chapter without the chatter.

Declaring variables

Variables can be declared explicitly or implicitly.

To implicitly declare a variable, just assign a value to it. The two statements that follow use two different commands to assign a string value to a variable whose identifier is *my_variable*:

```
set my_variable to "the value"
```

or

```
copy "the value" to my_variable
```

Properties

Properties are variables that are declared before the script's *run* handler. You have to assign a value to a property right from the start.

```
property identifier_name : "initial value"
```

The value of a property is available throughout the script including all subroutines, and will come back even between script runs.

Global variables

Much like properties, global variables are declared before the *run* handler. You don't supply them with an initial value, and you can declare multiple global variables with one statement.

```
global identifier_1, identifier_2, identifier_3
```

Once the value of a global variable has been set, it will be available throughout the script including all subroutines, and will come back even between script runs.

Local variables

Any variables you created and did not declare as either a global variable or a property are local variables. The value of a local variable is available only inside the handler it was defined in. To use the value of a local variable in another handler, you must pass it as a parameter.

Explicitly declaring local variables is not necessary, but is good practice.

```
on run
   local identifier_1, identifier_2
   --statements
end run
```

Naming variables

The basic variable naming rules are as follows:

1. An identifier can't start with a digit or contain spaces, dashes, or any other non-alphanumeric characters.

2. An identifier can't be a reserved word. You will know right away if it is.

3. An identifier can't have the same name as a handler identifier in the same script.

Use straight brackets at the start and end of a variable identifier, and you can break all the rules:

```
set |123 GO! Yes, this is a legal variable!| to "string value"
```

A good variable has at least two words to separate it from any other reserved word or predefined variable.

The words can be first letter capped or separated by an underscore.

Values and references

A variable can hold a value, but it can also hold a reference to an object.

In the first example, the value of x at the end will be "display dialog" since we set x to the text of document 1, which is "display dialog" at the time.

Script 8-13 (also includes following script)

```
tell application "Script Editor"
   set text of document 1 to "display dialog"
   set x to text of document 1
   set text of document 1 to "beep 3"
   set y to x as string
end tell
```

In the second example, the value of x at the end will be "beep 3" since we set x to a reference to the text of document 1, not the text itself. When we get x as string, the text of document 1 is already changed to "beep 3".

```
tell application "Script Editor"
    set text of document 1 to "display dialog"
    set x to a reference to text of document 1
    set text of document 1 to "beep 3"
    set y to x as string
end tell
```

No good variables

Variables whose values have not been set will generate an error if you try to use them.

Predefined variables

AppleScript has a few predefined variables that are mentioned and used throughout the book. These variables are

- *return*, which has the value of a return character
- *space*, which has the same value as a space character
- *tab*, which has the same value as a tab character
- *pi*, which has the real value of 3.14159265359
- *minutes*, which has the value of 60 seconds
- *hours*, which has the value of 3600 seconds
- *days*, which has the value of 86400 seconds
- *weeks*, which has the value of 604800 seconds

Reference variables it and me

The variable *it* is used to describe the currently targeted object. In the following script, the value of *it* is document 1 of Script Editor:

Script 8-14

```
tell application "Script Editor"
    tell document 1
        display dialog (text of it)
    end tell
end tell
```

The value of *me* is always the current script.

You use *me* to get the path to the script application.

```
path to me
```

You can direct handler calls to the script itself and away from the application's *tell* block.

Script 8-15

```
tell application "Script Editor"
   do_this_thing() of me
--or...
   my do_this_thing()
--or...
   tell me to do_this_thing()
end tell
```

Result

The *result* variable contains the result of the last statement that ran, given that the last statement returned a result. In the following example, the value of the *result* variable will be 12 after the first line and 36 after the second line:

```
5 + 7
result * 3
```

Details previously . . .

The last part of this chapter is a summary of the entire chapter. For more details on any of the items here, refer to earlier sections in this chapter.

8

CHAPTER 9
OPERATIONS AND COERCION

```
set my_age to 16
display dialog my_age & " candles"
```

```
display dialog "Enter your email addre:
set email to text returned of result
if not ((email contains "@") ¬
        and ¬
        ((email ends with ".com") or (ema
            and ¬
        ((offset of "@" in email) > 1)) ¬
        then
        display dialog "Invalid email, try a
else
        exit repeat
end if
repeat
```

```
application "InDesign CS"
    tell page 1 of document 1
        repeat with i from (count grap
            tell graphic line 1
                set swatch_name to
                set line_tint to stroke
            end tell
            if swatch_name is "None"
                delete graphic line 1
            end if
        end repeat
    end tell
tell
```

Since operators and operations are everywhere in AppleScript, they are covered extensively throughout the book. Mainly, you will find operations covered in the chapters devoted to numbers and math, text and strings, dates and time, etc.

This chapter tries to tie up the loose ends but not to cover what is extensively covered in the other, more targeted chapters.

What are operations?

I like to come up with my own definitions whenever needed, but in the case of operations, the AppleScript Language Guide describes it best:

"Operations are expressions that use operators to derive values from other values." (AppleScript Language Guide, page 161)

In simple terms, operations turn flower, milk, and sugar into pancakes, a few words into a sentence, some numbers into a meaningful result, etc.

In the pancake's case, the ingredients are the operands, mixing is the operator, the mixed batter is the expression, and the steaming pancake on your plate is the result.

While AppleScript doesn't have operators that can be used for cooking, it does have operators for comparing values, doing math with numbers, performing Boolean operations, calculating dates and times, etc.

Operations and coercion

Operations can only happen when the operand values are either from the same value class or from compatible value classes: strings can only be compared to and concatenated to other strings; math can only be done with numbers (reals and integers), date and time manipulations can have operands that are numbers in some cases, etc.

This restriction is very reasonable from the computer's standpoint. After all, the different value classes serve entirely different purposes.

AppleScript, however, is more a person's language than a computer language. Therefore, AppleScript is designed to try and deal with the value class restriction internally, and shield you from having to include some potentially irritating code.

Although my lazy side is delighted whenever the computer does anything for me, there is also a level of anxiety: what does AppleScript do behind the scenes, and what do I need to know about it? Is it true that what I don't know can't hurt me?

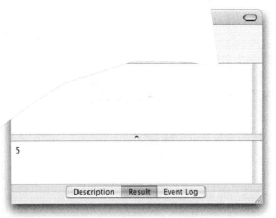

anyway?

over from one value class to another. For instance, the
'5" is a string. You can't do math with "5", and you can't
ng as it is an integer.

'", it must be converted, or coerced, into a number,
ng, it must be itself coerced into a string.

lues?

want to coerce values from one value class to

e left operand is a value of a specific value
ss you want the left operand coerced into.
s.

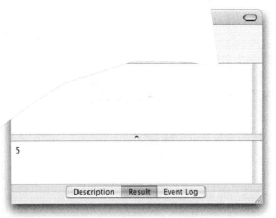

5

Description Result Event Log

Figure 9-1. A string value
is coerced into an integer.

Figure 9-2. An integer value
is coerced into a string.

A single statement can combine a few levels of coercion, as seen in Figure 9-3.

Figure 9-3. A single statement with two levels of coercion

In Figure 9-3 you can see that each of the operands had to be coerced into an integer individually before the multiplication could take place. However, since the result had to end up being a string, we had to coerce the entire statement into a string.

Notice the use of parentheses; you do not want to leave the order of evaluation up to AppleScript! While it might end up correctly, parentheses bring predictable results and help make your script legible.

The script in Figure 9-3 could have been broken down into a few lines, as seen in Figure 9-4.

Figure 9-4. The script from Figure 9-3 broken down into lines

Although AppleScript will attempt to coerce values for you, you should in many cases explicitly coerce values and operation results on your own. This makes your intention clearer and prevents potential problems down the road, especially with operators that can result in more than one value class such as the concatenation operator.

The reason for this is tied with AppleScript's core difference from other programming languages. Part of what makes AppleScript an easy language to use is its ability to coerce values between classes "on the fly," without your even thinking about it. So why doesn't every language do that? There's a very good reason. Once a programming language tries to guess your intention, it moves away from being transparent. AppleScript does take some of the work out of your everyday scriptwriting, but it does that with a heavy set of rules that you eventually have to learn.

What I prefer to do is coerce values myself whenever I remember. In the following statement, I don't have to explicitly coerce the result into a string, but if the composition changes, I would have. The possibility that AppleScript may coerce the result properly now, but won't do that if I make a small change, stresses me out enough to just take over coercion from AppleScript, even if it means some extra work. Here's the example:

Script 9-1 (includes the following two scripts)

```
set the_age to 35
set the_text to "I am " & the_age
--> "I am 35"
```

As you can see, the result for the preceding script is a string. However, what if I change the composition to the one shown here:

```
set the_age to 35
set the_text to the_age & " is my age"
--> {35, " is my age"}
```

Oops, now it's a list. If I counted on the result here to be a string, I would have gotten an error.

Coercion of values is everywhere and is part of many of your AppleScript statements, even if you're not aware of it. My suggestion is, become aware of it and do the extra work to take charge of it, as I do in the following script, which would be my preferred way to state the first script in the preceding example:

```
set the_age to 35
set the_text to "I am " & the_age as string
--> "I am 35"
```

Even though the result hasn't changed here, it will remain a string even if the statement changes, as it almost certainly will.

9

When does AppleScript perform coercion on its own?

AppleScript attempts to coerce values automatically during some operations.

In an operation there are three elements: left operand, operator, and right operand. In order for the operation to be successful, the left and right operands must belong to the same class, and the operator must be compatible with that class.

When an operation is encountered, AppleScript determines the value class of the left operand. If the left operand is of a legal class, and the operator can work with that operand, then the right operand is checked to see if it also matches.

If the left operand isn't compatible with the operator, AppleScript attempts to coerce it. If it can't, AppleScript will return error number -1700, which means that AppleScript can't coerce a value into the needed value class.

If the left operand is compatible with the operator, or AppleScript manages to coerce it, then the right operand is evaluated, and if needed, coerced to match the left operand.

Let's look at some script snippets:

In the script that follows, the left operand is compatible with the operator, but AppleScript will have to coerce the right operand to match:

```
5 + "12.3"
```

In the following script, AppleScript will first coerce the left operand into an integer to make it compatible with the + operator. Then it will coerce the right operand to match it as well.

```
"5" + "12.3"
```

The result will be a real number, since any operation that happens between a real number and an integer results in a real value.

One side effect of the left-to-right operation evaluation method is that an operation with the same values and same operator can produce a different class of results based on the order of the operands. Take for example the concatenation operator. If the left operand is a string, then AppleScript will attempt to coerce the right operand into a string as well, and return a string result. If the left operand is any other value class, the result will be a list, with each operand as an item in the list. Look at the following example:

The script in Figure 9-5 will result in an error since AppleScript evaluates the operation as a list, not a string, and the *display dialog* command requires a string.

The error message in Figure 9-6 shows the list value that AppleScript evaluated from the operation in the script in Figure 9-5.

Figure 9-5. The *display dialog* command fails since the operation evaluates as a list, not a string.

Figure 9-6. The error shows that the result was indeed a list, not a string.

As a solution to this problem, I go back to encouraging you to program a hot key on your Mac that types " as string" for you. Any operation where you want the result to be a string will be coded more quickly, giving AppleScript a little help in the coercion effort. Figure 9-7 shows the script the way it should be written.

9

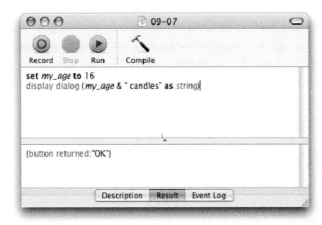

Figure 9-7. The *display dialog* command has no problem since the argument has been explicitly coerced into a string.

The following operation will return an error, since AppleScript can't coerce "sixteen" into a number:

```
"sixteen" + 2
```

Boolean operations

Boolean is a value class that allows only two possible values: true or false. Operating on Boolean values also produces a Boolean result.

The Boolean operators we discuss here should not be confused with comparison operators discussed later on. Although comparison operators produce a result in the Boolean value class, the operands are not Boolean values.

The three Boolean operators we will discuss here are *or*, *and*, and *not*. In operations that use these operators, both operands and the result are Booleans.

Using *and, not,* and *or* is pretty self-explanatory, much like the use of these words in the English language.

not

The *not* operator is used in operations with only a single Boolean operand to the right of it. The *not* operator simply reverses the value of that single operand.

The following script snippets show the *not* operator in action:

```
not true
--> false
not (1+2=3)
--> false
```

Since the expression *(1+2=3)* results in the Boolean value of true, putting the *not* operator before it reverses it to false.

The *not* operator is useful in a few situations. One is reversing a Boolean value when testing its value in a conditional statement, as shown here:

```
if (not log_file_exists) then create_log_file()
```

The parentheses are not needed here, but I use them to make the script clearer to read, as I do in my actual scripts.

and

The *and* operator produces one true result out of these four possible combinations:

```
true and true --> true
true and false --> false
false and true --> false
false and false --> false
```

Here are some better examples:

```
if (email_address contains "@") and (email_address contains ".") then
set valid_email_address to true
end if
```

Notice the use of the parentheses. They are not necessary, but they visually group the different operations.

To check if the value of the variable *x* is within a range of numbers, say between 10 and 20, you will use the following statement:

```
if (x ≥ 10) and (x ≤ 20) then do_something()
```

or

The *or* operator produces a false result only if both operands are false. If any of the operands are true, the result is true.

```
true or true --> true
true or false --> true
false or true --> true
false or false --> false
```

Here are some more examples:

```
if (email ends with ".net") or (email ends with ".com") or
(email ends with ".org") then...
```

The script in Figure 9-8 first assigns some color values of lines on an InDesign page to two variables: *swatch_name* and *line_tint*.

If either the value of *swatch_name* is "None" or the value of *line_tint* is 0, then the line is deleted.

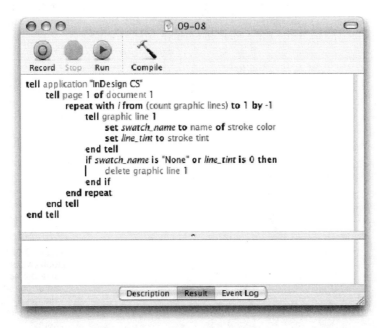

Figure 9-8. Notice the Boolean operation in the *if* statement to see the use of the *or* operator.

Mixing operators

Since the result of a Boolean operation is a Boolean value, you can create complex operations using many levels of Boolean operations.

Here's another one:

```
(email contains "@") and¬
((email ends with ".com") or (email ends with ".net")) and¬
((offset of "@" in email) > 1)
```

The preceding script includes four Boolean values:

- *email contains "@"*
- *email ends with ".com"*
- *email ends with ".net"*
- *(offset of "@" in email) > 1*

The final result is true if 1 and 4 are true, and either 2 or 3 are true.

Figure 9-9 shows a script that uses this Boolean operation to validate an e-mail address that a user types in. The script is in a closed loop and doesn't allow the user to leave unless a proper e-mail has been put in. Good use of Boolean, but very irritating for the user!

Notice that the conditional statement starts like this:

```
if not...
```

Everything after the *not* operator is in parentheses. If the operations in the parentheses evaluate as true, the *not* operator will reverse them, and the condition will not be met. The condition will be met if the e-mail isn't valid.

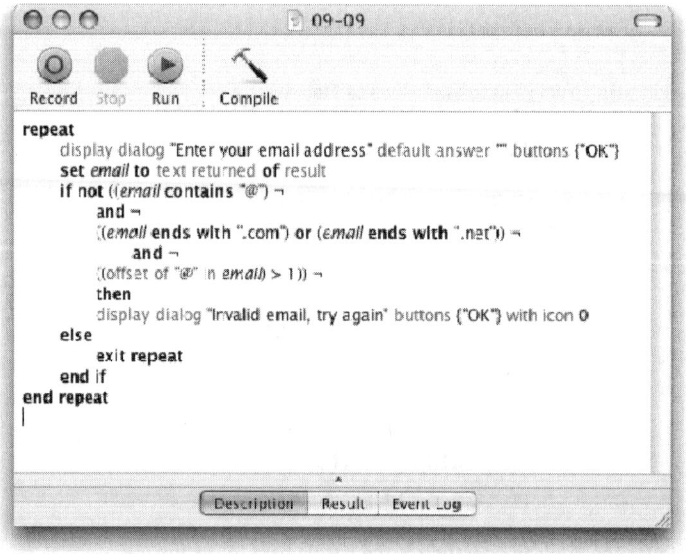

Figure 9-9. A Boolean operation using the *not*, *and*, and *or* operators validates a user-supplied e-mail address.

Comparison operators

Comparison operators basically ask a simple question: is the left operand the same as the right one, or not? There are, of course, some variations to this question.

The result of a comparison is always a Boolean value, and can be either true or false.

Let's look at how AppleScript deals with comparing values.

The basic comparison operator is the *equals* (=) operator. It returns true if the left and right operands are the same.

```
"a" = "b"
-->false
(5 + 5) = 10
-->true
```

The opposite of the *equals* operator is the *unequal* operator: ≠. You get it when you press OPTION+=.

```
17 ≠ 17.5
-->true
```

The last operation returned a true value because 17 is not the same as 17.5.

When comparing numbers, AppleScript acts as you would expect. However, when comparing text, things can get a little more complicated. We will look at the different possibilities in the "Consideration clauses" section later on.

The other comparison operators can help you figure out if the left operand is smaller or larger than the right operand.

```
5 > 3
--> true
12.1 < 12
--> false
```

A slight variation of the *greater than* (>) and *less than* (<) operators are the *greater than or equal to* (≥) and *less than or equal to* (≤) operators. You insert them by typing OPTION+. (period) to get ≥ and OPTION+, (comma) to get ≤.

These two operators have a built-in Boolean operator!

The ≥ operator checks to see if the right operand is greater than or equal to the left operand. The ≤ operator checks if the right operand is smaller than the left operand or equal to it. The two operators come in very handy, so make a mental note of them and put them to use.

9

Variations

AppleScript includes a few variations on the ways you can write the operators in your script. Some of the possibilities are very English-like, and have minute differences.

The table that follows shows the different comparison operators and their variations. Square brackets show optional words.

Note that some of these variations will compile differently from the way you typed them. If you type =>, for instance, AppleScript will compile it into "≥".

Sign	Variations	Shortcut
=	*is* *equal* *equals* *[is] equal to*	
≠	*is not* *isn't* *isn't equal [to]* *is not equal [to]* *doesn't equal* *does not equal*	Option+=
>	*[is] greater than* *comes after* *isn't less than or equal [to]* *is not less than or equal [to]*	Shift+. (period)
<	*[is] less than* *comes before* *isn't greater than or equal [to]* *is not greater than or equal [to]*	Shift+, (comma)
≥	*=>* *[is] greater than or equal [to]* *isn't less than* *is not less than* *does not come before* *doesn't come before*	Option+. (period)
≤	*<=* *[is] less than or equal [to]* *isn't greater than* *is not greater than* *does not come after* *doesn't come after*	Option+, (comma)

Here are some more comparison examples:

```
50 ≥ 50
--> true
51 ≥ 50
--> true
"Zebra" comes after "Armadillo"
--> true
50 is not greater than 50
--> true
date "Tuesday, January 1, 2002 12:00:00 AM" comes after (current date)
```

What value classes can be used?

While the result of the comparison operators is always a Boolean, the operands can be of other classes. Since AppleScript requires that both left and right operands are of the same value class (both are numbers, or both are strings, etc.), if the operands are of two different classes, AppleScript will attempt to coerce the right operand to match the value class of the left one.

The operators *equal* and *not equal* can be used to compare operators from any value class. In using these operators, AppleScript won't even try to coerce the right value into the class of the left value. If the values of the operands belong to two different classes, AppleScript will simply return a "not equal" verdict instead of returning an error. Examine the following script snippets:

```
5 = "lalala"
--> false
```

AppleScript didn't even try to coerce the string "lalala" into a number; it simply deemed the two values not equal and returned a false result.

We know that by trying the following line:

```
5 = "5"
--> false
```

If AppleScript would have just tried, it would have managed to coerce the right operand, "5", into an integer and seen that it was equal to the left operand.

For this reason, it is important to coerce the values before comparing to avoid letting AppleScript make these coercion decisions for you.

If your intention is to check whether the two operands do belong to the same value class, you should compare the value classes themselves in this manner:

```
(class of variable_x) = (class of variable_y)
```

or

```
if (class of variable_x) = string then...
```

In the same way that we used the *equals* operator, the result of the following operation is true:

```
5 ≠ "lalala"
```

The rest of the comparison operators, the ones that check for positional comparison, have to use two operands that are from the same value class. If not, the value of the right operand has to be able to be coerced to the value class of the left operand.

Since these operators check to see if the left operand come before or after the right operand, they only work on values from the value classes: string, real, integer, and date. If an operand is a single-item list, AppleScript will coerce it into either a string or a number if needed and possible. When comparing dates, AppleScript requires that both left and right operands are valid dates.

Containment operators

Containment operators is a name used to describe a group of six operators. These operators check whether one operand is a part of the other operand. Furthermore, some containment operators check whether one operand starts or ends with the second one.

Like the comparison operators, the result of operations using containment operators is always a Boolean.

The following table lists the different containment operators and the operand classes they support.

Syntax variations	Operand value classes
start with	*list* and *string*
starts with	*list* and *string*
begin with	*list* and *string*
begins with	*list* and *string*
end with	*list* and *string*
ends with	*list* and *string*
contain	*record*, *list*, and *string*
contains	*record*, *list*, and *string*
does not contain	*record*, *list*, and *string*
doesn't contain	*record*, *list*, and *string*
is in	*record*, *list*, and *string*

Syntax variations	Operand value classes
is contained by	*record*, *list*, and *string*
is not in	*record*, *list*, and *string*
isn't in	*record*, *list*, and *string*
isn't contained by	*record*, *list*, and *string*
is not contained by	*record*, *list*, and *string*

Containment operators don't work on numbers of any kind.

Following are some examples of operations taking advantage of containment operators:

```
"Apple Pie" contains "Apples"
--> false
"Apple Pie" starts with "Apple"
--> true
"art" is contained by "start"
--> true
{1, 2, 3} starts with 1
--> true
```

The following two operations show that you can test whether a list starts with another list:

```
{"abc", "def", "ghi"} starts with {"abc", "def"}
--> true
{"abc", "def", "ghi"} starts with {"abc"}
--> true
```

You can also test to see if a list starts with a value of any other value class.

```
{"abc", "def", "ghi"} starts with "abc"
--> true
```

In the following example, even though the first item of the list starts with the right operand, the result is false. The *starts with* and *ends with* operators only evaluate whole list items when comparing them.

```
{"abc", "def", "ghi"} starts with "a"
--> false
"the end" ands with "the end"
--> true
```

The preceding operation shows that when strings (or lists) are equal, the *starts with* and *ends with* operators will return a true result.

9

Contained by exception

The operator *is in*, which can be also written as *is contained by*, is really the same as the *contains* operator. Asking "Is the mouse in the trap?" is the same as asking "Does the trap contain the mouse?" Due to this, the order in which AppleScript evaluates the operands is reversed in operations using the *is in* operator. In operations using the *is in* operator, AppleScript checks the right operand first and only then checks to see if the left operand matches its value class, or can be coerced into that value class.

Math operators

The fourth group of operators contains all the math operators. I will list them briefly in this section, but for comprehensive coverage, you should look at Chapter 4.

All math operators can have operands that are either integers or reals. Integers and reals can be mixed as the left or right operands. The result of operations using these operators will always be a real if one of the operands is a real. Furthermore, and keeping with the book's nit-picking style, I should mention the following two facts: the integral division (*div*) operator always produces an integer, which makes sense. Also, the exponent (^) operator always produces a real.

The following table lists the math operators, their names, functions, and keyboard shortcuts.

Syntax	Name	Keyboard shortcut	Function
*	Multiply	*SHIFT+8*	Multiplies the left and right operands.
+	Plus	*SHIFT+=*	Adds the left and right operands.
-	Minus	-	Subtracts the right operand from the left operand.
/ ÷	Division	/ *OPTION+/*	Divides the left operand by the right operand.
div	Integral division		Returns the number of times the right operand fits whole in the left operand.
mod	Modulo, remainder		The right operand is subtracted from the left operand repeatedly until the remainder is smaller than the right operand. That final remainder is the result.
^	Exponent	*SHIFT+6*	The result is the left operand multiplied by itself the number of times indicated by the right operand.

Concatenation

Probably the most used operator in AppleScript is the concatenation operator, whose syntax is ampersand (&).

To concatenate means to link together or join. AppleScript's concatenation operator can concatenate two strings into a third string, two lists into a third list, and two records into a third record.

Trying to concatenate any other value class, or a mix of value classes, will return a list containing the left and right operands. More on that later in the chapter.

Following is a description and a few examples of the concatenation operator; however, for more complete coverage, see the individual chapters dealing with strings, and lists and records (Chapter 3 and Chapter 6, respectively).

Concatenating strings

When the left operand of an operation using the concatenation operator is a string, AppleScript tries to coerce the right operand into a string and produce a single string made up of three strings: the left operator, followed by the text item delimiter, followed by the right operand, after it has been coerced into a string, if possible.

The most common usage is concatenating two or more strings, where at least one is a variable. Take a look at this example:

```
set user_name to "Olivia"
set user_greeting to "Hello" & space & user_name
--> "Hello Olivia"
```

9

In the preceding example, I concatenated the literal expression " *Hello* ", the value of the *space* constant, which is by default a single space, and the value of the variable *user_name*, which happened to be "Olivia".

String rules

As with any other string operation, the same rules apply regarding constants such as *tab*, *space*, *return*, etc., and the need to escape certain characters such as quotes.

To produce the following string:

```
I said "Hello"!
```

you need to write

```
Set my_string to "I said \"Hello\"!"
```

Notice the backslashes before two of the quotes. The backslash is AppleScript's escape character. When you escape the quote marks by placing the backslash before them, they become a literal part of the text, instead of defining the string boundaries as the first and last quotes do. You can read more on this in Chapter 3.

Concatenating a string variable to itself

In many cases you will need to add text to the same string variable, for instance, if you're building a list or a report.

To concatenate a string variable to itself, simply include the variable identifier in the expression itself.

```
set my_var to "Hit"
set my_var to my_var & space & "the"
set my_var to my_var & space & "road"
```

In the following example we create a simple HTML file that has a title and some contents in a one-cell table. The contents and the title will be stored in the variables *the_title* and *the_contents*.

In this example we add a return at the end of every line. This isn't required by web browsers, but makes it more legible for people.

Here is the script:

Script 9-2

```
1. set the_title to "Welcome"
2. set the_contents to "Hello World!"
3. set html to ""
4. set html to html & "<html>" & return
5. set html to html & "<head>" & return
6. set html to html & "<title>" & the_title & "</title>" & return
7. set html to html & "</head>" & return
8. set html to html & "<body>" & return
9. set html to html & "<table border=\"2\">" & return
10. set html to html & "<tr>" & return
11. set html to html & "<td>" & return
12. set html to html & the_contents & return
13. set html to html & "</td>" & return
14. set html to html & "</tr>" & return
15. set html to html & "</table>" & return
16. set html to html & "</body>" & return
17. set html to html & "</html>" & return
```

And the finished HTML text:

```
<html>
<head>
<title>Welcome</title>
</head>
<body>
<table border="2">
<tr>
<td>
```

```
Hello World!
</td>
</tr>
</table>
</body>
</html>
```

While this is good, we can make another small leap towards readability by indenting the lines with tabs.

What we don't want to do, though, is to add *& tab & tab & tab & tab*, etc. to the script. This will make it hard to manage.

What we will do is create a little handler that will add the number of tabs we want to the script. The handler will simply repeat a given number of times and concatenate a tab character to an empty string in every repetition. The number of tabs needed will be passed to the handler as an argument, and the handler will simply return a string made of the number of tabs specified in the argument.

Here is the script:

Script 9-3

```
1. set the_title to "Welcome"
2. set the_contents to "Hello World!"
3. set html to ""
4. set html to html & "<html>" & return
5. set html to html & indent(1) & "<head>" & return
6. set html to html & indent(2) & "<title>" & the_title & ¬
   "</title>" & return
7. set html to html & indent(1) & "</head>" & return
8. set html to html & indent(1) & "<body>" & return
9. set html to html & indent(2) & "<table border=\"2\">" & return
10. set html to html & indent(3) & "<tr>" & return
11. set html to html & indent(4) & "<td>" & return
12. set html to html & indent(5) & the_contents & return
13. set html to html & indent(4) & "</td>" & return
14. set html to html & indent(3) & "</tr>" & return
15. set html to html & indent(2) & "</table>" & return
16. set html to html & indent(1) & "</body>" & return
17. set html to html & "</html>" & return

18. on indent(indent_level)
19.    set the_indent_string to ""
20.    repeat indent_level times
21.       set the_indent_string to the_indent_string & tab
22.    end repeat
23.    return the_indent_string
24. end indent
```

9

Notice the indent handler. It starts by creating an empty string, then loops the number of times given by the argument, and concatenates a tab to the string each time it loops.

In every line of the script where we want a tab indent, we just call the handler with the required indent level. The handler returns a string that becomes a part of the concatenation. There's no need for it to have its own line in the script.

More looping concatenations

Now let's imagine that we have two lists, one with names of people and one with their date of birth. We want to add these names to the table we created in the last script.

What we'll need is a repeat loop that adds both the text and the HTML tags to the main HTML string.

Here we go:

Script 9-4

```applescript
1.  set the_title to "Names and Dates"
2.  set name_list to {"George", "Silvia", "Ben", "Frank"}
3.  set date_list to {"October 15th", "December 6th", "May 11th", ¬
      "January 15th"}
4.  set html to ""
5.  set html to html & ¬
      "<html><head><title>" & the_title & "</title></head>" & return
6.  set html to html & "<body>" & return
7.  set html to html & "<table border=\"2\">" & return
8.  set html to html & "<tr>" & return
9.  repeat with i from 1 to count name_list
10.     set html to html & "<td>"
11.     set html to html & i & "<td>"
12.     set html to html & (item i of name_list) & "<td>"
13.     set html to html & (item i of date_list)
14.     set html to html & "</td>" & return
15.     set html to html & "<tr>" & return
16. end repeat
17. set html to html & "</tr>" & return
18. set html to html & "</table></body></html>" & return
19. set the_path to (get path to desktop as string) & ¬
      "names_and_dates.html"
20. open for access file the_path with write permission
21. write html to file the_path
22. close access file the_path
23. set the_alias to the_path as alias
24. tell application "Safari"
25. activate
26. open the_alias
27. end tell
```

Notice the repeat loop starting at line 9 and ending at line 16. It has an entire <td> tag that opens and closes, all the text for the row that includes items from the lists, and the <tr> tag that adds another row.

Lines 20, 21, and 22 save the text to a text file, and the rest of the line makes Safari open the HTML file and display it.

Concatenating records

When simply concatenating two records, the items from the second record are added to the first record. Figure 9-10 shows two records concatenating (in their natural habitat . . .)

Figure 9-10. Simple concatenation of records

When the second record contains a label that is identical to a label in the first record, the resulting record ignores the label and its value from the second, or right-side record operand, as seen in Figure 9-11.

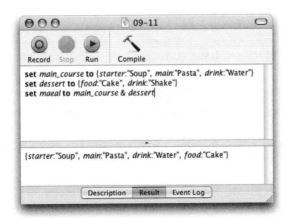

Figure 9-11. If a duplicate label is found in the second record, it is dropped from the resulting record.

Lists and concatenation

Concatenating two lists results in a single list containing the items of the left operand followed by the items of the right operand, as shown in Figure 9-12.

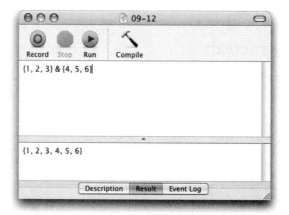

Figure 9-12. Two lists being concatenated

If one or more of the lists' items are lists themselves, these lists will remain intact and will not become a part of the main list. Figure 9-13 contains two lists. The items of the two lists are lists themselves, but they don't merge with the main list. The left operand is a two-item list, the right operand is a one-item list, and therefore the result is a three-item list.

Figure 9-13. Only the two main lists combine into a single list when concatenating. List items that are lists remain intact.

Adding an item to a list

Many times when working with lists, the intention is simply to tack on a value as the last item of the list. For instance, say we have a list of names, {*"Joe"*, *"Jill"*}, and we want to add a value to it to make {*"Joe"*, *"Jill"*, *"Bob"*}.

The inclination would be to set the list to itself plus the new item, like this:

```
set my_list to {"Joe", "Jill"}
set my_list to my_list & "Bob"
```

While this will work, there's another way to get the result you want. Adding a list to itself has to allocate temporary space in memory for the new list on top of the memory needed for the original list. This method can cause delays when adding items to long lists.

So in order to add items to a list faster, all you need to do is set the end of the list to the item, like this:

```
set my_list to {"Joe", "Jill"}
set end of my_list to "Bob"
--> {"Joe", "Jill", "Bob"}
```

With the second method, however, the list items will be dispersed in memory, while using the first method, the list items will occupy adjacent memory locations. This means that while creating the list may be slower using the first method, using the list later on may be more efficient, at least a few milliseconds faster.

Creating a list of lists

The syntax we saw previously, *set end of list*, is also useful for tacking on a list to the end of a list, but leaving the original list intact. This is useful when you need to create a list of lists.

In the following script, we attempt to create a list of three lists:

Script 9-5 (also includes the following script)

```
set the_list to {}
repeat 3 times
    set the_list to the_list & {1, 2, 3}
end repeat
the_list = {1, 2, 3, 1, 2, 3, 1, 2, 3}
```

Not exactly our intention. However, try this instead:

```
set the_list to {}
repeat 3 times
    set end of the_list to {1, 2, 3}
end repeat
the_list = {{1, 2, 3}, {1, 2, 3}, {1, 2, 3}}
```

Now that's more like it!

Insert to list handler

As a little example of list concatenation, here's a subroutine that adds a given item to a given list at a given position.

The parameters are, as mentioned earlier, the list you want to add to, the item you want to add, and the position.

Script 9-6

```
set the_list to {1, 2, 3, 4}
insert_to_list(the_list, "a", 2)

on insert_to_list(the_list, the_item, the_position)
    if the_position ≤ 1 then --add to start
        set the_list to (the_item as list) & the_list
    else if the_position ≥ (count the_list) then --add to end
        set end of the_list to the_item
    else --add in middle
        set the_list to ¬
            (items 1 thru (the_position - 1) of the_list) & ¬
            the_item & ¬
            (items the_position thru -1 of the_list) as list
    end if
    return the_list
end insert_to_list
```

Notice that in line 5 we have to coerce the item into a list. This turns the item into a list with a single item. The reason is that if the class of the item is a string, then the result of the operation is a string.

One of the shortfalls of the simplified handler shown previously is that if the item you want to add to the list is itself a list, the results will not be consistent. If the item is inserted in the middle or at the start (position 1), as follows, then the result will be one list containing all items of both lists:

```
set the_list to {1, 2, 3, 4}
insert_to_list(the_list, {"a", "b"}, 1)
--> {"a", "b", 1, 2, 3, 4}
```

In the preceding example we add the list {"a", "b"} to the beginning of the list {1, 2, 3, 4}. The result is a single list.

If the item is added to the end of the list, it will remain a separate list, as you see here:

```
set the_list to {1, 2, 3, 4}
insert_to_list(the_list, {"a", "b"},5)
--> {1, 2, 3, 4, {"a", "b"}}
```

As an exercise, change the preceding handler to make sure that, if the item that has to be inserted is a list, it is treated equally no matter what position it is inserted into.

Concatenating other value classes

Concatenating operands of value classes other than string, list, or record produces a list with two items, the left operand and the right operand. In the following code the concatenation operator is used with two date values. The result is a list with the two dates in it.

```
(current date) & (current date)
--> {date "Saturday, October 25, 2003 10:35:30 AM", ¬
    date "Saturday, October 25, 2003 10:35:30 AM"}
```

The reference to operator

We use the *reference to* operator when we want to include objects in our script that would just not fit, mainly objects from applications. Think about it: your script can include text and numbers, but what happens when you want to set a variable to a specific InDesign page, or a folder on the hard disk?

The *reference to* operator is most useful when the object you want to refer to has a value that AppleScript can get in one of the familiar classes such as number, text, list, etc. For instance, if you assign the text of a TextEdit document to the variable *doc_text*, you get the actual text in string form. Later on, even if the text of the document changes, the value of the variable *doc_text* will remain unchanged. See Figure 9-14 for an example.

Figure 9-14. The text of a TextEdit document is assigned to a variable, but AppleScript returns the result as a string.

Assigning the *value* of the document's text as string is OK if this is what you want, but what if you want a variable's value to be a reference to the document? This way you can use the variable to refer to the document anytime and get its current text. Figure 9-15 shows an example of how to do that.

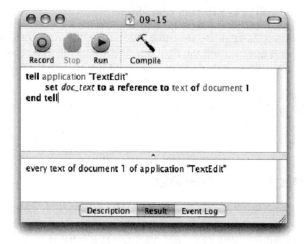

Figure 9-15. When the variable is set to a reference to the text,
you can always use it to get the current text of the document.

So now that we have a variable whose value is a reference to the document's text, in order
to get the actual string value of the object the variable refers to, we need to ask for the
contents of the variable, as shown in Figure 9-16.

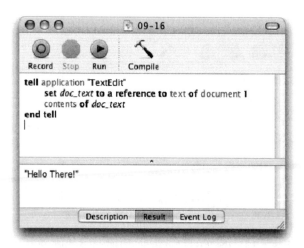

Figure 9-16. After we set a variable as a reference to an object,
we may be able to retrieve the value of the object by getting its content.

Implicit reference

When we assign an application's object to a variable, we don't always have to explicitly use the *reference to* operator. Any application object that is not meant to return a text or number value will automatically return a reference to the object.

For instance, look at the following line:

```
set the_doc to document "letterhead"
```

The value of the variable *the_doc* is a reference to the document.

The difference is, though, that when we use the *reference to* operator, the object we refer to doesn't have to actually exist. Also, the reference itself will look different and may affect its function in the script during runtime.

Let's evaluate the two following instances, both referring to a specific layer in an Illustrator document:

Script 9-7 (also includes the following script)

Instance 1:

```
tell application "Adobe Illustrator 10"
    tell document "brochure.ai"
        set my_layer to layer "images"
    end tell
end tell
--> layer 1 of document 1 of application "Adobe Illustrator 10"
```

Instance 2:

```
tell application "Adobe Illustrator 10"
    tell document "brochure.ai"
        set my_layer to a reference to layer "images"
    end tell
end tell
--> layer "images" of document "brochure.ai" of ¬
application "Adobe Illustrator 10"
```

In the first instance we do not use the *reference to* operator, but rather assign the object itself to the variable *my_layer*. Even though we mentioned the names of both the document and the layer, AppleScript (following Illustrator's scripting structure) assigned the variable the value layer 1 of document 1 . . . without the names.

In the second instance, AppleScript set the variable *my_layer* to a reference to a layer using the exact wording we used in the script: layer "images" of document "brochure.ai" . . .

Other applications may deal with that situation differently. The Finder, for instance, will also keep true to our language when we use the *reference to* operator, but if we simply write *set the_folder to folder 1*, the Finder will set the variable *the_folder* to a reference that includes the folder's name.

9

The best thing to do is test, test, and then test some more. Always know exactly what value you will get and what the implications are. If you refer to document 1, but then another document is added, the reference may not be pointing to the document you intended.

References and the tell block

Since references to application objects include the application itself, it is possible to use these references outside of the application's *tell* block.

Figure 9-17 shows how we can create a reference to a page item in InDesign inside the application's *tell* block, but then use the reference with the *delete* command outside the *tell* block.

Figure 9-17. The object referred to in the *my_object* variable contains the application, which allows you to use it even outside the application's *tell* block.

Consideration clauses

Although most AppleScript commands seem to speak for themselves, there are a lot of hidden assumptions that AppleScript makes by default in order to execute commands more smoothly.

All clauses, with the exception of the *application responses* clause, are relevant when making text comparisons.

The most common clause in text comparison is the *case* clause. You will notice it outside of AppleScript when you try your password for the fifth time wondering whether . . . the password is case sensitive. What does case sensitive mean exactly? Well, just by looking at two words we can see if they're the same, but are the words "free" and "FREE" the same? If you ignore the fact that one is uppercase and the other is lowercase, then they are the same.

This point is exactly what consideration clauses are all about.

In AppleScript, by default, the following statement is true:

```
"FREE" = "free" --> true
```

But what if you want to be a bit stricter and check to also see if the case is identical? What you have to do is put the statement in a consideration clause, like this:

```
considering case
    "FREE" = "free" --> false
end considering
```

Since the comparison operation in the preceding script happens inside the consideration clause block, AppleScript is forced to also check whether the case of the letters match, and therefore returns a false result from the operation.

Ignoring

While the letters' case is ignored during text comparison by default, some conditions you could possibly want to ignore are considered. Take for example white space and dashes: by default, the two statements that follow will return a false result:

```
"White-house" = "Whitehouse"
"Apple Script" =  "AppleScript"
```

But what if we want to see if the correct answer was provided to the question "Where does the president live?", and we want to allow some latitude? What we can do is make the comparison while asking AppleScript to return a true result even if there's an extra hyphen or white space. Here is how we would do that:

Script 9-8

```
Set the_quiz_question to "Where does the president live"
Display dialog the_quiz_question default answer ""
Set user_answer to text returned of result
ignoring white space and hyphens
   set answer_is_correct to (user_answer equals "Whitehouse")
end Ignoring
if answer_is_correct then display dialog "You got it!"
```

In the preceding example, even if quiz takers spelled "White house" or "White-house," they would still come up on top.

Now, what if we want to consider capitalization? For instance, the question is "Which is the smallest state?" and we want to accept Rhode Island and Rhode-Island, but not rhode island.

What we want to do is consider case during comparison, but ignore dashes. Here is how we do that:

Script 9-9 (also includes the following script)

```
considering case
   ignoring white space and hyphens
      "Rhode Island" is equal to "Rhode-Island" --> true
      "Rhode Island" is equal to "rhode island" --> false
   end ignoring
end considering
```

The reason that "Rhode Island" was found to be *not* equal to "rhode island" is that we asked AppleScript to consider the case of the letters.

Here's another way to make the same statement:

```
considering case but ignoring white space and hyphens
   "Rhode Island" is equal to "Rhode-Island" --> true
   "Rhode Island" is equal to "rhode island" --> false
end considering
```

Consideration attributes

So far we have looked at three attributes that AppleScript can consider when comparing strings: *case*, *white space*, and *hyphens*. Following is a detailed description of all possible consideration attributes.

case

If considered during string comparisons, AppleScript will check to see if the capitalization is equal in the two strings being compared. By default case is ignored, and therefore when making string comparisons without case consideration, AppleScript ignores the case of the different strings.

white space

By default, spaces, tab characters, and return characters are considered in string comparisons, which will make "whitehouse" different from "white house". If *white space* is included in the *ignore* clause, the preceding two strings would come out equal.

Script 9-10

```
"slow motion" is equal to "slowmotion" --> false
ignoring white space
   " slow motion" is equal to " slowmotion " --> true
end ignoring
```

diacriticals

Diacritical marks, or accents, can be either considered or ignored during string comparisons. (These are character accents such as ´, `, ^, ¨, and ˜.) Diacriticals are considered by default, so if you want the string "résumé" to be considered equal to "resume", then you have to ask AppleScript to ignore diacriticals.

Script 9-11

```
"resume" is equal to "résumé" --> false
ignoring diacriticals
    "resume" is equal to "résumé" --> true
end ignoring
```

hyphens

As we saw earlier, by default, strings with hyphens will evaluate to be not equal to the same string with hyphens.

Script 9-12

```
"Wall-Street" is equal to "Wall Street" --> false
ignoring hyphens
    "Wall-Street" is equal to "Wall Street" --> true
end ignoring
```

expansion

Expansion deals with letter combinations found in some European languages and their two-letter counterpart.

For instance, by default AppleScript would consider "Æ" not equal to "AE", " Œ" not equal to "CE", etc. Unless of course you tell AppleScript to ignore diacriticals.

Script 9-13

```
"AE" is equal to "Æ" --> false
ignoring diacriticals
    "AE" is equal to "Æ" --> true
end ignoring
```

> **NOTE**   *Note that the AppleScript reference manual states the opposite.*

punctuation

By default, AppleScript considers punctuation marks (. , ? : ; ! \ ' " `) when comparing strings. If the *punctuation* attribute is ignored, the strings are compared as if these punctuation marks were not there.

Script 9-14

```
"it's" equals "its" --> false
"1,000.00" equals "1.000,00" --> false
ignoring punctuation
    "it's" equals "its" --> true
    "1,000.00" equals "1.000,00" --> true
end ignoring
```

application responses

The *application responses* consideration attribute has nothing to do with comparing text, and little to do with operators. It is described here briefly and covered in detail in Chapter 16.

When AppleScript sends a command to an application, it waits until the command is through executing before moving on to the next script statement.

While this is good under normal operation, there are instances where you want to leave the application with a command and move on to other things.

Here is how you do that:

Script 9-15

```
ignoring application responses
    tell application "Adobe Photoshop CS"
        do action "convert all files to jpeg"
    end tell
end ignoring
doTheNextThing()
```

In the preceding example, AppleScript will tell Photoshop to perform the action and move on to the next statement.

Which value classes can be coerced?

As discussed before, coercing a value is converting it into a different value class by using the *as* operator.

```
13 as string --> "13"
"13" as real --> 13.0
```

In these two examples we coerced an integer value into a string and then coerced a string value into a real.

These operations worked for two reasons:

First, the value classes were interchangeable. That means that the value's original value class can be legally coerced to the value class we coerced it into. If it is not, an error will occur, as shown in Figures 9-18 and 9-19.

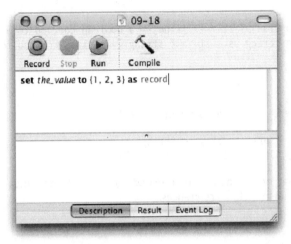

Figure 9-18. In this script we try to coerce a list value into a record.

Figure 9-19. The result of the script shown in Figure 9-18 is an error, telling you that you can't coerce a list into a record.

This is not to say, though, that the reverse wouldn't work; in this case it would have.

The second condition for a successful coercion is that the values themselves fit well with the new value class. For instance, here is what may happen when converting a string into an integer:

```
"3" as integer --> 3
```

The preceding one worked, but what about this one:

```
"Hello" as integer --> error number -1700
```

This didn't work because although the class itself is legal, the actual value we tried to coerce isn't.

So which classes can be coerced to which? Following is a list of each value class and the classes it can be coerced to, with some notes and exceptions.

boolean, *class*, *constant*, and *data* value classes can be each coerced into a single-item list only.

```
Set x to true as list--> {true}-- a boolean coerced to a list
Set x to string as list--> { string }--a class coerced to a list
```

Date

Dates can be coerced into strings, and into a single-item list:

```
Set x to (current date) as string--> ¬
"Tuesday, October 28, 2003 5:06:29 PM"
```

The exact format of the date is determined by the Date and the Time tabs in the International panel in System Preferences.

Integer

An integer can be coerced into a string any day without any restrictions.

An integer can also be coerced into a real, which will be the integer with a decimal point and a zero behind it.

```
Set x to 3 as real --> 3.0
```

And as with most other value classes, you can coerce an integer into a single-item list.

Single-item list

A single-item list can be coerced into any other class, given that the item in the list can be coerced into that class.

```
{3} as integer --> 3
{"lalala"} as real --> error -1700
```

Multi-item list

A list with multiple items can only be coerced into a string as long as all the items themselves are cool with the notion of turning into strings.

```
{1, 2, {"a", "b"}, (current date), "bumbum", 33.33} as string
--> "12abTuesday, October 28, 2003 5:22:03 PMbumbum33.33"
```

Real

A real value can be coerced into a string and a single-item list without any trouble.

If the real value has no fractional part, like 10.0 or 2.0, then it can be coerced into an integer as well; otherwise, it has to be rounded.

Record

Records can only be coerced into a list. All that happens is that they shed their labels.

String

Strings that match the required format can be coerced into integers or real values. Strings can also become a single-item list.

Mixing operators and the mighty parentheses

One of the fun things about creating operations is that the same operation with the same result can be spread over multiple lines in the script, or be crammed into a single line. While operations that are spread out are usually easier to read, in many cases you would want to create more complex operations that contain more than one operator and multiple operands.

What's important to remember is that an operation has one or two operands and a single operator. Complex operations, then, are really statements made up of many nuclear operations. Let's look at the following operation as an example:

    5 + 5 + 3

It appears to have three operands and two operators, right? Not really. The way AppleScript attacks this statement is by first resolving the leftmost operation: 5 + 5. The result is then the left operand for the following operation: 10 + 3.

So in a sense, AppleScript does this:

    5 + 5 = 10
    10 + 3 = 13

When resolving such statements, AppleScript uses the table of precedence to determine two things—the order in which operations should be resolved (shown in the Order column in the following table, which originally appeared in the AppleScript Language Guide), and what order in which to resolve operations whose operators have the same precedence level, such as multiply and divide (shown in the Form of association column).

9

Order	Operators	Form of association	Type of operator
1	*()*	Innermost to outermost	Grouping
2	+, -	Unary	Plus or minus sign for numbers
3	^	Right to left	Exponentiation
4	*, /, div, mod	Left to right	Multiplication and division
5	+, -	Left to right	Addition and subtraction
6	as	Left to right	Coercion
7	<, ≤, >, ≥	None	Comparison
8	=, ≠	None	Equality and inequality
9	not	Unary	Logical negation
10	and	Left to right	Logical for Boolean values
11	or	Left to right	Logical for Boolean values

Understanding precedence rules

While the order of precedence resolves some of the confusion, there are quite a few operators with the same order of precedence, like plus and minus. The Form of association column in the preceding table explains how AppleScript deals with statements that contain multiple operators that have the same precedence level.

Left to right and right to left

Operators marked "Left to right" are evaluated in that order when more than one operator from the same precedence exist. For instance, the operation

```
12 + 5 + 30 -- 7
```

will be resolved as follows:

```
12 + 5 = 17 -- leftmost
17 + 30 = 47
```

The result of the previous operation (17) is now the left operand.

Unary

A *unary* operator is one that takes a single operand to its left, for instance:

-7

The minus operator in this case turns the positive number operand to its right into a negative number, and a negative number into a positive one.

If you type multiple unary operators, they start evaluating from the one closest to the operator, going further and further away. Look at the following statement:

```
Not not not true
```

Here's how AppleScript looks at the preceding statement:

```
Not (not (not true))
```

In fact, if you do use the statement without the parentheses, when you compile the script, AppleScript will add parentheses for you!

None

The operators marked *none* can't be a part of a multi-operation statement that is not separated with parentheses.

```
3 > 4 > 5 --> error!
(3 > 4) = true --> works because of the... parentheses.
```

Use parentheses!

While it's important to understand the order of precedence, you should not get to a point where it matters. The reason is the number one operator on the list: parentheses.

If you write statements that contain more than one or two operations, you should wrap each operation in parentheses.

Since AppleScript evaluates parentheses the same way you learned in school, from the innermost out, it should be easy enough for you to use them.

There are two benefits for using parentheses: readability and predictability.

When working with complex multi-operation statements, you want to be able to analyze the intended result and tweak the order of operation in the most efficient manner. If you only use parentheses where you have to, the statement will require you to memorize the table of precedence (or constantly look it up . . .). Using parentheses for each separate operation will make it easier for you to arrive at the statement that produces the results you intended.

Oh, one more thing—did I mention you should use parentheses?

9

Power wrap-up

This section summarizes the chapter in an intensive-reference style. Use this part to look up facts related to the chapter without the chatter.

Operations

Operations are expressions that use operators to derive values from other values.

Coercion

Coercion is when a value changes over from one value class to another.

Explicit coercion

To explicitly coerce a value from one class to another, use the *as* operator.

```
set the_number to "120" as integer --> 120
set the_string to 75.5 as string --> "75.5"
(not true) as string --> "false"
```

Coercions that occur inside statements should be enclosed in parentheses. In the following statement, AppleScript will wrap at least the first coercion statement in parentheses if you don't:

```
("120" as integer) + ("120" as integer) --> 2
```

Coercion from list to string is common, especially when working with text.

```
set the_string to "Home"
set the_list to characters 3 thru 4 of the_string --> {"m", "e"}
set the_string to the_list as string --> "me"
```

You may coerce data multiple times in the same statement.

```
set the_price to ((characters 2 thru -1 of "$12.95") as string)  ¬
as real
--> 12.95
```

Automatic coercion

AppleScript will try to coerce values on its own when it sees fit. While such coercions are sometimes helpful, your script will be more legible and easier to change if you use the *as* operator explicitly.

AppleScript will coerce other values into strings in order to concatenate them with other strings, if needed. In the statement that follows, AppleScript has to coerce the integer 15 into a string:

```
"July " & 15 --> "July 15"
```

In this statement, however, the integer comes first, so AppleScript doesn't perform the coercion. Instead of a string, you get a list.

```
15 & " of July" --> {15, " of July"}
```

Boolean operators

Boolean operators operate on Boolean values and expressions. Any expression in a Boolean operation must evaluate as a Boolean. These are AppleScript's Boolean operators: *not*, *and*, and *or*. Following are some examples of using Boolean operators.

The *not* operator is a unary operator. It works by changing the operand to its right.

```
not true --> false
```

The *and* operator will return true if both left and right operands are true.

```
true and true --> true
(12 > 6) and (length of "Shaq" is 4) --> true
(5 = 5) and ("Yes" is "no") --> false
```

The *or* operator will return true if either the left or right operands are true.

```
true or false --> true
false or false --> false
(12 > 6) or (12 < 6) --> true
```

You can create complex Boolean statements that contain multiple Boolean operations.

```
if (email contains "@") and¬
((email ends with ".com") or (email ends with ".net")) and¬
((offset of "@" in email) > 1) then
set valid_email to true
end if
```

Comparison operators

Comparison operators can operate on many types of values, but the result of a comparison operation is always a Boolean.

AppleScript includes the following comparison operators: =, ≠, >, <, ≥, ≤.

Check out the variations table in this chapter for other text variations of each operator, such as *is greater than*.

9

Each value class uses a slightly different set of comparison operators. For class-specific operators, see the corresponding chapters: Chapter 3 for strings, Chapter 4 for numbers, Chapter 5 for dates, and Chapter 6 for lists and records. Following are a few comparison operations:

```
3 > 2 --> true
8 = "8" --> false
(current date) > date "1/1/2000" --> true
```

Containment operators

Containment operators also return a Boolean value. They check whether a particular value contains, or is contained by, another value.

The containment operator group includes the following operators: *starts with*, *ends with*, *contains*, *doesn't contain*, *is contained by*, and *isn't contained by*.

Each operator listed here has variations that can be seen in this chapter. Following are a few containment operator examples:

```
"Friendship" contains "Friend" --> true
{12, 14, 16} contains 14 --> true
{"ABC", "DEF"} contains "A" --> false (the list contains "ABC" but ¬
not "A").
```

Math operators

AppleScript allows you to use the following math operators:

- * (multiply)
- \+ (plus)
- \- (minus)
- / (division)
- *div* (integral division)
- *mod* (modulo, remainder)
- ^ (exponent)

Here are a few examples:

```
3 * 5 --> 15
72 / 12 --> 6
3 ^ 2 --> 9
```

For a complete explanation of math operators in AppleScript, see Chapter 4.

The concatenation operator

AppleScript uses the ampersand (&) as the concatenation operator.

You can concatenate strings, lists, and records, like this:

```
"Micro" & "Soft" --> "MicroSoft"
"Steely" &space & "Dan" -->  "Steely Dan"
{1, 2, 3} & 4 & {5, 6} --> {1, 2, 3, 4, 5, 6}
```

Adding items to a list

To add items to the end of a list, you can either use the concatenation operator or the following statement:

```
set end of {1, 2, 3} to 4 --> {1, 2, 3, 4}
```

This method works differently when adding lists to lists. When using the *end of* style operation, the lists are added as individual units.

```
set the_list to {}
set end of the_list to {1, 2, 3}
set end of the_list to {4, 5, 6}
set end of the_list to {7, 8, 9}
--the_list --> {{1, 2, 3}, {4, 5, 6}, {7, 8, 9}}
```

When using concatenation, the lists all merge.

```
set the_list to {}
set the_list to the_list & {1, 2, 3}
set the_list to the_list & {4, 5, 6}
set the_list to the_list & {7, 8, 9}
--the_list --> {1, 2, 3, 4, 5, 6, 7, 8, 9}
```

The reference to operator

The *reference to* operator returns a reference to an object, instead of the value of the object.

The following statement returns the string that is the second word of another string:

```
set the_string to "Double Impact"
to word 2 of the_string
```

The following statement, however, uses the *reference to* operator to get a reference to word 2. In this example, if the variable *the_string* changes, the variable *the_string_word_ref* will change as well.

```
set the_string to "Double Impact"
set the_string_ref to a reference to the_string
set the_string_word_ref to a reference to word 2 of the_string_ref
```

9

Consideration clauses

You can use a consideration block to alter the default result of a comparison operation. The consideration clause tells AppleScript to either consider or ignore specific attributes. The attributes that can be considered or ignored are *case*, *white space*, *diacriticals*, *hyphens*, *expansion*, and *punctuation*.

Following are two examples of using the different consideration clauses. For more examples, see earlier in this chapter.

For considering case:

```
"AppleScript" = "applescript" --> true
considering case
   "AppleScript" = "applescript" --> false
end considering
```

Or, for ignoring white space:

```
"800 555-1212" is equal to "8005551212" --> false
ignoring white space and hyphens
   "800 555-1212" is equal to "8005551212" --> true
end ignoring
```

Details previously . . .

The last part of this chapter is a summary of the entire chapter. For more details on any of the items here, refer to earlier sections in this chapter.

CHAPTER 10

TEACHING YOUR SCRIPT
TO MAKE DECISIONS

```
if sodas_left > 0 then
     set the_drink to "soda"
     set sodas_left to sodas_left - 1
else if beers_left > 0 then
     set the_drink to "beer"
     set beers_left to beers_left - 1
else if vodkas_left > 0 then
     set the_drink to "Vodka"
     set vodkas_left to vodkas_left -
else
     set the_drink to "nothing"
end if
return the_drink
get_drink
```

```
if car_color = "green" or car
     if mpg < 30 then
          if age ≤ 3 then
               if cost ≤ 1000
                    buy_car()
               end if
          end if
     end if
end if
|
```

```
_left to 4
_left to 1
rs_left to 5

_A to get_drink() --drink for me
_B to get_drink() --drink for a friend

rink()
das_left > 0 then
set the_drink to "soda"
set sodas_left to sodas_left - 1
if beers_left > 0 then
set the_drink to "beer"
set beers_left to beers_left - 1
```

The AppleScript language, like other programming languages, revolves around two things: a few simple concepts, and a lot of syntax. One of these concepts is the conditional statement. The concept behind conditional statements is so basic that most kids can master it by the time they can put a sentence together.

In AppleScript, the ability to make decisions is what gives your script artificial intelligence. The more conditional statements you use, attached to different sensors, the more organic and fluid your script is.

In AppleScript, we refer to an *if* statement as a conditional statement or a conditional statement block.

Conditions are everywhere! They do not need a conditional statement to exist. The state of every property of every object of every application, the text or buttons that are returned from a dialog box, the value and properties of any variable you use in your script—these are all conditions that you can test and use to your advantage. The only thing stopping you is your imagination (and how many hours you can bill for . . .).

The idea of a condition is that as complex as it may be, the result is primal: it can be either true or false. Even the most complex statements boil down to true or false.

The basic conditional statement

The basic syntax for a conditional statement, shown in Figure 10-1, is arranged in what we call a *tell* block. A *tell* block starts with the word "if," followed by the first condition, and ends with the line *end if*.

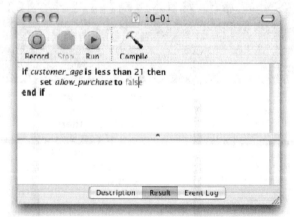

Figure 10-1. The basic *tell* block

In Figure 10-1 you can see the basic conditional statement. Line 1 has the condition. We test whether the value of the variable *customer_age* is less than 21.

The second line acts on the findings. That means that the code in line 2 will only execute *if* the statement in line 1 is true. If the statement isn't true, it is then false, and the script will skip the lines following line 1, until the script gets to either the end of the *if* statement block or a line that starts with the word "else."

In the case of the script in Figure 10-1, the third and last line indicates the end of the conditional statement.

From the dictionary

A bit later in this chapter we will go into the different ways you can use the *if* statement. Following is a dictionary-definition-style description of the different flavors of the *if-then* statement.

The variable we use is *boolean_expression*. The value of that variable can be either true or false, and it may be a complex expression replacing the variable.

1. The one-liner:

```
if boolean_expression then statement
```

2. The *if-then* statement block:

```
if boolean_expression then
    statement -- comment: execute if boolean_expression is true
end if
```

3. The *if-then-else* statement block:

```
if boolean_expression then
    statement -- comment: execute if boolean_expression is true
else
    statement -- comment: execute if boolean_expression is false
end if
```

4. The *if-then-else* statement block, where there are two or more different Boolean statements to follow:

```
if boolean_expression then
    statement -- comment: execute if boolean_expression is true
else if another_boolean_expression then
    statement -- comment: execute if another_boolean_expression ¬
is true
end if
```

5. The *if-then-else* statement block. Same as the previous one, but with a provision in case none of the Boolean expressions used are true:

```
if boolean_expression then
    statement -- comment: execute if boolean_expression is true
else if another_boolean_expression then
    statement -- comment: execute if another_boolean_expression is true
else
    statement -- comment: execute if no boolean expression was ¬
true thus far.
end if
```

10

Offering alternatives

In the script shown in Figure 10-1, there's a single conditional statement. If the condition is false, then line 2 of the script will be skipped, and the statement will be over without having anything happen.

AppleScript makes it easy to specify what happens if the condition set in the first line of the conditional statement happens to be not true.

Sometimes you will want to act only on a condition being true or false, but sometimes you will want to perform one or more actions if the condition is true, and other actions if it is false.

In that case you use the *else* clause. When used by itself, the *else* clause divides the conditional statement into two parts: what happens if the condition is true, and what happens if it is false. It's that simple!

If there's more juice, pour some for yourself; if there isn't, get some water.

The script in Figure 10-2 shows the *else* statement being used.

Figure 10-2.
A conditional statement is used with the *else* clause.

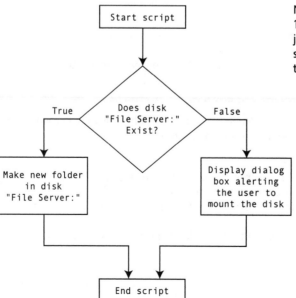

Note that the example in Figure 10-2 should be clear enough, but just to make sure, Figure 10-3 shows a flow chart that describes the script.

Figure 10-3.
A conditional statement's flow chart

More conditions

Many times, a conditional statement will be made out of multiple conditions. In this case, the first condition that is true will be executed and the conditional statement will be over.

Here's how it might work logically:

You're at a party and you want something to drink. If there's soda, you drink that. If there isn't, you look for the beer. If there's nothing else, go for the hard stuff. Although I know many people who may find my logic a bit backwards . . .

In AppleScript, the conditional statement for that search for liquid may look like this:

```
if exists "soda" then
    set contents of glass to "soda"
else if exists "beer" then
    set contents of glass to "beer"
else
    set contents of glass to "Vodka"
end if
```

The first condition checks for soda. If there is soda, it makes no difference if there's also beer or vodka. You will drink soda and skip the beer and vodka part. If there's no soda, the beer gets a chance. Again, if there's beer, the vodka is out of luck and it makes no difference if there is or isn't any left.

Now, suppose if you go to hunt for drinks for yourself and a friend. Your friend, for argument's sake, has the same preference as you do: he would rather get soda, then beer is OK, and so on.

To write a script that will fetch drinks for both of you, you will need to run the conditional statement twice.

10

Multiple condition script

You can do this in a couple of ways. If the script will always look for drinks for two people only, you can explicitly run the condition twice, as shown in the following script:

Script 10-1

```
1. local drink_A, drink_B

2. set sodas_left to 4
3. set beers_left to 1
4. set vodkas_left to 5

5. --drink for me
6. if sodas_left > 0 then
7.    set drink_A to "soda"
8.    set sodas_left to sodas_left - 1
```

```
 9. else if beers_left > 0 then
10.    set drink_A to "beer"
11.    set beers_left to beers_left - 1
12. else if vodkas_left > 0 then
13.    set drink_A to "Vodka"
14.    set vodkas_left to vodkas_left - 1
15. else
16.    set drink_A to "nothing"
17. end if
18. --drink for a friend
19. if sodas_left > 0 then
20.   set drink_B to "soda"
21.    set sodas_left to sodas_left - 1
22. else if beers_left > 0 then
23.    set drink_B to "beer"
24.    set beers_left to beers_left - 1
25. else if vodkas_left > 0 then
26.    set drink_B to "Vodka"
27.    set vodkas_left to vodkas_left - 1
28. else
29.    set drink_A to "nothing"
30. end if
```

How this script works

Let's examine the preceding script. Lines 2, 3, and 4 set the inventory. Each drink has a variable that indicates how many single servings are left in the category.

Later on, lines 6 through 17 contain the conditional statement block that determines your drink, or what the script calls *drink_A*. At the end of that conditional statement, the inventory has gotten updated to compensate for the drink you got.

Lines 19 through 30 do the same thing, but this time the result assigns a drink value to the *drink_B* variable.

Can this script be made better?

What instantly irritates me about the preceding script is that the two main chunks, lines 6–17 and lines 19–30, are nearly identical! This is wasteful coding, and will simply not do . . .

When you encounter two parts of your script that are very similar, there is usually a way to condense them, and make one of them take care of both tasks.

The two main forms of doing that are subroutines and repeat loops (or a combination of both).

In this case, we could either put the conditional statement into a subroutine and call it twice, or with a bit more thought we can create a list of people you want to get drinks for and loop through that list. Each loop will determine the drink for the next person in the list.

I know we are getting slightly sidetracked here, but we just can't leave the poor script looking like that. So what we'll do is put the conditional statement into a subroutine and call it twice, as shown in Figure 10-4.

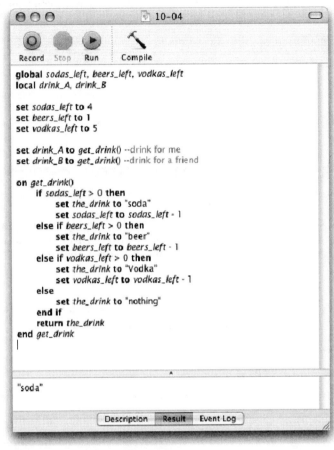

Figure 10-4. The conditional statement has been put in a subroutine. Now, it appears only once but can be called multiple times.

In a real-world situation, I would have wanted to start off by loading the inventory from a database (or user input) and then outputting the final inventory (i.e., after the drinks have been taken) at the end of the script.

Complex Boolean statements

What's important to remember when working with conditional statements is that the part of the statement that lies between the word "if" and the word "then" boils down to one thing: a Boolean value that can be either true or false.

Although the Boolean result may be simple, the logic used to arrive at it may be very complex. Until now we looked at a simple Boolean operation, *sodas_left > 0*, which simply evaluates one number.

Figure 10-5 shows a complex Boolean operation that is used in the conditional statement.

Figure 10-5. A conditional statement using a complex Boolean operation

To make this situation a bit easier to swallow, what I usually do is start by assigning the result of the complex Boolean operation to a well-named variable. Then I can use that variable in the conditional statement instead of the monstrous operation itself. Figure 10-6 shows an example of this.

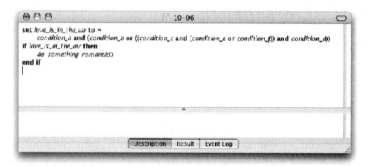

Figure 10-6. The same complex Boolean operation assigned to a variable before being used in a conditional statement

Nested conditional statements

A nested conditional statement is made of multiple conditional statements that are nested in a conditional statement block.

You put forth one condition; if it comes true, the next condition is tested, and so on.

Figure 10-7 shows a simple nested conditional statement.

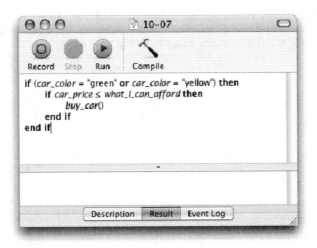

Figure 10-7. A simple nested conditional statement

By the nature of their functionality, some scripts will contain more conditional statement than others. Some scripts contain so many that their entire structure is one huge conditional statement.

One way to make working with complex conditional statements easier to handle is to use small conditional statements and nest them in other conditional statements. At first it may look like a waste of time and lines, but as the script becomes larger and more difficult to handle, you will start seeing the benefits of this style of writing.

Let's look at an example—say that you're in the market for a car. You travel from dealership to dealership and can present your requirements in two different formats:

The first format is this single statement: if you have a car that is yellow or green, uses less than 30 MPG, can fit five, is less than three years old, and costs less than $10,000, I'll take it!

The second format goes like this: do you have cars that are yellow and green?

Hmm, OK, of these cars, do any use less than 30 MPG?

OK now, out of these cars, are any three years old or younger?

And so on . . .

Format 1 is better since it'll get you out of the dealership more quickly. However, since it's in the nature of scripts to change around, what if new requirements pop up?

Let's say that if the car costs more than $8000, it also needs to have a CD changer. While you could build that into your Boolean operation, it would be much simpler to modify your script if the conditional statement is made up of multiple nested statements.

From looking at the two scripts in Figures 10-8 and 10-9, you can see that when you nest conditional statements inside other conditional statements, the script is longer, but it is also easier to read and will be much easier to add to later on.

Figure 10-8. The car search script in one conditional statement with a long Boolean operation

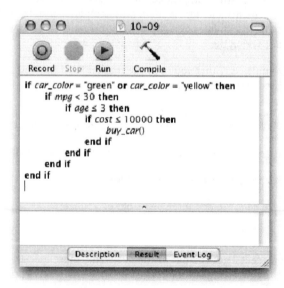

Figure 10-9. The same car search script with the Boolean operation broken down into multiple levels in the conditional block

Another big advantage of spreading out your conditions over multiple nested statements is that you can now add more statements in the different levels of the conditional statement, a thing you couldn't do with one Boolean operation.

Shortcuts

Here are some neat tricks to help you make the most out of conditional statements and save you some typing too.

Condition in a single line

What separates the conditional statement (and the *tell* command) from other control statements such as looping and error capturing (*try*) is that you can start and end it on a single line, like in the following script:

```
if time_left = 0 then set game_over to true
```

This form of conditional statement is useful when the statement is simple and has no foreseen potential for an *else* clause.

One place I use it a lot is when exiting repeat loops.

```
if (count text frames = 0) then exit repeat
```

Unnecessary conditional statements

Sometimes you want to check if a condition is true or false just in order to set the value of a variable to that true or false value. You may write the following:

Script 10-2 (includes the following script)

```
if the_stop_light_color is "green" then
   set walk_now to true
else
   set walk_now to false
end if
```

This does appear to make sense, but it is far too long. Instead try the following:

```
set walk_now to the_stop_light_color is "green"
```

The expression *the_stop_light_color is "green"* evaluates to either true or false. That value can be directly assigned to the *walk_now* variable without a conditional statement.

10

Is it true?

To check whether a Boolean value assigned to a variable is true or false, it isn't necessary to type the full statement. Simply use the variable itself, like this:

Instead of typing

```
if Boolean_variable = true then do_something()
```

type

```
if Boolean_variable then do_something()
```

If you want to find out if the value is false, simply add the *not* operator before the variable.

```
if not tired_yet then write_another_chapter()
```

This last line says that the handler *write_another_chapter* will be called if the variable *tired_yet* is false.

Shorthand writing

Like in other AppleScript statements, there are certain words you can omit that AppleScript will fill in for you. The only problem with this is that when you then switch to doing some programming in another language that doesn't have the same exact shortcut facilities (such as RealBASIC), you have to remember to write everything in.

One such shortcut AppleScript has is the word *then*. Simply omit it, and AppleScript will add it for you when it compiles. The other word you can omit in every control statement is the word after the word *end*.

Try this: start a new script window and write the script in Figure 10-10. Then compile the script, which will end up looking like the one in Figure 10-11.

Figure 10-10. The words *then* in the first line and *if* in the last line have been omitted.

Figure 10-11. AppleScript adds these words as the script compiles.

Power wrap-up

This section summarizes the chapter in an intensive-reference style. Use this part to look up facts related to the chapter without the chatter.

Basic conditional statement

When your script has to decide between executing one set of statements or the other, you use a conditional statement. There are a few ways of writing conditional statements, but they all include the two words "if" and "then."

Here is an example of a simple conditional statement:

Script 10-3 (includes following scripts)

```
if some_boolean_expression = true then
    display dialog "The answer is right"
end if
```

In the preceding example, only if the variable *some_boolean_expression* is true will the line containing the *display dialog* command execute.

The Boolean expression doesn't have to be a variable; it can be a complex Boolean operation, as in this example:

```
if (the_chip contains "G5") or (the_chip contains "G5") and ¬
    the_model contains "Power" and ((the_RAM ≥ 1000) or ¬
(the_MHZ ≥ 1000)) then
    buy_mac()
end if
```

10

No matter how complex, if the expression between *if* and *then* on the first line evaluates as either true or false, it is legal.

The two preceding scripts could have been written using one line only, like this:

```
if some_boolean_expression = true then display dialog ¬
"The answer is right"
```

if-then-else

If the script is going to choose from two options, the *else* part of the statement has to separate those choices, like this:

Script 10-4 (Includes following script)

```
if some_boolean is true then
   --perform these statements
else
   --perform these other statements
end if
```

To allow even more options, you can add branching with additional *else if* lines, like this:

```
if some_boolean is true then
   --perform these statements
else if some_boolean is true then
   --perform these other statements
else if some_boolean is true then
   --perform these other statements
else
   --perform these other statements
end if
```

The final *else* line is not required. If included, it handles all the cases that did not fall within the previous conditions.

Also note that if a variable is already a Boolean, you don't have to include the *is true* or *is false* part, simply use the variable itself, like this:

```
if document_exists then
   display dialog "The answer is right"
end if
```

Or from within an application's *tell* block:

Script 10-5

```
tell application "InDesign CS"
  if (exists of document 1) then
    display dialog (name of document 1)
  else
```

```
        display dialog "Create a document first"
    end if
end tell
```

Details previously . . .

The last part of this chapter is a summary of the entire chapter. For more details on any of the items here, refer to earlier sections in this chapter.

THE ASSEMBLY LINE:
CREATING REPEAT LOOPS

The repeat loop is one of the two concepts that make AppleScript so powerful (the other one being conditional statements).

These loops allow you to perform the same action multiple times. Figure 11-1 shows an example of a simple repeat loop.

Figure 11-1. A simple repeat loop

OK, so this didn't do much; it just beeped. Also, the operation was performed identically each time, without any variation. But, isn't that the idea: an assembly line that performs the same exact operation every time? Yes and no. See, if you have an assembly line in a soda can factory, for instance, you may want your repeat loop to punch in the top of the cans. The operation will be identical, but the can will be a different can every time. Identical cans, but different instances.

Or, what if you need to create a repeat loop that paints the white strips on the road? The road is the same road, but the position of the line changes.

There can in fact be many attributes that change from one repetition to the next to make the production line more intricate.

The most basic form of a repeat loop is this:

```
repeat
  --Do something...
end repeat
```

Notice that the statement starts with the word "repeat" and ends with an *end repeat* line. This is a requirement for all *repeat* statements.

What's sorely missing in the preceding *repeat* statement is a consideration the wizard's apprentice didn't take into account: what will make the repeat loop stop!

There are a few ways to tell AppleScript to stop looping. Some rely on an actual number, and some allow the specific situation to determine the stopping point. For instance, if you loop through folders and do something to each folder, the number of repetitions will depend on the number of folders, which is unknown at the time you write the script.

You can also include one or more statements inside the *repeat* statement block that either exit that repeat loop, or tell AppleScript to continue looping.

Following are the different variations of the *repeat* control statement, followed by a detailed explanation of each one.

From the dictionary

This section lists the different flavors of the repeat loop. These flavors are explained in detail later on in the chapter.

Script 11-1 (including the 6 following scripts)

Repeat forever:

```
repeat
   --statement/s to repeat
end repeat
```

Repeat a specific number of times:

```
repeat n times -- n is an integer
   --statement/s to repeat
end repeat
```

Repeat with a loop variable:

```
repeat with i from start_integer to end_integer-- i changes value ¬
with each loop
   --statement/s to repeat
end repeat
```

Repeat with a loop variable, jumping by intervals other than 1:

```
repeat with i from start_integer to end_integer by step_interval
-- i changes value with each loop by the step_interval
   --statement/s to repeat
end repeat
```

Repeat until a certain Boolean condition becomes true:

```
repeat until boolean_expression
   --statement/s to repeat
end repeat
```

11

Repeat while a certain Boolean condition is true:

```
repeat while boolean_expression
    --statement/s to repeat
end repeat
```

Repeat (forever)

Well, you never would really repeat forever, although I'm sure OS X is made to run continuously for that long . . .

By forever I mean that the *repeat* statement itself doesn't contain any provisions for ending the loop.

While looping forever does have a place in scripting, believe it or not, you can, and should, include an *exit repeat* statement inside the repeat loop block. More on that a bit later.

Just when would you repeat forever?

One instance that comes to mind is a script agent. An agent is a script that stays open and checks for a condition for as long as it's running. It repeats in an endless loop and may look at a hot folder or for a certain application to be running to kick in a process. When the process is over, you may want the script to exit the repeat loop and end, but you may not. You may want the script to continue looping all day waiting for that condition to occur again.

Interrupting a running script

A script that is in the middle of an endless loop can only be interrupted by pressing COMMAND+. (period), or by force quitting using COMMAND+OPTION+ESCAPE, but this isn't necessary.

Exiting a loop programmatically

Another way to use the simple *repeat* statement without specifying an end to it is by including an *exit repeat* statement.

This statement is contained for the most part in a conditional statement. If it isn't, the loop will end after the first repetition.

The advantage of using the *exit repeat* statement instead of some other *repeat* statement types is that the condition can be placed anywhere in the *repeat* block, not stuck in the first line.

Figure 11-2 shows an example of a repeat loop with an *exit repeat* statement inside a conditional statement.

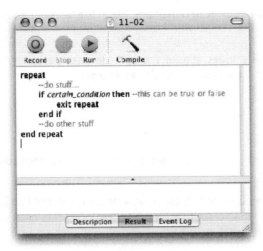

Figure 11-2. A plain repeat loop with a condition to exit the loop

You may be asking yourself what happens if the condition is never met. Well, then AppleScript will run the script forever. It is your job as a scripter to make sure your loops run their course and come to an end if and when appropriate. Remember, *Command+.* (period) will stop a script or quit a script application that's in the foreground. You will need to use that during testing.

Repeat a fixed number of times

This simple repeat variation doesn't offer much support, and leaves most of the work to you. It is useful when you want to perform the same operation with no variation from one loop to the other.

Figure 11-3 shows an example of a repeat loop that will repeat five times.

Figure 11-3. A repeat loop that repeats five times

You can use a variable to vary the number of repetitions, like in the following script:

Script 11-2

```
Display dialog "How many times should I beep?" default answer "5"
Set beep_count to text returned of result as integer
repeat beep_count times
    beep
    delay 1
end repeat
```

The preceding script asks the user to enter a number, and then repeats a *beep* command the number of times dictated by the user.

What's done is that the user's response (which comes as a string) is coerced into an integer. However, there's no verification to make sure the user doesn't cancel or enters a value that cannot be coerced into an integer.

Loop variables

The reason why the previous repeat loop flavor doesn't give us much to work with is that for a repeat loop to be versatile, you usually need at least one variable that will change with each loop.

Let's take a look at the following two examples:

You have a list of phone numbers, and you want to add the area code to the ones that have only seven digits. While we won't get into the details of this script, looking at the loop requirements, we see that each repetition will treat a different number from the list.

You want to write a script that loops through a folder's contents. It then takes every TIFF file and adds it to an image catalog in InDesign. Here we need a variable that will hold the path to a different item in the current folder with every repetition.

AppleScript gives us a couple of ways to integrate that variable into the loop from the outset.

The first one we'll look at is a repeat loop that hands you a counting variable, which holds an integer that changes value with every repetition. The second one is automatically set to the next item in a specified list.

Let's take a closer look at these two repeat loop variations.

Repeat with a variable

Repeat with a variable allows you to specify an integer variable and have that variable increase (or decrease) in value with each repetition, as shown in Figure 11-4.

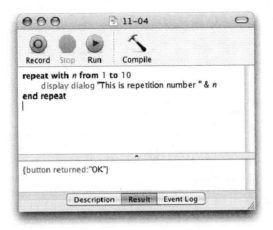

Figure 11-4. The variable *i* increases in value with each repetition, starting with 1 all the way to 10.

This repeat flavor also allows us to play with the way the *repeat* variable increases or decreases. Let's look at a few examples:

Using variables to define the range

As you may imagine, you can use any numbers, or integers stored in variables, to start and end the specified range.

Script 11-3

```
repeat with n from start_integer_variable to end_integer_variable
--do something with n...
end repeat
```

This is useful since you don't always know the number of repetitions you want to perform, and the starting number may not be 1. Many times, you want to treat the first item differently, or start from another number for any other reason.

This is one of the most widely used variations of repeat loops. What often happens is that you need to perform a certain operation on a range of application objects—for instance, all the pages of an InDesign documents, the records in a FileMaker's found set, or all the files in a particular folder. For that, you use the repeat loop along with the *count* command. The *count* command along with the object range returns the number of applicable objects, which in turn becomes your repeat loop's number of repetitions. Figure 11-5 shows an example of this. In the example, the script needs to add the word "folder" to the end of the folder name.

11

Figure 11-5. A repeat loop with a variable used for the range

Changing increments

The first variation of this repeat loop flavor lets you change the increments that the loop variable increases by. In the previous examples, the loop variable increased by 1 each time, but what happens if we increase it by another number? All we have to do is add the *by* argument along with the increments we want to use. Let's look at the following example:

Script 11-4

```
set the_list to {}
repeat with i from 1 to 50 by 5
    set end of the_list to i
end repeat
the_list = {5, 10, 15, 20, 25, 30, 35, 40, 45, 50}
```

If we take this concept a step further, we can create the entire multiplication table, and what the heck, let's make it in HTML:

Script 11-5

```
1. set html to ""
2. set html to html & "<html>" & return
3. set html to html & "<head>" & return
4. set html to html & "<title>Multiplication table</title>" & return
5. set html to html & "</head>" & return
6. set html to html & "<body>" & return
```

```
7. set html to html & "<table border=1 cellpadding=2>" & return
8. set html to html & "<tr>" & return

9. repeat with i from 1 to 10
10.     repeat with j from (1 * i) to (10 * i) by i
11.         set html to html & "<td>"
12.         set html to html & j
13.         set html to html & "</td>"
14.     end repeat
15.     set html to html & "<tr>" & return
16. end repeat
```

Now this is quite a repeat loop. For one, it is two repeat loops nested one inside the other.

The outer repeat loop simply counts from 1 to 10, assigning the loop value to the variable *i*, which becomes the driving force behind the inner repeat loop.

The inner repeat loop uses the variable *j*. What gives *j* the correct integer value for the multiplication table is that every time the loop executes, the start point and end point move up. Here is the inner *repeat* statement the way it appears in the code:

```
repeat with j from (i * 1) to (i * 10) by i
```

In the first loop, the value of the variable *i* is 1, and the inner repeat loop looks like this:

```
repeat with j from 1 to 10 by 1
```

In the second loop the value of *i* is 2, and therefore the *repeat* statement translates into this:

```
repeat with j from 2 to 20 by 2
```

The third loop is where *i* is 3 and the values of *j* are 2, 4, 6, 8 . . . 20:

```
repeat with j from 3 to 30 by 3
```

The values of j are 3, 6, 9, 12 . . . 30 and so on, all the way to the final loop where the value of the variable *i* is 10.

```
repeat with j from 10 to 100 by 10
```

The values of *j* are 10, 20, 30, 40 . . . 100.

Inside the loop, we add the *<td>* tag, followed by the actual value assigned to the variable *j*, followed by the closing *</td>* tag.

Figure 11-6 shows the resulting web page.

11

Figure 11-6.
The web page resulting from the multiplication table script

Counting backwards

AppleScript can also repeat backwards. This means that the value of the *repeat* variable is higher at the start than at the end. To do that, you must use a negative number in the *by* clause:

Script 11-6

```
Repeat with i from 100000 to 1 by -1
Display dialog "Shuttle launch in " & i & " seconds" giving up after 1
End repeat
```

While the preceding script won't land me a job at NASA, it shows how a repeat loop starts high and counts down. Note that it is not enough to specify from high to low numbers; you must add the *by* negative number at the end.

Counting forwards and backwards in the same loop

What if a loop calls for one variable to count both up and down? For that you will need some sort of a rig. You'll need to count up, and have the value of the *repeat* variable reversed inside the loop.

Script 11-7

```
repeat with i from 1 to 10
  set negative_i to -i
end repeat
```

The variable *negative_i* will start from -1 all the way to -10.

Repeat in a list

In many cases what you need is not an integer variable that goes up in value, but rather the value stored in the next item in a list.

For instance, if you have the following list of names:

    {"Ben", "Jen", "Stan"}

Figure 11-7 shows how you can create a variable that will have the next list item in every loop.

Figure 11-7. A repeat loop that repeats in a list

This script will display a dialog box with the value of the variable *the_name* in each repetition.

Naming repeat variables

Notice that before I used single-number variables such as *i* and *j* as the *repeat* variables. I did that because the variable's value had no special meaning other than being an integer. In this case, the variable actually holds a value that's an item from a list. So if the list is called *names_list*, then it's only fitting that the *repeat* variable will be called *the_name*.

Funny variable behavior

In AppleScript, we get used to the fact that an expression always returns its value as a result. When we run the statement *2 + 3*, the result is always 5. Also, when literally asking for a list value, we get the contents of the list item, as shown in Figure 11-8.

11

Figure 11-8. Item 2 of the *name_list* returned "Jen"

While we can count on that in normal AppleScript behavior, it is slightly different when repeating in a list. Look again at the script in Figure 11-7. The line that displays the dialog box goes like this:

```
Display dialog (the_name as string)
```

But wait a minute, isn't the value of *the_name* supposed to be a string? Nope, it isn't.

The value of it is a reference to the list item: item 1 of *name_list*, item 2 of *name_list*, and item 3 of *name_list*. To use it as a string, or any other value class for that matter, you have to coerce it to that class as I did in the script.

In the Panther release of AppleScript, the value of the *repeat* variable *the_name* would still be item 1 *of name_list*, etc. but the *display dialog* command now knows how to evaluate the reference into a string, so the *as string* coercion operation I used is no longer needed.

Another repeat in list example

Back to the name list we looked at earlier. Let's say that you have a report template called `report template.rtf`.

What your script will do is

- Open the template file in TextEdit.
- Set the first word in the document to the person's name.
- Save the document with the person's name plus the word "report."

Here is the script:

Script 11-8

```
set names_list to {"Ben", "Jen", "Stan"}
repeat with the_name in names_list
    set reportFilePath to (path to desktop) & the_name
    set reportTemplatePath to (path to desktop) & "report template.rtf"
    tell application "TextEdit"
        activate
        open file reportTemplatePath
        tell document 1
            set word 1 to the_name
            save in reportFilePath
            close saving no
        end tell
    end tell
end repeat
```

Notice that throughout the script we use the repeat loop variable twice: once to set the report file path and the other time when we do the variable data publishing. Well, sort of . . .

How useful is this, anyway?

In my opinion, repeating in a list isn't all that useful and doesn't save you much time.

What happens most of the time is that you eventually expand on the repeat loop functionality and you end up needing that variable that counts the loops. So here's what you do to get the same functionality without repeating in a list.

Instead of

```
set names_list to {"Ben", "Jen", "Stan"}
repeat with the_name in names_list
--> do something
end repeat
```

try this script:

Script 11-9 (includes previous script)

```
set names_list to {"Ben", "Jen", "Stan"}
repeat with i from 1 to (count names_list)
    set the_name to item i of names_list
--> do something with the_name
end repeat
```

Although the second method is one line longer than the first, it gives you the benefit of a loop variable (*i* in that case), which you will find useful later on.

11

repeat while and repeat until

In some situations, the number of repetitions will be determined by a condition that is fulfilled rather than by a number you know in advance or the number of items in a list.

Using *repeat while* and *repeat until*, you can attach a condition to the repeat loop that will exit the repeat loop when the result of the condition changes. For instance, if we have a cookie jar we're trying to empty (one cookie at a time), the condition is whether the jar is empty or not. Here's how we can script it:

```
Repeat until (jar is empty)
    Eat cookie
End repeat
```

In the preceding script, which won't run on any of my Macs, the condition *jar is empty* comes back false as long as there are still cookies in the jar. As soon as there aren't, the script exits the repeat loop.

Now in the preceding example, we could've theoretically counted the cookies and repeated a number of times that is equal to the number of cookies; however, in some cases, there's no number that can be easily determined in advance. We'll look at a couple of examples later on.

The opposite of repeating while a condition is true is repeating until a condition is true. In this case, we start with the condition being false and loop until it becomes true. This method is the exact opposite of the *repeat while* syntax.

Note that the *repeat while* and *repeat until* methods can be used interchangeably by adding the *not* operator before the condition. You choose one over the other simply by how it sounds and how well it fits what you do.

The syntax for the two examples goes as follow:

```
repeat while (condition is true)
-- do something
end repeat
```

The opposite of that is

```
repeat until (condition is true)
-- do something
end repeat
```

Figures 11-9 and 11-10 show simple examples of *repeat until* and *repeat while*.

In Figure 11-9 we have a virtual pile of playing cards. We want to see how many cards we flip before the card total reaches over 100. So we have a variable that adds the card values, and a variable that counts the cards. The script will loop *until* the cards total reaches 100, and will return the number of cards flipped so far.

Figure 11-9. Repeating until the total card value reaches over 100

In the script shown in Figure 11-10, the loop simply checks whether the file exists. When distilling a PostScript file into a PDF using Acrobat Distiller 5, for instance, Acrobat Distiller won't tell you when the PDF is complete. This loop can come in handy for delaying the script until the PDF file has been created.

Figure 11-10. Repeating while the file doesn't exist

The script in Figure 11-11 is a modification of the script in Figure 11-9. It repeats while the card total is less than 21. Look at the record that the script returns: it contains the card count, the total card value, and the cards themselves.

The problem? We asked the script to loop while the card value is *less* than 21, but the card value at the end is *over* 21. This happens because when the repeat loop condition executes, the card value has already been raised above 21! At that point, all the repeat loop can do is stop, but the damage has already been done, and the card total has climbed beyond 21.

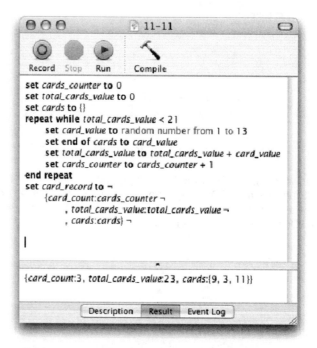

Figure 11-11. Does the *repeat until* continue one loop too many?

So how do we fix this problem? We use a simple repeat loop with a slightly more complex conditional statement, as shown here:

Script 11-10

```
repeat
    set card_value to random number from 1 to 13
    if (total_cards_value + card_value) ≥ 21 then exit repeat
    set end of cards to card_value
    set total_cards_value to total_cards_value + card_value
    set cards_counter to cards_counter + 1
end repeat
```

In the preceding script, the condition to stop the repeat isn't a part of the *repeat* statement, but rather a separate *if* statement. It checks whether the total goes above 21 before it actually adds the new card to the total.

Here's a neat example of the *repeat until* command. This example shows a script that arranges files in folders for archiving. The script has to make sure that each folder has files whose accumulated file size is almost, but not quite, 600MB (or any other specified size) so that they can fit on a disk.

The script combines two loops.

Script 11-11

```
1. set max_folder_size_in_mb to 600
2. set images_folder to path to pictures folder from user domain ¬
as string
3. set archive_folder to "Macintosh HD:archive:"
4. set subfolder_counter to 1
5. tell application "Finder"
6.    repeat until (count files in folder images_folder) is 0
7.        set folder_name to "folder " & subfolder_counter
8.        set archive_sub_folder to make new folder¬
          in folder archive_folder with properties {name:folder_name}
9.        set image_list to list folder ¬
          alias images_folder without invisibles
10.       set file_list to {}
11.       set total_MB to 0
12.       set file_counter to 1
13.       repeat while ((total_MB is less than max_folder_size_in_mb))
14.           set fileName to item file_counter of image_list
15.           set file_size to size of ¬
              (info for alias (images_folder & fileName))
16.           set file_size_in_MB to (file_size / 1024 / 1024)
17.           set total_MB to total_MB + file_size_in_MB
18.           set file_counter to file_counter + 1
19.           move file fileName of folder images_folder ¬
              to archive_sub_folder
20.           if (count files in folder images_folder) is 0 then
21.               return
22.           end if
23.       end repeat
24.       set subfolder_counter to subfolder_counter + 1
25.    end repeat
26. end tell
```

The first loop in the preceding script starts at line 6. It will repeat until the folder we're archiving is empty.

Notice that there's no mention of how many files there are or should be, only a simple condition: keep looping *while* there are more than zero files.

The second repeat loop starts on line 14, and relies on a variable called *total_MB*. This variable is a real value and is being added to incrementally. The size of every file that the script processes is added to the *total_MB* variable. The second loop repeats *while* the value of the *total_MB* variable is under the specified amount in the *max_folder_size_in_mb* variable.

In this script we also make use of two counters: the *file_counter* variable counts the files, and the *subfolder_counter* counts the subfolders.

Other ways of counting loops

The looping method of repeat with variables from x to y is the only one that has a built-in loop counter. This does not mean that you can't create your own loop counter.

It is common practice to use a counter variable in some instances with any of the other repeat loop flavors.

What you do is start by assigning an initial value to your counter variable, and then increase it, decrease it, multiply it, or divide it by any value you want.

This method gives you the most flexibility over your counter variable.

Here's an example:

```
Set counter_variable to 1
repeat
  set counter_variable to counter_variable * 2 - 3
    do something with counter_variable
end repeat
```

The variable *counter_variable* will have the following values: -1, -5, -13, -29, -125, -253, -509, etc.

Why would you need such an odd set of numbers? Well, I doubt you'll ever need this one, but it does demonstrate what flexibility you have with your counter variable, should you ever need it.

Avoid looping when possible

Although the repeat loop is a staple we can't do without, its use should be limited as much as possible. The reason for that is speed and efficiency.

What you can use instead of a repeat loop in some cases is the *whose* clause. The *whose* clause targets multiple items at the same time and allows you to apply an action to all of them together much faster than if you had a repeat loop target each one individually. Imagine standing in front of 100 people all wearing different color hats and having to ask all the red-hat wearers to take off their hats. With a repeat loop it would be first person with red hat, take it off; second person with red hat, take it off; third person with red hat, take it off, etc.

With a *whose* clause, it would be every person whose hat is red, take your hats off.

In the following example, we will delete all files that have the word "temp" in the name. First, the repeat version:

```
tell application "Finder"
    tell folder theFolder
        repeat with i from 1 to (count files)
            if name of file i contains "temp" then
                delete file i
            end if
        end repeat
    end tell
end tell
```

Or, the smart version that uses the *whose* clause:

Script 11-12 (includes previous script)

```
tell application "Finder"
    delete every file of folder theFolder whose name contains "temp"
end tell
```

It's not only that the code is shorter and more to the point, but the execution time will be shorter—much shorter in situations where there are many objects to loop through.

Power wrap-up

This section summarizes the chapter in an intensive-reference style. Use this part to look up facts related to the chapter without the chatter.

A simple repeat loop

The simplest repeat loop will repeat until stopped either by an *exit repeat* statement inside the loop, or by the user pressing COMMAND+. (period). With every repetition the script will be executing the statements between the *repeat* line and the *end repeat* line.

```
repeat
    --Do something...
end repeat
```

11

Exiting a repeat loop

You exit a repeat loop with the *exit repeat* statement. This statement usually sits in a conditional statement that determines when the loop has reached its potential. Here's how the *exit repeat* statement is used:

```
repeat
   --Do something...
   if time_to_stop_loop is true then
       exit repeat
   end if
end repeat
```

Repeating a fixed number of times

Use the following version of the *repeat* statement to repeat a specific number of times:

```
repeat 12 times
   --statements to execute repeatedly
end repeat
```

Loop variables

Loop variables are variables that automatically change with each repetition. In the following script, the variable *i* is the loop variable. It will start with the value of 1 and increment by 1 with every repetition. The loop will stop when the value of *i* has reached the number indicated at the end of the *repeat* line.

```
repeat with i from 1 to 10
   --The value of the variable i starts with 1
   --and grows by 1 with each loop
end repeat
```

Another example:

```
repeat with i from 1 to (count characters of user_name)
   --statement to execute repeatedly
end repeat
```

We can use the *by* parameter to change the *repeat* variable to any other number. The loop in the following script will have 20 repetitions:

```
repeat with i from 5 to 100 by 5
   --The value of the variable i starts with 5 and grows by 5 up to 100.
end repeat
```

You can also count backwards.

Script 11-13

```
repeat with i from 20 to 0 by -2
   --The value of the variable i starts with 20 and
   --decreases by 2 until it reaches 0.
end repeat
```

Repeat in a list

When you have a list whose items need to be processed in order, you can make the loop variable take on the value of the next item in the list every time. In the following example the value of the loop variable will be a different value from the *employee_names* list:

Script 11-14

```
set employee_names to {"Jena","Jack","Bonnie","Frank"}
repeat with the_name in employee_names
   --The value of the variable the_name
   -- starts with "Jena" in the first loop, then "Jack", etc.
end repeat
```

repeat while

You can repeat while a certain condition is true. This allows you to repeat the execution of statements without setting a predefined loop count. The following script will loop as long as there's an open document in FileMaker Pro. Since the repeating statement closes the front open document, all documents will be eventually closed, the Boolean expression *document 1 exists* will evaluate as false, and the loop will conclude.

Script 11-15

```
tell application "FileMaker Pro"
   repeat while (document 1 exists)
      close document 1
   end repeat
end tell
```

repeat until

The *repeat until* flavor of the repeat loop works the opposite way from the *repeat while* statement. You supply the repeat loop with a Boolean expression, and as soon as that expression evaluates as true, the loop will stop.

Script 11-16

```
tell application "FileMaker Pro"
   repeat until (count documents = 0)
      close document 1
   end repeat
end tell
```

11

Using counter variables

Counter variables are like loop variables, but you, the scripter, decide on their value. The typical counter variable will increase in value by 1 with every loop. You can have multiple counters that serve different purposes, as in the following script:

Script 11-17

```
set year_counter to 0
set dog_year_counter to 0
repeat
    set year_counter to year_counter + 1
    set dog_year_counter to dog_year_counter + 7
    set the_message to "After " & year_counter & ¬
    " years, your dog is really " & dog_year_counter & " years old."
    try
        display dialog the_message
    on error -128 -- user canceled
        exit repeat
    end try
end repeat
```

Avoiding loops

When automating tasks in applications, try to avoid using repeat loops in favor of using the *whose* clause. Besides ending up with a shorter and cleaner script, the script will also execute faster. The following two scripts perform the same action of changing the label of files that are over two weeks old. The first one will use a repeat loop and the second will use the *whose* clause.

Script 11-18

```
set the_folder to "Macintosh HD:Images Folder:"
tell application "Finder"
    repeat with i from 1 to (count files of folder the_folder)
        if (creation date of file i of folder the_folder) > ¬
            ((current date) - (days * 14)) then
            set label index of file i of folder the_folder to 1
        end if
    end repeat
end tell
```

And the *whose* clause version:

Script 11-19

```
set the_folder to "Macintosh HD:Images Folder:"
tell application "Finder"
    tell (every file of folder the_folder whose creation date > ¬
        ((current date) - (days * 14)))
        set label index of it to 1
    end tell
end tell
```

Details previously . . .

The last part of this chapter is a summary of the entire chapter. For more details on any of the items here, refer to earlier sections in the chapter.

Pick a city

New York
Providence
Atlanta
San Francisco
Seattle

Provide your information

Name ✓
  Mr.
  Ms.

Phone

E-mail

☐ New user

Happy

Help   Cancel

Colors

This chapter details the features related to user interaction. In various situations you need to get the user involved during the execution of your script.

While AppleScript does provide ways for the user to interact with the script and provide some input during script operation, these interaction facilities are minimal. AppleScript was designed for accessing data and manipulating it, and therefore doesn't include robust interface tools. If your solution calls for a more complex interface than the commands provided by the AppleScript (and detailed in this chapter), you have to look into other tools. These tools start from third-party scripting additions such as 24U that allow you to design more robust dialog boxes. To create solutions that include multiple complex windows with controls such as pop-up menus, images, movies, etc., you should look into using a development tool such as FaceSpan or the more complicated AppleScript Studio. Both FaceSpan and AppleScript Studio are explained in this chapter.

The best example for user interaction in AppleScript is, perhaps, the *display dialog* command, which can display a message, request the user to enter text, or click a button.

The *display dialog* command and other user interaction commands are all a part of the Standard Additions scripting additions that come installed as part of the Mac OS.

display dialog

The *display dialog* scripting addition is one of the most useful commands, and one of the first you will try in AppleScript, or in any other programming language.

The Standard Additions dictionary defines two display dialog–related items: the *display dialog* command and the dialog reply record.

From the dictionary: display dialog command

Following is the Standard Additions dictionary definition for *display dialog*:

```
display dialog: Display a dialog box, optionally requesting user input
    display dialog  plain text  -- the text to display in dialog box
        [default answer  plain text]  -- the default editable text
        [buttons  a list of plain text] ¬
         -- a list of up to three button names
        [default button  number or string]
            -- the name or number of the default button
        [with icon  number or string]
            -- the name or ID of the icon to display...
        [with icon  stop/note/caution] ¬
        -- ...or one of these system icons
        [giving up after  integer]
            -- number of seconds to wait before automatically dismissing ¬
            dialog
    Result:   dialog reply
        -- a record containing the button clicked and text entered ¬
        (if any)
```

From the dictionary: dialog reply

The following is the specification of the dialog reply record:

```
Class dialog reply: Reply record for the 'display dialog' command
Properties:
    button returned  plain text  [r/o]
        -- name of button chosen (empty if 'giving up after'
was supplied and dialog timed out)
    text returned  plain text  [r/o]
        -- text entered (present only if 'default answer' was supplied)
    gave up  boolean  [r/o]
        -- Did the dialog time out? (present only if 'giving up after' ¬
was supplied)
```

The most basic form

The basic form of the command allows you to display a simple message in a dialog box along with two buttons, OK and Cancel. Figure 12-1 shows that basic *display dialog* command and its resulting record, and Figure 12-2 shows the dialog box itself.

Figure 12-1. The script shows the simple *display dialog* command. The Result tab in the lower split view shows the record AppleScript returned once the user clicked OK.

Figure 12-2. The dialog box that was displayed when the script ran

If you look at the script result in the Result tab in Figure 12-1, you will notice that the result is a record with a single item. The label is button returned, and the value is "OK". This record will actually have more items in it when we add more parameters to the *display dialog* command.

For now, we can see that the button returned (the button the user clicked) was the OK button.

The erroneous Cancel button

Let's try to run the script and click the Cancel button.

Hmm . . . where's the result? No record this time? What happened is that AppleScript generates an error when the Cancel button is clicked. We can get more information about it if we trap it using the *try . . .on error* control block.

Create a new script and copy the text from the script in Figure 12-3.

Figure 12-3. Trapping the Cancel button error using the *try* block

Now run the script and click the Cancel button to the first dialog box. This will generate an error.

As explained in detail in Chapter 15, if you place an identifier after the *on error* line, AppleScript will create a variable with that identifier containing the error message. In simple terms, the variable *error_text*, which could have been *x* for all intents and purposes, will get the text of the error message.

The second dialog box will display that text. This will be, in effect, our own error message dialog box.

As you can see for yourself in the dialog box shown in Figure 12-4, the error AppleScript returned was a *User Canceled* error. This error has an error number of -128.

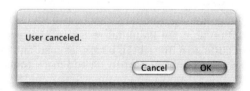

Figure 12-4. The dialog box showing the error message

Custom buttons

By default, AppleScript gives you the OK and Cancel buttons. However, you can easily define one, two, or three buttons of your own.

To define buttons, we use the *buttons* argument followed by a list of button names as strings. Each string will become a button.

A list with more than three items will generate a parameter error, and an empty list will prompt AppleScript to use the default OK and Cancel buttons.

When running the script in Figure 12-5, the dialog box shown in Figure 12-6 will be displayed.

Figure 12-5. You can create your own dialog buttons.

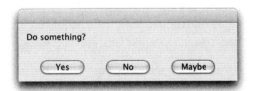

Figure 12-6. The dialog box with the custom buttons

If you use text that is too long for the button, AppleScript will produce a dialog box with wider buttons to try and accommodate your text. All buttons are stretched equally, and the widest button you will get can have about 20 characters.

There's no way to change the type font size or style of the dialog box. For that kind of control, you need to upgrade your skill to the "everything is possible" land of AppleScript Studio, FaceSpan 4.0, or other third-party scripting additions.

12

Default button

What's missing from the dialog box in Figure 12-6 is a button that will execute when the *RETURN* key is pressed. This is called the default button.

You can turn a button into the default button by using either the name or sequential number of one of the dialog box's buttons.

Running the script in Figure 12-7 will produce the dialog box shown in Figure 12-8.

Figure 12-7. The default button is specified.

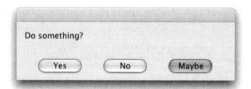

Figure 12-8. The dialog box with a default button

The *default button* argument may also take an integer between 1 and 3. 1 would be the leftmost button in the dialog box. This means that to get the same result as shown in Figure 12-8, you could have specified the default button as 3 instead of "Maybe".

Deciding which button is the default one can play an important role. What you have to assume is that for the most part, people don't read dialog boxes. There's even a phrase that says "It's a Mac, just click OK . . ." This aspect of human nature forces you to make the default button the button with the least harsh consequences. For instance, the default button in a dialog box that reminds users for the last time that the script is about to erase their hard disk should be the Cancel button, not the OK button.

Showing icons in dialog boxes

The right icon in a dialog box is a bit like the score in a movie: it sets the mood. A dialog box that informs the user that the process has completed should probably have the note sign, while alerting the user that something did or might go wrong can be aided with the stop icon.

There are four icon choices in all:

- Stop
- Note
- Caution
- And, the default choice, having no icon at all

You specify an icon by adding the *with icon* argument to the *display dialog* command, followed by the choice of icon.

For example:

    Display dialog "Are you sure you want to do this?" with icon stop

Notice that the word "stop" isn't a string; instead it's a constant defined in the *display dialog* standard scripting addition.

You can also specify an icon by number. The number 0 will give you the stop icon, the number 1 will display the note, and 2 will show the yellow-triangle caution sign.

Getting text input from the user

Beginning programmers derive special satisfaction from getting information back from users, and AppleScript makes that real easy to do.

All you need is to add a *default answer* parameter to your *display dialog* command, followed by a string. When you run the script shown in Figure 12-9, AppleScript will show you the dialog box that appears in Figure 12-10.

Figure 12-9. A command that will display a dialog box with a user text input field, shown in Figure 12-10

12

Figure 12-10. A simple dialog box with a text input field

Specifying the default text parameter in the *display dialog* command will tell AppleScript to add the input field to the dialog box. The string you supplied as part of the default text parameter is the text that appears by default in the field when the dialog box is displayed.

Out of the box, AppleScript allows only a single text field. With some creativity, you can stretch this field a bit, but you only get one.

There are a few ways to create custom dialog boxes. You may be able to find a third-party scripting addition with some more dialog box support. One such scripting addition is 24U from 24U Software (www.24usoftware.com/).

My favorite way to create custom dialog boxes is to create a standalone AppleScript Studio shell application. The application runs in the background, and has a few windows that can be shown or hidden.

Using user-entered text

Notice the result panel in Figure 12-9. Until now, the result record had a single item labeled *button returned*. Now, we have a new item added on: *text returned*.

The *text returned* item of the dialog reply record contains a string that is the text the user typed.

Only dialog box commands that include the *default text* parameter will have the *text returned* item in the dialog reply record.

Later on in this chapter we will look at different ways to validate the text users enter.

How long do dialog boxes display?

Dialog boxes may display forever when shown outside an application's *tell* block. Inside a *tell* block, the dialog box will expire after 120 seconds, or a different amount of time if specified using the *timeout* block.

You can, however, take control over the length of time the dialog box lingers by means of the *give up* parameter.

Consider the following *display dialog* command:

```
display dialog "Click this within ten seconds!" giving up after 10
```

If you clicked the OK button within ten seconds, the dialog would return this result:

    {button returned:"OK", gave up:false}

Otherwise, the dialog box would automatically close itself, and the result would be:

    {button returned:"", gave up:true}

As you can see, the use of the *giving up after* parameter is responsible for the *gave up* item in the dialog reply record.

The value of the *gave up* parameter is Boolean, and it is true if the dialog gave up since no one clicked any button, or false if the user clicked a button.

Following is an example of how the *giving up after* parameter can be used for speed-quizzing:

Script 12-1

```
set q to display dialog "5472 ÷ 57 =" buttons {"56", "76", "96"} ¬
    giving up after 7
if (gave up of q is true) then
    set qResponse to "Not fast enough!"
else
    if button returned of q is "96" then
        set qResponse to "You got it!"
    else
        set qResponse to "Wrong answer"
    end if
end if
display dialog qResponse
```

The preceding example places the dialog reply in the variable *q*. The script counts on the fact that the dialog reply record will contain a *gave up* item that will have a Boolean value.

More about dialog boxes

Although you can only display a single text field when including the default answer parameter, you do have some play with that text field.

The first thing you can do is to make the user text field larger.

To make the text field wider, force the button to be wider. You can do that by adding anywhere between 10 and 15 spaces before and after the name of one of the buttons.

You only need to pad one button since AppleScript will automatically make all buttons as wide as the widest one.

Running the script that follows produces the dialog box shown in Figure 12-11.

12

Script 12-2

```
display dialog "" default answer "" ¬
    buttons {"          yes              ", "Hmm", "No"}
```

Figure 12-11. A wide dialog box thanks to fake-wide buttons

Making the text field hold multiple lines is even easier. All you have to do is add a few returns in the *default answer* parameter's string.

The following script line produces a dialog box with an input field that has five lines, shown in Figure 12-12.

Script 12-3

```
display dialog "" default answer (return & return & return & return ¬
    & return)
```

Figure 12-12. A multiline text input box

You can also create a mini-form and then parse-out the returned text. This is not, however, a very reliable form.

The script that follows produces the dialog box shown in Figure 12-13.

Script 12-4

```
set form to ""
set form to form & "Name: xxxxxx" & return
set form to form & "Phone: xxx-xxx-xxxx" & return
set form to form & "E-mail: me@mac.com"
display dialog "Please enter your information:" default answer form
```

Figure 12-13. A dialog box acting as a form

Validating user-entered text

The nature of asking the user to enter data involves expecting a certain type of data back. When the data you expect is a string, such as the user's name, a city, or a company name, there shouldn't be any problems, since AppleScript returns a string as the *text returned* item in the dialog reply.

You may, however, run into issues when you expect the user to enter a value that has to be later coerced into a valid date, an integer, or a string with special formatting such as an e-mail address or URL.

The method I found most effective is to put the dialog box inside an endless repeat loop that won't relent until the user either enters a conforming string or cancels.

As an example, let's imagine that we want the user to enter a meeting date and that the date, besides being a valid date, has to be in the future.

What we'll need is a variable that will hold the final date.

We start the script by creating the loop, initializing the date variable, and displaying the dialog box:

```
set date_is_ok to false
set the_date to missing value
repeat
    set date_dialog to display dialog "Enter date" default answer ""
    ...more script here
end repeat
```

Next, we will try to coerce the string the user typed into a date. If successful, we will check whether the date is after today's date.

If it is, we will release the user from eternal bondage and exit the repeat loop.

If anything goes wrong, then the user is requested to reenter the date, and the loop repeats again.

Notice in the following script that we also put the initial dialog box in a *try* statement in case the user wants to cancel.

12

355

Script 12-5

```
1. set the_date to missing value
2. repeat
3.    try
4.       set date_dialog to display dialog "Enter date" ¬
           default answer ""
5.       set user_date to text returned of date_dialog
6.         try
7.           set the_date to date user_date
8.           if the_date comes after (current date) then
9.              exit repeat
10.           end if
11.         end try
12.         display dialog "Reenter date" buttons {"OK"} ¬
               default button 1 with icon 0
13.      on error
14.         --User canceled...
15.          return
16.    end try
17. end repeat
```

So, the *try* statement that extends from line 2 to line 15 is the *try* statement that checks that the user didn't cancel.

The *try* statement that extends from line 5 to line 10 is responsible for capturing the error generated in the event that the string the user typed doesn't want to be coerced into a date class. There's no *on error* in this case; the repeat loop simply doesn't end. Also, the *if* statement that starts on line 7 doesn't have an *else* clause. If the condition isn't fulfilled, the repeat loop simply makes another revolution.

We can take this script a step further and check once more with the user that the date AppleScript coerced his/her string into is indeed the date s/he intended.

We do that by inserting yet another layer containing a dialog box and a conditional (*if*) statement. The conditional statement will simply check to see if the button returned is Keep, which keeps the date, or Change, which changes it.

Following is the script with the new portion added on:

Script 12-6

```
1. set the_date to missing value
2. set dialog_text to "Enter date"
3. set dialog_icon to -1
4. repeat
5.    try
6.       set date_dialog to display dialog dialog_text ¬
              default answer "" with icon dialog_icon
7.       set user_date to text returned of date_dialog
8.         try
```

```
9.        set the_date to date user_date
10.        if the_date comes after (current date) then
11.            set msg to "You've entered the following date:" & ¬
12.                return & (date string of the_date) & ¬
13.                return & "Keep it or change it?"
14.            display dialog msg buttons {"Change", "Keep"} ¬
                    with icon 1
15.            if button returned of result is "Keep" then
16.                exit repeat
17.            else
18.                set dialog_icon to 1
19.            end if
20.        end if
21.        on error
22.            set dialog_icon to 0
23.        end try
24.        set dialog_text to "Re-enter date"
25.        --Following line no longer needed:
26.        --display dialog "Reenter date" buttons {"OK"} ¬
                    default button 1 with icon 0
27.    on error
28.        --User canceled...
29.        return
30.    end try
31. end repeat
```

Hmm . . . looks a bit different. The other change I made in the last script is that I put the initial dialog box's icon and message parameters in variables. The icon and message will change based on the different situations that the script encounters. For instance, initially we want the message to be just "Enter date", and we want no icon. Instead of creating a whole other dialog box statement with no icon, I set the icon to -1, which achieves the same result.

If the date checks OK, but the user chooses to change it rather than to keep it, then the text will read "Re-enter text", but the icon will be the calm note icon. However, if the user flunked on the entry and the returned text failed to be coerced into a string, then we will change the icon to 0, which will display the stop icon.

The nice thing is that we do all that with one dialog box. This is also better, since it makes the same impression with one instead of two dialog boxes.

Alert handler

One more dialog box–related thing I include in my script is the *alert* handler.

It so happens that a dialog style that repeats quite often is what I call alert. It is a simple dialog with one OK button and a stop icon. For this dialog box I create a special handler called *alert*, which has a single parameter: the text to display. I call that parameter *msg* (short for message).

12

> *I would normally prefer to stay away from shorthand and personal acronyms. They cause general confusion, and if you manage to remember what you meant two years ago when you wrote the script, your replacement certainly won't. Unless this is what you're aiming for, which is a language my ASP programmer buddy Steve Adler calls JSL (short for **J**ob **S**ecurity **L**anguage), you should spell things out AMAP (**A**s **M**uch **A**s **P**ossible).*
>
> *Acronyms are perfectly acceptable, however, when they are a part of a well-defined naming convention.*

Here's what my handler and the handler call look like:

Script 12-7

```
alert("Did it again!")--the call

on alert(msg)
    display dialog msg buttons {"OK"} default button 1 with icon 0
end alert
```

Now I could certainly spice it up a bit and add more parameters, such as one for the icon, etc. But the idea of my alert handler is that it's very simple. I have other dialog-related handlers that include more options. Not this one.

choose from list

The *choose from list* command is a scripting addition (part of the Standard Additions collection) that allows you to display a special dialog box that lists a number of strings. You can then choose one or more items from the list.

The dialog box has two buttons, which always perform the same OK/Cancel function; however, you can customize the titles of these buttons.

You can also determine which items are selected by default.

From the dictionary

The following is the dictionary specification of the *choose from list* command:

```
choose from list: Allows user to select an item from a list of strings
choose from list  a list of plain text  -- a list of strings
to display (an empty list if no selection)
[with prompt  plain text]
    -- the prompt to appear at the top of the list selection dialog
[default items  a list of plain text]  ¬
-- list of strings to initially select
```

```
[OK button name  plain text]  -- the name of the OK button
[cancel button name  plain text]  -- the name of the Cancel button
[multiple selections allowed  boolean]  -- Allow multiple items to be ¬
selected?
[empty selection allowed  boolean]
    -- Can the user make no selection and then choose OK?
Result:  a list of plain text  -- the list of strings chosen
Choose from list result
```

The Choose from List dialog box has two buttons: OK and Cancel. Although you can customize the titles of these buttons, you can't add buttons or change the function of these buttons.

The OK button, which is always the button on the right and the default button, will always return a list. By default, this list is always going to be a one-item list. You can use parameters (shown later on) to allow an empty selection or a multiple-item selection.

Clicking the Cancel button, however, will return a false result. The reason for that, I assume, is to spare you from a record result with the list and button in separate items, like in the dialog reply record.

It is, however, a bit frustrating not knowing the value class of the result you're expecting. This situation forces you to first check if you got a false answer. You can do that with one of these two solutions:

1. Check if the result is false:

```
set item_choice to choose from list {1, 2, 3}
if item_choice is false then
   --Cancel clicked
else
   --OK clicked
end if
```

2. Check if the result is a list:

Script 12-8 (includes two previous scripts)

```
set item_choice to choose from list {1, 2, 3}
if class of item_choice is list then
   --OK clicked
else
   --Cancel clicked
end if
```

12

Using choose from list

In its simplest form, the *choose from list* command takes a single parameter: the list you want the user to choose items from.

The result is always a list. If nothing is chosen, which is a possibility, the command returns an empty list. If the user selects one item, then the result is a single-item list.

Following is an example of the simplest use of the *choose from list* command. Figure 12-14 shows the dialog box that the following script line produces.

```
choose from list {"a", "b", "c"}
```

Figure 12-14. The simplest Choose from List dialog box

Notice how the list expands to fit the number of items.

Custom title

The first thing you will want to change about this dialog is the title. You do that with the *prompt* parameter.

For example:

```
choose from list {"a", "b", "c"} with prompt "Pick a letter"
```

Figure 12-15 shows the dialog box resulting from this script.

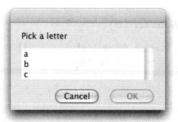

Figure 12-15. A Choose from List dialog box with a custom prompt message

Default selection

If there are items that you want to already have selected when the dialog box displays, you can specify them with the *default items* parameter.

In the following example, the user has to pick from a list of five cities. A property called *previous_city* captures the selection the user made the previous time the script ran.

This time, we will display the list, but have the city that was previously chosen selected by default.

Figure 12-16 shows the dialog box resulting from the following script:

Script 12-9

```
property previous_city : ""
set city_list to ¬
    {"New York", "Providence", "Atlanta", "San Francisco", "Seattle"}
set the_city to choose from list city_list with prompt ¬
    "Pick a city" default items {previous_city}
set previous_city to the_city as string
```

Figure 12-16. The second time this script ran, the list item "Providence" was selected by default.

Selection restriction

The *choose from list* command allows you to restrict the selection the user can make. You can choose to allow or disallow the selection of multiple items, and allow or disallow the user to select nothing. By default, the user must choose one item, and one item only.

To allow the user to select multiple items, set *multiple selections allowed* to true. This can be done by specifying the value true after the parameter, or having the parameter follow the word "with":

Script 12-10

```
set state_list to {"NY", "RI", "GA", "CA", "WA"}
set chosen_states to choose from list state_list with multiple ¬
selections allowed
--> -- Result: {"RI", "GA", "WA"}
```

In the preceding script, the user selected three items: RI, GA, and WA.

In a similar fashion, you can allow the user to click *OK* while making no selection at all.

12

Now, about selecting nothing, the user can always click Cancel, but by default, if the user hasn't picked any item from the list, the OK button will be disabled. You can allow the user to pick no items and still click OK with the *empty selection allowed* parameter.

```
set chosen_states to choose from list state_list with empty selection ¬
allowed
```

If the user selected noting and clicked OK, the result would be an empty list:

```
--> {}
```

Customizing buttons

The *choose from list* command has two buttons: OK and Cancel. As discussed earlier, the function and position of these buttons are set. The right-side button will return a list containing the selected items, and the left-side button will always return the value false.

You can, however, change the title of these buttons. To do that you can use the *OK button name* and *cancel button name* parameters. Each one of these parameters is followed with a string containing the new title for the button.

The following script will display the Choose from List dialog box shown in Figure 12-17.

Script 12-11

```
set state_list to {"NY", "RI", "GA", "CA", "WA"}
set chosen_states to choose from list state_list ¬
    OK button name "Make a Pick" cancel button name "Na..."
```

Figure 12-17. Choose from list with custom buttons

Choosing finder items

The Standard Additions give us a few ways to allow the user to choose files, folders, disks, etc.

Although they are user interaction functions and are discussed in the upcoming text, they will be covered extensively in the file management realm in Chapter 13.

Common results

All file-related *choose* commands, with the exception of *choose application*, return an alias to the chosen file.

You can ask to get the result returned as a string simply by adding the *as string* coercion parameter at the end of the command.

Operating system version

It's important to note that, while the command and result remain the same no matter which Mac OS you use, the look of the dialog box will change. OS X 10.1 will show the generic file-list dialog box, Jaguar (OS X 10.2) will let you choose a file using the outline style view, and Panther (OS X 10.3) adds the sidebar to the left of the Finder windows.

choose file

The *choose file* command has many uses. It allows the user to specify a file using the Open dialog box.

From the dictionary

The following text is the dictionary definition of the *choose file* command:

```
choose file: Choose a file on a disk or server
    choose file
        [with prompt  plain text]
            -- a prompt to be displayed in the file chooser
        [of type  a list of plain text]
            -- restrict the files shown to only these file types
            [default location  alias]  -- the default file location
            [invisibles  boolean]
                -- Show invisible files and folders? (default is true)
            [multiple selections allowed  boolean]
                -- Allow multiple items to be selected? (default is false)
        Result:   alias  -- to the chosen file
```

Result of choose file

The *choose file* command will return either a list, an alias, or an error, depending on the user action and parameters.

First off, the dialog box will generate a "user canceled" error if the user clicks the Cancel button.

12

If the user clicks OK, then the command will return a single alias by default. However, if the *multiple selections allowed* parameter is set to true, then the result will be a list of aliases, even if the user chose only one file.

That means that you probably have to put your *choose file* command in a *try* block, and know whether to anticipate a list of aliases or a single alias based on your use of the *multiple selections allowed* parameter.

When to use?

The *choose file* command is the AppleScript version of the Open dialog box. Not that the command opens anything, but it does present the user with the Open dialog box and allows him/her to specify a file. From that point on, what happens to the file is up to you and your script.

You use *choose file* when you need the user to specify a path to a file that the script has to deal with.

Allowing the user to choose a file has the same sort of effect as a script droplet. The user has the ability to specify a file that the script will then process.

Imagine you create a script that opens an InDesign file, exports all images, and catalogs them.

Sure, if you have a strict filing convention and folder hierarchy, the script may be able to find the files that need processing. However, if the file can be any InDesign file from any-where on the hard disk or network, you will want to use the *choose file* command to allow users to specify the file themselves.

One of the most important parameters of the *choose file* command is the ability to restrict the user to choosing files of specific file types. Just as when you use the *open* command from an application you are restricted to choosing files that this application supports, the same is true for the restrictions you can put on your script's users, and what files they can choose with the *choose file* command. More details on that later on.

The basic command

To invoke the basic *choose file* command, you don't need to specify any parameters, just the command itself.

This script line will produce the dialog box shown in Figure 12-18:

```
choose file
```

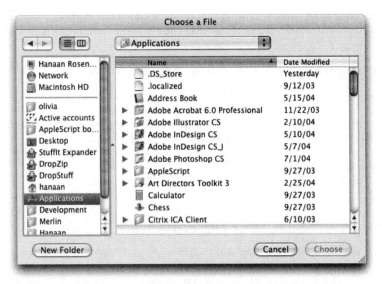

Figure 12-18. The basic dialog box produced by the *choose file* command

Custom prompt

The first parameter you can change is the prompt. The prompt is the text that appears at the top of the dialog box.

The default Choose File dialog box shown in Figure 12-18 has no prompt.

The script that follows produces the dialog box whose top is shown in Figure 12-19:

```
choose file with prompt "Pick a file to use as template"
```

Figure 12-19. The top of a Choose File dialog box with a custom prompt

Restricting to specific file types

One of the parameters that makes the *choose file* command so useful and powerful is the *of type* parameter.

12

The *of type* parameter takes a list of up to four strings, each representing a file type. When the dialog box is displayed, the user can only choose files whose file types appear in the list.

In the following example, we limit the user to choosing a text file:

```
choose file of type {"TEXT"}
```

The following script prompts the user to pick a background image (for something) and restricts him/her to choosing a JPEG, TIFF, GIF, or PSD file:

```
choose file with prompt "Choose a background image" ¬
    of type {"JPEG", "TIFF", "GIFf", "8BPS"}
```

How do I know the file's file type?

Looking at the list of four file types I used previously, you might be wondering how I figured them out. Getting TIFF and JPEG is kind of obvious, but how did I know that the PSD file type is 8BPS? Is there a list of file types somewhere? There might be a list, but I don't have it. To get the file type, I use . . . well . . . a script!

The following script line will return the four-letter string that is the chosen file's file type. It uses, as you can see, the *choose file* command.

```
file type of (info for (choose file))
```

> *Creating small scripts that give you results you need to use in your script, as I did here to get the file's four-character type, is one of the scripter's best tools.*

The preceding script is a combination of three commands: *choose file*, which returns an alias; *info for*, which returns the info record of the alias; and (get) *file type of*, which returns the file type item of the file info record.

As you can see in Figure 12-20, the script's result is the chosen file's four-character code.

Figure 12-20. The script's result is the chosen file's four-character type code.

To use, just copy the result from the Result pane and paste it in your list.

Here's a fun exercise for you: create a scripter's utility script that builds a list of file types for use with the *choose file* command. The script should be a repeat loop that loops four times. Every loop the user should be asked to choose a different file for the file type list. If the user clicks Cancel at any point, exit the loop.

The result of the script should be a list of file types of the files the user picked. To make it even better, make sure that the user is notified if a file with the same file type is picked.

Invisibles

By default, the *choose file* command will allow you to pick invisible files. To restrict the user to visible files only, add the *invisibles* parameter with a true value to its right, or add *without invisibles*.

The difference between the invisibles and file type restriction is that when you use the *without invisibles* parameter, invisible files won't even show. When you restrict to only specific file types, all files will show, but files with different file types will be grayed out.

The following script will show the Choose File dialog box, but will not allow users to pick invisible files:

```
choose file without invisibles
```

Setting the default location

The optional *default location* property allows you to set a starting point for the Choose File dialog box. As the dialog box is displayed, you may want to direct the user to a specific folder.

The following script lets users start the search at the documents folder in their home directory:

```
choose file default location (path to documents folder from user domain)
```

You can also specify a folder path the usual way. In the following script, the variable *jobs_folder_path* was set to a path referencing the jobs folder. Note that the variable itself is a string, not a file reference, therefore we need to add the word "alias" before it when we use it to specify the default location.

Script 12-12

```
set jobs_folder_path to "Macintosh HD:Clients:Jobs:New Jobs:"
choose file with prompt "Pick a job to process" ¬
    default location alias jobs_folder_path
```

If the folder you specify as the default location doesn't exist, the starting location will revert to the default, but no error will be generated.

12

Allowing multiple selection

You may allow the user to pick multiple files at one time. To do that, set the *multiple selections allowed* parameter to true. This can be done by adding the word "true" after the parameter, or putting the parameter after the work "with."

The natural restriction of the *multiple selections allowed* parameter is that all files have to be visible to you in the same Choose File dialog box. If you want to pick one file from the documents folder in your home domain and one file from some nested folder on the server, you may have a problem. OS X 10.3 does allow you to switch from list view to outline view in the Choose File dialog box. The list type will allow you to collapse and expand folders and therefore choose files from different locations. Still, it will be most comfortable for the user to choose multiple files from the same folder.

Adding the *allow multiple selections* parameter with a true value will alter the command's result from a single alias to a list of aliases. Even if the user ends up choosing one file only, this alias will be returned as the only item in a list.

The following script allows the user to choose multiple files:

```
choose file with multiple selections allowed
```

Two files were chosen:

```
--> {alias "Macintosh HD:image 1.gif", ¬
alias "Macintosh HD: image 2.gif "}
```

choose file name

The *choose file name* command is specified in the Standard Additions. It allows you to add a Save As–like dialog box to your scripts. The result is a path to a not-yet existing file.

From the dictionary

The following is the dictionary specification of the *choose file name* command:

```
choose file name: Get a new file reference from the user, ¬
  without creating the file
  choose file name
    [with prompt  plain text]
       -- the text to display in the file creation dialog box
    [default name  plain text]  -- the default name for the new file
    [default location  alias]  -- the default file location
  Result:  'file'  -- the file the user specified
```

choose file name vs. choose file

The difference between the *choose file* and *choose file name* commands is the same as the difference between the Open and Save dialog boxes. When you open, you can choose a file. When you save, you specify a file name and location, but the file doesn't yet exist.

When to use?

You use the *choose file name* command whenever you want the user to specify a file that the script has to create in some way—for instance, if the script creates a text log, and you want to let the user decide where that log is saved and what the log's name is. Or, if you're creating an InDesign project from a template, and you want the user to specify where the project should be saved.

Results of choose file name

The *choose file name* command can return one of two types of values based on the button that the user clicks. If the user clicks the OK button, the command returns a file reference to the yet-to-exist file. If the user clicks Cancel, then a "user canceled" error will be generated.

The reason why the *choose file name* command returns a file reference (*file "filepath"*) instead of an alias (*alias "filepath"*) as in the *choose file* command, is that AppleScript only allows alias references to files that actually exist, and the file you specify here does not yet exist.

The basic command

The basic *choose file name* command used in the following script will display the Save dialog box shown in Figure 12-21.

```
choose file name
```

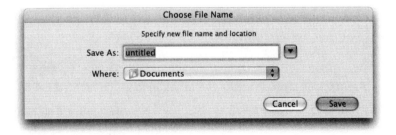

Figure 12-21. When used without any parameters, the *choose file name* command displays the basic Save dialog box.

Custom prompt

As with other file-related dialog box commands, you can add a custom title to your dialog box. As you can see in Figure 12-21, there is a default prompt saying "Specify new file name and location". Using the *with prompt* parameter, as in the following script line, will replace that prompt with your own custom message.

The following script will display the Choose File Name dialog box with a custom prompt:

```
choose file name with prompt "Save the log file"
```

Default name and location

As with the *choose file* command, the *choose file name* command also contains a parameter that allows you to set the default folder location. This location will be the first folder shown in the dialog box.

The *choose file name* command also allows you to set the default name for your file.

The following script lets the user choose a file name while directing the user to the log files folder and providing a default file name of log.txt. The resulting Choose File Name dialog box is shown in Figure 12-22.

Script 12-13

```
set default_log_folder to (path to documents folder from user domain ¬
    as string) & "log files:" as string
choose file name with prompt "Save the log file" ¬
    default location alias default_log_folder default name "Log.txt"
```

If the user accepted the defaults and clicked OK, the result would be

```
file "Macintosh HD:Users:hanaan:Documents:log files:Log.txt"
```

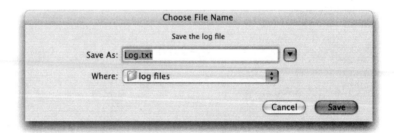

Figure 12-22. A Choose File Name dialog box with a default path and file name

Replace existing file

An interesting feature of the *choose file name* command is that you cannot choose a file name in a folder in which a file with the same name already exists. If you do, you will get the generic File Already Exists dialog box with an option to replace it.

What's interesting about it is that the *choose file name* command doesn't create any file, and therefore the same-name file that already exists in the selected location will not be replaced even if you choose the Replace option.

It is up to you, the scripter, to verify manually that a file with the same name doesn't exist in the chosen location, and delete it or move it if needed.

Example

As a simple example of using the *choose file name* command, we will create a new InDesign file and save it using a name and location the user chooses with the *choose file name* command.

The script is shown here first, followed by explanation:

Script 12-14

```
1. set jobs_folder_path to ":Jobs:"
2. try
3.    set new_file_path to choose file name ¬
            default location alias jobs_folder_path ¬
            default name "job name.indd"
4. on error e
5.    display dialog "Canceled"
6.    return
7. end try
8. set new_file_path to new_file_path as string
9. tell application "Finder"
10.    if exists file new_file_path then
11.        delete file new_file_path
12.    end if
13. end tell
14. tell application "InDesign CS"
15.    set new_doc to make new document
16.    tell new_doc
17.        save it to new_file_path
18.    end tell
19. end tell
```

12

The script starts with line 1 setting a variable to a string value that refers to the folder Jobs on the startup disk. In line 3, we use the variable *jobs_folder_path* to specify the default location.

The reason why the value for the default location folder path was placed in a string variable was that if we would try to use it literally, like this—*alias ":Jobs:"*—AppleScript would have compiled it into *alias "Macintosh HD:Jobs:"*, and the drive name–independent variable value would have vanished.

Lines 2 through 7 encompass the *try* command that captures the error generated if the user clicks the Cancel button.

In line 8, I coerce the file reference into a string. Strings are easier to work with since they can be later converted to aliases, file references, folder references, or also written to a text file themselves if needed.

In lines 9 through 13, we check whether the file reference returned by the *choose file name* command exists, and delete it if it does.

We take the liberty of deleting the file since if the file does exist, the *choose file name* command would have alerted the user and prompted him/her to replace the file.

In lines 14 through 19, we have InDesign create a new file and save it to the file path the user chose in line 2.

choose folder

The *choose folder* command allows you to make the user choose a folder using the Finder's Choose Folder dialog box. The *choose folder* command is a part of the Standard Additions scripting additions.

From the dictionary

The following is the dictionary definition of the *choose folder* command:

```
choose folder: Choose a folder on a disk or server
    choose folder
        [with prompt  plain text]
            -- a prompt to be displayed in the folder chooser
        [default location  alias]  -- the default folder location
        [invisibles  boolean]
            -- Show invisible files and folders? (default is false)
        [multiple selections allowed  boolean]
            -- Allow multiple items to be selected? (default is false)
    Result:   alias  -- chosen folder
```

What does it do?

The *choose folder* command presents users with the Choose Folder dialog box and allows them to choose a folder. The result is a reference to that folder.

If the user clicks Cancel, however, the "user canceled" error will be generated.

Figure 12-23 shows the dialog box that the *choose folder* command generates. The following script shows the basic form of the *choose folder* command, without any parameters:

```
choose folder
```

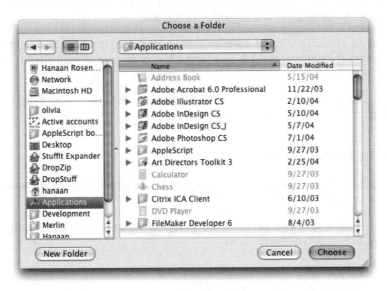

Figure 12-23. The dialog box shown by the *choose folder* command. Notice how files are grayed out.

When to use?

The *choose folder* command should be used when you need a reference to a folder and you want the user to choose the folder for you.

The folder can be chosen once and then stored in a property. You can then start the script by checking if the folder reference is still valid. If it's not, you can ask the user to "refresh" it. See this script's example in the "Choosing a folder once" section.

Parameters

The *choose folder* command is very similar to the *choose file* command.

Both allow you to choose Finder items.

Both will produce an error if the user clicks Cancel.

And, both share the same exact parameters: *invisibles*, *default location*, and *multiple selections allowed*.

To read more about these parameters, refer to the "Choose file" section earlier. Here are the descriptions in short:

The *invisibles* parameter determines whether invisible folders appear in the list or not. You can set *Invisibles* to true or false.

The *default location* parameter determines the location that the Choose Folder dialog box starts out in. By default, this would be the startup disk.

The *multiple selections allowed* parameter allows the user to select multiple folders at once. You set that parameter either by adding a true or false value right after it, or placing it after the *with* indicator.

If the *multiple selections allowed* parameter is turned on, then the *choose folder* command returns a list of aliases instead of a single alias.

Choosing a folder once

The script snippet that follows has a *folder_path* property. The property starts out having the value "missing value" assigned to it.

The script starts out by figuring out if the folder reference is valid. If it isn't, the user is prompted to choose a different folder.

Script 12-15

```
property folder_path : missing value
try
    alias folder_path
on error
    set folder_path to choose folder
    set folder_path to folder_path as string
end try
```

In the preceding example, we count on the script generating an error if the value of the variable *folder_path* does not contain a valid folder reference.

> **Aliases:** The alias value class requires that the string that follows the word "alias" is a valid path to a file or folder that actually exists. If the alias isn't pointing at a valid file, the file won't compile. If the string following the alias prefix is stored in a string variable, then a runtime error would occur. More on that in Chapter 13.

When the error occurs (which means that the folder reference isn't good), we quickly trap it in our *on error* net, and make the user choose a different folder.

Also notice that I keep the folder reference as a string. This helps me keep my options open.

choose application

The *choose application* command is defined in the Standard Additions dictionary. Its purpose is to let the user pick an application on the machine running the script. The *choose application* command can return either an alias pointing to the application, or the application itself, as you will see a bit later.

From the dictionary

The following is the dictionary definition of the *choose application* command:

```
choose application: Choose an application on this machine or the ¬
network
   choose application
      [with title  plain text]  -- the dialog window title
      [with prompt  plain text]
         -- the prompt to appear at the top of the application ¬
         chooser dialog box
      [multiple selections allowed  boolean]
         -- Allow multiple items to be selected? (default is false)
      [as  type class]
         -- the desired type of result.  May be application
(the default) or alias.
      Result:   app  -- the application chosen
```

Using the command

The *choose application* command, if used by itself with no parameters, displays the dialog box shown in Figure 12-24. The default result is an application object as shown here:

```
application "Finder"
```

Using the *as* parameter, you can ask for the result to be returned as an alias to the application, as shown here:

```
choose application as alias
--> alias "Macintosh HD:Applications:FileMaker Pro 7:FileMaker ¬
Pro.app:"
```

You can also use the *with title* and *with prompt* parameters to add a title and a prompt to the dialog box. In Figure 12-24 you can see the default title "Choose Application" and the default prompt "Select an application".

12

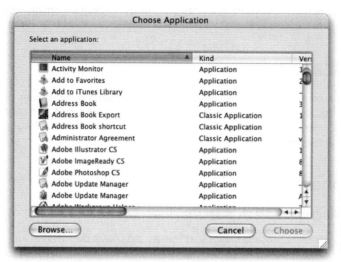

Figure 12-24. The default Choose Application dialog box with the default prompt and title

choose URL

The *choose URL* command is defined in the Standard Additions. It allows the user to specify a URL to a server in one of several protocols, such as FTP servers, file servers, remote applications, etc.

The result of the command is a URL that can be used as a parameter with other commands such as *mount volume* (described in Chapter 13).

From the dictionary

The following is the dictionary definition of the *choose URL* command:

```
choose URL: Choose a service on the Internet
    choose URL
        [showing  a list of ¬
            Web servers/FTP Servers/Telnet hosts/File servers/¬
            News servers/Directory services/Media servers/¬
            Remote applications]  -- which network services to show
        [editable URL  boolean]  -- Allow user to type in a URL?
    Result:   URL  -- the URL chosen
```

Using the command

The *choose URL* command has two parameters. The *showing* parameter allows you to specify a list of protocols that will appear in the protocol pop-up menu at the bottom. By default the list shows seven protocols (listed previously in the "From the dictionary" section). The following script restricts the command to three of the seven protocols.

The script also uses the Boolean parameter *editable URL* with a false value. This prevents the user from typing in a URL rather than choosing one from the list.

The dialog box resulting from the following script is shown in Figure 12-25.

```
choose URL showing {Web servers, FTP Servers, Telnet hosts} without ¬
editable URL
```

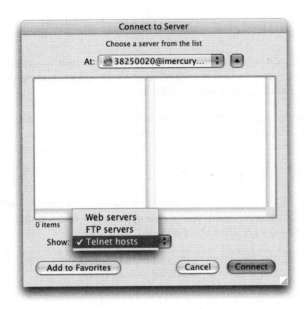

Figure 12-25. The dialog box resulting from the *choose url* command in the script

The following script will ask the user to specify a file server URL by either choosing it from a list or typing it, and then mount the specified volume:

```
set server_address to choose URL showing {File servers} with ¬
editable URL
mount volume server_address
```

choose color

The following is the dictionary definition of the *choose color* command.

From the dictionary

```
choose color: Choose a color (defined in: StandardAdditions.osax)
    choose color
        [default color RGB color] -- the default color
    Result: RGB color  -- chosen color
```

The result

The result is an AppleScript class called color specifications. It is no more than a list of three integer values, representing the red, green, and blue values of an RGB color.

Although the color picker the user is presented with does allow the user to specify HEX colors for web and CMYK colors, the result will always be the RGB color equivalent.

When to use?

Use this command whenever you're in a situation that the user has to specify a color. This feature wasn't intended for precise color use in production or design environments, but rather for picking colors in a more general way: pinkish, light blue, etc.

In Chapter 13, we look at an example where we create an RTF file. The *choose color* command is used there to specify RGB colors that are later used in the RTF file.

The basic command and parameters

The *choose color* command has one parameter: *default color*. It allows you to specify the color that is displayed by default when the dialog box appears.

The following script will display the Choose Color dialog box without a predefined default color:

choose color

The following script will display the Choose Color dialog box shown in Figure 12-26.

choose color default color {65535, 0, 0}

Figure 12-26.
The Choose Color
dialog box

User interaction and timeouts

AppleScript's timeout feature creates an error if you send an application a command and the application doesn't respond within a certain amount of time.

By default, that timeout period is 120 seconds, which is enough for 99% of any command an application has to complete. However, if your script is displaying a dialog box of any kind inside an application's *tell* block, but the user is out on a break or something, the dialog box will stick around and generate a timeout error.

The error will be generated and the script will stop, even though the dialog box will be still displayed.

In general, we can avoid timeout errors by extending the timeout period, like this:

```
tell application "Finder"
    with timeout of (3 * hours) seconds
        --do something that may take a long time...
    end timeout
end tell
```

However, with dialog boxes, there's no guarantee that anyone will be there to dismiss them. If your script displays a dialog box of any kind at, say, Friday afternoon, your time-out should be at least three-and-a-half days long, in case of a long weekend . . . Instead, you should try to capture the timeout error. If the dialog you're dealing with is a normal dialog box generated by the *display dialog* command, all you need to do is add the *giving up* parameter and either specify a number of seconds that is less than 120 seconds, or increase the timeout and set the *giving up* time to a number of seconds smaller than the timeout.

If you're displaying another type of dialog box, such as the Choose File or Choose Folder dialog boxes, however, you don't have the *giving up* parameter on your side. In these cases, you have a few other choices: you can either trap the timeout error using a *try* block, and simply stop the script if the dialog times out, or use UI scripting (also referred to as GUI scripting) to actually click the Cancel button and exit the script gracefully.

The *try* statement in the following script is designed to trap the timeout error, which is error number -1712, and use user interface (UI) scripting to click the Cancel button.

Script 12-16

```
try
    tell application "Finder"
        choose file
    end tell
on error number error_number
    if error_number is -1712 then
        tell application "Finder" to activate
        tell application "System Events"
            tell application process "Finder"
                click button "Cancel" of window "Choose a File"
            end tell
        end tell
    end if
end try
```

12

The preceding script is one big *try* statement. Line 5 is designed to not only trap the error, but also to figure out the error number.

The conditional statement from line 6 through line 13 will execute if the error is the time-out error, or in other words, error number -1712.

Lines 8 through 12 target the Cancel button of the Choose File window, and click it.

> **More on errors:** *Read more on errors, error trapping, and figuring out which errors have which numbers in Chapter 15. Also, look for the Chapter 19, which deals with UI scripting to see how to isolate the button you need in the jungle of UI elements.*

Quick custom dialog boxes for your script using AppleScript Studio

Undoubtedly the biggest boost AppleScript has gotten in the last few years is AppleScript Studio. With Studio you can create full-blown Cocoa applications for Mac OS X using Xcode and AppleScript.

AppleScript Studio is a set of classes that come with Mac OS X and enable any AppleScript Studio application to run on every Mac OS X computer. To develop AppleScript Studio applications of your own, you do have to install Apple's Developer Tools, which are included with OS X but are not installed by default. While we can use AppleScript Studio to create fully programmed applications, here I will teach you a neat technique for using an AppleScript Studio application with minimal AppleScript programming to create a series of rich custom dialog boxes that you can use in your scripts.

We are going to take advantage of one of the Cocoa programming environment's coolest features: any application you build is automatically scriptable. OK . . . so it doesn't have an object model with rich properties relating to the application's subject matter, but all of the UI elements are fully scriptable from external scripts such as the scripts you're writing in Script Editor.

What we will create here is a simple application with a minimal amount of programming (as little as four lines!) that will act as a repository for dialog boxes and panels.

Later, using our script, we can display those panels, return any buttons that were clicked, and extract any text from the text fields, status of check boxes, selections of pop-up menus, etc.

We can also utilize another new AppleScript feature and embed the dialogs application inside a script application bundle. This will mean that the user doesn't see multiple files, just your script application.

Now, why go through this trouble instead of just creating an AppleScript Studio application? Many times what you want is a script, and a simple AppleScript application is the best solution. Since adding AppleScript Studio–created dialog boxes is relatively easy, you may find it to be a cool alternative.

You also may have scripts you already created and you just want to enhance them with some extra dialog boxes.

How will it work?

Our dialog boxes will be windows in the AppleScript Studio application we're going to create.

All buttons in the application will do the same thing: they will copy their own title to a hidden text field called "button", and then make the window invisible. The rest of the elements will just have names that the script can later use to extract their contents or state.

From the script we will invoke the dialog box in three steps:

1. Tell the dialogs application to show the window we want.

2. Use a repeat loop to wait while the window is still visible.

3. Once the window has become invisible, the script will extract the values from the different text fields and other UI elements. Remember that the text fields and other UI elements retain their value even after the window is invisible.

We will start by creating the application and then we will create the script tidbits that will display the dialog box and get the dialog information.

Creating the application

We will create a new project in AppleScript Studio called "dialog". This project will be the application we'll use to edit and later show dialog boxes from.

Launch Xcode, which is an application that is part of the Developers Tools package, and start a new AppleScript Application project as shown in Figure 12-27. Name the project "dialogs", as you see in Figure 12-28.

Figure 12-27.
Create a new AppleScript Application project.

12

Figure 12-28.
Name the new
project "dialogs".

After the project has been created, locate the icon for the MainMenu.nib file (highlighted in Figure 12-29) and double-click it.

The MainMenu.nib file is the interface of your application.

> Nib stands for Next Interface Builder.

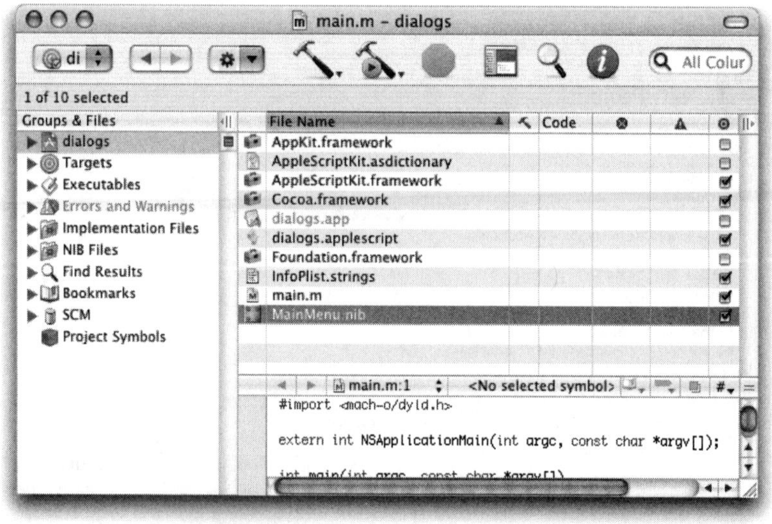

Figure 12-29. The MainMenu.nib interface file icon in your Xcode project

In the MainMenu file window (at the top of Figure 12-30), locate the icon for the default window, click it, and click Delete. We will create a panel to replace it.

At the top of the Cocoa panel, click the fourth icon to show the palette with the window elements, shown at the bottom of Figure 12-30.

Drag an instance of the panel object to your MainMenu file window, as shown in Figure 12-30.

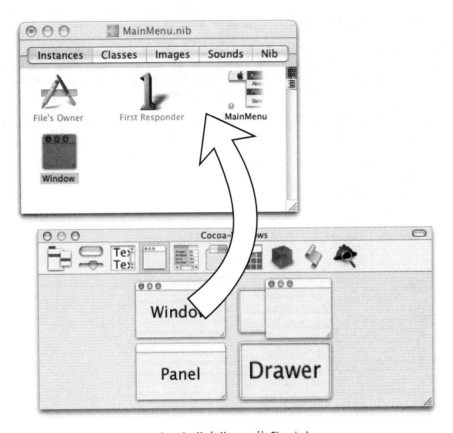

Figure 12-30. Dragging a new panel to the MainMenu.nib file window

Edit your first dialog box

In the MainMenu.nib file window, double-click the newly created panel to open it.

In Interface Builder (IB), go to the Tools menu and choose Show Info. This will display the Info palette. If not selected, select Attributes from the pop-up menu at the top of the Info palette.

In the Info palette you can give your dialog box a title and apply texture to it if you want. The texture will make it brushed steel. Many people poke fun at the brushed steel windows; call me uncool if you want, but I like them!

To give your panel the brushed steel look, check the Has texture check box.

Also, type a title in the Window Title field at the top. I used the title "Provide Your Information:".

The window's three controls, Miniaturize, Close, and Resize, should be checked off. This will help to ensure that the window stays up until one of the buttons is clicked.

If you didn't create a new panel but rather used the window that came with the application by default, you have to uncheck Visible at launch time. Remember, when the application launches, we don't want any windows to show; we only want the windows showing when our script specifically makes them visible.

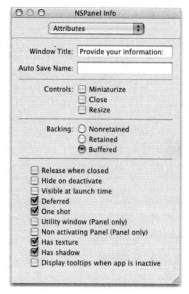

The Info palette with the appropriate settings is shown in Figure 12-31.

Figure 12-31.
The Info palette with our panel's settings

Giving your window its AppleScript name

The dialog box we designed must have an AppleScript name on top of its title. The panel's name will be used by our script to specify the window we want to show.

To name the window, choose AppleScript from the top pop-up menu in the Info palette.

If there are any controls on the window, such as buttons, etc., make sure that none of them are selected. If they are, you will be naming them, not the window.

Now, type the name in the Name field as shown in Figure 12-32.

Figure 12-32. The window Info palette with the new window name

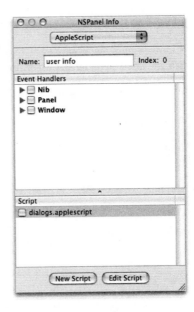

Add dialog elements

The dialog box we're going to create will be fairly simple, housing three text fields, a check box, a pop-up menu, a slider, and a few buttons.

The text labels are there for information only and don't serve any programming-related purpose.

The purpose of the dialog box we're creating will be to collect the user's information, but you're welcome to experiment with any other fields, labels, and UI elements.

If you want to just follow the example, then set up your panel the way I did, as shown in Figure 12-33.

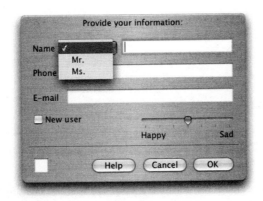

Figure 12-33. The finished dialog layout

Name and edit dialog elements

The dialog box we created has two types of elements: buttons and nonbutton elements. We will need to name the nonbutton elements only.

We name the elements in the AppleScript pane of the Info palette. Make sure that the Info palette is visible and choose AppleScript from the pop-up menu at the top, as shown in Figure 12-34.

To name an element, click it in the window and type the element's name in the Name text field on the Info palette, also shown in Figure 12-34.

The names I gave the text fields are "name", "phone", and "email".

The pop-up is named "salutation"; the check box is called "newuser", and the slider is called "mood".

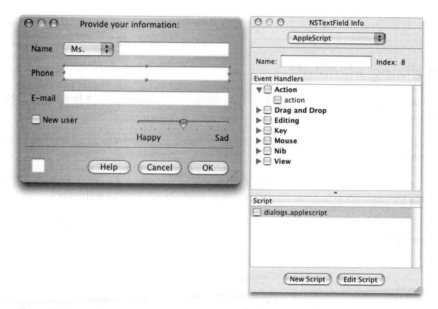

Figure 12-34. Naming user elements in the AppleScript pane of the Info palette

The hidden button field

Notice the label-free square text field at the bottom left of the window we designed, shown in Figure 12-35. That field is named "button" and is the way for us to know which button the user clicked.

When any button is clicked, our script will take the title of that button and place it in that field, which will be hidden. Later on, we can use our script to get the contents of the button text field to know which button was clicked.

You can make the button transparent by checking the Hidden check box in the Attributes pane of the Info palette.

Testing the interface

In IB, you can press *COMMAND+R* (or choose Test Interface from the File menu) at any point, to see how the interface will look, and try out all the controls you put on it.

Connecting the buttons to the script

One more thing we have to do in order to make the buttons perform is link them to the script in Xcode.

We link the buttons to the script in the AppleScript pane of the Info palette, as shown in Figure 12-35.

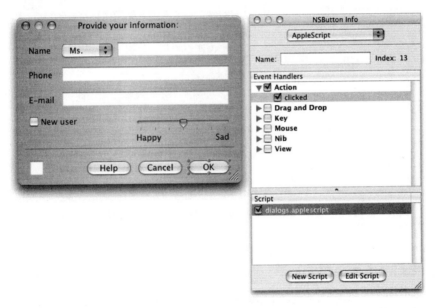

Figure 12-35. To link a UI element to a script, click that UI element (a button in this case), and check both the *clicked* action and the script.

1. Click the first button.

2. Choose AppleScript from the pop-up menu at the top of the Info palette.

3. In the Event Handlers pane, expand the Action triangle and check clicked.

4. In the script pane, check dialogs.applescript.

Notice that we didn't give the buttons names. We can, but it's easier to rely on their title instead, like we do in the *display dialog* command.

Repeat steps 1 through 4 for all buttons.

In AppleScript Studio, all those buttons will invoke the same event handler in the script.

To create that event handler in the script, click one of the buttons to select it (any one) and click the Edit Script button at the bottom of the Info palette.

Once you do, the script in the Xcode project will open, and the *clicked* event will be added, as shown in Figure 12-36.

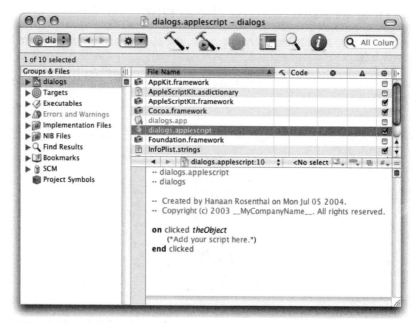

Figure 12-36. The Xcode project window with the script, and the *clicked* event that has been added by IB.

The clicked event

The *clicked* event will be invoked whenever a UI element that is linked to that event is clicked.

Since all of the buttons in the panel we designed are linked to the *clicked* event, clicking any of them will invoke the *clicked* event.

The way we structure the dialogs application will allow us to treat all buttons with one simple script. All we want is to copy the title of the button that has been clicked to the field named "button". Following is the script we will write between the *on clicked theObject* and *end clicked* lines:

```
on clicked theObject
   tell (window of theObject)
      set contents of text field "button" to title of theObject
      close
   end tell
end clicked
```

The script will start by identifying and focusing the attention on the window on which the clicked button sits.

Since the variable *theObject* is a reference to the button that has been clicked, when we talk to the window of *theObject* (line 2), we instantly identify the window that this button belongs to. Again, we can have the same script work for all dialog boxes we design in that application.

In line 3 we set the contents of the text field named "button" to the title of the clicked button.

Line 4 closes the window.

At this point, the dialog portion is done, and this is pretty much all the code your dialogs application will require.

The rest of the work will be up to the script itself—it will need to extract the values from the different text fields and other UI elements.

Testing the application

In Xcode, choose Build and Run from the Build menu, or press COMMAND+R. This will build the application and launch it.

Click the Save All button if Xcode prompts you to save changes.

The default location for the application is in the Build folder inside the project folder. Later on you can move it to any other location. You must beware, however, because if you leave a copy of it in the Build folder, AppleScript may try to launch this version of the application when it is mentioned in the script.

When you see the dialogs application in your dock, you can switch to your script editor, where you will complete the exercise.

To test the scriptability of your application, try something like this: create a new script window in Script Editor, or other script editing application, and type the following script lines:

```
tell application "dialogs"
   get name of every window
end tell
```

12

As a result you should get a list of one item, the name of your one window:

```
{"user info"}
```

Now, let's test for the text fields. Change the script to look like this one:

```
tell application "dialogs"
    tell window "user info"
        name of every text field
    end tell
end tell
```

And the result will be

```
{"name", "phone", "email", "button", missing value, ¬
missing value, missing value, missing value, missing value}
```

The reason for all the missing values is that you haven't named all of the text labels that are also considered text fields by AppleScript.

Using the custom dialog in a script

Now that you have created the application and tested its scriptability, let's see if we can put it to use.

Our strategy will be to start by telling the dialogs application to show the window we want to use as a dialog box. Then, we will wait until the window isn't showing anymore, and finally, when that happens, we will extract the values from the different controls.

Show the dialog box

The part of the script that shows the dialog box will look like this:

```
tell application "dialogs"
    activate
    tell window "user info"
        set contents of every text field to ""
        set visible of it to true
        --more to come here
    end tell
end tell
```

We start by activating the application. Then, we clear the text from all the text fields. This is important since we don't want the dialog box to retain the values from the last time you used it.

Instead of clearing the text fields, you could use this part to populate them with default values as well.

Then we say *set visible of it to true*, which simply displays the window.

Wait for the user to close the dialog box

Next we will create a repeat loop that will go on as long as the window is open.

Since we want to replicate the script's natural behavior, the script has to sit there until the user picks a button.

The script with the waiting repeat loop looks like this:

```
tell application "dialogs"
    activate
    tell window "user info"
        set contents of every text field to ""
        set visible of it to true
        --Wait for window to close:
        repeat while visible of it is true
        end repeat
        --more to come here
    end tell
end tell
```

You could, if you needed to, track the time the dialog box is up and bring it down after a while. This can replicate AppleScript's *give up* parameter in the *display dialog* command.

Extract user-entered values

Next we will go control by control and extract the values the user chose or typed in.

To figure out which button the user clicked, just use this line:

```
set buttonReturned to contents of text field "button"
```

Here's the script in its entirety:

```
1. tell application "dialogs"
2.     activate
3.     tell window "user info"
4.         set contents of every text field to ""
5.         set visible of it to true
6.         repeat while visible of it is true
7.         end repeat

8.         set buttonReturned to contents of text field "button"
9.         set userName to contents of text field "User"
10.        set userPhone to contents of text field "phone"
11.        set userEmail to contents of text field "email"
12.        set userName to contents of text field "User"
13.        set userSalutation to title of current menu item ¬
                of popup button "salutation"
14.        set userMood to integer value of slider "mood"-- 0=happy, ¬
                100=sad
```

12

```
15.        set userNew to integer value of button "new user"
                -- 1=checked or 0=unchecked

16.        tell me to activate
17.     end tell
18. end tell
```

FaceSpan for OS X

This section is by Shirley Hopkins of DTI, maker of FaceSpan.

Whether you want to develop a fully functional application or just provide an interface for an AppleScript you have already written, FaceSpan provides the tools you need.

What is FaceSpan? It is an integrated development environment that allows you to create the user interface, add resources (movies, graphics, etc.), define the code, and build a Macintosh application that looks and runs like an "off-the-shelf" application. FaceSpan 4.0 does this for you in an easy-to-use, high-level environment. Everything you need to build an application for OS X is at your fingertips. Its predecessor application, versions 1 through 3.5, works with earlier versions of the OS. This discussion will only cover the 4.0 version.

FaceSpan 4.0 is deceptively easy to use. But there is a lot of power "under the hood." With a full complement of objects from tables and tab views to a secure text field that hides user entries as they are typed, FaceSpan interfaces are created with simple drag and drop. Much functionality is built in, and handlers are provided that can be used as is or modified to suit your specific needs. You can even make calls directly to Cocoa if the need arises.

Best of all, FaceSpan takes advantage of AppleScript's object-oriented structure. Events generated at the window item level can be handled in the script for the item, in the script for its parent window, or in the Project Script. If an event is handled at the window item level, it can be continued to a same-named handler in a window or the Project Script. Properties assigned at the Project Script level can be "seen" by the window's scripts and by window item scripts using the *my* qualifier. It's like having a well-organized team at your command, with each item and each script working in concert. You can even add Script Object scripts (FaceSpan scripts) to your project to further the object-oriented functionality.

For the more advanced user, FaceSpan interfaces nicely with Script Debugger, which can be set to work as its editor and/or debugger (www.latenightsw.com).

Nine steps to success

Basically, the process of creating a project in FaceSpan can be outlined in nine easy steps:

1. **Start a new project.** Determine the project type and give it a name. Optionally, you may want to quick-start a project using a template (see Figure 12-37).

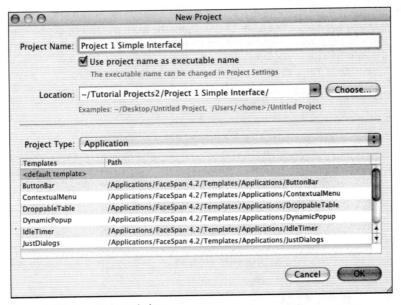

Figure 12-37. New Project window

2. **Add resources.** The project has a main window and main menu created by default. There is also a script for the project, the Project Script. Artwork, movies, sounds, and files can be added to your project using the Project window (see Figure 12-38) or by selecting Add Files from the Project menu.

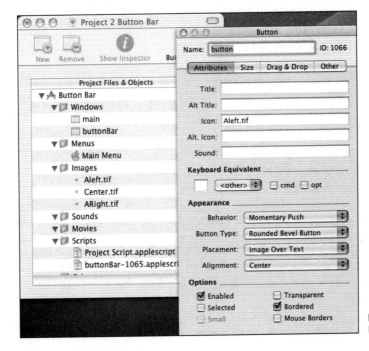

Figure 12-38.
Project window

3. **Set up windows.** For many scripts, the main window, provided by default, is all that you will need (see Figure 12-39). Open the main window by double-clicking its entry in the Project window. Define its properties in the Info palette provided. (If the Info palette is not open, you can open it from the Windows menu or press COMMAND+I.) You can add more windows (or panels) as needed.

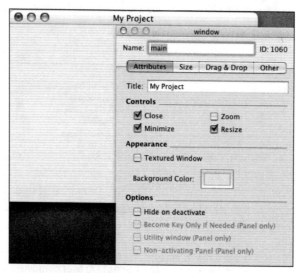

Figure 12-39.
Main window

4. **Design the user interface.** Objects are added to windows (and panels) by dragging objects from the Objects Palette and placing as needed (see Figure 12-40). As you move objects around in a window, guides appear to help in positioning.

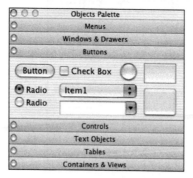

Figure 12-40.
Objects Palette

Clicking a title bar in the Objects Palette opens the object group. If you only need one object, use the small round button to open the group. This allows the group to close automatically once the item is placed on the window. You can also CONTROL-click (right-click) on a window to select an object from its contextual menu.

Hint: hold the cursor over an object in the Objects Palette to see its description (tool tip).

Set the properties for each object in the Info palette. If the Info palette is not open, it can be opened from the Window menu or by pressing COMMAND+I.

The Info palette shows information for the interface element currently selected and indicates its class in its title bar (see Figure 12-41). In naming objects, select names that are easy to remember. Names are used to reference objects in scripts and are case sensitive.

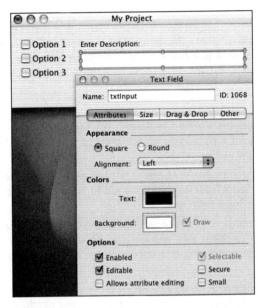

Figure 12-41.
Info palette

Hint: get in the habit of typing a tab after typing an entry in a text field for the Info palette.

5. **Edit main menu.** Change, add, or remove items from the main menu as needed (see Figure 12-42). To work with the main menu, double-click its entry in the Menus folder of the Project window.

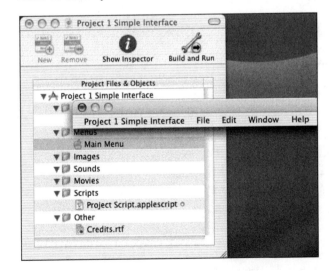

Figure 12-42.
Main menu

12

To change an item, click a menu title in the menu bar to disclose its menu items. Highlight an item and type over it. Change the behavior for a menu item in the Actions list of the Info palette. Items assigned "<execute script>" will need to have code written in the *choose menu item* handler in the Project Script to handle its being selected.

To add an item to the menu bar, drag an item from the Menus group of the Objects Palette (an insert line will appear where the item will be inserted). A Submenu item added to the menu bar will have one blank menu item by default. CONTROL-click (right-click) an item in a menu list (or on a blank item) to add, delete, or move items within a menu list.

Close the main menu when complete

6. **Attach scripts.** A project script is provided by default. You can put all of your code here, or you can manage your scripts in an object-oriented manner by attaching scripts to windows or window items.

To create a script, select the item to which the script will be attached and press COMMAND+E (or select Add Script from the Script menu). To open an existing script, double-click its entry in the Project window.

To get references to the window and to window objects, the Object Browser in the Scripting Help drawer of the Script Edit window can be used. Double-click an object in the Object Browser, and its full reference is placed at the cursor location in the script.

Create functionality by adding code to scripts. FaceSpan helps you by providing a wealth of handlers that can be used as-is or modified to suit your needs. Many are written as templates requiring that you replace placeholder text (designated by ALL CAPS) with references to objects or values.

Test your code by clicking the Compile button in the Script Edit window. Correct errors as needed. Most errors will be typographical in nature: forgot to end a quote with a quotation mark, misspelled a word, forgot to close a parenthesis pair, etc. (See Figure 12-43.)

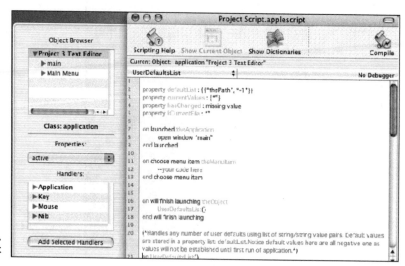

Figure 12-43.
Project Script

7. Test and debug. Click the Build and Run button in the Project window (or press *COMMAND+R*) to test run the script. Debug as needed. The Message window can be a great aid for simple debugging. To test values for variables at runtime, place log statements within code having the following format:

```
log variableValue
```

The value for *variableValue* in the preceding example would be printed to the Message window as the project runs (see Figure 12-44).

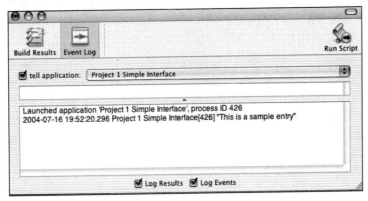

Figure 12-44. Message window

The Build and Run button changes to a Stop button while a project is running. Click this button to stop a test run.

8. Edit the Credits page. To add user instructions, comments, etc. to the Credits page, double-click Credits.rtf (see Figure 12-45) in the Other folder of the Project window. The page will open in your default text editor. A template is provided that can be modified as needed.

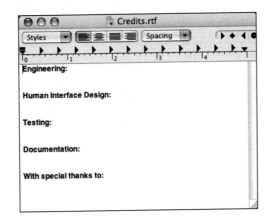

Figure 12-45. Credits.rtf

12

9. Save the project. You may wish to set the preference Save unsaved projects to Ask before building. This will remind you to save projects periodically as you work. Once the project is working as desired, save the project.

Establish settings for the executable (application created) if desired. The name of the executable will be the same as that of your project if you checked Use project name as executable name when you created the project. You can give your executable a different name. You can also assign a custom icon, an identifier, and an info string to be used by the system. These settings are found in the Executable Settings dialog box (see Figure 12-46), which is opened by selecting Executable Settings from the Project menu.

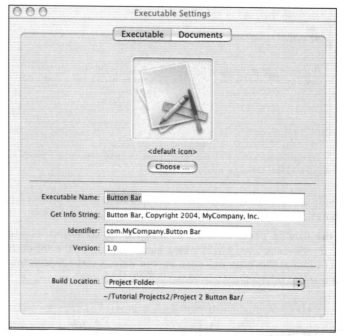

Figure 12-46. Executable Settings dialog box

Note: if you do use a different name for the executable than that for the project, you will need to change the name of the project in the various menu items for the Application menu.

Build and run (or build) your project after editing the Credits page.

You can now save and close the project (or throw it away, if you choose).

After completing the preceding steps, you should now have a folder that looks like the one in Figure 12-47.

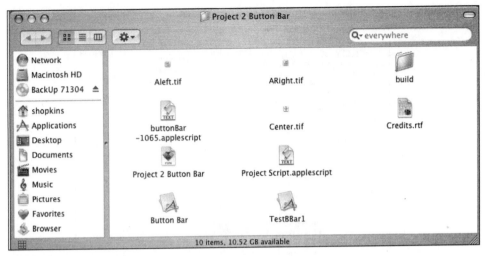

Figure 12-47. Project folder

The executable, which will have the default icon that resembles a letter "A" (or the custom one you assigned), can be double-clicked to run. The main menu is part of your application by default, allowing the user to quit the application by selecting Quit from the File menu or pressing COMMAND+Q.

As you can see, a lot of functionality is built into a FaceSpan project without your having to even think about it.

A word about FaceSpan's auxiliary resources

FaceSpan gives users a wealth of aids to make creating projects easier and to fit the way the user wants to work. Among these are the script library and template collection.

Library

One of the features of FaceSpan is a growing library of standard handlers that can be used to build scripts. The library is accessed by CONTROL-clicking (right-clicking) an empty line of the Script Edit window. Code found in this library includes comments documenting how the routine can be implemented (see Figure 12-48). Property declarations, a call statement for the subroutine, and supporting handlers, as needed, are also included.

12

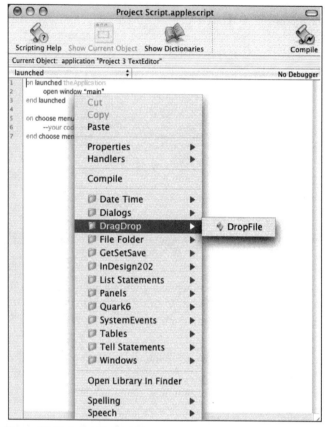

Figure 12-48. Script Library entry

If the code includes a property statement, this should be cut and pasted at the beginning of the script where the property will be managed (usually the Project Script). A call to the handler is often included and will need to be cut and pasted at the appropriate location in the script. Some entries act as templates, with placeholder text (indicated with ALL CAPS). These will need to be replaced with actual object references or values.

The Script Library folder is installed in the same folder as FaceSpan. You can add your own routines to this collection by saving scripts as text with the .applescript extension and placing in appropriate folders.

Templates

Another great resource is the Templates folder, which is also installed in the same folder as FaceSpan. Templates are a great way to quick-start a project. You can save a project at any stage as a template. Just save the project to the Templates folder using Save As. Take note that your current project is now the template project, so you will want to close out the current project and reopen the original project from which the template was created before continuing.

Keep up to date

As there are new templates and library scripts being added periodically, you may wish to check FaceSpan's downloads web page (www.FaceSpan.com) to make sure you have all of the latest.

The completed projects described in the tutorials following are also found on the downloads page.

Writing code

When writing a script in Script Editor, there is a strong tendency to write statements as one big monolithic piece of code. When you work with an interface, however, each action or event that can take place can potentially be "handled" in a separate "mini-script" or handler.

Handlers

Writing code for FaceSpan depends on the use of handlers. When an object in a window is clicked, it sends a *clicked* event. Statements included in the *clicked* handler for the object dictate what happens when the button is clicked. Many handlers include the variable *theObject* as part of the *on* statement. This variable is a reference to the object that sent the event. If you have a *clicked* handler in a script for the object, the *clicked* handler will only receive the event for its object. However, if you put a *clicked* handler in the script for a window or in the Project Script, the code will need to determine which object sent the event since any object belonging to the button class can send a *clicked* event.

Think of handlers (routines) as the building blocks for a project. The more you can "bundle" statements together into meaningful blocks of code that perform a singular function, the more reusable your code will become.

For the sake of consistency, the user-defined handlers used in the tutorials all use positional parameters. Positional parameters are those references, values, or variables that you find inside of parentheses in the first line of a handler. What you need to remember is if a handler has variables within parentheses, you need to provide a value for each item, and in the same order inside the parentheses for the calling statement. Handlers found in the Script Library should all have sample call statements that can be used as a model. Or, better yet, cut the statement (or statements) and paste where the call is to be made.

To get a template for a handler that responds to an event sent by an interface object, click the object in the Object Browser for the Script Help drawer. The handler choices for the object are then displayed in the Handler browser. Double-clicking an entry in the Handler browser will place the handler template in the script at the current cursor location. Make sure the cursor is in an open area of the Script Edit window before double-clicking.

12

FaceSpan scripts

If you like the idea of having reusable script handlers in a Script Library, you will love the concept of using FaceSpan scripts. With a FaceSpan script, you put a collection of handlers together into one script file. For instance, all of your handlers that work with text in your favorite scriptable text editor could be put in one file. Just stack the handlers in the file, as you collect them, but be sure to keep documentation handy to remind you of the handlers and if/or what parameters are required. Save the file as a text file with the .applescript extension.

When you want to use the handlers in the collection, add the file to your project. To add a file, select Add Files from the Project menu or drag the file to the Scripts folder in the Project window. The code inside of the file is not available to your scripts until you actually load the file. This is normally done in the Project Script so that all objects can have access to the code.

1. Define a global variable to reference the file's handlers in the Project Script. You might want to call it *gTextScripts*.

   global gTextScripts

2. Before you need to use the handlers, load the file into the variable using the name of the file as shown in the Project window but without the .applescript extension.

   set gTextScripts to load facespan script "FSTextScripts"

3. When you need to call one of the handlers in the file, first make sure that the script from where the call is being made has declared the global variable at the top of the script.

   global gTextScript

4. Now any statement in the script can reference a handler in the file as an element of the variable. For instance, if the FaceSpan script contains a *getText ( )* handler, you would call the handler using

   set theText to gTextScript's getText ( )

In all other respects, the handlers found in a FaceSpan script are used like handlers found in any other script within a project.

More advanced users will appreciate the simplicity with which one can create script object files using FaceSpan script. *CONTROL*-click the Script folder in the Project window and select New Script from the contextual menu. A new unattached script is created for the project. You can accept the default name or change the name by clicking the Show Inspector button. The code in these files is loaded and referenced within a project in the same manner as described previously.

Tutorials

The best way to examine how an application functions is to work with it. Following are several simple projects to demonstrate some of FaceSpan's features. The tutorials will follow the basic nine-step procedure outlined previously with further explanation as needed. Remember to refer to the nine-step outline as you work through the projects for more information.

Even if you do not currently have access to FaceSpan, the projects are short enough that you can mentally work through them to see how FaceSpan makes it easy to create working applications using AppleScript.

Preliminaries

Before you start putting your first project together, you might want to set up a folder where you want your projects to be saved. You may also want to establish some preferences for how you want to work.

Once you launch FaceSpan, select Preferences from the Application menu. If nothing else, you will want to establish the location for your projects. To target the folder that you set aside for your projects, select Other from the Default project location drop-down list in General Preferences and navigate to the folder you created. Most preferences are pretty self-explanatory. The following are suggested:

General:

When adding files: Copy files into project folder

Sync script names with object names

Windows and panels: Remember document states

When FaceSpan launches: Show Objects Palette

Show Info palette

Editing:

All options are checked. You may wish to uncheck allow text completion.

Building:

As defaulted

12

Starting a project

With FaceSpan running, select New from the File menu. In the New Project dialog box, give your project a name. For most applications you will want to click the Use project name as executable name check box. Select the application type from the pop-up and, if needed, designate where the project will be saved. Select a template from the templates list, if desired. Once you have given FaceSpan this information, click OK.

Project 1: Put a face on it

The first project will demonstrate adding a user interface to a script that is already written. The basic procedure outlined could be applied to any number of scripts you might have that could benefit from a user-friendly interface.

For demonstration, assume that the existing script presents users a list of options from which they must select one or more options (*choose from list*). There is also a text string that must be entered by users (*display dialog*). From there the script performs some functionality depending on the choices made. Putting this all in a FaceSpan project is a no-brainer. The structure for the current script could read something like the following:

```
set userChoiceList to {"Choice 1", "Choice 2", "Choice 3"}
set defaultString to "Input string here"
--calls routine that uses choose from list to return user's choices
set userChoice to getUserChoice (userChoiceList)
--calls routine that uses display dialog to get string entry
set userInput to getUserInput (defaultString)
--call main process using input from user
doMainProcess (userChoice, userInput)
--this is followed by routines that perform the various functions
```

Here are the steps (refer to the nine-step outline in the "Nine steps to success" section for details):

1. Start a new project.

Select application for type. No template will be used.

2. Add resources.

No resources will be added to the project; skip step 2.

3. Set up windows.

This project will only require one window, "main," which is provided by default.

4. Design the interface.

Analyzing the script should help in deciding the design for the project. The script dictates the need for a main window with one text field for text entry (see Figure 12-49). A check box matrix can be used in place of the *choose from list* command. The window will also require a push button for the user to push to "trigger" the functionality.

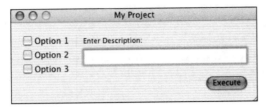

Figure 12-49. Project 1: main window

Open the "main" window and set its properties (use your discretion for settings, but don't change the window's name).

Check box matrix

To create the check box matrix, drag a check box from the Buttons group of the Objects Palette. Once placed on the window, hold down the *OPTION* key. Click and drag on one of the sizing handles for the check box to create three check boxes stacked vertically. The Info palette will display the word "Matrix" in its title bar. Use the Info palette to name the matrix "matCheck" (see Figure 12-50).

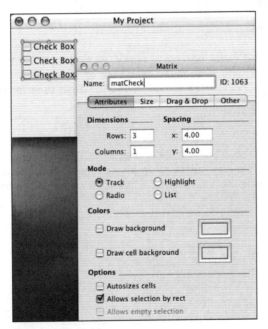

Figure 12-50. Matrix

Now double-click the first check box in the matrix. (The window will gray out, indicating that a nested object is selected, and the Info palette will display "Button Cell" in its title.) Set the name for the first check box to Option1. Set the title to Option 1 (see Figure 12-51).

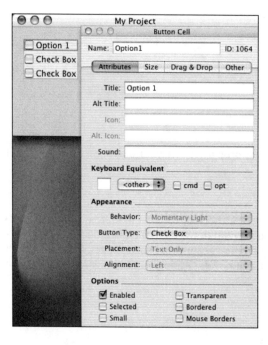

Figure 12-51. Button cell

Click each of the next check boxes and repeat, naming them "Option2" and "Option3" with titles "Option 2" and "Option 3." Click back on the window when finished. Note: names for the check boxes need to correspond to names used for reference in scripts; titles can be any title you choose.

Label

To create the label above the text field, drag a Small System Font Text from the Text Object group in the Objects Palette. Once placed, double-click the object. (The window will gray out, indicating that the text field editor is now active.) Type the text you want for the title (see Figure 12-52).

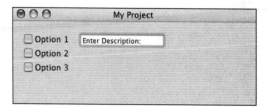

Figure 12-52. Label

Text field

The text field is the box in the Text Objects group that does not have a scrollbar. Add one to the window and resize as desired. Name the text field "txtInput" in the Info palette. You may want to set a text formatter for this field to ensure that only text can be entered. For this, select Add formatter from the Format menu. The formatter type should be Text by default. You may wish to experiment with the various format options (see Figure 12-53).

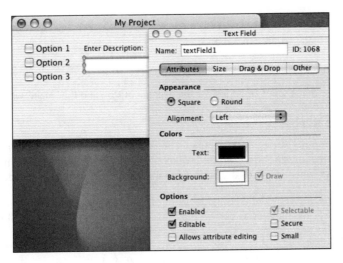

Figure 12-53.
Text field

Push button

Add a push button to the main window. Name the button "pshExecute." Label it "Execute". You may wish to give the push button default behavior to send it a *clicked* event when the user presses the RETURN key on the keyboard. For this, set Keyboard Equivalent in its Info palette to the Return option found in the pop-up (see Figure 12-54).

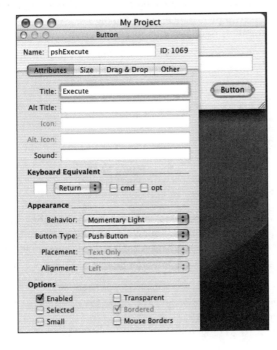

Figure 12-54.
Keyboard equivalent

5. Edit main menu.

No alterations will be made to the main menu.

6. Attach scripts.

This project will require that a script be added for the Execute button and the "main" window.

Execute button script

Create a script for the push button "pshExecute." The *clicked* handler for the button will call two user-defined handlers: (1) *getUserInput*, which gets the results of the user's input, and (2) *doMainProcess*, where most of the code from the existing script will be placed.

If FaceSpan preferences are set to Add code for standard handlers (in Editing Preferences), the script will have a *clicked* handler as part of the button's script. Complete it as follows:

```
on clicked theObject
    set {userOptions, userEntry} to getUserInput ( )
    doMainProcess (userOptions, userEntry)
end clicked
```

Main window script

Create a script for the "main" window. A handler in this script, *getUserInput*, will be used to collect the result of the user's interaction with the window items (see listing that follows). To write this user-defined handler, use the Object Browser in the Script Help drawer to add references to the objects. For instance, after typing set userOptions to name of every cell of in the first statement, double-click the entry for the matrix in the Object Browser (see Figure 12-55).

Figure 12-55.
Object Browser

Notice that a complete reference is entered, including a reference to the window. Finish the statement to read as in the following script. Follow this procedure for entering the reference for the text field in the next statement. The completed routine should be similar to the following:

```
on getUserInput ( )
    set userOptions to name of every cell of matrix "matCheck" ¬
        of window "main" whose state is on state
        set userEntry to string value of text field "txtInput" of ¬
        window "main"
    return {userOptions, userEntry}
end getUserInput
```

Main process subroutine

The main process subroutine (*doMainProcess*) will take care of most of the functionality from the existing script. This could be placed in the script for the "main" window, in the script for the push button, or in the Project Script. This is one of the nice things about FaceSpan: most routines can be placed wherever it makes the most sense to you (and perhaps the script). For demonstration, a user-defined routine has been "dummied up" to indicate how this handler would be written. Putting the procedure in the script for the "main" window allows the Script Help drawer to return the reference for the text field.

In the "main" window's script include the following:

```
on doMainProcess (userOptions, userEntry)
    if "Option1" is in userOptions then
        --statements to perform if Option1 checkbox is checked
    end if
    --add if/then statements for remaining checkboxes.
    set string value of text field "txtInput" of window "main" to ¬
    "Script completed successfully"
end doMainProcess
```

7. Test and debug.

If the project runs successfully, the message "Script completed successfully" will appear in the text field. As you test run a project, you may see the need to add additional code or functionality. Often this becomes apparent as you experience how user behavior might cause a project to fail.

In this project, should the user fail to check a check box, or fail to add information to the text field, the project could fail. This can be prevented by making sure that at least one option is checked and a default entry is placed in the text field. An opened handler for the window would be an appropriate place for such code.

Main window script opened handler

Open the "main" window's script. To create the handler, select main in the Object Browser and disclose the Window entry in the Handlers browser. With the text cursor on an open line in the script, double-click opened from the handler list. The handler wrappers are added to the script. Add statements to the handler so it reads as follows. (Use Object Browser to get the references to the matrix and text field.)

```
on opened theObject
    set state of cell 1 of matrix "matCheck" of window "main" to on state
    set string value of text field "txtInput" of window "main" to ¬
    "Default value"
end opened
```

8. Edit F page.

Refer to the outline in "Nine steps to success" for details.

9. Save project.

Although this project has no real functionality, the hope is that this introductory project will give you a quick overview of using FaceSpan to create a simple user interface.

12

Project 2: Multiple functionality for a button bar

This project demonstrates using a template to quick-start a project.

Perhaps you have a number of scripts that work in the same environment such as ones for automating InDesign or QuarkXPress. Think how handy it would be to have a floating button bar so that all you (or your user) need do is push a button to get script functionality. The following tutorial demonstrates this. You will want to have some graphics handy that measure 36 pixels by 36 pixels (or however large you want your buttons to be). These can be just about any common format; TIFF may be preferred.

1. Start new project.

In the New Project window, select the ButtonBar template from the template list to quick-start this project (see Figure 12-56).

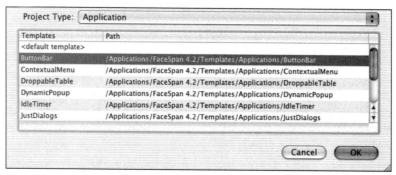

Figure 12-56. ButtonBar template

2. Add resources.

You can add a number of graphics to your project at one time by *SHIFT*-selecting and dragging them into the Images folder in the Project Window. Just make sure that you do not release the graphics until the line below the Images folder appears.

3. Set up windows.

The template provides all we will need for this project.

4. Design the interface.

Much of what is needed for the interface is provided by the template, but you can modify the project to fit your particular needs.

Bevel buttons

The template provides a panel "buttonBar" that is set up to float. It has one bevel button. Duplicate this bevel button to create the number of buttons that you want on your button bar. You may need to resize the window. To duplicate the bevel button, select it and press *COMMAND*+D. Enter values into the fields (the demonstration project used 39 in the

Horizontal Offset field, 0 in the Vertical Offset field, and 8 for Repeat Count). Click OK (see Figure 12-57).

Figure 12-57.
Duplicating an object

To assign an image to a button, click the button and enter the name of the graphic in the Icon field for the Info palette. Type the file name exactly as it appears in the Images list in the Project window.

Note: in version 4.2 you can drag the entry from the Project window to the button to assign the image.

Alternately, you could set it up so that a button works as a toggle with one graphic to display when in the "on" position and another to display when in the "off" position. To do this, set the Behavior for the button to Toggle and add a file name reference to the Alt. Icon field.

5. Edit main menu.

The title of the menu item Bring All To Front in the Window menu has been changed to Reopen panel in the template. Its action is handled in the *choose menu item* handler in the Project Script.

Note: projects created with a template inherit the name of the template. You will need to open the menu editor and change the title of each of the three menu items with the template's name. (Use the title field in Info palette to change the title.)

6. Attach scripts.

Now it's just a matter of adding scripts and code to the project to respond to the buttons being pushed. One way this could be done would be to put a lengthy *if/then* statement in a *clicked* handler inside the panel's script. This would test for the button being pushed and then call procedures depending on the button pushed. This has been started for you in the template and reads as follows:

```
on clicked theObject
    set theName to name of theObject
    if theName is "button" then
        --call to procedure for bevel button "button"
        processImage ()
    else if theName is "button1" then
        --call to next procedure
        --repeat for all buttons
    end if
end clicked
```

12

The routines called could be in the same script, in the Project Script, or could even be part of an imported FaceSpan script. The template provides a dummy routine.

```
on processImage ()
    --statements for called routine
    activate
    display dialog "Button was pushed"
end processImage
```

Code to accommodate the floating panel is part of the Project Script that is included in the ButtonBar template. This includes code to respond to the Reopen panel menu item in the *choose menu* handler:

```
on choose menu item theMenuItem
    if title of theMenuItem is "Reopen panel" then
        display panel thePanel
    end if
end choose menu item
```

7. Test and debug.

Click the Compile button to test your scripts. A project with this limited scope should run without a hitch.

8. Edit Credits page.

If you decide to save this project, you may want to put instructions to your user on the Credits page.

9. Save project.

Projects that use a template inherit the name of the template's executable. You will need to open the Executable Settings window (select Executable Settings from the Project menu). Change the name of your project there.

Project 3: Simple text editor

This project demonstrates how using scripts from the script library can reduce the amount of actual code writing required in a project to a bare minimum.

Our next project will create a simple text editor using scripts provided as part of FaceSpan's Script Library to work with User Defaults and the Open panel (see Figure 12-58).

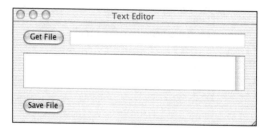

Figure 12-58.
Simple text editor

1. Start new project.

Select application for type. No template will be used.

2. Add resources.

No resources will be added to the project.

3. Set up windows.

Open the "main" window and set its properties. (Use your discretion in setting its properties.)

4. Design the interface.

The "main" window will be set up to allow the user to click the "pshGet" button or drop a file on it to open. The name of the file opened will display in the text field and the contents of the file will display in the text view (has scrollbar). When the user clicks the Save button, the text in the text view will be saved over the original file if changes have been made. We will add some push buttons, a text view, and a text field to the window.

Push buttons

Add a push button to the window and place it top left. Name the button "pshFiles" and give it the title "Get File".

Duplicate the button by pressing COMMAND+D with the button still selected. You will want a horizontal offset of 0; the vertical offset is not critical. Try 200 as a value. Rename the duplicated button "pshSave" and give it the title "Save File."

To handle a drop event (should our user drop a file on the "pshfiles" button), we need to set the "pshFiles" button up to accept a drop. To do this, click the button and select the Drag & Drop tab in the Info palette. Click the check box next to Filenames in the list. The button is now ready to accept a file name (see Figure 12-59).

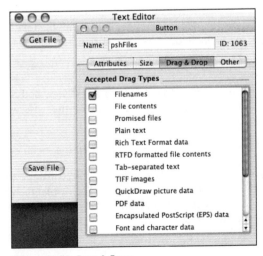

Figure 12-59. Drag & Drop

Text view

The text view is identified by a scrollbar on the right side. Add a text view to the window and resize by dragging resize handles as needed.

Several objects in FaceSpan 4 are nested inside other objects. The text view is an example. When you drag the text view onto a window, you will notice that the title for the Info palette is "Scroll View". The scroll view is the parent of the text view and gives it scrollbar behavior. Make sure you name the scroll view "txtScroll".

To access the text view, double-click the scroll view. Notice that the window grays to indicate that you are inside a nested structure. To "back out" of the structure, you can click the little up arrow in the lower-right corner of the text view, use the COMMAND-up arrow key combination, or click back on the window. If you want to set properties for the text view, make sure that the Info palette displays the words "Text View" at the top (see Figure 12-60).

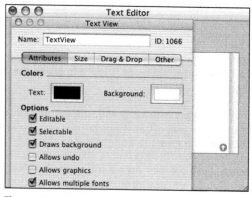

Figure 12-60. Text View

Text field

Add a text field to the window and resize as needed. Name the text field "txtFile". You will also want to uncheck the Editable option in the Attributes pane.

5. Edit main menu.

A contextual menu is connected automatically to a text view and a text field to provide access to text formatting and spelling functionality. You may also want to add this functionality to the main menu.

Double-click Main Menu in the Project window to open the menu editor.

Drag the Format item from the Menus group in the Objects Palette to the main menu bar (a line will appear where the menu will be inserted). The Format menu has a Font item and Text item that open to display submenus. Functionality for the menu items in the Format menu is built in (see Figure 12-61).

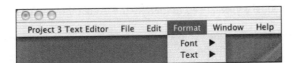

Figure 12-61. Main menu

Close the menu editor.

6. Attach scripts.

Open the Project Script. If Add code for standard handlers is checked in the Preferences Editing tab, the Project Script will include two handlers by default: *launched* and *choose menu item*. The Project Script is an ideal place to manage values that need to be available to various objects within the project.

Functionality for managing values that are permanently stored with the application is provided by User Defaults. User Defaults is a collection of key/value pairs that are stored as part of a project. Our demonstration project will use code found in the Script Library to manage User Defaults.

CONTROL-click or right-click an open line in the script window to open the Script Library. In the GetSetSave collection you will find the entry UserDefaultList. This provides the code for managing User Defaults as a list of values. When the entry is selected, the code is dumped to the cursor location in the script edit window.

Notice that the code includes property statements. These will need to be cut and pasted at the top of the Project Script. The comments suggest that the handler be called as part of the project's *will finish launching* event. Cut the call to the *UserDefaultsList* handler (it will be pasted in the next step into the *will finish launching* handler).

will finish launching handler

To add a *will finish launching* handler to the script, select the project name in the Object Browser. From the list of handlers presented, disclose the Application group. Make sure the text cursor is on an open line in the edit window, and double-click the will finish launching entry. Wrappers for the handler are added to the script. The call should still be on the clipboard, so highlight the single statement inside the *will finish launching* handler and paste.

Define the User Defaults by editing the *defaultList* property. For this project, leave the list as defaulted. Notice that there is only one item in the *defaultList*: *thePath* with a default value of -1. Each entry in User Defaults is a key/value pair. Each item in our default list is a list of two items: the key and the value.

The *currentValues* list needs to have a list of empty strings to correspond to each item in the *defaultList*. This variable will keep track of the values while in runtime. User Defaults normally are not saved back to the application until right before the application quits. Notice that a *will quit* handler is included as part of the code.

12

If you use User Defaults, you will need to identify the executable settings for the application.

Click the Compile button for the Project Script. Once compiled, you can close the script if you wish.

"pshFiles" button script

Create a script for the "pshFiles" button. This will need a handler to take care of a file name drop. In the DragDrop collection of the Script Library there is an entry called DropFile. Add it to the "GetFiles" button's script. Notice that the code includes a property, *kCurrentFile*. Cut and paste this property declaration at the top of the Project Script. It also makes a call to a *populateWindow* handler.

Should the user click the button (instead of dropping a file), the script will need a handler to let the user select a file from an Open Panel dialog box. In the File Folder collection of the Script Library, find the entry for *GetFileOpenPanel*. Add this to the button's script. The code includes statements to be provided as part of a call to the handler. Cut the call statements and paste them into the *clicked* handler for the button. The value for *thePath* (the default folder path) is item 1 of the *currentValues* list. The *theTitle* and *thePrompt* values can be any string value. Add a call to the *populateWindow* handler and update the value for the *kCurrentFile* property. The *clicked* handler should read similar to the following:

```
on clicked theObject
    set thePath to (item 1 of my currentValues)
    set theTitle to "Place Title Here"
    set thePrompt to "Select file"
    set theFiles to getFiles (thePath, theTitle, thePrompt, false)
    populateWindow (theFiles)
    set my kCurrentFile to theFiles
end clicked
```

Main window script

Create a script for the "main" window. Again, the script code will come from the Script Library. In the Window collection, the entry *Initialize Window* should be found. Add it to the "main" window's script. This handler can set up initial values and flag our project when a condition changes. Cut the *hasChanged* property and paste at the top of the Project Script.

PopulateWindow

The *PopulateWindow* routine will call a *readFileText* handler and place the contents of the file in the text view. The name of the file will be placed in the text field. This routine will be placed in the script for the "main" window. The *PopulateWindow* code, found in the Windows collection of the Script Library, is a handler template designed just for this purpose. Add it to the "main" window's script. Words shown in ALL CAPS need to be replaced with actual references and values pertinent to the script. Highlight TEXT FIELD REFERENCE in the first line and double-click the entry for *txtFile* in the Object Browser. For VALUE, replace this with the variable *fileRef*. Notice that the next line calls a handler that is included with the template. Highlight TEXT OBJECT REFERENCE, and double-click the entry for TextView in the Object Browser. (You may need to click the twisty triangle next to the *txtScroll* entry to see the entry for TextView.) Compile the script.

7. Test and debug.

This may be a good place to test what has been done so far. When the project runs, drag a text file onto the Get File button, or click the button and select a file from the Open panel. Stop the run. If nothing happened when you dragged a file to the button, check to make sure the name of the button is the same as is required by the *drop* handler.

```
if name of theObject is "pshFiles" then
```

Also, double-check to make sure you have set the button to recognize a file (check Filenames in the Drag & Drop tab of Button's Info palette).

Save button script

Create a script for the "pshSave" button. This will call a routine to verify if there is text in the text view. If the value of the application property *hasChanged* is found to be true, the routine will need to save the text to the current file. (The reference to the current file is in the *kCurrentFile* property.)

The routine that we will use, *GetTextandSave*, is found in the *GetSetSave* collection of the Script Library. Place this in the script for the "pshSave" button. The call to the *GetTextandSave* routine needs to be cut and pasted into the *clicked* handler for the Save Button script. The properties *hasChanged* and *kCurrentFile* are already defined in the Project Script, so they can be deleted.

All that is left is to add a reference to the text view in place of the TEXT VIEW REFERENCE placeholder.

One last detail

There is just one detail that needs to be attended to. The *hasChanged* property will have the value false until code is added that will (1) set the value of *hasChanged* to false when new text is placed in the text view, or (2) set the value of *hasChanged* to true when the text view gets a changed event.

Main window script

For the first step, the *populateWindow* handler in the script for window "main" would be a good place to initialize the value for the *hasChanged* property. Add the following statement as the last line:

```
set my hasChanged to false
```

For the second step, a changed handler can be added to the window's script. This will set the value of *hasChanged* to true when the window receives a *changed* event from the text view. The *changed* handler is found in the Editing group of handlers for a text object. Select the text view entry in the Object Browser and disclose the *Editing* handlers. Double-click the changed entry to add its wrappers to the window's script.

12

Add code so the handler reads as follows:

```
--toggles false to true for application property hasChanged
on changed theObject
    if name of theObject is "TextView" and my hasChanged is false then
        set my hasChanged to not my hasChanged
    end if
end changed
```

Compile the script. Again, after these additions have been made, you may wish to test run the project.

8. Edit Credits page.

Even though adding a Credits page may seem like an unnecessary step, it adds a touch of professionalism to your project.

9. Save project.

When you are satisfied, save the project.

This is just the beginning of what could be a fully functional text editing application. As is, it can be used to read text from a file and save the edited text. You may want to run it just to explore all of the text editing capability that comes with a text view without your having to write one line of code.

Tutorial wrap-up

The goal of the tutorials was to introduce you to some of the ways that FaceSpan can be used, and give a better understanding of what can be done with it. This is just the tip of the iceberg. There is so much more waiting for your creativity. The possibilities for creating stunning interfaces with custom views and the ability to nest objects within one another are just some of the options.

There is literally no right and wrong way to put a project together. The tutorial examples use a style that is referred to as a distributed approach, as code is "distributed" among the various objects. Not that there is anything wrong with putting all of your code in the Project Script, it's just that a distributed approach makes a project easier to read and maintain. There are no hard and fast rules for how this is done, but the following steps are a good guideline:

1. Variables whose values need to be used throughout the project are put in property statements for the application.

2. If FaceSpan scripts are used, define and initialize a global variable to reference the file in the application script.

3. Reserve the application script for managing persistent properties, handling menu actions, and for handlers that need to be available to more than one window.

4. Handlers that work with "outside" applications are often placed in the Project Script or are part of a collection that is loaded from a FaceSpan script.

5. All activity that is generated in a window should be handled in the window's script or in individual scripts for its window items.

6. If there are a number of similar buttons in a window, you may wish to handle their *clicked* events in a single clicked handler using *if/then* tests to determine which button sent the message.

7. Use prebuilt scripts from the Script Library when possible. There should be no need to re-create the wheel. Make sure that property statements are cut and pasted to the top of the Project Script. Place sample calls to the handlers in code where appropriate.

A word about my

Watch for the little qualifier *my*: it can make or break a project.

1. Use the *my* qualifier as part of a call to a handler when you are making the call within a *tell* statement.

2. Use the *my* qualifier to reference a property in a parent object. If a property statement is declared at the application level, *my* is needed to reference the property from a script at either the window or window item level.

Code in the Script Library assumes that property declarations will be made at the application level with the code at the window or window item level. Notice that references to properties include *my*.

The unsung heroes

Within FaceSpan are a number of functionalities and windows that can be used to facilitate project building. You may find them seldom-used or may wonder how you could work without them.

The dictionary viewer

Dictionaries are online references of an application's object classes and methods (commands). Besides being able to display its own, FaceSpan's dictionary viewer displays the dictionaries for other scriptable applications. You can even set it to show the information as raw event codes. And, a dictionary can be saved so it can be viewed without having to find it each time you want to use it (see Figure 12-62).

12

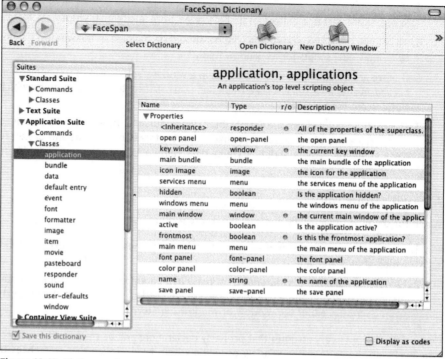

Figure 12-62. Dictionary viewer

Contextual menus

Just about every object in FaceSpan has a contextual menu to give an alternate method for creating and managing objects. CONTROL-click (or right-click) an object to see the options available. It's enough to make you want a three-button mouse (if you don't have one already).

Object Inspector

To get information about a resource in the project, the Object Inspector is the place to go. Click the Show Inspector button in the Project window and activate one of the three tabs. You can preview graphics and movies in the Preview tab (see Figure 12-63).

Figure 12-63. Object Inspector

Formatting helps

If you find yourself needing to align objects, the Alignment panel is a handy tool. COMMAND-select objects you wish to align and select Align from the Format menu (COMMAND+SHIFT+A). Hold the cursor over an icon in the tool to get its description (tool tip) if you can't discern its functionality (see Figure 12-64).

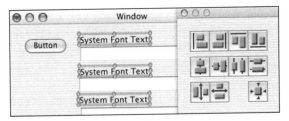

Figure 12-64. Alignment panel

The Format menu also has some handy formatting aids that respond to quick-key short-cuts: Shift Right (COMMAND+]) and Shift Left (COMMAND+[); Comment Selection (COMMAND+}) and Uncomment Selection (COMMAND+{).

Test interface

Objects have built-in behavior such as changing appearance when selected. These behaviors can be tested by putting a project in Test Interface mode. To indicate when a project is in Test Interface mode, FaceSpan's icon changes in the doc. To return to edit mode, press COMMAND+Q.

12

To explore further

To see the tutorial projects and other sample projects at work, visit FaceSpan's download page. Download the projects desired. We hope you will soon experience the variety of ways that AppleScript and FaceSpan can make a world-class application, or just a much-used utility, out of your AppleScript scripts.

Power wrap-up

This section summarizes the chapter in an intensive-reference style. Use this part to look up facts related to the chapter without the chatter.

User interaction and AppleScript

Since the AppleScript language was designed for data manipulation, the user interaction portion of it is minimal. This chapter deals with the few user-interaction commands AppleScript does possess.

All user interaction commands are defined in the Standard Additions dictionary.

display dialog

The *display dialog* command displays a simple dialog box with buttons and an optional text field. This is the basic *display dialog* command, which displays a dialog box with some text and two buttons, OK and Cancel:

```
display dialog  "Something interesting"
```

You can see screenshots of the different resulting dialog boxes previously in this chapter.

Canceling a dialog box

When clicking the Cancel button, the command will generate a "silent" error. The error is the "user canceled" error, number -128. It will stop the script if not captured in a *try* block, but will not generate an error message. Here's how to trap the cancel error:

```
try
    display dialog  "Something interesting"
on error number -128
    display dialog  "You canceled"
    return
end
```

Custom buttons

The *display dialog* command allows you to define up to three custom buttons. This is done with the *buttons* parameter. To specify custom buttons, you supply the *buttons* parameter with a list of up to three strings, where each string is one button's title. The buttons will be displayed in the dialog box in the same order they appear in the list.

The following script will display a dialog box with the buttons Yes, No, and Maybe:

```
display dialog  "Click a button:" buttons {"Yes", "No", "Maybe"}
```

To specify which button is the default button, use the *default button* parameter. This parameter accepts either a string that is the name of the button you want to make the default button or an integer that specifies the button by number.

The following script lines both define the Yes button as the default button:

```
display dialog "Click a button:" buttons {"Yes", "No", "Maybe"} ¬
    default button 1
display dialog "Click a button:" buttons {"Yes", "No", "Maybe"} ¬
    default button "Yes"
```

To extract the button the user clicked, get the *button returned* item of the dialog reply record (see the "Dialog reply" section that follows).

Dialog icons

AppleScript dialog boxes can have one of three icons, or no icon at all.

Icons are specified with the *with icon* parameter. The options are as follows:

For the stop icon, use the value "stop" or 0; for the note icon (face with speech bubble) use either "note" or 1; for the caution icon (yellow triangle) use either "caution" or 2. The noninteger values are not strings but rather reserved words you type without quotes. The following two script lines will display a dialog box with the stop icon:

```
display dialog "The script will now stop"  with icon  stop
display dialog "The script will now stop"  with icon  0
```

12

Getting user input

The *display dialog* command allows you to solicit user input by using the *default answer* parameter. The *default answer* parameter takes a string value. Including that parameter will cause the dialog box to include a text field. The string you provide as the parameter's value will be the default text in the text field. To have a blank text field, use a blank string ("") as the parameter's value.

The following script will display a dialog box with a blank text field for user input:

```
display dialog  "Enter your name:"  default answer ""
```

The following script will display a dialog box with default text:

```
display dialog  "Enter your date of birth:" default answer "MM/DD/YYYY"
```

To extract the text the user typed, get the *text returned* item of the *dialog reply* record (see the "Dialog reply" section that follows).

Dialogs that give up

The *gave up* parameter of the *display dialog* command allows you to specify a time period in seconds, after which the dialog box will "give up" and close itself.

If the *gave up* parameter is included, the dialog reply record will include the Boolean parameter *gave up*. A true value indicates that a button was not clicked and the dialog box gave up after the specified number of seconds.

The following script will give up after 20 seconds:

```
display dialog  "Click a button, quick!" giving up after 20
```

Dialog reply

The dialog reply is a record returned by the *display dialog* command. The dialog reply record is a bit different depending on the parameters you use. Following are pairs of statements using the *display dialog* command, followed by the resulting dialog reply record.

A simple dialog box:

```
display dialog  "Click a button"
--> {button returned:"OK"}
```

A dialog box with text input:

```
display dialog  "Enter your name" default answer ""
--> {text returned:"Joe", button returned:"OK"}
```

A dialog box with a *give up* parameter:

```
display dialog  "Click a button, quick!" giving up after 20
--> {button returned:"", gave up:true}
```

choose from list

The *choose from list* command is defined in the Standard Additions dictionary. It allows you to let the user choose an item from a list of strings. The result can be a list of items, or simply false if the user clicks the Cancel button.

The following script allows the user to choose from a list of three cities:

```
choose from list {"Los Angeles", "Boston", "Atlanta"}
```

The *choose from list* command has a few parameters that define the titles of the buttons and the item-selection behavior.

Prompt

Use the *with prompt* parameter to specify a prompt to the dialog box.

To specify alternate titles for the OK and Cancel buttons, use the *OK button name* and *Cancel button name* parameters, as you see in the following script:

```
choose from list with prompt "Pick a city" ¬
    {"Los Angeles", "Boston", "Atlanta"} OK button name "Get there"
```

Item selection

By default, the user must make a single choice. No empty selection or multiple selections are allowed. To change these defaults, use the *multiple selections allowed* and *empty selection allowed* parameters.

The following script will allow the user to click OK even if no selection has been made:

```
choose from list  {"Los Angeles", "Boston", "Atlanta"} ¬
with empty selection allowed
```

The following script will allow the user to select multiple items from the list:

```
choose from list  {"Los Angeles", "Boston", "Atlanta"} ¬
    with multiple selections allowed
```

You can also specify which items will be selected by default. The following script starts with the "US" item selected:

```
choose from list  {"US", "France", "Mexico"} default items {"US"}
```

choose file

The *choose file* command allows the user to specify an existing file using the Open dialog box. This command returns an alias to the chosen file, and generates an error if the Cancel button is clicked. The following script will display the basic Open dialog box using the *choose file* command:

```
choose file
```

12

Prompt

The *with prompt* parameter allows you to specify a custom prompt. By default, there is no prompt. The following script will display the dialog box with a custom prompt:

```
choose file with prompt "Pick a text file to clean:"
```

Restricting file types

The *of type* parameter allows you to specify a list of up to four file types. The *choose file* command will allow the user to choose only files whose type is mentioned in the list of types you provide. The following script will restrict the user to choosing text and word files:

```
choose file of type {"W8BN", "TEXT"}
```

Default location

The default location is an alias to a folder that the *choose file* dialog box will point to as it opens. The following script will ensure that the Open dialog box starts out by pointing to the desktop:

```
choose file default location (path to desktop)
```

Invisibles

The Boolean parameter *invisibles* determines if the *choose file* command will allow the user to choose invisible files.

Multiple selections

The Boolean parameter *multiple selections allowed* determines if the *choose file* command will allow the user to choose multiple files.

choose file name

The *choose file name* command displays a dialog box similar to the Save dialog box. It allows you to specify a file name and location of a nonexisting file. The command doesn't create any file, only returns a path to the new file the user specified.

The *choose file name* command has three parameters: *with prompt*, *default name*, and *default location*.

The *with prompt* parameter adds a prompt to the top of the dialog box.

The parameters *default name* and *default location* allow you to specify the default file name and default folder location that the Save dialog box will be pointing to. The following script will allow the user to choose a file name and location with a default location of the desktop and a default name:

```
choose file name default name "Image.JPG" default location path ¬
to desktop
--> file "Macintosh HD:Users:hanaan:Desktop:Image.JPG"
```

choose folder

The *choose folder* command is nearly identical to the *choose file* command (see the section "choose file" earlier), but instead of a file, the user will be only able to select a folder.

choose application

The *choose application* command allows the user to pick an application from the applications on the computer. The parameters *with title* and *with prompt* allow you to customize the *choose application* dialog box. The *multiple selections allowed* parameter allows the user to pick multiple applications.

The result is either an application as an application object as shown here:

```
application "Finder"
```

or you can use the *as* parameter to have the command return the result as an alias to the application file instead, as shown here:

```
choose application as alias
--> alias "Macintosh HD:Applications:FileMaker Pro 7:FileMaker Pro.app:"
```

choose URL

The *choose URL* command returns a path to a URL you either choose or specify in a special dialog box. You can use the *showing* parameter along with one or more of the following terms to limit the type of URL the user can choose. The possible values for that parameter are "Web servers", "FTP servers", "Telnet hosts", "File servers", "News servers", "Directory services", "Media servers", and "Remote applications".

The Boolean parameter *editable URL* determines if the user can specify a URL by typing it. A *false* value means that the user will not get a text field in which the URL can be edited or typed in.

choose color

The *choose color* command allows the user to specify a color using OS X's Choose Color dialog box. The color is returned as a list of three integers from 0 to 65,535, which describes the color as 16 bits per pixel. The command's one parameter, *default color*, allows you to specify the color that the dialog box will have when it first appears. The following script will allow the user to pick a color, and the default color in the dialog box will be red:

```
choose color default color {65535, 0, 0}
```

12

Details previously . . .

The last part of this chapter is a summary of the entire chapter. For more details on any of the items here, refer to earlier sections in this chapter.

In this chapter we will see how you can use scripts to manipulate files by copying, moving, and deleting them, by reading them and writing to them, and also how to refer to files and folders.

When we work with files, what we need is a way to refer to the files we work with. No matter if our goal is to create a text file, back up some folders, or delete the entire contents of a hard disk, the ways we refer to a file are the same.

There are a few ways AppleScript can refer to files, and our job is to choose the method that works best with the specific situation and with the application we're using.

Some of the methods used to refer to files are alias, file reference, POSIX file, URL, and a few more, including some that are only defined in the Finder and System Event applications' dictionaries.

File reference delimiters

The main part of a file reference is a string that contains the full name of the file. This full name starts out with the name of the volume the file is on, followed by the name of each folder in the folder tree that the file is a part of. The folder names, and finally the subject's file name, are separated by a delimiter.

This delimiter is one of two characters: colon (:) or slash (/). The colon is the Mac's original delimiter that is still being used by most disks, by most Mac users, and in most cases by AppleScript. The slash is used due to the integration of the UNIX OS with OS X.

For example, if you have a file called reference.pdf in a folder called documents on your hard disk whose name is "Macintosh HD", the full name, or the path name, is going to be "Macintosh HD:documents:reference.pdf".

When a situation calls for a UNIX-style path, then the path will be "/Volumes/Macintosh HD/documents/reference.pdf". Notice that the word "Volumes" was added. This addition will be there to identify files that are not found on the startup disk. More on that later on when we discuss UNIX file references.

The most descriptive-reading reference style is the Finder reference style. Although it works only within the Finder's *tell* block, it's easy to coerce it into an alias, string, etc.

In the following examples, you can see a few ways to look at a file path, starting with the Finder's reference, and then both Mac-style and UNIX-style path names. Figure 13-1 shows the Finder's window displaying the hierarchy leading to the final file.

Finder reference:

document file "InDesign CS Scripting Guide.pdf" of folder "Scripting" of folder "Adobe InDesign Technical Info" of folder "Adobe InDesign CS" of folder "Applications" of startup disk of application "Finder"

Mac-style path name:

Macintosh HD:Applications:Adobe InDesign CS:Adobe InDesign Technical Info:Scripting: InDesign CS Scripting Guide.pdf

UNIX-style path name:

/Applications/Adobe InDesign CS/Adobe InDesign Technical Info/Scripting/InDesign CS Scripting Guide.pdf

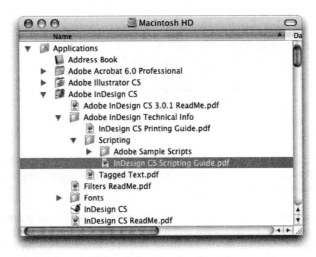

Figure 13-1. A Finder window showing the path names shown previously

In pre-OS X, the Mac allowed you to use slashes (/) in file names. While this was very useful for specifying dates in names of files and folders, it became a nightmare when files had to be backed up or looked at by other operating systems.

Now, Mac OS X doesn't allow the use of colons (:) or slashes (/) in names of files and folders.

File references, strings, and coercion

Most file reference types can be coerced into each other or into a string. In fact, most file reference types are a string preceded by the reference type. If, for instance, you wanted to refer to a file called Report.doc found on the hard drive, the string would be

    "Macintosh HD:Report.doc"

The alias reference would be

    alias "Macintosh HD:Report.doc"

13

The file reference form would be

```
file "Macintosh HD:Report.doc"
```

Notice that the prefix changes, but the string is the same.

What's more, you can use the *as* coercion to convert between one reference form to another. Following are a few examples (the following paths have to be changed to point to actual files on your hard drive in order to work):

Script 13-1

```
tell application "Finder"
file "Macintosh HD:Report.doc" as alias
   --> alias "Macintosh HD:Report.doc"
   a reference to file "Macintosh HD:Report.doc"
   --> file "Macintosh HD:Report.doc"
   file "Macintosh HD:Report.doc"
   --> error: Can't get file "Macintosh HD:Report.doc".
end tell
```

In this case, AppleScript generated an error, since the file reference isn't a class you can use by itself. The statements were put in a Finder *tell* block since using the file reference form outside the *tell* block will not compile.

Due to the relatively complex nature of file reference forms, I usually prefer to store file references as strings. You can coerce any file reference form into a string, and coerce the string back into different file reference forms by simply attaching the appropriate prefix to the string.

Script 13-2

```
set the_path to "Macintosh HD:Report.doc"
set the_alias to alias the_path
--or:
tell application "Finder"
   delete file the_path
end tell
--or:
tell application "System Events"
   set unix_path to posix path of file the_path
   --"/Report.doc"
end tell
```

Strings are also much more flexible when you want to store them. In order to store your path in a text file or in a database, you would most likely want to convert it to a string.

There are times, however, when you will need the power of the *alias* class, which is discussed later on in this chapter.

Alias and file reference

The two main forms of file reference are the file and alias. While their written forms appear similar, they do have significant differences, which we will look at here.

The written form of these references include the prefix word ("alias" or "file"), followed by a string that represents the path name.

> A path name is the full file name including the drive and subsequent nested folders going down to the file's name, all separated by colons.

Examples:

```
alias "Macintosh HD:AppleScript Reference.pdf"
file "Macintosh HD:AppleScript Reference.pdf"
```

Note that the second form using the term "file" will only compile if placed inside an application *tell* block such as a Finder *tell* block.

How aliases work

The first thing you may notice about using the alias reference form is that AppleScript goes out and checks if there's a file (that includes folders, applications, etc.) that corresponds to the supplied path name.

If you script includes the following statement:

```
alias "Macintosh HD:AppleScript Reference.pdf"
```

as you compile the script, AppleScript will check to see if there's actually a file named `AppleScript Reference.pdf` on a mounted volume named "Macintosh HD". If there isn't such a file, AppleScript will return a syntax error. When trying to compile the following statement, AppleScript will generate the error shown in Figure 13-2.

```
alias "Macintosh HD:Windows XP source code.TXT"
```

Figure 13-2. The script won't compile since the file referenced with the alias reference form doesn't exist.

13

Now why would AppleScript go through the trouble of checking the file's existence right away? The answer is that as soon as AppleScript finds the referenced file, it creates an internal reference to that file. This reference works much like the way file aliases work in the Finder: the file is found even if its name or location has been changed. Yes! As long as the script has been provided a valid alias, the script will retain a pointer to that file until it is deleted.

Alias file-tracking example

To test and demonstrate that alias capability, we will create a script that tracks a file you pick, and reports back if the location or name has changed.

For that, we will need two properties: one for the alias itself, which will change when the file is moved or renamed, and one that will keep track of the previous path name as string.

The application's script will start by checking if the *the_alias* property has been set (line 3). If the script is running for the first time and the *the_alias* property has not been set, then the script will ask you to choose a file (line 4). The *choose file* command will return an alias that will be assigned to the *the_alias* property.

From there, the script will compare the string variable containing the previous location to the alias to check if the file has moved (line 7). If the file has moved, AppleScript will show you the old path and the new path in a dialog box (line 10).

Here's the script:

Script 13-3

```
property the_alias : missing value
property last_pathname : ""
if the_alias is missing value then
   set the_alias to choose file
else
   set this_pathname to the_alias as string
   if this_pathname = last_pathname then
      display dialog "The file hasn't moved"
   else
      display dialog "Old file path:" & return & ¬
      last_pathname & return & ¬
      "New location: " & return & ¬
      this_pathname
   end if
end if
set last_pathname to the_alias as string
```

Run the script once to choose the file.

Now, change the name of the file you chose, or even move it to a different folder. Run the script again (without recompiling the script!). The script should show you the old path and the new path of the file you originally chose.

To force AppleScript to let go of the *the_alias* property, recompile the script.

Nontracked aliases

Can we use the alias reference form on a file that doesn't yet exist? Yes, however, you will be losing the benefit of AppleScript's file-tracking functionality described previously. The way to use an alias in AppleScript for referring to a nonexisting file is by describing the path name using an expression that is not a literal expression.

Either write

```
Set the_path_name to "Macintosh HD:Windows XP source code.TXT"
alias the_path_name
```

or

```
alias (get "Macintosh HD:Windows XP source code.TXT")
```

In both cases, AppleScript will only evaluate the alias at runtime. If the corresponding file still does not exist, then you will get error number -43, which means "file not found."

So what about file references?

File references are different from aliases in a few ways. For starters, an alias points to an existing file or folder, while a file reference can be pointing to a file that doesn't yet exist.

File references can't be assigned to variables just by tacking a string onto the word "file." For example, look at the following statement:

```
set file_reference to file "Macintosh HD:Some file.pdf"
```

or

```
set file_reference to file the_file_path
```

Running either line in a script will generate a runtime error number 10 (general script error).

The right way to store such references in variables is by using the *reference to* operator, or by using them in scripting additions or application-related commands.

Inside an application's *tell* block, the file reference can stand by itself.

```
tell application "Finder"
  set file_reference to file the_file_path
end tell
```

To assign a file reference to a variable, use the following:

```
set file_reference to a reference to file "Macintosh HD:Some file.pdf"
```

The result will be

```
file "Macintosh HD:Some file.pdf" of «script»
```

13

Or, you can simply use the simple file reference form as you would use *alias* in commands that support both file reference forms, such as the *read* command:

```
read file "Macintosh HD:Some file.txt"
```

Referring to folders and disks

When referring to folders or disks, use the same syntax you would use for files, but add a colon at the end, like this:

```
"Macintosh HD:Applications:"
```

The colon at the end of the file name indicates that the item is a container. When creating aliases, AppleScript will add a colon to the end if the referenced file is a container of sorts.

Using colons helps you when concatenating folders into a path name. If you have a colon at the end of the path name, all you have to do is tack on the name of the next folder.

Referring to packages

Packages, also referred to as bundles, are a funny breed of file. In a Finder window, they look like files. However, to the system, they're not much more than a folder with more folders and files inside of it. The most commonly known form packages take is Cocoa applications, but packages do exist in the Carbon world as well. The folders and files inside the package make up the different components of the application.

In the Finder's dictionary packages are just packages, not containers or files. In the System Events dictionary, however, packages are referred to as bundles.

Referring to these items becomes especially important when you work with your own AppleScript Studio applications. There, however, you need to refer to the package from the inside, which you can do with the bundle object.

From the outside, however, all you need to do is add a colon to the end of the application's path name, and then add the rest of the path of the enclosed file or folder you want to work with.

You know that an application is a package when you CONTROL-click it. If one of the menu items is Show Package Contents, as shown in Figure 13-3, then you know it's a Cocoa application you're dealing with, and you can open the package and look around.

Figure 13-3. The file contextual menu showing the Show Package Contents menu item

Figure 13-4 shows the package contents of the application Safari.

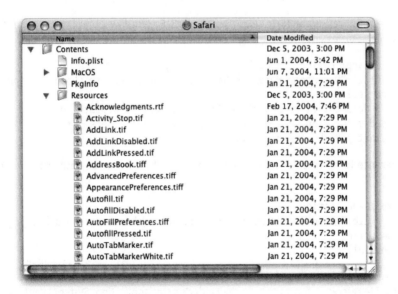

Figure 13-4. The open package of the application Safari

So, to refer to a file inside the package, you may have to do a couple of things:

First, you will have to check if the application has the .app file name extension. This extension has to be added to the path name.

After that, you have to add the colon, followed by the rest of the path. Packages always start with a single folder called Contents. From there, there are a couple of other folders called MacOS and Resources. Open them up and double-click some files. You will be surprised how much of your system you can mess up in a short period of time!

The following path points at a TIFF file in the resources folder in the Safari package:

```
alias "Macintosh
HD:Applications:Safari.app:Contents:Resources:AutoTabMarker.tif"
```

Finder references

So far we looked at the way different applications, scripting additions, and AppleScript itself refer to files. The Finder dictionary (and System Events dictionary) allow us to refer to files and folders as objects in a well-structured object model.

The top object (other than the application itself) is the hard disk. Every subsequent folder in the structure is an element of that object, and the folders also have their own elements: the files and folders they contain.

The Finder's file reference form uses AppleScript's English-like object reference form to refer to files. For instance, look at the following script and at the result:

```
tell application "Finder"
    file "Macintosh HD:Users:hanaan:Desktop:chocolate:chocolate.jpg"
end tell
--> document file "chocolate.jpg" of folder "chocolate" of ¬
folder "Desktop" of folder "hanaan" of folder "Users" of ¬
 startup disk of application "Finder"
```

This reference form, when still inside the Finder's *tell* block, may be easily coerced into a string.

```
tell application "Finder"
    file "Macintosh HD:Users:hanaan:Desktop:chocolate:chocolate.jpg" ¬
as string
end tell
--> "Macintosh HD:Users:hanaan:Desktop:chocolate:chocolate.jpg"
```

The same file reference form works in the Finder's sister application, System Events, as well.

With files and folders being objects, you can now create nested *tell* blocks for directing commands to certain files or folders. The following three examples have the same outcome:

Script 13-4 (includes two following scripts)

```
tell application "Finder"
    delete file "Macintosh HD:jobs:report.rtf"
end tell
```

or

```
tell application "Finder"
   tell startup disk
      delete document file "report.rtf" of folder "jobs"
   end tell
end tell
```

or

```
tell application "Finder"
   tell startup disk
      tell folder "jobs"
         tell document file "report.rtf"
            delete it
         end tell
      end tell
   end tell
end tell
```

Notice the word "it" after the *delete* command in the last example. The object *it* refers to the current *tell* target, in this case the file report.rtf. The use of *it* is optional for the most part, but does make your script a bit clearer than if you simply used the command *delete* by itself.

UNIX's POSIX paths

A POSIX path is a file reference form used in the UNIX OS, and therefore also in Mac OS X to some extent.

The main differences between the normal Mac file reference and the UNIX file reference are the delimiters used to separate folders, and the optional inclusion of the startup disk in the path name.

The most visible difference is the delimiters. If a path name is made out of names of folders followed by the name of the file at the end, the delimiters are the characters that separate the folder names.

In Mac operation and programming, path names use the color character as a delimiter. In UNIX, that delimiter is a slash. So, for a path name that looks like this on the Mac:

```
"Macintosh HD:Documents:Report.pdf"
```

the UNIX-style path name would look like this:

```
"Macintosh HD/Documents/Report.pdf"
```

13

In UNIX, a path name's beginning depends on the location of the file: any file on the startup disk may start with a slash while the name of the startup disk is omitted:

"/Documents/Report.pdf"

If the file is on another hard disk, let's say a disk named "External2000", the word "Volumes" has to be added at the start, like this:

"Volumes/External2000/Documents/Report.pdf"

Furthermore, in UNIX, any file that is found in the current user's home directory will start with a tilde (~). That means that if you have the file named report.rtf on your desktop, the UNIX path to it may be one of the following three POSIX paths:

~/Desktop/report.rtf
/Users/hanaan/Desktop/report.rtf
Volumes/Macintosh HD/Users/hanaan/Desktop/report.rtf

For now, you are on your own as far as adding the word "Volumes" or replacing the name of the home folder with a tilde. AppleScript may have a few ways to coerce the color-delimited path into a slash-delimited path, but the conversion isn't foolproof, and you may have to do some fixing.

Coercing paths to and from POSIX paths

AppleScript gives us a few ways to convert traditional colon-delimited AppleScript paths into UNIX POSIX paths, and vice versa.

You should know, however, that whenever you're using these paths, you will have to qualify them; and because they hardly work OK right out of the conversion, some adjustment is usually necessary.

POSIX path property

Aliases and file reference objects have a *POSIX path* property. This property can also work on nonexisting files, and in that case it isn't a hard reference to the file, but rather a "best guess" of how the conversion should work.

It is important to note that the *POSIX path* property exists so that scripters can make better use of the *do shell script* command.

You can get the *POSIX path* property of nonexisting files, which means that it is unsafe to assume that a file or folder exists because you've gotten its *POSIX path* property.

As one would expect, the *POSIX path* property was designed to work only with alias or file objects. However, when it was released, the *POSIX path* property also worked on strings. Unfortunately, people started relying on that "feature" and the AppleScript team couldn't remove it; now it's there for good.

The *POSIX path* property also works in reverse: you can ask for the *POSIX path* property of a slash-delimited path, and get its colon-delimited counterpart. Here too, however, the conversion is a best guess based on position of slashes, and doesn't represent a sure-fire path you can use in your script. The *POSIX path* property, however, was not intended to work in reverse. For that purpose the *POSIX file* object was created.

Here are some examples of the *POSIX path* property:

```
POSIX path of (path to startup disk)
--> "/"
POSIX path of (path to documents folder from user domain)
--> "/Users/hanaan/Documents/"
POSIX path of "lala:bombim"
--> "/lala/bimbim"
POSIX path of "/lala/bimbim"
--> "/:lala:bimbim"
POSIX path of file "~/report.xls"
--> "/~:report.xls"
```

Notice the last example: it has the tilde, but AppleScript somehow treats it as a folder name and places a colon between it and the file name; that's pretty useless, and hopefully will be fixed in future versions of AppleScript.

POSIX file straight-up

POSIX file is an object that converts a UNIX-style path that is returned from the *do shell script* command into a file reference. It is similar to the *POSIX path* property discussed previously, but it isn't identical in outcome.

POSIX file behaves a bit like the alias object does, where it will resolve itself into a file object if you hand it a file path as a literal expression instead of a string variable.

For instance, if you type this line:

```
posix file "/Applications/Chess"
```

When you compile your script, AppleScript will convert your text to

```
file "Macintosh HD:Applications:Chess"
```

Manual coercion using strings

Another way to convert colon-delimited file path names into slash-delimited file path names is to use string and list manipulation using AppleScript's text item delimiter. It is important to realize that AppleScript colon-style paths are different than UNIX paths, using slashes in more ways than simply the delimiter. For instance, to refer to files and folders inside the startup disk, you start with a slash instead on the startup disk name. For this reason, it is important to thoroughly test the manual conversion of paths from UNIX to Mac and vice versa before using them, because simply changing the delimiters will most likely result in a nonworking path. The example that follows shows how to manually change the delimiters:

13

Script 13-5

```
set the_path to "Macintosh HD:Users:hanaan:Desktop:report.xls"
set AppleScript's text item delimiters to ":"
set path_items to text items of the_path
set AppleScript's text item delimiters to "/"
set the_unix_path to path_items as string
--> "Macintosh HD/Users/hanaan/Desktop/report.xls"
```

Also in this case, however, the name of the hard disk isn't stripped; you still don't have the word "Volumes" before the path name, and there's no consideration to the fact that the file is in your user directory. More work is required here as well.

Where are UNIX-style POSIX paths used?

The main use of POSIX paths is in the *do shell script* command. This command allows you to perform a UNIX shell command and hit the heart of the UNIX-based OS X.

Whenever you perform any shell command of a file or folder, and many of the shell commands do just that, you specify the file using a POSIX path.

Here's an example of a shell script that generates an error if the file referenced in the shell script doesn't exist:

```
do shell script "test -f ~/Desktop/report.xls"
```

If the path includes a space, you will need to escape it with a backslash, which means that since it's coming through AppleScript, you need to escape that backslash with another backslash.

URL

The URL file reference is useful for opening local files using Safari or other web browsers.

You can get a file's URL by tapping to its *URL* property defined in the Finder and System Events dictionaries.

The script that follows gets the *URL* property of the file you choose:

Script 13-6

```
set the_alias to (choose file)
alias "Macintosh HD:Developer:Documentation:index.html"
tell application "System Events"
    set the_url to URL of the_alias
end tell
--> file://localhost/Developer/Documentation/index.html
```

While you can get the URL of any existing file, folder, or disk, it is only useful with Internet-savvy files such as HTML, JPG, GIF, etc.

You can use the URL in Safari, or you can use the *open location* command.

The following script will open a new window in Safari and display the URL in the variable *the_url* (from the preceding script):

```
tell application "Safari" to make new document with properties¬
 {URL:the_url}
```

You can also use the *open location* command to open a URL in the default browser:

```
open location the_url
```

The *open location* command is part of the Standard Additions.

```
open location: Opens a URL with the appropriate program
  (defined in: StandardAdditions.osax)
   open location [string]  -- the URL to open
      [error reporting boolean] -- Should error conditions¬
      be reported in a dialog?
```

File name extension

One more present the new UNIX-based OS X gave us is the introduction of file name extensions. Yup, just like that, say goodbye to years of taunting my PC programmer buddies about their antiquated dependency on easily changeable file name extensions . . . OK, enough of that. Now file name extensions are great! I love them.

Files can either have an extension, or not. Despite the irritation, it is always better to have a name extension. It makes it easier to spot the purpose of the files, and makes you a better network citizen.

If the file has a name extension, it might be hidden. In the Finder, you can see the name extension and its status in the Info panel.

Click a file, choose Get Info from the File menu, and expand the Name Extension pane. Figure 13-5 shows the Finder's Info box with the Name & Extension pane.

13

Figure 13-5. The Finder's Info box with the Name & Extension panel

Using AppleScript, you can check the status of the name extension in a few ways. The best way to gain information about the existence and status of a specific file's extension is by tapping into the file information record.

As seen later in this chapter, you can use the *get info* command to return records containing useful information about any files you wish. While OS 9 had one name-related property called *name*, OS X has four name-related properties. Three of them are Unicode strings: *name*, *displayed name*, and *name extension*. The fourth is a Boolean variable, *extension hidden*, which is true if the extension is hidden, and false if it is visible.

Following is a little script that goes through all the files that don't have an extension, and if the file type is PDF, it sets the name extension to PDF as well:

Script 13-7

```
1. set the_folder to (choose folder) as string
2. tell application "Finder"
3.    tell folder the_folder
4.       try
5.          set file_list to name of every file ¬
                whose name extension is ""
6.          repeat with the_file in file_list
7.             if file type of file the_file starts with "PDF" then
8.                set name of file the_file to (the_file & ".pdf")
9.             end if
10.          end repeat
11.       on error error_text number error_number
12.          if error_number is -1728 then --no matching files
13.             display dialog "No applicable files were found"
14.          else
```

```
15.          display dialog error_text
16.        end if
17.        return
18.      end try
19.    end tell
20. end tell
```

In line 5 of the script we isolate the files whose extension is hidden.

Since the Finder will generate an error if no applicable files are found, we have to prepare for that possibility with a *try* statement.

Once we trap an error, on line 11, we check to see the nature of the error. If the error number is -1728, we know that no applicable files were found, and we can gracefully exit the script. For more on errors and error trapping, see Chapter 15.

Getting file information

Whenever you need to get file information from a file or folder, the best place to go is the *info for* command.

The *info for* command is a scripting addition and a part of the Standard Additions.

The power of the *info for* command is in the information it returns to you. The information about a file is returned in a record whose properties are shown in the following section.

From the dictionary

Here's the dictionary entry for the *info for* command:

```
info for: Return information for a file or folder
   (defined in: StandardAdditions.osax)
   info for anything
      -- the alias or file reference to the file or folder
   Result: file information
      -- a record containing the information for file or folder ¬
specified
```

The record returned from the *info for* command is also described in the Standard Additions dictionary:

```
Class file information: Reply record for the 'info for' command
Properties:
   name Unicode text  [r/o]  -- the name of the item
   displayed name Unicode text  [r/o]  -- the user-visible name of ¬
the item
   name extension Unicode text  [r/o]
      -- the name extension of the item (such as "txt")
```

13

```
    bundle identifier Unicode text  [r/o]
        -- the item's bundle identifier (if the item is a package)
    kind Unicode text  [r/o]  -- the kind of the item
    default application alias  [r/o]
        -- the application that normally opens this kind of item
    creation date date  [r/o]  -- the date the item was created
    modification date date  [r/o]  -- the date the item was last ¬
modified
    file type string  [r/o]  -- the file type of the item
    file creator string  [r/o]  -- the creator type of the item
    short version string  [r/o]
        -- the item's short version string (from the Finder's ¬
'Get Info'box)
    long version string  [r/o]
        -- the item's long version string (from the Finder's 'Get ¬
Info' box)
    size integer  [r/o]  -- the size of the item in bytes
    alias boolean  [r/o]  -- Is the item an alias file?
    folder boolean  [r/o]  -- Is the item a folder?
    package folder boolean  [r/o]
        -- Is the item a package (a folder treated as a file?)
    extension hidden boolean  [r/o]
        -- Is the item's name extension hidden from the user?
    visible boolean  [r/o]  -- Is the item visible?
    locked boolean  [r/o]  -- Is the item locked?
    busy status boolean  [r/o]  -- Is the item currently in use?
    icon position point  [r/o]
        -- the coordinates of the item's icon in its window or on the ¬
desktop
    folder window bounding rectangle  [r/o]
        -- the coordinates of the folder's window (if the item is a ¬
folder)
```

Using info for

The nice thing about using the *info for* command is that, due to it being a scripting addition, you don't have to use it inside an application's *tell* block.

You should familiarize yourself with the *info for* reply record. The different elements can come in very handy at many situations.

Following is a script that uses the *info for* command to calculate the number of days a chosen file has not been updated. The script will do that by subtracting the modification date from the current date. The script is first shown in the legible format, written over a few lines, and then condensed to two lines only:

```
set the_alias to (choose file)
set file_info to info for the_alias
set seconds_old to (current date) - (modification date of file_info)
```

```
        set days_old to seconds_old div days
        set file_name to name of file_info
        display dialog "The file \"" & file_name & "\" hasn't been modified ¬
        for " & days_old & " days."
```

And, the same script on two lines:

```
        set the_alias to (choose file)
        display dialog "The file \"" & (name of (info for the_alias)) & ¬
            "\" hasn't been modified for " & ((current date) - ¬
            (modification date of (info for the_alias))) div days & " days."
```

The result of line 2 of the script (*set file_info to info for the_alias*) is

```
        {Name:"report.rtf",¬
        creation date:date "Thursday, November 20, 2003 11:04:20 PM",  ¬
        modification date:date "Thursday, November 20, 2003 11:04:30 PM", ¬
         icon position:{0, 0}, size:6.961535E+6, folder:false, alias:false, ¬
         name extension:"rtf", extension hidden:false, visible:true,  ¬
        package folder:false, file type:"RTF ", file creator:"MSWD",  ¬
        displayed name:"report.rtf", default application:¬
        alias "Macintosh HD:Applications:Microsoft Office X:Microsoft Word",¬
        kind:"Microsoft Word RTF document", locked:false,¬
         busy status:false, short version:"", long version:""}
```

Other useful bits of information you can get from the *info for* result are the file's size in bytes, whether the file is a folder or not, and whether it's an alias or not. You can see if the file is busy or locked, and more.

Reading and writing files

When I started using AppleScript, one of the things that fascinated me the most was writing text files. Man, that was almost as much fun as displaying my first dialog box.

AppleScript has a few commands for reading data from files and writing the data back. For the most part, these commands are used to read and write text, but you can pretty much read and write any data: graphic formats, PDFs, etc. The reason why we mostly use the read and write commands for text files is that we can easily create text in strings, see what we created, and understand it. Any other data is a bit more complex. You can't really look at the data of a PDF file and understand what's going on in there.

But text doesn't have to be dull. There are plenty of text-based file formats that allow you to create richly formatted files, such as XML, RTF (see the "Writing RTF files" section later in this chapter), SVG (another flavor of XML), etc. Also, both QuarkXPress and InDesign make use of their own tagged text file format, which you can create.

13

Commands for reading and writing files

Reading and writing files is done using the file read/write scripting additions, which are part of the Standard Additions. The main commands are *read* and *write*, but in order to use them, we use other commands that are used to open and close access to the files we want to read and write to, and get and set the **e**nd **o**f **f**ile (EOF) of the files we want to deal with.

Following is an explanation of the different file reading and writing commands.

read

The *read* command allows you to read the text data or binary data of a file.

From the dictionary

```
read: Read data from a file that has been opened for access ¬
    (defined in: StandardAdditions.osax)
    read anything
    -- the reference number, alias, or file reference of the file to ¬
read
        [using delimiters list of string]
          -- ...or a list of values that separate items to read
        [as type class] -- the form in which to read and return data
        [for double integer]
            -- the number of bytes to read from current position;
            -- if omitted, read until the end of the file
        [before string] -- read up to but not including this ¬
character...
        [until string] -- ...or read up to and including this character
        [from double integer]
          -- starting from this position;
          -- if omitted, start at last position read from
        [to double integer] -- stopping at this position
    Result: anything  -- the data read from the file
```

Using the read command

Reading files is fairly straightforward: you furnish the *read* command with the required file reference, and the result is the contents of the file.

Try the following:

Use TextEdit to create a text file. Make sure to convert the file to plain text (not RTF). Let's say that the file is named work.txt and we save it on the hard disk.

Type some text in the file, save it again, and close it.

Now, start a new script document and write the following line:

```
read file "Macintosh HD:work.txt"
```

The result of running the script is the text stored in the file.

Opening and closing access to files

The Standard Additions define two file-access-related commands: *open for access* and *close access*.

These commands allow AppleScript access to files for reading data from and writing data to.

Although we can read data from files without opening them for access, there's a difference in the way the *read* command operates when you do or don't open the files. This difference is illustrated in the "Reading files and open for access" section.

From the dictionary

Here's the dictionary definition of the *open for access* and *close access* commands:

```
open for access: Open a disk file for the read and write commands
(defined in: StandardAdditions.osax)
 open for access file
   -- the file or alias to open for access.
   -- If the file does not exist, a new file is created.
     [write permission boolean] -- whether to allow writing to the ¬
file.
   Result: small integer
     -- a file reference number; use for 'read', 'write', and 'close ¬
access'

close access: Close a file that was opened for access
(defined in: StandardAdditions.osax)
   close access anything
     -- the file reference number, alias, or file reference of the ¬
file to close
The open for access result
```

Notice the result section of the *open for access* command: it's an integer.

When you open access to a file, the result is not a file reference in the usual form of a path name, but rather an integer referring to the file. This integer can be used to specify the file when you read data from the file, write data to the file, use the EOF commands, and close access to the file.

The following script shows the use of the integer resulting from the *open for access* command:

```
set the_file to "Macintosh HD:work.txt"
set the_file_integer to open for access file the_file
--> 5680
set file_data to read the_file_integer
close access the_file_integer
```

You can use the original file reference for all these as well—after all, you had to have a normal file reference to the file for the purpose of opening the file for access. However, using the file reference number allows AppleScript to find the file faster. Really, at least a billionth of a second faster!

13

Seriously though, if you do a fair amount of reading and writing files, get used to extracting that integer from the *open for access* command and using it.

The number is referring to the file for as long as it is open, so there's no use in holding on to the value of this integer beyond that point. A new integer, one number up from the last one, is assigned every time you open a file for access, even if it's the same exact file.

File reference argument

Although you may use a plain string to refer to a file, it is recommended that you use a proper file reference.

```
open for access "Macintosh HD:new file.txt"
```

will work, but this is better:

```
open for access file "Macintosh HD:new file.txt"
```

This is OK too:

```
open for access alias "Macintosh HD:new file.txt"
```

The only problem with the last script line is that if the file doesn't exist yet, the script will refuse to compile. However, using the alias will work OK if the string defining the alias's path is a variable.

```
set the_path to "Macintosh HD:new file.txt"
open for access alias the_path
```

What if there's no such file?

The *open for access* command is used not only for reading existing files, but also for creating them!

Try the following script:

```
set new_file_path to (path to startup disk) & "not there yet.txt" as
string
open for access file new_file_path
close access file new_file_path
```

After running this script, look in your startup disk and see that a new file named not there yet.txt was created there. It does happen to be empty (has zero bytes), so reading it will generate an error, but you could write text to it.

Opening a file for writing

The *open for access* command has one parameter (with no arguments): *with write permission*.

This parameter allows you to write to the file. This would be the only way you can write text (or other data) to that file. Trying to write to a file that has not been opened using the *with write permission* parameter will generate an error.

The following line opens a file for access with write permission:

```
set the_file to "Macintosh HD:work12345222.txt"
open for access alias the_file with write permission
```

Close what you've opened

Every time you open a file for access you should use the *close access* command to close it down again. Not closing a file is a bit like leaving the phone off the hook.

So, the last command relating to reading or writing to or from a file should be followed by a command closing access to that file.

You shouldn't worry, however, that leaving a file open for access will cause any damage to the file. The file itself isn't actually affected by the *open for access* or *close access* commands.

Even if you open a file for access with write permission, the file's busy status remains unchanged. In fact, once you opened access to a file from one script, you can use another script to write to that file using the same file reference number.

Also you should know that quitting the script editor will close access to any files you opened.

Read command parameters

The *read* command can become even more powerful with a set of parameters.

Using a delimiter to read text into a list

The *using delimiter* parameter allows you to read a text file directly into a list. You do that by specifying a delimiter character. This character acts as the text delimiter, which separates the text read from the file into list items.

For example, if we have a multiline text saved in a file, we can read that file in to a list, where each list item is a paragraph, simply by setting the *with delimiters* parameter to the return character, like this:

```
set paragraph_list to ¬
    read file "macintosh HD:other work.txt" using delimiter return
--> {"First paragraph", "second paragraph", "next line"}
```

The *as* parameter allows you to read files that were saved especially to be read with the *as* parameter.

While we usually save strings and read them back as strings, we can also save lists and records using the *write* command, and then read them back as lists or records using the *as* parameter.

Look for more on that option later on this chapter when we discuss saving and loading lists and records.

13

Reading a specific number of characters

The *for* parameter allows you to read a specific number of bytes, or characters, from the current position.

For instance, the following script will read the first 10 characters of a text file, or the first 10 bytes of any other file type:

```
read file "macintosh HD:somefile.txt" for 10
```

The before and until parameters

The *before* and *until* parameters are similar: they both allow you to set a stopper character. The file will be read from the start (or from the number indicated after the *from* parameter) until the character indicated after the *until* parameter is reached. The *before* parameter reads up to the specified character while the *until* parameter includes the indicated character.

Let's assume that we have a text file with the contents "abcde-abcde".

The following scripts will illustrate the use of the *until* and *before* parameters:

```
read file "macintosh HD:work.txt" before "d"
--> "abc"
```

Notice that the character "d" is omitted, unlike in the next script:

```
read file "macintosh HD:work.txt" until "d"
--> "abcd"
```

Now, let's start from the fifth byte:

```
read file "macintosh HD:work.txt" from 5 until "d"
--> "e-abcd"
```

This time, the script started from the fifth character and continued up until the following instance of "d".

The from and to parameters

The *from* and *to* parameters allow you again to specify starting and ending points for reading data.

While the *for* parameter reads a certain number of bytes from the file marker (or from the start), the *from* and *to* parameters read data from a specific byte counted from the start of the file.

Let's assume that we have a text file with the contents "applescript".

The following script will use the *from* and *to* parameters to read characters 3 through 6:

```
read file "macintosh HD:work.txt" from 3 to 6
--> "ples"
```

Reading files and open for access

Two more commands in the *read/write* suit are the *open for access* and *close access*. These commands open read and write access to files.

As you saw in the first *read* example, the *read* command does not require that the file is first opened for access. Opening the file with the *open for access* command prior to reading changes the scene a bit.

For one, the *open for access* command places a file marker, which determines the position from which the read operation starts.

To understand that better, imagine reading a book. When you start the book, you start from page 1 and you read, say, five pages. When you put the book down, you mark it with a marker. When you pick it up again, you can't go back! You have to start reading from the point of the marker, and as you read more, the marker advances. When you get to the end of the book, you have to close it and put it away before you can read it again.

The same is true with reading a text file. As an example, open the file you saved before and type the alphabet: abcde . . . wxyz. Now save the file and close it.

We will write a script that uses the *read* command with the *to* parameter.

Start a new script and write the following:

Script 13-8

```
open for access file "Macintosh HD:work.txt"
repeat
    set the_text to read file "macintosh HD:work.txt" for 4
    display dialog the_text
end repeat
```

Now run the script.

The script will loop, each time reading the next four bytes, which is also four characters, until it gets to the end of the file. At that point, you will get an "end of file" error.

No matter what you do, you will not be able to read this file again until you use the *close access* command to close access to that file. Try to run your script again, and you will get the error to start with. To fix the problem, do the following:

Create another script file, then type this line and run the script:

```
close access file "Macintosh HD:work.txt"
```

Now, you can read more from that file.

Working with end of file (EOF) commands

EOF is an integer that signifies the number of bytes (or characters) there are in a given file. AppleScript allows you to both get a file's EOF and set it.

13

The end of file property of a file is the same as the file size as returned by the *info for* command:

```
set the_file to alias "Macintosh HD:work.txt"
size of (info for the_file) = get eof of the_file
--> true
```

From the dictionary

Following are the dictionary entries of the *get eof* and *set eof* commands

```
get eof: Return the length, in bytes, of a file opened for access
(defined in: StandardAdditions.osax)
   get eof anything
      -- a reference number, alias, or file reference of a file
      -- that has been opened for access
   Result: double integer  -- the total number of bytes in the file

set eof: Set end of file location for the specified file ¬
   (defined in: StandardAdditions.osax)
   set eof anything  -- Reference number or file to set end of file ¬
location of
        to double integer
   -- the new length of the file, in bytes.  Any data beyond this ¬
position is lost.
```

Getting a file's EOF

To get the EOF value of a file, we use the *eof* command. The *eof* command takes a single argument, a valid file specifications value, and returns an integer.

The following script returns the EOF value of the file work.txt from your hard disk:

```
set the_file to alias "Macintosh HD:work.txt"
set file_character_count to get eof of the_file
```

The *get eof* command returns a real value, although the digit after the decimal is always 0. The reason for that is that internally AppleScript uses a double-integer class to store the file size, which can get beyond the limits of a plain integer. As a result, AppleScript returns the value as a real. No big deal, though.

Setting a file's EOF

When you set a file's EOF, you in fact determine the new end of the file. Setting the EOF to a smaller number than it already is will permanently delete the data after the new EOF you set. For instance, if the text of your file is "I Love Christina", the EOF of it is 16. If you go ahead and set the EOF to 12, you will find your file saying "I Love Chris", which is still perfectly valid, but may not be what you intended.

On the other side of the coin, if you set the EOF to a larger number than it is, AppleScript will fill the extra characters with characters of ASCII number 0. These are invisible characters, but if you use the arrow keys, you can actually advance through them.

The following script sets the size of the file Work.txt to 10:

```
set the_file to alias "Macintosh HD:work.txt"
set eof of the_file to 10
```

The following script takes the same file and discards half the characters:

```
set the_file to alias "Macintosh HD:work.txt"
set file_character_count to get eof of the_file
set eof of the_file to (round (file_character_count/2))
```

Using EOF when writing files

To add text to the end of a file, do the following:

```
set file_ref to open for access file theTextFilePath with write
permission
write theData to file_ref starting at eof
close access file_ref
```

Writing files

AppleScript allows us to write data to files using the *write* command as defined in the Standard Additions.

Although we can write any type of data, for the most part, we stick to what we understand, which is text. We can see it, read it, and understand it. For writing JPEGs, I suggest that you use Photoshop :-).

From the dictionary

Following is the dictionary definition of the *write* command:

```
write: Write data to a file that was opened for access with ¬
write permission
    (defined in: StandardAdditions.osax)
    write anything  -- the data to write to the file
        [for double integer]
         -- the number of bytes to write; if not specified, write all ¬
the data provided
        [starting at double integer] -- start writing at this position ¬
in the file
        to anything
           --the reference number, alias or file reference of the file ¬
to write to
        [as type class] -- how to write the data: as text, data, list, ¬
etc.
```

13

Using the write command

The *write* command returns no result. It simply writes text or other data to a file.

To use the *write* command to write to a file, you must first use the *open for access* command with the *with write* permission parameter in order to grant yourself writing privileges.

You then have to specify the file you want to write to either by referring to it using file specifications or alias, or by using the reference number returned by the *open for access* command.

Since the *open for access* command will create a new file if none is there, you can easily create text files and write to them.

As you may remember from earlier, the *open for access* command returns an integer, which is a reference to the file. You can use that integer to refer to the file you want to write to.

The following example creates a new text file (if none is there) and writes some text into it:

```
set the_file_path to "Macintosh HD:work.txt"
set file_reference to open for access file the_file_path with ¬
write permission
write "abc" to file_reference
close access file_reference
```

The same script could be different, if we choose to forgo the integer result of the *open for access* command, and just use the original file reference.

```
set the_file_path to "Macintosh HD:work.txt"
open for access file the_file_path with write permission
write "abc" to file the_file_path
close access file the_file_path
```

Notice that, in both cases, we cleaned up after ourselves by closing the file.

How much to write and where to start

Two of the *write* command's parameters help you specify how much data or text you want to write to the file, and at which position in the file you want to start.

The *starting at* parameter takes an integer argument and is very useful for writing text or data to a file, when you don't want to start the writing from the beginning of the file.

One of the most common uses of the *starting at* parameter is adding data or text to the end of a file.

For that, you will simply tell the *write* command to write at the end of the file, or starting at EOF. Here's the example script:

Script 13-9

```
set the_file_path to "Macintosh HD:work.txt"
open for access file the_file_path with write permission
write "this is the beginning" to file the_file_path
write " and this is the end!" to file the_file_path starting at eof
close access file the_file_path
```

The resulting text file will have the text "this is the beginning and this is the end!"

Notice that the first text line started writing at the beginning of the file, and the second one, using the *starting at* parameter with the *eof* argument, stuck the second bunch of text after the first one.

Determining how much we want to write may be a bit redundant since AppleScript will write all of the text or data we supply in the *write* command. If you want to limit the written text or data, however, you can do that with the *for* parameter.

The *for* parameter takes an integer as argument, and will limit the number of bytes/characters written to that number.

In the following script, only the first five characters will be written:

Script 13-10

```
set the_file_path to "Macintosh HD:work.txt"
open for access file the_file_path with write permission
write "abcdefghij" to file the_file_path for 5
close access file the_file_path
```

TextEdit AppleScript style

The following script is a small AppleScript dialog-box-based text editor:

Script 13-11

```
1.  property file_name : "Untitled"
2.  property the_text : ""
3.  property the_file : ""
4.  repeat
5.     set paragraph_count to count paragraphs of the_text
6.     if paragraph_count is less than 20 then
7.        repeat (20 - paragraph_count) times
8.           set the_text to the_text & return
9.        end repeat
10.    end if
11.    set r to display dialog file_name ¬
           default answer the_text buttons {"Open", "Save As", "Save"}
12.    set the_text to text returned of r
13.    set the_button to button returned of r
14.    if the_button is "Save" then
15.       if the_file = "" then
```

13

```
16.              set the_file to choose file name with prompt ¬
                     "Save text file:"
17.          end if
18.          open for access the_file with write permission
19.          write the_text to the_file
20.          close access the_file
21.      else if the_button is "Save As" then
22.          set the_file to choose file name with prompt ¬
                     "Save text file as:"
23.          open for access the_file with write permission
24.          write the_text to the_file
25.          close access the_file
26.      else if the_button is "Open" then
27.          set the_file to choose file with prompt "Open file" ¬
                     of type {"TEXT"}
28.          set the_text to ""
29.          set the_text to read the_file
30.      end if
31.      set file_name to name of (info for the_file)
32. end repeat
```

From line 6 to line 10 we pad the text with returns to make sure that the window remains large.

Lines 16 through 20 treat the *Save* command. If the variable *the_file* is still empty, the user is prompted to choose a file name and location, and then the file is saved. If the file has been saved before, then it will just be saved again to the same file.

The *save as* command, lines 22 through 25, prompts you to pick a new file name and location every time.

Lines 27 through 31 operate the *Open* command. You choose a file, the file is read, and . . . the repeat loop starts over again, but this time with the new file name and contents read by the *read* command.

The text editor script allows you to compose text, save it, save it as another file, and open text files. Since it all happens in one big loop, it feels like an application.

Try to analyze it to see how it makes use of the different file commands. The script uses the following file-related commands: *open for access, close access, read, write, choose file,* and *choose file name.*

Using the write command to create a script log

In this little exercise we will create a handler that I personally use in all my systems. The purpose is to create a detailed log of script activity. This log will help you determine what went wrong if the script crashes and you're on the other end of the phone with a communicationally challenged individual trying to describe the problem to you.

The idea behind the logging system here is that instead of collecting all of the messages into a long string and writing the whole thing to a file at the end, the script constantly writes the latest information to the end of the file. This way, if the script gets an error, you can pinpoint the error location in the script. You can make the log as detailed as you want by calling the handler from more areas in your script.

The handler really is pretty simple. It receives a message to add to the log, and adds it along with the date and time.

You can make it more complex by incorporating a date-based folder structure, but we will avoid that. Instead, we will create a log file whose name will include the date and the file extension .log. We use .log because on OS X, files with this extension are automatically opened by the Console application, which adds a level of coolness to the mix.

Following is the finished handler. To use it, call it from anywhere in the script with a simple text message that describes your current location in the script. You can even use a number with several digits as a code for the script location. To find the script position of the last executed command, just search the script for that number.

Another technique I use is to include a property called *debug* that has a Boolean value. You can set it up so you call the *add_to_log* handler only if the *debug* handler is on.

Here's the handler:

Script 13-12

```
on add_to_log(the_message)
    set YY to year of (current date)
    set MM to month of (current date) as integer
    if MM < 10 then set MM to "0" & MM
    set DD to day of (current date)
    if DD < 10 then set DD to "0" & DD
    set log_file_name to YY & "_" & MM & "_" & DD & ".log" as string
    set log_file_path to (path to desktop) & log_file_name as string
    set full_message to return & (current date) & return & the_message
    set file_reference to open for access file log_file_path ¬
    with write permission
    write full_message to file_reference starting at eof
    close access file_reference
end add_to_log
```

In lines 2 through 8 we create the file path for the log file. You can either do that once and keep it in a property or have it created every time.

Line 9 puts the message together. Notice that the return characters are added before the text. Adding a return at the end to be used as a new line for the next time the script runs does no good.

Here's the handler call:

```
set the_message to "1044 Adding client name to job ticket"
if debug then add_to_log(the_message)
```

13

Saving and loading AppleScript lists and records

Another fantastic feature of the *write* command is the little-known *as* parameter.

Besides being able to save binary data, you can write AppleScript lists and records to files, and read them right back! This is great for saving script preferences and data that can be shared among scripts or backed up. It's true that you can coerce most things into strings and save them as text, but here you can save lists containing real numbers, date values, and more embedded lists, write them all to a file, and later read them back.

All you have to do is use the *as list* or *as record* parameter at the end of the *write* command.

The following script writes a simple list to a file, and the script following it reads it back:

```
set the_list to {"Anthony", 37, ¬
date "Sunday, December 4, 2067 12:00:00 AM"}
set file_path to (path to desktop) & "list file" as string
set f to open for access file file_path with write permission
write the_list to f as list
close access f
```

Now, let's read it back:

Script 13-13 (Includes previous script)

```
set file_path to (path to desktop) & "list file" as string
set f to open for access file file_path
set the_new_list to read f as list
close access f
--> the_new_list =
--> {"Anthony", 37, date "Sunday, December 4, 2067 12:00:00 AM"}
```

Reading and writing text files

By far the most useful function of the *read*, *write*, and other related commands is the ability to save and read plain text documents.

We will use text files as a way to introduce these commands, and later on see what other uses they may have.

Writing RTF files

RTF is the acronym for **R**ich **T**ext **F**ormat. RTF is a plain text-based file format that uses tags to specify type-style formatting. RTF is widely used on both Macs and PCs, by Microsoft Word and TextEdit, and it can be also imported into InDesign, QuarkXPress, and other programs.

Creating styled RTF files is actually pretty easy. All you have to do is apply RTF tags before the text, specify some colors and fonts, and you can create RTF files that can be viewed with Apple's TextEdit, MS Word, etc.

I was surprised to see how easy it was to format and create RTF files with AppleScript. You should know that I don't have a masters degree in computer science and have memorized the encoding and specifications for 125 different file formats. All I did was backwards-engineer a simple RTF file I created with TextEdit. After creating a new file with a single word and some basic formatting, I opened the file using BBEdit and tried to figure it out.

The first thing I did was remove any extraneous lines I didn't understand and check if Word and TextEdit still wanted to open them. I boiled the coding down to a bare minimum before I started looking at the formatting encoding.

In this part of the book I will give you a small head start. If you want to create more complex RTF files, you will need to get a good RTF reference, which can be found on the Microsoft support web site.

> **RTF reference:** *You can also find the RTF reference in a more Mac-friendly format at this web address:*
>
> www.ucmb.ulb.ac.be/documents/RTF-Spec-1.3.ps.gz
>
> *It is a PostScript file, but Preview will open it!*

RTF file formatting basics

Here are some of my (very basic, but useful) findings:

First off, the entire RTF text is surrounded by curly brackets.

Next, there are a couple of elements, also wrapped by curly brackets: These elements describe the fonts and colors used in the document. The fonts are each assigned a code, f1, f2, etc., that you can later use in the document for formatting purposes.

The colors are specified using red, green, and blue and are separated by semicolon. The colors are referred to by number: cf0 is black, and color f1 (color font 1) is the first color specified, f2 is the second color, etc. Other elements can also use colors: ulc2 will apply the second color to the underline of the following text.

After that, there were some lines describing document boundaries and paragraphs that I will leave as an exercise for you to explore on your own. Open up your own RTF with BBEdit and try getting them yourself.

Carriage returns

In order to include carriage returns in your document, you must escape them with the backslash (\) character. That means that only a return character that has a backslash right before it will register as a new line in the RTF document.

The header

The RTF file starts with this text:

13

```
\rtf1
```

and is wrapped in its entirety with curly brackets. Which means that the following text is a valid RTF file that will display the letter "a" when opened:

```
{\rtf1 a}
```

Try to type this in BBEdit or other text editor, and open it with Word or TextEdit.

Specifying fonts

We will start by specifying fonts:

Add a new line between the "rtf1" and the "a", and type the following:

```
{\fonttbl\f0\ Helvetica;\f1\ Helvetica-Bold;\f2\ Chalkboard;}
```

This line specifies the font table (fonttbl) with three fonts, and assigns each font a new name to be used in your file: Helvetica will be f0, Helvetica-bold is f1, and chalkboard is f2.

Specifying colors

Next, let's add some color. After the *fonts* line, add an additional line, and type the following:

```
{\colortbl;\red255\green0\blue0;\red0\green0\blue255;}
```

This starts the color table (*colortbl*) and adds two colors: red and blue. You will later refer to these colors by number: 1 for red and 2 for blue (color 0 is black, by default).

Our RTF file so far

So far, our RTF file looks like this:

```
{\rtf1
{\fonttbl\f0\ Helvetica;\f1\ Helvetica-Bold;\f2\ Chalkboard;}
{\colortbl;\red255\green0\blue0;\red0\green0\blue255;}
a}
```

Adding some formatted text

To format our "a", let's add some text before it.

To set the type size, use the code fs followed by the size in half-points. That means that size 18 should be written as 36. Also, the code must be escaped with a backslash: *fs36*.

To change the font we can just add the font name we assigned to the font in the fonts table, f1, f2, etc., like so: *f1*

To change the color to red, add the following to the formatting line: cf, followed by the color number. In our case, *cf1* is red, since the first color we specified is red.

I also changed the text "a" to "AppleScript".

Our complete formatted line will be

```
\f1\fs36 \cf1 AppleScript
```

And, the complete file so far:

```
{\rtf1
{\fonttbl\f0\ Helvetica;\f1\ Helvetica-Bold;\f2\ Chalkboard;}
{\colortbl;\red255\green0\blue0;\red0\green0\blue255;}
\f1\fs36 \cf1 AppleScript}
```

And the file with two lines, each formatted differently:

```
{\rtf1
{\fonttbl\f0\ Helvetica;\f1\ Helvetica-Bold;\f2\ Chalkboard;}
{\colortbl;\red255\green0\blue0;\red0\green0\blue255;}
\f1\fs36 \cf1 AppleScript\
\f2\fs24 \cf2 The language for the rest of us}
```

Notice the backslash at the end of the first line, escaping the return character.

Figure 13-6 shows the final formatted file opened with TextEdit.

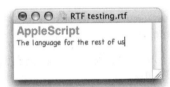

Figure 13-6. The final formatted file opened with TextEdit

Creating RTF with AppleScript

Creating RTF files using AppleScript is done in three stages:

1. Use AppleScript to concatenate actual text, header text, and formatting tags into valid RTF content.

2. Use AppleScript's *write* command to write the text to a new text file.

3. Use the Finder to change the file type and creator type, if you want a specific application to open your RTF document. For instance, if you want Word to open your file, you will change the file type to RTF, and the file creator to MSWD.

In this example, we will create a script that asks the user for some text, and then to pick a start color and end color, and the script will create an RTF file in which the color of the characters blend from the start color all the way to the end color.

We start by getting the user to choose some colors and specify the text:

```
set start_color to choose color
set end_color to choose color
display dialog "Enter document text:" default answer "AppleScript"
```

13

```
set the_text to text returned of result
```

We now have three variables: *start_color*, *end_color*, and *the_text*.

We move on by starting to collect the RTF text.

```
set rtf_text to ""
set rtf_text to rtf_text & "{\\rtf1" & return
set rtf_text to rtf_text & "{\\fonttbl\\f1\\ Helvetica-Bold;}" & return
```

In the three preceding lines, we initialized a string variable that will be used to collect the RTF text, and started building the RTF code itself.

Notice that we have to use a double backslash character instead of only one. We do that since in AppleScript, when you want to include a backslash character in a string, you must escape it with . . . another backslash character.

The returns we add after each line are strictly for legibility of the file. They have no bearing on the final outcome.

Next, we need to add the color specifications. This is going to be interesting since the number of colors will be based on the number of characters in the string assigned to the *the_text* variable.

We start by breaking down the color variable into 6 integers: r1, g1, b1, r2, g2, and b2 for the RGB values in the start color and end color.

We will also need to convert the colors from the 16-bit color spec AppleScript returned (0–65535) to the 8-bit color used in RTF (0–255).

The next portion of the script is a bit complex, but nothing that is beyond your bright self. I'm leaving it without detailed explanation to avoid turning this into an RTF book, but if you do want to follow it, follow one color component, say, the red, all the way through.

Script 13-14

```
1. --Split the color vars to separate components
2. copy start_color to {r1, g1, b1}
3. copy end_color to {r2, g2, b2}
4. --Convert the 16 bit AppleScript color to 8 bit RTF color
5. set r1 to r1 mod 256
6. set g1 to g1 mod 256
7. set b1 to b1 mod 256
8. set r2 to r2 mod 256
9. set g2 to g2 mod 256
10. set b2 to b2 mod 256
11. --Figure out the color difference for each component
12. set difference_red to r2 - r1
13. set difference_green to g2 - g1
14. set difference_blue to b2 - b1
15. --Find out how different each component is between characters
16. set step_red to round (difference_red / character_count)
```

```
17. set step_green to round (difference_green / character_count)
18. set step_blue to round (difference_blue / character_count)
19. --Create the color table component
20. repeat with i from 1 to character_count
21.    set next_red to r1 + ((i - 1) * step_red)
22.    set next_green to g1 + ((i - 1) * step_green)
23.    set next_blue to b1 + ((i - 1) * step_blue)
24.    set rtf_text to rtf_text & ¬
       "\\red" & next_red &¬
       "\\green" & next_green &¬
       "\\blue" & next_blue & ";"
25. end repeat
26. --Start the text formatting
27. set rtf_text to rtf_text & "}" & return
28. set rtf_text to rtf_text & "\\f1\\fs120"
29. --Add the text and color for each character
30. repeat with i from 1 to character_count
31.    set next_character to (character i of the_text) as string
32.    set rtf_text to rtf_text & "\\cf" & i & " " & next_character
33. end repeat
34. --Close the RTF code
35. set rtf_text to rtf_text & "}"
```

Next, we will need to save the resulting text to a file.

We will let the user pick a file for us using the *choose file name* command. After the file has been picked, we will save the RTF-encoded text as plain text to the file path the user had specified.

To make life easier for the user, we will predefine the default file name as the text of the file and the .rtf file extension.

Following is the final portion of the script:

Script 13-15

```
1. --Shorten the text to fit in the file name, if needed
2. if character_count > 26 then
3.    set default_name to characters 1 thru 26 of the_text as string
4. else
5.    set default_name to the_text
6. end if
7. --Let the user choose the RTF file's name and location
8. set final_rtf_path to choose file name ¬
       with prompt "Save RTF file:" default name (default_name & ".rtf")
9. --Write the RTF text to the file
10. open for access final_rtf_path with write permission
11. write rtf_text to final_rtf_path
12. close access final_rtf_path
13. --Open the RTF file in TextEdit
14. tell application "TextEdit"
```

13

```
15.    open final_rtf_path
16. end tell
```

The final script will produce an RTF file as the one shown in Figure 13-7. I used black as the start color and white as the end color, and my text was . . . "AppleScript".

Figure 13-7.
The final RTF document our script produced

Here is the final script:

Script 13-16

```
1. set start_color to choose color
2. set end_color to choose color
3. display dialog "Enter document text:" default answer "AppleScript"
4. set the_text to text returned of result

5. set character_count to length of the_text

6. set rtf_text to ""
7. set rtf_text to rtf_text & "{\\rtf1" & return
8.   set rtf_text to rtf_text & ¬
"{\\fonttbl\\f1\\ Helvetica-Bold;}" & return
9. set rtf_text to rtf_text & "{\\colortbl;"
10. --Split the color vars to separate components
11. copy start_color to {r1, g1, b1}
12. copy end_color to {r2, g2, b2}
13. --Convert the 16 bit AppleScript color to 8 bit RTF color
14. set r1 to r1 mod 256
15. set g1 to g1 mod 256
16. set b1 to b1 mod 256
17. set r2 to r2 mod 256
18. set g2 to g2 mod 256
19. set b2 to b2 mod 256
20. --Figure out the color difference for each component
21. set difference_red to r2 - r1
22. set difference_green to g2 - g1
23. set difference_blue to b2 - b1
24. --Find out how different each component is between characters
25. set step_red to round (difference_red / character_count)
26. set step_green to round (difference_green / character_count)
27. set step_blue to round (difference_blue / character_count)
28. --Create the color table component
```

```
29. repeat with i from 1 to character_count
30.     set next_red to r1 + ((i - 1) * step_red)
31.     set next_green to g1 + ((i - 1) * step_green)
32.     set next_blue to b1 + ((i - 1) * step_blue)
33.     set rtf_text to rtf_text & "\\red" & next_red & ¬
            "\\green" & next_green & "\\blue" & next_blue & ";"
34. end repeat
35. --Start the text formatting
36. set rtf_text to rtf_text & "}" & return
37. set rtf_text to rtf_text & "\\f1\\fs120"
38. --Add the text and color for each character
39. repeat with i from 1 to character_count
40.     set next_character to (character i of the_text) as string
41.     set rtf_text to rtf_text & "\\cf" & i & " " & next_character
42. end repeat
43. --Close the RTF code
44. set rtf_text to rtf_text & "}"
45. --Shorten the text to fit in the file name, if needed
46. if character_count > 26 then
47.     set default_name to characters 1 thru 26 of the_text as string
48. else
49.     set default_name to the_text
50. end if
51. --Let the user choose the RTF file's name and location
52. set final_rtf_path to choose file name ¬
        with prompt "Save RTF file:" default name (default_name & ".rtf")
53. --Write the RTF text to the file
54. open for access final_rtf_path with write permission
55. write rtf_text to final_rtf_path
56. close access final_rtf_path
57. --Open the RTF file in TextEdit
58. tell application "TextEdit"
59.     open final_rtf_path
60. end tell
```

Writing sound files with speech

Another fun file-related trick that has been introduced by the ever-busy AppleScript team is the ability to save sound files using AppleScript.

These aren't any sound files, but rather text that is read back by one of the Mac's voices.

13

The following script will allow you to choose a file, and it'll save a text file that is the voice of Ralph reciting a verse from the Bible:

```
say "The lord is my Shepherd, I shall not want" ¬
    using "Ralph" saving to (choose file name)
```

Working with the file system, the Finder, and System Events

This section deals with the different aspects of scripting the file system using the Finder and System Event applications.

Finder and System Events

One of the AppleScript improvements that came with Mac OS X is the faceless background application known as System Events.

System Events is a scriptable application that takes on some of the Finder's scripting capabilities.

The idea behind the introduction of System Events was to allow scripters to script the file system including files, folders, etc. without having to rely on the state of the Finder. While Finder conditions relating to the file system may change and break your scripts, the System Events application remains consistent.

While the System Events scripting responsibilities grow, the Finder still holds on to a few exclusive scripting features. For instance, System Events doesn't have access to Finder windows and icon positions.

You do have to refrain from assuming that the System Events scripting dictionary is merely a subset of the Finder's dictionary. Both dictionaries have subtle differences in their object model that can catch you by surprise.

Although some file-system-related functions are available through Standard Additions such as *list folder* and *info for*, these functions are informational only: they get information, but can't really do anything. To perform file-related actions such as creating folders and deleting files, you have to use either the Finder or System Events.

Files, folders, and disks

The first things that come to mind when scripting the file system are the different items you can control and the commands you can use on them.

Until OS X, AppleScript's object model for the file system was something to sink your teeth into, but at least it was all concentrated in one place: the Finder's dictionary. Now, to make matters more complex, we can also use System Events, which has a slightly different object model.

The following portion of the book will examine the object model of both System Events and the Finder.

The Finder's file system object model

The top of the food chain in the Finder's object model is a super class called *item*. The *item* class refers to anything you could possibly put on your hard disk. That includes all types of files, such as files, folders, disks, etc.

This is helpful when you want to script commands or get properties of items of unknown type. For instance, if you want to create a handler that deletes a Finder item, you can use the *item* class without having to worry if the item passed by the handler call is a file, an application, or a folder. This can work since all Finder items understand the same commands and have the same basic information.

The item class has three subclasses: *container*, *file*, and *package*.

Containers

The *container* class includes all Finder items that don't have any value on their own, but have the potential of containing other items, such as files or other containers.

The *container* object class has the following subclasses: *disk*, *folder*, *desktop-object*, *trash-object*. The last two, *trash-object* and *desktop-object*, are two special containers to which we can refer by name. Following are two examples using *trash* and *desktop*:

```
tell application "Finder" to set trashed_items to every item of trash
tell application "Finder" to move every file of desktop to trash
```

Notice how in the two preceding script lines (of which the second one you won't want to execute . . .) we used the words "trash" and "desktop" to refer to the two special Finder containers.

Using the *container* class is great when you want to execute any command on or get info about objects that you know are containers, but are not sure if they are disks, folders, etc. The script that follows backs up every TIFF file of a given container:

```
tell application "Finder" to duplicate every file of ¬
container the_container to folder "backup" of home
```

The preceding script will duplicate items from a given container, whether that container is a disk or a folder.

Notice the use of the word "home" in the preceding script. *home* happens to be a property of the application Finder, and so is *desktop*, *trash*, and *startup disk*. What make the *trash* and *desktop* objects different from the properties *startup disk* and *home* is that *desktop* and *trash* are actual objects with properties and elements. For instance, you can ask the Finder to get you the *bounds* property of *desktop*, but not the *bounds* property of *home*.

13

The *disk* and *folder* subclasses of *container* are familiar: *disk* is, for the most part, a top-level folder, and for many scripting purposes they are the same, unless you want to use a command such as *erase* or *eject*. These commands work only with disks.

Files

The *file* class has five subclasses: *alias file*, *application file*, *document file*, *internet location file*, and *clipping*.

Each subclass may add its own set of properties that no other class has. The *application file* class, for instance, has a Boolean property called *has scripting dictionary*. This property is true when the application is scriptable.

While for the most part you will just use the class *file* in scripts, distinguishing between the different subclasses may be useful when getting lists of specific items from folders.

For instance, we can create a script that goes through the hard drive and deletes all of the nonworking alias files. The script will loop through all of the alias files in each folder and try to fix them.

Heck, let's create that script right now!

We will create a script that will loop through folders and delete all the aliases whose original items no longer exist. Later on you can fix it to ask the user for a new original, but that is your homework.

The script has to be recursive, or in other words, a script that can execute itself. This isn't exactly like a repeat loop, although it has a repeat loop in it. Recursive means that if you're processing files in folders, the script will methodically go into every folder and process all the files in that folder too.

Make sure to distinguish between AppleScript's *alias* class and the Finder's *alias file*. Alias file is the file's shortcut on the desktop (or anywhere else you put it), and AppleScript's *alias* is a class that points to a file.

Following is the script:

Script 13-17

```
1. set the_container to (choose folder)
2. clean_aliases_from_container(the_container)
3. on clean_aliases_from_container(the_container)
4.    tell application "Finder"
5.       set alias_file_list to alias files of container the_container
6.       repeat with the_alias in alias_file_list
7.          set theItem to original item of the_alias
8.          if not (exists of theItem) then
9.             delete the_alias
10.         end if
11.      end repeat
12.      set container_list to (folders of container the_container)
13.      repeat with the_sub_container in container_list
```

```
14.            set the_sub_container to (the_sub_container as string) ¬
                  as alias
15.            my clean_aliases_from_container(the_sub_container)
16.       end repeat
17.    end tell
18. end clean_aliases_from_container
```

Line 1 of the script allows the user to choose a folder. This folder will be the top-level folder processed by the script. The script will then process all nested files in that folder.

In line 2 we call the main handler, *clean_aliases_from_container*. As you will see in a minute, what makes the script recursive is the fact that the handler calls itself.

The handler, which starts from line 3 through 18, treats only one folder.

First, all the alias files are treated. That happens from line 5 through 11. We start by creating a list, listing only the alias files in the folder:

```
set alias_file_list to alias files of container the_container
```

Then, we loop through the list, check the *original item* property of each alias file, and delete the alias files whose original item doesn't exist.

From line 12 to 17 we do a similar thing: we list the containers that are in the folder and loop through these. What we do with the containers, however, is very different. We use them, one at a time, as the argument in the call for that handler itself. That happens in line 15. When there are no more folders, AppleScript knows to get back to the spot it left off and continue running through more folders.

Packages

Packages are a cross-breed between files and folder: they appear as files in a Finder's window, but they can be opened up as a container that holds more folders and files.

In the System Events dictionary, they're referred to as bundles, not packages, but the object is the same.

The most common form of packages is the Cocoa application.

Packages can also be created by your using the script editor. In fact, you can create two types of packages: script application bundle and script bundle. More on that when we discuss saving scripts.

You can read more about packages earlier in the first section of this chapter.

System Event's file system object model

System Events has a slightly different object model than the Finder.

While the top dog in the System Events' object class hierarchy is *item* like in the Finder, the subclass of that *item* class that deals with Finder items is the class *disk item*. We will look at disk items now, and at other items later on.

> *The type of hierarchy we're looking at here isn't the containment hierarchy, but rather an inheritance hierarchy.*

The top object, the *disk item*, is also the most general object; any other object in the file system is a disk item: folders are disk items, applications are disk items, clippings are disk items, etc. Also, every folder is a disk item, but not every disk item is a folder.

The *disk item* object class has four subclasses: *folder*, *alias*, *disk*, and *file*. Note how different they are from the Finder's object class hierarchy. However different, the System Events' class hierarchy is pretty easy to understand. Let's look at the four different subclasses in detail.

Files

Files include any disk item that can't contain other disk items. Unlike the Finder, System Events does not distinguish between application files, clippings, document files, etc.

The file class has one subclass, which is *file package*. File packages are identical to what the Finder refers to as bundles. They are a breed of file that appear as files in a Finder window, but can be opened as a folder. One flavor of a file package is Cocoa applications, as seen in the following script:

```
tell application "System Events"
    every file package of folder "applications" of startup disk
end tell
```

The preceding script lists all applications and other bundles that may be there.

Folders

In scripting terms, folders are disk items that can have elements. These elements are simply files and other folders that are contained by the folder.

The *folder* class has no subclasses, which means that System Events just looks at them as folders.

Disks

In the Finder, *disks* are a subclass of the *container* class. In System Events *disks* are a direct subclass of the *disk item* class.

The following script lists the names of all available disks:

```
tell application "System Events"
    name of disks
end tell
--> {"Macintosh HD", "Number Nine", "Network"}
```

Aliases

Aliases may be a bit confusing. Unlike the Finder, which has the *alias* subclass of the *file* class, and refers to the shortcut aliases you can create with the *Make Alias* command in the Finder, aliases in System Events are the alias value class we use in AppleScript. The *alias* class is a reference form to any disk item. You can read more about it in the first section of this chapter.

System Events items

Up until now we looked at the objects and classes of System Events that directly deal with the file system. These are called disk items. The *item* class of System Events is an entirely different animal.

To start, the *disk item* class we looked at earlier is a subclass of the *item* class. The following is a list all the other types (or subclasses) of items System Events gives us access to: document, window, application, color, text, attribute run, character, word, paragraph, user, login item, disk item, domain, item, script, folder action, action, attribute, and UI element.

You can learn a lot about scripting your system by tinkering with the System Events dictionary. Let's look at a few of these items and see what information they hold.

User

No, not only you and your family members are privileged enough to be users on your OS X–equipped Mac. Try this script to see who else has an account on your Mac:

```
tell application "System Events"
    name of every user
end tell
--> {"nobody", "root", "daemon", "unknown", "smmsp", "lp", "postfix", ¬
"www", "eppc", "mysql", "sshd", "qtss", "cyrus", "mailman", ¬
"appserver", "johanne", "olivia", "hanaan", "aylam" }
```

Now, let's see what properties each user has. I'll first check the properties of user "hanaan":

```
tell application "System Events"
    properties of user "hanaan"
end tell
 --> {full name:"Hanaan Rosenthal", Name:"hanaan",    ¬
home directory:"/Users/hanaan",¬
picture path:"/Library/User Pictures/Animals/Dragonfly.tif",
class:user}
```

Hmm . . . I have access to the users' picture path. Maybe I'll create an AppleScript Studio application that automatically changes users' pictures based on their mood. Maybe not.

13

The following script looks for only the users whose home directory is in the Users folder:

```
tell application "System Events"
    full name of every user whose home directory starts with "/users"
end tell
```

Domain

Domain is yet another term Mac users have to get used to. Domains are a UNIX method of specifying regions in the startup disk relating to different system functions.

The following script lists the domains:

```
tell application "System Events"
    name of every domain
end tell
--> {"System", "Local", "Network", "User", "Classic"}
```

What other things are domains good for? For example, we know you can get the path to different system locations using the *path to* Standard Addition command. But what if you want to get the paths to all possible locations a scripting addition can be in, or get the paths for all font folders in the system? To do that the easy way, you need System Events.

```
tell application "System Events"
    scripting additions folder of every domain
end tell
--> {folder "Macintosh HD:System:Library:ScriptingAdditions:" ¬
    of application ¬
    "System Events", folder "Macintosh HD:Library:ScriptingAdditions:" ¬
    of application "System Events", missing value, ¬
    folder "Macintosh HD:Users:hanaan:Library:ScriptingAdditions:" ¬
    of application "System Events", ¬
    folder "Number Nine:System Folder:Scripting Additions:" ¬
    of application "System Events"}
```

If you don't recognize the result, it is a list of references to every scripting additions folder on your system.

Login item

Remember the good old OS 9 times, when all you had to do was pop an alias of a file in the startup disk's folder and it would launch when the system started?

The following script will prompt the user to pick an application, and will create a login item for that app, which means that the application will start by itself when that user logs in. (Remember, in UNIX land we don't start, we log.)

Script 13-18

```
set the_app to choose application with prompt ¬
    "Choose application to startup automatically" as alias
tell application "System Events"
    set app_name to name of the_app
```

```
    set app_POSIX_path to POSIX path of the_app
    make new login item at end with properties ¬
{name:app_name, kind:"APPLICATION", path:app_POSIX_path, ¬
hidden:true}
end tell
```

Now, after users have lots of fun with your script, they will have a surplus of unwanted login items. The following script will allow them to choose a login item from a list and have it deleted:

Script 13-19

```
tell application "System Events"
    set login_item_list to name of every login item
    choose from list login_item_list OK button name "Delete"
    set selected_login_item to result as string
    if selected_login_item is not "false" then
        delete login item selected_login_item
    end if
end tell
```

Your homework is to allow the user to delete multiple login items at a time, and warn the user before deleting ("Are you sure . . .").

What can you do to Finder items?

In this section we will focus not on all of the things you can do with the Finder application, but rather all the things you can do with and to Finder items.

Since the System Events commands are so similar to the Finder's commands, we will concentrate on the Finder.

open and close

The *open* command can open any Finder item that you can open from the Finder. It acts as if you double-clicked the item. If you use the *open* command on a folder, the folder will open. If you use it to open a file, you can actually determine ahead of time which application is going to be used to open the selected item. You do that by asking for the default application property found in the *info for* command reply.

This is one way to do it:

```
name of (info for (default application of (info for (choose file))))
```

The *close* command only works on folders.

Moving and copying files

The Finder gives you a few commands for moving and copying files to various places. The following five commands are variations of moving and copying files:

13

copy and duplicate

While you can use the *copy* command to make a copy of a file or a folder to a different location, the *duplicate* command gives you some very useful parameters.

To use the basic *duplicate* command, you have to specify a reference to the Finder item you want to duplicate and a reference to the container you want to duplicate it to:

```
tell application "Finder"
  duplicate file the_file_path to folder the_folder_path
end tell
```

You can use the *duplicate* command to simply replace the Finder's Duplicate command from the menu. In this case, all you have to specify is the path to the item you want to duplicate:

```
tell application "Finder" to duplicate file the_file_path
```

The most useful feature, however, is being able to decide what to do if an item by that name already exists in the container you duplicate to. To do that, use the *replacing* parameter with a Boolean value:

```
duplicate file the_file_path to folder the_folder_path replacing yes
```

delete

The *delete* command in the Finder's dictionary doesn't actually delete anything, it just moves the referenced Finder item to the trash.

```
tell application "Finder" to delete file the_file_path
```

would be identical to

```
tell application "Finder" to move file the_file_path to the trash
```

Or, delete multiple items with the Finder's powerful implementation of the *whose* clause:

```
tell application "Finder"
  delete every file of desktop folder whose label index is not
end tell
```

You can also empty the trash by simply using the *empty* command:

```
tell application "Finder" to empty
```

or

```
tell application "Finder" to empty trash
```

move

Moving files works just like dragging files in the Finder: you have the file or folder you want to move and the folder or disk you're moving it to. You can also specify whether you want to replace an existing item with the same name:

Script 13-20 (includes following script)

```
    tell application "Finder" to move file the_file_path to container ¬
    the_folder_path
```

or

```
    tell application "Finder"
       try
          move file 1 of folder source_folder to folder dest_folder
    replacing no
       on error number error_number
          if error_number is -15267 then
             display dialog ¬
             "Can't replace the file, replace the scripter instead..."
          else
             display dialog "An error occurred: " & error_number
          end if
       end try
    end tell
```

In the preceding example we asked AppleScript not to replace items if it encounters items with identical names in the destination container. This forced us to place the *whose* statement in a *try* block to capture the error. In the preceding example we also captured the error that the failed move generated and acted on it. If files already exist, AppleScript will generate error number -15267.

exists

The *exists* command is one of my favorites. It takes one parameter, the Finder item whose existence is in question, and returns a Boolean: true if the item exists or false if it doesn't.

```
    exists of file "I am here!" of the desktop
```

The fun thing about this ability to contemplate existence of files is that due to the clean Boolean result, you can incorporate the command directly into statements that call for a Boolean value, such as *if* statements:

> *Note that both the words "of" and "the" are optional in this commands. The word "the," actually, can be added in most places where it makes sense grammatically with no consequences to your script.*

13

make

The *make* command allows you to create Finder items such as files, folders, and Finder windows, although most places where the *make* command is used, it is used to create folders.

The *make* command is always followed by the word "new," and then by the class of the objects you want to create.

Following are a few examples of the *make* command.

The following script creates a new folder on the desktop. The script will use the *with properties* parameter to name the folder "My Files" and assign a comment to it:

```
tell application "Finder"
   activate
   make new folder at desktop with properties ¬
      {name:"My Files", comment:"Place to put stuff"}
end tell
```

The following script creates a new window in the Finder pointing to the startup disk. You can specify the folder the file will point to after the *to* parameter.

```
tell application "Finder"
   activate
   make new Finder window to startup disk
end tell
```

The *make* command can also be used to create text files.

```
tell application "Finder"
   make new file at desktop with properties ¬
      {name:"My File", comment:"Place to put thoughts"}
end tell
```

Managing files in windows

The following few commands work with files, but don't really do anything to them. For instance, selecting a file or sorting a window doesn't change any files or folders, only how you look at them.

Selecting and revealing files

The *select* and *reveal* commands work very similarly in the Finder. They both select a Finder item in the Finder window. If the container of the item is closed, both commands will open it, but slightly differently:

The *select* command will open the container to a window using the last viewing style (icon, outline, or browser). If the *reveal* command has to open a window to reveal the item, it will default the view browser view.

Revealing files and folders in Finder windows can come in very handy. In the interface of any system or script dealing with files, it is a pleasant surprise for the user to have a button that reveals a related file or folder in the Finder. That is, of course, if the intention of your script is to keep these users *out* of the file system . . .

eject

The *eject* command takes a disk reference as the parameter and ejects that disk.

```
tell application "Finder" to eject disk "Removable 4000"
```

The following script will use the *ejectable* property of a disk to eject only the disks that can be ejected:

```
tell application "Finder"
    eject (every disk whose ejectable is true)
end tell
```

Creating files

AppleScript allows you to create files in a variety of ways. One way, obviously, is using applications that create the kind of files you need to create.

To create text files, you can use one of two methods: you can use the Finder to create an empty text file, or you can use the *open for access* and *write* commands defined in Standard Additions to create text files and write text into them.

The *open for access* and *write* commands are explained in detail in this chapter in the "Reading and writing files" section.

Getting the contents of folders

AppleScript gives us several ways to get a list containing the items in a particular folder. The two routes you can take are using the *list folder* Standard Addition or use the Finder. Each way has its advantages.

list folder

list folder is a command defined in the Standard Additions dictionary. The *list folder* command returns a list containing the names of the files and folders in the container (either folder or disk) you specify:

```
list folder (path to startup disk)
--> {".DS_Store", ".hidden", ".hotfiles.btree", ".Trashes", ".vol", ¬
"Active accounts", "Applications", "automount", "bin", "client jobs",¬
"cores", "Desktop", "Desktop (Mac OS 9)", "Desktop DB", "Desktop DF",¬
"Desktop Folder", "Developer", "Games", "jobs", "Library", "mach",¬
"mach.sym", "mach_kernel", "Network", "obj", "Previous Systems",¬
"private", "sbin", "System", "TheFindByContentFolder",¬
 "TheVolumeSettingsFolder", "tmp", "Trash",¬
"User Guides and Information", "Users", "usr", "var", "Volumes"}
```

Oh no, what's all that stuff?! Do I really have all this junk right on my hard drive? Yes I do. Luckily, most of these files are invisibles. In case I didn't want to have them listed, I can omit the invisible files by giving the *invisibles* parameter a false value.

```
list folder (path to startup disk) without invisibles
```

OK now, this time I got less junk, and a list I can actually use.

Using the Finder to get the content of folders

While *list disks* is great because you don't need any application to use it, the Finder offers a much more powerful solution.

Using both *every* and *whose* clauses, we can filter out just the set of files we want to work with.

Let's look at a few examples of using the Finder to filter files in different folders.

The following script will list all files in a chosen folder that have not been modified for ten weeks and have no label attached to them:

```
set the_folder to choose folder
tell application "Finder"
  every file of the_folder whose ¬
    (modification date < ((current date) - (10 * weeks)) ¬
    and label index = 0)
end tell
```

Notice how in the preceding script we managed to use a single command to look for files (not folders) that are of a certain age and label.

In the next script we will look for files that are larger than 10MB and are not applications. Unlike the last script, this script will be recursive, starting from the folder selected by the user:

Script 13-21

```
1. global list_of_large_files, byte_limit
2. set list_of_large_files to {}
3. set mb_limit to 10
4. set byte_limit to mb_limit * 1024 * 1024
5. set the_folder to (choose folder) as string
6. set list_of_large_files to get_large_files(the_folder)

7. on get_large_files(the_folder)
8.    tell application "Finder"
9.       try
10.          set file_list to every file of container the_folder ¬
                whose size ≥ byte_limit and kind is not "Application"
11.          set list_of_large_files to list_of_large_files & file_list
12.       end try
13.       set folder_list to every folder of container the_folder
14.       repeat with the_listed_folder in folder_list
15.          set the_listed_folder to the_listed_folder as string
16.          my get_large_files(the_listed_folder)
17.       end repeat
18.    end tell
19.    return list_of_large_files
20. end get_large_files
```

Lines 7 through 20 of the script represent the main handler that makes the script recursive. In line 16, the handler calls itself.

Notice that we start by taking all the applicable files and adding a reference to them to the *list_of_large_files* list. That happens on lines 10 and 11. After that, we get all the folders in the current folder, which the handler treats, and feed each folder to that same handler as the argument.

What makes this script possible is the Finder's incredible ability to filter the right kind of files with the *whose* clause. See lines 10 and 13.

Entire contents

Another useful property of the *container* class in the Finder is the *entire contents* property. The *entire contents* property lists a reference to every file and folder contained in nested folders.

Here is something NOT to try:

```
tell application "Finder"
    get entire contents of (path to library folder from system domain)
end tell
```

This would give you a list of the system's library contents, which is comprised of one and a quarter gigabytes of mainly small text files.

The *entire contents* property can come in very handy, however. You can use it to quickly look for a file by name.

```
tell application "Finder"
    set fileString to  entire contents of folder "The:folder:path:" ¬
        as string
    fileString contains fileName
end tell
```

Listing disks

On a related issue, you can use the *list disks* command to get a list of all your disks.

Built-in file and folder paths

OS X is all about domains, permissions, and libraries where you have to be quite orderly, otherwise you get thrown out. In OS 9, your computer was your computer and the hard drive was your hard drive, while in OS X, the computer belongs to the system, and you are a mere user. But from down there you rise and slowly gain control, and realize that while you still have to ask permission where you need to go, it is worth the tremendous stability and the ability to get anything you want done.

Part of getting around in OS X is gaining an understanding of the different domains and special folders that organize the different domain-related files.

13

The best way to get to these folders is by using the *path to* command, as defined in the Standard Additions. Using the *path to* command, you can get the paths to the different font folders that sometime seem to be randomly scattered around the system.

The *path to* command has two main parts: the folder you're looking for, and the domain you want to find the folder in. Following are a few examples:

```
path to fonts
--> alias "Macintosh HD:System:Library:Fonts:"
path to fonts from user domain
--> alias "Macintosh HD:Users:hanaan:Library:Fonts:"
path to launcher items folder from Classic domain
--> alias "Number Nine:System Folder:Launcher Items:"
```

The *path to* command has two other parameters. The *as* parameter allows you to ask for the result as a string instead of an alias.

```
path to startup disk as string
--> "Macintosh HD:"
```

The other parameter is *folder creation*. According to the dictionary, *folder creation* means that if the folder you're asking a path for does not exist, the folder will be created. Also, the dictionary claims that the default is true. Nevertheless, I still got an error when trying to get the path to a nonexisting folder.

Startup disk and user directory

Two of the most useful paths you can get are the paths to the startup disk and the user's home directory. Using built-in paths that represent these two containers can take you a long way to having a system-independent script.

The idea is to make our script as portable and flexible as possible. I know what you're thinking . . . this is just a script that'll run on your Mac and has a small chance of going anywhere else. Not necessarily so. As you will discover, a small bit of code you write to perform a simple task suddenly grows into a full-blown script and then becomes a part of a larger scheme. It is at that point that you copy the script to some other Macs to test it, and wham! Nothing works since the other Mac's hard drive has a different name.

So, as much as you just want to get that pesky script quickly working, I urge you to take the time and replace the hard drive names using one of the few ways AppleScript has to refer to the startup disk, no matter what its name is.

Let's say for example that your script refers to a folder called Client Jobs on the hard disk. You need a variable in your script that'll reference that folder. If you use a literal expression, your script line may look like this:

```
set the_jobs_folder_path to "Macintosh HD:Client Jobs:"
```

If you move the script to a Mac with a differently named hard drive, your script will break. Instead, use the *path to startup disk* reference, like this:

Declare a global variable called something like "hd", and assign the name of the startup disk to it up front. From that point, anytime you want to refer to the startup disk, just use this variable.

```
global hd
set hd to (path to startup disk) as string
set the_jobs_folder_path to hd & "Client Jobs:"
```

Why did we coerce the hd variable to string? This way it's easier to concatenate it to names of other folders, colons, and other strings that make up path names. After the path name is complete, you can give it the correct designation, such as folder, alias, file, etc.

path to me

One of the most useful statements you can use in your quest for script-portability is *path to me*.

The expression *me* refers to the script application itself. You use *path to me* when you need to know where the script application is.

This comes in awfully handy when your script is a part of some sort of folder structure. The way I like to set it up is by having a folder I call the main folder. Inside I have all the folders the system needs (even small systems). The folders may be resources, templates, in/out, etc. One of my folders is always named *system*. In this folder I put my script, etc. Since the script is the application that the user will need to use for launching the system, I usually give the user an alias file in a more convenient place, just to keep his/her paws out of the system's folder structure. The script, however, needs to know where all the related files are. All the script needs for that is the path to the main folder. To get that I need to just get the container of the container of the script application's file. The container is the folder System, and that folder's container is the main folder. Here's the line in the script that assigns the main folder's path to a variable:

```
tell application "Finder"
    set main_folder_path to container of (container of (path to me))
end tell
```

The problem with using *path to me* is that when you create your script with Apple's Script Editor application, the *path to me* expression will return the path to the application itself. You can see that in Figure 13-8.

Figure 13-8. The *path to me* command in Script Editor returns the path to the Script Editor application.

13

For that, you can actually embed the path to the folder you're using in the development stages, and then remove it.

Late Night Software's Script Debugger allows you to choose whether the *path to me* expression returns the path to the application or to the script file. For our purposes, we usually want the path to the script file. For me, this feature alone was worth Script Debugger's price.

Using UNIX file commands

One of the biggest boosts for Mac users, and scripters in particular, is the whole new OS under the hood of OS X. I am of course referring to UNIX.

One of the most exciting additions to AppleScript comes in the form of a single command: *do shell script*.

Shell scripts are UNIX command-line-style scripting. There are a few flavors of shell scripting, hundreds of commands, and endless possibilities.

In this book I do not go into shell scripts in any sort of detail since there's no way I can do the subject any justice. Instead, I will show you how to use the *do shell script* command in AppleScript, and how to convert Mac-style color-delimited file paths to UNIX-style slash-delimited POSIX paths.

In this section we will look at the *do shell script* command for the purpose of managing the file system. Although we will only look at a couple of commands, I urge you to pick up a UNIX book that fits your level and get a good understanding of shell scripts and UNIX as a whole.

The do shell script command

The *do shell script* command is very simple: it takes a single string parameter and executes it as if you typed it in the Terminal application and pressed *RETURN*.

When the *do shell script* command requires a path to a file, that path is using a special slash-delimited UNIX format. This format, including conversion between UNIX and AppleScript style paths, is explained in detail in the "UNIX paths" section of this chapter.

Figure 13-9 shows the script in the Script Editor with a shell script and the result. Figure 13-10 shows the same shell script executed in the terminal followed by the terminal's result.

The command I'm showing is the shell *ls* command, which is similar to AppleScript's *list folder* command. Like the *list folder* command, the *ls* command takes a parameter describing the path of the directory whose contents you want to list.

Like many other shell script commands, the *ls* command may take no parameters, and in this case uses the current working directory as the directory to list. More on the working directory in a bit.

In the script shown in Figure 13-9, we call the shell script "ls". The result is a string listing the files and folders in the directory /Applications/AppleScript/. The slash at the start of the path name indicates that the path is an absolute path and not a relative path. More on that later on in this chapter.

Figure 13-9. The *ls* command passed using the *do shell script* command from the Script Editor. The parameter passed along with the *ls* command is a POSIX path pointing to the AppleScript folder in the Applications folder.

In Figure 13-10 you can see a breakdown of the *ls* command the way it is executed from the Terminal. You can compare the command and the result between Figures 13-9 and 13-10.

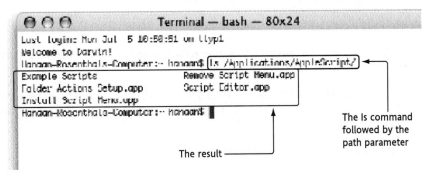

Figure 13-10. The *ls* command in the Terminal application with the result below it

Absolute paths, relative paths, and the working directory

When executing file-related shell script commands either in AppleScript or in the Terminal, you need to pass the path of the target file or directory as parameters. There are two ways to pass that file path parameter: either as an absolute path or as a relative path.

Passing an absolute path means that you disregard your current location and assume that the starting point (which is also the top directory, in this case) is either the startup disk or the current user's home directory. Relative paths start from the current working directory.

13

When specifying an absolute path starting from the startup disk level, as shown in Figure 13-9 and Figure 13-10, we start the path with a slash. To indicate the startup disk only, we pass a slash by itself. The following shell script will list the content of the startup disk:

```
do shell script "ls /"
```

> *I fully realize that the ls command is by AppleScript and that the use of the ls command through the shell script may be redundant. I'm using the ls command since it's simple to understand.*

In a way, when executing the *do shell script* command from AppleScript, it is easier to use absolute paths starting from the startup disk since this is the path that is returned by the *POSIX path* property of alias file references. In the following script, we first get the path to the user's documents folder using AppleScript's *path to* command, then we get the *POSIX path* property of the result, and use it with the *ls* command in a shell script:

```
set mac_path to path to documents folder from user domain
--> alias "Macintosh HD:Users:hanaan:Documents:"
set unix_path to POSIX path of mac_path
--> "/Users/hanaan/Documents/"
do shell script ("ls " & unix_path)
```

If you want to start from the current user's directory, you have to precede the slash with a tilde: "~/". The following script will have the same result as the previous one, listing the contents of the documents folder in the home directory:

```
do shell script ("ls ~/Documents")
```

To do this, however, you will need to build the path yourself without much help from AppleScript's various POSIX path amenities.

You can also refer to disks other than the startup disk. To do that, you need to precede the name of the disk with the word "Volumes". The script that follows lists the contents of the hard disk External2000:

```
do shell script ("ls /Volumes/External2000")
```

When writing shell scripts in the Terminal application, where they belong, the most common way to pass path arguments is as relative paths. Relative paths use an implied working directory for all your file-related commands. You can add on to that working directory, or change the working directory and work from there.

Imagine giving someone directions to the kitchen in your house. You may tell that person to go to the front door or his/her room and start from there (absolute paths), or you may ask that person where s/he is standing at the moment and give directions from that point. After all, s/he might be one doorway away, so why send him/her all the way to the front door and back.

We can change the working directory with the *cd* command, after which we can see the path to the working directory in the Terminal as the prefix to our commands. Figure 13-11 shows the Terminal after the working directory was changed with the *cd* command.

The first line (after the welcome line) shows the *cd* command change the working directory to the AppleScript folder in the application's folder in the startup disk. The following line starts with that directory as part of the command prompt.

Figure 13-11. The Terminal window shown after the *cd* command. Watch how the command prompt changes.

To describe the enclosing directory when using relative paths you can use ../. The following script lists the directory that encloses the current working directory:

```
do shell script to "ls ../"
```

The problem with using the working directory in AppleScript's *do shell script* is that, unlike the Terminal, AppleScript forgets the working directory between executions of the *do shell script* command. You could execute multiple commands by separating them with a semicolon. The following script will change the working directory with the *cd* command and list the working directory with the *ls* command:

```
set shell_1 to "cd ~/documents"
set shell_2 to "ls"
do shell script (shell_1 & ";" & shell_2)
```

The fact that AppleScript doesn't retain the working directory makes using working directories pretty useless and absolute paths the method of choice.

Using spaces

Since spaces in shell scripts are used to separate the command from the parameters and the parameters from each other, we can't just casually use spaces in file and folder names. The easy way to include spaces in names is to escape them with the backslash character. To refer to the folder name client jobs, for instance, we need to type clients\ jobs.

This brings up an issue when we try to use the *do shell script* command in AppleScript, since in AppleScript the backslash character is an escape character by itself. The solution is to precede the space character with two backslashes: the first one to escape the space, and the second one (right before it) to escape the first one. The following script lists the folder client jobs in the startup disk:

```
do shell script to "ls /client\\ jobs"
```

13

Why and when are shell scripts used in AppleScript?

There are a few reasons to entrust some of your file commands to shell scripts.

One is that shell commands don't produce a Finder progress dialog box when deleting or copying files. Shell scripts also deal much better with large number of files. If you have a folder with over 1000 files and you need to extract a few files out of there, or if you need to search for a file in a directory tree, UNIX shell scripts can do that much faster.

Sometimes it's not that the Finder scriptability lacks a command, it's just that the shell script equivalent is a bit more than you want. For instance, if you need to duplicate a file to a different folder and rename it, you need to use the *duplicate* command and the *set* command to change the name of the file, which may cause an irritating problem if the file you're duplicating exists in the target location. Using shell scripts you can copy a file to another file that will duplicate it and rename it in one shot.

Shell scripts' ability to use wild card characters make them ideal for some tasks as well. Since it is way out of the scope of this book, I urge you to pick up a good Mac OS X UNIX book and study it.

Another reason to use UNIX is that you can tap years of UNIX development. Digging a bit will yield an array of useful UNIX-based applications and shell commands that can plug the holes in the functionality you're trying to achieve.

Faking volumes with disk utility

One of the challenges you encounter when working on client scripts from your home office (another way to describe working from bed while watching football . . .) is tapping into the company's servers. Servers are often referred to in scripts, but are guarded behind firewalls and are inaccessible from your home.

To get around this problem, I use a mirror of the server I create using a disk image.

A mounted disk image will appear to AppleScript as if it was any other mounted server on the system.

Since it would be unreasonable to replicate the entire folder structure of the server, you would want to copy only the parts that your script will use.

To replicate a server on your hard disk, you start by creating an empty disk image the size you need.

Start up the Disk Utility application in OS X 10.3. In earlier versions you should use the standalone disk copy application.

Click the new image icon in the toolbar or choose New Blank Image from the Image menu.

In the Save As field type the name of the server you're replicating. From the dialog box choices at the bottom (shown in Figure 13-12), choose a size that is going to be sufficient for the files you will be testing in your scripts.

I usually use 100MB, but if you're working with large images, you need more. Just remember that the size of the disk image will be the size that you choose, so choosing 2GB will make the disk image huge.

Figure 13-12. The New Blank Image dialog box

Also choose read/write format.

After you click Create, the disk image will be created and also mount on your system, as shown in Figure 13-13.

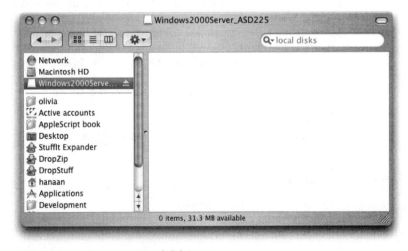

Figure 13-13. The new mounted disk image

13

In the mounted disk, create the needed folder structure and copy the needed files to the folders in the folder tree you've created.

Although you should test this solution in your own environment, AppleScript should not see the difference between that disk and the actual server, and the scripts that were created or modified using the fake disk should work smoothly when the real server is around.

You do have to watch, however, for features that may work slightly differently from your disk to the server, such as sorting of files and the availability of file labels, etc.

Mounting volumes

Mounting volumes from the server, remote computers, or iDisks is done with the *mount volume* command. That command is defined in the File Commands suite of the Standard Additions.

The main parameter of the *mount volume* command is a string that defines the server. This string is actually a URL that describes the server and the protocol used to connect to the server such as SMB or the more common AFP. While the user name and password can be defined using the *mount volume* parameters, you can also incorporate that information right into the URL string itself.

From the dictionary

Here's the *mount volume* command the way it appears in the dictionary:

```
mount volume: Mount the specified AppleShare volume
    (defined in: StandardAdditions.osax)
    mount volume string
        -- the name or URL path (starting with 'afp://') of the volume ¬
to mount
        on server string -- the server on which the volume resides
        [in AppleTalk zone string]
            -- the AppleTalk zone in which the server resides
        [as user name string]
            -- the user name with which to log in to the server;
                omit for guest access
        [with password string]
            -- the password for the user name; omit for guest access
```

Using the command

The basic command will look like the one right here:

```
mount volume "afp://serverNameOrIpAddress"
```

After running this command, the user will be shown a login dialog box to which s/he can enter his/her user name and password. That same dialog box allows the user to add that server to the keychain. Adding the server login info to the keychain should not be taken lightly because it will make access to the server much easier from the computer the script ran on. Adding the login info to the keychain can cause other issues as explained later in this chapter.

Adding login information to the command can happen in one of two different ways. You can either combine the information into the URL itself, or use the different command parameters.

The following two script lines will work the same under most circumstances. The first combines the login info into the URL and the second one uses parameters:

```
mount volume "afp://username:my_password@serverNameOrIpAddress/"
mount volume "afp://serverNameOrIpAddress" ¬
 as user name "username" password "my_password"
```

You can also use other protocols instead of AFP such as SMB. The protocol you use depends on the server setup.

The following subroutine can be used as a general subroutine for mounting server volumes:

```
on mountVolume(userName, pswd, serverIP, volumeName)
    set serverString to ¬
"afp://" & userName & ":" & pswd & "@" & ¬
 serverIP & "/" & volumeName as string
    mount volume serverString
end mountVolume
```

Mounting an iDisk

To mount an iDisk, use the following line of script:

```
mount volume "webdav://idskuser:idiskpassword@idisk.mac.com/idskuser/"
```

Mounting volumes and the keychain feature

One of the issues that may cause problems when trying to access volumes with the *mount volume* command is the keychain. If the volume info is already entered into a keychain but the password has changed, you may get an error. It has been reported that this situation happens when the login info is embedded in the URL. Manually deleting the keychain entry from the keychain can solve this problem.

13

Power wrap-up

This section summarizes the chapter in an intensive-reference style. Use this part to look up facts related to the chapter without the chatter.

File references

The basic form of referring to items on a hard drive or on the network is by using the colon delimiters. Referring to the file Reference.PDF in the folder Documents in the hard disk Macintosh HD is done like this:

```
"Macintosh HD:documents:reference.pdf"
```

Most commands that need a file reference as a parameter or return a file reference as a result use one of four main forms:

File reference is used by many applications and scripting additions. See the following reference form:

```
file "Macintosh HD:documents:reference.pdf"
```

Alias reference is probably the most common reference, mainly for commands that result in a file reference. Only files that exist and are accessible by AppleScript can be referenced with the alias reference form. The alias reference form remains accurate even if the file is moved on the same volume or renamed. See the following reference form:

```
alias "Macintosh HD:documents:reference.pdf"
```

POSIX path reference is used by the *do shell script* command.

```
"/documents/reference.pdf"
```

Some scripting additions and applications commands take a simple string as a valid file reference.

```
"Macintosh HD:documents:reference.pdf"
```

References to folders, disks, and other containers such as packages end with a colon, like this:

```
"Macintosh HD:documents:"
```

UNIX paths

UNIX paths are used in conjunction with the *do shell script* command. AppleScript has two primary ways to convert the traditional AppleScript path form, which is colon delimited, into a slash-delimited UNIX-style path.

The first method is by using the *POSIX path* property of a file, as shown here:

```
set unix_path to POSIX path of (choose file)
display dialog unix_path
```

The preceding script will display a dialog box showing the UNIX-style path of any file you choose.

The second method was created to convert UNIX paths back to AppleScript-style colon-delimited file references. This method uses the POSIX file object. This object converts a UNIX path into a normal AppleScript file reference, as shown here:

```
POSIX file "Macintosh HD:Applications:AppleScript:Folder Actions Setup"
--> "/Applications/AppleScript/Folder Actions Setup.app/"
```

File name extension

AppleScript allows you to get information about a file's name, displayed name, and name extension. You can get this information with the *info for* command. The *info for* command returns a large record with plenty of information about the given file.

The following four properties are connected to the name and name extension:

```
set file_info to info for file ¬
    "Macintosh HD:Applications:AppleScript:Folder Actions Setup.app:"
name of file_info --> "Folder Actions Setup.app"
displayed name of file_info --> "Folder Actions Setup"
name extension of file_info --> "app"
extension hidden of file_info --> true
```

Reading files

You can read files into a variable with the *read* command. The following script will read a chosen text file:

```
set file_text to read (choose file of type {"TEXT"})
```

You can also open the file for access before reading it. Opening a file before reading it has some implications detailed in this chapter.

Reading a file to a list

By default, when you read a file, you get all the text as a string. Using the *using delimiters* parameter, however, you can break the text into a list of items using a delimiter. The following script reads a file to a list, where each list item is a paragraph:

```
set text_paragraphs to ¬
    read alias "Macintosh HD:report export.txt"  using delimiters
{return}
```

13

Reading specific data

The *read* command has several other parameters that allow you to specify exactly the bytes (characters) you want to read from the file. The parameters are

- *For (integer)*: The number of bytes you want to read.
- *Before (string)*: Read all characters up to, but not including, the specified character.
- *Until (string)*: Read all characters until right after the specified character.
- *From (Integer)*: Start to read from this position and on. If omitted, start from character 1.
- *To (Integer)*: Read up to this point. If omitted, read to the end.

Reading different types of data

You can use the *as* parameter to read different types of data such as text, different image file formats, and raw AppleScript data such as a list. Refer to earlier parts of this chapter for more information about this.

Opening and closing file access

Before writing to files, and sometimes before reading files you have to open access to the file, which is done with the *open for access* command. After the file is opened and read or written to, it should be closed with the *close access* command.

The *open for access* command returns an integer that is used as a temporary reference to that file. That reference number can be later used by the *read, write*, and *close access* commands. The following script opens a file for access, and then uses the resulting file reference to read the file and close access to it:

```
set file_ref to open for access alias "Macintosh HD:report export.txt"
set report_text to read file_ref
close access file_ref
```

Note that opening and closing access to a file does not change its "busy" status. These files can be opened by any other application even after AppleScript has opened them for access.

In order to write to a file, you have to give it write permission. This is done as part of the *open for access* command:

```
set file_ref to open for access ¬
alias "Macintosh HD:report export.txt" with write permission
```

Writing to files

After you opened a file for access with write permission, you can use the *write* command to write any data to the file:

```
set file_ref to open for access ¬
    alias "Macintosh HD:report export.txt" with write permission
write "Today's special: Pea soup" to file_ref
close access file_ref
```

Writing a specified number of bytes

You can use the *for* and *starting at* parameters to specify how many bytes (characters) to write, and where to start writing. The following script writes text from a variable starting at the tenth byte of the file for 20 more bytes. Any part of the text in the variable beyond the twentieth byte will be omitted:

```
set file_ref to open for access ¬
    alias "Macintosh HD:report export.txt" with write permission
write the_long_text_variable for 20 starting at 10 to file_ref
close access file_ref
```

Writing different types of data

You can write data in different text and graphic file formats such as Unicode, GIF, TIFF, etc. You can also write data in native AppleScript format such as a list. You do that with the *as* parameter. For more information about that, refer to earlier portions of this chapter.

End Of File (EOF)

EOF is a file property that describes the number of bytes in the file. The EOF of a text file that has only the word "Apple" will be 5.

You can use EOF with the *read* and *write* commands. The following script writes text to the end of the file:

```
set file_ref to open for access ¬
    alias "Macintosh HD:report export.txt" with write permission
write the_long_text_variable to file_ref starting at EOF
close access file_ref
```

You can get and set the EOF of a given file with the *get eof* and *set eof* commands.

Details previously . . .

The last part of this chapter is a summary of the entire chapter. For more details on any of the items here, refer to earlier sections in the chapter.

13

In this chapter we will focus both on scripting clipboard operations such as copying and pasting between applications, and on manipulating data in the clipboard. As you will see, there are a few ways to get objects in and out of the clipboard, and it is used to move around objects that don't always fit well in native AppleScript variables.

Getting the clipboard data to AppleScript

The command *the clipboard* will return the contents of the clipboard. The class of the result of that command depends on the copied item; however, copying text usually returns styled text. See how to parse that style information later on in this chapter.

Setting the clipboard data

There are a few ways AppleScript or different applications allow you to set the content of the clipboard.

Copy in applications

Some applications will allow you to use the *copy* command with no parameters. Doing so will copy the selection to the clipboard.

In the following example, we copy the current selection in the front document in Microsoft Word to the clipboard:

```
tell application "Microsoft Word" to copy
```

The next example converts an RGB Illustrator document to a CMYK document.

Script 14-1

```
tell application "Illustrator CS"
    tell document 1
        set selected of every page item to true
    end tell
    activate
    copy
    close document 1 saving no
    make new document with properties {color space:CMYK}
    paste
end tell
```

Note that in the preceding example, the scripter is responsible for two critical tasks: the first is selecting the items that need to be copied, and the second is activating the application. The *copy* command only works on the application if it is the front-most process.

Using the set clipboard command

Use the *set* command to set the contents of the clipboard to a string.

```
set the clipboard to "Paste me!"
```

The following script sets the clipboard to the short version of the date:

```
set the_date_string to short date string of (current date)
set the clipboard to the_date_string
```

Using GUI scripting

You can usually copy selections from any application using UI scripting. The example in the "Saving clipboard data to a PDF file" section shows how this is done.

Clipboard info

The *get clipboard info* command returns some information about the contents of the clipboard, as shown in the following example:

```
set the clipboard to "Paste me!"
get clipboard info
--> {{string, 9}}
```

The list contains an item, also a list, that shows that the contents of the clipboard is a string containing 9 bytes.

The clipboard info can return some pretty complex results, which I will leave up to you to figure out. For instance, after copying one word from a Microsoft Word document, the clipboard info returns the following result:

{{*«class HLNK»*, 923}, {*«class OJLK»*, 132}, {*«class LKSD»*, 342}, {*«class LNKS»*, 874}, {*«class EMBS»*, 29184}, {*picture*, 258}, {*string*, 11}, {*scrap styles*, 22}, {*«class HTML»*, 30393}, {*«class RTF »*, 1719}, {*«class OBJD»*, 342}, {*«class MURF»*, 56}, {*«class DSIG»*, 4}}

Forgive me for not going there . . .

Parsing styled-text data

You must have seen styled text before: that pesky variation on the *string* class that appears in the most irritating situations just to throw us off. Countless times I found myself in situations where comparing two seemingly identical strings returned a false result. The problem was almost always not related to the text itself, but rather to the class: I was comparing plain strings with either styled text or Unicode text. By now, these two string class flavors are much better integrated into AppleScript, and comparing them with regular strings containing the same characters returns a true result.

14

So what else is styled text good for, and where is it used? Styled text is the primary format that AppleScript uses to describe styled text copied into the clipboard.

How was all that figured out?

The first one who published information regarding styled text was Arthur J. Knapp, who made his findings known in a post to the AppleScript Users mailing list.

From there, the information was further developed into a full-blown demo by Mark Munro, founder of Write Track Media, a consulting firm specializing in automation services and related products.

I took the information and turned it into the little tutorial you see in this chapter.

Getting styled text

Try the following:

Create a new document in Word and enter two words. Format them with bold, italic, etc. You can also format text in a FileMaker Pro cell.

Now, select the text and choose Copy from the Edit menu.

In a new script window, type the following two lines:

```
set clipboard_contents to the clipboard
class of clipboard_contents
--> string
```

AppleScript views styled text as a string when you try to get its class. However, let's pry open the data we got from the clipboard to reveal the style information.

Change the script to the following:

```
set clipboard_contents to the clipboard
clipboard_contents as record
--> {«class ktxt»:"This is it!", «class ksty»:«data ¬
styl0002000000000000C00090014
01000
00C00000000000000000005000C00090
0140300000C000000000000»}
```

When you ask for styled text as a record, AppleScript separates the text information from the style information. The text is placed in a record item labeled «class ktxt» and the style data is placed in a record item labeled «class ksty». This makes it easy to pluck the information we want. To get the text only as a plain string, which is the only way I know to get a clean (nonstyled) string from styled text, is by getting that «class ktxt» item. The following script ends up with two variables: *the_text* and *the_style*.

```
set clipboard_contents to the clipboard
set styled_text_data to clipboard_contents as record
set the_text to «class ktxt» of styled_text_data
-->This is it!
set the_style to «class ksty» of styled_text_data
--> «data styl000200000000000C0009001401000
00C00000000000000000005000C000900140300000C000000000000»
```

What we can do with the string is clear: anything we do with any other string. The style data, however, is a bit more challenging. With some testing and intuition we should be able to crack it down.

How is the style data organized?

We start with the understanding that the real data is broken down into 40-byte chunks, starting from the fifth digit and on. Each style-data chunk describes what's called an attribute run. An attribute run, also referred to as text-style range, is a set of characters that bear the same style. The 40 digits bear information about the location of the attribute run in the string, the font, the style, and even the text's color.

Following is a breakdown of the 40-digit code into functions. Most codes are four characters that have to be converted from hex numbers into normal numbers. For instance, the four digits responsible for the size may be 0009 for size 1, but 0010 for size 16—get it? Well, if not, don't worry. We will use a handy JavaScript call that will take our hex-encoded numbers and convert them into numbers mortals can understand as well. See the "Parsing hex numbers" section later on.

The following table breaks down the 40-digit style into components:

Digit Range	Function	Number Format
1–8	Range starting point	Hex
9–12	Line height	Hex
13–16	Font ascent	Hex
17–20	Font family ID	Hex
21–24	Style (bold, italic, etc.)	Hex
25–28	Type size	Hex
29–32	Red value	Hex
33–36	Green value	Hex
37–40	Blue value	Hex

14

As you can see, digits 9 through 24 are the style (including font, and styling type such as bold, italic, etc.), and digits 25 through 40 represent the color information.

Characters 21 and 22 represent the type style in this order:

00: Plain

01: Bold

02: Italic

03: Bold and italic

04: Underline

05: Underline and bold

06: Underline and italic

07: Underline, bold, and italic

. . .

10: Shadow

11: Shadow and Bold

etc.

Parsing hex numbers

To parse hex numbers into normal numbers, we use the JavaScript *parseInt* command with the hex number passed as integer.

```
set textDataStartAt to "00FF"
set textDataStartAt to ¬
    run script "parseInt( \"" & textDataStartAt & "\" , 16) " in ¬
"JavaScript"
--> 255
```

The largest 4-byte hex number is FFFF and its integer value is 65535.

Parsing the style data

Before we can tap all these goodies, we need access to the style data, and we need it as a string. Unfortunately, the style data isn't about to be coerced into a string without a fight, so a fight it'll be, and guess who's going to win? When AppleScript won't coerce a value into a string, all you have to do is force AppleScript to throw an error with the text you want in it, and then parse out the part of the error you want. This technique is explained in Chapter 15.

Back to style parsing: our first mission whose solution is shown next is to extract the group of 40-digit style range descriptions from the style's data portion. Here's how we do that, assuming that we continue the script from previously and the variable *the_style* has the style information in it:

```
try
    the_style as string
on error the_style_error
end try
Can't make «data styl000200000000000C000900140100000C000
00000000000000004000C000900140300000C000000000000» into a string.
set text item delimiters to {"«data style"}
set style_data to the_style_error's text item 2
set text item delimiters to {"»"}
set style_data to style_data's text item 1
set text item delimiters to {""}
style_data
--> 000200000000000C000900140100000C000000000000
00000004000C000900140300000C000000000000
```

The result is the data itself. Now, we need to remove the first five digits (or characters, since it is a string) from the style info.

```
Set style_data to (characters 5 thru -1 of style_data) as string
```

Next we will create a list where each item is 40 digits that describe a single text-style range:

```
set style_range_list to {}
repeat with i from 1 to ((length of style_data) / 40)
    set this_style_data to ¬
        characters (((i - 1) * 40) + 1) thru (i * 40) of style_data as ¬
        string
    set end of style_range_list to this_style_data
end repeat
style_range_list
--> {"00000000000C000900140100000C000000000000", ¬
"00000004000C000900140300000C000000000000"}
```

Next you will need to loop through the strings in the list and use the table shown earlier to extract the elements you want to use. Work with the text's size, style, or color—whatever you want.

14

The following example loops through the list of style ranges and creates a color palette that includes all the colors that exist in the file. It also assumes that you have a subroutine called *HexToNum* that takes the 4-byte hex string and converts it into an integer between 0 and 65535.

```
set color_palette_list to {}
repeat with the_style_range in style_range_list
    set red_info to characters 29 thru 32 of the_style_range as string
    set green_info to characters 33 thru 36 of the_style_range as string
    set blue_info to characters 37 thru 40 of the_style_range as string
    set color_specs to {HexToNum(red_info), ¬
        HexToNum(green_info), HexToNum(blue_info)}
    set end of color_palette_list to color_specs
end
```

Following is the complete script:

Script 14-2 (includes all script parts shown previously)

```
set clipboard_contents to the clipboard
set styled_text_data to clipboard_contents as record
set the_text to «class ktxt» of styled_text_data
set the_style to «class ksty» of styled_text_data

try
    the_style as string
on error the_style_error
end try
set text item delimiters to {"«data style"}
set style_data to the_style_error's text item 2
set text item delimiters to {"»"}
set style_data to style_data's text item 1
set text item delimiters to {""}
set style_data to (characters 5 thru -1 of style_data) as string

set style_range_list to {}
repeat with i from 1 to ((length of style_data) / 40)
    set this_style_data to ¬
        characters (((i - 1) * 40) + 1) thru (i * 40) of style_data ¬
        as string
    set end of style_range_list to this_style_data
end repeat
style_range_list

set color_palette_list to {}
repeat with the_style_range in style_range_list
    set red_info to characters 29 thru 32 of the_style_range as string
    set green_info to characters 33 thru 36 of the_style_range as string
    set blue_info to characters 37 thru 40 of the_style_range as string
    set color_specs to {HexToNum(red_info), ¬
```

```
      HexToNum(green_info), HexToNum(blue_info)}
   set end of color_palette_list to color_specs
end repeat
return color_palette_list

on HexToNum(hex)
   set parsed_hex to ¬
      run script "parseInt( \"" & hex & "\" , 16) " in "JavaScript"
   return parsed_hex
end HexToNum
```

Saving clipboard data to a PDF file

Following is an ultra-cool script in regard to utilizing PDF data in the clipboard. It takes a selection you make with the marquee in the application Preview and saves it to a file you specify.

The highlights of the scripts are as follows:

In line 1 the user chooses the name and location for the file.

In lines 4 through 8 we use UI scripting in System Events to deploy the Copy menu item of Apple's yet-to-be-scriptable Preview application.

In line 11 we verify that the *clipboard* class is a record. This is still not a guarantee for success, but it at least makes sure that something other than a string has been copied. In a script like that you'd most likely want to deploy a more comprehensive error trapping solution. I didn't do it here in order to not hide the important portions of the script.

In line 12 we create the file. In line 13 we write the data to the file, and then close it in line 14.

In lines 17 and 18 we use the Finder to set the file's type to PDF and creator to prvw, the creator type of the application Preview. This will ensure that Preview is the application that is launched when we open the file using the Preview application. Unfortunately, we have to use the Finder's *open* command, not Preview's, since it is not yet scriptable. (Did I mention that already?)

14

The complete script is as follows:

Script 14-3

```
1. set destination_file_path to choose file name default name ¬
   "Selection.pdf"
2. tell application "Preview" to activate
3. delay 1
4. tell application "System Events"
5.    tell application process "Preview"
6.       click menu item "Copy" of menu "Edit" of ¬
            menu bar item "Edit" of menu bar 1
7.    end tell
8. end tell
9. delay 1
10. set the_clipboard_data to the clipboard
11. if (class of the_clipboard_data) is record then
12.    set fileRef to open for access destination_file_path with ¬
       write permission
13.    write the_clipboard_data to fileRef as data
14.    close access fileRef
15.    tell application "Finder"
16.       tell file destination_file_path
17.          set file type of it to "PDF "
18.          set creator type of it to "prvw"
19.       end tell
20.       reveal destination_file_path
21.       open destination_file_path
22.    end tell
23. else
24.    set the_message to ¬
       "Make a selection with the marquee tool in Preview"
25.    display dialog the_message buttons {"OK"} default button 1 ¬
       with icon stop
26. end if
```

CHAPTER 15
TURN ERRORS IN YOUR FAVOR

An error occurred.
-128

E.T. could not phone home:
wrong number

There are two kinds of errors in AppleScript: compile errors and runtime errors. Since compile errors are very easy to discover and usually easy enough to fix, this chapter will concentrate mainly on runtime errors.

Compile errors

Compile errors are errors that prevent the script from compiling.

The bad news is that they happen a lot when you start to script simply because the syntax is still foreign to you. Later on, you still get them when your syntax is correct but some literal expression you used didn't take. For instance, type the following in a new script window:

```
Alias "Mammamia"
```

When you try to compile this script, AppleScript will return an error instead. The same happens when you try to compile a date with an illegitimate string.

The good news is that a compile error is a bit like losing your car keys at the gym. It's irritating, but you can't make it worse by driving away . . .

How runtime errors work in AppleScript

Runtime errors in AppleScript aren't an all-out unanticipated mistake that can't be recovered. Rather, runtime errors are designed to let you know that the data that was provided for a certain statement to chew on doesn't fit, and that AppleScript's next resort is to throw an error and terminate the script. Errors are the way out when the range of acceptable possibilities didn't come to be.

So are errors good or bad? Errors are actually a good thing, much like pain is a good thing for our health for the one reason, which is, we do our best to avoid it.

So can we avoid errors altogether? Not really. But while we can't avoid them, we can anticipate them, trap them, analyze them, and sentence them to community service.

The psychology of an error

Rule number 1: As the scripter, you subconsciously avoid doing things that will generate errors. Have someone else test your script for you.

Rule number 2: As the scripter, you think you know your script best. Wrong! Give it to the first novice user, and s/he will provoke errors within the first three seconds.

Rule number 3: People don't read instructions. If you think to yourself, "I wrote in the dialog to enter a date, it's not my fault if they don't," you're wrong, it is your fault. The blame does not lie with what the user entered, but with the fact that you didn't anticipate it.

Rule number 4: Anywhere in your script that can generate an error due to user incompetence will generate an error. Furthermore, the error yet again is reflected on you, the AppleScript genius, not the just-started-yesterday user.

The anatomy of an error

Every error that is thrown has a few components that help you identify its cause. The two main components are the error text that describes the error, and the error number, which we can use to make decisions, while the script is running, on what action we want to take.

The other components of an error are the partial result, which is the piece of result that the command did manage to return; the offending object, which is the object that is responsible for the error; and the expected type, which is the type of data the script would have liked to get instead of the offending object.

To understand a bit better, start a script and type the following:

```
1 + "abc"
```

In this case, the error is "Can't make data into expected type," which is error number -1700. There's no partial result, but we do have an offender. The offending object is "abc", and the expected type is number. AppleScript tried to coerce "abc" into a number, but couldn't.

Understanding the two main properties of an error, the number and the message, is important both when you want to trap potential errors and when you conspire to take the offender's role and throw an error yourself! More on that later in this chapter.

Trapping errors

How much effort you put into trapping errors really is up to you. You may be writing scripts for your own use, or for a limited use, and don't want to turn it into a big production. In this case, you may want to test the script and explain to the user how to write down any error and let you know.

On the other hand, if the script will have to be distributed among many users, or worst, distributed to unknown users all over the place, you want to take every precaution that no potential error will remain untrapped.

In the following section we will script as if trapping errors is a mission-critical entity, and look at all different ways to trap errors.

15

The try block

The one and only way to trap errors in AppleScript is by using *try* statement blocks, which start with a line containing a single word, "try," and end with a line containing two words, "end try." Most *try* blocks will also have an additional line in the middle that starts with "on error," but more on this one later.

The script that follows shows the basic *try* block:

```
try
    statement 1
    statement 2
    statement 3...
end try
```

If no errors occur in any of the lines containing statements 1, 2, and 3, then the *try* command is as much use as life insurance for a vampire.

If one of the three statements does decide to throw an error, then any of the statements from there until the *end try* statement will be skipped.

In fact, every time an error is thrown, AppleScript looks back in the script, line by line, to find a *try* statement. In this case, it will find that *try* statement. If no *try* statement is found, then AppleScript has no choice but to air our dirty laundry and let the user know that an error has occurred. If a *try* statement was found, AppleScript looks to see if there's an *on error* line associated with that *try* statement.

In our case, there's no *on error* line, just an *end try*. This means that AppleScript just continues to execute the lie following the *end try* line, and we may never know that an error has occurred.

Is not knowing an error occurred ever a good idea? Well, unless you have some control issues, it may be perfectly fine. Take for instance the following script:

Script 15-1

```
tell application "Finder"
    try
        delete file "Macintosh HD:temp"
    end try
end tell
```

In the preceding script, we specify to delete a temporary file. We may want to run these lines at the end or beginning of the script just to make sure we leave things neat. All we want is that the file will not exist after the lines execute. So if the file doesn't exist and the *delete* command in the Finder throws an error, we may not want to know about it. We could test for the error to see if it is any other error, but that will be a bit much.

So, just using the *try* and *end try* mandatory portions of the *try* block will simply skip the remainder of the script lines until the *end try*, and resume operation from there as if nothing happened.

The full try statement from the dictionary

Following is the dictionary definition of the *try* statement.

```
try
    --statement or statements that may throw an error.
on error [error_message] [number error_number] ¬
    [from offending_object] [to expected_type] ¬
        [partial result result_list]
    --the statement that will execute in case of an error...
end try
```

As you can see in this example, the *try* statement can be very involved. It is usually much simpler, though. Out of all the different parameters, all we really deal with are the error message itself and the error number.

What to do in case of an error

So far we dealt with the *try* statement as a simple block with a start and an end. Now, however, we're going to add the *on error* line in the heart of the *try* statement. From now on, our *try* statement block will have two compartments:

```
try
    compartment 1
on error
    compartment 2
end try
```

In compartment 1 we put all the statements that we want to execute under normal operation. In compartment 2 we want to put all the statements that we want to execute if anything goes wrong in compartment 1. Here's another way we can put it:

```
try
    light candles on cake
on error
    call fire department
end try
```

Do we usually invite firemen to birthday parties? I know my wife wouldn't mind, she has a thing for firemen, but they always seem so busy. However, it is a good idea to have a plan to call the fire fighters in case something goes wrong with the candles.

One of the most common uses of the *on error* clause is to trap error number -128. Error -128 is the user canceled error and it is thrown by the *display dialog* command when the user clicks the Cancel button. Any other button is simply returned in the dialog reply record; only the Cancel button generates an error. Error -128, however, will not generate an ugly error message to the user. All that'll happen if the Cancel button is clicked is that the script will exit, or if it is saved as an application, the application will quit.

15

One separate way to deal with this particular one is to rename the Cancel button with a space before and after. This, however, will deprive the user from being able to dismiss the dialog box with the ESCAPE key.

Following is a simple example of trapping the Cancel button error:

Script 15-2

```
try
    display dialog "What's next?" buttons {"Cancel", "Go", "Run"}
on error
    display dialog "I'm out of here..." giving up after 5
end try
```

Now this is OK, but what we want to do in many cases is take action only if the error is a specific error. In this case, we want the dialog box displayed only for the user-canceled error.

For that we need to know the error number. Just for adventure's sake, let's pretend we don't know exactly what error is thrown and what the error number is. To figure it out, we need to create a little script, make sure that AppleScript throws an error at us, trap it, and analyze it. We do that with the *error* and *error number* properties that are returned by the error.

To get information about an error, you can add a variable identifier right after the *on error* line. The error message will be assigned to this variable. Examine the following script:

Script 15-3

```
try
    display dialog "Do it?"
on error the_error_message
    display dialog "An error occurred. The message was:" & ¬
        return & the_error_message
end try
```

Figure 15-1 shows the message of the second dialog box. It shows that the value of the variable *the_error_message* we placed after the on error was "User canceled."

Figure 15-1. The error message trapped in the variable *the_error_message* is "User canceled."

To trap the error number, we add the word "number" before the variable. For now, add the word "number" as shown in the following script, run the script, and click the Cancel button. Figure 15-2 shows the dialog box displayed as a result of you clicking Cancel.

Check out the error number the dialog box revealed. (I also changed the text of that second dialog box, but that shouldn't matter.)

Script 15-4

```
try
    display dialog "Do it?"
on error number the_error_message
    display dialog "An error occurred. The number is:" & ¬
        return & the_error_message
end try
```

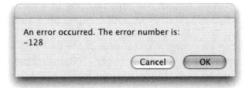

An error occurred. The error number is:
−128

Cancel   OK

Figure 15-2. The dialog box reveals the error number.

Ah, the satisfaction of attaining hard-earned knowledge! Now, let's mix the error message with the error number:

Script 15-5

```
try
    display dialog "Do it?"
on error the_error_message number the_error_number
    display dialog "An error occurred:" & return & the_error_message & ¬
        return & the_error_number
end try
```

Putting error numbers to use

Now that we know how to figure out the error numbers, we can start using them. To start, we will modify the preceding script to display the second dialog box only if the error number is -128. To do that we just have to replace the expression following the word "number" from a variable to a literal expression, or in other words, the actual error number. Here's how the script will look:

Script 15-6

```
try
    display dialog "Do it?"
on error number -128
    display dialog "You canceled the script. Bye!"
end try
```

15

The preceding script is OK, but it lets us act upon only one error. What if we anticipate two or more errors? For that there are two possible options: we have to either nest multiple *try* statement blocks one inside the other, or we have to put the error number into a variable and use an *if-else if* block to test for the different possible errors.

Testing for multiple errors

In many cases, the same statement may throw more than one type of error. In order to treat each error differently, you will need to use a simple conditional statement. Another thing you will need to do is identify the number of the errors you want to treat, and leave one last open *else* clause to deal with any other error that may occur. The script we will look at will take two variables: one with a path pointing to a folder, and one with a path pointing to a file. The script will attempt to duplicate the file into the folder.

Two of the things that can go wrong are that one of the paths point to a nonexisting file, in which case AppleScript will throw error number -10006; and the other error is that the file you're copying already exists in the destination folder, which is error number -15267.

Watch how we act differently based on the error:

Script 15-7

```
 1. try
 2.    tell application "Finder"
 3.        duplicate file source_file to folder dest_folder
 4.    end tell
 5. on error error_message number error_number
 6.    if error_number is -10006 then
 7.        display dialog ¬
            "Either the file or folder you specify doesn't exist"
 8.    else if error_number is -15267 then
 9.        display dialog ¬
            "The folder already has a file with the same name"
10.    else
11.      display dialog "The following message has occurred:" & ¬
            return & error_message
12.    end if
13.    display dialog "The script is going to stop now"
14.    return
15. end try
```

Nesting try handlers

Another way to achieve a similar result is to use a literal expression (a number, in this case) to describe the error number. This will force us to nest the *try* statements in the following fashion:

Script 15-8

```
1. try
2.    try
3.       try
4.          tell application "Finder"
5.             duplicate file source_file to folder dest_folder
6.          end tell
7.       on error number -10006
8.          display dialog ¬
              "Either the file or folder you specify doesn't exist"
9.       end try
10.   on error number -15267
11.      display dialog ¬
            "The folder already has a file with the same name"
12.   end try
13. on error
14.    display dialog "The following message has occurred:" & ¬
          return & error_message
15. end try
```

In the preceding example, the statement whose error we want to trap is actually inside three nested *try* statements. Each one of the first two will only trap a specific error. If the error that occurred is not that error, the error will trickle down to the next *try* statement. At the end, the error will get to the general error message that is designed to trap any error.

Be careful not to trap too much

Error trapping is not a solution to errors! Well, it kind of is, but either to errors you anticipate, or for freak-once-in-a-lifetime errors. During your testing and debugging stage, you should stay away from trapping errors. You want to see it as it comes and treat it. Once you've managed to account for almost all situations, go ahead and add some *try* statements just to be sure. See the "Script-wide try statement" section later in this chapter.

Another thing you may consider is deactivating any error-trapping *try* statements. Simply comment out the *try* statement components. When all is done, uncomment the *try* statements to make them active again. You do that since during the testing stages you actually want to see the errors so that you can possibly find better solutions for them.

Can errors serve a function?

Yes, we can train errors to serve a scripting function for us. While programmatically they may still be classified as something that an AppleScript command or statement couldn't handle, for us as scripters, they may present an opportunity. The key isn't whether the error is good or bad, but rather how reliably will AppleScript throw an error at a particular place. And just as AppleScript is reliable at executing statements correctly, if you plan things right, AppleScript will throw errors as anticipated.

15

Take for example the alias type file reference. If you put the word "alias" before a pathname of a nonexisting file, AppleScript will throw an error, every time! That means that we can use that as a way to check if a file exists or not.

Following is a handler that should be in every scripter's library. It returns true if the file path you pass to it exists and false if it doesn't.

Script 15-9

```
on file_exists(the_path)
    try
        alias the_path
        return true
    on error
        return false
    end try
end file_exists
```

In the preceding script we count on the fact that the script will throw an error if the path we used with the alias file reference is invalid. The error is thrown like clockwork, we trap it, and when we do, we gracefully return the value false to the statement calling the handler.

Script-wide try statement

One of the projects I'm working on is a bunch of scripts Sal wrote for Showtime Networks. The scripts automate the creation of the Upcoming shows menus for about ten of Showtime Networks's affiliate stations. Sal initially created the scripts for them as a PR campaign for Showtime and it really worked well. It also worked well for me to inherit the project, since besides billing for the time, I got to learn a lot from Sal's AppleScript mastery.

One of the neat features in these scripts was that, beside the localized error trapping that was implemented throughout the script, every script had one big *try* statement that covered it from head to toe.

The purpose of the *on error* handler wasn't to notify the user that something wrong went down. The script then displays the error message in a nice dialog box instead of the typical error message AppleScript displays in case of unhandled errors, with the dreaded Edit button that, no matter what I tell them, users always seem to want to click. The AppleScript application generic-style error message dialog box is shown in Figure 15-3.

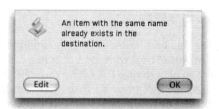

Figure 15-3. AppleScript's generic error message dialog box with the dreaded Edit button

Sal's script-wide *try* statement worked well, but I needed a way for the user to know exactly where things went bad. So I came up with the following solution: I added a global variable called *script_location* and assigned a different number to it throughout the script. Every two or three lines of real code, I'd add something like this:

```
set script_location to 64
```

At the end, part of the job of that script-wide *on error* handler was to report to me not only the nature of the error, but that script location variable, which allowed me to pinpoint the exact location of the error.

Scripts in which I implement this strategy do become about 40% longer in terms of lines, but the execution doesn't suffer: on a 1GHz G4 Mac, AppleScript can assign an integer to a variable 500,000 per second.

Logging errors to a file

An even better error hunting technique I use is to write the script's activity to a text file. Since by doing this every second or third line of the script really will hamper performance, you will only want the user to implement it when there's a persistent error. Find a way for the user to flag the script that should log errors. If you have an interface, then you can add a little check box caller "log activity." Otherwise, if your script has a dialog box that appears at the start, you may want to add a button there called Settings. Clicking this button will display another dialog box that will allow users to turn logging on for the following run of the script. This will turn a *log_error* global variable to true, which will then tell all the handlers in the script to log their activity.

The idea with logging activity is to create a text file on the desktop bearing the date and time, and add some text to that file every few lines. The text should describe the location and include some of the actual values used in the script. This can provide clues for the error.

I tell my clients to e-mail me that resulting text file, which comes in very handy in revealing the cause of the error.

Since you will be utilizing the error logging feature again and again, it is a perfect candidate for a handler with a couple of parameters such as line number, the part of the script it's called from, and maybe values of a few variables coerced into a string.

A handler call is much easier to embed multiple times in your script.

Generating errors

Having spent the last portion of the book trying to contain and control errors, why in the world, in our right mind, would we go around creating them ourselves?

15

Well, in some situations during the script's execution, you will realize that the user entered the wrong type of data, a file that was supposed to be found was not, or other items that your script could potentially deal with, but you feel that instead they call for the termination of the script.

To throw an error yourself, you have to go back to take a look at the few parameters that make up the error object.

The error message and error number are really the parameters that are usually used for throwing errors. The other parameters are offending object, expected type, and partial result.

To throw an error, add the following syntax to your script:

```
error error_message_string number error_number
```

Or, using literal expressions:

```
Error "E.T. could not phone home: wrong number" ¬
    number -91001 offending object phone
```

Figure 15-4 shows the error dialog box that this error, unhandled, will display.

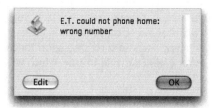

Figure 15-4. The error message shown in an AppleScript application error dialog box

Throwing your own errors is mainly a good idea if you deploy a script-wide error capturing strategy. This way this error will be logged somewhere and the client will get some feedback on what went wrong.

Using errors for string coercion

Several classes in AppleScript, such as records, for instance, just wouldn't coerce into a string. To force them to coerce, just force an error whose description will include the value you want. Next, trap the error's message (which is very much a string) and parse-out the values you want.

For instance, here's how you get a record as a string:

Script 15-10

```
set my_records to {dog:"Rufus", cat:"Fluff"}
try
    my_records as string
on error error_message
end try
--> Can't make {dog:"Rufus", cat:"Fluff"} into a string.
set text item delimiters to "Can't make "
set record_text to item 2 of text items of error_message
set text item delimiters to " into a string."
set record_text to item 1 of text items of record_text
set text item delimiters to ""
record_text
--> {dog:"Rufus", cat:"Fluff"}
```

Notice how we parse the record out of the error message. This is a perfectly valid form of tricking AppleScript into giving you what it doesn't want to give you. Now you just have to find a reason to get a record as a string . . .

List of error messages

The following part lists all AppleScript-related error messages that don't belong to third-party scripting additions or scriptable applications. The list is divided into sections: "Operating system errors," "Apple event errors," "Application scripting errors," and "AppleScript errors."

Operating system errors

An operating system error is an error that occurs when AppleScript or an application requests services from the Mac OS. They are rare, and more important, there's usually nothing you can do about them in a script. A few, such as "File <name> wasn't found" and "Application isn't running," make sense for scripts to handle.

0: No error.

-34: Disk <name> is full.

-35: Disk <name> wasn't found.

-37: Bad name for file.

-38: File <name> wasn't open.

-39: End of file error.

-42: Too many files open.

-43: File <name> wasn't found.

15

-44: Disk <name> is write protected.

-45: File <name> is locked.

-46: Disk <name> is locked.

-47: File <name> is busy.

-48: Duplicate file name.

-49: File <name> is already open.

-50: Parameter error.

-51: File reference number error.

-61: File not open with write permission.

-108: Out of memory.

-120: Folder <name> wasn't found.

-124: Disk <name> is disconnected.

-128: User canceled.

-192: A resource wasn't found.

-600: Application isn't running.

-601: Not enough room to launch application with special requirements.

-602: Application is not 32-bit clean.

-605: More memory is needed than is specified in the size resource.

-606: Application is background-only.

-607: Buffer is too small.

-608: No outstanding high-level event.

-609: Connection is invalid.

-904: Not enough system memory to connect to remote application.

-905: Remote access is not allowed.

-906: <name> isn't running or program linking isn't enabled.

-915: Can't find remote machine.

-30720: Invalid date and time <date string>.

Apple event errors

An Apple event error is an error that occurs when Apple events sent by AppleScript fail. Many of these errors, such as "No user interaction allowed," are of interest to users. Also of interest to users are errors that have to do with reference forms, as well as errors such as "No such object."

-1700: Can't make some data into the expected type.

-1701: Some parameter is missing for <commandName>.

-1702: Some data could not be read.

-1703: Some data was the wrong type.

-1704: Some parameter was invalid.

-1705: Operation involving a list item failed.

-1706: Need a newer version of the Apple Event Manager.

-1707: Event isn't an Apple event.

-1708: <reference> doesn't understand the <commandName> message.

-1709: AEResetTimer was passed an invalid reply.

-1710: Invalid sending mode was passed.

-1711: User canceled out of wait loop for reply or receipt.

-1712: Apple event timed out.

-1713: No user interaction allowed.

-1714: Wrong keyword for a special function.

-1715: Some parameter wasn't understood.

-1716: Unknown Apple event address type.

-1717: The handler <identifier> is not defined.

-1718: Reply has not yet arrived.

-1719: Can't get <reference>. Invalid index.

-1720: Invalid range.

-1721: <expression> doesn't match the parameters <parameterNames> for <commandName>.

-1723: Can't get <expression>. Access not allowed.

15

-1725: Illegal logical operator called.

-1726: Illegal comparison or logical.

-1727: Expected a reference.

-1728: Can't get <reference>.

-1729: Object counting procedure returned a negative count.

-1730: Container specified was an empty list.

-1731: Unknown object type.

-1750: Scripting component error.

-1751: Invalid script id.

-1752: Script doesn't seem to belong to AppleScript.

-1753: Script error.

-1754: Invalid selector given.

-1755: Invalid access.

-1756: Source not available.

-1757: No such dialect.

-1758: Data couldn't be read because its format is obsolete.

-1759: Data couldn't be read because its format is too new.

-1760: Recording is already on.

Application scripting errors

An application scripting error is an error returned by an application when handling standard AppleScript commands (commands that apply to all applications). Many of these errors, such as "The specified object is a property, not an element," are of interest to users and should be handled.

-10000: Apple event handler failed.

-10001: A descriptor type mismatch occurred.

-10002: Invalid key form.

-10003: Can't set <object or data> to <object or data>. Access not allowed.

-10004: A privilege violation occurred.

-10005: The read operation wasn't allowed.

-10006: Can't set <object or data> to <object or data>.

-10007: The index of the event is too large to be valid.

-10008: The specified object is a property, not an element.

-10009: Can't supply the requested descriptor type for the data.

-10010: The Apple event handler can't handle objects of this class.

-10011: Couldn't handle this command because it wasn't part of the current transaction.

-10012: The transaction to which this command belonged isn't a valid transaction.

-10013: There is no user selection.

-10014: Handler only handles single objects.

-10015: Can't undo the previous Apple event or user action.

AppleScript errors

An AppleScript error is an error that occurs when AppleScript processes script statements. Nearly all of these are of interest to users. For errors returned by an application, see the documentation for that application.

-2700: Unknown error.

-2701: Can't divide <number> by zero.

-2702: The result of a numeric operation was too large.

-2703: <reference> can't be launched because it is not an application.

-2704: <reference> isn't scriptable.

-2705: The application has a corrupted dictionary.

-2706: Stack overflow.

-2707: Internal table overflow.

-2708: Attempt to create a value larger than the allowable size.

-2709: Can't get the event dictionary.

-2720: Can't both consider and ignore <attribute>.

15

-2721: Can't perform operation on text longer than 32K bytes.

-2729: Message size too large for the 7.0 Finder.

-2740: A <language element> can't go after this <language element>.

-2741: Expected <language element> but found <language element>.

-2750: The <name> parameter is specified more than once.

-2751: The <name> property is specified more than once.

-2752: The <name> handler is specified more than once.

-2753: The variable <name> is not defined.

-2754: Can't declare <name> as both a local and global variable.

-2755: Exit statement was not in a repeat loop.

-2760: Tell statements are nested too deeply.

-2761: <name> is illegal as a formal parameter.

-2762: <name> is not a parameter name for the event <event>.

-2763: No result was returned for some argument of this expression.

Power wrap-up

This section summarizes the chapter in an intensive-reference style. Use this part to look up facts related to the chapter without the chatter.

Compile errors

Compile errors are errors that occur while the script tries to compile. Compiling scripts is what happens before the script even runs. Typical compile errors are aliases that point to a nonexisting file, two variables in a row, not using a *tell* block when using application-specific terms, etc.

Runtime errors

Runtime errors are errors that only happen while the script runs. An error that is thrown while the script is running has a few components that are either used by the scripter to debug the problem during development, or are used by the script itself to determine how it should precede, in case the error is trapped. Untrapped errors will cause the script to stop, and usually AppleScript will display a dialog box containing the grim details of the error to the user.

The error components are error text, error number, offending object, and expected type.

Trapping errors

Errors are trapped with the *try* block. Any runtime error that occurs in a statement inside a *try* block will not stop the script. Following is the basic *try* statement block:

```
try
    set x to 2 + "five"
end try
```

You can specify to the script what to do in case there's an error anywhere within the *try* block by adding the *on error* line to the *try* statement, like this:

```
try
    set x to 2 + "five"
on error
    set x to 0
    display dialog "Couldn't  get the value of x!"
end try
```

You can get the error components by placing variables after the *on error* line, like this:

```
try
    set x to 2 + "five"
on error error_text number error_number from offending_object to ¬
expected_type
    display dialog "There was an error, and here is what happened:" & ¬
        return & error_text
end try
```

Generating errors

You can use the *error* command to throw errors at any point during the script, like this:

```
error "Something happened" number 999
```

Although I only used the error text and number components, the other two can be used as well.

Be aware that negative error numbers are reserved by Apple.

Details previously . . .

The last part of this chapter is a summary of the entire chapter. For more details on any of the items here, refer to earlier sections in this chapter.

15

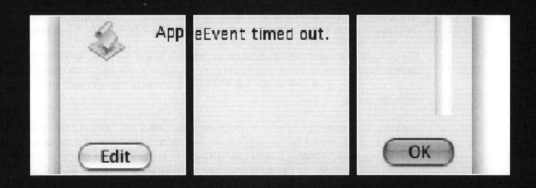

Whenever AppleScript sends a command to a scriptable application, it waits in order to get some communication back from the application. This communication may be information your script wanted from the application or an indication that a command has executed properly.

There are two issues related to the exchange between AppleScript and the scriptable application: how long should AppleScript wait for a response, and should AppleScript wait for a response in the first place? These two issues are handled in two ways, either by AppleScript's default behavior or by the means of two control statements: *application responses* and *timeout*.

These control statements act as wraps to code, as shown here:

```
considering/ignoring application responses
    tell application...
    ...code
    end tell
end considering
```

or

```
with timeout of 300 seconds
    tell application...
    ...code
    end tell
end timeout
```

Any code within the wrap will behave according to the instruction in the first line of the wrap. See details about the two statements in the upcoming sections.

Application responses

The *application responses* control statement controls whether or not AppleScript waits to see what response the application returned after AppleScript sent it a command.

By default, when you use AppleScript to tell an application to do something, AppleScript won't continue the script until it hears back from the application. While this is usually OK, there are times when you would want to send a command to an application and move on with the script.

Instructing AppleScript to ignore application responses will cause AppleScript to send the message of command to the application and ignore any error it may generate and any result that this command may return. Using this feature means that you either trust the application to complete the appointed task, or that you have other ways to verify that the task has been completed.

The following script tells Photoshop to play an action but does not hang around to see how things worked out:

```
tell application "Photoshop CS"
    ignoring application responses
        do script "Convert folder to JPG" from "Conversion action set"
    end ignoring
end tell
```

In the following script, we ask Acrobat Distiller to distill a PostScript file. Although we tell AppleScript to ignore any responses from Acrobat, we do go right away to check if the file has been generated.

```
set destination_pdf to "Macintosh HD:Users:hanaan:Desktop:final.pdf"
set dest_posix to POSIX path of destination_pdf
set source_posix to "/Users/hanaan/Desktop/temp_document.ps"
tell application "Acrobat Distiller 6.0.1"
    ignoring application responses
        Distill sourcePath source_posix destinationPath dest_posix
    end ignoring
end tell
tell application "Finder"
    repeat until exists file destination_pdf
        exit repeat
    end repeat
end tell
display dialog "PDF Done!"
```

Yes, Acrobat Distiller 6 now uses the command *distill* instead of *open*, and if you want it to take you seriously, you better supply it with POSIX paths for source and destination file paths.

Application responses and subroutines

The *ignoring application responses* command works through subroutine calls as well as when calling applications directly.

In the following script we call a *delete file* subroutine, but we ask it to delete a nonexisting file. The subroutine will usually generate an error in this case, but the *ignoring application responses* clause surrounding the subroutine call still tell AppleScript to proceed without waiting for a response from the Finder.

```
ignoring application responses
    delete_file("lala:bimbim")
end ignoring
on delete_file(file_path)
    tell application "Finder"
        delete file file_path
    end tell
end delete_file
```

In the preceding case, *ignoring application responses* acts as error trapping as well.

Timeouts

By default, when AppleScript sends a command to an application, it waits 120 seconds for a response. If the application returns no response by then, AppleScript throws a timeout error.

While *ignoring application responses* asks AppleScript to not wait for a response from an application it sends a command to, the *timeout* control statement asks AppleScript to hang around a bit longer than the default 120 seconds, or to cut it short and wait for a shorter amount of time.

The example script that follows will throw a timeout error since the Finder took longer than 120 seconds to perform the *duplicate* command:

```
tell application "Finder"
    duplicate disk "Macintosh HD" to folder "BU" ¬
        of disk "Backup Volume" replacing yes
end tell
```

Figure 16-1 shows the timeout error generated by the application script running the preceding script.

Figure 16-1. The timeout error generated by a command that took longer than the allowed timeout, 120 seconds by default

It is very important to understand that even though AppleScript gives up on the application and throws a timeout error, the application will still continue to perform the task assigned to it. In the case of the preceding script where we duplicate the entire hard drive to the backup folder, the duplication will still continue despite the fact that the script that initiated the command has already errored-out and stopped.

Setting a new timeout value

Increasing (or decreasing) the amount of time AppleScript allows an application to perform a task is done with the *timeout* control statement:

```
with timeout of 300 seconds
    --do some operation shorter than 5 minutes...
end timeout
```

The following script allows up to 20 minutes for a script to resize an image in Photoshop:

```
With timeout of (20 * minutes) seconds
    tell application "Photoshop CS"
        tell document 1
            resize image resolution 120 resample method none
        end tell
    end tell
end timeout
```

Trapping the timeout error

Even though we allow for extra time, that time may still not be enough. In this case you may want to provide extra protection by placing the *timeout* block inside a *try* statement.

The following script lets the user choose a file. It will allow the dialog box to remain up for one hour before exiting the script. The problem is that even though the script has stopped, the Choose file dialog box is still displayed. To deal with this issue, we will first verify that the error indeed is a timeout error (error -1712). If it is a timeout error, we will use UI scripting to gracefully dismiss the dialog box.

The script is as shown here:

```
1. try
2.     with timeout of 3000 seconds
3.         tell application "Finder"
4.             choose file
5.         end tell
6.     end timeout
7. on error number the_error_number
8.     if the_error_number is -1712 then
9.         tell application "Finder" to activate
10.         tell application "System Events"
11.             tell application process "Finder"
12.                 click button "Cancel" of window "Choose a File"
13.             end tell
14.         end tell
15.     end if
16.     return
17. end try
```

While subroutines aren't the first thing you create when you learn AppleScript, they are the one facet of scriptwriting that will have the most impact on your scripts. Subroutines are your tool for organizing scripts, making them efficient and giving you a perfect way to store and reuse your code.

What are subroutines?

Subroutines are bits of code that perform a certain task. Rather than being a part of the main body of the script, subroutines are organized away from it, and are called, or carried out, from the main body of the script.

Subroutines are commands that you write yourself. What is any other AppleScript command? A bunch of code that executes somewhere else in the system. A command you use in AppleScript can trigger a few or many lines of code, depending on its complexity.

Your subroutines aren't much different, it's just that subroutines are commands written using AppleScript, which means that you can easily write them and use them yourself.

To better understand subroutines, I want you to imagine making a list of tasks before throwing a party in your house. The list may include baking a cake, washing dishes, buying chips, and sending invitations. While this list is a great overview, it doesn't offer any detail. If the list actually included all the details of baking a cake or looping through dishes in the sink and washing each one, the list would no longer be a snapshot you could look at to see what needs to be done. For items that do require directions, such as the exact steps for baking the cake, which you'll most likely need, you know where to go. So when the day of the party finally arrives, you pick your list, and look for directions. Each item on the list, instead of being the specific instructions for the task, calls your attention to the task, whose details can be looked up somewhere else.

The same happens with a script that uses subroutines. The script in Figure 17-1 shows the party plan in the Script Editor the way you would organize it as a script with subroutines.

By looking at the script in Figure 17-1, you can easily differentiate between the master plan and the fine details.

Later on, as you gain experience, you can start spreading commonly used subroutines to different script files called script libraries. These libraries may have subroutines that all perform related tasks. In the preceding example, we could have a "baker" script library. In this case, we would use this line to bake the cake: *tell baker to bake_cake("chocolate cake")*.

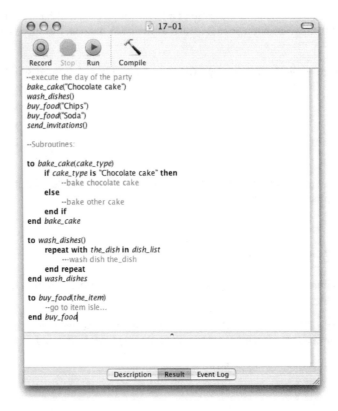

Figure 17-1. The party plan as a script

Subroutines have to be called in order to work

On their own, subroutines don't do a thing other than occupy bytes in your script file. A subroutine is only used when it is called from an active part of your script. That active part may start at the *run* handler (see the section "The run handler" later in this chapter) and continue through any subroutine that is called. Subroutines may call each other as well, which means that one subroutine will contain a call to another subroutine.

Imagine a job site without a foreman. You have a carpenter, electrician, landscaper plumber, and framer, but no one to take charge and say "OK, we start by digging a big hole . . ." This foreman will assign tasks to the other workers. Each worker may then, based on their function, assign tasks to other people on the site. As soon as all the tasks the foreman had in his list have been completed by all the workers, the job is considered done, and they can all go and have a drink (no matter what time of day it is . . .).

This job site with no foreman is the same as a script with a bunch of handlers but with no *run* handler (or other executing handler such as the *open* handler, but more on that later on as well).

The foreman may even come in, say, "OK, start," and leave. I created scripts like that; here's how they look:

```
go()
on go()
  --perform all commands...
end go
```

In this case, the *go* subroutine call is the only line in the *run* handler, but it's enough to ignite the script and get it going.

Your first subroutine

Before we go on about that subroutine thing, let's create one simple subroutine and a subroutine call.

We will create a little subroutine that displays a dialog box. At this point, the dialog box will display some literal text and not different text every time, as it could.

Figure 17-2 shows the most basic form of a subroutine.

Figure 17-2. The most basic form of a subroutine

By looking at the script in Figure 17-2, you clearly can see the two components that make up any subroutine: the subroutine definition and the subroutine call.

While the positioning of the subroutine call in your script is pivotal, the subroutine definition can live almost anywhere in your script, or even in other scripts.

Why is the position in your script from which you call the subroutine from so important? Simple: the subroutine call is actually the command that executes the subroutine. Its position in the script is as important as the position of any other command: it determines when in relation to the script it executes.

Subroutines can't be placed inside other subroutines.

The run handler

The *run* handler is any part of the script that is not a subroutine (or a script object, but more on that somewhere else . . .).

The *run* handler is the piece of code that actually executes when you run the script. If your script is saved as an application, after the *run* handler has completed executing, the *on quit* handler executes, if there is one, and then unless the *quit* handler stopped the quitting process, the script application quits.

There can be only one *run* handler per script, but some scripts may have no *run* handler at all.

I've never seen no run handler!

You may be wondering how come you already wrote a bunch of scripts, but none of them have anything that looks like a *run* handler. This is because the *run* handler doesn't have to be explicitly defined. Instead, AppleScript assumes that any code that is not a part of any other handler is a part of the *run* handler.

The scripts in Figures 17-3 and 17-4 are identical; it's just that the one in Figure 17-4 explicitly defines the *run* handler, and in the script shown in Figure 17-3, the *run* handler is implied.

Figure 17-3. The script has a *run* handler, but it is implied. The entire script shown is part of this *run* handler.

Figure 17-4. The *run* handler is explicitly written out.

Now, try this:

```
display dialog "You can run..."
on run
    display dialog "But you can't compile"
end run
```

Why won't this script compile? The first *display dialog* command is inside the implied *run* handler and the second dialog box command is in the declared *run* handler. Two *run* handlers don't get along.

When should you explicitly use the run handler?

While in many situations leaving the *run* handler implicit (not actually wrapping the code with *run/end run*) is OK, there are situations where you'd want to explicitly identify the *run* handler.

You would usually want to add the *run* handler when the script has some other unusual execution method. For instance, if the script is a droplet application, it will have another unique handler called the *on open* handler. This handler will be executed when a file is dropped on the script application. While for the most part the user will make use of the script by dropping a file on it, you may want to have some code in the *run* handler that will execute if someone double-clicks the droplet application.

The following script defines both the *run* handler and the *on open* handler in the same script. If you drop a file on the script application, it will show you the file's type, as defined in the *on open* handler, and if you double-click the script application, you will get instructions, as defined in the *on run* handler.

Script 17-1

```
on open these_items
    set the_item to item 1 of these_items
    set the_item_type to file type of (info for the_item)
    display dialog "You dropped a file of type \"" & ¬
    the_item_type & "\"" buttons {"OK"} default button 1
end open
on run
    display dialog ¬
        "Drop something on me and I'll tell you what type it is!" ¬
        buttons {"OK"} default button 1 with icon note
end run
```

We will discuss the *on open* handler in the Chapter 23, which covers droplets.

What are parameters?

Parameters, also referred to as arguments, give us the ability to explain to the subroutine how we want the different commands and statements executed.

When you stand at a coffee shop counter, asking for coffee may be the statement you use. The parameters are the main details you provide about how you like your coffee: "I'd like a large coffee, black with one sugar." There are three parameters in the "make coffee" subroutine: size, whitener, and sweetener. Anywhere you get coffee in the country you can add those parameters to the "make coffee" statement and people will understand, even though the exact way they'll go about making it may be different.

Following is the "make coffee" subroutine the way AppleScript would have it:

The subroutine call:

```
make_coffee(Large, none, 1)
```

The definition:

```
to make_coffee(size, whitener, sweetener)
    put size cup on counter
    fill with coffee
    if whitener is not none then add whitener
    add sweetener number of sugar baggies
    stir
    return cup of coffee
end make_coffee
```

What's the result?

In AppleScript, you may want your subroutines to return a value, or you may not.

A subroutine whose job is to close all open documents in InDesign may return no result. It will always just close any open documents and that's that. You may want to test whether the operation was successful and return a true or false, or you may return the number of documents you closed. This is entirely up to you.

AppleScript by default will return the result of the last statement the subroutine executed, even if you don't want to use it. To make it clearer which result the subroutine is returning, or to return a result in the middle of the subroutine, you can use the *return* command followed by the value you want to return.

The best way to capture the result of a subroutine is to assign the calling statement to a variable. This way, the result that the subroutine returns will be assigned to that variable. Let's look at a few examples.

The following four subroutines will return the sum of the two parameters:

First variation:

```
on add_up(a, b)
    return a + b
end add_up
```

Second variation:

```
on add_up(a, b)
    a + b
end add_up
```

Third variation:

```
on add_up(a, b)
    set the_sum to a + b
    return the_sum
    --any line beyond the return line will be ignored
end add_up
```

Fourth variation:

```
on add_up(a, b)
    set the_sum to a + b
end add_up
```

All four subroutines will act exactly the same way. Notice that the second and fourth subroutines don't explicitly use the *return* command, but AppleScript still returns the result of the last statement.

To call this subroutine, we will need to ensure that the result of it goes somewhere. The easiest way is to assign the call to a variable.

```
set the_sum to add_up(3, 7)
--> the_sum = 10
```

Returning a result midway

There are two reasons why you would return a result in the middle of a subroutine execution. One is if you trapped an error and the other is the use of a conditional statement (*if-then*):

Script 17-2

```
on do_math(a, b, the_operator)
   if the_operator is "+" then
      return a + b
   else if the_operator is "-" then
      return a - b
   else if the_operator is "*" then
      return a * b
   end if
end do_math
```

Returning results from subroutines

In other programming languages there are two kinds of subroutines you can define. One type of subroutine performs an action, and the other one performs some calculations and returns a result. In AppleScript we use subroutines for both purposes. We can have a subroutine that simply goes and performs an action where a result isn't needed, but other subroutines make themselves useful by performing some calculations based on parameters you provide, and return the result of those calculations.

In AppleScript, every subroutine you run can return a result; actually, most of them do even if you're not aware of it. This happens because a subroutine in AppleScript returns the result of the last statement that ran in the subroutine.

Let's start with a simple example. The following subroutine returns the sum of the two parameters you sent it:

```
on sum_it_up(a, b)
   a + b
end sum_it_up
```

Now we can call this subroutine:

```
sum_it_up(5, 12)
--> 17
```

The result of the subroutine call is 17 because the result of the last statement of the subroutine was 17.

We do, however, have a clearer alternative in dealing with subroutine results. To explicitly return a result from a subroutine, use the *return* command.

```
on sum_it_up(a, b)
    set the_sum to a + b
    return the_sum
end sum_it_up
```

Collecting results from subroutines

So we've just seen how generous subroutines are in returning results. What we need to do now is collect these results so that we can put them to use later on in the script. We do that by assigning the subroutine call to a variable. This variable is then assigned the result of the subroutine. Here's an example:

```
on cubic_feet(ft_tall, ft_wide, ft_long)
    return   ft_tall * ft_wide * ft_long
end cubic_feet
```

Now, we're going to call the subroutine, but we will make sure that the result it returns is assigned to a variable.

```
Set this_room_volume to cubic_feet(8 , 12 , 10)
--> this_box_volume = 960
```

Can a subroutine return more than one result?

By the AppleScript rules, a subroutine may return only one value as a result. This would have been too restrictive, since many subroutines you create produce more than one result you want to return to your script.

So, any thoughts yet on how to bypass this issue? Try returning the result in a list or a record.

All you do is collect the different values you want to return into a single list or record and return that list or record.

In the example that follows we will accept a full name as a string, and return the first name and last name separately.

To return the value to the calling statement, we will use a record.

Script 17-3

```
on split_name(the_name)
    set first_name to first word of the_name
    set last_name to last word of the_name
    return {first_name:first_name, last_name:last_name}
end split_name
set name_record to split_name("Paul Revere")
-->{first_name:"Paul", last_name:"Revere"}
```

In the preceding example we returned a record as a result. Personally, I like to use lists because they are more flexible.

The advantage of a list in this case is that you can map the result directly to individual variables. Here is how we do that:

Script 17-4

```
on split_name(the_name)
    set first_name to first word of the_name
    set last_name to last word of the_name
    return {first_name, last_name}
end split_name

set {first_name, last_name}to split_name("Paul Revere")
--> first_name = "Paul"
--> last_name = "Revere"
```

As you can see in this example, since the subroutine returned a list with two items, and the list we assigned the result to has two items, each item from the list was assigned to the corresponding item in the subroutine's returned result.

Now this is as close as it gets to returning multiple values.

Another thing that makes it easy to use is that the list of variables we used in the *return* statement inside the subroutine is the same as the list we assigned the subroutine to in the calling statement.

Subroutines' results can be used in an operation statement

Just like many other commands, you can call subroutines directly inside other statements without first assigning their result to a variable.

For example, let's create a little subroutine that formats a phone number. Just for this example we will keep it very simple. Here's our subroutine:

Script 17-5

```
on format_phone(the_number)
    set x to "(" & ¬
        (characters 1 thru 3 of the_number) & ") " & ¬
        (characters 4 thru 6 of the_number) & "-" & ¬
        (characters 7 thru 10 of the_number) as string
    return x
end format_phone
```

Now, let's create a statement that will make some use of that subroutine.

Script 17-6

```
set the_message to ¬
    "You can reach my office at: " & format_phone("8005551234") & ¬
    " or on my cell at: " & format_phone("2125551234")
display dialog the_message
```

As you can see in Figure 17-5, the preceding statement incorporated two calls to the *format_phone* subroutine. The downside is that the formatted results don't get stored anywhere, but it may not be a problem.

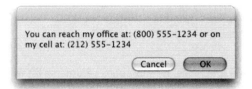

Figure 17-5. The dialog box produced by the two scripts using the *format_phone* subroutine

The other, more elaborate option would be the following:

Script 17-7

```
set formatted_number_1 to format_phone("8005551234")
set formatted_number_2 to format_phone("2125551234")
set the_message to ¬
    "You can reach my office at: " & formatted_number_1 & ¬
    " or on my cell at: " & formatted_number_2
display dialog the_message
```

Classes don't often mix

Another important consideration to make, especially if you value scripts that run their course, is for the person writing the subroutine call to know the intended class of the different parameters. For instance, what if the subroutine definition expects a string parameter for location, but the subroutine call provides a file reference or alias? In this case the subroutine will throw an error.

In the following example, the *path to* command returns an alias, but the subroutine expects a string:

```
create_folder(path to startup disk)
```

Subroutine definition:

```
on create_folder(folder_location)
    tell application "Finder"
        make new folder at container folder_location
    end tell
end create_folder
```

The command the Finder will try to execute here is

```
make new folder at container alias "Macintosh HD:"
```

This is sure to fail.

The two kinds of AppleScript subroutines

In AppleScript we can define and call two types of subroutines. While the functionality of the two types is similar (you can do in one everything you can do in the other), each provide advantages you will want to consider.

The two main differences between the two subroutines types is in the way the parameters are organized and the ease of use. The subroutine types are named after their parameter organization: one is called positional parameters subroutine and the other is called labeled parameters subroutine.

The easier-to-use subroutine type is positional. When defining and using positional subroutines, you decide on the parameters and on the order of the parameters. The subroutine will work properly only if the right values for the parameters are provided in that predefined order. While a bit limiting, this style of subroutine is very easy to pick up and start using.

Labeled parameters are more complex but provide you with greater flexibility in how the subroutine is called and a more command-like look.

Using the labels in the labeled parameter subroutine gives you an easy way to always remember what each of the parameters stand for. For instance, imagine the following call to an imaginary subroutine:

```
Do_this_thing("1:00 PM", true, true, "AAA", 100293)
```

Just what are all these values stand for? Does the string "AAA" stands for roadside assistance, or for the type of batteries the subroutine needs in order to work?

Now try this:

```
Do_this_thing from "1:00 PM" with do_it_right and ¬
    clean_up_after given battery_type:"AAA", number_to_use:100293
```

Ah! Now we can look at the subroutine call and see exactly what the different parameters mean (giving it makes sense to us . . .). I can't count how many times I've looked at subroutine calls I created in the past and had no clue what the different parameters did until I dug back into the subroutine definition.

Positional parameter subroutines

The claim to fame of positional parameter subroutines is that you can start using them quickly and they don't get any more complicated than what can be described in two paragraphs.

To understand positional parameter subroutines, imagine a cargo train where the cars aren't marked. The person loading the train knows in what order to organize the cars, and the person unloading is aware of the same order. If the first car is supposed to contain lumber and it contains straw instead, then your script will most likely end up trying to build a house of straw.

That's right: what's important in positional parameter subroutines is the order, or position, of the parameters.

From the dictionary

Following is the dictionary definition of the positional parameter subroutine.

Subroutine definition:

```
( on | to ) subroutineName ( [ paramVariable [, paramVariable ]...] ) ¬
    [ global variable [, variable ]...] [ local variable ¬
    [, variable ]...] [ statement ]... end [ subroutineName ]
```

Subroutine call:

```
subroutineName ( [ parameterValue [, parameterValue ]...] )
```

Defining and calling positional parameter subroutines

We will start by looking at another simple example of a positional parameter subroutine. The purpose of our subroutine will be to create a folder somewhere on the hard drive.

Let's start with the naked command:

```
tell application "Finder"
    make new folder
end tell
```

Now, let's add a subroutine wrapper for it. For that we will need the subroutine identifier. The subroutine identifier is a type of variable that will be used as the command name when we want to call the subroutine.

Here is the basic subroutine definition:

Script 17-8

```
on create_folder()
    tell application "Finder"
        make new folder
    end tell
end create_folder
```

The empty parentheses after the subroutine identifier *create_folder* are required. They are the now-empty home of any parameters the subroutine may use.

To call this subroutine we can use this line:

```
create_folder()
```

Note that in this case the call is identical to the definition with the exception of the word "on" (which can also be "to") before the identifier.

If the definition exists anywhere in the script, but not inside another subroutine, it will be executed whenever the call statement appears.

Adding parameters

As it is right now, the subroutine will create a folder named Untitled Folder on the desktop. This can't be what we want the script to do. What we want is to be able to specify a different location to the script, and possibly a different name for it as well.

As we talked about earlier, the important thing in adding these parameters to the subroutine is deciding on their order. We will do location followed by name.

Following is the new subroutine definition and call with the addition of these two parameters:

Script 17-9

```
on create_folder(folder_location, folder_name)
    tell application "Finder"
        make new folder at container folder_location ¬
            with properties {name:folder_name}
    end tell
end create_folder
```

Then, to call the subroutine from anywhere in our script, we can use

```
create_folder("Macintosh HD:", "My Stuff")
```

The result will be a folder named My Stuff placed at the root directory of the drive Macintosh HD.

> *When referring to the startup disk, it is almost always better not to use a literal expression such as the string "Macintosh HD:". If you are inside the Finder's tell block, all you have to do is use the term "startup disk." Outside the Finder block you have to use the path to scripting addition command like this: path to startup disk.*

Labeled parameter subroutines

Somebody please tell me, why? Positional parameters are so easy to use, they do everything we want, and they always work the same. So why complicate things by introducing labeled parameters? And if we don't figure them out, is anything wrong with us? Now you may not want to tie your self-esteem to your mastery of labeled parameters, because after all, if you never knew they existed, you could still script happily ever after. Nevertheless, they can be pretty cool.

While positional parameters are recognized only based on their position, labeled parameter subroutines have a couple of unique ways to recognize parameters. For starters, labeled parameter subroutines do away with the parentheses. Instead, they use a combination of special keywords and user-defined labels to define the subroutine, and a command-like treatment of Boolean values for calling the subroutine.

In order to understand the structure of labeled parameter subroutines, we will start with the very basic and move on to more complex features later on.

The definition and the call

The main struggle in subroutines is for the subroutine definition, the part that actually does the work, to properly use the parameters the user wants to feed it. This feeding of parameters to the subroutine happens in the subroutine call: the part that tells the script to execute the subroutine.

Hence, our main effort here will be finding a way to pass values from the call to the definition.

From the dictionary

Following is the definition of the labeled parameter subroutine.

Subroutine definition:

```
( on | to ) subroutineName ¬ [ [ of | in ] directParameterVariable ]   ¬
[ subroutineParamLabel paramVariable ]...   ¬
[ given label:paramVariable [, label:paramVariable ]...] ¬
[ global variable [, variable ]...] [ local variable [, variable ]...] ¬
[ statement ]... end [ subroutineName ]
```

Subroutine call:

```
subroutineName ¬
[ [ of | in ] directParameter ]  ¬
[ [ subroutineParamLabel parameterValue ]  ¬
| [ with labelForTrueParam [, labelForTrueParam ]... ¬
[ ( and | or | , ) labelForTrueParam ] ]  ¬
| [ without labelForFalseParam [, labelForFalseParam ]...] ¬
[ ( and | or | , ) labelForFalseParam ] ]  ¬
| [ given label:parameterValue ¬
[, label:parameterValue ]...]...
```

Start with the basics: Subroutine parameter labels

We start our labeled parameter subroutine discussion with the subroutine parameter labels. The subroutine parameter labels are 21 reserved words that you can use as labels to parameters. Let's look at the 21 words and at how we can use them.

The 21 labels are *about, above, against, apart from, around, aside from, at, below, beneath, beside, between, by, for, from, instead of, into, on, onto, out of, over, since, thru* (or *through*), and *under*.

We use these labels in both the subroutine definition and subroutine call in a coordinated way, which allows us to determine what values supplied by the subroutine call match up with which variables in the subroutine definition.

All 21 labels function the same, but you should choose them based on how well they fit into the context of the subroutine. The people who thought them up must have wanted your script to read more like a poem.

Say we have a subroutine that will return the highest number in a list of positive integers. The subroutine will require one parameter that is the list of integers. Out of the 21 labels, I chose the *out of* label to be most fitting for the subroutine parameter label assignment. Here is what my subroutine looks like:

Script 17-10

```
to find_highest out of the_list
   set highest_for_now to 0
   repeat with the_item in the_list
      if the_item > highest_for_now then
         set highest_for_now to the_item
      end if
   end repeat
   return highest_for_now as number
end find_highest
```

To call the subroutine I will use the following line:

```
find_highest out of {1, 4, 12, 5}
```

Let's compare the calling line with the first line of the subroutine definition, but let's change the subroutine identifier and label:

Definition:

```
to (name) parameter the_list
```

Call:

```
(name) parameter {1, 4, 12, 5}
```

As with positional parameters, the name lets the call locate the definition from all the other subroutines, and the parameter label specifies which variable *inside* the subroutine definition the parameter value will be assigned to. In the preceding example, you can clearly see that the value of the variable *the_list* in the subroutine will be {1, 4, 12, 5}.

Now let's try that with one more subroutine parameter. We will add a top number. This time, the subroutine will just return a Boolean value: true if the top number is higher than the highest number in the list, and false if the list contains a higher number than the top number we supply.

To make life easier for yourself, try to ignore the English meaning of the subroutine parameter labels (those 21 pesky words); instead just think about them as parameter 1, parameter 2, etc.

Here's the second subroutine definition:

Script 17-11

```
to find_highest above the_top out of the_list
   set the_top_is_highest to true
   repeat with the_item in the_list
      if the_item > the_top then
         return false
      end if
   end repeat
   return true
end find_highest
```

And the call:

```
find_highest above 16 out of {1, 4, 12, 5}
```

Making up your own labels

So far you had the chance to make up words for your variable and subroutine identifiers. Now you get a chance to label your parameters with your own words. All this means is that if you want, you can replace the 21 labels reserved by AppleScript with your own, hopefully a bit more descriptive terms to what the job of the parameter is.

There are three differences, however, from using the subroutine label parameters: you have to precede the use of your own labeled parameters with the word "given," your parameters must be separated by a comma, and you have to separate your labels from the variable (or value in the subroutine call) with a colon. A bit confusing, but together we can do it!

Let's start with a simple single-parameter subroutine. Our subroutine will take a word and return the reverse of it (word → drow).

We will need to invent three words for this subroutine: the subroutine identifier is going to be *reverse_word*, the parameter label will be *reversing_word*, and the identifier of the actual variable used in the subroutine will be *word_to_reverse*.

Here is how our subroutine definition will look like:

Script 17-12

```
to reverse_word given reversing_word:word_to_reverse
    set word_characters to characters of word_to_reverse
    set reverse_list to reverse of word_characters
    set new_word to reverse_list as string
    return new_word
end reverse_word
```

This really isn't as bad as it seems. You already know about the subroutine identifier and the parameter variable. All we did was added our own label to the parameter.

Here is the call for that subroutine:

```
reverse_word given reversing_word:"play"
--> result: "yalp"
```

Now let's try it with two parameters. The following subroutine will (yet again) calculate the area of a rectangle. Our parameters will be the *width* and *height*. Here we go:

```
to get_the_area given width:w, height:h
    return w * h
end get_the_area
```

What's nice in this situation is calling the subroutine. The parameter labels make it very easy to remember what the values stand for.

```
get_the_area given width:12, height:5
```

Calling subroutines with Boolean parameters

Another unique feature of the labeled parameter subroutines is the ability to specify Boolean values like you would in any other AppleScript command, using the *with* and *without* labels.

As an example we will create a subroutine that trims tabs and spaces from strings. As for parameters, we will have four Boolean parameters and one direct parameter.

The direct parameter is the first parameter used in a subroutine definition. The label of the direct parameter is either *in* or *of*, and it always has to be the first parameter. Our direct parameter will be the actual string we want to trim white text from. The four Boolean parameters will be *from_front*, *from_back*, *trimming_spaces*, and *trimming_tabs*. You can assume that for the subroutine to do anything, either one of the first pair and either one of the second pair of parameters must be set to true, but that's beside the point.

Now let's inspect the subroutine. Mainly pay attention to the first line in the definition and to the subroutine call.

The subroutine definition:

Script 17-13

```
1. to trim_characters of the_text¬
2. given from_front:f, from_back:b, trimming_spaces:s, trimming_tabs:t
3.     --assemble trim characters list
4.     set trim_character_list to {}
5.     if s then set end of trim_character_list to space
6.     if t then set end of trim_character_list to tab
7.     repeat (count trim_character_list) times
8.        repeat with the_character in trim_character_list
9.            --trim from front
10.           if f then
11.              repeat while the_text ends with the_character
12.                 set the_text to characters 1 thru -2 of the_text ¬
as string
13.              end repeat
14.           end if
15.           --trim from back
16.           if b then
17.              repeat while the_text starts with the_character
18.                 set the_text to characters 2 thru -1 of the_text ¬
as string
19.              end repeat
20.           end if
21.        end repeat
22.     end repeat
23.     return the_text
24. end trim_characters
```

Notice that this is a normal labeled parameter definition. We have our labels marking the four labeled parameters and we're ready to call the subroutine.

In the subroutine call, we're not going to supply values to the parameters in the fashion we learned earlier, which would go something like this:

```
trim_characters of the_text given ¬
    from_front:true, from_back: true, trimming_spaces: true,
trimming_tabs:false
```

Instead, we will treat the Boolean parameters like we would treat them in any other command, using the *with* and *without* keywords.

```
trim_characters of the_text with from_front, from_back, ¬
trimming_spaces and trimming_tabs
```

In the preceding call, all four Boolean parameters received a true value. In the call that follows, we will assign a false value to the *trimming_tabs* and *from_front* parameters:

```
trim_characters of the_text ¬
    with from_back and trimming_spaces without from_front and ¬
    trimming_tabs
```

Whose subroutine is it anyway?

First we learned about AppleScript commands and application commands. Then we saw that we can create our own commands, which is OK as long as we make up names for them such as *do_this_thing_now*.

Now, let's take it a step further.

It all starts when you want to call your subroutine from inside an application *tell* block. Let's assume that you created a subroutine for Valentine's Day called *foreplay*. If you call it from outside any *tell* block, all is well. But as soon as you try it from say, inside the Finder's *tell* block you get the following error: "Can't continue foreplay." Ouch! A second ago you were fine, but now we're trying it from the Finder and you can't? That hurts.

Don't worry, all the script is experiencing here is a bit of uncertainty on top of some performance anxiety. See, when you called the *foreplay* subroutine from inside the Finder's *tell* block, AppleScript looked to see if the Finder had a *foreplay* command in its dictionary. Since there was none, AppleScript couldn't continue. Next time, try to specify whose foreplay you're trying to perform. You do that with the *my* precedence word:

```
tell application "Finder"
  my foreplay()
end tell
```

Preceding the subroutine call with the word "my" tells AppleScript to look for the command in the script itself and not in the application that is the target of the *tell* statement you're in.

The other options relating to the matter is addressing script objects instead of the current script. If you have loaded a script into a variable, there are two ways you can use to execute the subroutine. For example, let's say that we have used the *load script* command to load a script file containing a *figure_average* subroutine to the variable *math_whiz*. We can either say

```
Tell math_whiz to figure_average(the_list)
```

or

```
math_whiz's figure_average(the_list)
```

The second option is more in line with what would be my *figure_average(the_list)* if the *figure_average* had been a part of the script and not loaded in.

Much more on that in Chapter 18.

Redefining AppleScript commands

You can redefine AppleScript and scripting addition commands. The code in your new definition will replace the code that usually runs when the command is called. For instance, let's try to meddle with the *choose from list* command defined in the Standard Additions.

In your script, type the following:

Script 17-14

```
on choose from list theList
    display dialog "I'll choose for you" buttons {"OK"}
    return some item of theList
end choose from list
choose from list {1, 2, 3}
```

In the preceding script, we changed the functionality of the *choose from list* command. If it is called from anywhere in the script, instead of allowing the user to choose, the script will let the user know that it will choose an item from the list, and indeed proceeds to pick a random item from the list using the *some item* filtering statement.

In the same situation, we can possibly add to the command, and then tell AppleScript to continue with the original command at some point. Look at the following script:

Script 17-15

```
on choose from list theList
    display dialog "Should I choose for you?" buttons {"No", "Yes"}
    if button returned of result is "No" then
        continue choose from list theList
```

```
        else
            return some item of theList
        end if
    end choose from list
    choose from list {1, 2, 3}
```

In the preceding script, AppleScript first offers to make the decision for the user. If the user declines, then the script will tell AppleScript to *continue* to execute the command the way it was designed originally.

Subroutines and variables

We talked a lot about variables being the memory of AppleScript. If you store a value in a variable, you can later use it anywhere in the script.

Well, this is almost all true.

As a refresher, in AppleScript we have two main kinds of variables: global variables and local variables. The main difference between the two comes to light when we work with variables.

Declaring variables

Although it is more organized and proper, you are not required to declare local variables. Only global variables require proper declaration.

You declare variables anywhere in the script's *run* handler, which mostly means that declaring global variables from inside other subroutine definitions will simply not work.

To declare a global variable, type the variable identifier following the word "global":

```
    global the_name
```

You can also declare multiple variables in the same statement, as follows:

```
    global x, y, z
```

although I think it is better to declare global variables one at a time, because this way you can add some comment for each variable in regard to its function.

The scope of local and global variables

In short, local variables are only good inside the subroutine they're used in, and local variables that were defined in the *run* handler (the main part of the script) have no meaning inside the subroutine definition.

Global variables, on the other hand, are good throughout any part of your script.

Let's look at an example.

In the following script we will have a subroutine that calculates the area of a rectangle. We will also use a local variable, which we will start by only declaring in the body of the script and not in the subroutine.

Script 17-16

```
local the_width, the_height --not needed, but nice
set the_width to 3
set the_height to 5
set the_area to get_area()
--subroutine definition:
on get_area()
    set the_area to the_width * the_height
    return the_area
end get_area
```

What happens when we run the script? We get the following error:

```
The variable the_width is not defined.
```

But how can that be when we had both variables defined in the script? Yes, but as soon as we started executing the subroutine, the local variables we declared and assigned values to were no longer valid.

So what are our options? First, let's look at global variables.

Let's run the same script with a slight modification: instead of declaring the variables *the_width* and *the_height* as local variables, we will declare them as global variables.

```
global the_width, the_height --Now it's needed, but is it nice?
```

Now that the variables are global, their reach, or in programming terms, their scope, spans the *run* handler and any other subroutine you defined.

Using local variables nevertheless

To use local variables in subroutines, all you have to do is pass them as parameters, like this:

Script 17-17

```
local the_width, the_height --not needed, but nice
set the_width to 3
set the_hight to 5
set the_area to get_area(the_width, the_height)
on get_area(the_width, the_height)
    set the_area to the_width * the_height
    return the_area
end get_area
```

They don't have to match the identifiers used in the subroutine itself, but they may. The subroutine definition may as well be

Script 17-18

```
on get_area(x, y)
    set z to x * y
    return z
end get_area
```

Don't yield to global temptation

It may be a wasted effort to try and explain that even though a couple of global variable declarations can spare you a lot of effort in passing parameters to subroutines, they can cause headaches later on. Nevertheless, I'm going to try, so here we go:

First, so you don't say no one ever told you: AppleScript global variables should not be used as a replacement to passing parameters in subroutines because you're too lazy to keep track of your parameters.

Global variables should be reserved for only the truly global values in your script. For instance, the path to the main folder in the automation solution you're creating, the variable whose value is the loaded script with many of the subroutines you use, and other such values that are used throughout the script—items whose usefulness covers many parts of the script, are used by many subroutines, and are global in nature.

If you overuse global variables, your scripts will become impossible to break apart later on, which will make reusing parts of them or different subroutines very difficult. Above all others, you as a scripter should know something about the importance of reusing your coded effort.

Scope of properties

In the eye of a subroutine definition, script properties are identical to global variables. You can declare a property once, and that value will be attached to that variable throughout the script, including subroutine definitions.

Storing individual subroutines

The identifier you use when you specify a subroutine automatically turns into a variable whose value is the content of the subroutine.

As an example, we will use the split name subroutine we created earlier.

After the subroutine is defined, we can ask the script for the class of the variable *split_name*.

Script 17-19

```
on split_name(the_name)
    set first_name to first word of the_name
    set last_name to last word of the_name
    return {first_name:first_name, last_name:last_name}
end split_name
class of split_name
--> handler
```

OK, so the variable has a handler value, what can we do with that? Watch:

```
set script_file_path to (path to scripts folder) & "script.scpt" as
string
store script split_name in file script_file_path
```

What will the two preceding lines do? They will create a compiled script file containing the *split_name* script. Figure 17-6 shows the resulting script file opened in the Script Editor application.

Figure 17-6. A subroutine that was stored as a script is open in the Script Editor application. Notice that the *on* wrapper is gone.

Moving script parts to subroutines

One way that subroutines are created in your script is when a portion of your script "evolves" into a subroutine.

It happens in the process of writing a script. You suddenly realize that the chunk of script you just created can be its own little thing. You may be able to use it somewhere else in the script, in other scripts, or maybe you just figured that it takes too much space in the body of the script and you want to move it out of the way.

What you need to do first is identify all the variables that this part of the script depends on. Some variables may be created inside the part you're trying to move, so you don't have to worry about them for the start.

After you have some idea of which variables you will need to pass as parameters, you can move the entire part of the script to your subroutine area and wrap it in an *on . . . end* subroutine wrapper.

This would also be a good time to create the subroutine call. If the result of the portion of the script you're porting into a subroutine returned a value result as a list, a number, or a few values, you will want to define this result as either a single variable or a list containing the different variables you want to return to the main script.

This list of variables can be used twice: once as the list you assign the result to when you call the subroutine, and once in the last line of the subroutine, which returns the value to the calling line.

In the following example, we will start with a script that part of gets the creation date and URL from a file's specifications. Then we will take the part of the script that gets the file properties and convert it into its own subroutine.

First the script itself:

Script 17-20

```
--some statement...
--some other statement...
set theFilePath to choose file
set theFilePath to theFilePath as string
set file_properties to info for file theFilePath
set file_creation_date to creation date of file_properties
set file_modification_date to modification date of file_properties
set file_age to file_modification_date - file_creation_date
set days_old to round (file_age / days)
--do something with days_old variable...
```

By looking at the script I can identify that the part I want to convert info a subroutine uses a few parameters but really requires one variable to start, which is the variable *theFilePath*.

The subroutine will return the *days_old* variable to the script.

It's important to check if the other variables used in that part of the script (like *file_age*, *file_modification*, etc.) are used later on in the script. If they are, you will need to have the subroutine return their values as well.

Following is the new part of the script and the subroutine definition:

Script 17-21

```
--some statement...
--some other statement...
set theFilePath to choose file
set theFilePath to theFilePath as string
set days_old to get_file_age_in_days(theFilePath)
--do something with days_old variable...
on get_file_age_in_days(theFilePath)
    set file_properties to info for file theFilePath
    set file_creation_date to creation date of file_properties
    set file_modification_date to modification date of file_properties
    set file_age to file_modification_date - file_creation_date
    set days_old to round (file_age / days)
    return days_old
end get_file_age_in_days
```

Creating your own programming language

Although all of us AppleScript users use AppleScript for programming, we all use it slightly differently. These differences come to light when we see the applications we use and the type of tasks we automate. It is safe to say that many scripters have a specialty beyond scripting, and that the AppleScript scripting language is a tool we use to perfect whatever else we do. I write scripts, but my true specialty is publishing workflows. A system administrator may use AppleScript, but his true function is to administer Macs.

After working with AppleScript for a while you will realize that you use the same types of functions that relate to your area of expertise. Your next step then is to create your own language that makes scripting *your* tasks easier.

No, I'm not suggesting you learn C++, put on rags, and walk barefoot from city to city preaching the new code. All I want you to do is start doing a few little things to make you into a better scripter:

Start collecting functions. Every collection starts small. My collection started with the subroutines I downloaded from the AppleScript website.

I collected them into a file, renamed them to fit my subroutine naming style, and saved them in a script file. I slowly added little subroutines to that file and started loading that file to every script I created.

Soon enough I realized that a large chunk of the volume of my scripts was code I called from my subroutine library. By now I have over ten libraries, each with its own function, and most of the boring side of my coding is taken care of by dragging and dropping subroutine calls.

For your naming convention, start with the large object such as the name of the application you're talking to and go from there. Give your subroutines long, clear names. Shorthand is great at the time of writing, but a month down the road the subroutines look like someone else wrote them, died, and never left the instructions.

So you see? Once you have many of these subroutines collected in one or more files, also referred to as script libraries, your main scripts will mostly use commands you created earlier (your subroutines) instead of AppleScript or scriptable applications commands.

Working smart with subroutines

The following few paragraphs contain tips for creating and using subroutines. Subroutines can be a boon for efficient script writing, and with the right organization, you will be able to spend more time on the function of the script and less time on messing with syntax.

Organizing scripts with subroutines

One of the brilliant factors subroutines add to your scripts is organization. They allow you to tell the story of your script in your language, rather than in a programming language.

You know those people who tell a story about something they did, but feel compelled to go into every last detail regarding each thing, until you lose the whole story? Well, without subroutines, AppleScript can be like that too. As you read through a script and try to understand it, you don't want to be bothered with the 50 lines of script that made a certain function of the script work. What you want is to quickly get a general idea of the script's organization, what happens in what order, and the basic branching that make up the script. That's true: out of 100 *if-then* statements and repeat loops in a given script, only a few actually play a part in the structure of the script and should be included in the main body (or, the *run* handler, as you'll see later on).

So how do we organize a script with subroutines? We think logically as we write the script. We also periodically read the script back, and pretend it's a story we're telling someone. If it sounds a bit heavy on the details, we may want to corral the code that has that extra detail we don't want to have in the main body of the script, and we turn it into a handler. We'll look at how to do that later on.

Reusing code with subroutines

Another big function of subroutines, if not the biggest one, is reusing code. The idea is that a subroutine is a closed nugget of code that, given the expected parameters, will perform reliably and return the expected result. Not the same result every time, but a result within the expected range.

Once you have such a subroutine, even if it has been written for a specific purpose, you may find that you can use it in other scripts. Another way to instantly know that a piece of a script will make a good subroutine is if you start copying chunks of script from one part of the script to another. If the same code, or similarly structured code, exists in more than one part of the script, you may want to consider turning it into a subroutine.

Think ahead

When creating subroutines, it is good to consider not only the script you're working on right now, but the wider scope of scripts you've created and are likely to create. Think about making your subroutines as general as possible without using any data specific to the subject matter your script is processing, but rather to the process it is performing.

Think small

Make your subroutines as small as you can (while keeping them longer than their own call). Small subroutines are much easier to reuse and integrate in other scripts.

What I personally use is a set of about 15 subroutine library files that have hundreds of subroutines that deal with different subjects. Some of the subroutines are long, but most have fewer than ten lines of script. This makes it so that most of my scripts are made up of subroutine calls instead of commands. I name my subroutines deliberately and descriptively so that I can easily identify what the script is doing at any given time.

Applications aside

Another thing I like to avoid is littering my scripts with application *tell* blocks. I know, I know, a 200-line script that talks to seven applications is much cooler to look at, but once you've passed the "look, ma" stage, you may want to consider chucking commands sent to applications into different subroutines, and storing them all in the same library. I have a library of commands for each application, and every time I use a new command, object, or property in that application, I turn it into a subroutine and add it to the library.

Script Debugger makes placing library and subroutine calls easy with its clipping palette.

Power wrap-up

This section summarizes the chapter in an intensive-reference style. Use this part to look up facts related to the chapter without the chatter.

What are subroutines?

Subroutines, also called handlers, are code-capsules that can be used by the main script multiple times. A subroutine that is not called by the main body of the script, also called the *run* handler, will never be executed.

The basic subroutine

The basic subroutine starts with the definition line and ends with the *end* line. The definition line starts with either the *on* or *to*, followed by the subroutine identifier, which is a term you make up to name the subroutine, and finally ends with the list of subroutine parameters.

```
on do_something(parameter_1, parameter_2)
```

The last line of the subroutine starts with *end* followed by the subroutine identifier:

```
end do_something
```

The body of the subroutine includes any statements that appear between the definition and *end* lines.

```
on do_something(parameter_1, parameter_2, etc)
--do this
--do that
end do_something
```

Subroutines can have multiple parameters or no parameters at all, in which case the subroutine identifier is followed by empty parentheses.

```
on do_something()
--do this
end do_something
```

Subroutine result

A subroutine returns the result of the last statement to execute in the subroutine. To make subroutines more legible, the final statement uses the *return* command to return the final value. Not every subroutine returns a value, however.

```
on calculate_numbers (a, b)
  set the_result to a + b
  return the_result
end do_something
```

To return more than one result, collect the different results in a list, and return the list as the result.

Calling subroutines

In order to be executed, the subroutine has to be called from the main script, or from another subroutine, like this:

```
do_something(parameter_1_value, parameter_2_value, etc)
```

If the subroutine is called from inside an application *tell* block, you have to specify that the subroutine is not an application command, but rather a script-defined command. This can be done in one of the following ways:

```
tell me to do_something()
my do_something()
do_something() of me
```

Positional parameter subroutines

The subroutine type seen previously is the positional parameter subroutine type. Each parameter is identified by its position within the other parameters. In this type of subroutine, the order of the parameters in the subroutine definition and the subroutine call must be identical.

Labeled parameter subroutines

Labeled parameter subroutines are a bit more complex to create and call. For more information regarding labeled parameter subroutines, read the corresponding section in this chapter.

Subroutines and variable scope

Any variable that is defined in one subroutine is only valid in that particular subroutine and not outside of it. To use a value of a variable from the body of the script in a subroutine that is called from the body of the script, the value has to either be passed as a parameter or defined as a global variable or a property.

Details previously . . .

The last part of this chapter is a summary of the entire chapter. For more details on any of the items here, refer to earlier sections in this chapter.

CHAPTER 18
SCRIPT OBJECTS

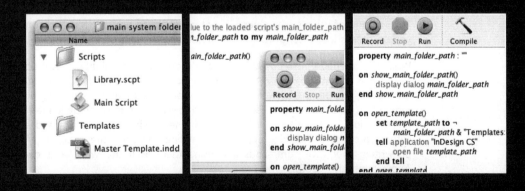

Script objects are probably the most underutilized complex feature in the AppleScript language. This chapter explains the idea behind script objects and how to use them, and discusses real-world techniques for putting script objects to use in your projects.

What are script objects and what are they good for?

So, you got through the basics and are now ready for the serious stuff.

Understanding script objects after creating many scripts is like understanding the solar system after living on earth. You have to imagine that each one of the scripts you created so far is not an entire entity, but rather an object that can be moved around, reproduced, and made to accept your commands. Not only can the script accept commands, so can any of its children, as you will soon see.

Initially, it is a bit difficult to see what's so great about script objects; after all, many, if not most, things can be done without them. In fact, there are scripters who will never start using script objects but still create some very useful scripts. So what's all the hoopla about script objects? Well, for a start, using script objects in your AppleScript will turn you from a scripter to a programmer; you are forced to deal with more advanced programming concepts.

Don't get me wrong now, starting out with script objects isn't that complicated and can become a useful tool very quickly. Like many other things in life, though, it takes some time and practice to really make the best use of them.

So what are script objects good for? Let's look at a few situations in which they are invaluable.

Simple: Loading script objects

This method of using script objects is not only easy to use, but highly recommended. All you do here is load a script to another script with the *load script* command.

While this method doesn't make use of the more advanced abilities script objects have to offer, it has an instant organizational benefit: you can now take all those handlers you keep on copying and pasting between your scripts, and give them a final resting place in one or more script files. These files, also referred to as script libraries, can be loaded into your different scripts. You can then call the subroutines in the loaded script and execute them without them actually taking place and crowding up your actual script. In effect, you will be writing your own commands and using them as if this were your own version of AppleScript (ah—cool!).

Serious stuff: Replicating scripts

When you get a bit more comfortable manipulating script objects, you can start preloading them into variables and calling them from your main script at will. One way of doing this is by loading script objects into a list. This allows you to use your script objects to manipulate and control any number of objects that can be controlled by a script. For example, you can use a list of scripts to work with a multidocument application in AppleScript Studio. Each document needs its own script with its own properties, but there's no way to know how many documents the user will create, so you start with an empty list, and for each document the user starts you add an item to your script list.

Declaring, initializing, and calling script objects

Script objects can be a rather complex matter to grasp, so we will start from the beginning and move along slowly. We will also try to stick to more doing and less talking.

We will start with script objects by creating the script code first. Start a new script file and type the following lines:

```
set x to "Hello"
display dialog x
```

Now run the script. The outcome is, as expected, a dialog box.

Next, let's turn this code into a script object. Wrap the two lines with the script wrapper, like this:

```
script
    set x to "Hello"
    display dialog x
end script
```

Now run the script. Nothing happens, but look at the result of your script: it's a script!

Try to add the following line to the end:

```
display dialog (class of result)
```

The dialog box displays "scpt". As you may imagine, this stands for script (with the "ri" in the middle suspiciously taken off . . .).

Now, replace the last line with the last line of the following script:

Script 18-1

```
script
    set x to "Hello"
    display dialog x
end script
run result
```

Aha! We got the script to run, but it's a bit awkward. Do we really have to ambush the script until it's done "passing through" just to capture it? Not really. What we have done previously is simply instantiate the script object, but we didn't leave ourselves a comfortable way to use that script.

What we will do next is give the script a name.

Naming the script object will create a neat situation: the script name will become a variable that has the script assigned to it. Now here is the punch line: the script is assigned to the variable while the script compiles! This is cool because you can start calling the script (by name) right from the beginning of the script—it has instantiated itself. Here's how we name a script (I use the name "simon"):

```
script simon
    set x to "Hello"
    display dialog x
end script
```

Now, we don't have to wait for the script to run as if it were a statement. Instead, we can give it commands from the beginning and push the actual code of the script to the end, as we do in the following script:

Script 18-2

```
Tell simon to run
script simon
    set x to "Hello"
    display dialog x
end script
```

Proliferating your script object

So far we met script *simon*. While script *simon* is very nice and has great intentions, it acts a bit too much like a simple subroutine. What is the difference between telling *simon* to run and calling any subroutine with the same code? Not much.

What we will do next, however, takes a script object. We will now give *simon* a couple of siblings: *jack* and *judy*.

The way we will do that is by copying *simon* to the variables *judy* and *jack*.

To make matters more interesting, we will also declare a property inside the script *simon*, and instead of a *run* handler, we will place the *display dialog* statement in a subroutine called *say something*. To start, let's look at the new *simon* script:

Script 18-3

```
script simon
    property x : "Hello"
    on say_something()
        display dialog x
    end say_something
end script
```

Now *simon* is a real script: it has a property and a subroutine like any script should. Let's see what we can do with it.

We will start by copying *simon* to *jack* and to *judy*. Then, we will set the *x* property of *jack* and *judy* to two different values. After that, we will tell both *judy* and *jack* to call the *say_something* subroutine and see what happens.

Here we go with the complete script:

Script 18-4

```
copy simon to jack
copy simon to judy

set x of judy to "Hi, I'm Judy"
set x of jack to "Hello, I'm Jack"

tell jack to say_something()
tell judy to say_something()

script simon
    property x : "Hello"
    on say_something()
        display dialog x
    end say_something
end script
```

In the first two lines we copy *simon* to *judy* and *jack*. How can we do that right at the start? Remember that *simon* was a script before the main script even started to run; *simon* was a script since the main script was compiled!

The following two lines set the *x* property of *judy* and *jack*. Remember, the script that was *simon* is now two separate scripts, each with its own *x* property that we can set to anything we want. And since *judy* and *jack* are objects, we can set their properties at will.

Lines 5 and 6 of the script actually call the *say_something* subroutine of *judy* and *jack*. As you can see for yourself when you run the script, each of them has something different to say.

So was what we just did parent and child scripts? Nope. They were more sibling scripts. To create a parent and child relationship between scripts, you need to actually tell the script who its parent is. More on parent/child script relationships and inheritance later on.

Using subroutines to create script object instances

So far we counted on the script objects being there, but we didn't really have control over when and where they became available. It was nice to have the script objects already in a variable upon recompiling the main script, but it can be a bit of a drag as well.

What we'll see now is how to tell the main script when to make the script objects available. We do that by placing the script objects in a subroutine. This way, only when we call that subroutine does the script become available.

Also, the script doesn't need to have a name. If we give the script a name by placing an identifier after the word "script" in the opening line, this name will have no meaning outside the subroutine scope. Instead, when we call the subroutine containing the script, we must assign the result the subroutine returns to the variable we want the script to be assigned to.

In the following script we will instantiate one out of two script objects contained in subroutines. During each execution of the main script, only one of the two script objects is needed. The following method will allow us to only load the needed subroutine and not take up space in memory.

In the following script, we let the user choose whether the template that needs to be created should be created in QuarkXPress or InDesign. The correct script is then loaded into the *new_template_script* variable, and that script is then executed using the *run* command.

Script 18-5

```
1. set application_selection to choose from list {"InDesign", "Quark"}
2. set application_selection to item 1 of application_selection

3. if application_selection is "InDesign" then
4.     set new_template_script to load_indesign_script()
5. else if application_selection is "Quark" then
6.     set new_template_script to load_quark_script()
7. end if
8. tell new_template_script to run

9. on load_indesign_script()
10.    script
11.       tell application "InDesign CS"
12.          make new document
13.          tell document 1
14.             save to file ¬
15.                ((path to documents folder as string) & "Template")
16.                   with stationery
17.             close
```

```
18.           end tell
19.         end tell
20.       end script
21. end load_indesign_script

22. on load_quark_script()
23.     script
24.       tell application "QuarkXPress"
25.         make new document
26.         tell document 1
27.           save in file ((path to documents folder as string) ¬
28.               & "Template1") with template
29.           close
30.         end tell
31.       end tell
32.     end script
33. end load_quark_script
```

Another benefit of the preceding arrangement is that if the applications aren't running before the script starts, the script will only launch the needed application. This also means that the applications needed for the script won't be forced to launch when the script is opened for editing.

Another way to do the same thing is to have both script objects in the same subroutine, but only return one of them as the calling statement's result. For that, we have to name the scripts:

Script 18-6

```
1. run load_script("x")

2. on load_script(script_name)
3.     script x
4.       display dialog "Hi, x here"
5.     end script

6.     script y
7.       display dialog "Hi, y's the name"
8.     end script

9.     script z
10.       display dialog "How can z help?"
11.     end script

12.     if script_name is "x" then
13.       return x
14.     else if script_name is "y" then
15.       return y
16.     else if script_name is "z" then
17.       return z
```

```
18.    end if
19. end load_script
```

Let's take another look at this script since it is a bit complicated.

In the *load_script* subroutine we do two things: first we define three scripts (named *x*, *y*, and *z*) and then we use the *user* parameter to decide which script to return.

In the calling statement we don't waste any time. Since we know that the result of the *load_script* variable is a script object, we use the *run* command to run that script in the same statement in which it is loaded.

Script objects and instances

Whenever you work with script objects, it is important to understand that the script object isn't an actual script, but rather an instance of that script.

This allows you to load the same script multiple times to multiple variables and use it slightly differently by setting the properties of the different instances to different values, and calling different subroutines in the different instances.

Remember the scripts *judy* and *jack* from earlier in this chapter? They were both instances of the same script, *simon*. After becoming an independent instance, each of them had their properties set to different values, although the properties themselves were the same.

Script objects, properties, and variables

The way script objects interact with variables and properties depends on how the script object got created. Script objects that were defined in the main script have access to all of the script's properties and global variables. They can also ask other script objects to share their property values and call their subroutines.

Properties and global variables are less available to scripts that have been loaded from files using the *load script* command.

In fact, loaded scripts don't have any access to properties of the script that loaded them nor to subroutines and properties of other script objects.

The only direction in which property-related interaction can happen is from the top down: the main script can get value from or set a property, and call a subroutine from the loaded script, but that is all the interaction that is allowed.

Loading script objects from files

Perhaps one of the most used and useful forms of script objects is the form that doesn't make specific use of the "object-oriented" aspect of script objects. Instead, the benefit of loading scripts from files allows you to organize your scripts and increase code reusability.

Loading scripts from files is very simple: you need to have a path to a compiled script file, and you have to have a variable identifier to which you want the script assigned.

Script loading basics

To avoid confusion, let's walk through all the steps:

Start by creating a new script. In it, type the following lines of code:

Script 18-7

```
display dialog "You can run but you cannot hide"
on do_something_else(the_thing)
display dialog "I'm now "& the_thing
end do_something_else
```

What we have done is created a script with a *run* handler that consists of a single *display dialog* statement and an additional subroutine that takes one parameter and consists of one *display dialog* statement.

Next, save your script on your desktop and name it "my script.scpt".

Close the file you've just created.

Now, start a new script file and type the following:

```
set script_path to ((path to desktop as string) & "my script.scpt")
set my_script_variable to load script file script_path
tell my_script_variable to run
```

What you should pay attention to here is the *load* command and the *run* command. The *load* command loads a script and assigns it as a script object to the *my_script_variable* variable.

In the following statement, the *run* command expects to find a script object assigned to the *my_script_variable* variable, and it executes this script object's *run* handler.

Now remember that the script you saved has more to it than just a *run* handler. It also has a subroutine you defined called *do_something_else*. To call this subroutine we can either call it in the script object's *tell* block:

```
tell my_script_variable
    do_something_else("cooking lunch")
end tell
```

or in this form:

```
my_script_variable's do_something_else("cooking lunch")
```

Either way, the result is that your main script has loaded a script file as a script object into a variable, and now you can call subroutines from that script object by using the variable it is assigned to.

Forming script libraries

The most common use people make of the *load script* command is to organize subroutines in script libraries. What that means is having compiled scripts that don't contain a *run* handler at all. Instead, those script files contain collections of subroutines that you can use in any script.

If you don't yet have a script library you're using, then start one right now. Working with script libraries is easy and addictive, although it does require an ounce of discipline. It forces you to evaluate every chunk of code you write. From now on, start writing scripts as small chunks that do one little thing after the other. Instead of creating one long script that interacts with many applications and is made out of hundreds of script lines, break it up into units.

Each nugget of code should have a small function and a name, such as *finder_delete_file* or *word_create_document*. The smaller the subroutines you put in your library, the more they will fit into your scripts, and the more modular your scripts will be.

Where should you save your library?

Another important aspect of a library is where you save it.

Of course, if you're writing scripts for yourself, the location of your library doesn't make too much difference. But sooner or later you will need to make your scripts available to other people or on other Macs. At that point, you must ensure that your script can always find the subroutine library, and that you don't go crazy with installation.

The best solution is to find a folder that you can later access using the *path to* command, preferably somewhere in the current user's library folder. Both Application Support and ScriptingAdditions folders are suitable. Placing your library in one of these folders allows your scripts to find them no matter which OS X computer they run on. For example, let's say that you named your script "command_library.scpt" and put it in the Applications Support folder in the user's home folder. To load that library, start your script with the following two lines:

```
set library_path to ¬
    (path to application support from user domain as string) & ¬
    "command_library.scpt"
set my_lib to load script file library_path
```

Since every Mac OS X has an `Applications Support` folder (and if it doesn't exist the command itself will create it), you are safe.

After that, all you have to do is type my_lib's before the command name to properly call it.

You still have to make sure that the computer the script is running on has your library in that folder. For computers running Panther, you can take advantage of script application packages. Just save your script as a package, place your library file in the resources folder in that package, and use the *path to me* command to access that resources folder. For a complete description, see Chapter 20, which explains how to install scripting additions.

18

Script objects and variables

Global variables and properties are good only in the script in which they are defined. If you created a script that has a *main_template* property, and then loaded a script object into that script, the loaded script will not have access to the loading script's *main_template* property, or any other property, for that matter.

The only connection these two scripts have to each other is from the loading script to the loaded script. That means that the loading script can set and get properties in the loaded script, but the loaded script has no way to speak to the script that loaded it.

That means that if there's a property in the loaded script that has to be set based on a variable value in the loading script, only the loading script can make that assignment, not the loaded script. Here's an example:

Let's say that you have a script application you run, which we will call "main script." This main script application has to process different files and use different templates and folders. All folders are located in a folder structure that the application is part of. To make life easier, you have a property in the script called *main_folder_path*, and you start the script by figuring out the main folder path and assigning it to the *main_folder_path* property.

To make things a little clearer, Figure 18-1 shows the system's folder structure.

Figure 18-1. The multiscript system folder structure

Figure 18-2 shows the two scripts used by the system: the main application script called *Main Script* and the loaded script called *Library.scpt*.

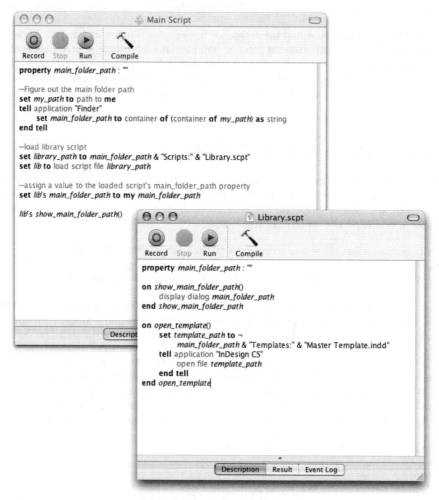

Figure 18-2. The two scripts used by the system: the main application script called *Main Script* and the loaded script called *Library.scpt*

The main script starts by figuring out the path for the main folder path. This allows it to find the path to the script library and load it to the variable *lib*.

After an instance of the *Library.scpt* script is loaded to the *lib* property, the *Main Script* assigns the loaded script's *main_folder_path* property.

The final thing the *Main Script* does is call a subroutine from the loaded script, which illustrates the fact the loaded script now has a value for the *main_folder_path* property.

Inheritance: When scripts start to have children

So far we have discussed how to create instances of script objects and how to call subroutines and set properties in them. Now, it's time to take it one step further.

Script object inheritance has more to do with inheriting traits than inheriting fortune. To better understand inheritance, imagine a book called *Mac OS X Unleashed* (so geeky, I get to pick any book, and here I go). You can read it because it has content. Now, imagine a second book: *Mac OS X Unleashed II*. However, when you open the second book to read, instead of contents, it says "Read the book *Mac OS X Unleashed*."

Since you happen to have that book, you read it.

In the case of the books, the first book is the parent. The second book is the child, which has inherited everything from the first book.

In AppleScript, script objects can inherit attributes from other script objects in a similar way. You define a parent to a script with the special *parent* property. In the example that follows we define the script *wilma*, and then we define the script *pebbles* with the *wilma* script acting as the parent:

Script 18-8

```
script wilma
    property hair_color : "red"
    property the_name : "Wilma"
    on say_your_name()
        display dialog "My name is " & the_name
    end say_your_name
end script
script pebbles
    property parent : wilma
end script
```

What we can do after defining the two script objects is call commands from the *pebbles* script as if it were the *wilma* script. Insert this line at the end of the script:

```
tell pebbles to say_your_name()
```

Now I know *pebbles* is pretty tiny, but there's no excuse for answering "My name is Wilma" when she was asked for her name. If we figure out why she did that we may be able to fix it. Pebbles said that her name was Wilma because the script *pebbles* inherits not only the *say_your_name* subroutine, but also the *the_name* property and its value.

One nice thing about script object inheritance is that you can choose which attributes (properties and subroutines) you want the child script object to inherit, and which ones you don't. In this case, the *say_your_name* subroutine fulfills its purpose well, but the *the_name* property should be restated in the child script, which should do wonders for Pebbles's sense of self.

To do this we will add the same property with a different value in the *pebbles* script. We will also add the words "of me" after the variable (see line 5) to specify that the variable *the_name* in the handler refers to the version of *the_name* that is defined in the script that calls the *say_your_name* handler. As you will see in a moment, if this handler is called from the *pebbles* script, it will use the value of *the_name* that is defined in the *pebbles* script, even though the handler is located in the *wilma* script, because the handler is called from the *pebbles* script. In other words, while the script is running, "me" means Pebbles, not Wilma, because *pebbles* is the current script. Using "of me" or "my" correctly when writing child scripts that inherit from parent scripts is critical to making them work correctly.

Script 18-9

```
script wilma
    property hair_color : "red"
    property the_name : "Wilma"
    on say_your_name()
        display dialog "My name is " & the_name of me
    end say_your_name
end script
script pebbles
    property parent : wilma
    property the_name : "Pebbles"
end script
tell pebbles to say_your_name()
```

Now, Pebbles will answer correctly, because while the subroutine is inherited from her mom, her name is different. To see the subroutine work from the parent script as well, try to change the last line of the previous script to

```
tell wilma to say_your_name()
```

In the preceding example, we saw that the *pebbles* script can redefine a property it inherited from the *wilma* script.

The child script can also redefine a subroutine that exists in the parent script. When the subroutine is called from the child script, the new, redefined subroutine will be called, as expected. In the following example, the *say_your_name* subroutine is defined in both parent and child scripts:

Script 18-10

```
1. script wilma
2.     property hair_color : "red"
3.     property the_name : "Wilma"
4.     on say_your_name()
5.         display dialog "My name is " & the_name of me
6.     end say_your_name
7. end script
8. script pebbles
9.     property parent : wilma
10.     property the_name : "Pebbles"
11.     on say_your_name()
```

```
12.        display dialog "Yabadabado!"
13.      end say_your_name
14. end script
15. tell pebbles to say_your_name()
```

Oh, come on now, Pebbles, that's not your name! At this point, Wilma can't take it any longer. She needs to help Pebbles say what she wants to. To help that happen, we can use the *continue* command in *pebbles*'s version of the *say_your_name* handler. The *continue* command tells the parent script to execute its own version of the called subroutine. To do that, add the *continue* command followed by the subroutine call inside the subroutine definition in the child script.

```
on say_your_name()
    display dialog "Yabadabado!"
    continue say_your_name()
end say_your_name
```

Now things seem to work OK. The dialog boxes we get are "Yabadabado" for Pebbles followed by "My name is Pebbles".

Got no life: Using inheritance to create a shoot 'em up game

One example we will talk about (but won't get into too much detail on) is the use of parent-child script objects and the inheritance of properties and handlers from the parent script to the child script.

The example I mentioned is an alien shoot 'em up game that makes a use of script objects to control every aspect of the game. In this script, among the many defined script objects, a few define the alien spaceships. One script object is the base ship; it defines the basic shape and behavior of the alien ships. In order to create variety, three other child scripts were created. Each one has a *parent* property, which defines the mother ship as its parent. The child scripts redefine some of the parent's subroutines and properties to create variety. For instance, the *score* property is different from one alien script to the other to make sure you get a different score for shooting different aliens.

Following is a small portion of the script that deals with the inheritance:

Script 18-11 (excerpt)

```
1. script masterAlien
2.     property currentSpot : 1
3.     property pointValue : 0 --assigned by individual children aliens
4.
5.     on advanceAlien(columns)
6.         if alive then
7.             --...
8.         end if
9.     end advanceAlien
```

```
10.    on explode(alienPositionInList)
11.        -- Explode alien...
12.    end explode
13.
14.    on firstRow()
15.        set r1 to " • "
16.        return r1
17.    end firstRow

18.    on secondRow()
19.        set r2 to "     "
20.        return r2
21.    end secondRow
22. end script

23. script greenAlien
24.    property parent : masterAlien
25.    property pointValue : 100
26.    on firstRow()
27.        if my cloaked then
28.            set r1 to continue firstRow()
29.        else
30.            set r1 to "0 0"
31.        end if
32.        return r1
33.    end firstRow
34.    on secondRow()
35.        if my cloaked then
36.            set r2 to continue secondRow()
37.        else
38.            set r2 to "000"
39.        end if
40.        return r2
41.    end secondRow
42. end script

43. script RedAlien
44.    property parent : masterAlien
45.    property pointValue : 200
46.    on firstRow()
47.        if my cloaked then
48.            set r1 to continue firstRow()
49.        else
50.            set r1 to " W "
51.        end if
52.        return r1
53.    end firstRow
54.    on secondRow()
55.        if my cloaked then
```

```
56.              set r2 to continue secondRow()
57.          else
58.              set r2 to "W W"
59.          end if
60.          return r2
61.      end secondRow
62. end script
```

The complete Script 18-11, the alien game script, can be found at the Downloads page on the Apress website (www.apress.com/book/download.html). To play, change the TextEdit preferences to create text documents by default.

Notice that the script named *masterAlien* has a point value of 0, but each one of the *redAlien* and *greenAlien* scripts define their own *pointValue* properties. Each of the two also defines the *masterAlien* script as its parent.

Another example of inheritance can be seen in line 27. The *redAlien* script decides whether to use its own version of the *secondRow()* subroutine or whether to *continue* the parent's version of that same subroutine.

Run script command

The *run script* command is very neat. It allows you to run plain text as if it were a string. Try this:

```
run script "beep 3"
```

You can also run text files as scripts.

Following is a little script that allows users to type in their own script into a plain AppleScript dialog box. After users enter their script, AppleScript tries to execute it using the *run script* command.

The script starts by collecting the user's entered text from a dialog box to a variable. After that, AppleScript tries to run the script and collect the script's result into another variable called *script_result*.

The end is a dialog box that has the script text and the result.

Script 18-12

```
display dialog "Script:" default answer return & ¬
    return & return & return & return & return
set the_script to text returned of result
try
    set script_result to run script the_script
    display dialog "Your script:" & return & ¬
    the_script & return & "had this result:" & return & script_result
on error script_error number error_number
```

```
      if error_number is not -2753 then
        display dialog "Your script didn't run because:" & return &
    script_error
      end if
    end try
```

Run script with parameters

If the script you're running with the *run script* command has parameters, you can supply those parameters with values.

The following script runs a small script and uses the (are you sitting down?) *with parameters* parameter to send a value to the script's parameter.

```
    run script "on run (x)
    display dialog x
    end " with parameters {"Hi"}
```

Folder stock example

In the this section, we will explore a script that uses script objects to track independent movement of stocks. The movement is, as can be expected, random, so if AAPL gets lower than MSFT, just restart the script . . .

Before getting into the specifics of the script, let's take a moment to understand its structure.

The core of the script is a list (*stock_script_list*) in which each item is a script object representing one stock.

The script object has a few properties and two subroutines: *start_stock* and *update_stock*. When the *start_stock* subroutine is called, the stock is initialized. For that reason we will call this subroutine only once at the start. The second subroutine, *update_stock*, changes the value of the stock and refreshes its view in the Finder window.

The part of the script that deals with the script objects is made out of three distinct parts. First the list of script objects is created (lines 16 through 19). This is rather simple: the script loops once for each item in the symbol list, and each repetition an instance of the script *stock* is tacked onto the scripts list.

The instances of the script object are created using the *stock_instance* subroutine. Since this subroutine returns an instance of the script object, I can add that object directly to the list (line 18).

After I have gathered a list of instances of the same script object, I can start working with them. To start, I will call the *start_stock* subroutine in each instance.

The *start_stock* subroutine holds the key to the future success of the stock. It assigns random values to the variables that will determine if the stock's general direction will be up or down. One of the parameters of that initialization subroutine holds the name of the stock.

To call the *start_stock* subroutine in each instance, the script loops through the script object instances list (lines 21 through 26).

Notice that in line 26 we address item I of *stock_script_list*. That's right: since every item of this list is an instance of a script object, I can tell it to execute a command defined in the script object definition.

The third and final part of the script (lines 28 through 35) has two nested repeat loops. The outer one is an endless loop with no way out. That's right: if you don't stop the script, the stocks will go up and down forever.

The inner loop is very similar to the last repeat loop. It loops in the list of script object instances and calls the *update_stock* subroutine for each script object instance in the list.

Script 18-13

```
1. set folder_name to "stocks"
2. set the_folder to (path to desktop as string) & folder_name & ":"
3. tell application "Finder"
4.    if not (exists folder the_folder) then
5.       make new folder at desktop with properties {name:folder_name}
6.    end if
7.    set w to make new Finder window to folder "Stocks" of desktop
8.    tell w
9.       set toolbar visible to false
10.       set current view to icon view
11.       set bounds of it to {30, 70, 1000, 770}
12.    end tell
13. end tell

14. set symbolList to {"IBM", "AAPL", "MSFT", "AOL", "ARC", ¬
       "AHT", "GLFD", "OXBC"}

15. --Create stock scripts list
16. set stock_script_list to {}
17. repeat (count symbolList) times
18.    set end of stock_script_list to stock_instance()
19. end repeat

20. --activate each item in the list
21. repeat with i from 1 to (count symbolList)
22.    set the_symbol to item i of symbolList
23.    tell item i of stock_script_list
24.       start_Stock for the_symbol out of the_folder beside i
25.    end tell
26. end repeat
```

```applescript
27. --advance each item in the list
28. repeat
29.    repeat with i from 1 to (count symbolList)
30.       set the_symbol to item i of symbolList
31.       tell item i of stock_script_list
32.          update_stock for the_symbol out of the_folder beside i
33.       end tell
34.    end repeat
35. end repeat

36. on stock_instance()
37.    script stock
38.       property negative_change_max : 0
39.       property positive_change_max : 0
40.       property stock_value : 0
41.       property start_y : 400

42.       to start_Stock for the_symbol out of the_folder beside n
43.          set negative_change_max to random number from -15 to -10
44.          set positive_change_max to random number from 10 to 15
45.          set X to n * 80
46.          set the_item to the_folder & the_symbol
47.          tell application "Finder"
48.             activate
49.             if not (exists folder the_item) then
50.                make new folder at folder the_folder ¬
                      with properties {name:the_symbol}
51.             end if
52.             set position of folder the_item to {X, start_y}
53.          end tell
54.       end start_Stock

55.
56.       to update_stock for the_symbol out of the_folder beside n
57.          set reverse_trend to random number from 1 to 5
58.          if reverse_trend = 1 then
59.             set temp to negative_change_max
60.             set negative_change_max to positive_change_max
61.             set positive_change_max to temp
62.          end if
63.          set the_item to the_folder & the_symbol
64.          set X to n * 80
65.          tell application "Finder"
66.             update the_folder
67.             set the_change to random number ¬
                   from negative_change_max to positive_change_max
68.             set stock_value to stock_value + the_change
69.             set Y to (-stock_value) + start_y
70.             set position of folder the_item to {X, Y}
71.             if stock_value < 0 then
```

```
72.                  set label index of folder the_item to 2
73.              else
74.                  set label index of folder the_item to 6
75.              end if
76.          end tell
77.      end update_stock
78.  end script
79.  return stock
80. end stock_instance
```

Alien invasion arcade game

The alien invasion game is an arcade game I created using AppleScript script objects. Every aspect of this game is a script object: the scoreboard, the spaceship, the aliens, etc.

The main use of script objects is the aliens themselves. They start as one mother-alien script object that produces children script objects with their own look and score. As the game moves on, more aliens are created. Each time an alien is created, an instance of one of the three alien "flavors" is added to a list. As the game moves on, every alien is advanced a bit. When each alien reaches the right side of the window, it is destroyed. This destruction is easy and very important. What we do is simply delete the item from the end of the list and off the alien goes to alien heaven. This helps us keep our memory use in check.

I urge you to download the script and check it out. The script file is called "Script 18-11 Alien Game", and you can find it among the hundreds of other scripts available for download with this book from the Downloads page on the Apress website (www.apress.com/book/download.html).

Case study: AutoGraph

AutoGraph is an automated publishing system I created for clients in the financial field. Besides making some neat use of XML, SVG, and InDesign Tagged Text, this system is made expandable by means of script objects.

The system uses script objects in two ways—one is for the basic purpose of organizing functions away from the main scripts. In fact, there are 11 such libraries, each one containing functions for a specific purpose. These script files (which I call engines) can be loaded independently to other scripts and provide functionality in the form of subroutines, each covering a slightly different area. One engine covers InDesign commands, one Illustrator commands, one interacts with SQL, one creates SVG contents, etc.

The second form in which script objects are used in the system is for processing the actual graph-bearing pages. Each script file has the code to create a unique type of graph: one creates a pie chart, one a bar graph, etc. The challenge in creating this system was that I knew that even after the system started being put to use I would have to add more of these graph scripts, for about 40 more types of graphs, but I didn't want to have to change the main script or have to update it every time with a call to a new script.

The solution was to make all the scripts share the same main subroutine. Each one of those graph-processing scripts has a subroutine called *process* with the exact same parameters. The main script starts out by loading instances of all of the scripts into a list of script objects. It also creates a sister list that contains a code name for each graph type in the same order in which they are stored in the script object list.

As the main processor runs, it is fed data for each one of the graphs. From that data it figures out the graph's code name, and uses it to get the offset in the script object list of the script object that can produce that graph type. Now, the main script has the data for the graph and it knows where in the script object list it can find the script that can process that graph. All that happens next is that the main script calls the *process* subroutine for the correct script object and waits for it to finish running (see the schematic drawing in Figure 18-3).

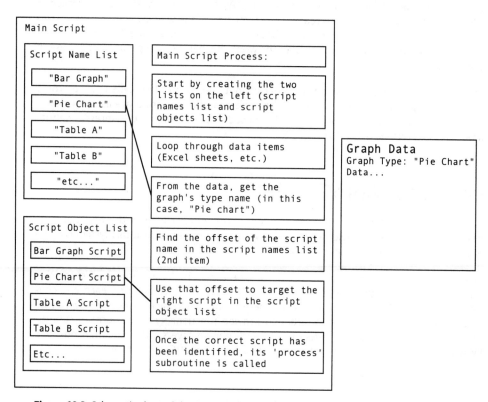

Figure 18-3. Schematic chart of the AutoGraph system

The advantage of this setup is that as long as I create the new graph-processing scripts using the same method, one main *process* subroutine with the same parameters, I can add them to the system without having to make any changes to the main script.

In addition, all of the graph-processing scripts load in these same "engine" library scripts for their own functionality.

Power wrap-up

This section summarizes the chapter in an intensive-reference style. Use this part to look up facts related to the chapter without the chatter.

What are script objects?

Script objects are special objects that contain a script. This script can then run independently from the main script and keep its own properties and subroutines.

Script objects can be scripts you load from another file, or script objects you declare inside the main script. A script object that exists in the same script document as your main script has to be wrapped in a script block, like this:

```
script simon
    property identifier : initial value
    on run
        --statements
    end run
    on do_something()
        --statements
    end do_something
end script
```

The preceding script has a *run* handler and a subroutine. It doesn't have to have both. This script is also named (*simon*). You are only required to name scripts in this way if they are not initialized with a subroutine.

In the case of the preceding script object, the script object is instantiated when the script is compiled.

Creating script instances with a subroutine

You can place your script object in a subroutine. In this case, the script object will not be instantiated when the main script is compiled. The script object will only become available when the subroutine in which it lives is called. Following is an example of a script object instantiated by a subroutine, and later called to run:

Script 18-14

```
set my_script_object to load_script()
tell my_script_object to run

on load_script()
    script
        display dialog "I'm running!"
    end script
end load_script
```

Declaring script objects

When named script objects appear in your compiled script, they become instantiated as soon as the script compiles. In this case you do not need to instantiate the script and you can refer to it by name, as shown here:

```
tell simon to run
script simon
    display dialog "I'm running!"
end script
```

Replicating script

Once you have a script object in a variable, you can make copies of it with the *copy* command:

```
set script_1 to load_script()
copy scipt_1 to script_2
```

If you use the *set* command instead of copy, you will end up with two variables referencing the same script object, instead of two separate copies.

Script object and inheritance

A script object can contain the property *parent*. The value of the *parent* property is usually another script. The script whose *parent* property is set immediately inherits all the properties and subroutines from the parent script (named as the value of the *parent* property). In some rare instances, an application is the parent; for instance, when embedding AppleScript scripts into a FileMaker Pro script, you can omit the *tell application "FileMaker Pro"* block, since the implied application is FileMaker.

The child script can redefine properties set in the parent script and also rewrite subroutines specified in the parent script. Such redefined subroutines can include the command *continue* followed by the name of the subroutine. This will cause the same subroutine to execute as it is defined in the parent. You can read much more about this earlier in the chapter.

Loading scripts

You can load script into variables in other scripts by using the *load script* command. The script you load has to be saved as a compiled script. The loading script must assign the loaded script to a variable. This variable will then be used to give the script commands. Here's an example:

```
set my_script to ¬
    load script file "Macintosh HD:Scripts:subroutine library.scpt"
tell my_script to do_something()
```

In the preceding example, the subroutine *do_something()* is defined in the loaded script.

Run script command

The *run script* command takes a script in the form of a string and tries to run it as an AppleScript. See the following example:

```
run script "on run (x)
display dialog x
end " with parameters {"Hello World"}
```

In this example the *run script* command runs a three-line script and passes it the string "Hello World" as a parameter.

Details previously . . .

The last part of this chapter is a summary of the entire chapter. For more details on any of the items here, refer to earlier sections in the chapter.

PART THREE
THE WILD WORLD OF APPLESCRIPT

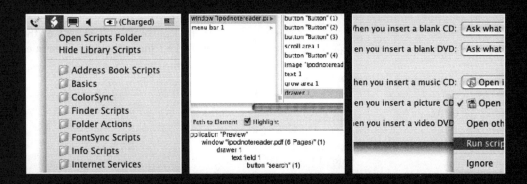

Following the great success companies had automating tasks with AppleScript in pre–OS X times, Apple has taken the time to make AppleScript even better, faster, and easier to integrate into applications. As soon as the OS X diagrams started circulating in 1999, it became clear that the days when AppleScript was a mere extension, riding on top of the code, begging for some CPU cycles were coming to an end. In Mac OS X, we were in.

The tight integration of AppleScript into OS X brought about some great stuff. For instance, applications created using Cocoa, Apple's new programming environment, are much easier to make into scriptable applications. Also, user interface element scripting (GUI scripting) became an integrated part of the OS, giving scripters access to almost all UI elements in any application. Other things didn't come as easily. For Finder recordability, we had to wait for several years until it finally emerged unannounced with OS X 10.3, also known as Panther. A bit earlier than that we saw the return of folder actions, but they also only became reliable with the Panther release.

In this chapter, we will look at some of the AppleScript amenities included with OS X. Since the latest version of the OS is 10.3, this is the latest version that the first edition of this book covers.

The script menu

Yet another optional OS X user interface item is the script menu. OS X does not come with the menu installed because the stylish black and white icons at the top right of the menu bar were meant strictly for hardware controls such as monitor control, volume, AirPort, etc. The script menu, however, blends in quite nicely, and installing it yourself is very easy.

Inside the AppleScript folder that is in your Applications folder you will find two small applications: Install Script Menu and Remove Script Menu.

After you double-click the Install Script Menu application, the script menu will appear to the left of the icons on the right side of the menu bar. Figure 19-1 shows the open script menu.

Figure 19-1.
The open
script menu

Preinstalled script

As you can tell from looking at the menu shown in Figure 19-1 (or by gazing at your own script menu), you can see that it already has quite a few scripts. There are actually two sets of scripts separated by a divider line with scripts above the divider and scripts below the divider. The scripts above the divider are those installed in the local domain's Scripts folder at /Library/Scripts, and those below the divide are those installed in the user domain's Scripts folder at ~/Library/Scripts. The divider may not have anything below it yet since the current user's Scripts folder is empty (see the text that follows).

The location of the scripts goes as follows: the preinstalled scripts are found in the Scripts folder in the Library folder from the startup disk. The user scripts shown in the menu are stored in the Scripts folder in the user's Library folder. Actually, what you will be seeing, especially if you haven't played around with the Scripts folders, is that there are no scripts in the script menu, only folders. This is because the script menu points to the Scripts folder, and shows its contents with the folders and all, where folders become submenus and the scripts themselves the menu items.

Other menu items

The script menu contains two additional items on top of the scripts and script folders. The first item, Open Scripts Folder, simply opens the system's Scripts folder in the Finder. This allows you quick access to adding or removing scripts.

The second item is toggled between Hide Library Scripts and Show Library Scripts. You use that in case you have your own scripts you use with the script menu and you don't want the scripts that came with your system to crowd the menu.

Running and launching scripts from the script menu

To run a script from the script menu, simply select it from the menu. To launch a script using the Script Editor, select a script from the menu while pressing the OPTION button.

Getting the path of the current script

Just for the record, it is not currently possible to get the path to the running script, unless it is saved as an application. This subject comes up around the issue of alternative script running venues such as the script menu.

Using the *path to me* statement in a compiled script running from the script menu will return the path to the System Events application.

Apple's sample scripts

One of the things that makes working with AppleScript great is the AppleScript community. You would think that competition in this small field would cause an unattractive "every man for himself" atmosphere, but not here! In the AppleScript community people are sometimes so eager to help you that they will share with you anywhere from chunks of code to entire scripts that will help you with your quest.

Beside handouts here and there, the AppleScript website contains many sample scripts, mostly written with the deliberate teacherly style of Sal Saghoian, AppleScript's product manager.

The first batch of scripts you have access to are the scripts in the Scripts folder I just spoke of in the section "The script menu." Following you will find more resources for free scripts. While many of these scripts aren't exactly what you need, they make a great starting point, and you are encouraged to open them and copy portions to your own scripts. There are two main places on Apple's website to look for sample scripts; one is the applications page in the AppleScript web page: www.apple.com/applescript/apps/. From there, go to the application of interest and look for sample scripts.

The following page also contains links to a great collection of utility subroutines: www.apple.com/applescript/guidebook/sbrt/.

Folder actions

Folder actions allow you to create hot folders on your Mac that respond to different events and trigger a script. You create a folder action by attaching a script to a folder. Such a script may contain special event handlers that activate when the folder opens, closes, moves, or when items are either added to or removed from the folder.

Folder actions are great for any hot-folder setup you need to create. Imagine any workflow in which files need to be processed automatically, but a person has to trigger the automation by telling the script which file or files to process. While the same workflow could have been created using a script application saved as a droplet (with the *on open* command), folder actions give you a wider variety of action-triggering events, and allow users to trigger scripts by dropping files into a folder, which may be more workflow-like than dragging and dropping files on an application droplet.

Another difference between droplets and folder actions is that dropping a file on a droplet triggers a script without moving the file anywhere. This may be good when the files are on the server, for instance, and the droplet is on the hard drive; using folder actions will actually copy the files to the hard drive, a thing you may or may not want to have happen.

In pre–OS X, folder actions worked reliably but with one problem: to trigger an action the folder had to be open. If you dropped a file into a closed folder, nothing happened, which for me was enough of a reason not to use folder actions. In OS X, on the other hand, although it took a few version updates for folder actions to return, and only become reliable in OS X 10.3 (Panther), they do work on open and closed folders.

Starting out with folder actions

In order for folder actions to work, a couple of conditions have to be met. First, you must have folder actions activated on the Mac that the actions should run on. Second, you must attach a script with at least one folder action event handler to a folder.

Turning folder actions on

There are three ways to start up folder actions. You can either run a script that will start them, use the Folder Actions Setup utility, or use the contextual menu.

To turn folder actions on or off using a script, look no further than the `Scripts` folder in your user's `Library` folder. In the folder called `Folder Actions`, you will find, among others, two files named `Enable Folder Actions.scpt` and `Disable Folder Actions.scpt`. You can run these scripts from either a script editor or from the script menu.

The scripts are very simple:

```
tell application "System Events" to set folder actions enabled to true
```

And to disable folder actions:

```
tell application "System Events" to set folder actions enabled to false
```

The Folder Actions Setup utility application also allows you to enable and disable folder actions as shown in Figure 19-2.

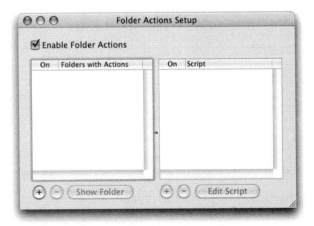

Figure 19-2. The Folder Actions Setup utility window. As you can see, this utility allows you to do much more than just enable folder actions.

To turn folder actions on with the contextual menu, CONTROL-click anywhere on the desktop and choose Enable Folder Actions from the pop-up menu. Unless you have some other utility installed, the folder action menu items should be at the end.

> Can't find the folder action items in your contextual menu? Folder action contextual menus are only starting to be available with the release of Panther.

You can also show the Folder Action Setup utility by choosing Configure Folder Actions from the Finder's contextual menu.

Your first folder action

After you enable folder actions, you may want to get started by creating a folder action script, attaching it to a folder, and testing it.

Let's start by creating a simple script that will change the label of the items you drop in the folder. We will use the Folder Actions Setup utility to administer the operation.

Step 1: Create your script

Start a new script with Script Editor. Your first lines will be the event handler that is triggered when a file is added.

Type into the script window the script lines shown in Figure 19-3.

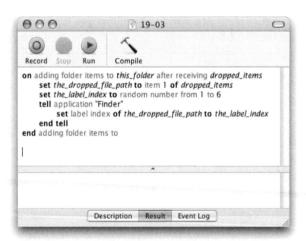

Figure 19-3. The event handler that gets activated when files are dropped into the folder

Let's try to analyze the script shown in Figure 19-3.

The script's one handler is the *adding folder items* handler. This handler will be called automatically when any file or folder is added to the folder that this script is attached to as a folder action—that is, after we turn the script into a folder action and attach it to a folder.

Step 2: Create your hot folder

> *Just how hot is the hot folder? The term "hot folder" refers to folders that aren't passive. Unlike with other folders, when you interact with hot folders, something happens. The term is used in workflow-related processes where files are treated in different ways based on the folder they are dropped in.*

Create a folder on the desktop and call it My Hot Folder. This will be the folder that will be the target of the folder action events.

Step 3: Save your script

In order for your script to become folder action material, you need to save (or move) it to the Folder Action Scripts folder. This folder is in the Scripts folder that is in your Library folder.

Step 4: Activate folder actions

If it's not already running, start up the Folder Actions Setup utility. It should be in the AppleScript folder in your Applications folder.

Once the utility is started, check the Enable Folder Actions check box, also shown in Figure 19-2.

Step 5: Attach the folder action to your folder

There are a few of ways to add a folder item to a folder. You can use a script or the Finder's contextual menu. Here, we will use the Folder Action Setup utility.

To attach the folder action script you created, you start by adding the folder to the folder list, and then you attach the script to it.

In the Folder Action Setup utility application, click the + button under the folder list on the left.

This will bring up the Choose Folder dialog box. Choose the hot folder you created on the desktop and click OK.

The folder will appear in the folder list.

Next, click the folder in the folder list, and then click the + button under the scripts list on the right.

This will present you with a list of scripts currently in the Folder Actions Scripts folder. Choose your script and click OK.

A couple of notes

Notice that you can check and uncheck folders in order to activate or deactivate them. Also, each hot folder may have more than one script attached to it, and the scripts can be activated and deactivated individually with the check boxes.

You can only see your scripts in the list when a folder is selected in the folder list.

Where are folder action scripts stored?

Folder action scripts are stored in the Folder Action Scripts folder in the Scripts folder of either your user library or the Library folder in the local library folder (in the startup disk). Out of the box, the Folder Actions Scripts folder already exists in the local domain, and it contains several samples of folder action scripts you can open and play with or attach to folders.

Using the contextual menus with folder actions

After some struggle, the folder action feature finally made it to the Finder's contextual menu in OS X 10.3. By default, the bottom of the menu has the options *disable (or enable) folder actions* and *configure folder actions*.

When you CONTROL-click a folder, however, you get more options, and yet even more options (as shown in Figure 19-4) if the folder has a folder action script attached to it.

Figure 19-4. The contextual menu after CONTROL-clicking a folder with a folder action attached to it

Using scripts to manage folder actions

You may be in a situation where you need to be able to set up multiple Macs with some folder action functionality. If you want to use scripts to automate the process of creating folder actions, you should open up and check out the scripts that come with the Mac in the `/Library/Scripts/Folder Actions` folder. In it you will find scripts for enabling and disabling folder actions as well as attaching to and removing folder actions from folders. All scripts, of course, are open, and you're encouraged to copy parts of them into your own scripts.

One of the features used in the folder action–related scripts is the *path to* command:

```
path to folder actions scripts
--> alias "Macintosh HD:Users:hanaan:Library:Scripts:Folder Action ¬
Scripts:"
```

Folder actions events

While the obvious thing to do with folder actions is to perform some action when items are added to the folder, folder actions provide you with four other events that can trigger handlers in your scripts. The five events in total are:

1. Adding items to a folder. With this event you get access to the path to the folder itself along with references to the items that were added as a list.

2. Removing items from a folder.

3. Opening a folder.

4. Closing a folder.

5. Moving a folder.

Scripting the user interface

When applications have good AppleScript support, a working object model, and a solid dictionary, scripting the graphic user interface (or GUI as I will refer to it here) is simply not needed. GUI scripting is used to plug holes in the scriptability of your system, including applications, utilities, and any other thing you'd want to automate.

Although GUI scripting is a bit of a newcomer to the AppleScript scene, it works really well and in a way is very satisfying, mainly because it allows you to automate almost any feature that can be invoked from the user interface. It can also be a bit frustrating, since the script sometimes works faster than the user interface and therefore trips over itself. This situation, however, is easily remedied with a small delay in the script.

Despite any issues it may have, GUI scripting is a very welcome addition, and in many cases the only option you have to bridge the scriptability gaps in the applications you use in your process.

GUI scripting also lets you get and set attributes of a UI element that are not defined in the System Events dictionary, and it also lets you perform actions that aren't defined in that dictionary, using technical terms defined by Apple and by third-party applications to support Apple's Accessibility technology—for example, *get value of attribute "AXPosition" of window 1* or *perform action "AXRaise" of window 1*. The Finder responds to several new technical terms of this nature, and GUI scripting can use this technique to get at them. You can use tools like Apple's UI Element Inspector and PreFab UI Browser to learn what these technical terms are.

Enabling UI scripting

By default, running scripts that make use of UI commands won't work. To enable UI scripting on any Mac, this Mac has to be running Mac OS X 10.3 Panther and has to have a little-known check box checked in a System Preferences panel.

To enable GUI scripting, launch System Preferences, and in the Universal Access panel, check the Enable access for assistive devices check box at the bottom of the window. You can leave it turned on all the time without ill effect.

GUI scripting dictionary

The GUI scripting commands and objects are defined in the System Events dictionary, under the Processes suite.

The Processes suite defines five commands and many elements.

The five commands are *click*, *perform*, *key code*, *keystroke*, and *select*.

The list of elements is a bit longer. It contains 45 elements, all of them being subclasses of the element named UI element. Even a window is a UI element. On top of that, each UI element has many elements and properties of its own. The values of many of the properties can be set using AppleScript's *set* command.

Although there's some logic that can apply to the hierarchy of the elements, such as a window element can contain a button element, but a button cannot contain a window, and a menu bar contains menus that contain menu items, the dictionary doesn't hint at any of that. In the eyes of the System Events dictionary, all elements are equal under the UI element super class, of course.

All this means that figuring out which element in the UI of a given application contains which other elements is very difficult. Unless, of course, you have the right tool.

Only after you discover the cryptic nature of UI elements can you understand that without a tool such as Prefab's UI Browser (created by Bill Cheeseman and available at www.prefab.com/uibrowser/), you wouldn't get very far. A less powerful but free utility called UI Element Inspector is available from Apple.

Some object structure

Even though the dictionary isn't any help when it comes to the UI object model, we can try and shed some light on the situation.

In GUI scripting there are two main types of objects that contain all others: windows and the menu bar. Windows, then, can contain all elements that belong in a window such as text fields, buttons, and pop-up buttons. Menu bars can contain menus, and menus contain menu items, etc.

It is also important to note that any object (such as a table) that appears to have a scroll bar, really doesn't. In reality, the scroll bar is part of a scroll view in which the object resides.

What can you do with GUI scripting?

Having only five commands makes it seem as if your options are limited; however, what you can do in this case has more to do with which object you perform the command on than with the command itself. On top of that, every UI element has many properties that can be set with AppleScript's *set* command. This by itself will account for a lot of what you can do with GUI scripting.

Before we see how to dig out the object you want from a pile of UI elements, let's look at four out of the five commands.

click

The *click* command makes the UI element behave as if you clicked it with the mouse. This applies to buttons, text fields, menu items, etc.

If you were going to the desert and could take just a single UI command with you, *click* would be it. Most UI tasks you will perform will boil down to clicking some UI element. It is finding that element that will pose the challenge.

perform

The *perform* command is a bit different than *click*, but can sometimes have the same effect.

The *perform* command will perform the action associated with a particular UI element. You use *perform* instead of *click* when the UI element whose action you want to execute is not one you can click, such as a text field. Clicking a text field will place the insertion point in it but will not perform any action that is built into it. Another example is that a window element may perform the *raise* action, which brings it to the front of other windows in the application.

19

keystroke

The *keystroke* command allows you to simulate the action of a user typing on the keyboard. All you have to do is follow the *keystroke* command with a string you want System Events to type on your keyboard.

This command comes handy in two situations: one is when you want to type text, and the other is for when you want to execute a keyboard shortcut with the COMMAND key (or other).

There are two ways to use modifier keys with your keystrokes. You can use the *using* argument to use the modifier key just for the next keystroke, like this:

```
keystroke "n" using command down
```

> *Be sure to use a lowercase letter when sending a keystroke as a COMMAND-key equivalent. Otherwise, GUI scripting will think you are also holding down the SHIFT key and it won't work as expected.*

Or, you can toggle modifier keys up or down with the *key down* and *key up* commands. If you use the *key up/key down* option, you will have to add a line of code before and after the *keystroke* command, like this:

```
key down command
keystroke "n"
key up command
```

This method works OK, until the script stops for any reason after the *key down* but before the *key up* command. If that happens, your keyboard's modifier key will be "stuck," like caps lock. To undo that, you will have to find a way to run a script that will unpress the modifier key. This may be difficult since you can't actually type anything with, say, the COMMAND key stuck in the down position.

Having the following script under the script menu can prove useful:

Script 19-1

```
tell application "System Events"
    key up command
    key up shift
    key up control
    key up option
end tell
```

On the other hand, if you want a coworker to be caught off guard, go to his/her Mac and run this script:

```
tell application "System Events" to key down command
```

Then, to add insult to injury, pass by that coworker's desk and fix it for him/her.

key code

The *key code* command is a bit like *keystroke*, but instead of typing based on a character, it uses the hardware-based integer key code of a particular key.

This method has the advantage of allowing you access to keys that aren't characters, such as the *DELETE* key, the arrow keys, and the function keys on the top row of your keyboard.

You can use the *using* modifier *down* as with the *keystroke* command.

For what it's worth, though, key code 123 through 126 are the arrow keys and code 51 is delete. Utilities such as Prefab's UI Browser can show you the key code of any key you press.

The following script will start a new document in TextEdit, type the word "Apple", and then go back one character, and select the one before last by using the left arrow with the *SHIFT* key:

Script 19-2

```
tell application "TextEdit"
    activate
end tell
tell application "System Events"
    keystroke "n" using command down
    keystroke "Apple"
    key code 123
    key down shift
    key code 123
    key up shift
end tell
```

In a few pages we will look at using the *set* command to set the value of UI elements.

Using UI Browser to locate elements

Working with GUI scripting is working with UI elements, and the only sane way to do that is by using Prefab's UI Browser (www.prefab.com).

The reason why you need a UI browser is because when the Mac GUI was created, it wasn't created with your scripting it in mind. It is a bit messy, and finding your way around means wasting a lot of time. For instance, if you want to know what's in the first column of the first row of Apple's mail, you have to use the following syntax:

```
value of text field 1 of row 1 of table 1 ¬
    of scroll area 1 of splitter group 1 of group 1 of window 1
```

So if you don't yet own UI Browser, go to www.prefab.com and download a demo. The version I'm using is 1.2, and it works with Panther.

19

The UI Browser interface

Using UI Browser is very simple. You start by picking the application whose interface you want to script from the Target pop-up menu. This pop-up menu shows all open applications and also allows you to choose an application.

Figure 19-5 shows UI Browser with the Target menu exposed.

Once you choose an application, the main browser view shows you the main set of UI elements. These usually are the menu bar and the main open windows.

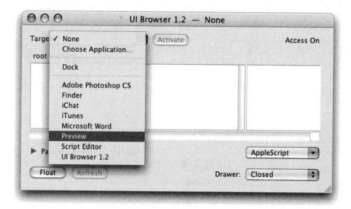

Figure 19-5. UI Browser with the Target menu exposed

In our first UI exercise, we will create a search script for Preview. We will first look at a simple script that enters a search string into the search field. Then, we will develop it further to catalog the search results it will pick right off of the interface.

Using UI Browser

We will start by opening a text PDF file with Preview. Try looking through the developer documentation for one.

Next, we choose Preview from the Target menu. If you already have, you may want to refresh your screen. I also expanded the *path to element* disclosure triangle to show the path.

Next, click the window element in the first browser block, and continue clicking the objects listed in the subsequent browser sections. If you check the very helpful Highlight check box, UI Browser will literally highlight the interface element with a yellow rectangle.

After we select the window, we click drawer 1, then text field 1. This is the search text field. We need to use the *keystroke* command to type something into that field.

To do that, we first need a *tell* block wrapper.

In UI Browser, choose Tell Block Wrapper from the AppleScript menu. Then, copy and paste the result in a new script window in Script Editor.

> *You can set the UI Browser preferences to automatically copy the script and/or place it in Script Editor for you.*

Although the *tell* block we get from UI Browser verifies that UI scripting is turned on, I will narrow it down to the bare script.

Targeting processes

In UI scripting we don't tell applications what to do. Instead, everything we do happens under the System Events application. We tell different processes of System Events what to do. Following is a typical *tell* block to start off a UI scripting script:

Script 19-3

```
tell application "Preview" to activate
tell application "System Events"
    tell application process "Preview"
        -- place script statements here,
    end tell
end tell
```

Targeting the UI element

After you clicked the last text field element, choose from the AppleScript pop-up menu set value of selected element. This will give you the following script line:

```
set value of text field 1 of drawer 1 of window "file name .pdf" to ¬
"<string>"
```

We will copy this line into our script, but since we will work more with this window, let's separate it and give it its own *tell* block, like this:

```
tell window 1
    set value of text field 1 of drawer 1 to "iPod"
end tell
```

Notice that I also switched the search string to a word I knew existed.

Now, we need to click the Search button. In the UI, the Search button is found inside the text field, and therefore will be shown in UI Browser in the browser column to the right of the text field, as shown in Figure 19-6.

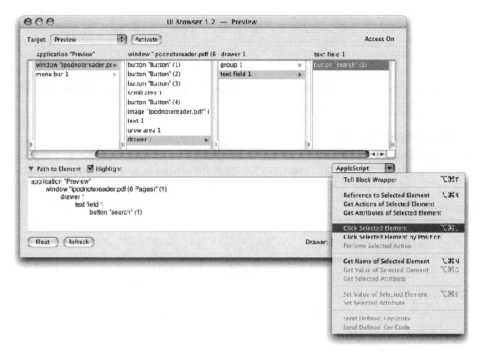

Figure 19-6. UI Browser's main browser with the Search button element selected

Following is our script so far, after we pasted the new *click* line into it and worked out the window's *tell* block:

Script 19-4

```
tell application "Preview" to activate
tell application "System Events"
    tell application process "Preview"
        tell window 1
            set value of text field 1 of drawer 1 to "iPod"
            click button "search" of text field 1 of drawer 1
        end tell
    end tell
end tell
```

This script is supposed to find the occurrence of the word "iPod" in the front Preview document.

Getting fancy with table data

As in many other applications, Preview makes a use of a table. The table we're interested in is the one containing the search results.

After digging a bit with UI Browser, we discover that the table object is

```
table 1 of scroll area 1 of group 1 of drawer 1
```

and that it has rows, and every row has two text fields.

If we just want a list of pages the text appears in, we can use the following line:

```
value of text field 1 of every row of table 1 ¬
of scroll area 1 of group 1 of drawer 1
```

You could also go row by row and validate the text as you go.

The Services menu

One of the nice features that OS X introduced is the Services menu. The Services menu is actually a submenu off of the Application menu. It allows software vendors to make their utilities available from within any application. You can see the Services submenu in Figure 19-7.

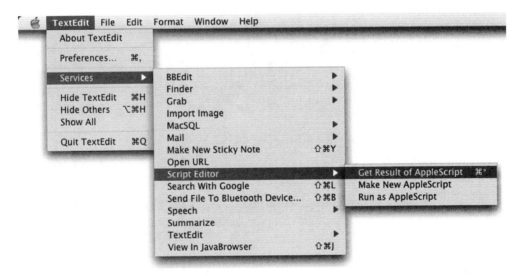

Figure 19-7. The Services menu with the Script Editor options shown

Some great services are Mail's Send Selection service, Search with Google service, and one of my favorites, Script Editor's three available services.

The services that get installed with Apple's Script Editor are Get Result of AppleScript, Make New AppleScript, and Run as AppleScript.

These services mean that you can highlight any text from an application that supports services, and try to perform the action you chose.

To try it, open TextEdit, type 12 * 7, highlight it, and choose Services → Script Editor → Get Result of AppleScript. This will replace the selected text with the result.

If you choose Make New Script, the text you highlighted becomes a new Script Editor script.

Digital hub actions

Digital hub actions can be set in the CDs & DVDs pane of System Preferences. The idea is that you can specify a script (or other action) that will be executed when different kinds of CDs are inserted into the Mac. This feature can be invaluable to people in the imaging, video, and graphics fields that have to deal with CD or DVD media on a regular basis. For instance, a script can be set to open a picture CD and process all the pictures, etc.

Example scripts can be found at www.apple.com/applescript/digitalhub/.

Figure 19-8 shows the CDs & DVDs pane of System Preferences.

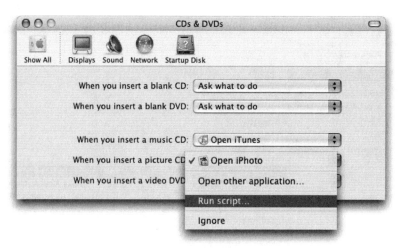

Figure 19-8. The CDs & DVDs pane of System Preferences

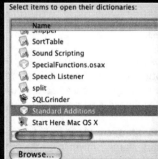

Select items to open their dictionaries:

Name
Snipper
SortTable
Sound Scripting
SpecialFunctions.osax
Speech Listener
split
SQLGrinder
Standard Additions
Start Here Mac OS X

Browse...

Please make your selection:

Al
Bill
Sara

Cancel   OK

Scripting additions, also referred to as OSAX (or osax), their technical term, are special little programs that add functionality to AppleScript. Usually written in a programming language such as C++, scripting additions take a bit more programming experience than possessed by the average scripter.

> *The acronym OSAX comes from the creator type and now, in Mac OS X, the file extension of a scripting addition, which is* .osax. *It stands for Open Scripting Architecture eXtension.*

There are three main reasons to get scripting additions: they may make your scripts run faster, they may make your development cycle shorter, and they may allow you to do things that vanilla AppleScript simply can't.

While there are those mega-additions that are widely used, most scripting additions are created by people who simply need their functionality and know how to create them. Many scripting additions are available as free downloads. You can find most, if not all, of them on www.macscripter.net and www.osax.com.

Scripting additions and the AppleScript language

When scripting scriptable applications, any command that is defined in the application's dictionary can only be compiled correctly and executed from inside that application's *tell* block:

```
open file "Macintosh HD:Jobs:1234.indd"
tell application "InDesign CS"
    open file "Macintosh HD:Jobs:1234.indd"
end tell
```

In the preceding script, since the first *open* statement is outside of the *tell* block, it will not run as intended.

The commands and classes defined in scripting additions, on the other hand, become integrated into your AppleScript scripts in a more natural way. You can script for a long time and not know that certain commands you use are not a part of AppleScript, but rather defined in the Standard Additions dictionary.

The fact that scripting additions lack a *tell* block forces developers to use the same command and class name universe with other scripting addition developers, and with AppleScript itself.

Scripting additions and Mac OS X

While scripting additions are supported by AppleScript shipped with Mac OS X, not many developers upgraded their additions. This phenomenon can be explained based on several factors.

One of these factors is the introduction of UNIX shell scripting in Mac OS X in general and shell scripting integration with AppleScript using the *do shell script* command. Much of the functionality that scripters used to rely on additions for is now available freely with different shell commands, which can be invoked right from AppleScript. Shell commands are fast, relatively easy to master, and are prolific in the variety of commands they offer.

Another contributing factor to the slow coming of new additions was that AppleScript was very slow under OS 9, making scripting additions very important. Using a scripting addition command instead of writing a vanilla AppleScript handler that will do the same thing could speed up execution by seconds or even minutes. Nowadays, however, AppleScript (and the Mac it runs on) is so fast that speed is not really an issue.

Installing scripting additions

Scripting additions simply need to reside in a ScriptingAdditions folder in one of your Mac's three domains in order to work. More specifically, these folders are as follows:

- System domain, to which you don't have write access: /System/Library/ScriptingAdditions/.
- Local domain, which makes a scripting addition available to all users: /Library/ScriptingAdditions/.
- And finally, the user domain, which is where you can place scripting additions that will be available to you only: /User/Library/ScriptingAdditions.

Note that the ScriptingAdditions folder in the user domain may have to be created by you. The name of the folder has no space between the two words.

The icon of scripting additions is an unmistakable Lego cube, shown here:

Standard Additions

Standard Additions are a collection of scripting additions that come preinstalled with AppleScript. They can be found in the system's domain ScriptingAdditions folder: /System/Library/ScriptingAdditions/StandardAdditions.osax/.

The commands in Standard Additions vary. Their collective theme is to extend scriptability to areas that AppleScript doesn't touch and aren't covered by the Finder or System Events dictionaries.

You can see the definitions of the commands and classes used in Standard Additions by selecting Open Dictionary from the File menu in Script Editor, and choosing Standard Additions from the list, as shown in Figure 20-1.

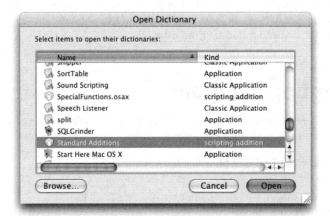

Figure 20-1.
Choose Standard Additions from the application list in the Open Dictionary dialog box.

In this section I will list the Standard Additions along with a short description, but will not get into a detailed explanation. The reason is that the book is structured around usability, not around the programming language structure. Therefore, the full explanation of each command in every one of the Standard Additions can be found in the appropriate part of the book.

Standard Addition commands are divided into nine suites based on functionality: user interaction, file commands, string commands, clipboard commands, file read/write, scripting commands, miscellaneous commands, folder actions, and Internet suite.

Following is the description of the Standard Additions that come preinstalled with every Mac, organized by suite.

User interaction

Some of the scripting additions that are described next are also explained in detail in Chapter 12, which discusses user interaction.

beep

Sounds a beep or a number of beeps.

```
beep 3
```

choose application

Displays the Choose Application dialog box shown in Figure 20-1. Returns either the name of the application or a path to it.

```
set application_path to choose application as alias
--> alias "Macintosh HD:Applications:Adobe InDesign CS:InDesign
CS.app:"
```

choose color

Displays the Choose Color panel. After the user chooses a color, the command returns a list of three integers specifying the 16-bit color values in red, green, and blue.

The following script will start with a default white color and return red:

```
set color_specs to choose color default color {65535, 65535, 65535}
--> {65535, 0, 0}
```

Figure 20-2 shows the Colors dialog box displayed during the execution of the *choose color* command.

Figure 20-2. The Colors dialog box shown during the execution of the *choose color* command

choose file

Displays the Open dialog box and allows the user to choose a file. The script can restrict the user to choosing files that are of specific file types. The result is either an alias or a string. Figure 20-3 shows the Choose a File dialog box displayed by the following script line:

```
set the_alias to choose file without invisibles
-->alias "Macintosh HD:test.xml"
```

Figure 20-3. The Choose a File dialog box

choose file name

Displays the Save dialog box. This command allows you to choose a location and specify a file name. It works for choosing a file that you want your script to create. Figure 20-4 shows the Choose File Name dialog box displayed by the following script line:

```
set the_alias to choose file name with prompt "Save..."
-->file "Macintosh HD:Users:hanaan:Desktop:job report.txt"
```

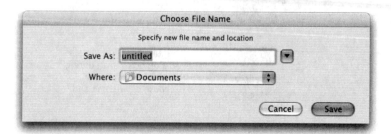

Figure 20-4. The Choose File Name dialog box

choose folder

Much like *choose file*, but will only allow the user to choose a folder.

choose from list

Displays a simple dialog box containing items from a list. The user can then choose no items or one or more items, based on different parameters. Following is a script line that shows the dialog box in Figure 20-5.

```
set chosen_name to choose from list {"Al", "Bill", "Sara"}
-->{"Al"}
```

Figure 20-5. The choose from list dialog box

choose URL

The *choose URL* command allows the user to choose a URL from Apple's URL browser. Can be used with the *mount volume* command.

delay

Delays the script by the specified number of seconds.

display dialog

Who knew that the good old *display dialog* command isn't a part of AppleScript, but rather defined in the Standard Additions?

class dialog reply

A record containing the result of the *display dialog* command. May contain information about the buttons returned from a dialog box, the text user typed in, or whether the dialog box gave up or not.

say

Speaks any text you provide using any one of Apple's built-in speech voices.

Note that the voice names are case sensitive.

File commands

Some of the file-related scripting additions shown here are described in detail in Chapter 13, which is dedicated to working with files.

info for

The *info for* command is very useful for getting information about files, folders, disks, and any other Finder item in your system.

The command will return the *file information* class record containing the file's name, type, creator, name extension, size, creation, modification dates, and more.

list disks

Returns a list of the currently mounted disks.

list folder

Lists the names of all items in a folder. The list may or may not contain invisible files.

```
set my_item_list to list folder
```

mount volume

This command is loved by Mac administrators everywhere! It allows you to mount a volume with or without a user name and password. If you don't provide login information, you will be prompted to enter it every time.

```
mount volume ¬
"afp://user_name:pass_word@server_name/volume_name/"
```

path to

The *path to* command is useful for getting the path to one of many special folders on your Mac.

Not only can you get the path to that specific folder, but when possible, the command will also create one if it doesn't exist.

When you use the *path to* command, you need to also specify the folder's domain, for instance, when you want the path to the Fonts folder, you have to decide if it's the Fonts folder in your Users folder, in the system, or in the local drive's Library folder. Here's how it works:

```
path to fonts folder from user domain
--> alias "Macintosh HD:Users:hanaan:Library:Fonts:"
path to fonts folder from local domain
--> alias "Macintosh HD:Library:Fonts:"
path to fonts folder from system domain
--> alias "Macintosh HD:System:Library:Fonts:"
```

Following are the other paths to command parameter values:

application support	modem scripts	trash
applications folder	movies folder	users folder
desktop	music folder	utilities folder
desktop pictures	pictures folder	voices
folder	preferences	apple menu
documents folder	printer descriptions	control panels
favorites folder	public folder	control strip
folder action	scripting additions	modules
scripts	scripts folder	extensions
fonts	shared documents	launcher items
frontmost	shared libraries	folder
application	sites folder	printer drivers
help	startup disk	printmonitor
home folder	startup items	shutdown folder
internet plugins	system folder	speakable items
keychain folder	system preferences	stationery
library folder	temporary items	

Class file information

This class includes the specifications of the file information record you get when you use the *path to* command.

Example:

```
info for alias "Macintosh HD:Users:hanaan:Desktop:results.doc"
--> {name:"results-all-1.doc", creation date:date "Tuesday, March 9, ¬
2004 2:06:41 PM", modification date:date "Tuesday, March 9, 2004 ¬
2:06:41 PM", icon position:
{0, 0}, size:2.71134E+5, folder:false, alias:false, ¬
name extension:"doc",
extension hidden:false, visible:true, package folder:false, ¬
file type:"W8BN",
file creator:"MSWD", displayed name:"results-all-1.doc", ¬
default application:
alias "Macintosh HD:Applications:Microsoft Office X:Microsoft Word", ¬
kind:
"Microsoft Word document", locked:false, busy status:false, short ¬
version:"",
long version:""}
```

String commands

Some of the file-related scripting additions shown here are described in detail in Chapter 3, which is dedicated to working with text.

ASCII character

Returns the character associated with the ASCII code you provided. Example:

```
ascii character 38
--> "&"
```

ascii number

The opposite of *ascii character*, the *ascii number* command takes a single character as an argument and returns the ASCII number associated with that character.

The following line of script will return the ASCII number of the tab character.

```
ascii number tab
--> 9
```

offset

The *offset* command takes two strings as parameters. It returns the position of the second string in the first string.

```
offset of "far" in "how far is it"
--> 5
```

The string "far" starts at the fifth character of the string "how far is it".

summarize

Returns a summary of a long string, using a specified number of sentences. Can also summarize a text file.

```
summarize file "MacHD:My Life Story.txt" in 1
```

Clipboard commands

Some of the file-related scripting additions shown here are described in Chapter 14 in detail, which is dedicated to working with the clipboard.

set the clipboard

Sets the content of the clipboard to anything a variable can hold. Here are a couple of examples:

```
set the clipboard to "Some text"
set the clipboard to (read file "Macintosh HD:Picture 1.pdf")
```

the clipboard

Returns the contents of the clipboard.

clipboard info

Returns information about the clipboard. The result can be quite cryptic at times.

The following example shows that the clipboard contains a styled string of six characters:

```
clipboard info
--> {{scrap styles, 22}, {string, 6}}
```

File read/write

Some of the file-related scripting additions shown here are described in detail in Chapter 13, which is dedicated to working with files.

open for access

Opens a file for access to reading it or for writing to it. This command returns an integer that is a reference to the file. That integer can then be used with the five other file commands.

You can open for access files that do not exist yet, which will in turn create the file for you.

```
open for access file "Macintosh HD:test.xml"
--> 1568
```

The integer result is a sequential number generated by the system. It does not refer to the file after the script is through executing.

If you want to write to a file, use this command:

```
open for access file "Macintosh HD:my text.txt"
```

close access

After you opened a file for access, you should close it back up.

```
close access file "Macintosh HD:my text.txt"
```

Or, if you have the associated integer returned by the *open for access* command, you could also use it as a parameter.

```
set file_reference to open for access file "Macintosh HD:test.xml"
set the_text to read file_reference
close access file_reference
```

read

As seen previously, the *read* command reads the content of any file to a variable.

write

Writes any data to a file. In order to use this command, you must open the file for access with write permission. The following script writes the contents of the clipboard to a file:

```
Set the_path to "Macintosh HD:clipboard"
set file_reference to open for access ¬
    file the_path with write permission
write (the clipboard) to file_reference
close access file_reference
```

get eof

EOF is the acronym for end of file. The *get eof* command returns the number of bytes in the specified file.

```
get eof file "Macintosh HD:test.xml"
--> 524
```

set eof

Sets the end of file of a file. This command can wipe out the contents of a file by setting the EOF to zero:

```
set eof file "Macintosh HD:test.xml" to 0
```

Scripting commands

Some of the file-related scripting additions shown here are described in detail in Chapter 18, which is dedicated to working with script objects.

load script

Loads a compiled script from a script file to memory.

store script

Stores a script in a file as compiled script.

run script

Executes a string as an AppleScript.

```
run script "5+5"
--> 10
```

scripting components

Returns the scripting components installed on your Mac.

```
scripting components
--> {"JavaScript", "AppleScript Debugger", "AppleScript"}
```

Miscellaneous commands

Some of the file-related scripting additions shown here are described in detail other chapters.

current date

Returns the current date and time in AppleScript's date format. This command likes to be wrapped in parentheses when used in a statement.

```
Set now to (current date)
--> date "Wednesday, March 10, 2004 7:25:27 AM"
```

set volume

Sets your Mac's volume to a value from 0 to 7.

```
set volume 0
```

system attribute

Used by experienced programmers to call what is known as the Gestalt command. The command takes a selector code that is usually a four-character code and an optional integer, and returns the corresponding piece of information regarding the system's hardware and software.

For example, to get the version of Mac OS X that is running on your computer, use this script statement:

```
system attribute "sysv"
```

The resulting value will be the ten-based number 4147. That number translates into the hexadecimal number 00001033, which indicates that the current system version is 10.3.3.

There are many resources that list the different descriptors and the results they return.

time to GMT

Returns the number of hours the current location is from Greenwich mean time. The result is in seconds, of course.

```
time to GMT
-->-18000
(time to GMT) / hours
-->-5.0
```

random number

Returns a random number. You can specify a range, or get the default result, which is a random number between 1 and 0.

```
random number
--> 0.918785996622
random number from 1 to 100
--> 39
```

round

Rounds a given real value.

```
round 5.2 rounding up
--> 6
round 5.2 rounding as taught in school
--> 5
```

do shell script

Performs a UNIX shell script. One of the new commands with the most explosive use, the *do shell script* command gives you unparalleled access to commands available in the UNIX operating system under the Mac OS X hood.

For instance, the shell script command *wc* returns the number of lines, words, and bytes (characters) in a text file. Here's how we can use this functionality from AppleScript:

```
do shell script " wc /some_file.txt"
--> "      66      158     1448 / some_file.txt"
```

It is your responsibility to parse the test, however.

```
copy (words 1 thru 3 of result) to {line_count, word_count,
character_count}
--> {"66", "158", "1448"}
```

Ah, this is better . . .

Still think that *do shell script* is just for geeks? Well, you may be right, but now you may also want to become one . . .

class: POSIX file

This command works upon compiling when you give it a literal path to a file. It converts a UNIX path into an AppleScript file reference for that same file.

Folder actions

The folder action commands are a part of the Standard Additions, but they are not really commands—they are event handlers used with AppleScript's folder actions feature.

To learn more, see Chapter 19.

opening folder

The event that is executed when the folder is opened.

closing folder window for

The event that is executed when the folder is closed.

moving folder window for

The event that is executed when the folder window is moved.

adding folder items to

The event that is executed when an item or items are added to the folder.

removing folder items from

The event that is executed when an item or items are removed from the folder.

Internet suite

The Internet suite of commands is a collection of Internet-related commands.

open location

Opens a URL with the default web browser.

```
open location "http://www.apple.com"
```

handle CGI request

This command allows you to use AppleScript to create CGIs that can run with Mac OS X web server.

Internet-related classes

There are four Internet-related classes that allow you to break down various Internet address types into components.

The first is the *URL* class.

```
set my_url to "http://www.apple.com" as URL
--> {class:URL, scheme:http URL, path:"http://www.apple.com", ¬
host:{class:Internet address, DNS form:"www.apple.com", port:80}}
```

The other three are the *Internet address* class, *Web page* class, and *FTP item* class.

Third-party scripting additions

Until now we looked at the scripting additions that are put out by Apple and are yours for free. In this section we will look at some third-party scripting additions. Although there are many third-party scripting additions on the market, only a handful of them ever got upgraded to work with OS X. Nevertheless, the ones that did make the transition are worth looking over.

Where to find third-party scripting additions

The one-stop place to shop (or more likely, browse) for scripting additions is MacScripter.net (www.macscripter.net, or www.osax.com). The folks at MacScripter.net are mostly volunteers who put a good bit of effort into a well-organized and fresh AppleScript website. Among other things, they boast the most complete and up-to-date searchable collection of scripting additions.

Following are some of the scripting additions that made it to OS X and are worth looking at.

ACME Script Widgets

ACME Script Widgets by ACME Technologies (www.acmetech.com) has been around for over ten years, and is one of the most successful commercial scripting additions out there.

ACME Script Widgets is known for its sorting, string replacement, and list manipulation commands.

Following is a brief description of some of the commands included with ACME Script Widgets.

ACME replace

ACME replace makes string replacement a snap. While it is not that difficult to create your own text-replacement handler using AppleScript, this command can do it for you faster and with some additional features. Here's a simple example of the *ACME replace* command:

```
Acme replace "Boston" in "Go to Boston by train" with "New York"
--> "Go to New York by train"
```

Using different parameters you can choose whether to replace all occurrences and whether the search is case sensitive or not.

change case

If you need to change the case of text in your scripts on a regular basis, this command just might be worth the price of admission. The *change case* command allows you to change the case of text in a string to uppercase, lowercase, title case, sentence case, or to toggle the current case of each letter.

```
change case of "THAT DAMN CAPS-LOCK KEY DID IT AGAIN." to lower
--> "that damn caps-lock key did it again."
```

Satimage

Satimage is a French company that is responsible for the development of SMILE, the free AppleScript script editor. Another thing Satimage developed and keeps on improving is a great set of commands bundled in the Satimage scripting additions.

My favorite two commands in the Satimage collection are the *find text* and *format* commands.

find text

What separates *find text* in Satimage from anything you could easily do yourself is the use of regular expressions. Sure, we can create a handler that replaces one word with another, but regular expressions take text replacement to a whole other level.

You can read more about it in Chapter 28.

format

The *format* command can also save you a lot of frustration in formatting numbers. You can use it to format numbers and return them as strings with the right number of decimal places, commas, parentheses, etc.

```
format 1234.5678 into "#,###.00"
"1,234.57"
```

ScriptDB

ScriptDB is a scripting addition written from scratch for OS X. It is put out by Custom Flow Solutions (www.customflowsolutions.com), which is a company operated by yours truly.

ScriptDB's main goal was to give scripters a set of built-in database commands and tools. The scripting addition doesn't use a database file to maintain the data, but rather keeps the whole database in memory.

The purpose of such a database is to assist you in manipulating data in a table-like structure during script execution.

As scripters, we constantly make lists, some of them synchronized with each other to form sorts of tables, and then we loop through to get the data we need out of them. ScriptDB allows you to take these lists, or data from text files or FileMaker Pro XML files, and manage them like a database.

See Chapter 26 for more about ScriptDB.

Missing additions and garbled scripts

Anytime you're counting on a third-party addition, you should also count on the day that you (or someone else) will open the script on a Mac that doesn't have those scripting additions installed.

In that case, needless to say, the script will error out on the lines that rely on the scripting addition's commands. Your script will compile; however, instead of the scripting addition commands you will see the Apple Event four-letter codes.

If it's important to you not to get an error in these cases, you can check to see if the scripting addition is installed. You can do that by looking for it in the various scripting addition folders in the system. You can do that using the scripting additions folder object of the domain object defined in the System Events dictionary.

Script 20-1

```
on is_sa_installed(sa_name)
    set sa_installed to false
    tell application "System Events"
        set sa_folder_list to scripting additions folder of every domain
        repeat with the_sa_folder in sa_folder_list
            try-- the_sa_folder may be missing value...
                if exists (file sa_name of the_sa_folder) then
                    set sa_installed to true
                    exit repeat
                end if
            end try
        end repeat
    end tell
end is_sa_installed
```

Scripting additions and script portability

Just as we like to travel light, so do our scripts. They just don't like to have too many strings attached. If you use scripting additions in your script, installing your script may not be as easy as copying it over anymore. Now, if the scripting addition is not available on the Mac your script is trying to run on, the script will return an error when it gets to the line where a command from that scripting addition is used.

This situation became a bit more manageable in Panther with the introduction of script bundles. With script bundles, you can save your script as a bundle that can contain other files such as scripting additions. This way, you can start the script by installing a scripting addition that is embedded into the actual script package.

Let's pretend that you need to create a script application that makes a use of the ScriptDB scripting addition.

Start a new script and type

```
display dialog "test"
```

Now, save the script as an application bundle, as shown in Figure 20-6.

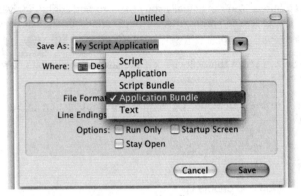

Figure 20-6. Saving a script as a bundle

After the script is saved, go to the Finder and locate it. *CONTROL*-click it and choose Show Package Contents, as shown in Figure 20-7.

Figure 20-7. Choose Show Package Contents from the contextual menu.

Figure 20-8 shows the contents of the package.

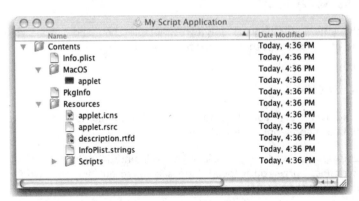

Figure 20-8. The contents of the package

The file `main.scpt` in the `Scripts` folder is your compiled script.

Back to scripting additions. You can actually copy the scripting addition (given your license allows you to) to the Resources folder of your application bundle, and it will be distributed with your script application.

What you need now is a script that will check if the scripting addition is already installed, and if not, install it.

First, test the *path to me* command. Open the script application in Script Editor and change the script to

```
set my_path to path to me as string
display dialog my_path
```

Now save the application and double-click it.

The dialog box should show you that the path to the application actually looks like a path to a folder.

Other faceless scriptable utilities

Another method of adding functionality to AppleScript is by using faceless scriptable applications. These applications are similar to scripting additions in their functionality. The main differences are that these applications can reside anywhere on your hard disk, and to use their commands, you have to refer to them using a proper *tell* block.

In this section we will explore three such faceless applications. All three are not only free, but come preinstalled with every Mac, so you don't run a risk that someone won't have them installed.

URL Access scripting

Although this little application has only two scriptable commands, it is a great one! It allows you to use AppleScript to download files from the Internet.

ColorSync scripting

If you use ColorSync on a regular basis to assign profiles to images or detect profiles, you may want to take a good look at this little utility.

In the Library/Scripts/ColorSync folder you will find 18 scripts that make use of ColorSync scripting. I urge you to open them and figure out how they work (it is a bit beyond the scope of the book).

Image Event scripting

Image Event scripting is another scriptable utility that has only a handful of commands and classes, but can be invaluable when you don't want to use a full-blown application such as Photoshop or Image Converter to perform basic operations such as rotate, flip, and resize.

One of the things Image Events is great for is not changing images, but rather getting information from images. You can open a file and then use the properties in the *image* class to get that image's bit depth, resolution, size, color space, file type, and more. This can prove invaluable in publishing workflows.

The following script changes the comment of a chosen file into a description of the image containing resolution, file type, bit depth, etc.

Script 20-2

```
1. set image_file_path to (choose file) as string
2. tell application "Image Events"
3.    try
4.        set my_image to open file image_file_path
5.    on error
6.        display dialog "The file you picked couldn't be analyzed"
7.        return
8.    end try
9.    tell my_image
10.       copy dimensions to {the_width, the_height}
11.       set file_type to file type
12.       set color_space to color space
13.       set bit_depth to bit depth
14.       set res to resolution
15.    end tell
16. end tell
17. set the_comment to "Image information:" & return & ¬
18.    "File type: " & file_type & return & ¬
19.    "Width: " & the_width & ", height: " & the_height & return & ¬
20.    "Resolution: " & res & return & ¬
21.    "Color space: " & color_space & return & ¬
22.    "Bit depth: " & bit_depth as string
23. tell application "Finder"
24.    set comment of file image_file_path to the_comment
25. end tell
```

The main things to notice in the preceding script is that the *open* command returns a document reference. After that, we can get information from that document by referring to its properties.

THE FUNDAMENTALS OF
AUTOMATING APPLICATIONS

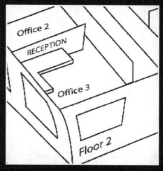

One point I have made again and again throughout the book is that the AppleScript language is pretty small on its own. It has merely five commands and a handful of objects and properties. What gives life and substance to AppleScript is the scriptability of various applications and scripting additions.

As you become an experienced scripter, you will learn specific statements that relate to specific applications that you need to script. Also you will learn the common structure applications share, which will help you tackle new scriptable applications.

In this chapter, we will look at how to attack a new application you want to start scripting. We will start with the structures of objects, elements, commands, and parameters, and move on to understanding dictionaries and using the *whose* clause.

Scripting dictionary basics

Every scriptable application has a scripting dictionary that exposes all of the application's commands and classes available for use with AppleScript. To view an application's dictionary, go to the Script Editor application and choose File → Open Dictionary. Then, choose the application whose dictionary you want to open and click Open.

You can also drop the application's icon over the icon of the Script Editor application. These two methods also work with Script Debugger.

The nicest way, however, to keep track of your scriptable applications and their dictionaries is by using the new Library window in Script Editor 2.0 (or later). The Library palette, shown in Figure 21-1, lists scriptable applications whose dictionaries you like to view often.

Figure 21-1. The Library window

You can add applications to the Library window with the + (plus) button and open an application's dictionary with the third button whose icon looks like books on a shelf.

A similar feature has existed long before in Late Night Software's Script Debugger.

In any means shown previously, you can open scripting dictionaries of both applications and scripting additions.

Figure 21-2 shows the dictionary for FileMaker Pro.

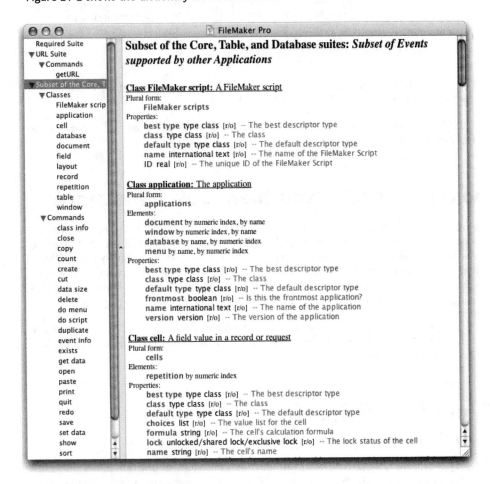

Figure 21-2. The dictionary for FileMaker Pro

While a scripting dictionary is an invaluable source of information, you still need additional documentation in order to script a given application. This is because while the dictionary lists all of the application's related commands and classes (object types), it doesn't explain the connection between them. For instance, while the iTunes dictionary will reveal the *Make* command and the *Track* class, you still can't use AppleScript to create a track—for that you need a recording studio.

Nevertheless, whenever you get any new application, the first thing you do is drop it on the Script Editor (or Script Debugger) icon to see if it is scriptable. Figure 21-3 shows the disappointing dialog box you get when the application you just got is not scriptable.

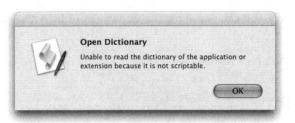

Figure 21-3.
The dialog box you get when you try to open the dictionary of a nonscriptable application

The Script Editor dictionary viewer window clearly separates between classes and commands. Classes are in effect the objects we work with.

In the following sections we explore commands and classes and the way they appear in the application dictionary.

Look, look again, and then look some more

While companies that put out scriptable applications try to make the commands and property names as descriptive as possible, sometimes the names can be a bit misleading. The property or command, despite having a funny name, can be exactly what will fill in that gap in your script. Before searching the Web or posting messages on Apple's AppleScript Users list in search of an answer, explore the dictionary. Any property or command that appears to not have any obvious purpose might be the one you need.

Try to teach yourself a new property or command every week by reading the dictionary, looking up information from the Net, and reading the scripting reference for that application. Doing this will help you keep moving forward.

Things (objects) and things to do (commands)

An application's scriptability is made out of two realms: objects and commands. Commands are generally things you tell the application to do, and objects are the things that will change in the application after you give certain commands.

For instance, the *open* command is designed to open a document in the application. After it runs successfully, a new instance of the object of class *document* is available. This object is an instance of the class *document*, it has all the *document* class properties, and as you are aware, you can have multiple such objects. We'll look at objects, classes, and properties in the section ahead.

The object model

A well-thought-out object model in an application is what separates applications with good AppleScript support and not-so-good AppleScript support. Even though most applications have some sort of a built-in object model, it takes a good amount of effort on the behalf of the development team to translate this object model into an AppleScript object model.

While different applications have different types of objects (the Finder has files and folders, InDesign has pages and text frames, etc.), most applications' object models follow the same structure.

To understand this structure, imagine a large office building. The building is divided into floors, each floor into offices, and an office may have desks and people in it. Every object has a specific address that anyone in the building can use to find it. For instance, the receptionist's desk can be found in the third office of the front office row on the second floor. The office also has a name: "Reception". So you could say, "the reception office on the second floor." The diagram in Figure 21-4 can help you visualize it.

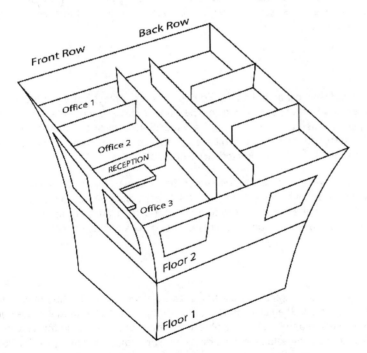

Figure 21-4. The office building described as an object model

Notice that we used both the numerical position of the desk and its name to identify it. Locating objects in order to script them is the first order of the day.

Scriptable applications use a similar method of addressing their objects: the Finder has disks that can contain files and folders. Folders can have files or more folders. In InDesign, we have a document that contains pages. The pages may contain, among other things, text frames that can contain words and characters. In FileMaker we have a database that can have tables with fields and records. Addressing the objects in these applications is also similar to our building example: in the Finder we can refer to the file `report.txt` in the third folder of the disk Server; in InDesign we can refer to the fifth text frame on page 2 of the document `Annual Report.indd`, and in FileMaker we can talk to cell Last Name of record 5 of table Contact of database 1. All are different types of objects, but the object model is pretty much the same.

On top of addressing, each object in an application has three other sides to it. An object is made up using the DNA of a specific class; an object can have properties that describe the object such as size, name, etc.; and an object can have elements. Elements are the objects that the object in question contains.

In scripting dictionaries, classes (object definitions) are listed separately from commands, and they are also structured a bit differently.

Every class shows a little description followed by the list of other classes that may be an element (see the "Elements" section later in this chapter). The list of elements is followed by a list of properties.

Classes

A class is what defines how an object should behave. Every object is the product of a class. In nature, we are all objects derived from the *human* class. When we are born, we get human traits such as an upright posture and a disposition towards talking too much. When you create an object, say, a document in InDesign, this document is an instance of the document class and it takes all its characteristics from that class.

Classes can also have subclasses. In the Finder, for instance, there's a super class called "item". This *item* class has subclasses such as *files*, *folders*, and *disks*. Each one of these subclasses inherits all of the traits of the *item* class, and then adds some on its own. For instance, a *file* class has a file type property but the *folder* subclass doesn't.

Properties

Properties are the object's traits. If your car was an object in the application of your life, its properties would include the car's color, manufacturing year, make, model, plate number, etc. Unlike elements in an object, every object may have only one value for a given property, even though that one value can be a list or a record containing many values. Your car can't have more than one plate number or multiple model names (this is a Toyota Camry, and . . . Celica).

An InDesign image object's properties may include the rotation angle, resolutions, and bounds, while a file on the Finder may have properties such as the size, creation date, and icon position.

The more properties listed in dictionary under the different classes, the better the scripting support is. Every listed property stands for another feature you can script in this application. In InDesign CS, for example, the *application* class and *document* class have combined over 100 properties, while FileMaker lists about 13. Granted these are different applications, but when InDesign was designed, there was a deliberate attempt to make it the most scriptable application it can be, which makes it a favorite among scripters.

Following is a list of properties of the *playlist* class as specified in the iTunes dictionary:

```
duration  integer  [r/o]  -- the total length of all songs (in seconds)
index  integer  [r/o]  -- the index of the playlist in internal
                          -- application order
name  Unicode text  -- the name of the playlist
shuffle  boolean  -- play the songs in this playlist in random order?
size  double integer  [r/o]  -- the total size of all songs (in bytes)
song repeat  off/one/all  -- playback repeat mode
time  Unicode text  [r/o]  -- the length of all songs in MM:SS format
visible  boolean  [r/o]  -- is this playlist visible in the Source
                            -- list?
```

Notice that each property in the list represents a true attribute of an iTune playlist.

Also notice that the name of each property is followed by the expected value type (shown in italics). That value type specification is helpful, but is not always a complete disclosure of all data types or values expected. Sometimes figuring out the property value takes some investigation. The best way to figure out the value of a particular property is to investigate an existing object. Whether it's a folder in the Finder, an image document in Photoshop, or a track in iTunes, open it, make it active, and ask to see its properties. The *properties* property will return, in most cases, a record with all of the properties of a given object. Examining the *properties* property of an object can prove to be an endless source of education. You can compare the result with the dictionary to learn even more about the scriptability of a particular object.

The best way to explore an object's properties (and elements, for that matter) is by using Late Night Software Script Debugger's Explorer window shown in Figure 21-5. The difference between the Explorer window and the dictionary is that while the dictionary shows classes, which are object prototypes, the Explorer window shows actual objects that currently exist in the application along with their properties, property values, and elements.

21

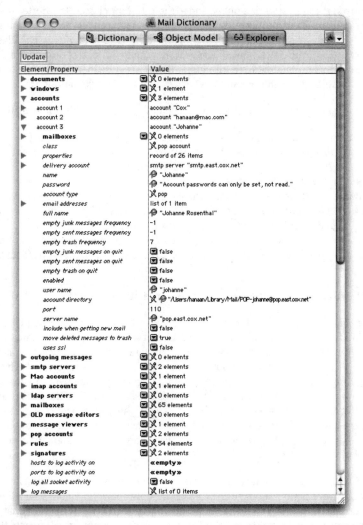

Figure 21-5. Late Night Software's Script Debugger has an Explorer window, which allows you to explore objects, properties, and object elements in an expandable outline view. This window is one of the many features that make Script Debugger worth the price.

Let's take another look at the properties list shown previously. Some properties have [r/o] after them, for example:

```
duration  integer  [r/o]  -- the total length of all songs (in seconds)
```

The r/o stands for read only, and indicates that the value of the property can only be read, not set. In some situations, it is the software developer's discretion—the developer simply decided that you shouldn't be able to change that specific property, and usually for a good reason. For instance, creation and modification dates are read only, or in applications dealing with images, the *image size* property is read only since you can't simply change the byte size of an image. Other times, the property simply doesn't lend itself to your manipulation, like the *duration* property shown previously; will changing the duration property of a playlist really change the length of time it takes to play the songs?

Another typical type of property value is *song repeat*.

```
song repeat  off/one/all  -- playback repeat mode
```

Notice that the possible values can be *off*, *one*, or *all*. These are not strings but rather special application code words. You probably want to avoid using these words as subroutine or variable identifiers. Many application dictionaries make use of special values such as these, so look out for them.

Working with properties

When it comes to scripting object properties in applications, there are two commands that do most of the talking: *set* and *get*.

The *get* command allows you to get properties from objects, even if you don't ever spell the command out. Whenever you want to use any object property in your script, such as the width of a Photoshop image or the modification date of a file in the Finder, you have to use the *get* command. This can get a bit confusing, though. Let's look at the following statement:

Script 21-1 (includes the following two scripts)

```
tell application "Finder"
    set the_size to physical size of file the_pdf_file_path
end tell
```

By looking at the preceding statement, it appears as if we used the Finder's *set* command. In fact, we used the *get*, not *set*, command. We know this because we got the *physical size* property of the file. We could have written the statement in the following way, which would have exposed the usage of the different commands:

```
tell application "Finder"
    --Use the Finder's get command:
    get the physical size of file the_pdf_file_path
    --Use AppleScript's set command:
    set the_size to the result--apl command
end tell
```

See, in the first example, the *set* command was just AppleScript setting its variable to the value that was returned by the Finder's *get* command.

Special property values

While the values of many properties adhere to AppleScript's own data types such as text, number, list, etc. many properties don't. Instead of using AppleScript's built-in data classes, these properties use constants defined in the application dictionary. Take for instance InDesign's *local display setting* property used by different page items. There are four possible values to that property. By looking in the InDesign dictionary you can tell that the possible values are *high quality*, *typical*, *optimized*, or *default*. These aren't strings, but rather keywords that are a part of InDesign's scripting terminology.

21

You can get it, but not set it

Objects in scriptable applications are divided into two categories: read only and editable. As you may imagine, the object model of an application doesn't always let you change every property of every object. For instance, the *creation date* property of a *file* object in the Finder can't be changed. Some other properties can't be changed simply because the developers decided that they shouldn't be.

Read-only properties are marked [r/o] in the dictionary, but if you really need to be able to change a read-only property, try to change it anyway; although rare, it is possible that the dictionary information is not fully accurate.

Create object with properties

An understanding of a class's properties can come in handy when creating an object from that class. In many situations, when creating an object, you can use the *with properties* parameter of the *create* or *make* command in order to specify the properties you want to start with. This method isn't always allowed, but is much faster than the alternative of changing properties once the object has been created.

The most common example of creating an object with properties is probably creating a folder in the Finder.

Script 21-2 (includes the following two scripts)

```
tell application "Finder"
    make new folder at desktop with properties¬
    {name:"my files2", label index:1}
end tell
```

Notice that while we set two legal properties to the folder while creating it, the Finder chose to use the *name* property but completely ignore the *label index* property.

To add the label to the folder after the fact, we can use the rule of thumb that when you create an object with the *make* or *create* command (in most applications), the result of that operation will be a reference to that object. Knowing that, we can complete the operation by setting the label index to the resulting value of the Finder's *make* command.

```
tell application "Finder"
    set myFolder to make new folder at desktop with properties ¬
    {name:"my files"}
--myFolder is:
folder "my files" of folder "Desktop" of folder "hanaan" ¬
    of folder "Users" of startup disk
    set label index of myFolder to 1
end tell
```

Elements

The elements listed in the dictionary under a specific class are not elements of an actual object, since the class is not an instance of an object, only its definition. The element listing is there just to let you know that objects created after this class could contain elements of the listed classes.

For instance, the class *folder* in the Finder's dictionary lists the following elements:

```
item by numeric index, by name
container by numeric index, by name
folder by numeric index, by name, by ID
file by numeric index, by name
alias file by numeric index, by name
application file by numeric index, by name, by ID
document file by numeric index, by name
internet location file by numeric index, by name
clipping by numeric index, by name
package by numeric index, by name
```

21

The text after the word "by" in each element's description shows the possible ways to reference an object from this class. For instance, the *file* class shows that it can be referenced by index and by name. This means that if you want to do anything with this folder in a script, you must either know its name:

```
folder "Jobs"
```

or know its order in the list:

```
folder 3
```

Notice that the *folder* class itself is also on the list, because folders in the Finder may contain other folders.

Hey, you! Referencing objects

Even the best-placed command with perfectly positioned parameters isn't very useful if you can't direct it at the right object.

Targeting objects can be tricky at times, but there are a few things you can do to make it better.

For starters, you have to understand your application's object model. An application with a solid object model makes it easier to identify objects.

Generally, there are three ways to talk to objects directly: by name, by index, and if you're lucky, by ID property, if the object's class has one.

Starting with the parents

Every object is an element of another object, other than the application itself, of course. Armed with this fact, you can go around asking different objects to identify its element objects. This can go a long way to finding the object you're looking to work with. Whether it is asking for every item of a folder in the Finder or every text frame in an InDesign page, the result will be a list in which each item is an object.

After you got the list, you can either loop through it in order to target each object, or better yet, command them all to dance at the same time. Whenever you can avoid looping (and you can't always), the faster your script will work.

Following are a few scripts that target a bunch of objects together:

Script 21-3 (includes the following two scripts)

```
tell application "Finder"
    tell every file of the desktop
        set label index to 2
    end tell
end tell
```

or

```
tell application "InDesign CS"
    tell page 1 of active document
        set stroke weight of every graphic line to 4
    end tell
end tell
```

You can either narrow down or expand your object collection by referring to higher- or lower-level classes. For instance, in the Finder, referring to "items" of a specific folder encompasses all items including folders, files, applications, etc. You can narrow it down to files, which will not include any containers such as folders, or even further by referring to specific file types such as application files or document files.

The dictionary shows you which class is on top by listing a special property called *inheritance*. This property shows the super class to which the class you're looking at belongs.

Figure 21-6 shows the Finder's dictionary with two classes highlighted: *file* and *folder*. You can see that the file inherits all of its properties from the *item* class, and the folder inherits its properties from the *container* class, which in turn also belongs to the *item* class.

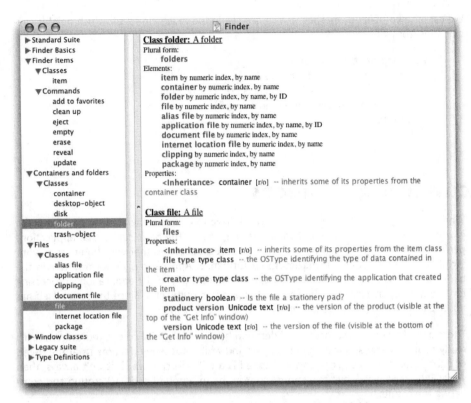

Figure 21-6. The Finder's dictionary with two classes highlighted: *file* and *folder*

"Whose" hot and who's not . . .

This kind of wholesale-object manipulation is fast and powerful, but wait, there's more! You can push it even further by isolating the objects you want to work with even more using the *whose* clause.

The *whose* clause allows you to only work with the objects that share specific properties. For instance, what if we want to change the line weight of the lines like we did previously, but only to lines that are thinner than half a point? Here's how we can do that:

Script 21-4 (includes the following two scripts)

```
tell application "InDesign CS"
    tell page 1 of active document
        tell (every graphic line whose stroke weight ≤ 0.5)
            set stroke weight to 0.5
        end tell
    end tell
end tell
```

We can also combine properties, as you can see in the following script, which deletes specific files from a folder:

```
tell application "Finder"
    tell every file of the desktop
        delete (every file whose size < 1000 and ¬
            name extension is not "pdf")
    end tell
end tell
```

Activating applications

When scripting different applications, you will have to decide if the applications should be in the foreground or background when the script runs. The basic rule is that applications perform better in the background, not in the foreground, and that you should bring your script to the foreground for maximum performance. Applications perform better in the background since this way the Mac OS doesn't allocate any of the application's processing time to the display tasks, which can slow things down quite a bit. Since the script itself has no display tasks or user interface, it does better in the front.

There are a few issues that need consideration here, starting with screen redraw. While it's really cool to see an application jumping around while processing documents at the speed of light, it does run slower this way. If speed is a critical issue, which it isn't always, then you will be served well by timing your script in the foreground and background and comparing the results.

There are some commands, such as *copy* and *paste*, that require that the application be in the foreground, so you don't really have a choice there, but you can perform the operation and then send it back again.

What I usually do is create a *should_activate* property. Then, instead of just using the *activate* command, I do this:

```
tell application "Some Application"
    if should_activate then activate
end tell
```

This way, when I know some VP will be checking out the system, I turn this property on, and all hell breaks loose on the screen. The system may run a few paces behind the usual speed, but no one cares at this point.

CHAPTER 22
DEBUGGING SCRIPTS

My Script

```
                    set report_string to rep:
                    set report_string to repr
            end if
          end repeat
        end tell
    end get_report

on get_file_info(file_path
    local file_size, file_date, file_type
    tell application "Finder"
        set file_size to size of file file_pa
        set file_date to creation date of
        set file_type to file type of file f
    end tell
    return {file_size, file_date, file_type}
end get_file_info

Mac ▶   Line: 15 Size: 2K      AppleScript Debugger
```

Class application: The application
Plural form:
   applications
Elements:
   document by numeric index, by name
   window by numeric index, by name
   database by name, by numeric index
   menu by name, by numeric index
Properties:
   best type type class [r/o] -- The best de
   class type class [r/o] -- The class
   default type type class [r/o] -- The defa
   frontmost boolean [r/o] -- is this the fro
   name international text [r/o] -- The nam
   version version [r/o] -- The version of th

Class cell: A field value in a record or request

Debugging your scripts is not something you do as the final step of script writing. You should do your debugging while you're writing the script, every step of the way. As your mom always told you: it is better to clean up as you go along.

While there are many tricks to debugging, there's no better overall way than to do it with Script Debugger (www.latenightsw.com). I know, it does cost about US$190, but if you spend a good chunk of your time writing scripts, it will pay for itself. It is currently the only script editor written for Mac OS X that gives you step-by-step debugging.

Script Debugger, as the name suggests, has useful tools for debugging scripts. The main debugging feature, and the one Script Debugger is most known for, is the ability to run through the script step by step and set breakpoints where the script pauses. We will get back to some Script Debugger debugging techniques later on in the chapter. In the meanwhile, let's look at some other ways you can get the bugs out of your scripts with any script editor.

Don't try to understand the problem, just solve it!

Fixing scripts does not always require you to know what caused them to break. Fixing scripts requires you to know *where* they break, and what part of the script isn't working anymore. This way you can find a way around the problem without ever fixing it.

My clients always crack up when they ask me what the problem was and my reply is, "I don't know, but I did make the script work again."

Of course, understanding the source of the problem can be extremely beneficial, but it may be far beyond your reach—for instance, say the client is switching servers and suddenly the script can't delete files. You can't change the server's behavior, but you can provide a workaround. Also, if a specific application acts buggy when you script one of its features, you don't have to get to the bottom of it and spend a week on the phone with the developers of this application. File a bug with the developer and then find a suitable workaround for your script.

Don't confuse user errors with bugs

There aren't many scripts that don't rely on any user action whatsoever, and as long as the user's action is required, some user at some point will cause your script to break. With complex scripts, it can be difficult to figure out whether the script broke or some file the script is expecting or other required element is not in place.

Although it may be tempting to get right into your script and find a workaround, you should stop and think. If the script has been operating successfully for some time, it is most likely still working OK, and the user is probably the cause. If fixing the script is not needed in this case, you may want to trap the error and ensure that the next time this specific error-causing condition occurs again that the user is notified gently with a dialog box. See more on capturing errors in Chapter 15.

Values are a window to your script statements

When you write a script statement, there's a chance that somewhere in that statement there's a bug. The bug can be in one of two levels: it's either a syntax error that will prevent the script from compiling or a runtime error. The first error type is in a way nicer, since AppleScript lets you know right away where the issue is. Runtime problems are a different issue altogether. The script's syntax is OK, but somewhere along the line, the code was unable to run. Imagine telling AppleScript to delete a file that doesn't exist, or trying to get the value of the fifth item in a four-item list. The script may be well written, but what it tries to do is impossible.

Script bugs revolve around two areas: application objects and AppleScript values.

Assuming that all application objects exist, and the problem is somewhere in your script logic, the only way you can spot the problem is by examining the values that contributed to the problematic statement.

To do that, we will look at a few ways of exposing values while the script is running. We will be relying on the fact that even though values that commands return aren't visible to us while the script is running, they do exist and can be exposed.

22

Using the return command

The first value-exposing debugging method we'll use is the *return* command. Using the *return* command allows us to return any value currently set in the script. The downside is that it will also stop the script right then and there. Using *return* within subroutines doesn't work the same, since it will simply return the value from the subroutine to the main script. However, using *return* is nice because it will return the value in a pure AppleScript format for us to examine.

To use the *return* command for debugging, create a new line somewhere in the middle of your script, before the place where the error happens but after the place where the value in question has been created. Let's assume that we have the following script that is supposed to remove some text from the name of files. Since all the files in the folder are named by another script, we can count on them being of the same length. Here's the start of our script:

Script 22-1

```
set file_name_list to list folder alias the_jobs_folder
repeat with the_file_name in file_name_list
    set new_name to characters 1 thru 12 of the_file_name as string
    tell application "Finder"
        set name of file (the_jobs_folder &the_file_name) to new_name
    end tell
end repeat
```

When we run our script, we get an error. We realize that there's some issue with the file list the script is using, so we add a line of script returning the value of the *file_name_list* after it has been created.

```
set file_name_list to list folder alias the_jobs_folder
return file_name_list
repeat with the_file_name in file_name_list
    set new_name to characters 1 thru 12 of the_file_name as string
    ...
```

By looking at the list in the result panel of Apple's Script Editor window (shown in Figure 22-1), we can clearly see that the list includes the OS X–generated .DS_STORE invisible file. We then trace the problem to the statement that assigned the file list value to the *file_name_list* variable. The solution will be to add the *without invisibles* parameter to the *list folder* command.

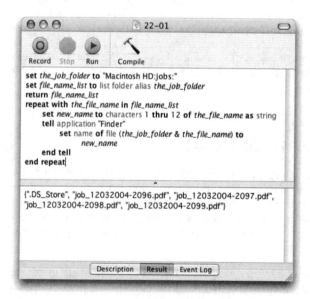

Figure 22-1. The *return* command stops the script and places the value of the *file_name_list* in the result panel in Script Editor.

One pitfall with using this form of debugging is that you may forget the *return* command in your script. This is not very likely, but if it happens, your script will stop in the middle, and this time it is going to be your fault . . .

Dialog boxes to the rescue

One of the most basic forms of debugging is the use of the *display dialog* command. All you do is display a dialog box showing the value in question.

The *display dialog* command is best for debugging string values, or other values that can be coerced into strings such as numbers, Booleans, and dates.

For the most part, you can just insert a line of code that looks like this:

```
display dialog variable_in_question
```

with the identifier of the real variable you want to test, of course.

The main advantage dialog boxes have over the *return* command we looked at before is that after you click the OK button, the script goes on. This allows you to check multiple items in the same debug session. Also, the dialog box gives you as much time as you need to make notes or do some good old thinking before you're ready to move on.

Using the dialog box debugging technique is great for checking the value of variables that change in a repeat loop. While the loop is crunching statements with slightly varying values in every repetition, a dialog box on every loop can reveal a lot of what's going on in there.

If you like the idea of debugging with dialog boxes, you may want to facilitate it a bit. The first thing you will need is a *debug* property. This property will be set to true when you're debugging and false when you're not. It is mainly a fail-safe mechanism to make sure you didn't leave any dialog box surprises for the script end users.

The subroutine itself should have a very short name, like *msg* (short for message, and a bit like the *msgbox* VB command).

The contents of the subroutine can be very simple.

```
on msg(the_value)
    if debug then display dialog the_value
end msg
```

If you want to get a little more fancy, here is a beefed-up subroutine that uses dialog boxes for debugging all sorts of values:

Script 22-2

```
1. property debug : true
2. msg({1, 2, 3, 4})

3. on msg(the_value)
4.     if debug then
5.         set the_class to class of the_value
6.         set the_class_string to the_class as string
7.         if the_class is in {integer, real} then
8.             display dialog the_class_string & return & the_value
9.         else if the_class is string then
10.            display dialog the_class_string & return & "\"" & ¬
                   the_value & "\""
11.        else if the_class is date then
12.            set the_string_value to the_value as string
13.            display dialog the_class_string & return & ¬
                   "date \"" & the_value & "\""
14.        else if the_class is list then
15.            set text item delimiters to ", "
```

22

```
16.          set the_string_value to the_value as string
17.          set text item delimiters to ""
18.          display dialog "List of " & (count the_value) & ¬
                " items" & return & "{" & the_string_value & "}"
19.      else
20.        try
21.          set the_string_value to the_value as string
22.          display dialog the_class_string & return & ¬
                the_string_value
23.        on error error_text
24.          display dialog "Debug error:" & return & ¬
                the_class_string & return & error_text
25.        end try
26.      end if
27.   end if
28. end msg
```

The preceding subroutine will give you a slightly more descriptive dialog box based on the class of value you're testing. Figure 22-2 shows the dialog box that will be displayed if a list is passed to the subroutine.

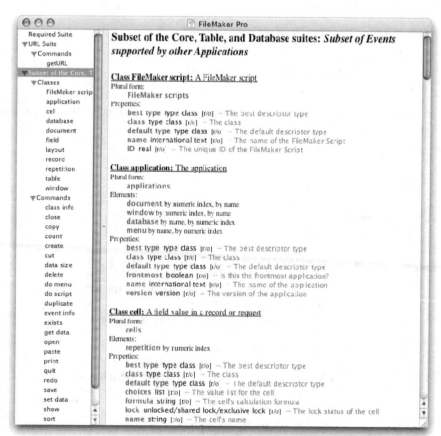

Figure 22-2.
The debugging subroutine handles a list that was passed on to it for display.

Error messages tell a story

A mix between the return value and the dialog box methods is the error method. Simply throw the value as an error. Say you want to see the value of the variable *my_file_list* in the middle of the script's execution; simply type the following:

```
error my_file_list
```

AppleScript will display the value of the variable *my_file_list* in an error message.

This method is very useful when you want to test your script when it is running as an application. In such cases, the return value method simply won't work.

Using the event log

The event log is the one debugging feature actually built into AppleScript.

Debugging with the log includes the use of the event log window in Script Editor (or Script Debugger), and the use of three log-related commands: *log*, *start log*, and *stop log*.

Let's start with the event log itself. When the event log pane is open in Script Editor, AppleScript logs the running statements and their results. Figure 22-3 shows a simple script and the results that the event log has captured.

Figure 22-3.
A simple script and the results that the event log has captured

Anything missing? The event log skipped some value assignments. The first and last statements, or results, aren't shown in the event log. The event log only logs events that are external to AppleScript. Statements that are taken care of inside AppleScript, such as *set y to x * 12*, are not logged.

Logging anything

While the event log in AppleScript will skip internal statements, you don't have to. You can force anything to be added to the event log by using the *log* command.

The *log* command, followed by a value, will add the given value to the log, wrapped in comment brackets: *(*value*)*.

The value is wrapped in a comment because anything that appears in the event log is actually legally compiled AppleScript code.

Figure 22-4 shows how we can force the result of *x * 12* to appear in the log.

Figure 22-4. By using the *log* command, we can force the result of *x * 12* to appear in the log.

Log history

Apple's Script Editor version 2 actually creates a history for the event log. You can check out the event log history by choosing Event Log History from the Window menu.

Figure 22-5 shows the Event Log History window. The left column allows you to select the script whose log you want to see, and the right side displays the actual log.

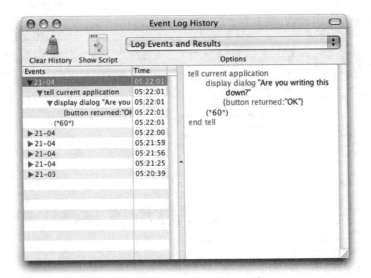

Figure 22-5. The event log history in Script Editor 2

Debugging with Script Debugger

As mentioned, Script Debugger is the best debugging tool for AppleScript. If you own Script Debugger, then check this section out for a few debugging how-to's; if you don't, read on and consider getting it.

Script Debugger doesn't really allow you to debug AppleScript. Instead, it converts your entire script into a special debugging language called AppleScript Debugger. This language is similar to AppleScript in any respect having to do with running the scripts, but you have to switch back to normal AppleScript before deploying your script in any way.

The Script Debugger script window

The most notable part of the Script Debugger script window is the Properties panel, shown at the top right of the window in Figure 22-6. This window shows all of the script's properties, variables, and their values.

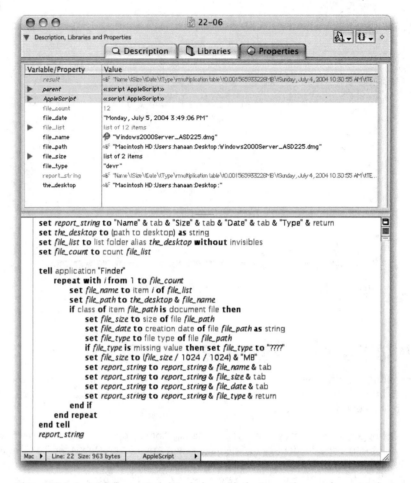

Figure 22-6. Script Debugger's script window with the Properties panel open at the top

Beside the value, you can see what type of string the value is by the little icon to the left of the value. Unicode text has a little globe with a T next to it, and styles text has a red, blue, and green "abc" icon.

This properties and variables list is great when you want to take a glimpse into the script's current state. The top value shown is always the result variable. This one comes handy when stepping through the script during debugging.

Script Debugger's debugging mode

Next, we will convert our script to AppleScript Debugger language. You do that by choosing Enable Debugging from the Script menu.

When the script is in Debugger mode, the Properties panel turns into the Debugging panel.

The most notable addition to the main scripting window is a row of diamonds to the left of the script. Each diamond represents a potential breakpoint next to a line of code. Clicking that diamond turns it red, and indicates that the script should stop at this line next time it runs. The script's "playback head," shown as a blue arrow, stops at the line with the breakpoint before this line is executed.

Figure 22-7 shows Script Debugger's script window in AppleScript Debugger mode.

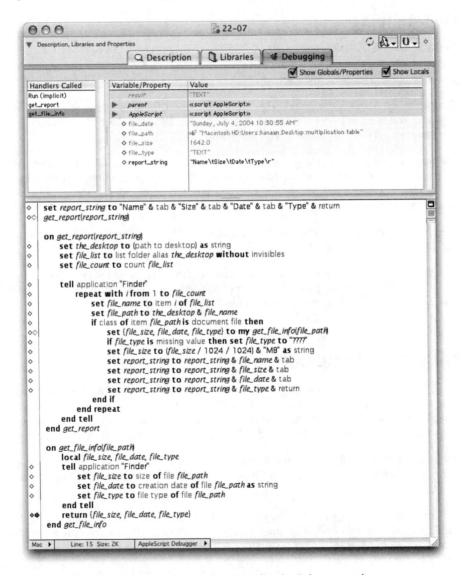

Figure 22-7. Script Debugger's script window in AppleScript Debugger mode

The left side of the debugging panel is now a list of handler calls. When the playback head is stopped inside a subroutine, then that subroutine is selected in the list, and all of its variables show in the property area to the right.

By default, only the values of the local variables passed as arguments to the subroutine will be shown in the list. If you want to examine values of other local variables, you have to declare them as local variables at the top of the subroutine definition. After doing so, these declared local variables and their values will appear in the yellow-shaded area in the Properties panel.

Script stepping

When in AppleScript Debugger mode, Script Debugger allows you to perform four additional script-navigation commands beside the usual *run* and *stop*. The commands are *pause*, *step into*, *step over*, and *step out*.

The *pause* command (*COMMAND+SHIFT+.* [period]) is good for scripts that run for a long time and you want to pause just to see where you are. Otherwise, there's no way to use this command in order to pause at an exact point.

Stepping is really where things heat up. The *step into* (*COMMAND+I*) and *step over* (*COMMAND+Y*) commands allow you to execute one line of script at a time. The difference is that *step into* will go into subroutine calls and step through every line there, while *step over* will skip the subroutine call and move right on to the next line.

The *step out* command comes in handy if you happened to have stepped into a subroutine but you want to get out of it.

In any case, the blue arrow will always show you where you are, and the *result* variable at the top of the Properties panel in the script window will always show you the result returned from the last line the script executed.

Divide and conquer

One of the best ways to avoid bugs is to make sure you don't introduce them into your scripts in the first place. To do that, don't write new code directly into your already over-complicated bowl of spaghetti code, but rather test your new code on the side first—just as you would crack an egg into a small bowl before adding it to the mix, just in case it is rotten.

If you create little script chunks on the side, and only integrate them into the main script once they are tested, you will have much less of a need to go around fixing bugs in your script.

This also goes for debugging. If there's a problem in the script, try to isolate it, copy the code to a different script window, and try to resolve it there. Besides having less code to deal with, you can quickly try a few scenarios without messing with that mammoth script.

When your scripts are used by clients

Ho, the joy of writing scripts for cash. The problem is that those scripts never seem to forget their creator, and they call out to him from all around the globe. Yes, once you created a script that is used by someone, they will hunt you down whenever anything goes wrong. I still have clients I wrote scripts for years ago calling me with questions about them.

The best defense against being swamped with fixing old scripts is to create good scripts to begin with. Not that good scripts don't break—they do—but the trick is to know exactly where they stopped, even years after you created them.

Error log

The best way I know to allow me to troubleshoot scripts remotely (other than Timbuktu, of course) is to give the script the ability to create a log that records its activity. This log can be triggered somehow by the client, and when triggered, will create a file where it will add lines of text each time certain things happen in the script.

This may sound like overkill, but truly, once you create the log subroutine, you can put it to use in any script you create.

The most important thing in the log subroutine construction is to not make the mistake of creating a string variable, adding log text to it, and writing it to a file at the end. What will happen is that the script will stop in the middle due to the bug, the string variable with all that good log info will be erased from memory, and you will still be clueless.

Instead, use *write log_test to the_file at eof*. This will ensure that each line you want to log will be added to the end of the text file right away.

22

CHAPTER 23

A SCRIPT BY ANY OTHER NAME . . .

While any script you write using AppleScript still looks the same and generally utilizes the same system resources in order to run, there are a few different ways that the Mac makes that AppleScript functionality available to you.

The most common forms used to save and run scripts are as a script application, a script droplet, and a compiled script. This chapter will look at the different ways we can put scripts to work.

Most of the options for saving scripts can be found in the Save dialog box of whichever script editor you're using. Figure 23-1 shows Apple's Script Editor's Save dialog box.

Figure 23-1. Apple's Script Editor's Save dialog box

The following table shows the different file formats available for saving AppleScript files.

Type	Description	Options	Features	Name Extension	Icon
Application	A normal application that runs when you double-click it	Run Only Stay Open Startup Screen		.app	run me
Droplet application	An application containing the *on open* handler	Run Only Stay Open Startup Screen	Allows your script to process files dropped on it	.app	drop me a file
Application bundle	An application saved as a Cocoa bundle	Run Only Stay Open Startup Screen	Can also be saved as a droplet by including the *on open* handler; bundle can hold any files such as templates, etc.	.app	Bundle

Type	Description	Options	Features	Name Extension	Icon
Compiled script	The native AppleScript file format Can be executed from within the script editor or loaded into other scripts	Run Only	Can also be run from the Script menu or other "script runner" utilities	.scpt	Basic.scpt
Compiled script bundle	The same as compiled script, but uses Cocoa's bundle format	Run Only	Script bundle can hold any files such as templates, etc.	.scptd	basic bundle.scptd
Text file	An ASCII text file that contains the noncompiled version of the script	Line Endings	Opens without requiring referenced applications to be open	.applescript	plain text.applescript

Compiled scripts

A compiled script file is AppleScript's default file format—it is used when you save a script you started writing in order to open it the next time and continue writing.

What is the difference between a compiled script and plain text? When you compile the script, a few things happen. The first thing you may notice is that the script text gets formatted based on the AppleScript formatting settings you specified in Script Editor's preferences.

Another thing you may have noticed is that if AppleScript didn't recognize any of the applications you used in the script, it asks you to locate them, and then it launches them in order to compare the commands and classes you used in this application's *tell* block with the ones defined in the application's dictionary. In the compiled script, AppleScript actually includes a sort of an alias to that application, which allows it to recognize that application even if it is renamed, moved, or even upgraded. That's right, if you created a script a year ago with Illustrator 10, and you're opening it now, AppleScript may recognize Illustrator CS as the target.

AppleScript also converts the syntax from AppleScript's hallmark English-like syntax into what appears to be cryptic text that is actually tokens that can be understood only by the OS Scripting Component. The simple script *display dialog "Hello"* generates the following compiled script text (when opened with BBEdit):

```
FasdUAS 1.101.10
ˇˇˇˇ
lˇ
I ˇˇˇ ˇˇ.sysodlogaskrTEXT
m\\ Helloˇ ˇ ˇˇˇ ˇˇˇ ˇˇˇˇ
.aevtoappnullÄê****  ˇˇˇˇˇ
ˇˇˇˇ.aevtoappnullÄê****
kˇ1ˇ1ˇˇˇˇ
\ˇÙˇÙ.sysodlogaskrTEXTˇˇ\‡jascr
ˇfifi≠
```

From a system standpoint, forcing you to compile a script before saving it can prevent many runtime issues such as syntax errors, missing applications, etc. It also brings the script one step closer to the language understood by the OS Scripting Component.

Having said all that, the reverse is also true: Script Editor acts as a decompiler. Whenever you open a script with Script Editor, it has to decompile the script, locate all the referenced aliases and applications, and apply the AppleScript formatting.

Another function of compiled scripts not saved as applications but rather as scripts is that they can be loaded into other scripts and act as subroutine libraries. As discussed in Chapter 20, loading scripts into other scripts is fairly easy and can help you reuse your code in an efficient way.

Script applications

What's easier to use than a script application? You write AppleScript code, test it, and save it as an application. All the user has to do is double-click it. When the script is done executing all the code in the *run* handler, it quits.

A script application has two events that execute: *run* and *quit*.

When you launch an application, the first thing that happens is the immediate execution of the *run* handler. Since you may have not included an actual *run* handler, any code that is not a part of any other handler is by default part of the *run* handler. Once the *run* handler runs to the end, the program executes the *quit* handler, is specified, and then quits.

There is another handler used by the script application: *on idle*. The *on idle* handler only gets executed if you have saved the script application as a stay-open application. Otherwise, there's no idle moment for the *on idle* handler to be called. More about the *on idle* handler and the *idle* event later on in this chapter.

Droplets

Droplets are script applications with a twist: they can process files that are dropped on them. Using droplets allows you to create script applications that apply certain processes to dropped files.

To turn an application into a droplet application, simply include the *on open* handler somewhere in it. The one parameter of the *on open* handler is a variable that will contain the paths to all of the files and folders dropped on the droplet. That means that the *on open* handler doesn't actually do anything; it doesn't move the dropped items to any particular place, unless, that is, you write the script to do that. All that happens is that your script gets a wakeup call with a reference to a bunch of files: "Hey, wake up, here are the files you will be processing . . ."

Following is a small (and rather crude) example of the *on open* handler. The example, which appears in Figure 23-2, shows a script that tells you how many files and how many folders were dropped on it. The only purpose of it is to show the basic operation of the *on open* handler and the function of its parameter.

Figure 23-2.
The basic droplet
application script

Notice a couple of things about the script in Figure 23-2. I named the variable *the_items_list*, and it can have any identifier name you want (as long as it adheres to variable naming rules, of course).

In the script, I use this variable as I would use any other list. This time, I'm looping through the items in the list.

Also notice that there's a *run* handler. While not required, it is nice to have something happen when some unsuspecting user tries to double-click the droplet. Remember, the droplet is just an application and will execute the *run* handler if double-clicked.

You can find some more templates and examples of droplets on the AppleScript web page. Go to www.apple.com/applescript/resources/, click Essential Subroutines, and then click Finder Droplets. There are some cool droplets you can copy and use.

Stay-open applets

So far we looked at normal applications and at droplet applications. The third kind of application we will look at are script applications that don't quit when they are done executing the *run* handler, and instead become idle and wait.

While a normal script application can only make use of the *run* and *quit* handlers, the stay-open application has two more: *reopen* and *idle*.

Let's look at a brief description of all these event handlers before we get into some more details regarding the *idle* handler and its function.

The handlers listed next are not really handlers you call, but rather handlers that respond to natural events in the life of a script application. The code inside the event handlers will execute, or be called, when the specific event occurs.

run

The *run* event handler is called once after the script application is launched, and never again. You can use this handler to initialize values, give instructions, or anything else that the application has to do once. After the *run* handler has completed, the *on idle* handler will be called.

reopen

The *reopen* event handler will be called when an already-launched script application is relaunched using the dock or by double-clicking it again.

quit

The *quit* event handler is called when the user chooses Quit from the File menu of the script application's menu, and when the scripter calls the *quit* handler (done by using the *quit* command).

If you include an *on quit* event handler in your application, you are in effect taking over the *quit* command. That means that the application will not quit; instead it will do what you ask it to.

You can use the *continue* command to let the script finish the self-destruct sequence, but you don't have to.

The following *on quit* event handler asks the user if s/he's sure s/he wants to quit, and only quits if the answer is yes:

```
on quit
    display dialog "Are you sure you want to quit?" buttons {"No", "Yes"}
    if button returned of result is "Yes" then
        continue quit
```

```
      end if
   end quit
```

In the preceding example, if the user quits the application but then clicks the No button, the application will remain open.

idle

The *on idle* event handler is really where the bulk of the script happens. As we saw earlier, the *run* handler executes once at the start, the *quit* event handler executes once at the end, and the *reopen* handler is really a "just in case" handler.

The *idle* event, however, happens all the time. Does that mean that the *on idle* event acts like a huge repeat loop? Well, sort of. The *on idle* event handler is a repeat loop by function, but you can tell it to cool off for a given period of time before it starts again. You do that with the *idle* event's version of the *return* command.

At the point where you want the handler to be done executing code for a while, use the *return* command, followed by a number of seconds you want to wait until the next time the *idle* event handler is called.

For instance, the following script, if saved as a stay-open application, will remind you to take a break every 15 minutes:

```
on idle
   tell me to activate
   display dialog "Time to stretch!" giving up after 30
   return (15 * 60)
end idle
```

In the preceding script, the *on idle* event handler will happen once to start; during that run it will activate the application, then it will display the dialog box, and then it will instruct the script application to invoke the *idle* event when 15 minutes (*15 * 60 seconds*) have passed.

Call handlers from other scripts

Another cool thing about stay-open scripts is that you can call their handlers from an outside script while they are running.

Let's say that the stay-open script application shown in Figure 23-3 is running. Another script can call its *tell_time* subroutine like it would call a command defined in any other application.

```
tell application "My Clock"
   activate
   tell_time()
end tell
```

23

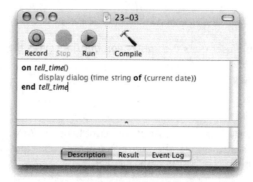

Figure 23-3.
The script of the
My Clock script
application

Bundle up

In Panther, you can now save both compiled scripts and script applications as application bundles. Bundles are the format used for all Cocoa applications, and more recently Carbon applications as well. It is more of a folder than an application, however—it looks like an application and behaves like one when you double-click it, but it can be opened like a folder.

To open it like a folder, CONTROL-click the bundle with the mouse, and choose Show Package Contents from the contextual menu.

Once you show the bundle's content, you can browse the application's folder structure.

Saving scripts as bundles makes much more sense with applications than with compiled scripts, mainly because there's no way for a compiled script to figure out its own path, making any use of the package's folder structure worthless to the script (unless it is in a folder known to the system through the *path to* command).

Bundles can come in very handy when your script needs to use external files such as templates, icons, sounds, scripting additions, or some text files containing data the script needs. After saving the script, place these files inside the Resources folder inside the bundle, and refer to it using the *path to me* statement:

```
set template_path to (path to me as string)&"Resources:Template.indd"
```

Locking scripts with run only

Unless you are saving your script as text, you can choose the Run Only save option to lock the contents of your script. Doing so will strip your script from the data it would later use to be decompiled and read by a script editor.

This feature may have severe consequences: if the locked script is the only version of your script, you will never gain access to it, other than for the purpose of running it. It is always advised to save a copy of your scripts as text for backup or you risk losing them. You should also consider saving scripts as run only right before deployment.

I personally never lock any of my scripts. As a consultant, I want my clients to open my scripts and look at them. All they can say is, "Wow, we better not touch that stuff!" For me, locking a script would be like Apple locking the containers of their computers so you couldn't open them.

There are, however, some situations where saving scripts as run only is a good idea. The obvious reason is protecting your scripting secrets, especially if your scripts are distributed to a mass audience. Another reason is to prevent the users of the scripts from messing them up intentionally or unintentionally.

Startup screen

When saving a script application, you can check the Startup screen check box, found in the Save dialog box. The next time the application runs, the text you typed in the description panel of your Script Editor script window will display in a rather crude dialog box that resembles more of an error dialog box than a welcome window.

Figure 23-4 shows the script's description panel, the options of the Save dialog box, and the dialog box displayed by AppleScript when the script application is launched.

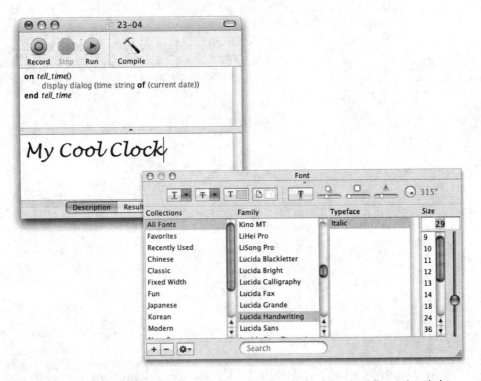

Figure 23-4. You can add formatted text to the description pane in the Script Editor script window. This text will be displayed when the script application starts up.

CHAPTER 24

HEALTHY SCRIPTWRITING PRACTICES

Once the euphoria of running your first script settles (hold on, it has been eight years and I'm still not over it . . .) there are a few things you can do to turn yourself from a mere scripter into a lean, mean, scripting machine. This chapter is dedicated to taking you through a few good practices that can help you turn scripting into more of a business, not from the business part, but more from the product-management viewpoint. When you script, someone benefits from your scripts financially. I get there by applying the simple "time is money" rule. It is amazing that, even with the immense time savings a single script can account for, there are things you can do to improve things for yourself as the scriptwriter.

There are no bad scripts, just bad scripters

Well, not really—catchy title though! What makes a script "bad" is when the scripter thinks of the code s/he is writing as a dead end. When you are a painter, every stroke of oil you put on the canvas is a dead end—it will serve the rest of its life as a part of that painting on that very canvas. An AppleScript statement you write, on the other hand, can be much more. If you work it right, much of your code can be reused in other scripts. Any part of any script is a potential part for future scripts you would write. If you feel that you spend a good part of your scripting time copying, pasting, and modifying script chunks from one script to another, you are on the right track, but on the wrong train. This chapter discusses some of the code optimization and other healthy scriptwriting habits that can make you a better scripter.

Naming conventions

One more sign of becoming a grown-up scripter is understanding the importance of naming conventions. Usually that understanding hits you when you should have already come up with a system and are now struggling with the find/change feature in Script Editor or Script Debugger to try and make sense of thousands of variables you named when you didn't know any better.

Before I go into detail and lay out a comprehensive naming convention system, let's look into some of the simple things you can do.

First and foremost, you have to follow AppleScript's rules for naming variables and subroutines (also called identifiers). These are defined in detail in Chapter 8 and Chapter 17. These include not starting an identifier with a digit, and not inserting any spaces or other special characters. One special character that is allowed and used quite a bit is the underscore (_).

There are in fact two main forms of naming identifiers: one is the intercap method, where the words are not separated, but each word starts with a capital letter:

```
totalPageCount
```

or

```
TotalPageCount
```

The other is the underscore method, where the words in the identifier are separated by underscores:

    total_page_count

In this chapter we will assume that you know the basic naming rules defined by AppleScript, and that what I refer to here as "wrong" may actually be a legal variable or subroutine name.

A comprehensive naming convention system

For any type of conventions relating to AppleScript, there's one source of information I always go back to: Mark Munro. Mark is the founder and president of Write Track Media (www.writetrackmedia.com), and has created some incredible automation systems for the Associated Press, Sony Music, and others. Mark is obsessed with the process of script writing and has dissected and categorized every aspect of his scripting process.

Among other things, Mark has come up with the following description of his naming conventions for subroutines and variables.

Naming subroutines

Write Track Media's standards for naming subroutines are discussed in the following sections.

Basic formula

The basic formula for subroutine naming is as follows:

«Group»«Entity»«Action»

«Group»«Entity»«Action»«Attribute»

Group is typically the application or functional group the subroutine deals with. If the subroutine deals with a single application and contains code that is as generic as possible, it should get the application name (*finder*, *filemaker*). If instead it deals with a single type of process that may involve several different applications, it should get the function name. For routines that are not typically open-ended enough to be harvested, I tend to make the group be the client name or code to help distinguish these routines as being exclusive to the client's project. The primary group serving as the first part of the name helps to keep you thinking in a structured way, encouraging you to keep a subroutine focused on one primary task or function. It also aids in sorting the subroutines when viewing them in a list.

24

The *Entity* (or noun) is the item or thing upon which action will be taken. This can be something straightforward such as a *folder* or a *file* in the Finder, a *record* or a *database* in FileMaker, or it can be something more complex like a department (*accounting*). While many people tend to want to put the action in the second place and the entity in the third place (*delete folder* rather than *folder delete*), I'd advise against it. Why? Sorting a list by entity first and action second makes it far easier to locate the subroutine you want. If you have any questions on this, or would like to discuss it further, ask me. I can post examples of this issue in a separate e-mail.

The *Action* is the type of processing that will be undertaken upon the *Entity*.

The *Attribute* is an optional naming position that is reserved for identifying the attribute of the *Entity* that will be modified in a manner described by the *Action*. For example, you might say *finderFolderSetName()* to denote which of the folder's properties will be changed. The attribute can also be an item that is further down the hierarchical chain. For example, you might say *finderFolderCreateFile* to indicate that you are going to create a file within the folder. The file is not really an attribute of the folder exactly . . . but this position in the naming formula can be used this way.

Simple examples:

filemakerFieldGetData()

filemakerFieldSetData()

filemakerRecordDelete()

finderFolderDelete()

finderFolderOpen()

finderItemCopy()

finderItemDelete()

finderItemMove()

More complex examples:

calendarDatesCreate()

clientDataParse()

Complex formulas

Sometimes the preceding basic formula is not sufficient to convey all the information necessary about the activity within a subroutine. Therefore, there are some additional rules to guide the exceptions. This is especially true with complex applications such as desktop publishing. With Finder or FileMaker routines, you are typically changing one attribute of a primary item. For example, you might change the name of a file or its file type. In FileMaker Pro you might change the contents of a cell.

In QuarkXPress, however, you may need to change the leading of some text of a paragraph of the contents of a text box, etc. More levels of hierarchy in the *Entity* and *Attribute* involved require more.

When required, you can simply add another level:

«Group»«Entity»«Action»«Attribute»«SubAttribute»

An example of this might be *quarkTextSetParagraphTabs()*.

Another example of a complex exception is a combination of items. This is somewhat rare but can be accommodated by simply adding a conjunction as follows—*finderFolderSetNameAndLabel()*.

Remember, the idea is not to limit your description . . . just to make it as formulaic as possible. If you need to be more specific, just add additional words to the end of the basic formula—while trying to keep the basic formula intact. A crazy example might be *quarkDocumentReplaceWordsStartingWithTECWithTECSoft()*.

Case sensitivity

I always make the *Group* (the first part) lowercase. All other parts of the name are title case. I avoid using an underscore to separate naming sections because it removes the possibility of double-clicking the name to select it.

Properly named subroutines:

finderAppActivate()

finderFolderCreate()

finderFolderDelete()

Improperly named subroutines (though legal by AppleScript):

FinderAppActivate()

finder_folder_delete()

FINDERFOLDERCREATE()

Stay consistent

If one subroutine creates a new record in FileMaker and another creates a text file in the Finder, it can be helpful to use the same action term such as *Create* or *Make*. When you start mixing these terms, it can become a little confusing. I know, because this is one area in which I have had difficulty staying consistent.

Single words

Each part of the formula should be a single word. This is especially important with automated harvesting, when you want to pull out the application name, and for sorting considerations.

Spell it out

Avoid what I call "hyper-abbreviation." This is a remnant from the days when memory was limited and every byte of space was like gold. People write *docChgeClr()* instead of *documentChangeColor* or, worse, *setTOD* instead of *SetTimeOfDay*. Abbreviations like this will always come back to haunt you, since you are very likely to forget the initial meaning of the abbreviation. As a rule, try to spell everything out except for very common things that are actually long. If confronted with a long word, try using a different word before a cryptic abbreviation.

Avoid "cute" expressions

I always try to avoid "cute" expressions. Instead, I try to keep things very serious and professional. *cdPLayThatFunkyMusic()* might show your personality, but isn't *cdPlayTrack* more accurate, serious minded, and helpful to others as well as to yourself in the future? I once saw a script with a subroutine called *MakeHTMLWhoopie()*. What the hell?

Conclusion:

```
Turn this --> into this
setMyGroovyDesktopColorBlue() --> finderDesktopSetColor()
MakeFileMakerRecordsSorted() --> filemakerRecordsSort()
crunchSomeFunkyNumbers() --> numberCalculatePercentage()
```

Naming variables

Write Track Media's standards for naming variables are given in the text that follows.

Variable naming formula

Variables should always be named in an efficient manner without compromising a clear description of what the variable contains. If a variable is too long, it should be reworded in such a way so as to not lose the general meaning in a manner similar to editing a long sentence. If it is too short and will not be easily understood, it should be expanded a little. Most importantly, all variables should have a descriptive prefix that helps to quickly identify the contents they hold or the type of window object whose name they contain. Some variable names require a "super prefix" to help establish their relationship to the script and their placement and usage within it. The basic formula for naming a subroutine is

«Optional Super Prefix»«Prefix»«Description»«Etc»

As with subroutine naming, lowercase the first prefix, title case the rest, don't include "cute" words, be descriptive without being too verbose, etc. The *Description* can be as many words as you need to describe the contents of the subroutine and can follow any pattern you choose. There are no current standards for how this part of the name should be configured besides general brevity and clarity.

Variable naming prefixes

Prefixes allow you to easily distinguish the use and purpose of the variable. You can tell the variable's purpose simply by glancing at it.

Primary variable prefixes

Primary variable prefixes are used to denote the most basic type of data that is contained within a variable. You will find that once you start using these, you will be almost instantly hooked. Variables become more quickly recognized, and you can deal with your code more efficiently.

bln: Identifies variables that contain Boolean (true or false) values.

data: Identifies variables that contain some unknown data type, i.e., any data type. This is useful when receiving a value from a subroutine that could be a text string, a list, or a number depending on the operations carried out. Typically this implies that you should check for the presence of certain values such as "Error" where you might be expecting a list.

list: Identifies variables that contain any list values. While it can be used to identify lists containing sublists, it should not be used to denote records.

name: Identifies variables that contain a name of an item.

num: Primary prefix that identifies variables containing numeric values. If a number is converted to a string, this prefix should not be used. Rather, *text* should be used—e.g., *textNumServerItems* or *textServerItemCount*.

path: Identifies variables that contain a path to an item. Typically, for readability, this should take the form of *pathTo«Item»* (*pathToTemplate* or *pathToProjectFolder*).

rec: Identifies variables that contain records.

script: Identifies variables that contain a loaded AppleScript or script object.

text: Identifies variables that contain any kind of text values including numbers that have been converted into text. *path*, *name* should be used in place of *text* to allow for more specific identification of certain types of text.

Secondary variable prefixes

Secondary variable prefixes are a little more specific than primary variable prefixes. At the moment they all deal with a more specific type of path or the path to a disk or mounted server volume. These are optional and can be interchanged with their primary counterparts.

disk: A secondary type of text prefix for paths that can be used to identify variables containing text values indicating the path to a disk. It should include the full path, i.e., *Server Name:*, and not just the name of the disk. This is slightly more specific than the *path* prefix, but either may be used.

file: A secondary type of text prefix for paths that can be used to identify variables containing text values indicating the path to a file. This is slightly more specific than the *path* prefix, but either may be used.

folder: A secondary type of text prefix for paths that can be used to identify variables containing text values indicating the path to a folder. This is slightly more specific than the *path* prefix, but either may be used.

vol: A secondary type of text prefix for paths that can be used to identify variables containing text values indicating the path to a server volume. It should include the full path, i.e., *Volume Name:*, and not just the name of the disk. This is slightly more specific than the *path* prefix, but either may be used.

Variable super prefixes

A super prefix is a prefix that goes in front of a primary or secondary prefix to help identify additional information about the status of the variable. The remainder of the variable name should be formatted as if the super prefix were not present.

c: Used for current item in any *repeat* statement. For example, if a variable contains the current item in a list it might be named *cNameFile*, *cNumToProcess*, or *cPathToStatusFile*.

g: Used for all globals (except standard wtm template globals, which may not follow this standard).

p: Used for all properties.

db«DatabaseName»: May be used when a variable contains something relating to a database. The database super prefix has a slightly different rule in terms of the formatting of the rest of the variable. Rather than use a primary or secondary prefix after the super prefix, the name of the database should be used first. Then, following that, the type of data should be used and then the descriptor of that data. The formula is db«DatabaseName»«DataType»«Descriptor»—for example, *dbContactsFieldFirstName* or *dbProjectsScriptBuildCatalog*. At the present time, this super prefix is optional because it is aberrant from the normal standards. At some time in the future this prefix may be modified to conform to the primary and secondary prefix requirements.

Development variable prefixes

dev: Used to denote a variable containing data that is only used when in development mode and should not be accessed or used in any way for the final release of a solution or product.

Script templates

Script templates are scripts you don't create from scratch, but rather from starter scripts that include basic code.

No one can create AppleScript templates for you—in order to fit your needs they have to be created by you and perfected over time. If you only sit down to create a template and can only come up with a few lines of basic common items, then this is all you need for now. The idea is that items you add to your template are added because System Events have a need for them.

Some items that can be useful in your templates are general global variables and properties. I have properties such as *main_folder* and *debug* in my template. Your template can also include either subroutines or the *load script* statement for loading your script library or libraries.

As time goes by, you will develop a few templates for different needs.

Storage solutions

Using global variables and properties in your scripts is power you should not abuse. In small scripts it may not be an issue, but as your scripts grow, the use of properties and global variables will cause your scripts to become entangled: you will either forget that a certain variable you use is global, or try to move a subroutine to another script and realize that you can't because it uses a global variable or property that you first have to isolate. Think about script properties as properties of the script, not a convenient method of passing values (or not having to) between subroutines. Even if a few of the subroutines in your script make use of the same variable, it still does not make it a candidate for a property or global variable. It may be a property of those few subroutines, and if it is, you should get them all into a separate script file and load them as a script object using the *load script* command. Once these subroutines are isolated and have their own secret society, they can have their own properties inside that script object.

It's also important to realize that the values of global variables and properties are saved when the script quits and are read again when the script launches again. If you store large lists or large script objects in global variables or properties, they can slow down the loading and quitting time of your script, and also bloat its size.

Separate functions from commands

This may sound funny, but the commands are not really the script's function. Getting dinner ready is the function; then one of the commands is *put pasta in pot*. Big functions such as make dinner should be written as a series of subroutines calls, not applications commands. Furthermore, complex scripts should be broken down into two or more levels of subroutines, like this:

```
on make_dinner()
    make_pasta()
    buy_icecream()
    serve_food()
    eat()
end make_dinner
on cook_pasta()
    boil water()
    cook_pasta()
    make_sauce ()
    strain_pasta()
end cook_pasta
on make_sauce()
    cut mushrooms ()
    cut vegs()
    ...
end make_sauce
```

In the preceding example, you can see how each subroutine is not littered with details; instead it gives an overview in the form of subroutine calls. Each subroutine level contains just enough details to show a clear objective and steps, but if there are too many details and actual application *tell* blocks, then you may not be able to see the script for the statements.

Commenting scripts

You don't comment scripts in case some other scripter opens them a few years from now. You comment your script so that when you open it a few months from now you won't have to rack your brain trying to figure out what that absolutely brilliant code that doesn't seem to work anymore actually meant.

For me personally, discipline and organization came with a great deal of pain and took a long time to be ingrained in my scripting, but I can say that I have been sloppy and I have been disciplined, and disciplined is better. I feel much better not wasting time dealing with my own scripts that I can no longer understand, descriptive variable names that don't make that much sense a month later, or rationale behind a certain subroutine.

Comments can seem to be dumb:

```
--This subroutine cleans blank data cells from the data for the page.
```

or

```
--This subroutine was create to prevent files from being created if
--the job is old
```

But man, you can seem much dumber to yourself when you can't understand your own code, which happens quite often.

Another important type of comment is one that dates itself. Every time I go back to an old script and make an adjustment, I comment out a copy of the old code, and add a visible comment such as this:

```
--•••-- Changed by Hanaan on 4/12/2004. Reason: include date in
-- report file name.
```

This leaves a trail of evidence for what was a part of the original script and what other statements were added later on.

Literal expressions can bring you down (dramatization)

Even if you're certain that a specific value in your script will never change, you should still not embed it directly into the operations or statements it is used in. This will make your scripts much less debugging friendly. Instead, just before the operation the value is used in, assign it to a descriptive variable name.

Enhancing performance

John Thorsen of TECSoft, the original AppleScript training company (www.tecsoft.com), claims that the value AppleScript automation adds to any workflow is so drastic that the actual speed in which the script runs doesn't really matter. After all, does it really matter if the process that used to take 3 hours takes 20 seconds or 30 seconds?

While this is true, some scripts do need to perform as fast as possible, since after a while, people start comparing them to how fast they are, not how fast the manual process was. People forget quickly . . .

For instance, a script that processes jobs in a queue can process that many more jobs an hour if it is made to run faster.

Following are some things to consider when trying to speed up your scripts.

OS X, baby!

If you're still limping along with OS 9, you are running scripts slower than you could. I know that there are many other considerations for upgrading the OS, but if you're looking for reasons to upgrade, then you should know that due to the tighter integration of AppleScript in the OS, your scripts are likely to run faster on OS X.

Who's on top?

One of the first considerations in the endless search for a faster script is which application is in the foreground and background.

The rule of thumb is that applications for the most part run faster when they are not the foreground application. When applications run in the background, the OS doesn't feel the need to update their display and other UI-related events that don't change the result of the script, but can slow down your script.

So if the application you're targeting is in the back, which application should be the active application? Your script application, if you're using one. Activating your script using the *tell me to activate* statement can speed things up quite a bit.

Faster syntax

There are a few script writing methods that can help speed up your code:

Adding items to lists

When you have a list and you want to add an item to it at the end, you can do it in two ways.

One way:

```
set the_list to the_list & the_item
```

The other way:

```
set end of the_list to the_item
```

Since adding items to a list usually happens multiple times inside a repeat loop, it is important that you realize the implication of the method you choose.

In the first way, adding items will take a bit more time, but the list will be cleaner, and working with it later on will be faster. The second method, where you tack on items to the *end* of the list, allows you to add items to a long list very quickly, but the list items will be scattered in memory and using the list will be slower.

Using every . . . whose vs. looping

Chapter 21 discusses using the *whose* clause when filtering objects in applications. Using the *whose* clause instead of looping through objects can add a real time boost to the script execution.

Imagine the following:

Script 24-1

```
tell every file whose name starts with "job"
    set label index to 2
    move to folder "jobs"
end tell
```

instead of this:

```
repeat with i from 1 to (count files)
    if name of file i starts with "job" then
        set label index of file i to 2
        move file i to folder "jobs"
    end if
end repeat
```

Exit looping after a result is gotten

While some repeat loops are meant to go through every item in a list or object in an application, the function of some repeat loops is to find a specific item or object and move on after it is found.

If this is the case, use the *exit repeat* statement to exit the loop right after you found the information desired.

In the following example, the repeat loop looks for a match in the list and returns the index in the list of the matching item:

Script 24-2

```
repeat with i from 1 to (count the_list)
    set the_item to item i of the_list
    if the_item is equal to the_other_item then
        set item_index to I
        --mission accomplished!
        exit repeat
    end if
end repeat
```

Reduce application interaction

One thing that slows AppleScript down is interacting with applications. While we can't eliminate this interaction altogether, we can try to limit it. We do that by getting as much data from the application as we can in one visit, and then parsing that data in AppleScript.

For example, when working with Excel, get the value of an entire range of cells and then loop through them and process that data in AppleScript, instead of going to Excel for the value of each individual cell.

Using subroutine libraries

Possibly one of the most efficiency-boosting practices you can follow is collecting subroutines in library files and loading these libraries into your other scripts. Libraries aren't special files, so you will not find a "Library" file format in the Save dialog box. A library is simply a compiled script that usually has no *run* handler, only subroutine definitions. You then use the *load script* command to load the file with the subroutine definitions into other scripts, which gives you access to all their subroutines.

Many little chunks

How you organize your scripts' code can help you make it more reusable and more efficient. One of the best ways to organize scripts is by means of subroutines.

The more of your scripts that are made of many subroutine calls instead of long, drawn-out conditional statements, repeat loops, and *tell* blocks, the better. Subroutines are really AppleScript commands that perform several smaller AppleScript commands, but are already tested and will always work. Using the same subroutines in multiple scripts can save you a lot of time.

When you write any script, you should always be asking yourself if the actual functionality you're scripting, as small or large as it may be, can be used somewhere else in any future scripts. If yes, give it a name and declare a subroutine—it's a bit more work, but will pay for itself many times over.

Loaded at the start and out of the way

If you use many subroutines in your scripts, you may want to dump them all in a separate file and load them in. The main consideration for this process is where these external files should be kept so that your scripts can find and load them every time. Other than that, using handlers stored in script objects is really a snap.

Creating and managing your own script libraries

Once you get over the initial mental barrier of using script libraries, you will want to facilitate their use.

As mentioned previously, the most important aspect is where those files should live. The two main options here are whether each script should be using its own set of libraries, and you should duplicate all your library files for each "system" or find one place on the Mac where all script libraries are shared by all scripts.

Even though it is more efficient to have a global set of script libraries, it may be easier to start out by having each "system" use its own set. This decision also has a lot to do with the scope of your projects. In my line of work, I create a few large systems for large clients, so for me it makes sense to have a separate `libraries` folder for each system. However, if you work for the one company that will be using your scripts, it may be smarter to store all your subroutine libraries in the `Application Support` folder, the `ScriptingAdditions` folder, or anywhere else that can be accessed with the *path to* command.

Load objects upfront, keep in properties

Loading a large number of handlers can be a bit time consuming. What you may want to do is have the scripts that are using the library load them into script properties. Then, every time you run the script, you will only have to load these scripts if the property that holds them is empty.

> **Empty values:** *there are a few ways in AppleScript to indicate an empty variable: null, missing value, or for strings and lists you can use "" and {}.*

Keep on top of things: Code buried in script objects can be time consuming

Once you have multiple scripts calling subroutines that are buried in other script files, and these subroutine calls are embedded in lengthy repeat loops, you may want to watch out that you don't lose track of your subroutine calls. It is fairly easy to forget a benign subroutine call inside a loop, which then loops itself a few times, and in the process causes the script to complete thousands of unnecessary operations.

Feedback

Most people who will run your scripts are used to performing small commands and getting instant feedback from the Mac. Running a script that takes more than ten seconds without knowing if it is still working or not can be frustrating. Your scripts must keep even the most anxious user informed.

Keep the users informed

With scripts that are taking longer than one minute to run, which is rarer now that both AppleScript and the Macs it runs on are so much faster, your users may get agitated if the only feedback they get from your script is the occasional color wheel and a "done" dialog message at the end.

The best thing to do is create a little face-only application in Studio, as explained in Chapter 12, to be used by your script for the sole purpose of telling the user what general process the script is going to. Time your processes in a way that the message updates every one to two seconds.

This way, instead of the users thinking, "This is taking so long," they are finally made aware of the sheer volume of things the script is doing for them.

The following script is a quick way to display a dialog box over the process that happens in a different application:

Script 24-3

```
tell application "System Events"
    activate
    ignoring application responses
        display dialog "Moving files to server..." giving up after 3
    end ignoring
end tell
```

Timing scripts

You may want to make a habit of timing portions of your scripts. This can come in handy in finding and fixing hang spots.

Timing scripts is easy. At the point in your script where the "stopwatch" should start, add the following line:

```
set start_timer to current date
```

Then, at the end of the timed process, use this line:

```
set run_time to (current date) - start_timer
```

It always makes a good impression to display the number of seconds a script took to run, especially if the process has been recently done manually.

Delivering scripts to other sites

Things can change dramatically once your children leave home. Managing scripts in other locations can be a drag, especially when they break for any reason, and your only source of information is a person with a distinct inability to form meaningful sentences.

In this case, a program like Timbuktu can be a real lifesaver; you can log in remotely and see the problem for yourself.

When this is not possible, you will want to make solid arrangements regarding the support of your off-site scripts. Following are a few tips.

Managing script preferences that the user can change

While writing scripts for other people to use, you have to always keep in mind that some of the values you defined in your script will be subject to change. Font names, type sizes, folder paths, user names—the list goes on.

There are a few ways to manage these script user preferences. Picking the format that works for you has to do with the frequency of the changes and the savvy of the users.

For not-so-savvy users who need to change settings more frequently, you can use a dialog box startup screen. Every time the script starts, a dialog box is displayed letting the user know what is about to happen. The dialog box sneaks in a button called "Settings" that, when clicked, takes the user through a set of dialog boxes with text input or buttons that account for the different settings they can change. These settings are then stored in properties for the next time the script runs. This is useful also for the first time the script runs when the user may have to initialize a few values.

The option for savvier users with scripts that may need to change every few months is to simply place the well-named properties at the top of the script and teach those users how to open the script and change these properties.

Updating and upgrading your solutions

One aspect of deploying script solutions in other location or multiple systems that can become a nightmare is version control. Keeping track of script versions to track updates and system disparity can be challenging, and there is room for many things to go wrong.

One thing that you have to do when version control becomes an issue is to sit down and work out a simple system for dealing with it.

Should you lock your code?

Locking your AppleScript code is done by saving your scripts as run only. They can still run and be loaded into other scripts, but they can never be opened.

There are two reasons for locking scripts: the first is to protect clients from themselves. If they can't open the scripts, they can't mess things up, and give you the work you dread most.

The other reason for locking your scripts is to protect your code from unauthorized access. There is nothing that prevents any scripter at the installed location from opening your scripts and copying your subroutines into his/her own scripts.

Nevertheless, I always leave my scripts unlocked. Yes, I do have clients who like to poke around in them, but I just explain the possible consequences, and they usually do it on a separate machine designated as a test environment. Another benefit it can give me is that I can use a person as a remote-controlled AppleScripter to help me fix scripts on site when they break. Besides, I'm an open source guy. Sharing code is what makes the AppleScript community so great, and I want to be a part of that. If someone can open my scripts and actually learn something, more power to them. Of course, there's that whole competition thing, but really, what are the chances that a script I wrote will be used against me if it falls into the wrong hands? In my eyes this is a very unlikely hypothetical situation.

You may also use a combination by locking your general cache of subroutines and leaving the main scripts unlocked for easy access.

Adding a debug mode to your scripts

One trick that can help you debug scripts from afar is making up your own debug mode. There are two reasons for running a script: to get things done with it (which is the reason why you wrote it in the first place), or to debug and fix it. There are several steps you may want the script to go through while debugging that you wouldn't want it to go through while doing live work.

24

You can facilitate this debug mode with a Boolean property called something like *debug*. Any part of the script that should only run while debugging can be conditional on the *debug* property being set to true:

```
if debug the log myVariable
```

or

```
if debug then
    set log_text to "Now running subroutine 'main_process'"
    log_to_file(log_text)
end if
```

The *debug* property can be either set manually inside the script or externally. Earlier we discussed a settings button in a greeting dialog box for your script. Asking whether the user wants to turn on debugging can be one of the settings indicated there.

Creating detailed text logs

One of the debugging operations I like to use in my scripts is the creation of a detailed runtime log. Every few operations I write a little blurb to a file describing the current position of the script. I later have the clients e-mail me that log file, which I use to quickly determine where the script had an error.

Wrap-up

Getting to be an experienced scripter is a funny thing: the more I work with AppleScript, the slower and more deliberate I become at writing the scripts, but due to that the systems I create are more solid and thought-out. I used to rush into things by writing scripts, but now I jot down diagrams and flow charts before I even get to the script editor.

Furthermore, I can appreciate the time I spend on writing better scripts when I have to refer to some of my older work. It spreads out on a sort of an evolutionary timeline, with older scripts looking a bit childish and "bad habits" slowly disappearing from them the more current they are.

The takeaway from here is that it's OK to take your time and plan things out as soon as you feel on top of things enough to do so. Channel your new-project excitement not through writing new code but through figuring out the best way to lay out that code and what things did or did not work for you in the past. Soon enough, this by itself will become the exciting part of the project.

In OS X's first year or two of existence, things were a bit hectic. Apple Computer was in the midst of its largest OS rollout ever, and it was scrambling to get applications out to hungry users. Us AppleScripters, we were just happy that AppleScript was going strong in OS X and improvements were made on a monthly basis. What we didn't like so much was that none of the shiny new applications called iApps were scriptable. Now, a few years later, things have changed for the better: not only are iTunes, iPhoto, iCal, Mail, and Address Book are all scriptable, but the implications are that scripters now have access to the databases used by Apple to manage contacts, music, and mail.

The subject of this chapter, as you can imagine, could fill its own little book. Therefore the intention here is not to cover every aspect of scripting Apple's applications, but rather to give you a solid start in scripting the five most important ones: iTunes (and the iPod), iPhoto, Mail, Address Book, and iCal.

iTunes + iPod

Starting with version 3, iTunes became a scriptable application with a solid dictionary and a fine object model describing tracks and various playlist types.

Scripting iTunes falls under two categories: maintenance scripts and usability scripts. Maintenance scripts are great for using every so often to clean up your library and managing your tracks and playlists. With the ability to have thousands of tracks, some from CDs, some from the music store, and some, well, from less respectable places, AppleScript can be a saving grace when you want to organize the iTune part of your life.

The other type of scripts can help you enjoy music on a day-to-day basis. You can easily create little AppleScript Studio utilities that control iTunes and perform tasks that would require several steps in the iTunes interface.

Examples from Apple

As always, you can find related sample scripts on Apple's AppleScript web page. Go to Apple.com/applescript, click scriptable applications, and then click iTunes. You will find a collection of about 30 scripts you can use and mainly open up and learn from.

iTunes scriptable objects

iTunes has a well-designed object model, a quality that can make scripting a given application easier. When examining the iTunes dictionary, you will see that there are more objects than commands, which is also an attribute of a well-crafted scripting environment. To complement how we think about music organization in general, iTunes has two main types of objects: playlist and track. Most other object types are variations of these two. In fact, there are five types of playlists and five types of tracks.

Before accessing these known goodies, you will have to go through an object class known as *source*. The source you will work with most is the library source. In the library source you will find your playlists and in there, your tracks.

Other sources may be very useful as well. If an iPod is connected to your Mac, for example, it becomes its own source with playlists and tracks. Some other source types are audio CD, MP3 CD, and shared library.

The library source, however, doesn't have direct access to all your tracks, as you may imagine: these tracks, which amount to every track iTunes is aware of, are elements of a special playlist named *Library* as well. So, in order to work with a particular track that is not part of what iTunes defines as a user playlist, you will have to go through the special playlist of type *library playlist*, called "Library." In the following example we play a random song from the library:

```
tell application "iTunes"
    play some track of playlist "Library" of source "Library"
end tell
```

Source *Library* has many playlists, which include your user playlists, but it has only one playlist of the subclass *library playlist*. That means that the following script would work as well:

```
tell application "iTunes"
    play some track of library playlist 1 of source "Library"
end tell
```

Working with tracks and playlists

One action you can't perform in iTunes is create a track. For that, you will have to wait until GarageBand is scriptable. You can, however, create new playlists. To add tracks to a playlist, you don't use the *add* command, but rather the *duplicate* command. The *add* command is used to add song files to the library or directly to a playlist.

The following script allows the user to type in a keyword. It then creates a new playlist based on that word, and duplicates (adds) to that new playlist every track whose name contains that keyword.

As an example, I used the word "Yellow." See Figure 25-1 for the resulting playlist.

Script 25-1

```
display dialog "Enter a key word" default answer ""
set track_criteria to text returned of result
tell application "iTunes"
    set my_playlist to make new playlist
    set name of my_playlist to "Songs with " & track_criteria
    tell playlist "Library" of source 1
        duplicate (every track whose name contains track_criteria) ¬
            to my_playlist
    end tell
end tell
```

25

Figure 25-1. The playlist created by the preceding script

Scripting the equalizer

iTunes allows us to control the equalizer using AppleScript. The equalizer contains properties for each one of the 12 bands, and one for the preamp, which is the leftmost slider in the equalizer.

Although it could be nicer if every band in the equalizer was an element of the equalizer, it makes sense to have them as properties since the number of bands can't change from one preset to the other.

The following script will be music to your ears, especially if you value alternative forms of music. It will, until stopped, change the bands of the manual equalizer preset to random numbers from -12 to 12.

Script 25-2

```
tell application "iTunes"
    activate
    set current EQ preset to EQ preset "Manual"
    repeat
        tell EQ preset "Manual"
            set preamp to random number from -12 to 12
            set band 1 to random number from -12 to 12
            set band 2 to random number from -12 to 12
            set band 3 to random number from -12 to 12
            set band 4 to random number from -12 to 12
            set band 5 to random number from -12 to 12
            set band 6 to random number from -12 to 12
            set band 7 to random number from -12 to 12
            set band 8 to random number from -12 to 12
            set band 9 to random number from -12 to 12
            set band 10 to random number from -12 to 12
        end tell
    end repeat
end tell
```

iPod scripting

No, the iPod is not scriptable. Apple does provide some iPod-related scripts from its website, but most of these simply help manage the iPod notes, etc.

iTunes' iPod-related command is the *update* command, which updates the track contents of a connected iPod.

As discussed previously, when an iPod is connected to your computer, iTunes regards it as another source.

Mail

Scripting Mail can be fun, but also a bit frustrating due to the obvious omission of certain functions, such as accessing attachments.

The structure of Mail's object model is very simple: we have accounts, mailboxes, and messages. Each account has mailboxes, and mailboxes can contain both messages and other mailboxes.

This script lists the mailboxes of the first account:

```
tell application "Mail"
    return name of every mailbox of account 1
end tell
--> {"INBOX", "Drafts", "Sent Messages", "Deleted Messages", "Junk"}
```

Mailboxes can also be elements of the application itself without having to belong to a specific account. Any mailbox in Mail that is created "on your Mac" can be accessed directly, like this:

Script 25-3

```
tell application "Mail"
    tell mailbox "lists"
        tell mailbox "applescript-users list"
            count messages
        end tell
    end tell
end tell
```

Unlike the *account* class, which can be manipulated quite a bit with AppleScript, the *mailbox* class contains only one writable property, which is *name*. The *account* class allows you to manipulate the account attributes set in Mail's account preferences.

25

Referring to a message

To get information from a message, you have to specify its account and mailbox. Let's say that I'm canceling my e-mail account with my service provider. I will want to notify every person who sent me mail to that address. Here's how I can get a list of their addresses:

Script 25-4

```
tell application "Mail"
    tell account "Flybynight.net"
        tell mailbox "INBOX"
            set address_list to sender of every message of it
        end tell
    end tell
end tell
```

If the message is in the "On your Mac" special account, you can just use the mailbox path without specifying the account, like this:

Script 25-5

```
tell application "Mail"
    tell mailbox "lists"
        tell mailbox "applescript-users list"
            count messages
        end tell
    end tell
end tell
--> 12374
```

Creating a message

Creating a message is pretty straightforward; you use Mail's dictionary to figure out the different properties, and assign their values in the newly created message. Following is an example of a script that creates a new e-mail message:

Script 25-6

```
set the_subject to "Hello there"
set the_body to return & "Please read the attached file"
set the_file_path to (choose file)
tell application "Mail"
    set new_message to make new outgoing message ¬
        with properties {subject:the_subject, visible:true}
    tell new_message
        set content of it to the_body
        --add recipients
        make new to recipient at end with properties ¬
            {name:"George", address:"george@cox.net"}
        make new cc recipient at end with properties ¬
            {name:"Georgia", address:"georgia@cox.net"}
```

```
        --add attachment
        tell first paragraph of content
            make new attachment at end with properties ¬
                {file name:the_file_path}
        end tell
    end tell
end tell
```

The preceding message has two recipients. Although *recipients* is a class, when we add recipients to a message we have to specify if they are to, cc, or bcc recipients.

Notice that when we create the attachment, we point at the first paragraph. This is because the attachment class is not an element, but rather a text item. It is used primarily for creating new messages, and not for manipulating attachments that are part of existing messages. A bit clunky, but it works.

Message headers

For some, message headers are the inexplicable gibberish text that appears above any e-mail message you get. For others, it is a treasure of information, tracing the e-mail message path from its origin, through each mail server, all the way to its destination. Apple made a nice effort to break each header into its own element, giving you fairly clean access to the information.

One thing you can extract from headers, if you care to, is the IP addresses of the different servers the message traveled through.

To do that, you first have to get a list of all the headers, and then parse out the IP address from the content of each header.

Here is how it can be done:

Script 25-7

```
tell application "Mail"
    set the_message_selection to selection as list
    set the_message to item 1 of the_message_selection
    tell the_message
        set header_list to content of every header of it ¬
            whose name is "received"
    end tell
end tell
set ip_address_list to {}
repeat with header_text in header_list
    set ip_address to extract_ip(header_text)
    set end of ip_address_list to ip_address
end repeat
set text item delimiters to return
set ip_address_list to ip_address_list as string
set text item delimiters to ""
```

25

```
            display dialog "This message visited the following IP addresses:" ¬
                & return & ip_address_list

        on extract_ip(header_text)
            set ip_start to (offset of "(" in header_text) + 1
            set ip_end to (offset of ")" in header_text) - 1
            set ip_address to characters ip_start thru ip_end ¬
                of header_text as string
            if ip_address starts with "[" then
                set ip_address to characters 2 thru -2 of ip_address as string
            end if
            return ip_address
        end extract_ip
```

String utilities

For your convenience, Mail's dictionary includes two string-related commands that can be very helpful when you need them. These are *extract name from* and *extract address from*. These commands will accept a full e-mail address containing the full name and the address in brackets (<>). Here are two examples of how they work:

```
set the_full_address to "Mickey T. Mouse <mickey@disney.com>"
extract name from the_full_address --> Mickey T. Mouse
extract address from the_full_address --> mickey@disney.com
```

Address Book

One of the hidden jewels scripters got with OS X is the ability to script Address Book, the contact management software. The reason why it is so nice is that we get access to the operating system's contact database. This database is used by other Apple applications such as Mail, and is open to any developer who wants to make use of it, including you and I.

What makes Address Book scripting so nice is the well-structured object model, which reflects the database structure itself. The structure of the object model in Address Book is open and flexible. It does not limit you to a specific number of addresses or phone numbers per person. Instead of numbers and addresses being properties of the person, they are elements. As you are aware of, properties have to be predefined, while we can add as many elements as the application allows.

The main entry in Address Book is a person. A person may have contact info elements and address elements.

Contact info elements are phone numbers, e-mails, related people, and other type of contacts that can be described in a label-value pair. For instance:

Work phone: 401-555-1212

The label is Work phone and the value is 401-555-1212.

Addresses are similar, but contain more specific properties such as city, state, etc.

This structure allows the Address Book to contain entries without any phone number but with three e-mail addresses, and others with no e-mails, but several phone and fax numbers, and any mix in between.

In the script that follows, I created a little utility that allows you to quickly look up contact information by a person's first or last name. The script taps the contact database structure and only shows the available phone numbers and e-mail addresses.

The script will start by letting the user pick a character from the alphabet. Then it will get the full name of all entries in the Address Book database whose either first or last name starts with the chosen character.

Once the name was chosen, the script will show the e-mail and phone numbers of the chosen contact, and create an e-mail message for that person if the user wants.

Let's look at the complete script and then dissect it line by line:

Script 25-8

```
1. set character_list to characters of ¬
      "ABCDEFGHIJKLMNOPQRSTUVWXYZ"
2. set chosen_character to (choose from list character_list) as string
3. set name_list to {}
4. tell application "Address Book"
5.    tell (every person whose last name starts with chosen_character)
6.       set name_list to name_list & name of it
7.    end tell
8.    tell (every person whose first name starts with chosen_character)
9.       set name_list to name_list & name of it
10.   end tell
11. end tell
12. if name_list is {} then return
13. set chosen_name to (choose from list name_list) as string
14. tell application "Address Book"
15.    tell (every person whose name is chosen_name)
16.       set chosen_person to item 1 of it
17.    end tell
18.    tell chosen_person
19.       set email_label_list to label of every email
20.       set email_value_list to value of every email
21.       set phone_label_list to label of every phone
22.       set phone_value_list to value of every phone
23.    end tell
24. end tell
25. if email_label_list is {} and phone_label_list is {} then
26.    display dialog "The contact you selected has no email or phones"
27. else
```

```
28.     set the_message to "Contact information for " & ¬
            chosen_name & ":" & return
29.    if email_label_list is not {} then
30.       repeat with i from 1 to (count email_label_list)
31.          set the_label to item i of email_label_list
32.          set the_value to item i of email_value_list
33.          set the_message to the_message & the_label & ¬
                " email: " & the_value & return
34.       end repeat
35.    end if
36.    if phone_label_list is not {} then
37.       repeat with i from 1 to (count phone_label_list)
38.          set the_label to item i of phone_label_list
39.          set the_value to item i of phone_value_list
40.          set the_message to the_message & the_label & ¬
                " number: " & the_value & return
41.       end repeat
42.    end if
43. end if
44. if email_label_list is {} then
45.    display dialog the_message buttons {"Thanks"} default button 1
46. else
47.    display dialog the_message buttons {"e-mail", "Thanks"}
48.    if button returned of result is "e-mail" then
49.       tell application "Mail"
50.          activate
51.          set newMessage to make new outgoing message ¬
                with properties {visible:true}
52.          tell newMessage
53.             make new to recipient with properties ¬
                {name:chosen_name, address:item 1 of email_value_list}
54.          end tell
55.       end tell
56.    end if
57. end if
```

After the user picks a letter from the alphabet, the script needs to create a list of names that start with that letter. This is done in two steps; in lines 5 through 7 the contacts whose last name starts with the letter are added, and in lines 8 through 10 the names that start with the first name are added.

In the Address Book dictionary, the *person* class has several name-related properties assigned to it: *first name, middle name, last name, nickname, maiden name*, and then phonetic *first, middle,* and *last* names. That makes nine different name options; better safe than sorry, I guess. Actually, there are only eight name-related properties you control. The property *name* is a read-only property that is comprised of the *first, middle,* and *last name* properties.

Once we collect the list of names, the user gets to pick the one s/he wants. That happens in line 13.

In lines 15 through 17 we get the reference to the person based on the full name the user picks from the list. Note that if there are two identical names, the script will arbitrarily pick the first one. Just make sure you fix that little issue before you package this script and sell it as shareware.

Once we assign the person to a variable, we can collect the phone numbers and e-mails assigned to that person. As we've seen earlier, the contacts database is a simple relational database in which the phone numbers and e-mail records are related to the person records.

Since we need both the label and the value of the e-mails and phone numbers, we collect both. This is done in lines 18 through 23, where we create two sets of list pairs: one pair is the e-mails label list and the e-mail values list, and the other one has the phone label and values list. The list pairs are only virtual, of course. The way the script is structured ensures that the e-mail labels list has corresponding items to the e-mail value list, but the lists themselves are completely independent.

Between lines 29 and 43 we collect the data for the string variable we call *the_message*. This variable will be used to display the collected information to the user.

At the end, if the script has detected one or more e-mail addresses, it will display a dialog box that has an email button. If the user clicks that button, the script will create a new e-mail message in Mail with the selected person's e-mail address.

iCal

The next iApp I will cover is iCal. iCal also has a small but well-crafted scripting dictionary.

In iCal we have calendars that can have to-do's and events. A to-do is a simple object with mostly a completion date, a due date, and a summary. Events, however, are more complex. Unlike to-do's, members of the *event* class can have their own attendee and various alarm elements.

Calendars in the iCal dictionary correspond to the different named calendars you can specify in iCal. Each calendar has *todo* class elements and *event* class elements. In iCal's window, you can identify which events belong to what calendars by their color.

25

> *While iCal can have multiple calendars, they are all seen, by default, in the same calendar window.*

Calendars

The *calendar* class is the core element of the iCal application. Any event you want to manipulate or create has to belong to a calendar.

To create calendars in iCal, you have to explicitly specify where you want the new calendar created.

```
tell application "iCal"
    make new calendar at end of calendars ¬
        with properties {title:"Sports"}
end tell
```

Result:

```
calendar 9 of application iCal
```

The *calendar* class's title (there is no calendar *name* property) is the only property that is not read only.

You can set the *tint* property of the calendar, but it will have no effect.

Events

As you can imagine, one of the most useful classes in iCal is the *event* class. Events are what make the calendar useful in the first place: dinner party Tuesday at 6, sales meeting Friday at 3:00 to 4:30 p.m., etc.

The *event* class has a few obvious properties such as *start date* and *end date*, both of which accept AppleScript's date value. You can also set the summary to the text you want displayed in the iCal window.

Following is a simple script that creates a new event and assigns it a few basic properties:

Script 25-9

```
tell application "iCal"
    tell calendar 1
        set new_event to make new event at end of events
        tell new_event
            set start date to date "Monday, May 3, 2004 4:00:00 PM"
            set end date to date "Monday, May 3, 2004 4:30:00 PM"
            set summary to "Feed ferret"
            set location to "Providence"
            set allday event to false
            set status to confirmed
            set recurrence to ¬
                "FREQ=DAILY;INTERVAL=2;UNTIL=20040531T035959Z"
        end tell
    end tell
end tell
```

Let's look at the four event properties set in these examples.

The first two properties are *start date* and *end date*. These are probably the most important properties that define the date and time boundaries of the event.

The *summary* and *location* properties are two strings that provide information about the event.

The event's *status* property can be *none*, *confirmed*, *tentative*, or *cancelled*, and the all-day event's value is a Boolean that determines whether the event appears as a single-day block or as a multiday banner that can be stretched around in the iCal UI.

The *recurrence* property is where Apple engineers could have definitely spent more time. Right now, as of iCal version 1.5, the *recurrence* property is an ugly string that includes information about the recurrence frequency, intervals, and duration of the event's recurrence. It also has a bug that makes the property appear with a colon at the start, but this can be ignored. Here is an example of the string again:

```
FREQ=DAILY;INTERVAL=2;UNTIL=20040531T035959Z
```

The string has three properties in it, which are shown next along with their possible values.

Frequency

Represented with *FREQ*, this can be followed by the value DAILY, WEEKLY, MONTHLY, or YEARLY.

Interval

If the frequency is set to DAILY, for instance, *INTERVAL* specifies how many days between event occurrences. In the preceding example, the intervals are 2, which means that the *feed ferret* event will recur every two days.

Duration

Duration can either be the word "UNTIL" followed by a funny date-time string, or the word "COUNT" followed by the number of occurrences that will happen before the event repetition expires. In the example I used the following *UNTIL* value: 20040531T035959Z. It means that the event will stop recurring on May 31, 2004 at 3:59:59 PM. It appears that the time in the *UNTIL* portion of the string is always one minute to four.

An *UNTIL* duration of -1 indicates that the event never expires.

Event elements

The *event* class can have elements of its own. An event can have attendees, and four types of alarms: open file alarm, sound alarm, display alarm, and mail alarm. We will not get into these in detail right now, but the script in the next section should shed some light on their use and creation.

25

New event based on Mail

In this sample script we will parse an e-mail that is sent by Microsoft Exchange Server when a new meeting is scheduled. We will take the text from the e-mail message and attempt to convert it into a new event in iCal.

The script is broken down into three parts: getting the information from Mail, extracting the dates and other information from the message, and finally creating the new event.

Please note that due to bugs in iCal 1.5 scriptability, the last portion of the script, which adds the attendees to the event, doesn't work, but should work once iCal is fixed (hopefully by the time you read this).

Let's look at the finished script and then examine certain portions of it.

Script 25-10

```
1.  --Get message information from Mail
2.  tell application "Mail"
3.     set selection_list to selection
4.     set my_message to item 1 of selection_list
5.     tell my_message
6.        set attendee_count to count every recipient
7.        set attendee_name_list to ¬
              name of every recipient -- of my_message
8.        set attendee_address_list to ¬
              address of every recipient -- of my_message
9.        set message_subject to subject -- of my_message
10.       set message_text to content --of my_message
11.    end tell
12. end tell
13. --parse text
14. set message_paragraph_list to paragraphs of message_text
15. repeat with the_paragraph in message_paragraph_list
16.    if the_paragraph starts with "When:" then
17.       set time_string_end to offset of "(" in the_paragraph
18.       set when_string to characters 7 thru (time_string_end - 2) ¬
              of the_paragraph as string
19.       set date_word_list to words of when_string
20.       set text item delimiters to space
21.       set date_string to items 1 thru 4 of date_word_list as string
22.       set time_start_string to items 5 thru 7 of date_word_list ¬
                 as string
23.       set time_end_string to items 8 thru 10 of date_word_list ¬
                 as string
24.       set text item delimiters to ""
25.       set start_date to date (date_string & space & ¬
              time_start_string)
26.       set end_date to date (date_string & space & time_end_string)
27.    else if the_paragraph starts with "When:" then
```

```
28.          set where_string to characters 8 thru -1 of the_paragraph ¬
                  as string
29.      else if the_paragraph starts with "*~" then
30.          exit repeat
31.      end if
32. end repeat
33. --Create event in iCal
34. tell application "iCal"
35.      set my_cal to calendar 1
36.      set new_event to make new event at end of my_cal ¬
                  with properties ¬
37.          {summary:message_subject, start date:start_date, ¬
                  end date:end_date}
38.      tell new_event
39.          make new mail alarm at end of mail alarms ¬
                  with properties {trigger interval:-30}
40.          --make attendees
41.          repeat with i from 1 to attendee_count
42.              set attendee_name to item i of attendee_name_list
43.              set attendee_address to item i of attendee_address_list
44.              set new_attendee to make new attendee at end of attendees
45.              tell new_attendee
46.                  set display name to attendee_name
47.                  set email to attendee_address
48.              end tell
49.          end repeat
50.      end tell
51. end tell
```

In the first portion of the script, between lines 1 and 12, we extract information directly from the mail message. Figure 25-2 shows the original mail message that we got.

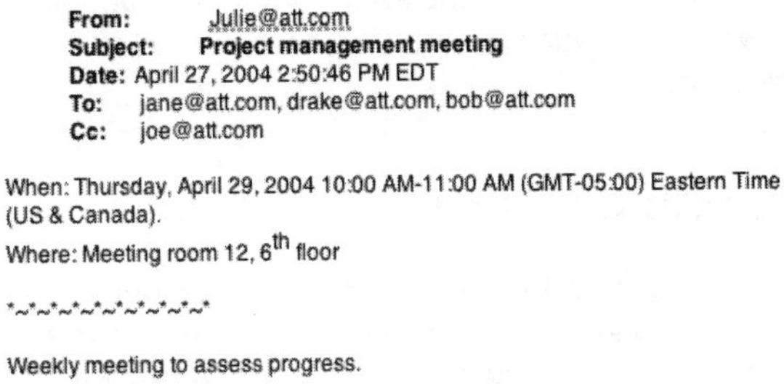

From: Julie@att.com
Subject: **Project management meeting**
Date: April 27, 2004 2:50:46 PM EDT
To: jane@att.com, drake@att.com, bob@att.com
Cc: joe@att.com

When: Thursday, April 29, 2004 10:00 AM-11:00 AM (GMT-05:00) Eastern Time (US & Canada).
Where: Meeting room 12, 6th floor

~~*~*~*~*~*~*~*

Weekly meeting to assess progress.

Figure 25-2. The original mail message we need to parse

The information extracted is the message subject that we will use as the summary of our event, the list of recipients that will be used to add attendees to the event, and the body of the message from which the start and end date for the event will be extracted.

In the second part, lines 13 through 32, we parse out the information we need from the mail message. There are many ways to do that, but the result has to be pretty much the same. We need to end up with three pieces of information for the iCal event: start time, end time, and location.

The way I tackled it in the script is by breaking the message into paragraphs and then examining each paragraph using a repeat loop.

If the paragraph starts with "when:", then I know it has the date info; if it starts with "Where:", then it has the location.

More specifically, I parse out the date information from the "When:" paragraph in two steps. I start by getting all the text from the seventh character to the first instance of a parenthesis.

The full line is as follows:

When: Thursday, April 29, 2004 10:00 AM-11:00 AM (GMT-05:00) Eastern Time (US & Canada)

But I needed this:

Thursday, April 29, 2004 10:00 AM-11:00 AM

The problem I had then is that the date included both the start time and end time. I solved that by getting the words only (line 18), and then attached them to new dates (lines 21–23): for instance, the date is always words 1 through 4. This situation works as long as the number of words is constant, and it appears to be.

The final part of the script is to create the event (lines 33 through 51). We create the actual event in lines 36–37, where we assign the summary and different date properties during the creation process. We also assign the result of the *create* command to the variable *new_event*.

In lines 38–49 we add the elements to the event. We start by adding a single e-mail alarm element, and then we loop through the list of attendee e-mail and name lists to add them as attendees to the event.

Use iCal to schedule scripts

Another neat thing you can do with iCal is to schedule the launching of scripts. To do that, create a new event in iCal and set the start date, time to the date, and time you want the script to execute on. Then use the open file alarm and specify the script file you want to execute.

iChat

iChat is a small application, so it's not surprising that there are only three classes and three commands defined in the iChat suite.

iChat classes

Besides the *application* class, iChat has an *account* class and a *service* class.

Different account elements in the iChat application correspond to different people you chat with. Accounts can be referenced either from the service they belong to or directly from the application.

There are only a handful of properties in iChat, as you may imagine, and most can't be changed. In fact, the only two significant properties belong to the *application* class, and they are *status* and *status message*. All properties of the *account* and *service* classes are read only.

One of the properties scripters like to have fun with is the *status message* property. This is the message that appears both at the top of your iChat window and as your status on your buddies' iChat windows.

The property is very simple; you can simply set it to any string.

```
tell application "iChat" to set status message to Honey, I'm Home"
```

The script that follows acts as an iChat status message agent. It is saved as a stay-open application and makes use of the *on idle* handler.

The script will check to see the current track name and playlist name and alternate them every five seconds as the status message. This way your buddies can know you're available, and know what song you happen to be listening to at the moment. Here's the script:

Script 25-11

```
1. property flag : true
2. property original_message : ""
3. on run
4.     tell application "iChat"
5.         set original_message to status message
6.     end tell
7. end run

8. on idle
9.     try
10.        tell application "iTunes"
11.            set this_track to name of current track
12.            set this_playlist to name of current playlist
13.        end tell
14.        set status_message to "Available and listening to "
```

25

```
15.        if flag then
16.            set status_message to status_message & ¬
                  "track: " & this_track
17.        else
18.            set status_message to status_message & "playlist:" & ¬
                    this_playlist
19.        end if
20.    on error
21.        set status_message to "Available and listening to nothin'"
22.    end try
23.    tell application "iChat"
24.        set status message to status_message
25.    end tell
26.    set flag to not flag
27.    return 5
28. end idle

29. on quit
30.    tell application "iChat"
31.        set status message to original_message
32.    end tell
33.    continue quit
34. end quit
```

The script uses two properties: *original_status* and *flag*. The *flag* property changes from true to false to indicate to the script whether the next status should be the name of the playlist or the track.

The *original_status* property is set in the *on run* handler, which executes once when the script application is launched. It holds the original status message. This original message is reinstated in the *on quit* handler, which is called when the script application quits.

A minimal amount of error handling is there in case iTune has no playlists open at the time, or no selected track.

Also notice that if you want your script application to be able to quit, you have to end the code in the *on quit* handler with the *continue quit* line. Otherwise, the quit operation will be stopped by your own *quit* handler.

CHAPTER 26

SCRIPTING DATA AND DATABASES

Take a piece of paper and make a simple shopping list: one column for the items you need and one column for the number of items you want. Did you just create a database? I think you did: you can sort it and find items in it, you can cross-reference items in the store's price list, which makes it a relational database, and you can add it to a longer list of all the shopping you've ever done. OK, so it's not that fast or efficient, but it has data organized in fields and records.

There are three factors that make a database what it is: the data structure, which is basically the fields and field definitions, the data itself, and the functionality, such as sorting, searching, and exporting.

AppleScript itself has no built-in database tools, but there is a bit you can get done with lists. For instance, you can collect data in two or more corresponding lists whose data relate item for item. Later on you can loop through those page items as if each list were a field and each set of items across the lists (item *n* of every list) for a single record. While this works for basic operations, it will fall short when you need to sort the data or perform less-than-sluggish searches.

In this chapter, we will look at three ways AppleScript can connect to or be used as a database.

We will start with scripting FileMaker Pro 7, then move on to connecting to SQL databases using MacSQL, and finally look at a scripting addition that acts as a built-in database engine for AppleScript.

Automating FileMaker Pro with AppleScript

FileMaker Pro is one of the oldest and most loved applications used on the Mac. It started out through Claris, an Apple subsidiary, and is now created and sold by FileMaker Inc. (www.filemaker.com). FileMaker Pro is known for its ease of use, robust scripting, and layout tools, which give developers the ability to develop database-driven applications quickly.

Out of the 50-something properties of the 12 or so classes that are defined in the FileMaker Pro dictionary, only one meaningful property is not read only. That property is the *cellValue* property, which allows you to access the data in the cell. Some other properties can be set as well, such as the window's bounds, and a couple of others, but nothing in the structure of the database such as field definitions, layout elements, object names, or FileMaker scripts is scriptable. So why do I even bother with it? Well, the beauty of scripting FileMaker Pro is not really in how we can control the database itself, but rather how we can use the already established database to help us with script execution. As a scripter I like the fact that I can use FileMaker to put together a back-end database for my script with minimal effort. I can give the users a nice user interface, set up reports and control security in a jiffy, and best of all, have full access to the underlying data.

While this section describes the important aspects of FileMaker scripting, it is by no means a comprehensive guide. FileMaker Pro does come with a database that explains the different events and commands available to scripters.

Versions

FileMaker Pro was never known for comprehensive AppleScript support; however, it gave scripters consistent support through the years. Even now with the introduction of the all-new FileMaker Pro 7, the scripting dictionary remains virtually unchanged.

One thing that did change with FileMaker Pro 7 is the introduction of the *table* class. Up to now, FileMaker's tables were synonymous with database files. Now, however, database files can have multiple tables, so the *table* class is an element of the *database* class, along with layout.

Having multiple versions of FileMaker Pro on the same Mac, all with the same exact name, may be a problem. To ensure that your script editor points to the right version of FileMaker, you can change the name of the application to FileMaker Pro 7, or change the name of the old one.

The FileMaker object model and the commands you can use

The FileMaker Pro object model is very simple, as described previously. In the following text, I get into it in more detail.

Databases, documents, and windows

The top objects inside the *application* class are *database*, *document*, and *window*. There's also *menu*, but we will not deal with it here.

The *database* and *document* classes are almost the same thing: they both represent the container of all the tables, fields, layouts, records, and cells. The difference between them used to be such that the *database* class contained every record, and the *document* class contained only the found set of records. Now, things are a bit different, since neither the *database* object nor the *document* object contains records; only layouts and tables contain records. In the new FileMaker 7, to get the found set you have to work with layouts versus tables. Read on.

This used to be easier to deal with in pre-FileMaker 7 versions. In FileMaker 7, not only can a file have multiple tables, but you can also have multiple windows open. That means the following:

To access records in a database, always use the *table* object; otherwise FileMaker will only allow you to access the data in the first table.

```
tell application "FileMaker Pro"-- 7.0
  get records of table "contacts" of database 1
end
```

If you want to refer to databases by name, use the database's file name.

26

To get access to the found set, on the other hand, we have to use the *window* class. It can be any window or a window of a specific document:

```
tell application "FileMaker Pro"-- 7.0
    get records of current layout of ¬
        window "contacts" of document 1
end
```

Remember, the found set of a database is circumstantial and changes all the time, so you have to make sure you're referring to the right window that contains the found set you're looking for.

Tables and layouts

The next level of object classes contains the *table* and *layout* classes. The difference between them is in the context of the data you can get from them. You refer to the table to get full access to all the fields in that table, and to the data in every cell of every record. The layout, on the other hand, gives you access to the same information the user can see on that layout. To better access a layout, you have to specify the window the layout is in, since different windows can now show the same layout with different found sets of records.

Let's look at two scripts that should illustrate the difference between a table and a layout. First we will get the data from a date field and a number field from the table they are in, then we will get the same values from the layout. In our example, the data returned is the same from the layout and from the table.

Here's the script for getting data from a layout:

Script 26-1

```
tell application "FileMaker Pro"
    tell document "Inventory "
        tell window 1
            tell layout "equipment"
                go to it
                tell current record
                    set the_date to get cellValue ¬
                        of cell "date purchased"
                    set the_cost to cell "value"
                end tell
            end tell
        end tell
    end tell
end tell
```

In the layout, the order of the fields is determined by the way they are organized graphically on the page, and you can only access the data of the cells that exist on that layout, including related fields. In a table, the fields are always ordered by their creation date. This is not an issue, however, if you ask for the value by field or cell name.

You can use the *layout* class with the *show* and *go to* commands for changing the currently displayed layout. You can't show or go to a table.

Now here's the script for getting data from a table:

Script 26-2

```
tell application "FileMaker Pro"
    tell document "Inventory"
        tell table "equipment"
            tell record 1
                set the_date to cell "date purchased"
                set the_cost to cell "value"
            end tell
        end tell
    end tell
end tell
```

Also note that the *table* class does not support the current *record* object. There is no current record, because for a table all records are just as current. Thus, the following line will error out:

```
current record of table 1 of database 1
```

Layout 0

Layout 0 is an object used in earlier versions of FileMaker Pro and is still there, but will give you access only to the first table in the database, so avoid using it.

Records, fields, and cells

In FileMaker Pro you can get and set the data of a cell or of an entire record or field at once.

While the cell class has a *cellValue* property, just referring to the *cell* object returns its value, as can be seen here:

Script 26-3

```
tell application "FileMaker Pro"
    tell document "applescript test"
        tell record 3 of table "equipment"
            cell "value" = cellValue ¬
                of cell "value" --> true
        end tell
    end tell
end tell
```

Getting either the cell or the *cellValue* of the cell always returns a string, no matter what field type the data comes from.

The following script sets the value of a cell in a table. The script first does a virtual "find" by changing only the records that match certain criteria.

Script 26-4

```
tell application "FileMaker Pro"
    tell database "Inventory"
        tell table "equipment"
            tell (every record whose cell "type" ¬
                is "222")
                set cell "model" to "AB-222"
            end tell
        end tell
    end tell
end tell
```

The preceding script represents more than merely a way to set data. In fact, this is AppleScript's simplistic answer to relational database searching. More on that later in the "Using the whose clause to retrieve relational data" section.

You can also set or get data of an entire field or record.

When you work with the *table* object, you will have to be aware of the order FileMaker uses when it sets and returns data.

As explained earlier, the field order in a table is the field creation order and the record order is the record creation order. There's no way to change that order, even by sorting the records.

When you get data from the layout instead of the table, the records will be returned from the found set in the current sort order. That means that although the *table* object is more flexible and has greater access to the data, it may be beneficial sometimes to use the *layout* object to get or set the same data, since you can set the sort order and found set before you change or get the data, and this way have more control over what you do.

The following script first does the AppleScript version of the *find* command and then sorts the data before retrieving the data:

Script 26-5

```
tell application "FileMaker Pro"
    tell table "equipment"
        show (every record whose cell "type" ¬
            is "222")
    end tell
    tell layout "equipment" of window 1
        sort by field "value"
        set value_list to field "value"
    end tell
end tell
```

In the preceding script, the *show* command acts as the *find* command. The actual *find* command in FileMaker Pro's AppleScript dictionary will perform a find using the most recent find settings.

Notice that for the *show* command we turn to the *table* object, not the *layout* object. Remember, the *layout* object only knows about the currently found set, so it will show the records that fit the criteria you set, if they are already in the found set. Even if you use the following line, FileMaker will not show all the records in the table:

```
show every record of layout "equipment"
```

To show all records in the table, you will need to do the following:

```
show every record of table "equipment"
```

To sort records, on the other hand, you have to use the *layout* command since the *table* object doesn't handle the *sort* command.

Just as you get data from the database a whole field at a time, you can also insert data a field at a time.

The following script sets the cell "serial number" of every record in the found set to values from a list. The values will be applied to the records in the order they happened to be sorted in at the time.

Script 26-6

```
set serial_list to {"AB-222", "AB-223", ¬
   "AB-224", "AB-225", "AB-226"}
tell application "FileMaker Pro"
   tell layout "equipment"
      set field "serial number" to serial_list
   end tell
end tell
```

If the second *tell* block had been directed at the *table* object instead of the *layout* object, then the data in the field would apply to the records in the table, starting from the first one in the creation order, going up until the last record, or the last item in the list (whichever comes first), completely ignoring the found set and the sort order.

set data

Unlike the *set* command, *set data* doesn't change any data property, but rather sets the data of a cell, record, or field to either a single value or a list of values. Using *set data of (cell/record/field)* is the same as simply setting the object itself to the string or list value.

Finding data quickly with the whose clause

We all know the *find* command in FileMaker, and have used it many times. When writing scripts for FileMaker, however, you may want to avoid using either the dictionary's *find* command or any reference to a FileMaker script that performs a *find* command—not necessarily because they don't work, but rather because there's a better way to refer to the set of records you want to work with. That way is AppleScript's powerful filtering *whose* clause.

26

For most operations such as get data and set data, you don't even need to actually find the data and display the found set, but rather isolate the records you want to work with inside your script. The *whose* clause is great for that.

As you've seen previously, you can use a single *whose* clause to retrieve complex sets of data. Here's an example:

Script 26-7

```
tell database "campaign"
    tell table "donors"
        tell every record whose ¬
            (cell  "State"  = "RI") and ¬
            (cell  "Income"  > 100000)
            set address_list to "address"
            set phone_list to cell "tel01"
            set name_list to cell "full name"
        end tell
    end tell
end tell
```

The preceding script allows us to get data very quickly from a very specific set of records without any interface changes, running any scripts, or invoking any FileMaker *find* commands.

Using the *whose* clause for filtering records is great in many cases, but FileMaker still may have search criteria that performs filtering functions not available in AppleScript, such as searches for duplicates and searches for Japanese characters.

Using the whose clause to retrieve relational data

Using the *whose* clause search techniques you saw previously, you can perform complex relational searches with minimal effort, and without having to set up or refer to any FileMaker Pro relationships.

The idea is to first find the key field, and then use the value in that key field to find related files. For example, let's say that we have a contacts database. In that contacts database we have two tables: people and numbers (much like the Address Book application). The numbers table contains all the fax and phone numbers for all the contacts, and every number is linked to the contacts with the person id field. Each number has four fields then: number id, person id, number label, and number value.

Now let's imagine that I have a person named John L. Smith from Boulder, CO, and I need to get all of the numbers related to his record. All I have to do is find the value of the person id field in the people table, and then find all the records in the numbers table that have that same number in that table's person id field. Here's how the script goes:

Script 26-8

```
tell application "FileMaker Pro"
    tell table "people" of database 1
        tell every record whose¬
            (cell "first name" = "John") and¬
            (cell "middle name" starts with "L") and¬
```

```
               (cell "last name" = "Smith") and¬
               (cell "city" = "Boulder") and¬
               (cell "state" = "CO")
                  set person_id to cell "person id"
            end tell
         end tell
      tell table "number" of database 1
         tell every record whose¬
            (cell " person id " = person_id)
            set person_number_list ¬
               to cell "number" of it
         end tell
      end tell
   end tell
```

Running AppleScripts from inside FileMaker

FileMaker Pro allows you to run AppleScripts that are embedded in FileMaker scripts. To
do that you use the *Perform AppleScript* script step in a FileMaker Pro script.

Figure 26-1 shows the dialog box in FileMaker that allows you to specify the AppleScript
script you want to run.

This script step is used to execute AppleScript code in the middle of a FileMaker script.

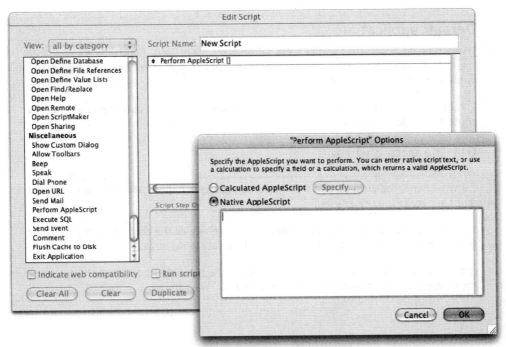

Figure 26-1.
The *Perform AppleScript* script step in a FileMaker Pro script

As you can see in Figure 26-1, there are two ways to perform AppleScripts from FileMaker scripts. You can either specify a calculation, whose text result is a valid AppleScript script, or dictate the actual script text.

If you dictate the actual AppleScript text, FileMaker will attempt to compile your script and check your syntax when you click the OK button. You will only be able to exit the dialog box if the script you entered compiles, or if you cancel out. However, FileMaker will not fill in any shortcuts you used as script editors do. For instance, if you used *tell app...* instead of *tell application*, that is the way your script will remain.

In the case of calculated fields, FileMaker compiles the script right before execution, since the script can change any time leading up to that point.

It is almost always preferred to use calculation fields rather than just entering or pasting the script text. If you choose to enter or paste the native AppleScript text right into the provided box, you will have to dig up that FileMaker script step every time you want to make a change. On the other hand, using a calculation to specify the AppleScript text allows you to refer to a field that contains the AppleScript script text.

See the next section for a few tips regarding the use of calculation fields with *Perform AppleScript* script steps.

Working smart with FileMaker

There are several ways you can make scripting FileMaker easier and cleaner. Here are a few of them.

Default application

When running AppleScript scripts from a FileMaker script step, FileMaker is considered the default application. That means that if you choose, you don't have to use the *tell application "FileMaker Pro"* line.

I recommend that you do, though, in order to make your scripts also usable outside the context of a FileMaker script.

Get the data and run

While AppleScript interaction with applications such as FileMaker Pro is necessary to get the work done, you want to limit this interaction to the minimum. This can speed up your script and make it more efficient.

The way I like to interact with FileMaker is by first getting all the data I need from it using as few commands as possible, and then using that data in my script.

It is better to let AppleScript access the data using the *table* object and make heavy use of the *whose* clause in order to filter the record set you want to use.

Work from behind

AppleScript scripts that interact with FileMaker Pro work much faster when FileMaker is in the background and the script is in the foreground. This is somewhat true for many applications, but makes a big performance difference in FileMaker.

The best way to put FileMaker in the background is to send the script the *activate* command, like this:

```
tell me to activate
```

Use a dedicated AppleScript scripts table

One structural piece I include with some solutions is a separate FileMaker table I call "AppleScript". In that table, each record contains the text for a different AppleScript script used by the entire database. This allows me easy access to the scripts from a central location.

External debug check box

One thing that FileMaker is not that good at is debugging AppleScript scripts. For that reason I deploy a scenario that allows me to halt any FileMaker script at the point where the AppleScript script has to take over.

To do that, I need to add to the AppleScript scripts table an additional field, which I call "debug". The debug field is formatted as a check box with a single value. This field acts as a flag that determines whether FileMaker should execute the actual text in the field containing the AppleScript text or execute a simple AppleScript that calls yet another FileMaker script that halts all FileMaker scripts. This sounds complex, but it isn't really. All I want to do is be able to check the debug check box and have the FileMaker script halt instead of having the actual AppleScript execute. This allows me to check that box and run the script from Script Debugger, where I can debug it more easily.

This method is good, but it requires FileMaker to search for the record containing the AppleScript you want to run and copy it to a global field that FileMaker can then execute using the *Perform AppleScript* script step.

Calling external libraries for easy debugging

Even better than the dedicated AppleScript table I described previously is the method of loading an external AppleScript file and running it. This way is great especially if you are supporting different solutions remotely. You can work on improving the scripts on a test environment and then send the improved AppleScript files to the live location and have the administrator there install them in the external scripts folder.

Read and write commands

Due to the fact discussed previously, that FileMaker acts as the default application when you run AppleScript scripts from inside FileMaker, some commands don't compile. The *read* and *write* commands, for instance, don't compile unless you place them in another application's *tell* block, such as the Finder.

26

Scripting Runtime Labs' MacSQL

In many cases your AppleScript scripts have to connect to different enterprise SQL databases. These databases span Microsoft SQL Server, MySQL, Oracle, FrontBase, OpenBase, Sybase, and others.

When your AppleScript solution calls for integration with an SQL database, one product stands out: Runtime Labs' MacSQL (www.runtimelabs.com).

MacSQL is a simple program that gives you GUI access to many flavors of SQL databases, including the few I mentioned previously. On top of helping you create queries and view the schema of the SQL database, MacSQL is AppleScript-able to a point that you can perform any SQL command with AppleScript code. You will, of course, have to have the proper SQL statements that will get the job done, but these are usually easy to get. The best thing to do, if you are not familiar with SQL syntax, is to find a good reference book that details the syntax of the specific SQL flavor you're using, and ask someone from IT to help you get a handle on the SQL statements you need.

Getting connected

The biggest challenge you will face when scripting an SQL database with MacSQL is the initial stage of getting access to your database. Once you're over that part, it's usually smooth sailing.

To get connected, you will need database access settings such as the host, database name, and user login information.

Start by choosing New Connection from the File Menu.

In the New Connection dialog box, shown in Figure 26-2, choose the database type you will be working with. Once you do that, MacSQL will display the fields you need to fill in order to establish a connection with your database. Write down the settings you will require and ask someone from IT for the values to enter.

Figure 26-2. MacSQL's New Connection dialog box

After some back and forth action with IT, you will hopefully be able to establish connection with the database. This connection will represent itself in the form of a MacSQL document. Save this document to the hard drive and keep a note somewhere with the settings the administrator gave you.

This document you saved is your new best friend. Every time your script needs to connect to that database, all you have to do is open that document. Then, you will direct any SQL statement to MacSQL's front document object, which has all the settings.

Speed

I always knew that SQL databases were generally very fast, but what surprised me was just how fast I could execute SQL commands with AppleScript in the middle. It would execute tens of operations per second, which may sound very slow in SQL terms, but usually fast enough for AppleScript projects that don't need to access the database that often.

Simple select command

Interacting with SQL databases with MacSQL is a bit more complicated than just using the *do query* command. Following is a script that gets data from two fields from the entire contact_table table. We will look at the script and then analyze it line by line:

Script 26-9

```
set query_text to ¬
    "SELECT contact_first_name, ¬
        contact_first_name FROM contact_table"
tell application "MacSQL"
    tell front document
        do query query_text with prefetching results
        set the_result_set to last result set of it
    end tell
    set theData to value of ¬
        every row of the_result_set
    delete the_result_set
end tell
```

The first line of the script is simply the string that makes up the SQL command. Usually, you will be concatenating strings in AppleScript to get to the final SQL statement you want.

Next, we will talk to our front document. Remember, this is the document we saved in the "Getting connected" section. This script assumes that this document is open.

In the following line, we do the query. We supply the *do query* command with one string parameter that contains the raw SQL command. The SQL statement we use has been put in the variable *query_text* in the first line of the script.

26

The result of a successful *do query* command is a result set. A result set is a MacSQL class that can contain rows and columns (more on that later). In this script we simply set the variable *the_data* to every row of the variable *the_result_set*, which contains the result set that was returned by our *do query* command.

Now, the value of the variable *the_data* is a list of lists, and it contains all the data we fetched from the SQL table.

The last line before the *end tell* line deletes the result set. This is essential housecleaning. If you don't delete the last result set in some way, MacSQL will jam after a couple of queries.

More on result sets

The result set is not like a list, and is not always as straightforward. Sometimes, the rows of the result set are indeterminate, so you can't really get every row of it. What you do in that case is loop an unlimited number of times, and get the next row of the result set until the script errors out. You should, of course, trap that error.

In our script we used the *prefetching results* parameter with a true value, which made sure that the value of every row of the result set could be extracted in one step.

Following is one of the sample scripts that come with MacSQL, which forces you to loop through the rows, and then through the items in each row for the purpose of generating a tab-delimited string.

Script 26-10

```
set theQuery to "select * from foo"
tell application "MacSQL"
    set theSession to front document
    tell theSession to set numRows ¬
        to do query theQuery
    set rs to last result set of theSession
    set the_data to ""
    set rowNum to 1
    try
        repeat
            set ro to value of row rowNum of rs
            set rowNum to rowNum + 1
            set the_data to the_data & first item of ro
            set ro to rest of ro
            repeat until ro is {}
                set the_data to the_data & tab & ¬
                    (first item of ro)
                set ro to rest of ro
            end repeat
            set the_data to the_data & return
            --the last five lines could have been:
            -- set the_data to the_data & ¬
                tab delimited values of ro
```

```
        end repeat
    on error err
    end try
    delete rs
end tell
```

While this is a good example of the *row* and *result set* objects, know that each *row* object has not only the *value* property whose value is a list, but also the *tab delimited values* and *comma separated values* properties, which contain the string versions of the data in the row.

When working with Microsoft SQL Server, for instance, you have to use the *with prefetching results* parameter, as I did in my examples.

Clean up or go overboard

As discussed previously, deleting the last result set is essential. If you don't, you will get the error "connection pool limit reached."

In the next section, note in the subroutine in Script 26-11 that the script attempts to delete the result set if there has been any error in the script. If the error occurred after the result set has been established but before it has been deleted, then you will eventually get that "connection pool limit reached" error.

MacSQL subroutines

Following are two subroutines I created for my own use. They use a document pointing at a Microsoft SQL Server database.

The first one returns data that the SQL statement gets from the database, and the other one sets data, so it doesn't need to return anything other than true or false to indicate success or failure.

Following are the subroutines, each with a sample subroutine call.

This script gets data from MacSQL:

Script 26-11

```
set query_text to "SELECT " & field_1 & ¬
    ", " & field_2 & " FROM " & theTable
set the_result to sql_query_insert(query_text)

on sql_query_select(query_text)
    try
        tell application "MacSQL"
            set theDoc to front document
            tell theDoc to set numRows to ¬
                do query query_text ¬
                with prefetching results
```

26

731

```
                set rs to last result set of theDoc
                set theData to value of every row of rs
                delete rs
            end tell
            return theData
        on error err
            --display dialog err & return & query_text
            try
                delete rs
            end try

            return false
        end try
    end sql_query_select
```

And here's the *Insert* command:

Script 26-12

```
    set query_text to ¬
        "INSERT INTO " & theTable & ¬
        " ("& field_1 &", "& field_2 & ") ¬
        VALUES ('" & value_1 & "', " & value_2 & ")"
    set the_result to sql_query_insert(query_text)
    on sql_query_insert(query_text)
        try
            tell application "MacSQL"
                set theDoc to front document
                tell theDoc to set numRows to ¬
                    do query query_text ¬
                    with prefetching results
                    set rs to last result set of theDoc
                    delete rs
                end tell
                return true
            on error err
                try
                    delete rs
                end try
                --display dialog err & return & query_text
                return false
            end try
        end sql_query_insert
```

ScriptDB

ScriptDB (www.applescriptdb.com) is a new scripting addition that gives you powerful database capabilities within AppleScript. It is created by Custom Flow Solutions, which I own, and is sold as a commercial product; it is also possible to download a demo of it from the preceding URL.

Although you can export and import a ScriptDB database to a file, the purpose of it is really to be used in memory. The ScriptDB object is a part of your script, and any operation you perform on it returns the ScriptDB object as the result.

You would use ScriptDB to replace any data in your script that needs to be stored in a more comprehensive manner than a list or a record. Among other things, it replaces all those clunky routines you have for sorting lists and finding items in lists, although this is only the tip of what ScriptDB can do.

All commands in the ScriptDB suit start with the letters "DB". This makes some commands read a bit funny, but ensures that the commands don't collide with other scripting addition or AppleScript commands.

ScriptDB is also fully Unicode compliant, so databases can contain text from different languages without any special setup.

In this section we will look at some of the capabilities of ScriptDB and see why it should be a staple in anyone's tool chest.

Classes and commands

In ScriptDB there are custom classes that represent a database, a field, a record, and other smaller related objects. The ScriptDB is the main object in the scripting addition. Its main properties are *DBName*, *DBFields*, and *DBData*.

The *DBFields* property is a list made of field definitions. You specify those definitions when you create the database.

Creating a database

There are two ways to create a ScriptDB database: you can either create it from scratch or load an existing file. The file can be a tab-delimited text file, or an XML file exported from either ScriptDB or FileMaker Pro. ScriptDB can also export data to these formats.

The script that follows creates a simple database called "contacts" with three fields: first name, age, and date of birth:

```
set field_list to ¬
    {{"first name", string}, {"married", boolean}, ¬
    {"age", integer}}
set my_db to DB create with properties ¬
    {DBName:"contacts", DBFields:field_list}
```

26

This is the resulting database object:

```
{class:ScriptDB, DBName:"contacts", ¬
    DBFields:{{DBFieldName:"first name",
DBFieldClass:string}, {DBFieldName:"married", ¬
    DBFieldClass:boolean},
{DBFieldName:"age", DBFieldClass:integer}}, ¬
DBData:{}}
```

While the resulting class is a bit complex, it is very easy to extract data out of it when you need to.

In the result, each field is no longer a simple list, but rather a record. This, however, shouldn't concern you at this point.

Database management and variables

Almost every operation you perform with ScriptDB returns the modified ScriptDB object. That means that after we use the *DB add record* command, the result of the statement will be the same database object with some records added.

As with other AppleScript statements, if you keep on assigning the result to the same variable, you will write over the last version of the database.

In the preceding example, we assign the resulting database to the variable *my_db*. From now on, whenever we want to perform any operation on that database, we will need to use the *my_db* variable.

Adding data to our database and deleting it

We can either add one record at a time, one field at a time, or multiple records at once.

To add a single record, we use the *DB add record* command. The following statement adds a single record to our database:

```
set my_db to DB add record ¬
    {"James", true, 28} to db my_db
```

The *DBData* property of the ScriptDB object will now be

```
DBData:{{"James", true, 28}}
```

You can also add multiple records with the *DB add records* command. You use the *DB add records* command the same way, only you supply a list of lists, with each list a record, like the one shown here:

```
{{"James", true, 28},{"Joan", false, 24},{"Mario", false, 15}}
```

So let's assume that we added these three records to the database. To delete a record, we can use the *DB delete records* command. The *DB delete records* command can be very simple, but also very powerful. In the following statement we delete the second record from the database:

```
set my_db to DB delete records from db ¬
    my_db number 2
```

To delete multiple records by their number, simply supply a list of records.

But what if you want to delete records based on their data? For instance, what if you want to delete all records of people under 18? Here's how you'd do that:

```
set my_db to DB delete records from db my_db ¬
    where {field(age), "<", 18}
```

Finding data

ScriptDB allows you to find data subsets that can be returned as a list of lists, as a new ScriptDB object, or as row numbers, representing the rows that the matching data exists in.

All that is done with the *DB get data* command, which has some unique parameters for maximum flexibility.

Narrow the field

The first way to restrict your search is by specifying the records and/or fields you want the data from. This may be all you need to do.

For instance, if you want just the second record, you can write

```
DB get data from db my_db in records 2
```

For record ranges, use a string with dashes to specify a range and comma to separate ranges.

```
DB get data from db my_db in records ¬
    "20-30, 45-55"
```

This can be very useful since you can use AppleScript to create the range string on the fly.

Use the *fields* parameter to restrict the returned result to specific fields:

```
DB get data from db my_db fields "age"
--> {28, 24, 15}
```

Or specify multiple fields by name or position:

```
DB get data from db my_db fields {1, "married"}
--> {{"James", true}, {"Joan", false}, {"Mario", false}}
```

You can also mix the *in records* and *fields* parameters, like this:

```
DB get data from db my_db in records "1,2" fields {1, "married"}
--> {{"James", true}, {"Joan", false}}
```

Search by criteria

The most powerful search option is the use of the *where* parameter. The *where* parameter takes an argument in the form of a list. This list may seem a bit awkward at first, but it does give you some great flexibility for finding data in your ScriptDB database object.

The list is made of fields names, operators, values, and Boolean operators such as *OR* and *AND*. Following are a few examples of searches:

```
DB get data from db my_db where {"field(age)", "<", 55}
```

And also:

```
DB get data from db my_db ¬
where {{"field(married)", "=", false}, "AND", ¬
    {"field(age)", ">", 18}}
```

Now, match that with the previous parameters in records and fields and you can pinpoint any data in your lists. For instance, to get the name of the only single person over 21 in our database, use the following search:

```
DB get data from db my_db ¬
    fields "first name" ¬
    where {{"field(married)", "=", false}, "AND", ¬
        {"field(age)", ">", 18}}
--> {"Joan"}
```

Search result formats

When you perform a search, you can ask for the data either as a list of lists, a list of row numbers, or as a ScriptDB object. To specify the result, you use the *as* parameter. The *as* parameter can have the following values, which correspond to the items mentioned previously: as database, as data only, or as row numbers.

When you ask for the result as data only, which is also the default, you have the choice of transposing the data.

If the result would have been

```
{{"James", true}, {"Joan", false}, {"Mario", false}}
```

then asking for it transposed would return

```
{{"James", "Joan", "Mario"}, {true, false, false}}
```

Sorting data

The *DB sort* command sorts the records in your database object. You can sort by any number of fields, and refer to them by name or number.

Here is an example of a database sorted by the first name field:

```
set my_sorted_db to DB sort db my_db by "first name"
```

In order to sort by descending order, you can put a minus sign before the field name or number. If you specify fields by name, then the minus sign has to be inside the quotes, like this:

```
set my_sorted_db to DB sort db my_db by "-first name"
```

You can also supply a list of fields to sort by.

```
set my_sorted_db to DB sort db my_db by {2, "-first name", -3}
```

The preceding example will sort first by the second field, then by the field first name in descending order, and then by the third field in descending order.

Adding and deleting fields

When we write scripts, we keep a lot of the script data in lists. The lists we use conform more to database fields than to records. Each list has a name that describes the data inside of it, like a field name would describe the contents of the field in the database table.

This is why it is very useful to be able to add fields to and delete them from a ScriptDB object.

Let's say that we created the database with three records that look like this:

```
{{"James", true, 28}, {"Joan", false, 24}, {"Mario", false, 15}}
```

The data here is really three fields: first name, married, and age. To add the gender field, we can use this command:

```
set my_db to DB add field to db my_db with data {"M", "F", "M"}
```

This will result in the following data:

```
{{"James", true, 28, "M"}, {"Joan", false, 24, "F"}, ¬
{"Mario", false, 15, "M"}}
```

If we want to, we can get the data transposed, like this:

```
{{"James", "Joan", "Mario"}, {true, false, false}, ¬
{28, 24, 15}, {"M", "F", "M"}}
```

26

We can also specify a default value, in case the list is not long enough, or we provide no data at all.

To delete a field, use the *DB remove field* command, like this:

```
DB remove field "married" from db my_db
```

Working with files

ScriptDB allows you to save and load database files. You can use either XML or tab-delimited formats. The *DB save* and *DB load* commands allow you to specify the format and delimiters for the text file. The neat thing is that ScriptDB uses a FileMaker Pro–compliant XML format, so you can load XML files exported by FileMaker Pro and have all the field formats preserved. You can also export the data from ScriptDB in XML, and then import that XML file right into a FileMaker database, or just open it with FileMaker Pro.

CHAPTER 27
AUTOMATING MEDIA WORKFLOW

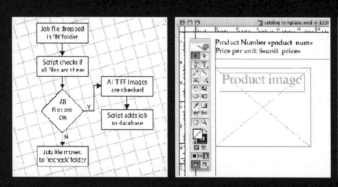

This chapter contains fewer actual scripting examples and more general discussion regarding the design and execution of workflow automation systems.

Building a hot folder API

In this section we will discuss a neat AppleScript system architecture that uses script objects to achieve a truly scalable solution. While I have created several successful systems that make use of the methods described here, there is no single available script that illustrates its points. The information in this chapter is offered as a basis for you to create your own systems.

I call it an API because the idea is to create an AppleScript-based system that is not only flexible, but also a system to which you can add an unlimited number of scripts and processes that integrate with it, without having to tell the system about those scripts.

For example, let's say that we created a system that uses data from a FileMaker Pro database to produce simple printed material such as postcards and mailers. The system is set up in a way that the information in the database and a template is all the system needs to create a finished product. The system may include a main script and a library or two of subroutines, and have the capability to produce three types of products for printing purposes. So it's now a few months after the system started working, and it's a success, saving the company time and money. You are now asked to upgrade the system to produce more types of products. What you have to do is open the "guts" of the script and add a whole new part that can process the same basic information but for a slightly different purpose. This development cycle means that the system has to be debugged again, and worst than that is the fact that you know that more product types will be added later on.

What if instead of just charging ahead with the system, you sat down and imagined all the different products the system could have possibly produced? I'm not saying you should predict the future, just try to anticipate it. Could the system possibly be used for producing static web content? What about presentation slides? There are so many options that you're going to pop. Instead of planning for everything, try to plan for anything! You can do that with a system that acts as a processor, but can have different scripts link to it. The central processor of the system is in charge of the workflow, and has facilities for getting the data and interacting with the publishing applications. That main processor, however, would not create any actual products. This will be the job of the specific product scripts. If the system is well designed, you will be able to create additional product-specific scripts without having to tinker with the main script.

The anatomy of the homegrown API

At the heart of our system lies the concept that the main script loads and runs other scripts whose exact purpose isn't known to it. It figures out which script to load based on some settings, but it never actually becomes aware of the scripts' purpose, and has a limited knowledge of their output. How can we do that? Let's start with defining the main purpose of the system and making up a list of three products our system would create.

The system's purpose is to turn client information into one-of-a-kind marketing pieces. The first three products our system will create will be a postcard, a flyer, and a custom e-mail.

Your next task is to design the products themselves. As you do, you will notice that all products use the same general data set, taken from the same database. Since they all use the same data, one of the jobs of the system could have a subroutine library for getting the data for the different product scripts.

As you work on your products, you will figure out which functions belong with the "system" and which ones belong with the actual product script.

Linking the product scripts to the system

So how will the system know which product script to call and when? Well, the "when" part depends on the specific workflow. In our particular situation, we need to make the operator make two choices: the type of product and the person the product will go to. The list of all the people is found in the FileMaker database, so it makes sense that we initiate the process from there. We could also build a hot folder workflow, but there aren't really any files to process beyond the templates that the system knows about.

Our next task is to figure out how the system will know which product we want to create. Knowing this will allow the system to choose the correct template and call the right product-specific script. But wait, we decided earlier that a truly expandable system can't know about the different product scripts, since we don't want to have to change the main script for every new product.

There are a few solutions for this. One solution is to have a product table in the system's FileMaker database. This way, every time we add a new product that the system can process, we can add a record to that table. Another way is to have a folder for each process. Deciding how to name the folder is the unexpected place where things turn interesting. This is because every product will have a short code name: postcard_01, text_email_01, etc. This code name is going to be the thing that will tie the product scripts with the system. The system will not know how many or what products there are, but it will know that when a request comes in for a product of type postcard_03, it needs to open the template in the folder named `postcard_03 folder`, and most importantly, run the script named `postcard_03.scpt` from the `product scripts` folder.

Now we have a solution: the code name for the product will drive the system to the appropriate template and the appropriate script file. This will allow us to add more products to the system later on without changing the main processor script, but have that main script and associated subroutine libraries for common functions.

27

Separate I/O from process

I/O stands for input-output. Essentially, the description of most systems could be this: "The process that turns the input into the output." You start with data, a few templates, and some settings, and you end up with a booklet, a job ticket, a clean folder, or folder full of processed files, etc.

When designing a workflow system, it is important to not only identify the four aspects of the system, but also know how to separate between them.

The four aspects are input, output, process, and workflow.

It is easy, especially for beginners, to start hacking at a problem with a small script and slowly build it up until it is a code monstrosity that mixes the Excel sheets you use for the data, the dialog boxes that allow the users to input settings, and the InDesign documents that make up the final product.

In my early years I used to create systems much faster, without really thinking the process through. Of course, I didn't have the experience that would allow me to think it through, so I learned the only way I knew how: from my many mistakes. These mistakes, however, were not the types of mistakes you find out right away, but rather later on when the project starts to get out of hand.

Back again to the four aspects of the system. The easy-to-understand part is input/output. Any job requires both data and settings. The data is the raw material, the numbers that will go into the catalog, the client job that has to be cleaned up, etc. At the start of the process you will need to convert this data into AppleScript data, such as lists, records, and other data types, all neatly stored in variables. The wrong way to do this is to sort of go and get the chunk of data you need when you need it in the script. The reason is that at some point, the source of the data will change: the company will move away from Excel to SQL tables, from paper forms to PDF forms, from no database to a FileMaker Pro database, etc. What you want it to be able to do is "detach" the old data connection from your system and "dock" the new one. The process that uses this data will not have to change since your new data source will feed the same AppleScript lists and other variables.

The same concept goes for your output. Now all you have to produce is, say, an Illustrator page with some data in a graph with a title, placed as a PDF in an InDesign page. Next year, however, the web team will get hooked on your automation genius, and you will need to output the same pages as GIFs for the company web site. If your system is well separated, this may not be difficult to do, but tearing apart the spaghetti code of an amateurish system can be a disaster.

Another aspect we mentioned is workflow. The workflow is the way in which the input and settings make their way through the process to become the output. The workflow may answer questions such as these: Is the original file dropped on the script? Will the script watch a folder for incoming job files? Will the users go to the company intranet and click a button that will start the process? Or all of the above? If the workflow piece is separated, your job of adding triggers and workflows become much easier, and many times it makes sense to have the same process triggered by different ways, and therefore creating different workflows.

Variable-data systems

How do you define a variable-data system? For starters, it needs to use data that varies from one cycle to the next. So what about a script that takes data from a text file to create a personalized mailer—is this a variable-data system? Well, besides not really being a system, it does come close.

Although variable data is a term more often associated with big expensive systems, there are compelling reasons for using AppleScript for the same purposes. In the following sections I outline some of the reasons why AppleScript can beat almost any dedicated variable-data system.

Cost

When you write an AppleScript system, you only write the code you need, and you write it to fit a specific need in a controlled environment. This makes for a shorter development cycle with a small team, usually with no more than one or two developers. These developers can easily undersell any large system while still making good money.

Another reason why AppleScript development is cheaper is that many large variable-data systems include their own integrated page layout and database programs. These programs cost a lot of money to develop, a cost that is added to the total cost of the system. In AppleScript, we automate the applications the client already owns.

Results are open

While any automated variable-data system can get most of the job done in a very short amount of time, no system can ensure that the products it produces are 100% finished. There are always some tweaks that the designers need to apply to make it perfect.

One of the downfalls of these monster proprietary systems is that their file format usually isn't compatible with QuarkXPress or InDesign. This means that to make tweaks designers either have to use the system's own layout program or start the job over, and I'm not sure which is worse.

In an AppleScript system, the page layout system is the same system the designers use for anything else, so any job the system finishes can be tweaked in its native format.

This page layout integration also means that the automated process can pick up and let go at any point in the process.

Custom fit without compromise

No matter how flexible a proprietary system is, the client's needs will always have to be compromised to fit the system. With AppleScript, the system is made from scratch to fit the client needs. With AppleScript, anything is possible as long as the client is willing to either pay for it or have someone learn how to create it internally.

27

Data vs. information

Another important thing to understand in regard to variable-data systems is the difference between data and information.

The data is the raw text and numbers that make their way from the data source to the product. Data is the number representing the item's price, which starts in a database somewhere and ends up in a catalog page.

By information, I mean the options that make the product what it is—for instance, whether to use the logo with the company name, the plain logo, or no logo at all. Any information that is used by the script to make decisions should be treated differently than data. This information is usually represented by check boxes, pop-up menus, and other form controls, unlike data, which is usually entered into text fields. These settings are usually set by other people, and not as often as the actual data.

It is important, as you write the script, to think through any constants you embed in the script. Some of these constants are perfect candidates for settings that can be pulled out from the script and be made available from an interface. It is easy to bury constants such as font names, style names, master page names, etc., in your script, but sooner or later you will have to either dig them out, or be forced to open the script and change it on a regular basis.

Find and replace routines

The center of any variable-data system is the ability to find variable text in a graphic document and replace that variable with the final data. These search-and-replace operations are functions you want to perfect and save in a subroutine library that is available to all scripts. This will allow you to keep the variable-data functions of the system in a central location, which can make the system easier to manage.

Years ago, to create a search-and-replace routine in AppleScript, we had to go through statements such as *tell every word of every text box of every page whose content = the_variable to set text of it to the_data*, or something like that. Today, at least in regard to the Adobe applications, the search-and-replace features are highly scriptable. In InDesign, for example, you can perform searches and change literally any aspect of the text you found. You can search for text that has specific type styles attached to it, and replace it with different text and different attributes.

Adding a nonscriptable application

When automating a workflow that includes scripting applications, one of the big factors in how easy the process will be depends on how good and complete the dictionaries of these applications is. The 20-80 rule works here: 80% of the process takes 20% of the time to develop, and the final touches take the longest.

One of the things that can get the best of any scripter and stretch any project's timeline is a missing command parameter or object property. If an option is available in the UI, it should be available in the scripting dictionary. If it is not, the scripter's job has just been made more miserable.

One of the last-resort options for such missing items is UI scripting. UI scripting allows you to use AppleScript to control almost any aspect of the Mac's user interface. UI scripting is great when the application comes up with unwanted dialog boxes, features that are not scriptable. It is also great for automating applications that are downright unscriptable.

While UI scripting can be a bit convoluted, much like the underpinnings of the user interface itself, PreFab's UI Browser (www.prefab.com/uibrowser) makes it much easier to deal with. Read more on scripting the user interface in Chapter 20.

27

SMILE: THE APPLESCRIPT INTEGRATED PRODUCTION ENVIRONMENT

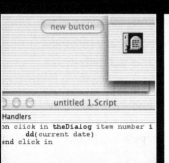

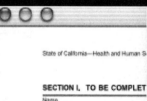

This chapter was contributed by Emmanuel Lévy from Satimage-software of Paris, France, creator of Smile.

Smile is an integrated development environment (IDE) for writing and executing scripts, and much more. Smile can be downloaded from www.satimage.fr/software.

Smile's integrated engine architecture

Smile can perform lots of different tasks for you, some of which you couldn't even think of without Smile. Yet the interface of Smile looks simple—the menu lists are not especially long, the windows do not carry a load of buttons and pop-ups—and Smile is not a huge download: how does that fit?

The reason is that most of Smile's features—including some of the more powerful—are not given an interface. They are just sitting here in the terminology, waiting for you to call them in a script.

However, Smile does have an interface: Smile's interface is designed in the first place to help you edit and test your scripts with efficiency. For instance, if you are writing a script to process text files, Smile lets you test it in a text window first. And when you make a graphic document, you view the graphic in a window as you are building it; the special thing is that the window does not show any tools palette.

Smile's technologies

Smile's architecture enables it to offer a particularly wide range of well-implemented technologies. Indeed, when you work with Smile, you work simultaneously with the following:

- An editor (and runner) of scripted Aqua interfaces
- A text editor supporting styled text and Unicode *
- A text search-and-replace tool supporting text and Unicode
- A regular expression engine supporting text and Unicode
- An XML engine
- A graphic generation engine capable of producing high-quality vectorial PDFs, JPGs, and movies
- A scientific environment with fast computational libraries on numbers and on arrays of numbers

---

* Specifically, styled text refers to styled Mac-Roman ASCII and Unicode refers to UTF-8 and UTF-16. This being said, Smile can convert between the various high-ASCII encodings such as ISO-8859-1, the "PC" encoding.

- A data visualization environment with the finest features: ready-to-publish vectorial PDF production, default settings of professional quality, 1D-2D-3D plots, 3D objects library, easy animations, easy customization of figures using the graphic generation engine, Unicode support, and more

- An industrial interface able to handle RS232 serial communication and some digital I/O USB devices

Since you control everything by script, you can use any of the preceding technologies in any automated process.

Smile's shell

In order to operate the various technologies available in Smile, you communicate with your machine through the AppleScript language. To that effect, Smile includes a unique command-line interpreter for AppleScript. Smile's command-line interpreter is somehow a modern version of the Terminal window.

It may be worth insisting that Smile's AppleScript shell is something other than a script editor. Smile does include a script editor for AppleScript, but here we are concerned with the AppleScript shell, an interactive command-line environment.

In fact, even if you use none of Smile's own power, you may choose to use Smile's AppleScript shell as the environment in which to control your machine—the Finder, the shell commands, the OSAX, and your preferred applications.

About this chapter

Not any language could have made Smile possible, only AppleScript. You may want to read a few lines about what makes AppleScript so special in the next section, "The perfect complement to AppleScript."

When you use Smile, you work in its AppleScript shell. This implies being familiar with the command-line interpreter, which the "Get familiar with Smile" section presents and demonstrates. If you want to run the script samples or the tutorial, please read that section first.

If you are curious about one or several of Smile's main technologies, read the presentations and test the samples provided in "An introduction to Smile's technologies."

If you want to experiment—or if you have some PDF forms to fill—read "A tutorial: making a tool to write text over an existing PDF document." This tutorial demonstrates step by step a project in which you will make a tool intended to fill PDF forms.

28

The perfect complement to AppleScript

Apple presents AppleScript as the language of interapplication communication. AppleScript is that, and it is more than that. Here are a few of the specificities of AppleScript at work in Smile that you may not be aware of at first.

AppleScript is an interpreted language. In AppleScript you can compile and execute in one operation a line, or a block of lines. You use this in Script Editor, yet you may regret that you cannot run "more lines." Instead you must run all lines every time. This is because Script Editor does not implement a persistent context.

AppleScript supports persistent contexts, which Smile uses. Smile embeds you in a context that augments as you work. You can see the benefits right away, and also in the long term: once a routine is programmed, it is straightforward to include it in the context as a library. Smile's context is itself a script, and you can dynamically load new handlers into that context—by the simplest means.

AppleScript is somehow auto-referential. Any script, be it running or not, is itself an object (it owns handlers and properties) and is scriptable too. A script can send commands to another script and change its properties. Furthermore, be it running or not, a script retains its current state.

An AppleScript program supports handling quantities belonging to any class, including classes that did not even exist at the time the program was written. For instance, it seems natural to the AppleScript user that the same commands that used to work with ASCII now work transparently with Unicode text.

Get familiar with Smile

This section will get you a bit more familiar with Smile and some of its components.

The download

Smile is available in two possible distributions: the standard edition (free) and the full edition (which includes SmileLab). I recommend that you download the full edition, since the full edition is required for some of the script samples. The full edition requires a paid registration; however, if you download the full edition and you do not register, Smile will run in demo mode, which is enough for testing the samples that follow.

Then you can experiment with the samples and if you wish you can practice with the tutorial that I provide in the last section.

To download Smile, do the following:

You may first want to visit Smile's home page at www.satimage-software.com/en/smile.html.

Download the full edition of Smile at www.satimage-software.com/en/downloads_software.html.

Install the software as instructed in the Read me file. Installing the software may include installing scripting additions. Do install them as described in the Read me file.

The script samples that I present later in the chapter were gathered into one text file, available at www.apress.com/book/download.html or at www.satimage-software.com/downloads/hr_book_samples.html.

Download the file. If the file does not expand by itself once downloaded, double-click its icon: it will expand into a (Smile) text document named hr_book_samples.

The AppleScript command-line environment

Smile's primary tool is its unique AppleScript shell: any text window is an interpreter for AppleScript; pressing the *ENTER* key executes the current line or the selected lines. To run a single line, you do not need to select the line: when no text is selected, the *ENTER* key runs the line where the insertion point is located, and then the insertion point moves to the beginning of the next line, making it natural to run a script line by line (see Figure 28-1).

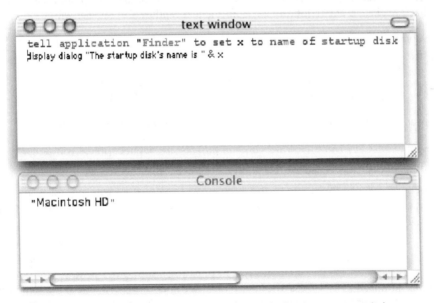

Figure 28-1. When you press *ENTER* after having entered a line in a new text window, the line gets compiled and then executed in the same operation, and the result of the script prints in the Console.

Next, launch Smile by double-clicking the saucer icon in /Applications/Smilexyz/ ("xyz" stands for the version number).

If this is the first time you are launching a copy of Smile, the Worksheet—Smile's auto-saving text window—proposes several script lines that you can run on the fly. You may practice a moment with those, and then proceed.

Double-click the icon of hr_book_samples. Click somewhere in the first uncommented line:

```
tell application "Finder" to set x to name of startup disk
```

Now the caret is blinking somewhere in the line. Press the *ENTER* key: this is the key that stands for "OK" but is not the key for inserting a carriage return. The result (the record returned by *display dialog*) by default prints in the Console—Smile's never-saving text window.

Now the caret is blinking at the beginning of the following line:

```
display dialog "The startup disk's name is " & x
```

Press the *ENTER* key again. As you can see, Smile remembers the value of x, which you would not expect if you were working in a regular script editor.

The preceding example was possible because Smile maintains a persistent AppleScript context. When you run one line or a block of lines in the AppleScript shell, i.e., in a text window, the variables and handlers remain defined until you quit. They are available at a global level, i.e., to any script running from any text window. Get familiar with this.

Now type in these two lines:

```
set pdf_url to ¬
    "http://www.satimage-software.com/downloads/mc0306.pdf"
set pdf_file to ((path to desktop) as text) & "mc0306.pdf"
```

Click anywhere in the first line, in order to put the insertion point in that line.

Press the *ENTER* key twice. Now *pdf_url* and *pdf_file* are defined: unless you assign them different values later, their contents are preserved.

If your computer is connected to the Internet, you can now execute the following line. Choose to copy it first in a new text window: you can check that all text windows share the same context.

```
tell application "URL Access Scripting.app" ¬
    to download pdf_url to file pdf_file replacing yes
```

This will download a PDF file that the tutorial discussed later will use. As long as the command executes, the script is suspended: the insertion point will blink again once the download is complete. As you see, the latest line makes use of the variables that were defined in a previous run. Actually, the tutorial will later use the *pdf_file* variable again.

Such variables compiled on the fly in text windows live in a script that is permanently available (persistent). This is called Smile's "global context."

An introduction to Smile's technologies

This section will introduce you to the different technologies embedded into Smile.

Smile's custom dialog windows

Smile includes an editor—and a runner—of graphical interfaces, known as Smile's custom dialog windows. Later (in the tutorial), I'll show you how to create a graphical interface, but I suggest that you experiment rapidly now with custom dialog windows. In fact, you are going to make your own user interface in less than one minute.

To create the user interface, do the following:

Select File → New dialog. This opens a new dialog window, and also the Controls palette (actually, a Smile dialog window itself).

Click the button entitled New button in the Controls palette and drag it to the empty dialog window.

Close the Controls palette.

Double-click New button and change its name to "Date & time".

The interface of our first dialog window is final; let's program it now. Click anywhere in the dialog window (far from the button) with the COMMAND and OPTION keys pressed. This opens a new colored window, the window of the dialog's script.

By default the dialog window's script contains two empty handlers: *prepare* and *click in*. Remove the *prepare* handler. In the *click in* handler insert the following line:

```
dd(current date)
```

Now your handler looks like this:

```
on click in theDialog item number i
dd(current date)
end click in
```

Next, select File → Save to save the script, and then File → Close to close the script's window.

Select Edit → Edit mode to toggle your dialog window from edit mode into normal mode.

Optionally, you can save the dialog window to disk: select File → Save and provide a name. The dialog window and script are shown in Figure 28-2.

28

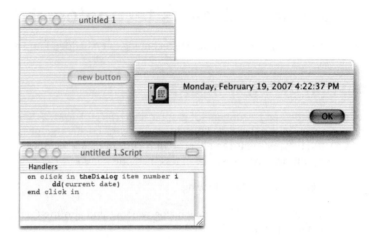

Figure 28-2. The simplest working dialog window ever: one button, one line of script

You can now test your first dialog window by clicking the button. Doing this will send the *click in* event to the dialog window, which will execute your script line.

Note that your script uses *dd*, a term not included in the native AppleScript. Smile's built-in libraries includes a number of handy terms, which are documented in the Help menu. To get information about a specific term such as *dd*, select the term and then select Edit → Find definition (or press *COMMAND+SHIFT+F*). Find definition is also available in the contextual menu.

Regular expressions

Smile offers an AppleScript implementation of the regular expressions, which supports both ASCII text (Mac-Roman) and Unicode.

Regular expressions (known as "grep" in the UNIX systems) are the basic tool for most text processing tasks, such as extracting a given substring or finding all the e-mail addresses contained in a file, so they are useful at one step or another in a wide range of situations.

The Find dialog window understands the regular expressions: the Find dialog window is the best place to test a regular expression on text windows before using it in a script. The same Find dialog window works both in the text windows and in the Unicode windows.

Next, we will try the Find window:

1. Select Edit → Find. This will open the Find dialog window.

2. Enter "[0-9]+" as the Find: string.

3. Enable the regular expression check box.

4. Click Find.

This will find the next sequence of several ("+") digits ("[0-9]") in the front window.

The script to perform the same task implies using the *find text* command. Make sure that the window just behind *hr_book_samples* is a text window, and execute the following line:

```
find text "[0-9]+" in window 2 with regexp, string result ¬
    and all occurrences.
```

Figure 28-3 shows an example of a regular expression script statement that looks for non-Latin text.

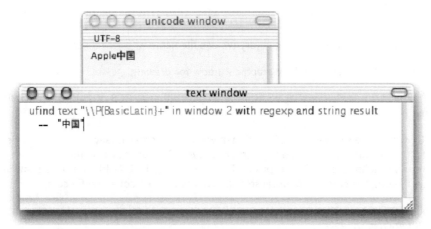

Figure 28-3. In Smile, the regular expressions understand Unicode.

If you are curious to experiment further with regular expressions, you will want to have the list of the regular expressions' metacharacters handy: you will find one in the pop-up in the Find dialog window, on the right of the regular expression check box.

Satimage's website provides the exhaustive documentation of the regular expressions. You can find it in www.satimage-software.com/en/smile.html.

The graphic engine

Smile includes an AppleScript PDF graphic library.

This is the facet of Smile that you will get a chance to explore in the tutorial. Let's get a small taste of it first:

In the *hr_book_samples* window, select the following block and press the *ENTER* key:

Script 28-1

```
set c to {250, 250}
set r to 100
set i to first character of (system attribute "USER")
BeginFigure(0)
SetPenColor({1 / 8, 1 / 4, 1 / 2})
```

28

```
SetFillColor({1 / 4, 1 / 2, 1, 1 / 2})
CirclePath(c, r)
DrawPath(3)
TextMoveTo(c)
SetTextSize(1.5 * r)
SetTextFont("Courier")
SetFillGray(1)
DrawString("[h]" & i)
DrawPath(0)
EndFigure()
```

Here we are using Smile's graphic library (whose file name is Graphic Kernel).

BeginFigure(0) prepares a default graphic window for drawing.

SetPenColor and *SetFillColor* let you specify a color, either as RGB or as RGB-alpha (alpha being the opacity).

In PDF you define shapes ("paths"), and then you draw them—usually in "stroke" mode or in "fill" mode, but there are other options. Here *CirclePath* defines a circular path, with the center and radius as specified in pixels (1 pixel equaling 1/72 inch), and then *DrawPath* draws it, using the current graphical settings such as the pen color and fill color.

Finally, *EndFigure* is what terminates the PDF record and displays the final graphic in the default graphic window.

Running this script will create the image shown in Figure 28-4.

Figure 28-4.
The image created by the preceding script. By default, saving a drawing in Smile makes a PDF document. Alternatively, you can produce JPGs, BMPs, PNGs (often an optimal solution for synthetic graphics), etc., and QuickTime movies.

Again, if you are curious about a particular term, select the term, then press *COMMAND+SHIFT+F* (Edit → Find definition). To open the documentation for the graphic engine, use the Help menu and follow the hypertext links.

SmileLab

Smile includes graphical objects for numerical data visualization and additional libraries that sum up to what is named SmileLab.

The graphical objects can make curves, plots, color maps, 3D surfaces, etc., to represent numerical data, and for making them into PDF—vectorial—graphics.

Smile also has a set of mathematical functions that allow you to program in AppleScript C-fast computations on numbers and on arrays.

Next, we will generate some data and then plot it. The results can be seen in Figure 28-5.

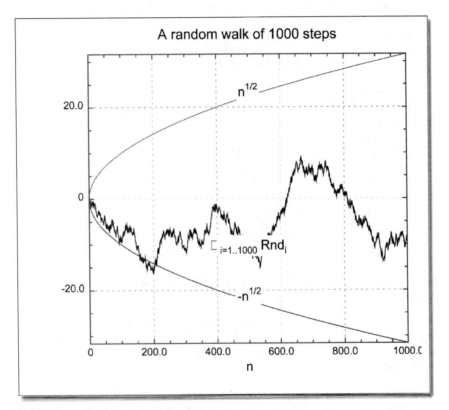

Figure 28-5. In many situations the default settings are perfectly adapted, which makes scripts shorter.

(The script that follows requires the full version of Smile. Demo mode is enough.)

28

In the *hr_book_samples* window, consider the following script.

Script 28-2

```
-- create data
set n to 1000
set x to createarray n
set y to runningsum (randomarray n range {-1, 1})
set y to multlist y with sqrt (3)

-- display data as a curve
set c to QuickCurve(x, y, 0)
set v to c's container -- the curve belongs to a plot ...
set w to v's container -- ... which belongs to a window

-- display equations as curves
set c1 to QuickCurve(x, "sqrt(x)", v)
set c2 to QuickCurve(x, "-sqrt(x)", v)

-- customize appearance
set name of v to "A random walk of " & n & " steps"
set legend kind of v to 3
set legend abscissa of v to n / 2
set legend text size of v to 14
set legend fill color of v to {1, 1, 1, 1}
set label text size of v to 14
set xlabel of v to "n"
set name of c to "\\Sigma_{i=1.." & n & "}\\ Rnd_i"
set name of c1 to "n^{1/2}"
set name of c2 to "-n^{1/2}"
draw w
```

Run the script block after block. You run a block by pressing the *ENTER* key once the lines are selected.

Block 1 creates the data. Smile introduces a data type equivalent to an AppleScript list of numbers such as {1.0, pi, 300}, the array of reals. Computations on arrays of reals are fast, and arrays of reals have virtually no size limit (AppleScript native lists are not adapted for extensive calculations).

createarray is one way of making a new array of reals. By default *createarray n* creates an array of the *n*-first integers. The dictionary shows that *createarray* accepts optional parameters. To view the entry for *createarray* in the dictionary where it belongs (namely, the dictionary of the Satimage OSAX), select *createarray* and then press *COMMAND+SHIFT+F* (or select Edit → Find definition, or use the contextual menu).

As its name suggests, *randomarray* returns an array of reals containing random numbers in the given range [-1 .. 1].

y contains*, as its item of rank *k*, the sum of the previous *k* random numbers. This is called a random walk (on the line): after *k* steps, the random walker's position may be any value between -*k* and *k*.

Block 2 will display the random walk as a curve: position vs. time. QuickCurve belongs to QuickPlotLib, a library included with SmileLab: COMMAND+SHIFT+F opens the documentation for QuickCurve.

As you see, the curve you made lives in a plot view, which in turn requires a graphic window to exist.

Which class of objects may contain what other class of objects is part of the information that the dictionary supplies: select Smile → Smile dictionary, and then use the Index menu in the dictionary's toolbar to view the entry for *curve*. Be aware that the entry for a given class shows which classes of objects it can contain (its elements), not which class of object can contain itself (its container).

Scientists know that a random walk (with *n* steps chosen randomly in [-1 .. 1]) will essentially scale like $\sqrt{n}$. Let's confirm the fact and plot the two curves $-\sqrt{n}$ and $+\sqrt{n}$: this is what the two lines in block 3 do. You may run the script several times: you will observe different draws. Also, you can increase *n*.

Finally, the fourth block is about cosmetic settings: each visual feature of an object can be adjusted by setting the corresponding property to the desired value. The list of the properties of an object of a given class is provided in the dictionary, in the entry for that class. To view the entry for a given class, you do like you do to view the entry for a given command: select the class's name, for instance *plot view*, and then press COMMAND+SHIFT+F.

Smile is one of the few software packages that implement AppleScript's *properties* property feature, intended for setting multiple (and getting all) properties in one instruction.

Here's an example:

```
set properties of v to ¬
    {name:"A random walk of " & n & " steps", ¬
    legend kind:3, legend abscissa:n / 2, legend text size:14, ¬
    legend fill color:{1, 1, 1, 1}, label text size:14, xlabel:"n"}
```

This can be used as a shortcut for the following:

```
set name of v to "A random walk of " & n & " steps"
set legend kind of v to 3
set legend abscissa of v to n / 2
set legend text size of v to 14
set legend fill color of v to {1, 1, 1, 1}
set label text size of v to 14
set xlabel of v to "n"
```

28

---

* Except for a scaling factor, which I do not mention for the sake of simplicity.

A tutorial: Making a tool to write text over an existing PDF document

As a first experience, we'll make a program in Smile to add some text to a PDF. Usually, this is done with Adobe's Acrobat software, which is not free.

So that we can test on a real document as we develop it, we have been given clearance by the state of California to use one of their forms from the Department of Health Services.

However, you may use any other PDF document as well.

Preparing the scripts

If you have run the first samples, the PDF file is already on the desktop, its path is stored in the *pdf_file* variable, and you can skip the following action.

Otherwise, or if you have quit Smile since, and if your machine is connected to the Internet, execute the following lines to download the PDF file to the desktop:

```
set pdf_url to ¬
    "http://www.satimage-software.com/downloads/mc0306.pdf"
set pdf_file to ((path to desktop) as text) & "mc0306.pdf"
tell application "URL Access Scripting.app" to ¬
    download pdf_url to file pdf_file replacing yes
```

If you want to use another file, store its path (as a string) into the *pdf_file* variable. Here you may want to know that dropping a file into a text window inserts its path in the window.

Now we'll open the PDF file in Smile (see Figure 28-6). If we double-click the file's icon, Finder will choose to open it in Acrobat Reader or in Preview; let's explicitly tell Smile to open it. Execute the following line:

```
set w to open pdf_file
```

As you can see in the Console window, the result returned (the value of *w*) is a graphic window. Let's get some information about that object class. Select graphic window, and press COMMAND+SHIFT+F; this displays the entry for the *graphic window* class. For our project we focus only on the two properties *back pdf* and *front pdf*: those are where the graphic window stores PDF data.

```
Class graphic window : (inherits from window) a window ¬
    where you can draw pictures of various kinds by script, ¬
    and that you can save as a PDF file or as a tiff file.
Plural form:
    graphic windows
Properties:
    frame a list of small real -- {x origin, y origin, width, height} [...]
[...]
    back pdf string -- The PDF data for the background of the window.
```

```
-- Can be set to a file, to some Graphic Kernel output or to raw PDF
data as string.
   front pdf string -- The PDF data drawn after the background and the
graphic views of the window. Can be set to a file, to some Graphic
Kernel output or to raw PDF data as string.
```

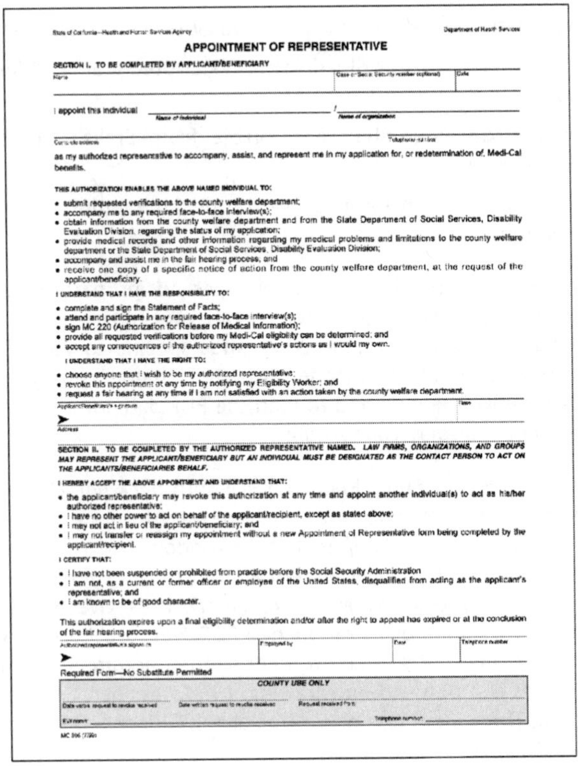

State of California—Health and Human Services Agency   Department of Health Services

APPOINTMENT OF REPRESENTATIVE

SECTION I. TO BE COMPLETED BY APPLICANT/BENEFICIARY

Name | Case or Social Security number (optional) | Date

I appoint this individual ______ (Name of individual) / ______ (Name of organization)

as my authorized representative to accompany, assist, and represent me in my application for, or redetermination of, Medi-Cal benefits.

THIS AUTHORIZATION ENABLES THE ABOVE NAMED INDIVIDUAL TO:

- submit requested verifications to the county welfare department;
- accompany me to any required face-to-face interview(s);
- obtain information from the county welfare department and from the State Department of Social Services, Disability Evaluation Division, regarding the status of my application;
- provide medical records and other information regarding my medical problems and limitations to the county welfare department or the State Department of Social Services, Disability Evaluation Division;
- accompany and assist me in the fair hearing process; and
- receive one copy of a specific notice of action from the county welfare department, at the request of the applicant/beneficiary.

I UNDERSTAND THAT I HAVE THE RESPONSIBILITY TO:

- complete and sign the Statement of Facts;
- attend and participate in any required face-to-face interview(s);
- sign MC 220 (Authorization for Release of Medical Information);
- provide all requested verifications before my Medi-Cal eligibility can be determined; and
- accept any consequences of the authorized representative's actions as I would my own.

I UNDERSTAND THAT I HAVE THE RIGHT TO:

- choose anyone that I wish to be my authorized representative;
- revoke this appointment at any time by notifying my Eligibility Worker; and
- request a fair hearing at any time if I am not satisfied with an action taken by the county welfare department.

Applicant/Beneficiary's signature | Date

➤

Address

SECTION II. TO BE COMPLETED BY THE AUTHORIZED REPRESENTATIVE NAMED. *LAW FIRMS, ORGANIZATIONS, AND GROUPS MAY REPRESENT THE APPLICANT/BENEFICIARY BUT AN INDIVIDUAL MUST BE DESIGNATED AS THE CONTACT PERSON TO ACT ON THE APPLICANTS/BENEFICIARIES BEHALF.*

I HEREBY ACCEPT THE ABOVE APPOINTMENT AND UNDERSTAND THAT:

- the applicant/beneficiary may revoke this authorization at any time and appoint another individual(s) to act as his/her authorized representative;
- I have no other power to act on behalf of the applicant/recipient, except as stated above;
- I may not act in lieu of the applicant/beneficiary; and
- I may not transfer or reassign my appointment without a new Appointment of Representative form being completed by the applicant/recipient.

I CERTIFY THAT:

- I have not been suspended or prohibited from practice before the Social Security Administration
- I am not, as a current or former officer or employee of the United States, disqualified from acting as the applicant's representative; and
- I am known to be of good character.

This authorization expires upon a final eligibility determination and/or after the right to appeal has expired or at the conclusion of the fair hearing process.

Authorized representative's signature | Employed by | Date | Telephone number

➤

Required Form—No Substitute Permitted

COUNTY USE ONLY

Date verbal request to revoke received | Date written request to revoke received | Request received from

EW name ______ Telephone number ______

MC 306 (7/99)

Figure 28-6. Smile opens PDF files in graphic windows, where you can make custom graphics.

Making a PDF drawing consists of filling the *back pdf* and/or the *front pdf* fields of a new graphic window with PDF data (a string, actually). Here is an excerpt of the PDF data in the file you just opened:

```
%PDF-1.3
%ƒÂÚÂÎßÛ -ƒΔ
2 0 obj
<< /Length 1 0 R /Filter /FlateDecode >>
stream
xú+T_T(_c}Σ\C_ó|dæ_ú_
endstream
[...]
xú•Ωk"-Σm&˙Ω ≈:ÛIûrñöwrÊì,ÀâO˘_KI*)WMŸgíÂ_..._ÌH_Â◊_>Ï^k_Ïáç~ÀÂ*K[__lÇ
[...]
```

You see, PDF is not as intuitive as AppleScript. Thus, you will not make PDF data directly; rather, Smile's graphic library will. You will use natural commands such as *MoveTo*, *LineTo*, and *DrawString*, and Smile's graphic library will make them into a regular PDF.

When you program the graphic library, you use the documentation, which is available in three forms:

- The hypertext documentation for all commands is available via the Help menu.
- A PDF document is included in the download: "Smile—Scripted graphics" (includes guide and reference).
- A chapter in the online documentation is available from Smile's home page (includes guide and reference).

However, to enjoy the tutorial, you do not have to use the documentation: the tutorial includes all the information you need.

To have Smile generate the PDF and provide it into the *back pdf* property of a given graphic window *w*, your script proceeds in three steps. First, you initiate the PDF with *BeginFigure(w)*, and then you include the graphic commands specific to your graphic. Finally, you close the PDF with *EndFigure()*. This is the instruction that will notify Smile to compile the graphic commands into PDF data and to load the PDF data into the *back pdf* field of *w* so as to have the window display your graphic.

When we open the PDF file mc0306.pdf, Smile loads the PDF into *back pdf*. On our side, we do not want to replace the original graphic, but rather we want to draw over it. Here we have to use the foreground layer, the *front pdf* field of the window. The instructions are the same as for drawing in the background layer, except we must call *BeginFrontFigure()* and *EndFrontFigure()* instead of *BeginFigure()* and *EndFigure()*. Let's give it a try and draw a line from one corner to the other, over the opened PDF. Here we'll use very basic graphic commands: *MoveTo* and *LineTo*. Both want a point as their argument, a list {x, y} of two numbers (*MoveTo* moves the pen without drawing; *LineTo* defines a line starting from the current pen location). The scale is one pixel (1 pixel = 1/72 inch ≈ 0.35 mm). x/y-coordinates increase rightwards/upwards.

```
BeginFrontFigure(w)
LineTo({0, 0})
MoveTo({600, 840})
EndFrontFigure()
```

As usual, select the text, press *ENTER* . . . ouch! Nothing happens.

This is because our program does not draw! All it does is define a shape (a "path")—here, the diagonal line. Indeed, after having defined a path we have to draw it: this is what *DrawPath* is for. The parameter of *DrawPath* will specify whether to draw the stroke of the path or not, whether to fill the path or not (which makes little sense for our line, of course), and proposes more options such as using the path, not to draw but as a mask. The most often used values are *DrawPath(3)*, which draws the stroke and fills the path, and *DrawPath(2)*, which draws the stroke only.

Usually, before firing a *DrawPath* command, you specify the pen and fill settings you want it to use. Here we'll use the default settings: by default the pen and the fill color are black and the pen size is 1 pixel.

```
BeginFrontFigure(w)
MoveTo({0, 0})
LineTo({600, 840})
DrawPath(2)
EndFrontFigure()
```

Select the text, press *Enter*. Here we are: evidently a diagonal is barring our page (see Figure 28-7).

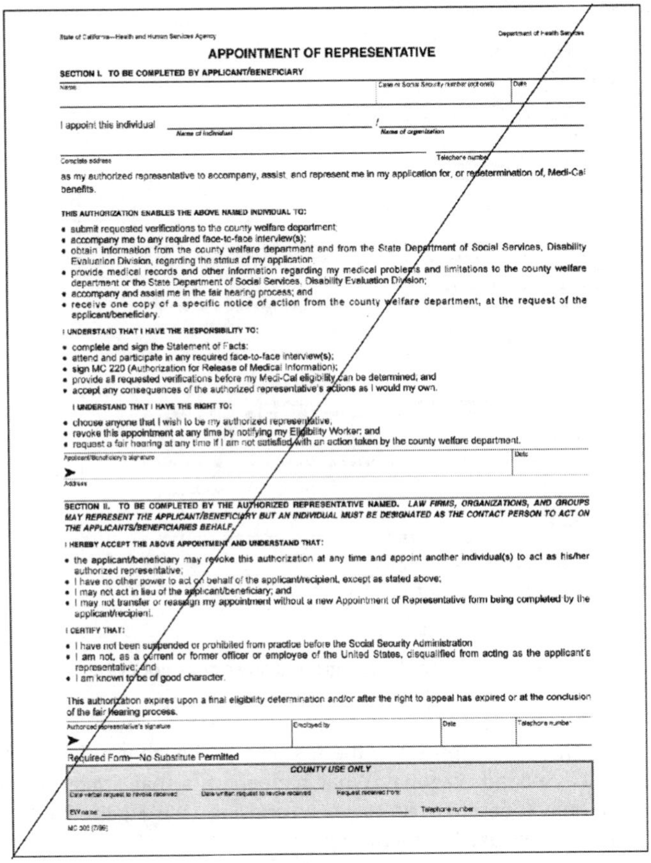

State of California—Health and Human Services Agency

Department of Health Services

APPOINTMENT OF REPRESENTATIVE

SECTION I. TO BE COMPLETED BY APPLICANT/BENEFICIARY

Name | Case or Social Security number (optional) | Date

I appoint this individual ______ Name of individual / ______ Name of organization

Complete address | Telephone number

as my authorized representative to accompany, assist, and represent me in my application for, or redetermination of, Medi-Cal benefits.

THIS AUTHORIZATION ENABLES THE ABOVE NAMED INDIVIDUAL TO:

- submit requested verifications to the county welfare department;
- accompany me to any required face-to-face interview(s);
- obtain information from the county welfare department and from the State Department of Social Services, Disability Evaluation Division, regarding the status of my application;
- provide medical records and other information regarding my medical problems and limitations to the county welfare department or the State Department of Social Services, Disability Evaluation Division;
- accompany and assist me in the fair hearing process; and
- receive one copy of a specific notice of action from the county welfare department, at the request of the applicant/beneficiary.

I UNDERSTAND THAT I HAVE THE RESPONSIBILITY TO:

- complete and sign the Statement of Facts;
- attend and participate in any required face-to-face interview(s);
- sign MC 220 (Authorization for Release of Medical Information);
- provide all requested verifications before my Medi-Cal eligibility can be determined; and
- accept any consequences of the authorized representative's actions as I would my own.

I UNDERSTAND THAT I HAVE THE RIGHT TO:

- choose anyone that I wish to be my authorized representative;
- revoke this appointment at any time by notifying my Eligibility Worker; and
- request a fair hearing at any time if I am not satisfied with an action taken by the county welfare department.

Applicant/Beneficiary's signature | Date

Address

SECTION II. TO BE COMPLETED BY THE AUTHORIZED REPRESENTATIVE NAMED. *LAW FIRMS, ORGANIZATIONS, AND GROUPS MAY REPRESENT THE APPLICANT/BENEFICIARY BUT AN INDIVIDUAL MUST BE DESIGNATED AS THE CONTACT PERSON TO ACT ON THE APPLICANTS/BENEFICIARIES BEHALF.*

I HEREBY ACCEPT THE ABOVE APPOINTMENT AND UNDERSTAND THAT:

- the applicant/beneficiary may revoke this authorization at any time and appoint another individual(s) to act as his/her authorized representative;
- I have no other power to act on behalf of the applicant/recipient, except as stated above;
- I may not act in lieu of the applicant/beneficiary; and
- I may not transfer or reassign my appointment without a new Appointment of Representative form being completed by the applicant/recipient.

I CERTIFY THAT:

- I have not been suspended or prohibited from practice before the Social Security Administration
- I am not, as a current or former officer or employee of the United States, disqualified from acting as the applicant's representative; and
- I am known to be of good character.

This authorization expires upon a final eligibility determination and/or after the right to appeal has expired or at the conclusion of the fair hearing process.

Authorized representative's signature | Employed by | Date | Telephone number

Required Form—No Substitute Permitted

COUNTY USE ONLY

Date verbal request to revoke received | Date written request to revoke received | Request received from

EW name | Telephone number

MC 306 (7/99)

Figure 28-7.
With five script lines we programmed our first graphic.

Let's experiment with the other diagonal:

```
BeginFrontFigure(w)
MoveTo({600, 0})
LineTo({0, 840})
DrawPath(2)
EndFrontFigure()
```

Our page is now barred with two lines, as you can see in Figure 28-8.

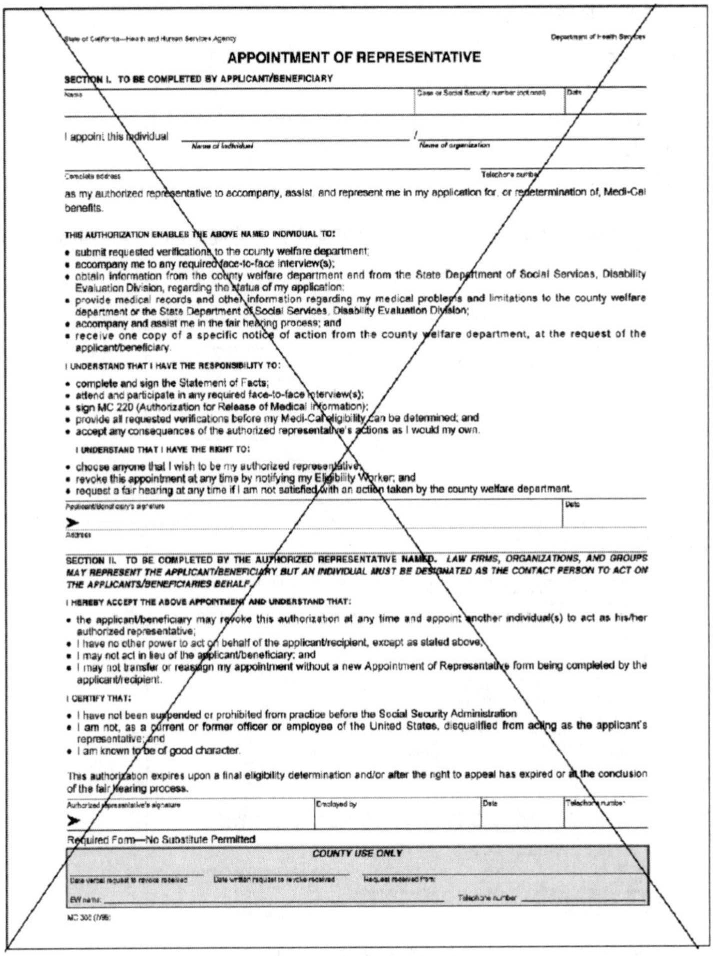

State of California—Health and Human Services Agency

Department of Health Services

APPOINTMENT OF REPRESENTATIVE

SECTION I. TO BE COMPLETED BY APPLICANT/BENEFICIARY

Name | Case or Social Security number (optional) | Date

I appoint this individual ____ Name of individual / ____ Name of organization

Complete address | Telephone number

as my authorized representative to accompany, assist, and represent me in my application for, or redetermination of, Medi-Cal benefits.

THIS AUTHORIZATION ENABLES THE ABOVE NAMED INDIVIDUAL TO:

- submit requested verifications to the county welfare department;
- accompany me to any required face-to-face interview(s);
- obtain information from the county welfare department and from the State Department of Social Services, Disability Evaluation Division, regarding the status of my application;
- provide medical records and other information regarding my medical problems and limitations to the county welfare department or the State Department of Social Services, Disability Evaluation Division;
- accompany and assist me in the fair hearing process; and
- receive one copy of a specific notice of action from the county welfare department, at the request of the applicant/beneficiary.

I UNDERSTAND THAT I HAVE THE RESPONSIBILITY TO:

- complete and sign the Statement of Facts;
- attend and participate in any required face-to-face interview(s);
- sign MC 220 (Authorization for Release of Medical Information);
- provide all requested verifications before my Medi-Cal eligibility can be determined; and
- accept any consequences of the authorized representative's actions as I would my own.

I UNDERSTAND THAT I HAVE THE RIGHT TO:

- choose anyone that I wish to be my authorized representative;
- revoke this appointment at any time by notifying my Eligibility Worker; and
- request a fair hearing at any time if I am not satisfied with an action taken by the county welfare department.

Applicant/Beneficiary's signature | Date

Address

SECTION II. TO BE COMPLETED BY THE AUTHORIZED REPRESENTATIVE NAMED. *LAW FIRMS, ORGANIZATIONS, AND GROUPS MAY REPRESENT THE APPLICANT/BENEFICIARY BUT AN INDIVIDUAL MUST BE DESIGNATED AS THE CONTACT PERSON TO ACT ON THE APPLICANTS/BENEFICIARIES BEHALF.*

I HEREBY ACCEPT THE ABOVE APPOINTMENT AND UNDERSTAND THAT:

- the applicant/beneficiary may revoke this authorization at any time and appoint another individual(s) to act as his/her authorized representative;
- I have no other power to act on behalf of the applicant/recipient, except as stated above;
- I may not act in lieu of the applicant/beneficiary; and
- I may not transfer or reassign my appointment without a new Appointment of Representative form being completed by the applicant/recipient.

I CERTIFY THAT:

- I have not been suspended or prohibited from practice before the Social Security Administration
- I am not, as a current or former officer or employee of the United States, disqualified from acting as the applicant's representative; and
- I am known to be of good character.

This authorization expires upon a final eligibility determination and/or after the right to appeal has expired or at the conclusion of the fair hearing process.

Authorized representative's signature | Employed by | Date | Telephone number

Required Form—No Substitute Permitted

COUNTY USE ONLY

Date verbal request to revoke received | Date written request to revoke received | Request received from

EW name: | Telephone number

MC 306 (7/98)

Figure 28-8. By default, a new drawing in the foreground layer does not erase the previous one.

However, the preceding program really suppressed the first line in the *front pdf* property: the window is storing only the second diagonal. What happened is that Smile did not refresh fully the window, it only superimposed the new drawing (see Figure 28-9). To refresh the window request explicitly, use the following:

```
draw w
```

State of California—Health and Human Services Agency
Department of Health Services

APPOINTMENT OF REPRESENTATIVE

SECTION I. TO BE COMPLETED BY APPLICANT/BENEFICIARY

Name | Case or Social Security number (optional) | Date

I appoint this individual ______ (Name of individual) / ______ (Name of organization)

Complete address | Telephone number

as my authorized representative to accompany, assist, and represent me in my application for, or redetermination of, Medi-Cal benefits.

THIS AUTHORIZATION ENABLES THE ABOVE NAMED INDIVIDUAL TO:

- submit requested verifications to the county welfare department;
- accompany me to any required face-to-face interview(s);
- obtain information from the county welfare department and from the State Department of Social Services, Disability Evaluation Division, regarding the status of my application;
- provide medical records and other information regarding my medical problems and limitations to the county welfare department or the State Department of Social Services, Disability Evaluation Division;
- accompany and assist me in the fair hearing process; and
- receive one copy of a specific notice of action from the county welfare department, at the request of the applicant/beneficiary.

I UNDERSTAND THAT I HAVE THE RESPONSIBILITY TO:

- complete and sign the Statement of Facts;
- attend and participate in any required face-to-face interview(s);
- sign MC 220 (Authorization for Release of Medical Information);
- provide all requested verifications before my Medi-Cal eligibility can be determined; and
- accept any consequences of the authorized representative's actions as I would my own.

I UNDERSTAND THAT I HAVE THE RIGHT TO:

- choose anyone that I wish to be my authorized representative;
- revoke this appointment at any time by notifying my Eligibility Worker; and
- request a fair hearing at any time if I am not satisfied with an action taken by the county welfare department.

Applicant/Beneficiary's signature | Date

➤

Address

SECTION II. TO BE COMPLETED BY THE AUTHORIZED REPRESENTATIVE NAMED. ***LAW FIRMS, ORGANIZATIONS, AND GROUPS MAY REPRESENT THE APPLICANT/BENEFICIARY BUT AN INDIVIDUAL MUST BE DESIGNATED AS THE CONTACT PERSON TO ACT ON THE APPLICANTS/BENEFICIARIES BEHALF.***

I HEREBY ACCEPT THE ABOVE APPOINTMENT AND UNDERSTAND THAT:

- the applicant/beneficiary may revoke this authorization at any time and appoint another individual(s) to act as his/her authorized representative;
- I have no other power to act on behalf of the applicant/recipient, except as stated above;
- I may not act in lieu of the applicant/beneficiary; and
- I may not transfer or reassign my appointment without a new Appointment of Representative form being completed by the applicant/recipient.

I CERTIFY THAT:

- I have not been suspended or prohibited from practice before the Social Security Administration
- I am not, as a current or former officer or employee of the United States, disqualified from acting as the applicant's representative; and
- I am known to be of good character.

This authorization expires upon a final eligibility determination and/or after the right to appeal has expired or at the conclusion of the fair hearing process.

Authorized representative's signature | Employed by | Date | Telephone number

➤

Required Form—No Substitute Permitted

COUNTY USE ONLY

Date verbal request to revoke received | Date written request to revoke received | Request received from:

EW name | Telephone number

MC 306 (7/99)

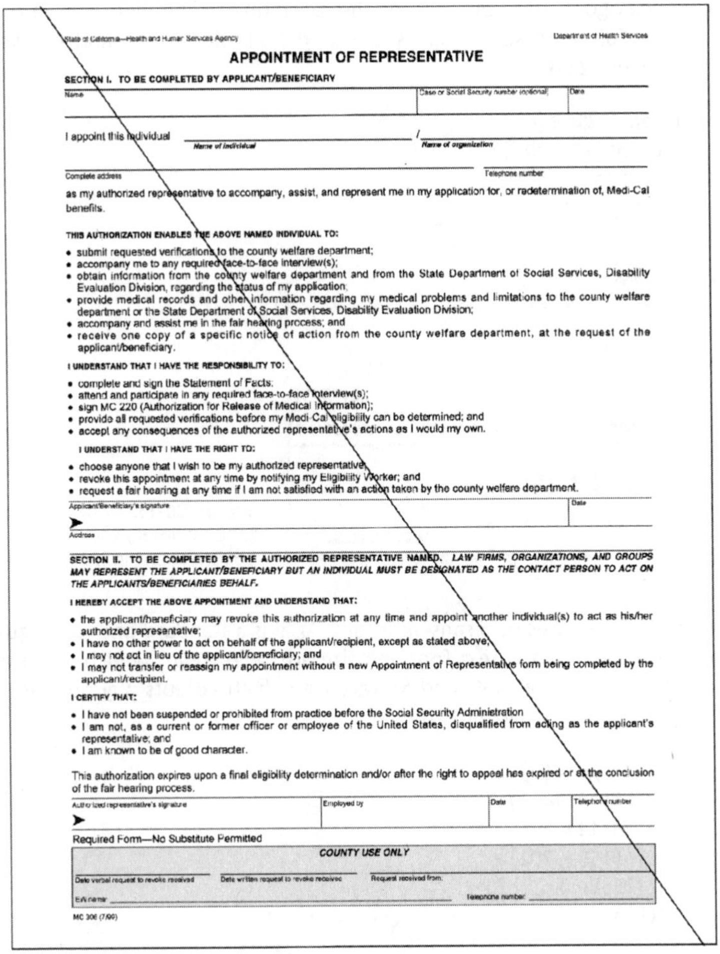

Figure 28-9. Smile is designed with scriptability in mind. In a script, often you do not want the display refresh at each step. This is why in several circumstances Smile does not refresh spontaneously the display; you have to request so explicitly with the *draw* verb.

Now let's experiment with the real thing: drawing text.

First we have to position the text. Let's click in the form, under the Name prompt: the toolbar of the window displays the values for *x* and *y*—values close to 55 and 702, respectively (see Figure 28-10).

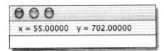

Figure 28-10. The graphic window's toolbar displays information regarding the location of the mouse pointer.

28

A command analogous to *MoveTo* sets the position of the pen for writing: this is *TextMoveTo*. The following script makes use of the simplest command for writing text: *DrawText* (see Figure 28-11).

```
BeginFrontFigure(w)
TextMoveTo({55, 702})
DrawText("John Smith")
EndFrontFigure()
```

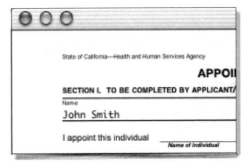

Figure 28-11. By default the graphic library's text drawing routines start in Monaco 10.

We'll improve the look by using a sans-serif font: Arial is a standard one (see Figure 28-12). The commands for setting the text font and size are *SetTextFont* (which wants a string as its argument, the name of a font) and *SetTextSize* (which accepts any positive real number). Our script is now the following; run it.

```
BeginFrontFigure(w)
SetTextFont("Arial")
SetTextSize(12)
TextMoveTo({55, 702})
DrawText("John Smith")
EndFrontFigure()
draw w
```

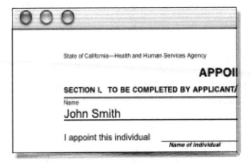

Figure 28-12. Now the string is in the right place with the right font and size.

We still have one thing to do. Once a string is correctly placed and printed in the window, and before we address another string, we have to merge the front graphic (the string) into the background. Otherwise, our next attempt to draw in the foreground layer will just remove the first string.

Appending a new graphic to an existing PDF is not merely concatenating two strings. You have to use a specific command (provided in the dictionary of Smile, in the Smile drawings suite) to merge the two graphics: *addpdf*. *addpdf* accepts input, either PDF data (a string) or a file—which has to be a regular PDF file. Here we'll merge the PDF stored in *front pdf* into the *back pdf* of the window.

```
addPDF (get front pdf of w) in back pdf of w at {0, 0}
close back pdf of w
```

When you manipulate directly the *front pdf* or *back pdf* property of the graphic window, you have to *close back pdf/front pdf* before any attempt to refresh the display.

Now that the string is in both layers, we can empty the front layer.

```
BeginFrontFigure(w)
EndFrontFigure()
```

Finally, let's check we did everything right by refreshing the display:

```
draw w
```

We have fulfilled our contract: we have a (small) script capable of writing any text in any location of a PDF, using any font. We can gather the lines once and for all in a new text document: create a new text document, copy the lines that follow, and then save.

```
-- replace with actual document's path
set pdf_file to ((path to desktop) as text) & "mc0306.pdf"
set w to open pdf_file
-- run the following block as many times as needed,
-- adapting the parameters to suit
BeginFrontFigure(w)
SetTextFont("Arial")
SetTextSize(12)
TextMoveTo({55, 702})
DrawText("John Smith")
DrawPath(2)
EndFrontFigure()
draw w

-- run the following block to validate the string once it
-- prints where and how you want
addPDF (get front pdf of w) in back pdf of w at {0, 0}
close back pdf of w
```

Productivity sometimes means making the minimal effort required to have the work done. Here we are not implementing any error checking, user warning, or any of the bells and whistles for an application that you would distribute: we just add a few comments to make the program reusable later.

28

Rolling up the scripts into a graphical interface

In this section, we will add a user interface to the script we created earlier.

Introduction

Once you have made a task doable in Smile, you may want to make it available also to nonscripters. This is one of the reasons why you would want to make a custom interface to your script.

Smile makes graphical interfaces known as "custom dialogs." When you save a custom dialog window, you get a document that will open in Smile when double-clicked: each graphical interface can be seen as a separate application able to run in Smile's environment.

To make or to edit a custom dialog window, you use the documentation, which is available in three forms:

- A summarized guide is provided in the built-in help: select Help → Smile help, and then click Custom dialogs.
- A PDF document is included in the download: "Smile—GUI editor" (includes guide and reference).
- A chapter in the online documentation is available from Smile's home page (includes guide and reference).

However, to enjoy the tutorial, you do not have to use the documentation; the tutorial includes all the information you need.

For a first experience of a custom dialog window, we'll keep it simple: we'll have the user enter each quantity as a string, in text fields. So far we identified the following inputs: the string itself, the font, the text size, and the location, which consists of two numbers, so we need five text entry fields ("editable text boxes"), and as many "static text boxes" to let the user know what to type there.

In our tests, we obtained a reference to the graphic window (w) because we opened the PDF file ourselves. In a real situation, the user opens a PDF file and then uses (or does not use) the custom dialog window to edit the PDF. So that the user will be able to target any open PDF file (any graphic window), we'll add a sixth text field where the user will type the name of the window to target. Obviously we could design a more user-friendly way of targeting the desired window, but for the purposes of this example, let's restrict ourselves to a very simple tool.

The user will trigger the actions with buttons. We won't update the window's display each time the user changes any quantity in the text fields, but rather we'll have the user decide when to show the result: a first button will display the new string with the current settings. We also saw that we have to take a specific action to validate the current drawing before editing a new string; we need a second button for that.

In order to have the dialog window open at one click, we'll install it in the User scripts menu (the menu with a parchment icon). Installing a new item in the User scripts menu really consists of copying it into a specific location in the user's domain, namely in /User/<login>/Library/Application support/Smile/User scripts/.

This makes us ready to create our Smile tool. In the first step, we'll build the interface, the dialog window as the user will see it. Then we'll provide the scripts that will bring the dialog window to life.

Building the interface

The first action is to make a new dialog window. Select File → New dialog. This opens a new dialog window, and also the Controls palette, from which you will copy the desired widgets (see Figure 28-13). Note that the Controls palette is merely a dialog window itself. It is part of Smile's philosophy to define a limited number of window classes, so that you script Smile more easily.

Figure 28-13. The Controls palette is where you find one copy of each of the widgets you can install in your dialog window. The Controls palette is in edit mode: you copy a widget into your dialog window by drag-and-drop.

As you can check by pulling down the Edit menu, both windows are in edit mode, the mode where you can make structural changes to the dialog window. This is because we used File → New dialog. When you open an existing dialog window by the usual means, it opens in running mode, the normal use mode: the Edit → Edit mode command lets you toggle the dialog window into edit mode and immediately make any change.

You can also check that, since the dialog windows are in edit mode, the menu bar displays a Dialog menu with several commands to help with editing a dialog window.

28

Now we'll populate the empty new dialog window. Enlarge generously the new dialog window. Click the new static text widget in the Controls palette, hold down the mouse button, and drag the widget to the new dialog window, close to the upper-left corner. You have installed your first widget.

Sooner or later we'll save the dialog window to disk; let's do so now. Select File → Save, and save the dialog window as "Add text to a PDF file" (our suggestion) in /User/ <login>/Library/Application support/Smile/User scripts/.

This changes the dialog window's name into the file's name. You can check that the User scripts menu now offers one new item, with the name you supplied. Now, choose File → Save (or press COMMAND+S) to save the dialog window from time to time as you would do with any document.

Proceeding as we did for new static text, install a new editable text widget into the dialog window. Place it to the right of new static text. It is better that the two widgets do not overlap: drag the new editable text widget sufficiently to the right, and/or resize the new static text widget to a shorter size: select it with the mouse, and then move its frame's bottom-right corner.

Instead of dropping more items, we'll duplicate the two existing items (see Figure 28-14). Select them both, in the creation order (new static text, then new editable text), using the SHIFT key. Or, deselect any item by clicking in an empty spot in the dialog window, and then select Edit → Select all. Now press COMMAND+D—or select User scripts → More Smile commands → Edit → Duplicate. (Duplicate is better than Copy-Paste, because Duplicate leaves the clipboard untouched.) The duplicated items are created with an offset of 20 pixels to the right and to the bottom. You can move them with the arrows of the keyboard: press the SHIFT key to have the items move by 20 pixels, and use the left and the bottom arrows to align the new widgets with the first ones.

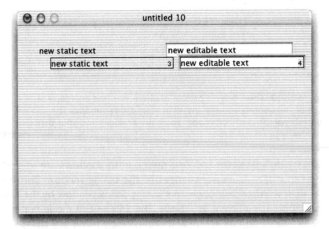

Figure 28-14. New items are created with increasing indexes. The Duplicate command creates new copies at an offset of (20, 20) with respect to the original: use the arrow keys with the SHIFT key pressed to align the copies with the original.

Repeat this step again four times (so as to end up with six copies of each).

Still using drag and drop from the Controls palette, create (for instance, both at the same height, under the array of text fields) two new button buttons. Now you can resize the dialog window so as to enclose exactly the widgets.

When we write the script for the dialog window, we'll refer to the widgets by their indexes. A widget's index is the number that its frame displays in the bottom-right corner when selected. Check that the indexes are in the natural order, that is, from left to right then from top to bottom. The rightmost button in the bottom should assume the index 14. If you have more items, use Edit → Clear to suppress the extra widgets. If the order is not what it should be, proceed as follows. Unselect any item by clicking an empty spot. Then, press the SHIFT key, and click each item once in the desired order, so as to finally select them all. Now, select Edit → Cut then Edit → Paste; the widgets will be pasted in the same order as you selected them.

The contents of the editable text boxes will be handled by the script, but we have to name the other eight widgets. For the editable text boxes we suggest the following names: "string to display:", "text font:", "text size:", "x (pixels):", "y (pixels):", and "current target:", and for the buttons: "refresh" and "validate" (see Figure 28-15). For each of the eight widgets to be renamed successively, double-click each so as to open its Control dialog window ("control" here means "widget"), set its name to the desired string, and close the Control dialog window.

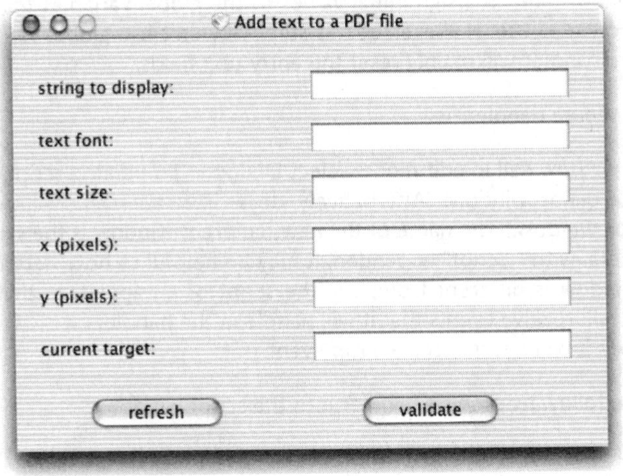

Figure 28-15. When a dialog window is in edit mode, the bottom-right corner shows a grow box, which resizes the dialog window. Here no grow box is visible. The dialog window was toggled into running mode, the normal use mode.

28

You will not need another new widget for the moment: close the Controls palette.

The interface of the dialog window is now operational—if not fully finalized from the cosmetic point of view. I won't demonstrate more cosmetic-oriented features here. It may be enough to say that in addition to moving and resizing, you can, using the Dialog → Align items menu item, copy the sizes from a widget to another and align and/or distribute the widgets vertically and/or horizontally.

Programming the dialog window

Last but not least, we have to program our dialog window by providing it with scripts. All the lines we wrote for our first test are still available, so our task will have much to do with Copy/Paste.

In Smile, when the user acts on a widget (for instance, typing a character in an editable text box, or clicking a button), Smile notifies the script of the widget's container—the dialog window; the widget itself is not notified. More precisely, the script of the dialog window will receive the following event:

```
click in d item number n
```

where *d* is a reference to the dialog window itself (the owner of the script) and *n* is the index of the widget that the user's action addresses. Thus, we won't write as many *click in* handlers as we have active widgets, only one.

The other handler that we have to write is *prepare*. When a custom dialog window opens, Smile, just before making it visible, sends to its script the following event:

```
prepare d
```

where *d* is a reference to the dialog window. Any initialization should be performed in the *prepare* handler. Most often, the job of the *prepare* handler is to prepare the appearance of the dialog window and to assign initial values to the global variables that the script of the dialog window may use. However, at this step we won't use global variables (*properties*); the *prepare* handler will mainly reset the entry text fields.

Let's write the *prepare* handler first.

With the dialog window still in edit mode, select Dialog → Edit dialog script: this will open the script of the dialog window. (Alternatively, do a COMMAND+OPTION-click in an empty spot of the dialog window.) The name of the new (colored) window is the same as the dialog window's name, with ".Script" appended. It may be helpful to note here that the script of the dialog window is different from, say, the script of an applet, in that it will never "run": the script will receive events that it will handle in the handlers we'll write, but under normal conditions it will never receive a *run* event.

Type or copy the following *prepare* handler into the script window:

```
on prepare theDialog
    repeat with i from 2 to 12 by 2
        set contained data of dialog item i of theDialog to ""
    end repeat
end prepare
```

(By default, the script of the dialog window already includes the first and last lines of the handler, so you have only three lines to type. A script may not contain two handlers with the same name.)

Now let's save the script into the dialog window. Select File → Save. If you introduced a typo, Smile throws an alert to notify you of a compilation error, and the script does not get saved; fix the typo and try again.

In Smile, you test as you develop: let's test our handler. Bring the dialog window to the front, and then bring the *hr_book_samples* window to the front—the dialog is now the second window. Execute the following line in the *hr_book_samples* window:

```
set d to window 2
```

This returns to *d* an absolute reference to the dialog window, which will remain valid even when the dialog window is no longer the second window, and until it gets deleted. Now to test the handler, execute the following:

```
tell d to prepare it
```

This should clear the editable text fields.

If it does not, the first thing—if you are sure that the script was saved—is to install an error output. Indeed, in the spirit of a behavior ready for automatic applications, an error triggered in a *prepare* handler remains silent unless the scripter explicitly handles it. Here is how you would install an error handler; on purpose we introduce a typo in the script that follows.

To experiment with the error handler, bring back the dialog's script window to the front and replace its content with the following lines:

```
on prepare theDialog
    try
        repeat with i from 2 to 12 by 2
            set contained data of dialog item i of theDlog to ""
        end repeat
    on error s
        FatalAlert(s)
    end try
end prepare
```

Do not forget to save the script with File → Save to make the change effective. Now, as you have done already, put the cursor in the following line and press ENTER:

```
tell d to prepare it
```

AppleScript attempts to run the *prepare* handler. But in the *set contained data . . .* line, it will choke on a variable that was not defined before: *theDlog* (the variable passed as the argument to *prepare* is *theDialog*, not *theDlog*). This is a typical runtime error. AppleScript thus jumps to the first line after the *on error* clause. There you see *FatalAlert*; *FatalAlert* is nothing but a shortcut that Smile defines for convenience, which is really one option of *display dialog* (with a stop icon and one OK button).

Now correct the typo (replace *theDlog* with *theDialog*) and save the script with File → Save.

28

We are finished with the *prepare* dialog window; now let's program the *click in* handler. It is a good practice not to handle directly the event in the *click in* handler, but to write routines that *click in* will call: AppleScript was thought to be a rather strongly procedural language.

Reviewing our sequence of test scripts, we identify the block that draws the new front graphic and refreshes the whole window, and the block that merges the current front graphic into the background graphic. It will be a good idea, as a visual confirmation, to blank the "string to display" once the current front graphic is merged in the background graphic.

Bring the script of the dialog window back in view if needed and type (or copy) the three following new handlers. Remove the built-in sample *click in* handler, but keep the *prepare* handler that you entered previously.

Script 28-3

```
on RefreshDisplay(d)
    tell d
        set s to contained data of dialog item 2
        set text_font to contained data of dialog item 4
        set text_size to contained data of dialog item 6
        set x to contained data of dialog item 8
        set y to contained data of dialog item 10
        set w_name to contained data of dialog item 12
    end tell
    set w to graphic window w_name
    BeginFrontFigure(w)
    SetTextFont(text_font)
    SetTextSize(text_size)
    TextMoveTo({x, y})
    DrawText(s)
    DrawPath(2)
    EndFrontFigure()
    draw w
end RefreshDisplay

on MergeCurrent(d)
    set w_name to contained data of dialog item 12 of d
    set w to graphic window w_name
    addPDF (get front pdf of w) in back pdf of w at {0, 0}
    close back pdf of w
    BeginFrontFigure(w)
    EndFrontFigure()
    draw w
    set contained data of dialog item 2 of d to ""
end MergeCurrent

on click in d item number n
    if n = 13 then
```

```
        RefreshDisplay(d)
    else if n = 14 then
        MergeCurrent(d)
    end if
end click in
```

Now your dialog window should look like Figure 28-16 (with possibly an additional *try . . . on error . . . end try* structure in the *prepare* handler).

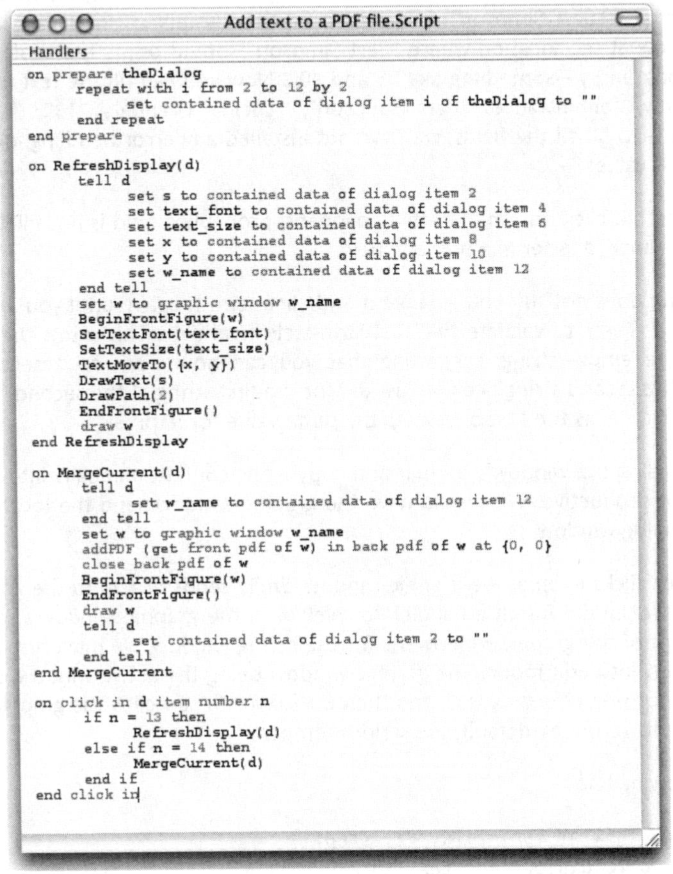

Figure 28-16. Our whole dialog window works with one script only, and that script is not very long. Yet, our dialog window does not handle any error, and its features are very basic.

Select File → Save to save the script, and select File → Close to close its window. Bring the dialog window to the front and select File → Save. This will save to disk the changes that we made to the dialog window, including the script we just wrote.

We are now ready to test and use our new Smile tool. If it is still open, close the PDF file, discarding the changes. If it is still open, close the dialog window, too.

Now, open the PDF file in Smile like a user would do normally: drop its icon on the icon of Smile, or use File → Open in Smile, or use a script as shown here:

```
open pdf_file
```

Open the dialog window. If you followed the instructions verbatim, your new dialog window should be available as an item in the User scripts menu. Otherwise, just double-click the icon of the dialog window in Finder.

Now we can use our new tool. Let's add a first string to the document; say we want to set the Name info to "Bart Simpson". In order to fill the x/y (pixels) information, click the graphic window at the location where "Bart Simpson" should print. The toolbar displays the values for x and y—something like 55 and 702. Now you can fill the text fields in the dialog window, for instance, "Bart Simpson", "Lucida Grande", "13", "55", "702", "mc0306.pdf". Do fill all the fields; we have not installed any error handling, nor any system of default values.

To view the result, click refresh. If nothing happens, probably a field is not filled, or badly filled—for instance, a letter in a numeric field.

If some setting does not suit you, change it and click refresh again, until you are satisfied with the result. Then, to validate that first string, click validate. This resets the "string to display" to the empty string, suggesting that you can now work on a second string. Proceed for the second string like you just did for the first string. If the second string is on the same horizontal as the first one, keep the same value for y (pixels).

Obviously, reading the window's toolbar and copying its content manually into the dialog window is not productive. We should have the graphic window send the location of the click to the dialog window.

When the user clicks in an active graphic window, Smile sends *pick in* to the graphic window's script: we should install a handler for *pick in* in the graphic window's script. Let's open the script of the graphic window. As for the dialog window, we must first toggle the graphic window into edit mode. The graphic window being the active window, select Edit → Edit mode (or press COMMAND+Y), and then COMMAND+OPTION-click the graphic window. This will open its script; by default, the script is empty.

Type the following lines:

```
on pick in w at {point:{x, y}, step:i}
    set d to dialog "Add text to a PDF file"
    set contained data of item 8 of d to x
    set contained data of item 10 of d to y
end pick in
```

(This is assuming that you named the dialog window "Add text to a PDF file". Otherwise, change the string in the script accordingly.)

Note that *pick in* passes a *step* argument. The value of *step* is 1 when the user presses the button down ("mouse down"), 2 when the user is moving the mouse while the button is down ("drag"), and 3 when the user releases the button ("mouse up").

For more sophisticated handling, for instance, if we wanted to implement constraining the drag with the SHIFT key, we would use the value of *step*.

Also, if you look carefully at the script, you'll observe that we set the *contained data* property of an editable text field, not to a string, but to a number. This is something special to Smile: since Smile targets the scientific audience, text fields can be filled with numbers, and you can customize the way they will display numbers by setting their format property (editable in the contextual menu in edit mode).

On the other side, reading the *contained data* property of an editable text field always returns a string—unless you coerce the string to a number by specifying *as real*.

Select File → Save then File → Close to close the script's window, and then select Edit → Edit mode (or press COMMAND+Y) to toggle the PDF's graphic window back into running mode.

Now click and drag the mouse; the dialog window should display the mouse's location in the x/y(pixels) fields.

Note that you can hide the toolbar; it does not display the coordinates when you drag the mouse. This is because we did not supply a *continue pick in [...]* line in our handler, so our handler overrides the standard behavior.

If we expect that nonprogrammers will use our tool, we should have the script installed auto-magically. We'll make a third button that will implement the *pick in* script in the target graphic window. For this, toggle the dialog window into edit mode (Edit → Edit mode), click the validate button to select it, move it a little to the left with the left arrow key, duplicate it (User scripts → More Smile commands → Edit → Duplicate), and align it (arrow keys with or without the SHIFT key pressed). Double-click the new button and name it "auto click".

Now let's program the new button. COMMAND+OPTION-click the dialog window to open its script (or select Dialog → Edit dialog script). Add the following handler to the script (in addition to *RefreshDisplay*, *MergeCurrent*, and *click in*) at any location in the script.

Script 28-4

```
on InstallScript(d)
    set w_name to contained data of item 12 of d
    set w to graphic window w_name
    set script of w to "on pick in w at {point:{x, y}, step:i}
    set d to dialog \"" & name of d & "\"
    set contained data of item 8 of d to x
    set contained data of item 10 of d to y
end pick in"
postit ("Loaded")
    smilepause 5
    postit ("")
end InstallScript
```

28

In this handler we use a sophisticated feature, scripted scripting. In Smile you can dynamically provide a script to an object: you can set the *script* property of an object to a string—provided the string is a compilable AppleScript source. Smile lets you manipulate—by script—scripts as well as the individual handlers and properties of a script.

We have chosen to display feedback when the action is done: the floating Message window will display "Loaded" for 5 seconds (*postit ("")* closes the Message window).

The handler uses a unique command of Smile's: *smilepause*. Inserting *smilepause* in a script pauses the script (for the time specified, which can be 0) while letting the application be fully responsive. *smilepause* may be used for a wide variety of occasions. Here we use it to have the message go away after five seconds, yet letting the user work normally as soon as the action is done.

Of course we must have our new handler called when the user clicks auto click. This is the job of the *click in* handler, where we should install (before *end if*) the two following lines:

```
else if n = 15 then
    InstallScript(d)
```

You can check that your script conforms to Figure 28-17, where the script is given as two pages. The order of the routines is arbitrary. If there is no error, select File → Save, and then File → Close to save and close the script. Once the dialog is the front window, select File → Save.

Now you can click the new button and finish filling in the form if you wish, and then you can save it with File → Save. Finally, you can view the file by double-clicking its icon. Depending on your settings, this will open the file in Preview or in Adobe Reader (or Acrobat Reader), and you can see the strings you have added. You can use a high magnification to check that you have vectorial graphics.

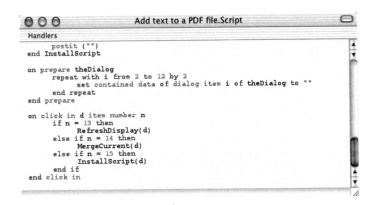

```
● ● ●                Add text to a PDF file.Script
Handlers
on RefreshDisplay(d)
    tell d
        set s to contained data of dialog item 2
        set text_font to contained data of dialog item 4
        set text_size to contained data of dialog item 6
        set x to contained data of dialog item 8
        set y to contained data of dialog item 10
        set w_name to contained data of dialog item 12
    end tell
    set w to graphic window w_name
    BeginFrontFigure(w)
    SetTextFont(text_font)
    SetTextSize(text_size)
    TextMoveTo({x, y})
    DrawText(s)
    DrawPath(2)
    EndFrontFigure()
    draw w
end RefreshDisplay

on MergeCurrent(d)
    tell d
        set w_name to contained data of dialog item 12
    end tell
    set w to graphic window w_name
    addPDF (get front pdf of w) in back pdf of w at {0, 0}
    close back pdf of w
    BeginFrontFigure(w)
    EndFrontFigure()
    draw w
    tell d
        set contained data of dialog item 2 to ""
    end tell
end MergeCurrent

on InstallScript(d)
    set w_name to contained data of item 12 of d
    set w to graphic window w_name
    set script of w to "on pick in w at {point:{x, y}, step:i}
    set d to dialog \"" & name of d & "\"
    set contained data of item 8 of d to x
    set contained data of item 10 of d to y
end pick in"
    postit ("Loaded")
    smilepause 5
    postit ("")
end InstallScript

on prepare theDialog
```

```
● ● ●                Add text to a PDF file.Script
Handlers
    postit ("")
end InstallScript

on prepare theDialog
    repeat with i from 2 to 12 by 2
        set contained data of dialog item i of theDialog to ""
    end repeat
end prepare

on click in d item number n
    if n = 13 then
        RefreshDisplay(d)
    else if n = 14 then
        MergeCurrent(d)
    else if n = 15 then
        InstallScript(d)
    end if
end click in
```

28

Figure 28-17. The first page gathers our special handlers, which we call ourselves in script. The second page gathers the event handlers, which handle the events that Smile sends to the script.

Exercises

Obviously, we have made a working tool, yet a minimal one. What we should do now depends mostly on who will be using the tool and how often they will use it.

Here are some standard improvements that you may want to implement later. All of them can be implemented; for the sake of brevity, they are left as an exercise for you to do on your own.

- Have the dialog window systematically work on the first graphic window (even if the window is not the second window)—yet displaying its name as a visual feedback. Or, install a load window 2 button.
- Install a menu for the text font. For the text size, install the small arrows control.
- The pick in script should support the SHIFT key to pin one coordinate.
- The user should be allowed to type a numeric expression such as "55+200" as x or y.
- Install a live check box for live update.
- Rewrite the whole program to use picture views instead of working directly in the graphic window, so that all texts remain editable until the user saves as PDF.
- Graphic windows support widgets that you can use like scriptable handles to an object. Rewrite Adobe Illustrator using the widgets.

CHAPTER 29
AUTOMATING UNIX APPLICATIONS

The world of UNIX offers scripters an endless source of free scriptable applications. There are so many free UNIX applications out there, each performing little commands and actions. You can utilize most of these applications in your AppleScript solution by means of the *do shell script* command.

In this chapter, we explore one UNIX command and one such UNIX application. This should give you some idea of what is involved in making use of UNIX in your scripts.

In order to incorporate UNIX into your scripts, you have to be familiar with the UNIX-style path names. Unlike the AppleScript path names that are colon delimited, UNIX paths are slash delimited.

AppleScript path:

```
"Macintosh HD:Applications:Finder.app"
```

UNIX path:

```
"/Applications/Finder.app"
```

To learn more about the UNIX path and how to manipulate it with AppleScript, turn to Chapter 13.

Changing permissions

One of the biggest headaches the UNIX integration brought to the Mac platform is permissions. I know, it's all for the best, but it is still a pain.

Since this is not a UNIX book, and there are many UNIX books out there, I will not go into it too deeply, but I do want to cover the shell command *chmod*, and how to integrate it with AppleScript. *chmod*, which is short for change mode, changes the permission modes of a file or folder. Besides the file you want to change, it takes a mode parameter, which is a single code that describes the new permissions settings for the file.

Another important parameter is *-R*, which determines whether folders are processed recursively, and the same options you applied to the folder apply to all the files and folders in it.

The mode parameter itself is a bit more complicated, but we can look at one facet of it.

Imagine a three-digit number in which the first digit represents the owner, the second digit represents the group, and the third represents anyone else. Now, let's look at one of these digits, and see that the number 4 stands for "allow to read," number 2 stands for "allow to write," and 1 is for "allow to execute." Now let's put a simple one together: the mode number 444 means allow the owner to read, the group to read, and anyone else to read.

What if, however, we want to let the owner read and write? Well, read is 4 and write is 2, so read and write is 6. The mode number in that case would be 644. You can refer to the following table for a quick reference:

Permission Level	Mode Number
Read	4
Write	2
Execute	1
Read/Write	6
Read/Execute	5
Write/Execute	3
Read/Write/Execute	7

Looking at the preceding table, you can tell why a popular choice is 777, which allows anyone to do anything. Also 775 is useful, as it prevents anyone other than the group and owner from writing to the file.

To learn more about *chmod*, use the man page: type man chmod in the Terminal application. After a lengthy explanation of the command, you will find one bug mentioned. The bug is that there's no perm option for the naughty bits. Now, does that mean that if the bits are naughty their hairdresser appointment will be canceled? Couldn't resist.

The script that follows is a droplet that loops through nine dialog boxes that represent the nine options: owner read, owner write, owner execute, and the same for group and others.

After collecting the information from the user, including an administrator's password, the script assembles a string that will be used as a shell script.

The script is followed by brief explanation at the bottom.

Script 29-1

```
1. on open the_item_list
2.     set error_count to 0
3.     try
4.         display dialog ¬
               "Enter administrator password" default answer ""
5.         set admin_password to button returned of result
6.     on error
7.         return
8.     end try
9.     repeat with this_item in the_item_list
10.        set the_path to this_item as string
11.        set the_posix_path to ¬
               POSIX path of alias the_path

12.        set action_value_list to {4, 2, 1}
```

29

```
13.      set action_list to {"read", "write to", "execute"}
14.      set entity_value_list to {100, 10, 1}
15.      set entity_list to {"owner", "group members", "others"}
16.      set this_mode to 0
17.      repeat with e from 1 to (count entity_list)
18.         set entity_name to item e of entity_list
19.         set entity_val to item e of entity_value_list
20.         repeat with a from 1 to (count action_list)
21.            set action_name to item a of action_list
22.            set action_val to item a of action_value_list
23.            set the_message to "Allow " & entity_name & " to " & ¬
                  action_name & space & return & the_posix_path & "?"
24.            display dialog the_message ¬
                  buttons {"No", "Yes"} default button "Yes"
25.            set should_allow to button returned of result
26.            if should_allow is "Yes" then
27.               set this_mode to this_mode + (entity_val * action_val)
28.            end if
29.         end repeat
30.      end repeat
31.      set shell to "chmod "
32.      if (folder of (info for alias the_path)) then
33.         set the_message to ¬
               "Change all enclosed files of " & ¬
               return & the_posix_path & " as well?"
34.         display dialog the_message buttons {"No", "Yes"} ¬
               default button "Yes"
35.         set change_enclosed to button returned of result
36.         if change_enclosed is "Yes" then
37.            set shell to shell & "-R "
38.         end if
39.      end if
40.      set shell to shell & this_mode
41.      set shell to shell & " '" & the_posix_path & "'"
42.      try
43.         do shell script ¬
               shell password admin_password ¬
               with administrator privileges
44.      on error
45.         set error_count to error_count + 1
46.      end try
47.   end repeat
48   if error_count is 0 then
49.      set the_message to ¬
            (count the_item_list) & " files were processed" as string
50.      else
51.      set the_message to error_count & ¬
            " files out of " & (count the_item_list) & ¬
            " were not processed" as string
```

```
52.    end if
53.    display dialog the_message
54. end open
```

The preceding script is made of a few parts. The first part allows the user to enter a password. It also starts looping through the files and folders dropped on the applet.

Next, the script loops through four lists, two in the outer loop and two in the inner loop. Since there are three items in each list, the script loops three times.

Every loop represents a combination containing an entity (owner, group, or other) and a permission context (read, write, or execute). In each loop, a dialog box asks the user to choose whether to allow or disallow permission. It starts with owner read permission, then owner write, etc.

In line 27 of the script, the choices are collected into the mode number described earlier.

In lines 32–39, the script determines if the current Finder item in the loop is a folder. If it is, then the user can choose whether to apply the settings to all of the contained files. As you can see in line 37, this is done by adding the *-R* option to the *chmod* command.

In line 41 the shell script string is assembled. Notice that the POSIX path is put in single quotes. This is done to avoid having to escape, or in other words place a backslash before the spaces in the file's path name.

In line 43 the shell script is executed, which is really the purpose of the entire script.

Working with UNIX applications

There are many free UNIX applications out there, and you can figure out how to script many of them with the *do shell script* command.

After you download any UNIX application, you will need to make sure that you have executing rights to that application file.

Use the preceding explanation to change the permissions on the file, or run this shell script:

```
chmod 777 /path/to/unix/app
```

You can also use a free application called BatChmod (http://macchampion.com/arbysoft/). This little application can change the owner and permissions using a graphical user interface.

As a small example, I will show how to script a UNIX application called PDFfonts (www.glyphandcog.com/). PDFfonts takes the path of a PDF file and returns detailed information about the fonts in that PDF file—whether the font is embedded, the font type, etc. Following is a sample output from PDFfonts:

29

Name	Type	Emb	Sub	Uni	Object ID
TZJIIJ+Palatino-Roman	CID Type 0C	yes	yes	yes	17 0
RJPWGN+Palatino-Bold	CID Type 0C	yes	yes	yes	23 0
QBFQSP+Palatino-Italic	CID Type 0C	yes	yes	yes	9 0

While the preceding table has been formatted, the real result from PDFfonts looks more like this:

```
Name                                  Type          Emb Sub Uni Object ID
------------------------------------- ------------- --- --- --- ---------

TZJIIJ+Palatino-Roman                 CID Type 0C   yes yes yes    17  0

RJPWGN+Palatino-Bold                  CID Type 0C   yes yes yes    23  0

QBFQSP+Palatino-Italic                CID Type 0C   yes yes yes     9  0
```

The meaning of the different columns is as follows:

- **Name:** The font name, including the subset prefix, which is the text before the "+".
- **Type:** The font type. This can be Type, Type 3, TrueType, CID Type 0, CID Type 0C, or CID TrueType.
- **Emb:** Whether the font is embedded in the PDF.
- **Sub:** Whether the font is a subset.
- **Uni:** Whether the PDF contains an explicit "to Unicode" map. For details, see www.glyphandcog.com.
- **Object ID:** The font dictionary object ID, which includes the number and generation.

It is up to you to parse it out into components and extract the information you want.

The script we will look at is a small AppleScript interpretation of PDFfonts. We will create a droplet that accepts a PDF file. The droplet will tell us how many fonts there are and how many are embedded.

To start, we will need to convert the path of the dropped file from a Mac path using colons into a UNIX path with slashes. We'll do that with the *POSIX Path* property. We will also place the path in single quotes in case it has a space in it.

Script 29-2

```
1. on open thePDF
2.     set thePdfPath to item 1 of thePDF
3.     set thePdfPath to POSIX path of thePdfPath
4.     set shell_script_text to "~/Documents/pdffonts '" & thePdfPath & "'"
5.     try
6.         set shell_result to do shell script shell_script_text
```

```
7.    on error error_text
8.        display dialog "Error" & return & error_text
9.        return
10.   end try
11.   if shell_result is "" then
12.       display dialog "No fonts were found"
13.   else
14.       set font_info_list to paragraphs 3 thru -1 of shell_result
15.       set font_count to 0
16.       set embedded_font_count to 0
17.       repeat with i from 1 to (count font_info_list)
18.           set font_count to font_count + 1
19.           set this_font_info to item i of font_info_list
20.           set is_embedded to characters 51 thru 53 of ¬
                  this_font_info as string
21.           if is_embedded is "yes" then
22.               set embedded_font_count to embedded_font_count + 1
23.           end if
24.       end repeat
25.       set the_message to "This PDF contains " & ¬
                  font_count & " fonts, out of which " & ¬
                  embedded_font_count & " are embedded."
26.       display dialog the_message
27.   end if
28. end open
```

In lines 2–4 of the script we get the path to the dropped PDF, convert it to a UNIX-style POSIX path, and construct the *shell* command.

Between the lines 5 and 13 we run the *shell* command and compensate for two possibilities: one is that the file dropped is not a PDF. This situation will be trapped as an error. The other option is that there are no fonts at all in the PDF, and in that case the user will be notified as well (line 12).

In line 14 we create a list that includes all the paragraphs of the result, starting from the third paragraph (paragraphs 1 and 2 are the title and underscore).

Once we have the list, we loop through each font information line and pick off the information we need.

After a short examination, I realized that the result is not a tab-delimited text, but rather, every column has a System Events number of characters. The first column uses 37 characters, the second 13 characters, followed by the 3 Boolean columns, each taking 4 characters, and at last the 9-character font info column.

29

Using this information led me to the fact that if characters 51 through 53 say "yes", then it means that the font is embedded (see line 20).

If the current font is embedded, I add it to the count of embedded fonts.

In lines 25 and 26 the final message is created and displayed.

CHAPTER 30
SCHEDULING SCRIPTS

So far we dealt with the scripts themselves: how to write them, save them, and run them. But what if you want a script to run automatically at any time of the day or night?

In this chapter, I cover a few options for scheduling scripts to automatically run at any time on your Mac.

iDo Script Scheduler

Perhaps the most well-known option for automating the launch of scripts is iDo Script Scheduler by Sophisticated Circuits. You can buy it or download a demo from Sophisticated Circuits' website: www.sophisticated.com.

iDo Script Scheduler allows you to select a script file and specify when it should run. Your choices are Once only, Repeating, Day of week, Day of month, Hot key, and System idle.

The Repeating, Day of week, and Day of month choices are all variations of the *Repeating* option. They allow you to specify in what intervals your scripts will run.

The System idle option lets you set a number of minutes that the system can be idle before your script executes.

Hot key is also a neat alternative to attaching key combinations to script execution.

You can have iDo Script Scheduler run scripts from many languages, including Perl, UNIX shell, Python, and others. These scripts have to be identified with special file name extensions.

iDo Script Scheduler is a reliable and easy-to-use utility, and most of its windows and dialog boxes are self-explanatory.

The main window, shown in Figure 30-1, lists the scheduled events and allows you to add, delete, or edit an event.

Figure 30-1. The scheduled events in iDo Script Scheduler's main window

Clicking the New or Edit button will bring up a simple Event window, which allows you to set the trigger for the script and specify the script file. You can also specify parameters for the script, but for that your script must be saved as a compiled script with a *run* handler containing parameters, like this:

```
on run (parameter1, parameter2...)
--script
end run
```

Using iCal to schedule scripts

Another neat way of scheduling script execution is by using iCal.

To do that, create a new event in iCal and set the start date and time to the date and time you want the script to execute on.

After you have the event, choose the Open file alarm, and choose the script file you want to run. This can be either a compiled script or a script application. Set the alarm to execute 0 minutes before the event.

The example in Figure 30-2 will run the script "Backup user folders" every night at 12:20 a.m.

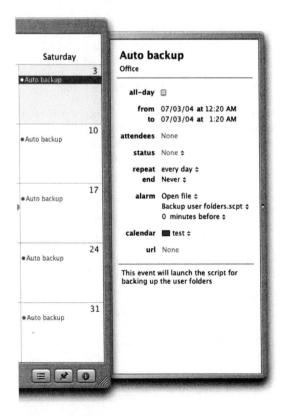

Figure 30-2.
The event shown will run the script "Backup user folders" every night at 12:20 a.m.

30

Managing stuck scripts

In Chapter 22 we looked at many ways to avoid having our script error out. As much as we try, however, we can never eliminate the possibility that our script will crash.

The consequences of your script hanging or crashing may be small; someone will eventually find it and restart it. In other cases, however, it may control an automated system that processes critical jobs that people are waiting for, and has to be up 24/7. In these cases, a crashed script has to be attended to immediately.

I encountered this situation in a recent project I worked on. The project was a system that produces financial documents in a fully automated fashion. Users drop source files into hot folders, and the finished PDF is e-mailed to them within minutes. Not only that, but the system is used by the company's offices in Australia, Japan, and the UK, so it was critical to have it start itself up if needed.

The solution for this problem was Kick-off, a hardware-software combination made by Sophisticated Circuits, the company that makes iDo Script Scheduler. Kick-off is a part of a family of products that allow you to control the computer power from scripts, among other ways.

Kick-off connects between the power strip and your Mac's power cord, and also connects to the USB port. You can configure it to restart your Mac in the event that a particular script gets hung.

The way it is done is by using an application called PowerKey Daemon. PowerKey Daemon is a scriptable utility that has a built-in timer. To use it, you include the command *tickleAppTimer* with the number of seconds the timer should be set to, like this:

```
tell application "PowerKey Daemon" to tickleAppTimer 300
```

After the PowerKey Daemon gets the "tickle," it starts the timer. If the timer expires, meaning the number of seconds you set in the timer pass before you tickle the timer again with *tickleAppTimer*, Kick-off starts the restart sequence. First, Kick-off tries to restart your Mac the nice way a specified number of times. If it can't restart, the hardware part takes over and the power to your Mac is stopped and then started again.

All you have to do is make sure that you have a startup script in the startup items that restarts your system.

To make sure Kick-off doesn't restart your Mac after the script quits normally, add this *quit* handler:

```
on quit
    tell application "PowerKey Daemon"
        tickleAppTimer 0 -- clear the timer before exiting.
    end tell
    continue quit -- let the script quit normally.
end quit
```

UNIX cron

The UNIX *cron* and *crontab* commands allow you to schedule UNIX commands, including the launching of scripts.

The freeware application CronniX puts a graphical interface on the *cron* command, which "allows scheduled execution of scripts, programs, applications—in short anything that can be started from the command line. This includes OSX applications and AppleScripts." You can download CronniX and read more about it at www.koch-schmidt.de/cronnix/.

Other such applications are MacAT (http://gimr.garvan.unsw.edu.au/gerham/macsos/macat/index.html), piTime from piDog Software (www.pidog.com/piTime/), Scheduler 3 (www.macscheduler.com/), and T-Minus Ten from MK Software (http://home.austin.rr.com/mk/tmt).

If you aren't intimidated by UNIX, you may want to try to schedule your scripts with the *cron* application, which allows you to schedule shell scripts on the Mac.

You can use the *osascript* shell command along with the path to the script you want to run. *osascript* is a shell script command that will execute a script either from a file or from text.

To find out exactly how to use the *cron* application to create *cron* tabs, pick up a UNIX book that deals with the subject.

CHAPTER 31
CONTROLLING REMOTE
APPLICATIONS

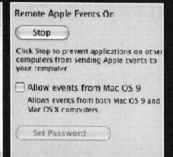

Did you know that you can use AppleScript to control applications across the network or across the world? This chapter discusses scripting remote Macs and remote applications.

Scripting remote Macs over IP

One of AppleScript's features is the ability to run script on one Mac that controls applications on another Mac. This is done with Remote Apple Events over IP.

Beside a couple of extra lines you have to wrap your code with, the scripts themselves are the same as if they were made to run locally.

Enabling Remote Apple Events

Before you can even start scripting remote Macs, the Mac you want to script has to be able to accept them. By default, Macs are set to not allow access by Remote Apple Events. This issue is crucial to security: imagine the risk if anyone who knew your IP address could control your Mac from afar. Well, they would also need you user name and password, but in a multi-Mac environment those may not be the most difficult things to get.

To activate Remote Apple Events on any OS X Mac, check the Remote Apple Events check box in the Services tab of the Sharing pane of System Preferences, as shown in Figure 31-1.

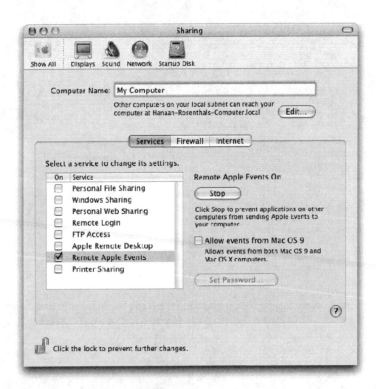

Figure 31-1.
System Preferences Sharing pane where you turn on Remote Apple Events and check the user's Rendezvous name

While you're in the Sharing pane, check out the user's Rendezvous name. It is noted under the computer name with the ".local" name ending. This name may come in handy later on.

Talking to machines

When you write scripts that run locally, the scripts run on the default machine, which is your Mac—therefore specifying the machine is unnecessary. When scripting other Macs over IP, however, you need to specify what Mac, or *machine* as it is referred to in the script, you want to send events to.

The remote machine can be specified either by using its IP address or, if it is on your local network, its Rendezvous name. You can find the Rendezvous name in the Sharing pane of System Preferences, as noted earlier. The IP address can be gotten from the Network pane of System Preferences.

Once you figured out the IP address or Rendezvous name of the target machine, you can compose the *tell* block. Let's say that you want the Finder of the target Mac to create a folder. For argument's sake, we are talking to a Mac whose IP address is 101.2.3.4. We'll need to tell the application Finder of the machine in this way:

```
tell application  "Finder" of machine "eppc://101.2.3.4:3031/"
    make new folder...
end tell
```

The beginning of the machine name string is always "eppc://" followed by either the IP address or the Rendezvous name. The IP address can be followed by the port number 3031, the port that is used for sending Apple Events over IP.

The *tell* block for a Mac on the same local network would be

```
tell application  "Finder" of machine "eppc://rendezvous-name.local"
```

Authentication

And you thought for a second that OS X security would let you by without identifying yourself? Not a chance. In fact, even if the target Mac allows incoming Apple Events over IP, you will still need to have a user name and password of a user on that Mac with administrator privileges.

You can embed the user name and password for that Mac in your machine name string, like this:

```
machine "eppc://username:password@101.2.3.4:3031/"
```

or in the case of using the Rendezvous name:

```
machine "eppc://username:password@rendezvous-name.local"
```

If you don't use the name and password, when you run a script for the first time you will have to enter the login information in a dialog box, and ask to keep it in the keychain. While the first method of embedding login info in the machine name is a bit easier, using the keychain is more secure, since the login info isn't hardcoded in a script somewhere.

terms from

While you can connect and talk to applications on remote Macs, you may not want to have a live connection to them while you're writing and compiling the script. For that purpose, we enclose any script that is aimed at a remote application with the *using terms from* block. This tells AppleScript to compile the script intended to be execute by a remote application, using terms from the same application locally. This makes our *tell* block look like this:

Script 31-1

```
tell application "Finder" of machine "eppc://101.2.3.4:3031/"
    using terms from application "Finder"
        --script aimed at the remote Finder
    end using terms from
end tell
```

Launching applications

Another caveat of scripting remote applications is that if the application isn't running when you target it with a script, your commands won't go through, even if you use the *launch* command.

What you have to do is use the Finder on the remote machine to first launch the application file, and only then target it with commands. You use the Finder since it is almost certain to be running.

Using aliases

The alias file-reference form is useful on the local Mac since it keeps track of files even as they move or change names. In scripting remote applications, however, using the alias reference form can cause AppleScript to get confused. Instead, store file paths in variables as strings.

Controlling XML-RPC and SOAP

AppleScript has taken a bold step to integrate the XML-RPC and SOAP technologies into its core language. XML-RPC and SOAP are web services, or types of applications that communicate with users by means of XML.

With AppleScript, however, you don't need to know or write any XML, since AppleScript does all the communication with the remote application for you. What you do have to know are the service's URL, function name, and some other parameters.

A few websites, such as XMethods (www.xmethods.com), list many such services along with their settings. Converting that information into a fruitful AppleScript call is a different story.

You can use AppleScript to make a call to a SOAP service or an XML-RPC service. Both call types are done using syntax similar to that for targeting any other application.

SOAP

The syntax for making a call to a SOAP service looks like this:

Script 31-2

```
tell application "http://url-to-soap-service"
    call soap {method name: the_method, method namespace uri: uri}
end tell
```

If the service requires parameters, you can supply them using the *parameters* item in the call record shown previously. The parameter for a service that requires a single parameter can be included as is, like this:

```
call soap {method name: the_method, method namespace uri: uri, ¬
parameters: "02909"}
```

The preceding call needs to be a five-digit zip code as a string.

If more parameters are needed, you can supply them as a record.

XML-RPC

The syntax for XML-RPC service calls looks like this:

```
tell application "http://url-to-soap-service"
    call xmlrpc {method name: the_method, parameters: parameter_list}
end tell
```

Sample code

So you went to the XMethods website and found a service you want to test. If you find it difficult to marry the service specification listed on that website with the parameters AppleScript needs, don't despair: you're not alone. Very little documentation exists on taking just any service and calling it with AppleScript.

Following is an example of a service that uses no parameters but returns a record as a result.

I first list the service specifics exactly as they appear on the XMethods website, and then the way the same information should be turned into an AppleScript statement.

The service, called *getRandomBushism*, simply returns a record with two items: the bushism and the context.

On the website, the service's specifications are listed as follows:

Method Name:	*getRandomBushism*
Endpoint URL:	http://greg.froh.ca/fun/random_bushism/soap/index.php
SOAPAction:	*urn:RandomBushism#bushism#getRandomBushism*
Method Namespace URI:	*urn:RandomBushism*
Input Parameters:	
Output Parameters:	
return:	*RandomBushism*

The AppleScript syntax for calling that service looks like this:

Script 31-3

```
tell application ¬
   "http://greg.froh.ca/fun/random_bushism/soap/index.php"
   set {bushism_text, bushism_context} to call soap ¬
      {method name:¬
         "getRandomBushism", method namespace uri:¬
         "urn:RandomBushism", SOAPAction:¬
         "urn:RandomBushism#bushism#getRandomBushism"}
end tell
display dialog  "Bush: " & bushism_text buttons {"context", "OK"}
if button returned of result is "context" then
   display dialog bushism_context buttons {"OK"}
end if
```

Wrap-up

Even though AppleScript supports XML-RPC and SOAP calls natively, there's still a usability gap that makes it difficult for any scripter to look up a SOAP or XML-RPC application on the Web and quickly put it to use with AppleScript. Regardless of that fact, the promise of such web services should keep you interested; they are slowly turning into a valuable, and mostly free, resource for the scripting community. You can use these web services to get weather information and stock quotes, verify e-mail addresses and credit card numbers, get ample data on places in the U.S. based on their zip code, and also find TV listings in Iceland, and obtain a list of famous people whose birthday is on a given date. This list is endless and it keeps on growing all the time.

There are quite a few websites that list useful web services, which you can call from AppleScript, as well as XML-RPC and SOAP specifications, such as Xmethods (www.xmethods.com) and Userland's XML-RPC's website (www.xmlrpc.com).

Another place to find information and help is from Apple's AppleScript website (www.apple.com/applescript/resources/). From there, look for the XML-RPC and SOAP references.

```
set shell to "chmod "
if (folder of (info for alias the_path)) then
        set the_message to "Change all enclc
            " & return & the_posix_path & '
        display dialog the_message buttons {
            default button "Yes"
        set change_enclosed to button return
            result
        if change_enclosed is "Yes" then
            set shell to shell & "-R "
        end if
end if
set shell to shell & this_mode
set shell to shell & " '" & the_posix_path &
try
        do shell script shell password admin_
            with administrator privileges
```

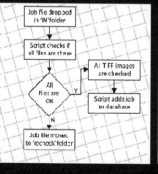

If you use AppleScript for more than the occasional script you write for yourself, then you are saving someone time and increasing their productivity. All that goodness translates into money that someone is either saving or making. An AppleScript return on investment study published a few years ago by GISTICS suggests that media producers saved over $100 million during 1998 alone (for more info on this study, see the "Taking the next step" section).

As the scripter, there are things you can do to get in on the action. You can do that by either pushing your position as a scripter within your organization, or becoming an independent automation consultant and writing scripts for living, as I have been doing for almost ten years. In any case, you need to understand what makes AppleScript automation unique, and how you can use it to dramatically improve workflows of companies that use Macs for their business.

This chapter discusses some of the business aspects of AppleScript, and gives advice to those who want to capitalize on this incredible technology.

Starting to make an impact

As in any other business, when you're just starting out, you have to stand out from the crowd in order to be noticed. Luckily for you, you are not trying to direct a major Hollywood film or sell your paintings to a museum. What you're trying to do is write scripts for your organization, and slowly get recognized, and then slowly get paid. What may make this very possible is part of what makes AppleScript so great: you can make a substantial impact without too much work.

Before jumping to asking for a budget or writing up a six-figure proposal for a project, you have to remember a simple rule: what you can do for others always comes before the reward you get back, or at least the monetary reward.

Rolling up your sleeves

To make it as a scripter, you can't sit around waiting for someone to promote you to that position; it has to be all you. If there's very little automation going on in the company you work for, then it is a typical company. You have to be the one that looks around for scripting opportunities, and when you find them, don't ask if you should try to automate them, just do it. In your spare time, during lunch, or on your work hours—no matter what it takes, find a problem or task that can be helped with scripting and work on solving it. Wait as long as you can before revealing your work—the more complete it is when you show it, the better off you will be.

Now that you have something to show, make sure that you have a clean demo arranged in order to show off your script. Collect some basic numbers such as "This used to take three hours, but now it can be done in six minutes," or something to that effect.

Before long, you will find that little automation issues come to you: could you script this, could you automate that . . .

Taking the next step

If you have what it takes to script and you decide that you want to take a more serious crack at it, start by looking around your own company, but this time with a bit more ammunition. To start, you have to be fully aware of the value and impact that scripting and automating can have on your department and company. A good starting point is a return on investment study published by GISTICS. To get the full study, go to Google and type AppleScript ROI GISTICS; you will encounter numerous websites that have the full study posted. Among other facts, the study claims that companies saw their investment in AppleScript returned 2.4–4.3 times during the first year of adaptation; usually, the expectation is to return the investment once within a few years. This information can help you convince your company, or other companies, to give you a nudge upwards on the pay scale.

Joining Apple's Consultants Network

Apple's Consultants Network is a network of certified consultants that is maintained by Apple Computer. The consultants are "skilled in the setup, use, and maintenance of Apple products and solutions," and prospective clients can search for them by geographic location and area of expertise. The Consultant Network's website is at consultants.apple.com.

In order to become a consultant, you need to pass a few tests and pay the membership fee. Membership doesn't make sense for everyone, but if you're looking to become an independent consultant, you should look into it.

Figuring out the value of automation

It is quite difficult to figure out the monetary value of a scripting project, since it can stretch across many areas in a company and have impact that is far greater than the time saved by having AppleScript do the work instead of a person.

In fact, the time saved estimates is where you have to be the most cautious. Let's assume that you ran some tests and some numbers, and you've figured out that the catalog takes 20 hours to produce in the current manual workflow, but you can create scripts that will produce it in 1 hour. Let's also assume, for argument's sake, that you are right. Will that mean that the company can lay off 95% of the employees working on the catalog as soon as the script is working? No. The company won't be able (and shouldn't want to) lay off anyone for a while.

By manual workflow, I don't refer to X-Acto knives and tape, rather to workflow that uses Macs, but is not (yet) automated.

The reality is that even with the type of drastic results you can get with AppleScript, change is always slower. This is good in a way, since you can now avoid those nightmares about having your coworkers lose their jobs because of you. In reality, if you save your company or department 10% of the workforce after a year, which can happen through attrition and promotion instead of layoffs, you have done a great job. It is important, however, to have realistic expectations as far as the immediate impact your scripting work will have on your department.

The broad impact

Let's get back to the catalog you are working to automate. If you can shorten the production time from 20 hours to 1 hour, you can imagine that the production lead time, which is the amount of time you have to start the work before the catalog has to be ready, will shorten by, say, 50%. Even though production sees a direct improvement of 95%, the lead time has to take into account much more than just the raw production. An improvement of 50%, however, is huge. It means that all the information in the catalog can be much more up to date, which is essential in some markets. The fact that a script will now be placing the prices in instead of a person means that errors will be down drastically, which means much less work for proofreaders and graphic designers. An automated process also means that you in effect taught the Mac how to do all the boring repetitive work, and that all those designers who spent days and nights correcting copy and retyping prices can now concentrate on design instead.

The art of prototyping

Back to selling your work. One of the things you will come to realize is that with AppleScript development, the 80-20 rule applies: you can finish 80% of the project in 20% of the time. This by itself doesn't mean much, since you will have to spend the rest of the 80% of the time on the small things (believe me, it is unavoidable). Where you do take advantage of it is that you can create a working prototype of the project in a very short amount of time.

The key is to have a meeting with a prospective client, be it in your company or as a consulting job somewhere else. In that meeting, try to gain an understanding of the terms they use and of their workflow. Pay special attention to the raw material, the documents, and the final output: raw material being the data that they use to produce whatever it is they produce, the material being their templates, etc., and the output being the finished job. Try to take as much of it with you, with permission of course; sign a confidentiality agreement if you have to. Then, make a meeting with them a couple of weeks from that point.

At this point you should get busy: make sure you have a good prototyping tool such as AppleScript Studio, FileMaker Pro, or FaceSpan to use for a basic interface. Now, create some basic scripts that take their material and turn them into parts of the final product. I like to have a dialog box come up at the end that says, "The process is complete, and took 23 seconds" or something to that effect. It is very impressive for people at a company see their product or part of it created automatically, and so fast.

Is it possible?

A question you will get again and again is whether one thing or another is possible to automate. In reality, anything is possible, as long as the client is willing to pay for it. As far as your experience goes, unless they're asking for things that are way beyond your ability, you should assume that you can figure out how to get anything done, even if you haven't done it yet.

Charging for automation

Automation is very valuable, and unless you're in the process of starting out and trying to get any experience, you should charge good money for it. Along with charging money comes the question of how much to charge.

To figure out how much to charge, you have to look at two variables: one is the value of your services to the client and the other is the value of your time. The ultimate situation is where the difference between the two is the greatest—for instance, if you figure out that the job will save the company approximately $200,000 over two years, and it will realistically take you 50 hours to create. Now, even if you figure your time is worth $250/hour, you come out at $12,500. The ratio is huge. You can easily ask for $20,000 to $30,000, and know that even at less than that you will do fine.

Another way to charge is for time. You can charge either hourly or by the day. Hourly, you can expect $120–$225/hour, depending on whom you deal with. Although this may appear to be less than what you get if you charge by the project, you are covered if you run over your estimates. Charging by the day is also possible. Try not to place yourself under $1000/day, or $500–$700 or so if you're starting out.

Always keep in mind that the value of your work will be far greater than anything you will ever dream to ask, so don't be afraid to ask what you want.

Scope creep

You may or may not have heard the term scope creep (also called feature creep), but the problem is very real, and as a sole developer, you have to protect yourself from it. Scope creep is bound to happen sometimes during development: clients periodically realize that the system or script you're creating can do just a wee bit more than initially thought. They approach you with the idea and see if they can squeeze it in.

Usually, these requests are small enough that you don't feel like you can say no to them. A half-hour here or an hour there really isn't much, especially for a project of a particular size. In reality, the larger the project, the more you have to avoid this creep. Anything you agree to will mean more benefit to the client, more work for you, more features for you to later support, and not any more reward. The only reward is that this client now knows that they can get more out of you for less money.

Here's how I deal with scope creep: I start by defining what the system will do, and make the description as tight as I can, not leaving open-ended items such as "may connect to SQL database" or "could have intranet interface." Then, I encourage the client to come up with more features they want to add, but instead of agreeing to them, I write them down. My point to the client is this: we have to keep our eye on the target. After we're done, or at some point during the development, we can look at all the proposed additions and adjust the price accordingly. This way the additional features are added in a more organized way, instead of just creeping in, and mainly you get paid more for adding them.

Another reason to avoid bloating the project is that as much fun as it is to be useful to your client, anything you agree to do, you own. By own, I mean owning the problem; if that feature ends up being a problem in any way, you are stuck with having to solve it. It doesn't matter that you were nice enough to suggest it; you can't take it back without taking a hit.

Supporting your solutions

Another facet of creating scripts for clients is that those scripts depend on the client's environment remaining static. There are many things that can go wrong, and 99% of them have nothing to do with you. For that reason, you have to be ready to support your scripts, and the client has to be willing to pay for this support.

The way I calculate the cost of support is by adding up the cost of the entire system, taking 20% of that amount and spreading it over 12 months. If the client is more than 60–90 minutes away, I charge extra for being on site. Using this formula, if you had a $24,000 project, the annual support agreement will be $4,800, which will be $400 a month.

This should cover everything you have to do to make sure their system works. Having that on your head also helps you create a system that is as maintenance free as possible.

Also insist that the client will have one point person for contacting you in order to avoid having a few people contacting you with the same problem.

INDEX

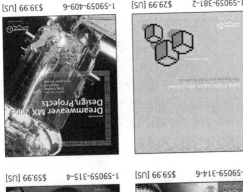

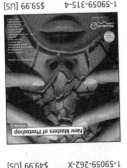

friendsofed.com/forums

Join the friends of ED forums to find out more about our books, discover useful technology tips and tricks, or get a helping hand on a challenging project. Designer to Designer™ is what it's all about—our community sharing ideas and inspiring each other. In the friends of ED forums, you'll find a wide range of topics to discuss, so look around, find a forum, and dive right in!

- **Books and Information**
  Chat about friends of ED books, gossip about the community, or even tell us some bad jokes!

- **Site Check**
  Show off your work or get new ideas.

- **Digital Imagery**
  Create eye candy with Photoshop, Fireworks, Illustrator, and FreeHand.

- **ArchiveD**
  Browse through an archive of old questions and answers.

- **Flash**
  Discuss design issues, ActionScript, dynamic content, and video and sound.

- **Web Design**
  From front-end frustrations to back-end blight, share your problems and your knowledge here.

◄ HOW TO PARTICIPATE ►

Go to the friends of ED forums at **www.friendsofed.com/forums.**

friendsofED™
DESIGNER-TO-DESIGNER™
an Apress® company

Visit **www.friendsofed.com** to get the latest on our books, find out what's going on in the community, and discover some of the slickest sites online today!